The I–D–E–A Model of Data Analysis and Interpretation

48 ± 7,
$d = 0.52$,
< .05

ESTIMATE
using information from these statistical tools to complement each other

- the width of the confidence interval to assess precision

- the magnitude of the effect size to compare with other research findings

- the degree of chance variation if the null hypothesis were true (to assess Type I error)

- the probability of correctly rejecting a false null hypothesis (power)

- the likelihood of replicating a finding at the .05 level

ANNOUNCE

- in a clear and complete fashion using standard (e.g., APA) conventions

- drawing appropriate conclusions

www.wadsworth.com

wadsworth.com is the World Wide Web site for Wadsworth and is your direct source to dozens of online resources.

At *wadsworth.com* you can find out about supplements, demonstration software, and student resources. You can also send email to many of our authors and preview new publications and exciting new technologies.

wadsworth.com
Changing the way the world learns®

DATA

ANALYSIS

AND

INTERPRETATION

IN THE

BEHAVIORAL

SCIENCES

Eugene B. Zechmeister

Emil J. Posavac

Loyola University of Chicago

THOMSON

™

WADSWORTH

Australia ▪ Canada ▪ Mexico ▪ Singapore ▪ Spain
United Kingdom ▪ United States

THOMSON

WADSWORTH

Publisher: Vicki Knight
Assistant Editor: Dan Moneypenny
Editorial Assistant: Lucy Faridany
Marketing Manager: Lori Grebe
Marketing Assistant: Laurel Anderson
Project Manager, Editorial Production: Paula Berman
Print/Media Buyer: Nancy Panziera
Permissions Editor: Joohee Lee

Production Service: Janet Vail
Text Designer: Andrew Ogus
Copy Editor: Tom Gillen
Illustrator: Richard Sheppard
Cover Designer: Denise Davidson
Cover Image: Eric Evans/Image State
Cover and Text Printer: Phoenix Color Corp.
Compositor: UG / GGS Information Services, Inc.

For more information about our products, contact us at:
Thomson Learning Academic Resource Center
1-800-423-0563

Library of Congress Control Number: 2002108866

ISBN 0-534-52986-0

Wadsworth/Thomson Learning
10 Davis Drive
Belmont, CA 94002-3098
USA

Asia
Thomson Learning
5 Shenton Way #01-01
UIC Building
Singapore 068808

Australia
Nelson Thomson Learning
102 Dodds Street
South Melbourne, Victoria 3205
Australia

Canada
Nelson Thomson Learning
1120 Birchmount Road
Toronto, Ontario M1K 5G4
Canada

Europe/Middle East/Africa
Thomson Learning
High Holborn House
50/51 Bedford Row
London WC1R 4LR
United Kingdom

Latin America
Thomson Learning
Seneca, 53
Colonia Polanco
11560 Mexico D.F.
Mexico

Spain
Paraninfo Thomson Learning
Calle/Magallanes, 25
28015 Madrid, Spain

To Al Erlebacher,
who taught me more about statistics than I ever demonstrated in his classes

E.B.Z.

To Austin Graham Posavac,
who is still too young to understand how he benefits from statistics, but someday he will

E.J.P

ABOUT THE AUTHORS

EUGENE B. ZECHMEISTER (Ph.D., Northwestern University, Evanston, IL) is a professor of psychology at Loyola University of Chicago, where he has served as Director of the Graduate Experimental Psychology Program, Assistant Dean for Social Sciences, and Director of the Undergraduate Psychology Program. He has published extensively in the field of human learning and memory, as well as the teaching of psychology, and has authored five books, including *Research Methods in Psychology* (2003) (with J.J. Shaughnessy and J.S. Zechmeister). In 1994, he was the recipient of the Sujack Award for Teaching Excellence in the College of Arts and Sciences. Professor Zechmeister is a fellow in the American Psychological Society and the American Psychological Association (Divisions 1, 2, & 3).

EMIL J. POSAVAC (Ph.D., University of Illinois, Champaign) is a professor of psychology at Loyola University of Chicago where he has served as Director of the Applied Social Psychology Program and chairman of the psychology department. He has published sixty papers and chapters, edited or co-edited six volumes on program evaluation and applied social psychology, and written numerous reports for health care and educational institutions. He is the author (with R.G. Carey) of *Program Evaluation: Methods and Case Studies* (2003). He has consulted with a number of public and private organizations, and, in 1990, he was awarded the Myrdal Award by the American Evaluation Association for his contributions to the advancement of program evaluation practice.

BRIEF CONTENTS

CONTENTS

PART 2
I-D-E-A FOR A STUDY INVOLVING A SINGLE MEAN 105

PART 3
I-D-E-A WHEN THERE ARE TWO MEANS 141

PART 4

I-D-E-A WHEN THERE ARE MORE THAN TWO MEANS 239

PART 5
I-D-E-A WHEN EXAMINING THE RELATIONSHIP BETWEEN TWO VARIABLES 325

PART 6

I-D-E-A FOR STUDIES WITH NOMINAL DATA 447

To the Instructor

This book is about the *process* of statistical decision making. It reflects what we have learned from the recent and continuing discussion among social scientists about the nature of statistical inquiry and, most notably, about the role of null hypothesis significance testing (NHST) in the behavioral sciences. This discussion has clarified misunderstandings surrounding traditional approaches to data analysis and interpretation and has suggested new ways of looking at data. (See, e.g., Abelson, 1995, 1997; Cohen, 1994; Estes, 1997; Loftus, 1996; Hunter, 1997; Schmidt, 1996.) A committee appointed by the Board of Scientific Affairs of the American Psychological Association (APA) summarized many of these issues and provided guidelines for researchers. (See Wilkinson & the Task Force on Statistical Inference, 1999.)

Our understanding of these issues led us as teachers to change the way in which we introduce statistics to students in their first statistics course. For example, the traditional separation between descriptive and inferential statistics (i.e., NHST) does not fit well with recent recommendations. Inference is not linked simply to hypothesis tests; rather, it begins with exploratory and descriptive analysis as one gets a feel for what the data are telling us. It seems clear that common misinterpretations of (and a fixation on) NHST have handicapped students who seek to understand their data. Early prophets (e.g., Meehl, 1967) have seen their concerns vindicated in recent statements on the use and interpretation of statistics (e.g., Wilkinson et al., 1999).

In many situations, confidence intervals may be the best way to conduct statistical estimation. Yet confidence intervals often are taught to undergraduates almost as an afterthought, and students seldom are shown how to use them effectively. (See Friedrich, Buday, & Kerr, 2000.) Many observers demonstrate that examining confidence intervals along with traditional tests improves interpretations (e.g., Loftus, 1996). Measures of effect size are not always mentioned in introductory texts (see, e.g., Friedrich et al., 2000), although most effect size indices provide a more intuitive way to understand data than do inferential tests (Hunter & Schmidt, 1990). We emphasize both confidence intervals and effect sizes in our first course.

We suggest that the following three approaches to understanding data are complementary:

(a) confidence intervals for estimating the precision of our findings,

(b) effect sizes for estimating and describing the strength of our findings, and

(c) NHST to discipline ourselves from claiming more than our data can support and to provide information on the likelihood of successful replications.

We discuss the particular benefits (and limitations) of these three approaches and attempt to show how they are interrelated in our quest to understand the data we collect.

Abelson (1995) reminds us that we do statistics to support a claim about behavior. Yet this reason for doing statistics can be lost on undergraduates in their first course. Students learn a variety of procedures and tests that are supposed to be the tools they use for making decisions about research results. Our experience in the classroom, however, has been that, by the end of the traditional first statistics course, students have considerable difficulty approaching statistical decision-making in a systematic fashion, that is, in a way that makes it clear they know how to go about supporting a claim about behavior. In fact, during their first statistics course, we have observed that many students seem to lose the common sense we believe they had when they began the course. Instead of looking at data (something we feel they would intuitively do *before* the typical statistics course), they leap to "*p* levels" and ignore means, not to mention standard deviations. A major goal of our course—and of this book—is to get students to pay much more attention to the data and to consider statistics as providing a reasoned (albeit imperfect) approach to making a claim about what the data mean.

To give students a dependable process to follow when making decisions about their data, we provide a model we call *I-D-E-A*. For each of several kinds of "claims," we take students through the process of data inspection (*I*), description (*D*), estimating (*E*) confidence, and announcing (*A*) results. Thus, the I-D-E-A model emphasizes the *process* of analyzing and interpreting data. (It is outlined at the end of the prefaces.) We rehearse students using the I-D-E-A model as they proceed through the course.

Many introductory statistics courses try to do too much. Our approach is to use the I-D-E-A method to focus students on a limited number of research situations. We want students to learn to analyze and interpret data in an appropriate fashion for those situations that they are most likely to meet when asked to apply their statistical skills; they can later learn to deal with other kinds of data and to make other kinds of decisions. The APA Task Force was clear in its recommendation to researchers: keep it simple.

Yet another assumption guiding our approach is that students will no longer be doing calculations for various statistical tests: computers will. Therefore, more emphasis should be placed on interpreting data and analyses and less emphasis placed on performing calculations. This doesn't mean that students shouldn't be asked to work with formulas (at least the definitional ones). In fact, they should especially know the definitional ones, but it does mean that less emphasis should be placed on working through the computation. We believe that students do not need to be drilled in the calculation of various statistical procedures for them to understand how to make statistical decisions. Not everyone agrees, of course. Nevertheless, the question is most likely moot because computers are not going to go away and students (and researchers) are using them. The *Statistical Package for Social Sciences*, *SPSS*, is available to most college students, and there are several very good, brief, "how to" books for this program (e.g., Kirkpatrick & Feeney, 2001). We have relied on this software for our examples.

Throughout the book, we ask students to focus on real issues facing people who are working with a data set. By following the steps of data analysis and interpretation that we recommend (i.e., I-D-E-A), we believe students will be less apt to attempt to explain observations that are most likely just random effects of sampling or to claim more (*or less*) than the data support. They will, in other words, be able to appropriately support or not support a claim about behavior.

ACKNOWLEDGMENTS

We'd like to acknowledge the support and encouragement from our colleagues at Loyola University when writing this book. Several classes of students patiently put up with draft materials and loose-leaf copies of this book. Members of our undergraduate classes also helped by identifying typos and other mistakes, as well as when we were just not clear. We are especially indebted to Elizabeth Hudzik, who carefully checked many of the answers to problems appearing at the end of the chapters. However, if there are any errors remaining, we assume all responsibility. We have also been supported during this project by wonderful spouses, one of whom went so far as to help us prepare the ancillary materials while she was working on her own book. Thanks, Jeanne.

In addition, we'd like to thank the publishing professionals at Wadsworth who saw this book into being. In particular, thanks to Vicki Knight, our publisher, for her support and friendship over many years. Paula Berman, project manager, was calmly efficient in overseeing the publishing process; Janet Vail, production editor, deciphered our scribbled comments and shepherded the book through production with aplomb; and thanks to Richard Sheppard who created all the artwork.

Last, thanks to the following reviewers: Mark Stasson (Metropolitan State University, Twin Cities), Joan C. Ballard (State University of New York College at Geneseo), Winona Cochran (Bloomsburg University), David Basden (California State University–Fresno), Gerald Ritter (Alcorn State University), Tim Goldsmith (University of New Mexico), Virginia Diehl (Western Illinois University), Charles Reichardt (University of Denver), Jody Meerdink (Nebraska Wesleyan University), Maxwell Twum (Fayetteville State University), Darwin Hunt (New Mexico State University), Malina Monaco (Georgia State University), Charlotte Mandell (University of Massachusetts at Lowell), Richard Topolski (Augusta State University), Elizabeth Krupinski (University of Arizona), Eva Szeli (Mental Disability Rights International), Bonnie Walker (Rollins College), Michael Biderman (University of Tennessee at Chattanooga), and Anna Smith (Troy State University).

To the Student

Needless to say, students sometimes approach their first statistics course with some degree of anxiety. "I'm not very good at math" is a common refrain of students we advise. Well, statistics is not so much about math as it is thinking in new ways about numerical data. Besides, with the easy access we all have to computers, much of what used to pass for math is no longer necessary in a statistics course. But, yes, you will have to learn to think about numbers in ways you might not have previously.

We want to let you know that this book was written with you, the student, in mind. We present a new model of data analysis and interpretation, one that is in no other statistics book. We call it the I-D-E-A model because each letter is the first letter in one of the four major stages of data analysis. You'll learn more about that later, but we wanted you to know that the goal of this model is to provide you with a systematic way to think about data. Students in the introductory course sometimes get confused with details and miss the big picture. Our I-D-E-A model is a way of approaching statistical analysis that we believe will help you see how the parts complement each other. It is a new way to think about statistics.

In addition to this new model, throughout each chapter we have sprinkled *Your Turn* exercises so you can check your learning as you go along. Please use them! We also have listed major points at the end of each chapter where they can serve as summaries of what you learned. Of course, each chapter has problems and exercises, too. We selected problems and exercises like those that you might face in later courses or in a career that requires statistical analysis.

Although you might not have thought about it, you have been benefiting from statistics for as long as you have been alive. Statistical analyses lie behind all scientific research. Research in the fields of education, medicine, public health, psychology, sociology, and economics (to name but a few) depend on statistical analyses. So, too, do political polls and the many surveys you see reported in the media ("How Often Do You Eat Out?"). It isn't too far fetched to say that you are alive today because of statistics. Certainly, the progress we have made as a society can in some real sense be seen as the result of statistical analyses. Although using and understanding statistical techniques are essential for modern life, actually doing statistics is often viewed as drudgery. Well, prior to computers it often was. At the start of the 21st century, however, these mindless but extremely capable machines have taken the tedium out of statistical analyses. We don't mean that computers have made statistical analysis easy; in fact, the hardest part has always been to understand what the analyses reveal. But computers have freed us to do what people can do best when performing statistical analyses: use our judgment to understand and draw conclusions. The I-D-E-A is to help you do just that.

The *I-D-E-A* Model of Data Analysis and Interpretation

Inspect (each data point, as well as the overall data set with graphs):

- for errors
- for outliers
- for distribution problems (skewness, including floor or ceiling effects, and kurtosis)

Describe (with graphs as well as with numbers):

- central tendency
- variation
- covariation

Estimate (using information from these statistical tools to complement each other):

- width of the confidence interval to assess precision
- magnitude of the effect size to compare with other research findings
- the degree of chance variation if the null hypothesis were true (to assess Type I error)
- the probability of correctly rejecting a false null hypothesis (power)
- the likelihood of replicating a finding at the .05 level

Announce (in a clear and complete fashion):

- using standard (e.g., APA) conventions
- drawing appropriate conclusions

CHAPTER 1

Introduction to the I-D-E-A Model of Data Analysis and Interpretation

Some researchers have the impression or have been taught to believe that some of these [research] forms yield information that is more valuable or credible than others. . . . In fact, each form of research has its own strengths, weaknesses, and standards of practice.

Wilkinson and the Task Force on Statistical Inference
(1999, p. 594)

INTRODUCTION

Try to imagine yourself in one or more of the following research situations. We will be referring to these scenarios as we begin this introduction to data analysis and interpretation.

- Karen is a senior psychology major working with a clinical psychologist doing research on suicide. She and her professor are gathering data that show the frequency of suicides for each month of the year as a function of age.

- Brandon is a graduate student doing a master's thesis on students' memory for complex information that is presented using various multimedia formats.

- Tim is taking part in an internship course offered at his university. Students in the course find positions with various organizations in the community that can benefit from help by someone with the skills students such as Tim have developed while an undergraduate. He is working with the staff at a homeless shelter to evaluate the impact of a program to bring the homeless off the streets.

- Carla graduated from college several years ago and is now working for an advertising firm. Her company just launched a new ad campaign for a client's product. Carla has been asked to determine if the new campaign is working to increase sales.

- Mary is a child psychologist looking at the relationship between infant temperament and later (adult) cognitive and emotional development.

- Joshua works for a local school district. One of his jobs is to survey parents in the district regarding their satisfaction with the school curriculum and to obtain suggestions for changes.

Research takes many forms and occurs in myriad locations. It isn't something that only scientists do, and it isn't something that takes place only in laboratories. Nor is research limited to scholarly pursuits and theoretical questions. Behavioral scientists (e.g., psychologists, sociologists, and criminal justice specialists) do research "to find something out," and often they will use statistical methods to help learn what it is that was found, how the results compare with those of others, how confident one can be of the findings, and what it all really means. In short, to find something out, we frequently must become involved with data analysis and interpretation. This book is to help you with that process no matter what your goals when doing research or where you do the research.

WHAT IS/ARE DATA?

A dictionary will tell you that *data* are facts. *Data* also means information, for example, as used to aid decision-making. Because of these somewhat different uses of the word *data*, people frequently don't know whether to give it a plural verb (as in *facts are*) or a singular verb (as in *information is*). Do we say the *data are* or the *data is*? Generally speaking, in psychology the word *data* is most often used to refer to facts obtained as part of a scientific study. In this case, you would treat *data* as a plural noun and give it a plural verb. Nevertheless, *data* also appears sometimes as synonymous with *information* and is treated as singular. In this book, we will adhere to this distinction and try to be consistently correct in our usage, as should you.

The facts obtained in a research study take two forms. **Qualitative data** are records of behavior that are characterized by a lack of quantification. These data are typically in the form of written descriptions and summaries of behavior. Qualitative data are the basis of case studies (intensive descriptions of individuals), field notes (written records of an observer), verbal narratives, and interviews—that is, "findings not arrived at by means of statistical procedures or other means of quantification" (Strauss & Corbin, 1990, p. 17). In short, qualitative data are not numbers. The second kind of data is the quantitative variety. **Quantitative data** are represented by numbers and require statistical methods to analyze and interpret them. That is what this book is about. To be precise, the title of this book should have been, *Quantitative Data Analysis and Interpretation in the Behavioral Sciences*. Although qualitative research is important and has grown in sophistication over the past couple of decades, research that yields quantitative data is more common in the behavioral sciences. Should you choose to pursue a research career in a behavioral science, at some point you will need to become familiar with qualitative research methods and data analysis (see, for example, Miles & Huberman, 1994). Here, however, we will be focusing exclusively on quantitative facts.

The word *statistic,* by the way, is usually defined in a dictionary as "a numerical fact." We typically describe our height and weight, for instance, using statistics expressed in inches and pounds, respectively. The plural form, *statistics,* also means the science of dealing with numerical information or, as behavioral scientists typically use it, the methods of analysis and interpretation of quantitative data (and in this case takes a singular verb). As you will soon see, behavioral scientists use the word *statistic* to refer to a particular type of quantitative data.

WHY (SPECIFICALLY) AND HOW (GENERALLY) DO SCIENTISTS DO RESEARCH?

This book is mainly about the use of statistics in the behavioral sciences; however, the statistical methods you will learn about are used in many disciplines and can be important well beyond a college career. Research methods and statistical methods are intimately linked. A particular research methodology "delivers" the data for analysis and interpretation. For the most part, we will assume that the data for analysis have been obtained using a sound research methodology. Data obtained from a poorly done research study may tell us nothing of importance or, worse, lead us to think something is important when it isn't. Because this book focuses on statistical methods, we cannot also focus on research methods to the same degree. In the usual plan of things, you either have been already introduced to research methodology or a course with that emphasis is yet to come. Some students are fortunate enough to take research methods and statistics courses simultaneously. With apologies to those who previously have had an introduction to research methods, we'll begin with a brief overview of the goals and types of research carried out by behavioral scientists. This will provide an important background to our presentation of statistics.

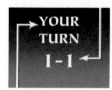

Suppose you were interested in how students study. Can you briefly show how you might investigate student study habits by collecting both quantitative and qualitative data? (Answers to *Your Turn* are at the end of the chapter.) ■

The **goals of scientific research** are generally one or more of the following:

- to provide a description of organisms and events
- to permit prediction
- to understand (discover the causes of) phenomena
- to effect change

Description frequently is the first step in any research endeavor; however, for some studies, the major goal is simply a description of what is there. Karen and her adviser were seeking to describe the number of suicides by different age groups for each month of the year. Knowing this information will tell us more about fluctuations in the seasonal occurrence of suicide. Mary, a child psychologist, was looking for a relationship among various measures of infant temperament and psychological measures obtained in adulthood. She no doubt used a longitudinal design, one in which measures are taken from the same individuals at two or more different points in time. Her goal is to use measures obtained at time 1 to predict measures of behavior at time 2. The basis for prediction is the correlation (covariation) between sets of scores. If knowing about a child's temperament permits Mary to successfully predict adult development, we say that the measures *covary,* or are *correlated.*

To understand a phenomenon is to know what causes it (see, for example, Shaughnessy, Zechmeister, & Zechmeister, 2003). Discovering the causes of a behavioral phenomenon is a tricky business and generally requires a degree of control over situations and events that is difficult to accomplish outside a laboratory environment. The graduate student, Brandon, is trying to understand memory processes by investigating whether different multimedia presentations cause differences in students' retention. We also do research to make changes in the status quo. In one manner or another, the results of Tim's, Carla's, and Joshua's research may effect a change in the way that things are now being done. This goal of research is often associated with what is called *program evaluation* and is an important concern of many institutions and organizations (see, for example, Posavac & Carey, 2003). It is very likely, for example, that you have been asked to complete a questionnaire as part of a survey of customer satisfaction when you bought a big-ticket item from a store. This is a form of program evaluation. Companies often change the way they produce and market goods on the basis of information obtained in such surveys. Similarly, colleges and universities may institute curriculum reforms on the basis of survey results obtained from their students.

How behavioral scientists do research is related to the research goals we just described. That is, particular research methodologies generally are better suited for meeting certain goals. No one research method is inherently better than another; each has its own strengths and weaknesses (Wilkinson et al., 1999). It is important to select a method that best meets the goal of the research study. Table 1.1 illustrates common links between the goals of scientific research and the methods used to meet those goals. These are not hard-and-fast rules for doing research, however. Survey questionnaires, for example, are often used to obtain data for correlational studies, such as those seeking correlations between various personality characteristics and self-reports of depression. Identifying such relationships may permit psy-

TABLE 1.1 ■ Goals of Scientific Research and Related Methodologies

Scientific Goal	Research Methodology
Description	Observation, case studies, surveys, interviews
Prediction	Surveys, longitudinal designs, correlational techniques
Understanding	Experiments, quasi-experiments
Effecting Change	All of the above

chologists to predict likelihood of depressive episodes for particular kinds of people. Surveys, however, also are frequently used for description (e.g., determining attitudes of today's college students) and even for discovering the causes of a phenomenon using experimental methods. Survey researchers, for instance, sometimes vary the order of items on a questionnaire to see if this causes a difference in people's thinking (Krosnick, 1999). Thus, the information found in Table 1.1 is meant to be mainly illustrative of some common associations between research goals and methods used to meet them. In the next sections, we define these methods more fully.

YOUR TURN 1-2

If you were a researcher interested in the relationship between the size of children's vocabulary and their performance on standardized school achievement tests, how would you likely describe the scientific goal of your research?   ■

WHAT IS AN EXPERIMENT?

As you have seen, experimental methods are linked with the goal of understanding or discovering the causes of a phenomenon. Although we might call any research endeavor "an experiment" in the sense that we are trying to find out something new, scientists give special meaning to the term **experiment.** In doing an experiment, we seek to control all the factors that might influence a phenomenon except one, and we systematically vary that one factor to see if it influences behavior. A **factor** or **variable** (the words generally are used synonymously) is the term that behavioral scientists use for properties of people or objects that can take on different values. For example, height is a variable frequently used to describe people (or plants, buildings, etc.), color is a variable useful for describing balloons, and we traditionally use points as a variable describing a football game. As you move through this book, you will see the word *variable* (or *factor*) over and over again, sometimes alone and sometimes with an adjective for special kinds of factors or variables, as we will now illustrate.

Let's look a bit more closely at what our hypothetical graduate student, Brandon, might do to investigate the effect of type of multimedia presentation on students' memory. A factor that the researcher systematically varies to determine if it has an effect on behavior is called an **independent variable.** Because it is something that varies, an independent variable must be defined using two or more conditions. Thus, in the simplest case, an independent variable has two conditions or levels. Sometimes this represents the presence of something (frequently called an *experimental condition*) and the absence of something (sometimes referred to as a *control condition*), but this is not always the case. The independent variable may just as easily be defined as two or more levels of something, but with different "amounts" (degrees) of that something, as when a researcher compares the effect on behavior of three levels (dosages) of a drug using 5, 10, and 15 mg. Because Brandon was interested in the factor of multimedia presentation, we can presume that he varied this factor using two or more levels (kinds) of presentation format. Let's assume that his independent variable had three levels: (a) information presented using videos, (b) information presented using slides, and (c) information presented without videos or slides.

A measure of behavior used to assess the effect of an independent variable is the **dependent variable.** In our example, a possible dependent variable would be scores on a test of students' retention of the information presented in the experimental conditions. For instance, recall (short answer) or recognition (multiple choice) tests could be used. Thus, the goal of the experiment is to determine if the independent variable (type of presentation) produces a change in the dependent variable (scores on a test of retention).

In a true experimental comparison, only one factor—the independent variable—is permitted to vary. In this way, if we observe a change in the dependent variable as a function of the independent variable, then (assuming the independent variable was the only thing that varied among conditions) logically the change must be due to the effect of the independent variable. This means that Brandon must make sure that factors such as the specific information presented (e.g., psychology facts), the length of the presentation, the time of day of the presentation, and other factors that might influence students' memory are controlled so that they do not influence behavior. One way in which this is accomplished is by holding these factors constant. For instance, exactly the same information must be given to students using the three presentation conditions. Otherwise, students may remember more or less depending on the difficulty of the material or because they found one type of information more interesting than another. If a factor is held constant, it cannot logically influence behavior differentially across the levels (conditions) of the experiment.

One factor that the experimenter typically cannot hold constant across conditions of an experiment is the nature of the participants. To perform the experiment, Brandon will have to assign students to the various experimental conditions. How should he do this? What if brighter and more motivated students get assigned to one of the conditions more than to the others? If such were the case, then the reason for any differences among students' retention scores across the conditions of the experiment would be unclear. Was a difference due to type of presentation (the independent variable), or was a difference due to the fact that students in some conditions were likely to remember more information no matter what the presentation format? The solution to this problem is to randomly assign participants to conditions of an experiment.

The goal of **random assignment** is to achieve essentially equivalent groups. Equivalent on what? Anything. That is, researchers use random assignment to establish groups of participants that are, as a group, similar on all important characteristics that might influence the dependent variable under study. Random assignment balances individual differences across conditions of an experiment. A random process of assigning participants typically will result in similar proportions of bright, motivated, not so bright, not so motivated, hungry, not hungry, tired, not so tired (and so forth) participants in all the conditions. Thus, on average the groups will not differ on the dependent variable prior to the introduction of the independent variable. If groups are similar in all important characteristics prior to any treatment, and if all other factors except the independent variable are controlled (e.g., by holding them constant), then we have met the criteria for a true experiment.

Random assignment permits the strongest possible causal inference given that other extraneous factors are controlled (Wilkinson et al., 1999). If the conditions of a true experiment are met, and if our hypothetical graduate student finds a difference in retention associated with type of presentation format, then we can reasonably conclude that presentation format caused the difference. We have thus grown in our understanding of what is good (or not good) for student retention of information.

When an experimenter cannot assign participants randomly to conditions of an experiment, we typically refer to the procedure as a **quasi-experiment.** Such a situation often presents itself when researchers move out of the laboratory into the real world. Research done in organizations, businesses, and various institutions may not permit the researcher the degree of control over experimental procedures that might be found in a laboratory setting. For instance, Tim, who is doing research at a homeless shelter, may not have the freedom (nor may it be judged right ethically) to randomly assign some homeless people to a treatment program and others to a no-treatment condition. He may find it necessary to compare the behavior of people who volunteer for a treatment program at one shelter with the behavior of people observed at another homeless shelter with no program. Doing research on such societal issues as care of the homeless is important, and researchers must do the best that they can under the circumstances presented to them. A quasi-experiment (of which there are many forms) may be conducted in these situations (see Shadish, Cook, & Campbell, 2002). It is important to note that quasi-experiments generally do not permit the same degree of confidence in what caused a phenomenon as do true experiments.

There is another type of behavioral experiment that poses serious problems when drawing causal inferences, namely, that when the levels of the independent variable represent so called "natural groups." A researcher cannot assign subjects randomly to be male or female, schizophrenic or non-schizophrenic, divorced or married, or 4 years old or 10 years old. Subjects are that way naturally. Yet, as you can imagine, these individual differences are of interest to researchers, and many scientific studies make use of such variables. In one sense, these studies are quasi-experiments in that subjects are not randomly assigned to the conditions of an experiment. However, the term *quasi-experiment* generally is reserved for studies in which practical or ethical constraints deter random assignment. We will have more to say about research designs that make use of natural groups later in this book.

Sally is a sport psychologist. She designs an experiment to examine the effect of different relaxation instructions on basketball free-throw performance. Volunteers from several high school basketball teams are randomly assigned to a control group (no relaxation instructions) or to one of two different relaxation groups (imagery based or non-imagery based). Her subjects then make 100 free throw attempts, and she records the number of successful attempts. Identify the independent and dependent variables, and then explain the role of random assignment in her experiment. ∎

HOW ARE BEHAVIOR AND EVENTS MEASURED?

The numbers we use to measure behavior and events are obtained using various types of measurement scales. We don't really know what a number means until we know what scale was used to produce it. Consider the number 23. We might initially think of 23 as nearly two dozen (of something), or slightly more than 20 (of something). But fans of professional basketball will always associate 23 with Michael Jordan, who wore that number jersey when he played for the Chicago Bulls. On the other hand, finishing 23(rd) in the Boston marathon is quite an accomplishment, and no doubt it is a meaningful number in that sense for some people. These meanings of the number 23 differ not simply because they refer to different things (amount, a person, a position) but because the number 23 in these examples is the product of different scales of measurement.

There are four major **scales of measurement.** The name, characteristics, and example measures of each scale are found in Table 1.2.

One way to think about these scales is in terms of increasing amounts of information as you proceed from nominal to ordinal to interval to ratio scales. *Nominal scales* simply tell you whether an event belongs to one class of events or another. The number 23 on Michael Jordan's basketball jersey, for instance, merely indicated that he was not the same as other players. (We might know that Jordan was better than other players, but the number does not tell us that.) In some sports, such as football, a range of numbers is used to indicate certain positions on the team. Quarterbacks on a football team, for example, typically wear numbers between 1 and 10. If a player has a number within this range, we usually assume this person is a quarterback. A nominal scale represents qualitatively different categories and may or may not be expressed using numbers. Gender, with the values *male* and *female,* is a nominal scale, but, when working with a computer, we might assign a value of 1 to women and 2 to men in order to "code" these categories. In this case, the 1 and 2—like the numbers on football players' uniforms—merely indicate categories. Classifying someone as male indicates that person is the "same" as others in that category, and saying someone is female means that person is "different" from males (and, for purpose of data analysis, is treated the same as those persons in the female category).

An *ordinal scale* adds information about relative order. Finishing 23rd in a marathon not only assigns us to a particular category (the 23rd position among the finalists) but indicates that we are faster than people who finished 24th or higher and slower than people who crossed the line in the 22nd position or lower. Ordinal scales permit us to place people and events in rank order. These scales do not tell us how much faster, taller, heavier (and so forth) anyone is from the people or events above and below a particular rank. Ordinal scales

TABLE 1.2 ■ Scales of Measurement

Scale	Characteristics	Example Measures
Nominal	Classification, categorical (same or different)	Gender, eye color, race, marital status
Ordinal	Rank, magnitude (greater than or less than)	Rank order in class, top 10 soccer teams
Interval	Distance between events measured without an absolute zero	Temperature (Celsius or Fahrenheit), aptitude tests
Ratio	Distance between events measured with an absolute zero	Height (e.g., in), weight (e.g., lb), distance (e.g., mi)

measure events only in terms of relative magnitude (greater, heavier, farther, etc.); they do not tell us the distance between events.

When we can specify the distance between events on a scale, we have an *interval scale.* Equal intervals (differences between numbers) on the scale represent equal differences on the characteristic being measured. A good example of an interval scale is temperature measured on a Celsius or Fahrenheit scale. A temperature of 20° Fahrenheit, for example, is lower (colder) than one of 40° Fahrenheit. In fact, there is a 20° difference between these temperatures, and this is the same difference as 120° to 140°. Distance between events (temperatures) is measured. However, temperature measured in this way is a good example of an interval scale for another important reason: there is no absolute zero point. The zero on a Celsius or Fahrenheit scale does not indicate the absence of temperature; in a sense, it is an arbitrary value. Interval scales permit us to add and subtract measures and to perform particular statistical operations that are important for describing and interpreting these numbers. Nevertheless, without an absolute zero, we cannot legitimately speak of ratios between scale values on an interval scale. It is not appropriate, for example, to say that 100° Celsius is twice as hot as 50° Celsius. This is a tricky point but an important one because many scales used in psychology are of an interval nature. The question to ask is does the "zero" on a scale really mean "zero" (that is, the absence of something). A zero temperature on a Celsius thermometer does not mean that there is no temperature. Similarly, a zero on an intelligence test would not mean that the person taking it had zero intelligence, nor would a zero on a clerical aptitude test mean that someone had no clerical aptitude whatsoever (e.g., they might at least know what a filing cabinet is).

If our scale includes all of the information found in an interval scale but also includes an absolute zero, then we have what is called a *ratio scale.* Measures of height, weight, and distance are good examples of ratio scales. A zero measurement means just that: the absence of height, weight, or distance. The term *ratio* should remind you that ratios of scale values on this scale are meaningful. It is perfectly correct, of course, to say that a box weighing 100 pounds is twice as heavy as one weighing 50 pounds.

How data analysis is accomplished depends importantly on the kind of data (nominal, ordinal, interval, or ratio) that was obtained. We'll have more to say about measurement scales when we describe specific techniques for data analysis.

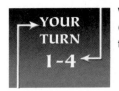

What level of measurement would most likely be associated with measures of (a) reaction time, (b) ethnic/racial identity, (c) 20-item verbal fluency test, and (d) finishers in a sorority/fraternity tricycle race? ■

WHAT IS THE ROLE OF STATISTICS
IN BEHAVIORAL SCIENCE RESEARCH?

By now, you no doubt are able to recognize the role of statistics in behavioral research. Statistical methods are used to analyze data and to aid in our interpretation of what the data mean.

Perhaps the most important distinction in all of statistics is that made between a population and a sample. A **population** represents all the data of interest; a **sample** is anything less than that. Note that a population is defined by what you are interested in and not according to some absolute standard. If you are interested in reading scores of 4th graders, then the population is defined as scores of "all 4th graders." If you are interested in parking tickets given to motorists in a large city, then your population is represented by "all the parking tickets" written in that city. How the results of a research study are interpreted depends on how the population under study is defined, and therefore it is important to define clearly the characteristics of your population (Wilkinson et al., 1999).

Although we conduct research about populations (remember, that represents the data of interest), we typically must work only with something less than what we are interested in, namely a sample. Practical considerations—including those related to time, resources, and the availability of subjects—usually make it impossible to obtain all the data of interest. Assume that your population of interest is the student body at a university. Consider the problems you would have if you attempted to contact every student at a single large university, let alone the problems that would accompany an attempt to contact every college student in the country should your data of interest happen to be "U.S. college students." A sample is what we will seek, and how that sample is obtained will determine what we can say about the population. A major goal of statistics is to relate sample data to the population. To help keep these kinds of data separate, researchers usually refer to characteristics of samples as **statistics** and characteristics of populations as **parameters.** (You may remember we said that behavioral scientists use the word *statistics* to refer to a particular kind of quantitative data. This is what we meant: statistics are characteristics of samples.) Let's presume that we are interested in the average weight of people in the United States. Weights of people in the United States represent our population of interest, and the average weight of this population is a parameter. Weights of people in Illinois, or Chicago, or in one of your classrooms, would be examples of samples because they are something less than what we are really interested in (namely the weights of everyone in the United States). The average weight of any of these samples would be a statistic.

HOW DO I GET A SAMPLE OF BEHAVIOR?

Samples are obtained in one of two ways: randomly or not randomly. Sampling is done in a random manner to achieve a **representative sample,** that is, one that is like the population on all important characteristics (but proportionally smaller, of course). Consider the population of registered voters in a city. If 40 percent of the population are registered Democrats and 30 percent are registered Republicans, with the remaining 30 percent Independents, then a representative sample will have close to 40 percent Democrats, 30 percent Republicans, and 30 percent Independents.

Keep in mind that samples are not what we are really interested in; populations are. But populations are difficult—and often impossible practically speaking—to work with. If the population is defined as "eligible voters in a U.S. election," how would one begin to obtain data on all U.S. citizens who are registered to vote? Fortunately, it isn't necessary to contact every eligible voter if one can obtain a representative sample. And the best way to do that is to use a procedure that ensures randomness. The goal of random sampling is a representative sample. A **random sample** is one in which every individual (item, event, etc.) in the population has an equal chance of being selected for the sample. If we were to write 30 names on 30 small pieces of paper, fold the pieces to approximately the same size, place the names in a box, shake vigorously, and then draw blindly a name from the box, we would satisfy the conditions of random selection. On any draw, each name would have an equal chance of being selected. Pollsters can predict election results with a high degree of accuracy by talking to a sample of the country's electorate when that sample is representative of people who will be voting. In other words, we don't need to contact all the members of a population if our sample is representative.

Samples that are not random pose serious problems for data analysis and interpretation. And, although it's easy to define what a random sample is, actually obtaining one is frequently not so easy. Think of the problems that would arise if you were trying to personally interview a random sample of homeowners in a city neighborhood. Many people work odd hours and are difficult to contact, others are rarely at home when they are not working, still others are on vacation, some may not open their doors to strangers, and so forth. Any of these factors may bias a sample by ruining its representativeness. True random samples are golden nuggets for the behavioral prospector.

Nonrandom samples are, nevertheless, frequently the basis for a research study, and this may occur for a couple of reasons. First, researchers (perhaps to make things convenient for themselves) do not even attempt to obtain a random sample. They instead select individuals or events that just happen to be available, such as a classroom of students or familiar coworkers on the job. Imagine that the management of a mall asked you to sample shoppers and get their opinions about the availability of stores in the mall. A representative sample could be achieved by using a random selection procedure that identified, say, every fourth person entering the mall at random times and through all entrances during the hours when the mall is open. It may be easier, however, to stand at only one entrance and only during the morning hours. Such samples are called **convenience samples** and typically would be treated as "biased," that is, nonrepresentative. A **biased sample** is one that over- or under-represents segments of the population. People who shop in the morning are likely to be different than those who shop later in the day (e.g., they are not working full time or are mainly parents with kids in school). Similarly, students who happen to be enrolled in a particular class are not likely to be representative of all students at a school (e.g., they may represent mainly one major or year in school), nor are students enrolled at one college or university necessarily representative of all college and university students. Because college students are not necessarily representative of non-college students, or for that matter of older or younger people, and because much psychological research is done with college student samples (because it is convenient), there has been criticism of this procedure. Convenience samples may be convenient, but they are unlikely to be representative.

Another reason that researchers sometimes end up with samples that don't represent the population of interest is that they sample the wrong population. This isn't done on purpose, and the reasons for such a mistake can be subtle and the outcome exasperating (to say the least). For example, sampling people who say they will vote in an upcoming election is not the same as sampling people who actually voted. Many people, perhaps to look good, say that they will vote, but then never get around to actually doing it. Their views will not necessarily be the same as those who actually get up the energy to vote.

It is also possible that random samples can end up being nonrepresentative even when a random selection process was initially followed. This may occur if a researcher is unable to obtain data from all the members of a randomly identified sample. We previously gave one example of this when discussing the problems that a survey researcher might experience when trying to personally interview homeowners in a neighborhood. This problem frequently also arises when other kinds of surveys are conducted. Mail surveys, for example, may be based on a perfectly good random sample of addressees. However, the response rate from a mail survey is often not greater than 30 percent, and those people who take the time to complete a questionnaire may not be representative of the entire population. Note that it is not because the sample is smaller than anticipated that creates the problem (i.e., that only 30 percent of those contacted reply); a biased sample results due to the fact that those ending up in the sample are likely to differ from others in the population in important ways (e.g., they are more conscientious, more educated, wealthier, etc.). Truly representative samples, even when relatively small, are more useful to learn about populations than are biased samples, however large. The Gallup organization typically is quite accurate when predicting election outcomes (and other social behaviors) of the American voting population, which consists of millions of people. Yet the sample size is usually no larger than 1,500.

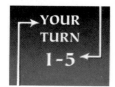

It is important to note that random sampling is not the same as random assignment. Each procedure has a different goal. At this point, you should be able to state the goals associated with each random procedure. Can you? ∎

WHAT QUESTION ARE YOU ASKING?

Research begins with a question, and we began this chapter with examples of questions asked by different kinds of researchers. (What is the suicide rate for different age groups for each month of the year? Are children's temperaments predictive of adult behavior?) This book is organized around questions typically asked by researchers. We begin with questions that might be answered with data obtained from a single random sample. Other questions require a comparison between groups that are treated differently, as when we conduct an experiment. Another common question concerns the relationship (correlation) between measures, and this, too, is discussed. It is of the utmost importance to state the question of your research before beginning to collect data. What do you want to learn from your research study? The more clearly your research question is articulated, the easier it will be to make appropriate decisions about what measures to use, what research design to employ, and what statistical methods are necessary to analyze and interpret your findings.

HOW CONFIDENT CAN I BE OF MY ANSWER?

We employ statistical techniques to provide answers to questions. Although we would like to be certain of our answers to various questions, most of the time we will find that our answers have a probability of being true that represents something less than perfect certainty. Research findings, in other words, typically leave us with a certain degree of uncertainty about the "truth," and statistical methods help us to say how sure we are of a research finding. One reason for our uncertainty may be apparent to you: we don't have access to what we are really interested in (the population). We must make do with what we find out using a sample. And what we find out varies from one sample to another, what is called **sampling variability** (or **variation**). Consider a simple example.

Imagine a bag with 100 numbers, fifty 1s and fifty 2s. Suppose we take a random sample of 20 numbers from the bag. If the resulting random sample is perfectly representative of what is in the bag, we should have ten 1s and ten 2s in our sample. It doesn't take much thought to realize that, although this may happen with some regularity, we also know that sometimes a sample, even when drawn randomly, will have some distribution of 1s and 2s that is different from 50:50. It is just something that happens by chance. Now, if we are using sample information to describe the population, our description of the population will vary somewhat from sample to sample. There is the dilemma. How can we be certain that the sample information we are using represents exactly the population we are interested in? The answer, unfortunately, is that we can't be certain. But we can determine a level of confidence in our finding. This confidence will indicate to us (and to those who look at our data) just how certain we are (even when we can't be absolutely certain) that our sample values represent the population values.

If you are facing an important decision and the answer is uncertain, are you not interested in knowing which of several answers has the highest probability of being correct? Of course you are. You'll take what you can get to aid your decision-making. (If a doctor tells you that drug A has an 80% chance of making you feel better, but the odds of drug B helping you are only 50%, which drug will you ask for?) Therefore, even when we can't arrive at certainty, it is important to know what the odds are of being right. When those odds are appreciable and point us in a particular direction, then we would be unwise to ignore the information even if we can't be absolutely sure it is right. Life gives us little in the way of certainty, and statistics is a way to guide our thinking when we are in doubt.

By using a deck of cards, it is easy to get a feel for sampling variation. A normal deck has 52 cards, 13 each of four suits (spades, hearts, diamonds, and clubs). Let the cards in the deck represent a population of college students with each of the four suits being a different class (freshman, sophomore, junior, senior). Shuffle the deck well and then draw blindly (randomly) 16 cards from the deck. If the sample is perfectly representative of the population, how many of each class should be in your sample? (It will be most informative if you actually do this little demonstration a couple of times and compare your samples with one that is perfectly representative.) ■

AN I-D-E-A FOR DATA ANALYSIS AND INTERPRETATION

There are four major steps in data analysis and interpretation. The first step is *inspection*. Once data are collected, we must make every effort to make sure that our data are "clean," for example, that the data set is free of errors. Consider for a moment the many ways that errors can creep into a data set. A researcher (e.g., observer, interviewer) may mistakenly report the wrong number when making a measurement. A respondent filling out a questionnaire may misread a question and supply an inappropriate response (e.g., when asked about the number of children in her family, the person being surveyed writes "yes"). A machine used to record data automatically (e.g., measuring heart rate) may malfunction and give erroneous information. The person coding data and entering it in the computer for analysis may make a typographical error. These mistakes in data recording should be corrected before continuing the analysis.

We also want to examine our data looking for outliers, that is, numbers that just don't seem to go with the other numbers in our data set. Outliers may be present for many reasons. One reason is that an error of the kind we just discussed has occurred. At other times, an outlier may be a truthful value; it is simply extreme relative to other numbers in the data set. (Maybe at your school there is a college student whose income is above $1 million a year. When completing a questionnaire asking about financial resources, her reported income may stand out in a student sample if others have incomes that are more typical of the starving student.) Extreme values can produce problems for analysis and interpretation. We will have more to say about the identification of outliers, and what to do about them, in the next chapter.

The second step in data analysis is *description*. Data description actually begins as we inspect the data for errors and outliers, but in this second step we focus on summarizing the data. What does the distribution of data look like? Is it symmetrical or asymmetrical? How much dispersion (variability) is there? What are the numbers around which most of the numbers tend to center? Does the data set have obvious trends that we can see just by looking at summaries of data across conditions of an experiment? Data description is done using descriptive statistics (e.g., reporting an "average" number in our data set) as well as using figures (e.g., graphs showing the relative frequency of occurrence). How we use numbers and pictures to describe data is a major topic of this book.

Estimating confidence in our results is the third major step. An important task at this point is to carry out appropriate statistical procedures to help decide whether the results are likely to have occurred simply due to chance (e.g., as the result of normal variation among samples). Let's say that you have done a research study to answer one or more specific questions. How confident can we be that your results answer the question you asked at the beginning of your study? What do the results mean? Are the findings really different from those of others? Estimating confidence in the results of a research study is necessary to convince others (and yourself) that your data are worth talking about, that you have found something that others will be interested in.

Announcing the results of our investigation is the final step. When announcing findings, we will need to use various statistical measures, and perhaps figures or graphs, as well as appropriate verbal commentary. There often will be many pieces to put together to present your data in an interesting and convincing way. Telling an accurate and informative research story is as important as doing the actual data analysis. At this stage, we need to demonstrate that we know what the data mean and that we correctly interpreted the findings. Like a good lawyer, we must assemble the evidence and present our case before the jury. In this case, the jury is that body of interested people who await our results (e.g., journal editors, corporation executives, heads of research foundations, PTA members, managers of not-for-profit organizations, laboratory instructors). In what follows, we will help you to make this announcement in a way that hopefully will allow you to win your case.

Students of psychology are asked to follow the recommendations of the *Publication Manual of the American Psychological Association* (5th ed.) when reporting research results (see American Psychological Association, 2001). The kinds of statistical information that should be part of any research report, as well as the specific format in which the results should be reported, are part of these recommendations. We will illustrate the American Psychological Association (APA) rules for statistical presentation of research results as we discuss various statistical procedures.

TABLE 1.3 ■ An I-D-E-A for Data Analysis and Interpretation

I Inspection	Make sure data are free of errors; look for anomalies and outliers. "Get a good feel for the data."
D Description	Determine what the data set looks like; examine variability and find measures of central tendency. Look for trends and possible relationships.
E Estimating confidence	Construct confidence estimates for your findings: how likely are the results due to chance? Do the results differ from those of other researchers? Are your findings "interesting"?
A Announcing results	Use words along with statistical measures and "pictures" of your data to tell your audience what was found and what it means.

These steps can be remembered as the **I-D-E-A** model (*Inspection - Description - Estimating confidence - Announcing results*), and should be used in data analysis and interpretation whenever you are presented the results of a quantitative research study. A general outline of the I-D-E-A model is found in Table 1.3, but don't be concerned if you are not familiar with some of the terms and procedures that are shown there. We are just beginning! By the end of this book, you will have a good idea of how to analyze and interpret data using the I-D-E-A model.

WHAT YOU HAVE LEARNED AND THE NEXT STEP

This chapter has laid the foundation for our discussion of data analysis and interpretation. Some of the major points discussed in this chapter are as follows:

- The goals of scientific research are generally to (a) provide a description of organisms and events, (b) permit prediction, (c) understand (discover the causes of) phenomena, and (d) effect change.

- How scientists do research is related to the research goal. Particular research methodologies generally are better suited for meeting certain goals. For example, experiments are best for discovering cause and effect relationships. No one research method, however, is inherently better than another; each has its own strengths and weaknesses.

- A *factor* or *variable* is a term for properties of people or objects that can take on different values.

- In doing an experiment, we seek to control all the factors that might influence a phenomenon except one, and that one factor we systematically vary to see if it influences behavior.

- A factor that the researcher systematically varies to determine if it has an effect on behavior is called an *independent variable*. A measure of behavior used to assess the effect of an independent variable is the *dependent variable*.

- Researchers use random assignment to establish groups of participants that are, as a group, similar on all important characteristics that might influence the dependent variable under study.

- When an experimenter cannot assign participants randomly to conditions of an experiment, we typically refer to the procedure as a *quasi-experiment.*

- The numbers we use to measure behavior and events are obtained using nominal, ordinal, interval, and ratio measurement scales.

- A *population* represents all the data of interest, whereas a *sample* is anything less than that. Characteristics of populations are called *parameters,* and characteristics of samples are called *statistics.*

- A random sampling procedure is used to achieve a representative sample, one that is like the population on all important characteristics.

- The more clearly your research question is articulated, the easier it will be to make appropriate decisions about what measures to use, what research design to employ, and what statistical methods are necessary to analyze and interpret your findings.

- We generally don't have access to what we are really interested in, which is the population. We use sample information to infer characteristics of a population, but information varies from one sample to another, which is known as *sampling variability* or *variation.*

- The four major steps of data analysis and interpretation are inspection, description, estimating confidence, and announcing results. We call this the I-D-E-A model of data analysis and interpretation.

In the next chapter, we begin a discussion of the inspection stage of data analysis, particularly as it applies to inspecting data from a single sample. Inspection is a critical first step as we seek to get a feel for exactly what our research study produced.

Key Concepts

qualitative data	random assignment	parameters
quantitative data	quasi-experiment	representative sample
goals of scientific research	scales of measurement:	random sample
experiment	nominal, ordinal, interval, ratio	convenience samples
variable (factor)	population	biased sample
independent variable	sample	sampling variability (variation)
dependent variable	statistics	I-D-E-A

Answers to *Your Turn* Questions

1–1. Qualitative research does not involve numbers; cases studies and other written descriptions of behavior are examples. Quantitative research does involve numerical facts and is the most popular method of doing research in psychology. We might investigate student study habits by interviewing students and then summarizing in writing what was learned from the interviews (qualitative). We might also investigate student study behavior by asking students to complete a questionnaire asking about the number of hours they spend in the library, how much time they study for a final exam, and so forth. A summary of these numbers would represent quantitative analysis.

1–2. Although description would be part of your research, we can assume that your major goal is that of prediction because your research focuses on the relationship between vocabulary scores and test scores. How well do vocabulary scores predict test scores?

1–3. The independent variable is type of instructions. It has three levels: none, imagery, and non-imagery. The dependent available is a measure of free-throw performance, specifically, in this case, the number of suc-

cessful free throws out of 100 attempts. Random assignment is used to "equate" free-throw ability (motivation, experience, etc.) across the groups before the introduction of the independent variable.

1–4. (a) ratio, (b) nominal, (c) interval, (d) ordinal

1–5. The goal of random assignment is "equivalent groups," whereas that of random sampling is a "representative" sample.

1–6. A perfectly representative sample of 16 cards would have 4 cards of each suit. Should you actually perform this demonstration a few times, you will find that your random samples will not always be perfectly representative, sometimes yielding too few and too many of a suit. Random sampling has the goal of achieving a representative sample, but a random sampling procedure does not guarantee a representative sample.

Analyzing and Interpreting Data: Problems and Exercises

1. A psychologist is investigating children's aggression toward one another on the school playground. Provide an example of both qualitative and quantitative data that might be collected.

2. For each of the following situations, describe the scientific goal of the research study as description, prediction, or understanding:
   a) A researcher seeks to identify attitudes of college students toward gun control in various parts of the United States.
   b) Brian works for a pharmaceutical company that is testing a new cancer drug on rats with tumors. He measures tumor reduction after giving groups of rats 0, 10, or 20 mg of the drug.
   c) As part of a program evaluation project of a city-wide recreational program for senior citizens, Alicia interviews elderly participants in the program to find out their degree of satisfaction.
   d) Mira helps a health psychologist examine the relationship between women's self-reported degree of concern about body image and various measures of self-esteem.

3. Give an example of a research project in which the goal clearly is to "effect change."

4. For Brian's study (2b), what is the independent variable? The dependent variable?

5. Suppose that you wished to do an experiment examining the effect of lightly touching people on their arm before asking them to do a small favor. Can you design a simple experiment to test the effect of touching on people's willingness to respond to a small request? What would be your independent variable? The dependent variable?

6. Briefly explain the logic and rationale of the experimental method.

7. Why are experiments usually considered the best way to determine cause-and-effect relationships? What role does random assignment play?

8. Random assignment and random sampling have different goals; however, "chance" operates to interfere with these goals in similar ways. Explain.

9. When is an experiment a "true" experiment and when is it only a "quasi" one?

10. For each of the following measures, identify the scale of measurement:
    a) body weight (pounds)
    b) scores (10 to 100) on a paper and pencil test of "relationship" anxiety

c) ranking of arousal producing pictures shown to a person with agoraphobia (fear of open spaces)

d) eye contact (seconds) made by passers-by to someone in a wheelchair

11. Suppose that you wished to conduct a study of students' academic achievement. Provide examples of nominal, ordinal, interval, and ratio scales of measurement that might be used in such a study.

12. When first learning about scales of measurement, students sometimes have difficulty with the concept of an "absolute zero" as part of the definition of a ratio scale of measurement. Why, for example, is a person's height (inches) an example of a variable measured on a ratio scale even though someone can't possibly be "zero" inches tall?

13. In a study investigating the performance of 3rd-grade school children from a local elementary school, an educational psychologist compares the students' average scores with the average score based on nationwide testing of 3rd graders. What is a "statistic" and what is a "parameter" in this example?

14. What makes a sample "representative"?

15. What is the defining characteristic of a random sample?

16. What is the defining characteristic of a "convenience" sample.

17. Describe two ways that a sampling procedure may produce a biased sample.

18. Why is it important to clearly articulate the research question you are asking before doing the research?

19. Why do the results of a research study usually leave us with a certain degree of uncertainty about "what happened"?

20. Briefly describe what happens at each of the four major steps in data analysis and interpretation: I-D-E-A.

Answers to Odd-Numbered Questions

1. We will assume that the researcher has a clear definition of what constitutes "aggression." The psychologist might make written notes of who was involved in an aggressive episode, how it started, whether it was verbal or physical aggression, and descriptions of the severity of the aggression. Quantitative data might be collected by recording how many times (over a long period) a child is involved in an aggressive episode, the length of time of the episode, the severity of the episode as indicated on a 7-point scale, and the number of times a teacher must break up a "fight."

3. There are, of course, numerous examples. Research that has the goal to effect change is just that: research that seeks to find different (and perhaps better) ways of doing things. A survey questionnaire might be designed to determine students' attitudes toward the food service on campus with the goal of making changes in the way, for example, a cafeteria serves food. A clinical psychologist may conduct an experiment investigating several methods of psychotherapy attempting to find out which is the best way to treat clients with a particular disorder.

5. An experiment could be conducted by asking the same person to approach many different people and request a quarter for an important phone call. For half the people, randomly determined, the person would touch them lightly on the arm just before the request was being made. For the other half of the people, there would be no touching but the same request would be made. The independent variable would be "degree of touching" or "type of touch," and it would have two conditions (or levels): touch and no touch. The dependent variable would be a measure of whether a person did or did not give a quarter to the individual seeking a favor. (The investigator may or may not want to record those people who apparently tried to honor the request but did not have the correct change.)

7. Experiments provide the best way to arrive at cause-and-effect conclusions due to the degree of control that is exercised by the investigator over factors that might influence the behavior under study. All those factors that might influence behavior are controlled except one (the independent variable). Random assignment is particularly important as a way to control indi-

vidual differences between subjects by "balancing" the effect of these individual differences variables (e.g., gender, attitude, motivation) across conditions of the experiment.

9. A true experiment is one in which all the variables (factors) that might influence a phenomenon are controlled (e.g., held constant) except for one factor that is varied systematically to see if it has an effect on behavior. Random assignment is used to balance the characteristics of subjects prior to the introduction of the independent variable. Thus, in a true experiment, the groups are on average equivalent before treatment. On the other hand, a quasi-experiment is one in which the groups are not necessarily equivalent prior to beginning the experiment. For example, two different psychology classes might be assigned to a control and an experimental condition, respectively. It is unlikely that the two classes would be equivalent on all important characteristics, and thus this would be a quasi-experiment.

11. Nominal data would be obtained if students were classified as having a major or being undeclared, or as withdrawing from a course or not withdrawing. It is tempting to suggest pass/fail as a nominal classification, but we would argue it is an ordinal scale in that the pass/fail distinction is based on relative order of magnitude (of grades). Rank in class also would certainly qualify as ordinal data, as might letter grades unless linked directly to number correct on tests with equal intervals between numbers. An interval scale of measurement is usually associated with performance measures (i.e., class examinations) related to knowledge of the content of lectures and readings. We say this because we do not believe that a "zero" on a class quiz always indicates that a student knows absolutely nothing about the material. Grade point average appears to satisfy the requirements of a ratio scale, but we must keep in mind that the underlying letter grade may be ordinal at best. Certainly, number of credits earned toward graduation constitutes a ratio level of measurement.

13. The statistic is the average score from the sample of local 3rd graders; the parameter is the average of the population of 3rd graders obtained from nationwide testing.

15. A random sample is defined by the procedure and not the outcome. A random sample is guaranteed if every element has an equal chance of being selected on any given draw. Most of the time the outcome will be representative, but it is not guaranteed to be.

17. A sampling procedure can be biased if (a) a sampling procedure based on convenience is used, (b) the wrong population is sampled, (c) not all the data from a random sample are obtained.

19. We typically must live with a degree of uncertainty about our research findings because we usually work with data from samples and not with the data we are really interested in (i.e., from the population). Characteristics of samples will vary from sample to sample, and thus we are left with some degree of uncertainty about the exact relationship between the characteristics of our sample and the features of the population that we are interested in.

 Go to http://psychology.wadsworth.com/courses/statistics/ and test your knowledge of this chapter by taking the online quiz. Another resource to check is the online workshops that provide a step-by-step guide through a number of topics at http://psychology.wadsworth.com/workshops/workshops.html.

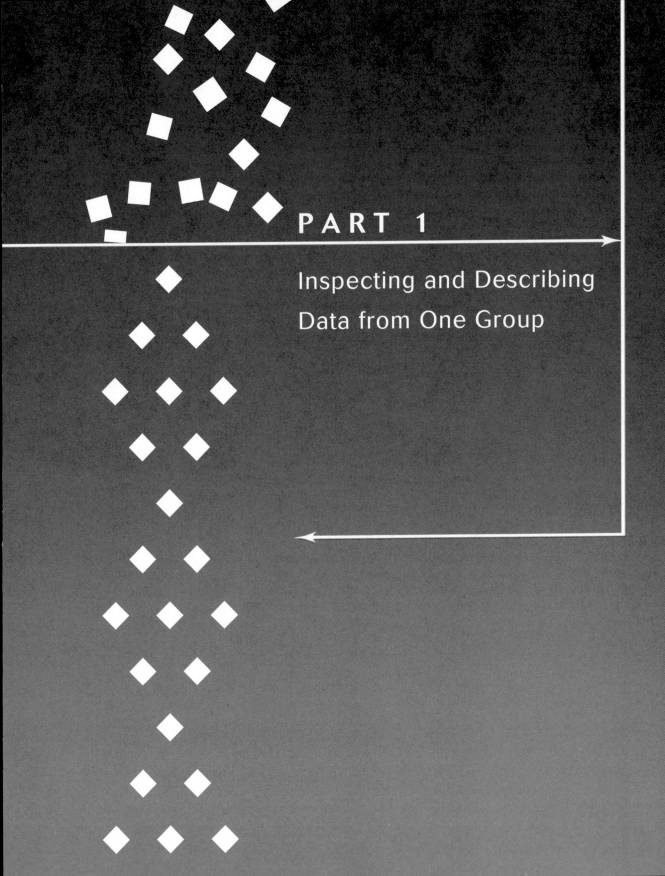

PART 1

Inspecting and Describing
Data from One Group

CHAPTER 2

Inspecting Data Point by Point

. . . . *Rule 1 in the analysis of data is "look at the data"*
Good (1983, p.138).

INTRODUCTION

Once data are collected, it is tempting to hurry to find trends and patterns in a data set without checking whether there are any problems that could distort or hide the findings. But looking carefully at the data is always wise. This is why the first step in the I-D-E-A model is inspection. Following are several situations in which the value of inspecting the data is particularly apparent. You will notice (if not now at least by the end of the chapter) that there is a warning bell in each of these situations that signals the researcher that the data may have a problem or two.

- Sheila measured how long it took 20 children to complete a simple wooden puzzle. Most of the 4-year-old children completed the puzzle in less than 15 sec.; however, two worked on the puzzle for about 3 min. before finishing. She wondered if these long times would affect her analyses.

- For her honors project, Latoya surveyed 215 students using a 200-item attitude test. When she mentioned to her friends how long it would take to make a computer file of her data, several of them volunteered to help. They seemed to have a good time, and the file was completed much more quickly than if she had done it herself. Yet, she worried about the accuracy of their work.

- Four fraternities agreed to complete questionnaires for Professor Chan. Each house agreed by majority vote that all the brothers would complete the materials, and each house would receive $1,000 from the professor's grant. A couple members from Zeta Omega complained to their president. He told them that they had better go along with the agreement because "we really need the money." These displeased members did complete the surveys along with the other members, but Prof. Chan sensed that some members seemed to be angry. As he gathered the materials at the end of the session, he wondered whether he could trust the answers of those members.

The first step in data analysis is data inspection. Checking on the quality of the data itself comes first; this chapter could be subtitled "Looking Before You Leap." Data interpretation will be more accurate if we devote time to becoming very familiar with the data. Some writers call this process *making friends* with your data (Hoaglin, Mosteller, & Tukey, 1991). We call these efforts *inspecting* the data, the "I" in the I-D-E-A model of data analysis. This step is not emphasized in many statistics textbooks, but it is the essential first step in analysis. The present chapter focuses on examining one variable, data point by data point. The next chapter emphasizes inspecting the overall distribution of a variable. In later chapters, additional approaches to inspection will be addressed.

In each of the three preceding hypothetical situations, the researchers sensed that there might be something about the data they gathered or the way in which it was handled that could create problems. It would be especially wise for these researchers to inspect their data before continuing because they each had hints that something might be wrong. But, even when there are no obvious danger signals, it is crucial to inspect data. Carefully considering how to inspect data for possible errors and to identify data points that would misrepresent the population will serve you well anytime that you are asked to use data to test the validity of an idea or to inform a practical decision.

CLEANING DATA

Data errors can occur in many ways. Even when preparing the data for inspection, one should be alert for problems. The actual data sheets (forms or pages) should be carefully examined. It is rare but not unknown for people to indicate their displeasure with being asked to complete a survey by selecting answers randomly; the most blatant may express their dissatisfaction by making designs on standard, fill-in-the-bubble answer sheets. If there is good reason to believe that respondents are not taking data collection seriously, it may be wise to discard data from those respondents. At times, some research participants fail to understand the directions in an experiment; their data should be discarded as well. It is important to emphasize that data are not discarded on the basis of whether the answers match our expectations. It is simply wrong to discard some data so that the findings make more sense to us, even if good reasons can be developed supporting that decision. The correct and ethical approach is to inspect the data as the first step in all analyses and to remove those data points that are obviously inappropriate.

Perhaps Professor Chan's fraternity sample includes a few members who have only gone through the motions to fulfill the chapter's commitment to provide data. If the surveys are completed anonymously, these dissatisfied individuals might be tempted to answer in rather silly ways or to answer without reading the items. But what might reveal that a person was uncooperative? Imagine an attitude survey given to students in a statistics class with items such as the following:

Statistics class is the most enjoyable class I have this term.

1	2	3	4
Strongly Disagree	Disagree	Agree	Strongly Agree

A few participants may create patterns on standard answer sheets, selecting option 1, then 2, then 3, then 4, then 3, then 2, and so on. Less rarely, participants will select the same answer for all items. This is a behavior that one can most easily detect by looking at the data sheets themselves; once entered in a computer file, such patterns are very hard to notice.

More often, when answering a questionnaire, participants get a little lazy or hurried and do not clearly mark their surveys. For example, instead of clearly circling 4 (on a 4-point scale), they might place a big circle that covers 3 and 4. Or, they might have made a vertical line between 3 and 4. Some people do this because they cannot decide between the two choices. Because only 1, 2, 3, and 4 are valid answers, we do not want to enter 3.5 for some people. We can deal with such problems in several possible ways. First, we can discard that item for that person. (It is treated as if the item had been omitted.) Or we could alternate between entering the left or the right value. What is most crucial is that we apply the convention we've selected with absolute consistency. It is wrong, of course, to choose the alternative on the basis of whether the value supports the hypothesis of the research. If there are relatively few such data points, the overall findings will not be affected by alternating between left and right answers.

Researchers using self-report surveys sometimes insert items that all participants are expected to answer in a particular way. No normal person paying attention to the survey will endorse such items as "I rarely breathe during weekends" or "I make all my own clothes." Sometimes a person marks down an unusual answer in error, but several such impossible answers mean that the respondent is not paying attention to the content of a questionnaire or to what a test item requires. Given this evidence, it may be best to exclude that person's data.

Once the data have been cleaned, the data are usually entered into a computer file. Perhaps it goes without saying, but considerable care must be devoted to catch errors that are made in transferring data from questionnaires and recording sheets to computer files.

HOW TO SPOT SUSPICIOUS DATA POINTS

Once we have verified that the data have been entered into our computer file correctly, we look for data points that are markedly different from the bulk of the data set, errors, and data that just don't "fit." What exactly are we looking for?

Klinkers

First, we are looking for what Abelson (1995, p. 68) called *klinkers,* "defective observations" that are caused by failures of recording equipment; respondents who clearly misperceive, misunderstand, or misrespond; or experimenters who fail to follow the experimental procedure. **Klinkers,** in other words, are errors or invalid data points. If a keyboard fails to record all the responses, or if some surveys were assembled in an incorrect order, there will be errors in the data set. Some klinkers might be detected as we examine the data sheets prior to entering the data into a computer file. The person entering the data into the computer may also introduce klinkers. One might misread a response or type the code incorrectly. Careful inspection of the data file is required to spot these problems.

Missing Data

Another serious problem for data analysis is caused by **missing data.** It is not unusual for some data points to be missing. A respondent may mistakenly skip an item; a research assistant may not record a participant's response; an answer may be illegible, obscured by a coffee spill, lost after a paper tear, and so on. Consequently, there may be no option but to code a data point as missing.

Dealing with missing data can be a little tricky. One option (the radical option) is to discard all data from someone who omitted any response. We seldom need to do that. The other option is simply to enter a code into the data file to indicate that the research participant did not supply an answer. With many computer programs, a dot (or period) can be entered for missing data. If data for variables are missing, all analyses involving those variables will be conducted without the participants who skipped those items. If the last answer is missing from a standard, fill-in-the-bubble answer sheet, it is possible that all the answers are invalid because the participant is off one item.

Note that, if a variable consists of answers to test questions that are scored right or wrong, missing values would be listed as wrong, just as teachers do for class tests. If the variables are self-descriptions or attitude measures, we usually can tolerate a few missing data points. At some point, however, the proportion of missing items will prompt one to discard all of the data for a participant. We know of no rule about what proportion dictates doing this. Perhaps we can suggest that it would be appropriate to discard the data from a participant when 10% of the items from a questionnaire are missing. On the other hand, the loss of data from a key variable might mean that the participant's data must be discarded.

A particular problem occurs if one had intended to combine a number of individual variables into a single index. Imagine having 10 items that each deal with a political position.

Typically, the researcher would combine the 10 items into an attitude scale showing how favorable people are toward, say, space exploration. If that is what you are doing, we suggest that you check with some books dealing in detail with attitude surveys (see, for example, Babbie, 1989); a number of options are available, but they are more complicated than simply coding an item as missing.

One should discard data that appear to be klinkers and code missing data appropriately. However, careful researchers make notes about all decisions so that they can explain how these data points were dealt with and why the decision was appropriate. Sometimes, however, some data points may well reflect the feelings or behaviors of the respondent accurately that, nevertheless, ought to be discarded also; we call them *outliers*.

Outliers

Some people provide data that are indeed quite different from what others provide. If asked to make estimates of a particular target value, for example, some people will make estimates that are very different from those of others. As a class exercise, undergraduates were divided into two groups. Each student estimated within 5 sec. the answer to one of two multiplication problems. The problems were (a) $1 \times 2 \times 3 \times 4 \times 5 \times 6 \times 7 \times 8 \times 9$, or (b) $9 \times 8 \times 7 \times 6 \times 5 \times 4 \times 3 \times 2 \times 1$. Note that the problems are really the same and have identical answers. However, when asked to make a decision quickly, people are often influenced by the way in which a problem is presented (see Kahneman, Slovic, & Tversky, 1982).

Table 2.1 contains the students' estimates. Note that many of the students in the "$9 \times 8 \times 7 \ldots$" group gave larger answers than those in the "$1 \times 2 \times 3 \ldots$" group. It is also clear that one answer in each column is very different from all the others. These answers are bigger—way bigger—than any of the other answers. Such unusual data points are called **outliers.** The students who made those estimates may have felt that they were giving plausible answers. Regardless of the intent of the respondent, outliers present problems for analysis and are usually removed before analyses continue. Later in this text, we will suggest some mathematical ways to identify outliers and show how outliers affect our statistical analyses. (Note that the term is not *outliar* as some students have thought.)

Outliers often occur when a variable has no fixed maximum value. Unlike a class exam that has, say, 50 questions (making 50 the highest score possible), the estimates in Table 2.1 were not limited by the measurement procedure. Other variables have no set maximum as well. Imagine for a moment that an experimental psychologist is studying the effect of a hormone on learning speed. White rats are given the hormone or a placebo and trained to escape from a maze to a food dish. The dependent variable is the time to find the food dish. Time is a variable that has no end—well, at least no end relative to the length of time to conduct an experiment. If normally intelligent rats find the end of the maze and the food within 30 sec. or less, a particularly dull rat who took 10 min. and 22 sec. (a total of 622 sec.) to finally stumble onto the food dish would distort the average for his or her group. Scrupulously including the 622 sec. with all the 12, 15, and 17 sec. times would so affect the average time (that is, adding up all the times and dividing the total by the number of rats) that comparisons of the two groups are no longer interpretable. The 622 sec. is an outlier, being so far outside of the distribution of scores that we can conclude only that the rat that produced it was so unusual that its score should not be used. For instance, some children will similarly take much longer to complete a puzzle than the majority of a sample, as Sheila observed in the example given in the introduction to this chapter.

TABLE 2.1 ■ Estimates for the Answer to a Multiplication Problem Presented in Two Ways

$1 \times 2 \times 3 \times 4 \times 5 \times 6 \times 7 \times 8 \times 9 =$	$9 \times 8 \times 7 \times 6 \times 5 \times 4 \times 3 \times 2 \times 1 =$
81	124
100	150
100	190
130	200
172	250
256	350
306	500
1,200	987
3,645	1,250
4,125	2,898
5,500	6,761
8,000,000	10,000
	560,000,000

Note: The correct answer is 362,880.

YOUR TURN 2-1 Think about your habits and life style. On what variables might you be an outlier compared to your classmates? To get you thinking, how far is your home from campus? What are the ages of your parents? How many pets have you had? How many pairs of shoes, CDs, Beanie Babies, telephones, etc., do you own? How many letters does your name have? If you think about it, you ought to find a couple of ways, perhaps trivial ways, in which you are an outliner. ■

Discarding data makes ethical investigators uneasy. If the 622 had been from a member of the control (placebo) group, which is the group that is expected on the average to take longer to get through the maze, retaining the 622 time would serve to make the hormone group look like the quicker learners, supporting the hypothesis. If, on the other hand, the 622 had been from the hormone group, it could make the hormone look detrimental to learning. Discarding data without adequate justification is a serious breach of ethics.

To avoid the appearance of bias in discarding outliers, some writers suggest routinely discarding the largest and the smallest values in a data set (Rosnow & Rosenthal, 1999). In a small data set such as Table 2.1, only the single highest and single lowest values in each condition would be discarded. In larger samples, the largest and smallest 5% of scores might be discarded. In this way, outliers are discarded in a systematic way without appearing arbitrary.

A HYPOTHETICAL SET OF DATA

As you go through this text, our hope is that you will become eager to look at numbers, searching for interesting or distressing patterns. The only way to learn to swim or ride a bicycle is to try (and, perhaps, try, try again); similarly, the only way to become comfortable with statistical analyses is through experience. Beginning in this chapter, you are going to see many sets of data. Some are hypothetical, and some represent real people or events, but all have been chosen to illustrate the points we are making. Just as you would not expect to learn philosophy if you skipped every other page in a philosophy textbook, you should not expect to learn statistics if you skip over the tables, graphs, and equations in this book. We will always point out the important features of tables, graphs, and equations, but it is essential to examine the tables and graphs for yourself and to relate the words to equations and other statistical indices. Working with equations will go a long way toward your remembering and understanding them.

A number of techniques are available for use in data inspection, and it will be easier to understand these approaches with illustrative data. Imagine that you are working as an intern for a community group in a poor community, perhaps in the center of a city or in a rural setting. Suppose that the director of the agency learned of a federal program to help new parents with young children. The director (your boss) decided that the agency would apply for a $500,000 grant to develop a parent education program. To prepare the proposal, it is necessary to describe the population of the community to show that a portion of its residents has sufficient unmet needs to qualify for service under this federal program. A survey of people in need of the supported services is to provide part of the data in the proposal, and the proposal would present a plan for meeting these needs. (We will not be discussing how to plan services; that's for other courses.) The Department of Education awards committee must be convinced that the people served by your agency definitely need assistance. (The committee members must be convinced that your agency can effectively serve the population also, but that's another issue.)

As we discussed in Chapter 1, the sample should be representative of those in your community who would benefit from the federal program. You also learned that we seek a representative sample by sampling randomly. Suppose that the agency randomly selects and surveys 100 parents of young children in the community to demonstrate need for the program. Undoubtedly, many characteristics of the mothers would be measured, but, for our purposes, five variables illustrate our points. The planning group believed that information about the following variables would be important to know:

- the mothers' ages
- years of schooling completed
- the number of children in the family
- racial/ethnic background
- scores on the Parenting Skills and Attitudes Survey (PSAS)

The scores on the PSAS could vary from 0 to 75. Let's assume that this instrument had been used previously with groups of skilled and successful mothers. The typical parent in these groups scored between 50 and 62. Consequently, a score below 50 suggests that a respondent is lacking some skills that successful parents have.

Table 2.2 contains the ID numbers and the data that are part of the information gathered from the survey. The response forms were examined to look for obvious problems and missing data. Table 2.2 contains two kinds of variables: *continuous* and *discrete*. The

TABLE 2.2 ■ Hypothetical Data for a Survey of Mothers Prior to Inspection

ID	Age	No. of children	Parenting Test	Yr of education	ID	Age	No. of children	Parenting Test	Yr of education
1	23	2	21	6	51	18	1	21	12
2	25	1	40	11	52	26	3	52	14
3	25	2	47	10	53	22	2	32	12
4	26	2	51	14	54	30	2	23	11
5	24	3	16	12	55	18	1	29	13
6	20	1	28	12	56	32	1	35	9
7	21	1	24	9	57	27	2	24	11
8	20	2	38	8	58	31	1	32	7
9	27	0	36	12	59	23	1	39	9
10	22	1	33	9	60	23	1	24	11
11	20	1	0	10	61	28	2	36	9
12	20	2	38	11	62	22	1	28	7
13	17	1	30	16	63	19	1	48	14
14	20	1	29	9	64	20	1	40	9
15	19	2	10	12	65	18	2	11	10
16	19	9	21	10	66	24	1	34	13
17	20	2	16	9	67	22	1	37	8
18	30	3	85	14	68	18	2	39	14
19	17	1	37	15	69	30	1	46	10
20	29	2	23	11	70	23	1	27	10
21	20	2	19	9	71	19	1	22	11
22	18	1	25	12	72	28	1	35	7
23	54	1	40	11	73	15	1	18	9
24	22	1	27	6	74	25	1	29	8
25	25	1	26	12	75	19	1	19	14
26	22	2	33	12	76	26	2	32	12
27	30	4	31	8	77	24	1	26	12
28	29	3	35	12	78	28	2	23	14
29	19	1	36	12	79	25	1	31	10
30	25	1	21	7	80	21	2	14	8
31	26	1	44	9	81	22	1	20	12
32	29	3	46	12	82	20	1	23	12
33	28	2	34	8	83	29	3	43	11
34	17	1	38	9	84	18	1	28	7
35	18	1	9	13	85	22	1	26	12
36	22	2	22	14	86	27	2	41	15
37	29	1	17	8	87	21	1	28	14
38	24	1	18	9	88	16	2	25	12
39	17	2	31	8	89	31	1	36	13
40	19	2	28	10	90	28	1	21	7
41	22	1	31	9	91	26	1	23	6
42	28	1	34	12	92	20	2	26	10
43	16	2	41	12	93	20	1	43	11
44	21	2	38	7	94	23	1	36	10
45	16	1	18	13	95	20	1	30	10
46	18	1	9	9	96	24	1	25	13
47	21	1	33	12	97	25	2	44	10
48	19	1	33	11	98	24	1	27	12
49	23	1	23	9	99	18	1	29	14
50	18	1	8	11	100	23	2	31	14

mothers' age, years of education, and score on the PSAS are **continuous variables.** If a variable is continuous, we can imagine a value between any two values on the measurement instrument. Even though age has been recorded without decimal values, age is actually a continuum because we can imagine that someone could be over 23 but under 24 years of age. Likewise, even though scores on the PSAS can take on only 76 different values (i.e., 0 through 75), the agency intended to measure parenting skill, which is a continuum and not a variable that progresses in 75 steps from incompetence to perfection. We could imagine having a more detailed test with more items, leading to a greater number of possible values that would permit one to make finer distinctions among the skills of the parents who take the test; thus, score on the PSAS is a continuous variable.

In contrast to continuous variables, **discrete variables** cannot have certain values. Number of children is a discrete variable because the variable cannot have fractional values. We cannot imagine a third value between any two given values; for example, there is no intermediate point between one and two children. Unlike parenting skills, family size does grow in steps (one-child steps). This is why some people smile when they hear that the average woman in North America has 1.9 children (Potts, 2000). Where are those homes with 1.9 kids running around?

List some continuous variables that describe you. Now list some discrete variables. Discrete variables might initially seem harder to think of; here are two: How many people form your family? How many CDs do you have? Think of some more. ■

TABLE 2.3 ■ Techniques Used to Organize Data from One Variable Prior to Inspection

Technique	When Used	Scale	Examples
Place values in order of their magnitude	With any quantitative variable	Ordinal, interval, or ratio	Judgments of brightness of lights, ages, grades test scores
Stem-and-leaf	For any variable when the original values of the scores are to be retained in the table; works best when data are in 2 or 3 digits. With more than 3 digits, it is often not possible to extract the original values of the data points.	Interval or ratio	Age, grades, scores on personality tests, test scores
Simple frequency distribution table	With variables that have only 20 or fewer values	Nominal, ordinal, interval, or ratio	Diagnoses, age, years of education of employees
Grouped frequency distribution table	With variables that have many different values	Interval or ratio	IQ scores, test scores, age of citizens of a town

USING TABULAR INSPECTION METHODS

Spotting errors and outliers is facilitated by ordering the data and by using tables and graphs. It is inefficient to look through each line of data when tabular and graphical methods can easily show us the odd data points that we need to recheck, correct, or even discard. Table 2.3 describes some common techniques for organizing data using tabular methods. These techniques will be more fully defined and illustrated in what follows. Keep in mind that data inspection, like all of statistical analyses, requires making choices. There is often more than one way to correctly conduct an analysis (and even more ways to do it incorrectly). You must choose which method of organizing your data is best for the purposes of your analysis.

What might you think is the simplest way that one could start inspecting the values of a variable? As you probably would guess, the simplest thing to do is to arrange the values from lowest to highest. This can be done by placing the lowest value at the top of a page and progressing to the highest at the bottom. One can order values by hand, but, with large sets of numbers, it is recommended that data be entered into a computer file. A computer will order the numbers with a couple clicks of a mouse. The scores on the PSAS have been reordered this way in Table 2.4. Note that you immediately have a better sense

TABLE 2.4   ■   PSAS Scores Ordered from Low to High

0	21	25	30	35	40
8	21	26	30	35	40
9	21	26	31	35	41
9	21	26	31	36	41
10	22	26	31	36	43
11	22	27	31	36	43
14	23	27	31	36	44
16	23	27	32	36	44
16	23	28	32	37	46
17	23	28	32	37	46
18	23	28	33	38	47
18	23	28	33	38	48
18	24	28	33	38	51
19	24	29	33	38	52
19	24	29	34	39	85
20	25	29	34	39	
21	25	29	34	40	

of the distribution of the scores; you can get a sense of the highest, the lowest, and the middle scores. And, you can see that the values of nearly all the scores of this sample are markedly lower than the 50–62 range, which was said to be typical of parents thought to have good parenting skills. Note that, at the inspection stage, we begin to learn about our research findings.

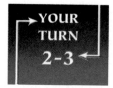

YOUR TURN 2-3

Here are the 1998 murder rates per 1,000,000 people for the 13 states that were the original 13 colonies: CN, 41; DE, 28; GA, 81; MA, 20; MD, 100; NH, 15; NJ, 49; NY, 51; NC, 81; PA, 53; RI, 24; SC, 80; and VA, 62. Place these rates in order. What do the data tell you? ■

Stem-and-Leaf Display (Plot)

Although placing the scores in order is one way to obtain information about a data set, it is only a preliminary step in inspection because we can represent the scores in ways that are far more compact and easier to use. Figure 2.1 is a stem-and-leaf display of the scores on the PSAS. A **stem-and-leaf display** or **plot** permits examining all the values of a variable in a manner that provides information on the group as a whole, but yet permits one to see all the original data points as well. It is very easy to construct a stem-and-leaf plot either by hand or with a computer.

First, imagine values as split into two parts. One part (the leading digit or digits) becomes the stem, and the other part (the trailing digit) is the leaf. Because PSAS scores are in two digits, we split each number into the tens' digit and the ones' digit. For example, we can think of the PSAS score values of 24 and 52 as shown in the following:

Value	Split	Stem	and	Leaf
24	→ 2 4 →	2	and	4
52	→ 5 2 →	5	and	2

Data values with the same stem are plotted on the same line with each leaf entered to the right. In Figure 2.1, the tens' digits of the PSAS scores are written down a column (a branch, if you will) that supports the stems. The units' digit of each score is written to the right of the stem, forming the leaves. (The number of leaves for each value in the stem is given on the left side of the figure.) For example, the score 24 is represented by a 2 identifying the stem and a 4 as a leaf. Note the three bold **4**s that indicate that three mothers had scores of

FIGURE 2.1 ■ Stem-and-leaf plot of the scores on the PSAs.

Frequency	Stem	Leaf
4	0	0899
11	1	01466788899
36	2	011111223333334**444**5556666777888889999
33	3	00111112223333444555666677888899
13	4	0001133446678
2	5	12
0	6	
0	7	
1	8	5

24 in our sample. (If scores were three digits long, such as 156, the stem would have two leading digits (15) and the leaf would have one trailing digit (6).)

As you can see from Figure 2.1, there were 36 scores between 20 and 29 and no scores between 60 and 79. More details about stem-and-leaf plots will be mentioned later; at this point, just note what the stem-and-leaf display tells us about the PSAS scores we obtained.

The stem-and-leaf display reveals two problems in the data. Did you notice them? First, there is a score of 85. The possible range of the test was given as 0 to 75. So, 85 is larger than possible. Suppose that a review of the interviewer's records shows that the score was 58; the person making the file transposed the digits. At the other end of the plot, we notice a 0. Although this is within the possible range, the next lowest scores are 8 and 9. The 0 just seems unlikely. Suppose that a check of the original forms shows that the interviewer noted that mother #11 was suddenly called away during the interview and did not take the PSAS. We need to correct the file so that the score for respondent #11 is coded as missing, not as 0. Notice, by the way, while we are looking at Figure 2.1, the bulk of the scores are in the 20s and 30s. Remember that the norm information from the test developer suggested that successful parents scored within the 50–62 range. The mothers tested tend to be lower than the range of successful parents, which is something we began to appreciate when we first ordered the data from lowest to highest.

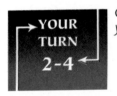

Construct a stem-and-leaf plot of the murder rates in the 13 states given in the preceding *Your Turn*. ■

How the data are entered into a stem-and-leaf display is quite flexible. In Figure 2.1, each stem represented 10 different possible values (viz., 20–29 or 30–39). However, it is not necessary to keep all scores in the 20s, 30s, and so forth, in one group; if scores were particularly closely bunched, we could, for example, place the 20s (and 30s, 40s, etc.) into two stems. Thus, the scores 20–29 would be divided as follows:

Frequency	Stem	Leaves
17	2*	01111122333333444
19	2·	5556666777888889999

The stems now cover only five different possible values; 2* stands for scores of 20 through 24 and 2· stands for scores of 25 through 29. The use of the asterisk and the dot are arbitrary: any symbols could be used. When the scores are bunched even more closely together than the PSAS scores are, a stem-and-leaf plot could split all the 20s into five groups: 20 and 21, 22 and 23, and so forth. Of course, each stem must include the same number of values. If we used stems of two values each, the section of the stem-and-leaf for scores of 20 through 29 would be as follows:

Frequency	Stem	Leaves
6	2*	011111
8	2 t	22333333
6	2 f	444555
7	2 s	6666777
9	2·	888889999

Perhaps you have decoded the symbols already: the *t* stands for twos and threes, the *f* for fours and fives, and the *s* for sixes and sevens.

The number of unique values represented by each stem of a stem-and-leaf plot determines the number of stems because, to be useful, each stem must include the same number of values. We would not use these more detailed presentations for the PSAS data in Figure 2.1 because that would have given us too many stems. If one used stems representing only two possible values each, the plot would have had to include 38 stems to cover 0 through 75, the possible range of scores. (To cover 76 values, we divide 76 by 2 to get the number of stems needed: 38.) This is far too many stems for 100 data points.

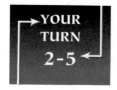

How many stems would we need to cover 76 values if it were planned that each stem should represent 5 values? ∎

Stem-and-leaf displays let us see the actual values of the data points. This feature is quite valuable when inspecting data. Any suspicious points can be spotted in a stem-and-leaf plot and reexamined for verification. No other data exploration technique has this feature.

The use of stem-and-leaf plots has some limitations though. When data are measured very precisely, it becomes harder to see the overall pattern of scores. Stem-and-leaf plots also become unwieldy when the values range widely and are given in many digits, such as 124.53°F through 283.66°F. If the values of the variable are that precise and yet have a large range, stem-and-leaf displays may be made by ignoring the digits to the right of the decimal point. The point of inspection is to find evidence of errors or outliers; inspection procedures will not normally detect errors in the third, fourth, or fifth digits of data points.

Frequency Distribution

Another tabular technique for inspecting data is a frequency distribution. A distinction is often made between simple (or ungrouped) frequency distributions and grouped frequency distributions. In a **simple (or ungrouped) frequency distribution,** the frequency of each value in the number set is identified. Table 2.5 is a simple frequency distribution table of the number of children of the mothers represented in Table 2.2. Because there were so few different values for the variable "number of children," it is both convenient and informative to give each value its own entry. In this frequency distribution, we can learn about the number of data points of each possible value just as we could in the stem-and-leaf display.

Note what we can learn from Table 2.5. We can see two suspicious data points. First, there is one mother listed as having nine children. Although nine children in a family is possible, it is very unusual in the USA, especially in recent decades. One would want to find the original data record and check to be sure that the nine is correct. Second, we note that one "mother" has zero children. Either this person is not a mother and should not be in this data set or a mistake has been made and we have found a klinker. Remember, one of the reasons for data inspection is to discover these problems before putting time into further data analyses that would need to be redone when findings suggest that there is something wrong with the data (or, worse, making decisions on the basis of inaccurate findings because we never spotted the problems in our data set).

TABLE 2.5   ■   Frequency Distribution of the Number of Children in the Families Sampled

Value	Frequency	Percentage
0 (No children)	1	1.0%*
1 (One child)	61	61.0%
2 (Two children)	30	30.0%
3 (Three children)	6	6.0%
4 (Four children)	1	1.0%
9 (Nine children)	1	1.0%
Total	100	100.0%

* Because the sample contains exactly 100 mothers, the percentages and the frequency columns are the same; that would not be true for most samples.

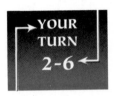
YOUR TURN 2-6

Comment on the pattern of the following scores that 20 students earned on an essay: 54, 98, 62, 86, 97, 70, 86, 96, 74, 72, 85, 78, 95, 94, 77, 94, 93, 75, 83, and 80. What tools would facilitate getting a sense of the distributions of the data?   ■

If there were many different values represented in a set of data, a simple frequency distribution table in which every value is listed (as in Table 2.5) would be very lengthy and, consequently, not very useful. For example, a table that listed the frequency of each individual PSAS value would be too long to work with. A general guide when organizing a data set might be as follows: when more than 20 different values are represented, intervals of values should be created before making a frequency distribution. When a frequency distribution is based on intervals rather than individual values, the table is called a grouped frequency distribution. Intervals are much like ranges or categories of scores used with stem-and-leaf displays; for example, 20–24 would be an interval. A **grouped frequency distribution** is similar to the left column of the stem-and-leaf display in Figure 2.1; it is simply the number of scores observed in each range of values, but without the information about the value of each individual data point. In statistical analyses, we lose detail as we summarize. Our job is to make it more possible to understand the data without losing essential information. In Figure 2.1, for example, we learned that the frequency of scores in the 40s was 13, but we no longer can tell what the exact scores were. When a grouped frequency distribution is constructed some conventions make the construction job easier and the frequency table easier to interpret.

Grouped frequency tables are constructed when there is a wide range of values to present in the graph. If the range of the original observations had been small, such as 10 or 12, one would seldom form groups, but use the simple (ungrouped) frequency distribution.

When faced with a large range the analyst faces three decisions:

1. Choosing the number of groups.
2. Setting the number of values in each interval.
3. Selecting the value that defines the lower end of the lowest interval.

Decisions 1 and 2

The first two decisions are interrelated; deciding one determines the other. Textbook authors differ somewhat in how many groups of scores are to be used. However, using fewer than five groups would lose too much information and using more than 20 seems overly detailed, making interpretation cumbersome. To get started, one uses a simple ordering of the data to find the largest and smallest values. The range gives us the number of different values of the variable that the table needs to include; subtract the smallest score from the largest score and add 1 to that difference. Note that the number of values to be included is not the number of participants whose data are to be included in the table.

Then, we divide the number of values to be included by 2, or 5, or 10, or a multiple of 10 depending on the size of the range. This step shows how many groups will be needed. If a class of premed students scored from 52 to 84 on a chemistry examination, 33 values would need to be included in a table ($84 - 52 + 1 = 33$). Tentatively, consider groups that include 10 different values (such as 50 through 59). Divide 33 by 10 (yielding 3.3). That means we would need four groups of 10 scores each to cover 52 through 84. Four is too few because four provides little detail. If we divide 33 by 5, we get 6.6, or seven groups. Seven would seem to be fine; there are to be seven groups each including five values.

Decision 3

Now we need to determine the ranges of scores to define the seven groups. It may seem reasonable to begin the first interval at the lowest observed test score (52), resulting in an interval that includes the values of 52 through 56. (Note, by the way, that an interval from 52 to 56 covers five different chemistry test values: 52, 53, 54, 55, and 56.)

There is a good reason why the lowest interval should not be 52–56: starting at 52 would create intervals that would be awkward to use. If one had started at 52, the intervals would have been 52 to 56, 57 to 61, . . . , 82 to 86. It is easier to interpret tables with intervals whose lower boundaries are multiples of 5. Values that are evenly divisible by 5 and lower than the lowest chemistry test score include 40, 45, and 50. Because the lowest test score is 52, we would begin the table at 50. If intervals are to include five values, the lowest interval would be 50 to 54. The other intervals would be 55–59, 60–64, 65–69, 70–74, 75–79, and 80–84. These groups of scores are called *intervals of width 5*. The interval boundaries (e.g., 50 and 54) are called *stated limits,* and stated limits are given in tables. The low boundaries are called the *lower stated limits,* and the high boundaries are called the *upper stated limits*. Note that the upper stated limit is not the lower stated limit plus the interval width ($50 + 5 = 55$). For this example, such an interval would include six possible scores: 50, 51, 52, 53, 54, and 55.

Because there can be intermediate values between any two values of continuous variables, one might wonder where a data point of 54.7 would go if it became possible to measure chemistry knowledge more precisely than only to whole numbers. The intervals not only have stated limits (such as 50 to 54), but also *real limits*. The real limits of the 50–54 interval are 49.5 and 54.5. By convention, the real limits of a number are defined as those points falling one-half a measurement unit above a number and one-half a unit below a number. For example, if whole numbers are used, then one-half a unit is .5; if numbers are expressed in tenths, then one-half a unit would be .05. Once one thinks about real limits, the interval into which to place a score of 54.7 is obvious.

BOX 2.1 ■ Summary of the Steps in Constructing a Grouped Frequency Distribution

1. **Find the Range.** Highest score minus lowest score plus 1 equals the range. This is the number of values that needs to be included in the distribution.

2. **Find the Interval Width.** Divide the range by 2, 5, or 10 until you have an answer that when rounded up to the next whole number (e.g., 4.2 becomes 5) is between 10 and 20. The number you divided by is the interval width.

3. **Find the Lower Stated Limit of the First Interval.** Find the smallest value in the data set. The largest number that is evenly divisible by the interval width and is smaller than the smallest value in the data set is the lowest stated limit of the distribution.

For the hypothetical chemistry examination, the intervals would be as follows:

Stated Limits	Real Limits	Interval Width
50–54	49.5–54.5	5
55–59	54.5–59.5	5
60–64	59.5–64.5	5
65–69	64.5–69.5	5
70–74	69.5–74.5	5
75–79	74.5–79.5	5
80–84	79.5–84.5	5

Because there are no test scores larger than 84 or smaller than 50, no other intervals would be listed in the table. The finished table would not include the real limits or the interval size. But it would include a column giving the numbers of students whose examination scores fell within each interval.

A major advantage of grouped frequency distributions is economy of presentation. Once researchers have completed the data-point-by-data-point inspection phase of research and no longer require the detail provided in stem-and-leaf plots, grouped frequency tables are concise ways of presenting findings. As Table 2.6 shows, the number of possible values in each interval should be a convenient number, such as 2, 5, or some multiple of 2 or 5. Grouped frequency distributions are easier to use if the boundaries of the intervals have convenient values as just shown. Table 2.6 is a grouped frequency distribution of PSAS scores following the conventions we recommend. Box 2.1 is a summary of the steps to use in making up a grouped frequency table.

The grouped frequency distribution in Table 2.6 still permits detecting the error on the high end of the scores, but the grouped frequency distribution does not reveal the exact value of the invalid high test score, 85. Furthermore, it would be easy to overlook the problem at

TABLE 2.6 ■ Grouped Frequency Distribution of the Scores on the PSAS

Interval	Frequency	Real Limits
0–9	4	−0.5–9.5*
10–19	11	9.5–19.5
20–29	36	19.5–29.5
30–39	33	29.5–39.5
40–49	13	39.5–49.5
50–59	2	49.5–59.5
60–69	0	59.5–69.5
70–79	0	69.5–79.5
80–89	1	79.5–89.5

* The lower real limit of −0.5 may be somewhat confusing. Zero is indeed the lowest possible score; however, PSAS is a variable with the qualities of an interval scale having no absolute zero point. Thus, the negative lowest real limit reflects the fact that a score of 0 simply means the lowest score on the scale, not zero parenting skill.

the low end of the range. The score of 0 is simply within the first interval, 0–9. That problem was easy to spot with the stem-and-leaf plot, but it's easy to miss in the grouped frequency distribution. Because the first step in inspection is an examination of data point by data point, it is very helpful initially to place the data points in order and to construct a stem-and-leaf plot. If the stem-and-leaf plot is done on a computer, ordering the data is not necessary because the data are ordered in the plot. After one can be sure that all suspicious individual data points have been verified or corrected, a frequency distribution can then be constructed.

YOUR TURN 2-7

Construct a grouped frequency distribution using the 20 paper grades you have placed in order (see *Your Turn* 2-6). Use intervals that include 10 scores each; make the highest interval 90 to 99. ■

WHAT YOU HAVE LEARNED AND THE NEXT STEP

Following the procedures in this chapter facilitates the beginning steps of data analysis. The central point is to first look at the data. As some have said, make friends with the data. By carefully inspecting data, we begin to learn what happened in the study. Major ways to inspect data points and important ideas covered in this chapter include the following:

● Examine the original data sheets for clues that participants did or did not take the research seriously.

● Remove data of uncooperative or confused participants.

- Identify and decide what to do with illegible or ambiguous notations.
- Decide how to treat missing data.
- Keep complete records of the decisions to delete data and the conventions used to deal with ambiguous notations.
- Order scores of a variable according to size (magnitude).
- Klinkers (invalid data points) and outliers (data points that are very discrepant from the rest of data points) can be detected from an inspection of ordered data as well as from tabular presentations.
- Stem-and-leaf plots reveal all the individual values of the data, permitting one to easily detect outliers and potential klinkers.
- When a variable is continuous we can imagine a value between any two values on the measurement instrument; in contrast, a discrete variable (e.g., number of children) cannot have certain values.
- A simple or ungrouped frequency distribution is an ordered list of all the unique data points from the smallest to the largest scores, accompanied by the frequency of each unique value.
- A grouped frequency distribution is an even more compact tabular presentation, but its compactness comes at a price because individual data points are no longer listed individually. Grouped frequency distributions are not often used as an initial description of the data.
- Tabular presentations can be used for both continuous and discrete variables; however, they are more critical with continuous variables that often have more unique values than do discrete variables.

The focus of the next chapter is on the distribution as a whole rather than the individual data points. Even when all the data points are correctly recorded, there can be problems with the distribution of the variable that could require correction or might mean that some analyses would be inappropriate. The next chapter shows how frequency distributions can be turned into graphs for more compact, visual presentations of the distribution of a variable.

Key Concepts

klinker	continuous variable	simple (ungrouped) frequency distribution
missing data	discrete variable	
outlier	stem-and-leaf display (plot)	grouped frequency distribution

Answers to *Your Turn* Questions

2-1. College professors probably own more books than most people do. But we don't know how you are an outlier. Note that, with respect to one group (e.g., your swim team), you might seem just average on some variables (e.g., number of hours spent in the water per week), but with respect to some other group (e.g., your chess club), you would be an outlier on those same variables.

2-2. Continuous variables: height, weight, degree in favor of a tax cut, et cetera. Discrete variables: number of parking tickets last year, number of intramural teams you are on, number of credit hours completed.

2-3. Southern states (GA, MD, NC, SC, and VA) were higher than middle states (DE, NJ, NY, and PA) or northern states (CN, MA, NH, and RI).

2-4.

Frequency	**Stem**	**Leaf**
1	1	5
3	2	048
0	3	
2	4	19
2	5	13
1	6	2
0	7	
3	8	011
0	9	
1	10	0

2-5. 16 stems (76 values divided by 5 is 15.2, which would require 16 stems).

2-6. You should place the numbers in order, and you should then notice that they are clustered toward high numbers. Constructing a simple frequency distribution or a stem-and-leaf plot would make this very clear.

2-7. Simply ordering the scores would help. A stem-and-leaf plot would show the traditional breakdown of letter grades if the scores were percentage values. More students were clustered in the highest level than in the lowest levels.

50–59	1
60–69	1
70–79	6
80–89	5
90–99	7

Analyzing and Interpreting Data: Problems and Exercises

1. What is data "cleaning"?

2. Define and distinguish between "klinkers" and "outliers."

3. Describe some ways in which invalid data points (i.e., klinkers) could be produced by an unhappy or uncooperative person completing a survey.

4. Although some klinkers initially may appear to be outliers, not all outliers are klinkers. Explain.

5. Suppose that you were conducting interviews with shoppers at a mall. You ask a sample of shoppers the following questions: What is the size of your household? How often does someone in the household shop for clothes? How much money does your family spend on clothes each month? In addition, you estimate the respondent's approximate age and sex. Identify at least three ways in which a klinker (invalid data point) might appear in your data.

6. What is one method that researchers sometimes consider as they plan their study to help detect respondents who are not paying attention to questionnaire or test items?

7. What are two strategies to use when respondents provide responses with decimals when only whole numbers were requested (e.g., responding 3.5 when valid scale responses are 1, 2, 3, or 4)?

8. What is often the first, and perhaps simplest, way to begin data inspection?

9. What should a researcher do when data points are missing?

10. Consider the following data set showing 26 students' scores (percentage correct) on a class exam: 70, 92, 93, 94, 76, 84, 44, 68, 71, 72, 87, 86, 95, 95, 94, 75, 84, 91, 98, 91, 81, 85, 85, 94, 96, and 86.

   a) Prepare a stem-and-leaf display of these data.

   b) Is there evidence of an outlier?

11. a) Suppose that Agnes randomly selects 20 students from the sophomore class and weighs them. If one of them weighs 375 lbs., may she report that 5% (i.e., 100 times 1/20) of the sophomore class weighs more than 350 lbs.?

   b) Suppose that the admissions director needs to report applicant SAT scores to the college president, but the director does not have time to do a careful study. Suppose that, to save time, he randomly selects 15 applications to learn what the SAT scores are for applicants to his college. If one applicant had an SAT verbal score of 780, is it fair for the director to report that nearly 7% (i.e., 100 times 1/15) of applicants to the college have SAT verbal scores greater than 760? Would you change your answer if you knew that the range of SAT scores for the other 14 applicants in the sample was 360 to 580?

12. What are the usual conventions for creating intervals for a grouped frequency distribution?

13. It is important to identify real limits when constructing intervals for a grouped frequency distribution using a continuous variable; real limits are not appropriate when the variable is discrete. Explain.

14. Use the data set from question 10 to answer these two questions. (a) Prepare a grouped frequency distribution identifying the interval width and the stated and real limits of each interval. (b) What information is "lost" in a grouped frequency distribution that is available in a simple frequency distribution as well as a stem-and-leaf display?

15. Prepare a stem-and-leaf display for the scores obtained from college students who were asked to report the number of alcoholic drinks they had during a week: 5, 3, 0, 1, 12, 5, 8, 2, 0, 15, 9, 10, 20, 2, 3, 15, 8, 6, 9, 13, 4, 0, 1, 6, 11, 12, 4, 2, 1, 3, 0, 4, 7, 6, 8, 10, 18, 2, 7, 6, 8, 0, 4, 10, 12, 13, 22, 4, 5, and 12.

16. Create a grouped frequency distribution for the data in problem #15. Use an interval width of 2.

17. Suppose that two research assistants for a large research project handle missing data differently. Assistant A did not use any data from participants who did not provide data for any single item (e.g., if Mary did not report her age, all of Mary's data would be discarded). Assistant B, on the other hand, entered a "dot" to indicate missing data and entered all the other data from every participant. What problem might be caused by this difference in handling missing data?

18. Imagine that a smiling research participant hands you a standard, multiple-selection answer sheet saying, "It took some effort, but I found the answer pattern you put into your survey." As he turns and walks out of the room, what should you do with his answer sheet?

19. Suppose that a stem-and-leaf display has been constructed, but additional data become available. (a) Explain why the additional data might not require adding stems to the display. (b) Explain why adding the additional data to the display might require more stems. (c) Is it possible that fewer stems would be required?

20. (a) Define a simple frequency distribution. (b) What determines the number of rows in a simple frequency distribution?

Answers to Odd-Numbered Questions

1. Analysis begins with a careful inspection of the data. One looks for outliers and klinkers.

3. People have been known to concoct impossible data, to misunderstand questions and to answer questions without reading them, and to answer randomly rather than using the rating scale provided.

5. Klinkers might occur if (a) a shopper decides to impress the interviewer by claiming to spend much more than his/her family indeed spends, (b) the person interviewed does not know the answer but gives an answer anyway, (c) the interviewer makes an error in estimating the person's age, (d) the interviewer might note down an incorrect value in the confusion of the mall.

7. One strategy is to drop that data point from the record and make a written record why this data point is now missing; a more common strategy when a scale is used is to record alternately the higher and lower values when encountering fractional responses. This decision, too, should be noted for later explanation of the data.

9. When assuming many possible items and only one data point, or at most a few data points, are missing, a researcher may simply code the response as missing and then conduct analyses without these data points. However, a written record should be made of the exact data points that are missing so that variations in data totals may be explained later. Care must be taken so that a missing data point is not treated as a "wrong" response to a test. Also, if several responses are being

summed to produce an index of some sort, missing data can create serious problems and other strategies may have to be considered. When many data points are missing (e.g., more than 10%) from a respondent, a researcher should consider dropping all of the respondent's data from the data record. Of course, a written record should be made of this decision to explain later why a respondent's data were dropped.

11. (a) Agnes had found an outlier. It would be incorrect for her to conclude that 5% of the students in her college weigh that much.

(b) One should be very cautious before proceeding. Ordering the 15 data points would tell you whether the 780 was an outlier or not. If you found that the other 14 students had scores ranging from 360 to 580, you would conclude that the 780 was an outlier and the director should not make the claim.

13. Real limits are important to describe the continuous nature of a variable. Just because we record height or weight, for example, using whole numbers does not mean that finer gradations of these variables are not possible. The real limits show that the variable is considered to be continuous and that, if finer measurements were made, where these responses would fall in the distribution. When constructing a frequency distribution using discrete variables, there is no need to define real limits because no finer discrimination is possible.

15.

Frequency	Stem	Leaf
20	0 *	00000111222233344444
15	0 .	555666677888899
10	1 *	0001222233
3	1 .	558
1	2 *	02

17. These two different strategies should not be mixed in a single study. If a respondent is rejected for even one missing answer, the sample will be different from that used by a researcher who uses more of the data. It is critical to be able to describe how missing data were handled; if two strategies were in use, it is impossible to do this.

19. The number of stems is determined by how fine the scores are subdivided. If the additional data include values that were already represented in the smaller sample, then a new stem-and-leaf plot might contain the same number of stems even though the sample is larger. However, with a larger sample size one might decide to include fewer different values in each stem. For example, instead of placing scores of 10 through 19 in one stem, one might use two stems (e.g., one for 10 through 14, and one for 15 through 19). In that case, the number of stems would increase with a larger sample size. The number of stems cannot decrease as sample size increases.

 Go to http://psychology.wadsworth.com/courses/statistics/ and test your knowledge of this chapter by taking the online quiz. Another resource to check is the online workshops that provide a step-by-step guide through a number of topics at http://psychology.wadsworth.com/workshops/workshops.html.

CHAPTER 3

Inspecting Distributions of Data

If "a picture is worth a thousand words," surely a graph is worth a couple hundred numbers.

Posavac, (2000)

INTRODUCTION

Once a data set has been inspected point by point, it is helpful to inspect the entire distribution by drawing a graph. The best graphs are informative without confusing readers with unnecessary detail. Here are two situations that would require a careful look at the distribution as a whole.

- Jim made a computer file of the reaction times of 317 junior high students. He had intended to analyze the data after he had completed his statistics course. His adviser asked him how the students did, but all Jim could say was, "Some of them are really quick." He wanted to tell his adviser something more meaningful than that, but he did not know what to say, so he handed his adviser a list of the 317 reaction times listed in order from longest to shortest. His adviser looked puzzled. "Can't you summarize these reaction times?" his adviser asked.

- As part of her work-study job with the registrar of her college, Maura was asked to develop a presentation on the size of the classes in the college. After checking on the accuracy of the data that she was given and verifying that she did not add any klinkers when she made the data file, she intended to summarize the data in an economical fashion. When she showed a stem-and-leaf plot to the chair of one of the departments, Maura was asked, "What are all these numbers? This doesn't look like any kind of graph that I have seen before."

Inspecting distributions with stem-and-leaf plots is particularly helpful when searching for outliers and klinkers (errors introduced during data compilation); however, stem-and-leaf plots are not commonly presented in reports or used to show others how a variable is distributed. Although frequency tables are sometimes used, graphs are even more likely to be used. Table 3.1 identifies several common techniques for displaying data using graphs. We will

TABLE 3.1 ■ Common Graphical Techniques Used to Organize Data

Technique	When Used	Scale	Examples
Histogram	With continuous variables that have many different values. Histograms are not needed when a sample includes only a few different values.	Interval or ratio	SAT scores, age, weight, height, time to complete a task
Frequency Polygon	Whenever a grouped frequency distribution or histogram is appropriate, but a line graph is preferred rather than the columns of a histogram.	Interval or ratio	SAT scores, age, weight, height, time to complete a task
Bar Graph	Best when discrete variables can take on 20 or fewer values. If there are more than 20 values, it is often best to combine several values into groups when appropriate.	Nominal	Religious identification, racial background, college major

examine these techniques to show how to convey the shape of a distribution in a manner that is readily understood.

USING HISTOGRAMS TO INSPECT DISTRIBUTIONS

Histograms are graphical presentations of frequency distributions of continuous variables. The frequency (or number) of each score is plotted as a column rather than listed in a table. Figure 3.1 is a histogram of the heights (rounded to the nearest inch) of the male employees of a company. Note that the histogram is based on a simple, ungrouped frequency distribution. Each value of height between the highest and lowest values in the data is represented by a column. Notice how this histogram provides a way to get a sense of a distribution very quickly. Because height is a continuous variable, the graph is drawn without spaces between the columns. The x-axis is labeled with the values of the heights; however, because height was rounded to the nearest inch, we know that the employees represented by a particular column are not all exactly that tall. That is, the column labeled "66" really refers to all employees who are taller than 65.5 in. but shorter than 66.5 in. These values are the real limits of 66 as defined in Chapter 2, where we described the conventions in constructing grouped frequency distributions. (See Box 2.1.) Instead of giving the upper and lower real limits (that is, the values of the edges of the columns of a histogram), histograms provide on the x-axis the number midway between the real limits. It is called the **midpoint** of the interval. The midpoint is defined as halfway between the lower real limit and the upper real limit.

Figure 3.1 shows that there was at least one employee at every height between the shortest and the tallest employees in this company. Suppose that there had been no one at a particular height. If there had been no employees, let's say, 73 in. tall, the histogram should still contain a place for a column at 73. Of course, one would see only a space between 72.5 and 73.5, not a column. Because we prepare graphs to obtain a sense of the distribution, it would be misleading if the heights on the x-axis were to jump from 72 to 74. If there is just one gap in a histogram, there is no problem. However, if there were many gaps between the lowest and highest scores, the graph would have a scattered and disjointed appearance. It is not

FIGURE 3.1 ■ A histogram with the midpoints of the intervals given on the x-axis.

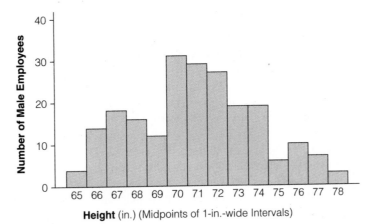

TABLE 3.2 ■ Grouped Frequency Distribution of Class Sizes

Frequency	Stated Limits	Real Limits	Interval Width	Midpoint
10	10–19	9.5–19.5	10	14.5
12	20–29	19.5–29.5	10	24.5
26	30–39	29.5–39.5	10	34.5
12	40–49	39.5–49.5	10	44.5
23	50–59	49.5–59.5	10	54.5
10	60–69	59.5–69.5	10	64.5
5	70–79	69.5–79.5	10	74.5
9	80–89	79.5–89.5	10	84.5
7	90–99	89.5–99.5	10	94.5
0	100–109	99.5–109.5	10	104.5
1	110–119	109.5–119.5	10	114.5
1	120–129	119.5–129.5	10	124.5
1	130–139	129.5–139.5	10	134.5
0	140–149	139.5–149.5	10	144.5
0	150–159	149.5–159.5	10	154.5
1	160–169	159.5–169.5	10	164.5

likely that there will be many gaps when the range of scores is small. In Figure 3.1, the range of heights (78 − 65 + 1, or 14) is small, so this frequency histogram works quite well. If there were a large range, a frequency histogram based on a simple frequency distribution may be hard to read because there will be many columns and perhaps many gaps.

Maura discovered this problem when she tried to prepare a frequency histogram for the class size data at her college. She found that class sizes ranged from 14 through 164 students. She realized that a frequency histogram of section enrollments using every value within the range in her data set would be hard to read because it would contain 151 columns (that is, a column for every value from 14 through 164). Furthermore, unlike Figure 3.1 in which there were many employees having the same height, only very few sections had the same number of students enrolled. Thus, most columns would represent just one section— hardly a very informative graph. There's a better way. Histograms can also be plotted for grouped frequency distributions. In this case, each column represents the number of sections (or, whatever is being studied) whose scores are within an interval.

Maura followed the suggestions in the previous chapter (Box 2.1) and used intervals of 10 units wide. An interval width of 10 resulted in 16 intervals, and her grouped frequency distribution is in Table 3.2. We have included the real limits and interval midpoints in this table so that you can become familiar with them; these are usually omitted when grouped frequency distributions are used in reports. Note that some of her intervals do not contain any sections.

Figure 3.2 is the histogram based on Table 3.2. The columns are centered around the midpoints of the intervals. For example, the second column represents the number of sections with 20 to 29 students. Although there cannot be any "half" students enrolled, the real limits of that interval are 19.5 to 29.5 with a midpoint of 24.5. For ease of interpretation, the column could be labeled with the stated limits of 20 to 29. Because Table 3.2 had several

FIGURE 3.2 ■ A histogram representing a grouped frequency distribution. The midpoints are given for every other interval.

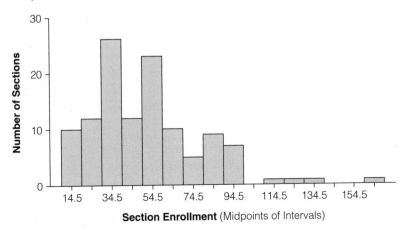

Section Enrollment (Midpoints of Intervals)

empty intervals, the histogram contains several gaps that correspond to these empty intervals. Keeping spaces for those intervals in the histogram even through they contain no class sections makes it clear that the distribution contains four rather large sections that are quite a bit bigger than the others.

Figure 3.3 is a grouped frequency histogram of the PSAS scores of the 100 mothers given in Table 2.7 of Chapter 2. The sides of adjacent columns touch each other because, when using continuous variables, the upper real limit of an interval is essentially equal to the lower real limit of the next higher interval. If you are provided with a histogram with only the midpoints of the columns labeled on the x-axis (as in Figure 3.3), the real limits of intervals can easily be calculated. To do so, one merely adds up the midpoints of two adjacent intervals and divides by 2. For example, the midpoint of the interval containing the most PSAS scores is 27. Its real upper limit is the sum of its midpoint (27) plus the midpoint of

FIGURE 3.3 ■ A frequency histogram of the PSAS scores for the mothers represented in Table 2.2, after the corrections to the file had been made.

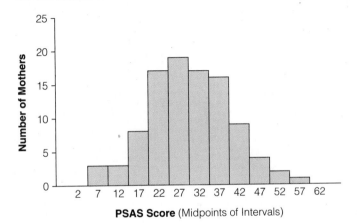

PSAS Score (Midpoints of Intervals)

the next higher interval (32), divided by 2, or (27 + 32)/2 is 29.5. The real lower limit of that interval is the sum of its midpoint (27) plus the midpoint of the next lowest interval (22), divided by 2, or (27 + 22)/2 is 24.5. Thus, the real limits of the interval including the most scores are 24.5 to 29.5.

YOUR TURN 3-1

Why do the midpoints of Maura's histogram in Figure 3.2 include fractions (viz. 24.5), but the midpoints of Figure 3.3 for the PSAS scores are whole numbers (viz. 22)? ■

Histograms are particularly important when examining the distribution as a whole; they provide a visual sense of the distribution of scores over the entire range of the variable. In later chapters, you will learn that many variables studied by behavioral scientists follow a predictable pattern: more scores appear in the middle of the distribution with fewer very large or very small scores away from the middle. Furthermore, these distributions tend to be balanced or symmetrical; that is, there is roughly the same number of scores above the middle as there are below. In these cases, frequency distributions take on the shape of a cross section of a bell. When other criteria are also met, we will call this "bell shape" the **normal distribution** or **normal curve.** Figure 3.4 is a histogram that shows a normal or bell-shaped distribution of 1,500 scores. Knowing whether a distribution is normal is of more than casual interest: some statistical analyses were derived assuming a normal distribution of the variables. Gross violations of that assumption mean that certain kinds of analyses may not apply. Therefore, we are particularly interested in detecting distributions that depart markedly from a normal distribution. Characteristics of the normal curve will be discussed at greater length in following chapters. For now, we simply want to emphasize that, when examining the shape of a distribution, it is important to note whether the distribution is generally "bell shaped."

FIGURE 3.4 ■ A histogram based on a large sample and drawn with narrow intervals showing the bell shape that is expected from normally distributed variables.

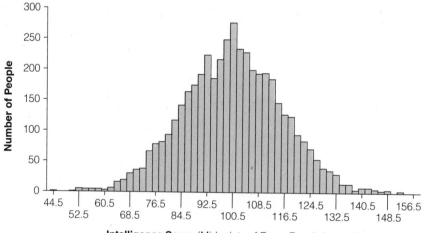

Intelligence Score (Midpoints of Every Fourth Interval)

Skewness

When some scores are bunched at either the high or low end of a distribution and thus the distribution does not look bell shaped, the distribution is said to be **skewed.** For example, typical incomes of Americans are around $39,000 per year (Goozer, 1999). The lowest incomes can be $0; however, the difference between the typical income and the highest income is essentially unlimited. This means that the horizontal axis of a histogram of yearly income levels for all Americans must range from $0 to perhaps $50,000,000 or more to account for the incomes of Bill Gates and Oprah Winfrey. A distribution of a variable such as income is said to be *positively skewed* because, although most values are bunched at the lower end of the scale, there will also be some much greater values trailing out toward the high end of the scale. A distribution showing the number of children in a family is also positively skewed because the typical family with children in developed countries includes two or three children. Most families have relatively few children, and thus the frequency of these values will be greatest. However, although a family can have no fewer than zero children, a value not that different from the typical value, a family can include considerably more than two or three children. Thus, a distribution of the number of children in a family, like income, will be positively skewed. Attendance at Chicago Cubs baseball games measured each day of the baseball season is *negatively skewed* because, if you plotted the frequency of attendance for different games during the season, you would find that on a typical day the stadium is usually filled or close to it. On the other hand, some days the weather is so cold that only a few fans show up. Thus, most attendance figures will represent those days when the stadium is close to capacity, and these values will be bunched at the high end of the scale, but there will be some attendance figures trailing toward the low end of the scale.

Figure 3.5 provides examples of positively and negatively skewed frequency distributions. It is essential to examine distributions for skewness before doing further analyses because, if highly skewed data are mindlessly analyzed, some analyses will become absolutely meaningless or, worse, misleading. Note that the distribution of PSAS scores in Figure 3.3 is a bit positively skewed; however, the amount of imbalance is not severe and would not cause problems during additional analyses.

As the examples show, scores can be skewed for natural reasons; however, data can be skewed also because there is a flaw in the way a variable was measured. Ideally, items on a test are chosen so that the typical score is toward the middle of the range of scores with a roughly normal distribution. Imagine a set of items that measure attitudes regarding physical fitness and exercise patterns among a college-aged population. Senior citizens with typical limitations would probably cluster toward the low end of such a measure with only a few very hearty persons holding attitudes similar to typical college students. Furthermore, the items that apply to college students in general may not apply to Olympic-level athletes. Olympic-level athletes using this questionnaire would probably cluster together with very high scores, with very few athletes having scores as low as the typical college student's score.

The senior citizens would produce a positively skewed distribution as a result of a *floor effect.* A floor effect occurs when scores bunch near the lowest values in the distribution due to a limitation of the measuring device. In this example, we may assume that many items would not be relevant to the lives of most senior citizens because few of them can do what college-age people can do. Hence, their scores may be artificially low. If a gerontologist wanted to learn about the range of attitudes toward physical activities held by senior

FIGURE 3.5 ■ Variables that are highly skewed, whether positively like income, or negatively like attendance at home baseball games in cities with many loyal fans but some very cold days, cannot be used in some analyses because the extreme values have a disproportionate and, perhaps, misleading effect on interpretations.

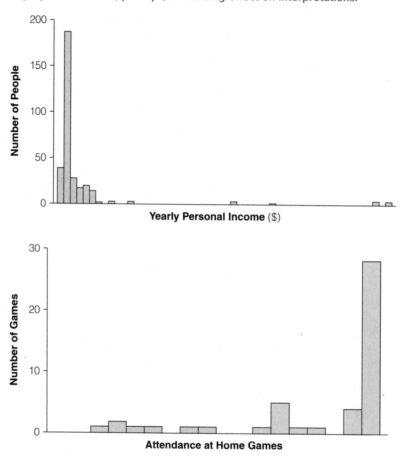

citizens, a very different set of items would need to be developed. In contrast to the seniors, the distribution of scores of Olympic-level athletes would show a *ceiling effect* because many of them would get the highest score possible. A ceiling effect occurs when scores are bunched at the high end of the distribution due to a limitation of the measuring device. If a sports psychologist wanted to learn about the attitudes of supremely gifted athletes, a set of items relevant to college students in general would not be appropriate.

YOUR TURN 3-2

Suppose an athletic director at a college wondered how students felt about having a college football team. After designing the survey (higher numbers represent more positive attitudes), suppose she administered it to the current members of the college's football team. Would the scores of the members of the football team show a floor or a ceiling effect? ■

Ceiling effects are common. In applied research, it is sometimes a surprise to learn that the vast majority of patients at a hospital, alumni of a college, and shoppers at a store are quite satisfied with the care, the instruction, or the service they have received. If the writer of the survey questions were unaware of the high level of overall satisfaction, the data likely would be markedly negatively skewed. If given a choice to rate satisfaction as Poor, Fair, Good, or Excellent, most people select the most favorable option. Although such findings might please those who manage hospitals, colleges, and stores, information that does not distinguish among the people tested or observed is seldom very useful in helping managers choose among possible improvements. And such data will violate assumptions of statistical tests with which you will soon be working.

If there is bunching of scores at either end of the range, the range has been reduced by an artifact of the measurement procedure. Any measurement limitation that restricts the range of scores reduces the validity of findings and may make some analyses inappropriate. As we move through this text, you will see why bunching at end points violates the assumptions of some statistical tests.

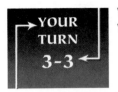

Would you call the distribution of section sizes (Figure 3.2) negatively or positively skewed? Would you say that there is a floor or ceiling effect? ∎

Kurtosis

Skewed distributions are not symmetrical. However, a distribution can deviate from a bell-shaped or normal distribution in other ways. One could imagine taking a normal curve and cutting some scores off the top of the middle of the bell and packing them onto both sides, halfway down both slopes. See the top panel of Figure 3.6. The resulting distribution is flatter than the normal curve and is called **platykurtic.** If one kept rearranging the scores in this fashion, the distribution would end up with a rectangular shape. Another way to distort the normal curve would be the reverse of the changes just mentioned. Instead of adding to the sides, one could carve into the sides and add those scores to the middle region and to the tails. The lower panel of Figure 3.6 illustrates this pattern; such a peaked distribution is called **leptokurtic.** Distributions in Figure 3.6 are perfectly symmetrical, but they are neither bell shaped nor normal. The distributions are said to show **kurtosis** (DeCarlo, 1997). The process of inspection should detect when distributions, even though symmetrical, deviate markedly from the normal curve in these ways. A normal distribution is called **mesokurtic.**

Here are some concrete examples to help you visualize situations in which a problem with kurtosis would be found. Suppose we asked students in a liberal arts college to report the number of years of education they had completed. A first-year college student would report 12 because most students have completed 12 years of education before entering college. Most sophomores would report 13, juniors 14, and seniors 15. We would find roughly the same number of students reporting 12, 13, 14, or 15 with only a handful of very gifted freshmen having fewer than 12 years of formal education and a handful of students completing a second major and those seniors who are on the "five-year plan" and are yet to graduate. The resulting distribution would not be normal, as is clear in Figure 3.7. Similar numbers of students are in the middle four categories, and very few students are in the tails.

FIGURE 3.6 ■ Compared to normal distributions, platykurtic distributions have fewer scores in the middle of the distribution and fewer in the tails; it is flatter. Compared to a normal distribution, leptokurtic distributions have a greater number of scores in the middle and in the tails; it is more peaked. (Normal distributions are given in the blue lines.)

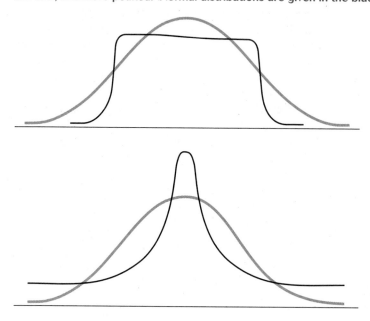

Consequently, the histogram resembles a rectangle rather than the silhouette of a bell and is said to be platykurtic. If our only goal was to describe the students in the college, such a distribution would not cause any problems. At this point, we want you to notice that the distributions of some variables can be expected to be platykurtic.

Some other variables produce distributions that would yield a different kurtosis problem. Suppose we asked for the ages of all the freshmen at Knox College, a traditional liberal arts college located in a rural area of Illinois. If on December 1 we recorded the ages of all the freshmen, we would expect nearly all of them to be 18 years old. Only a few would be younger or older. The distribution would be very concentrated at 18 with rapid dropoffs for both lower and higher ages. This leptokurtic distribution would look like a mountain peak with essentially no foothills. See the right side of Figure 3.7.

You might have noticed that these illustrations of platykurtic and leptokurtic distributions were based on variables that were in some way severely constrained. That is the point. When a variable can take on only certain values, its distribution is seldom normal. In contrast, skewed distributions occur when there is a limit for either high or low scores, but little constraint on scores at the other end of the range. We are most likely to run into positively skewed distributions, with a long tail out toward high values, when we measure such variables as income, time to complete a task, or estimates of some value. Such variables are limited at the low end, namely at zero, but not limited at the high end.

That a distribution is not roughly bell shaped is less of a concern if we are simply seeking to describe a sample. One simply reports whatever one has measured. However, for drawing conclusions from a sample in order to learn about a population and for conducting addi-

FIGURE 3.7 ■ Some variables can be expected to form distributions that are decidedly not normal. (Normal distributions are illustrated by the dashed lines.)

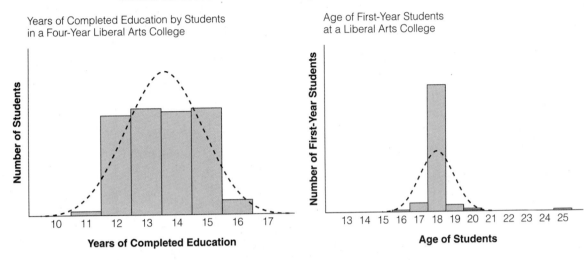

tional analyses, some preliminary work on decidedly leptokurtic or platykurtic distributions may be required. These strategies would take us beyond the topics that are covered in the first statistics course. At this point, the lesson to remember is that we cannot analyze variables with *severe* problems of kurtosis, such as years of education and age as shown in Figure 3.7, in the same way as we would analyze variables that are approximately normally distributed (such as PSAS scores). Fortunately, serious problems of kurtosis arise infrequently. Problems of skewness are more common, but there are some easy approaches to dealing with skewed variables that will be discussed later in this chapter.

Glance back at the histogram of the heights of employees given in Figure 3.1. That distribution is not skewed, but it is not exactly normal either. Would you say the distribution is more leptokurtic or platykurtic? ■

FREQUENCY POLYGONS

If you understood histograms, you know almost all you need to know to construct another type of graph that's often used by investigators to describe distributions: a **frequency polygon.** A frequency polygon is a line graph (instead of a graph made of columns) in which the lines connect the frequency of scores in adjacent intervals; it is an adaptation of a histogram. Figure 3.8 includes a histogram of the PSAS scores showing the parenting skills of the hypothetical mothers introduced in Chapter 2. The errors detected by examining the stem-and-leaf plot have been corrected; that is, the original 85 was changed to a 58 because we are pretending that the data entry person reversed the original 58 and we are pretending that the original 0 should have been missing.

The lower panel of Figure 3.8 includes a frequency polygon of the same PSAS data with the histogram's bars shown in dotted lines. We have included these dotted bars so that it is

FIGURE 3.8 ■ A histogram (top) and a frequency polygon with the bars of the histogram in dotted lines (bottom). A frequency polygon indicates the number of scores in each interval with a point above the midpoint of the interval. Because the graph looks better attached to the horizontal axis, we also place points at zero for the two intervals adjacent to the intervals that contain scores, one below and one above. The line connecting the points is added to aid in reading the graph and suggests the name, polygon.

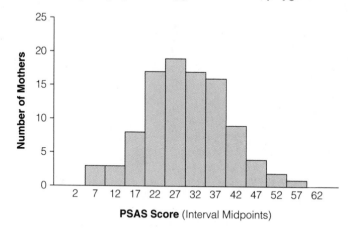

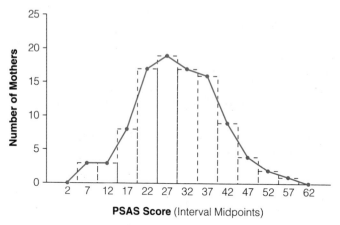

easier to see the simple relationship between the two types of graphs. In a frequency polygon, dots are placed above the midpoints of the intervals at the appropriate frequencies for each interval. Dots are also placed at midpoints in the intervals below and above the intervals defining the range of values plotted in the polygon. This is done to indicate a frequency of zero for these intervals, that is, to indicate that no scores were observed at the next lowest interval and none in the next highest interval. Doing this serves to "anchor" the polygon on the x-axis. Adjacent dots are connected with straight lines. Some students initially connect the dots with curved lines. They may have gotten that idea from graphs drawn for mathematics classes that were composed of a selection of points from an equation that related values of X to values of Y. In contrast, we use straight lines because the lines in frequency polygons are drawn only to provide a visual sense of the distribution, not to suggest a mathematical function.

Here are the 1998 murder rates (per one million residents) from the 13 states initially given in Chapter 2: CN, 41; DE, 28; GA, 81; MA, 20; MD, 100; NH, 15; NJ, 49; NY, 51; NC, 81; PA, 53; RI, 24; SC, 80; and VA, 62. With only 13 data points, one would not normally construct a histogram; however, for practice, go ahead and place the murder rate data in a histogram. You should use no more than five or six groups. Once you have your histogram, sketch in a frequency polygon on top of your graph's columns. Why are histograms and frequency polygons appropriate for this variable? ■

There is one important exception to what we just said about using only straight lines in a frequency polygon. Imagine for a moment having 10 million PSAS scores based on a revised PSAS comprising 500 items. When plotting a frequency polygon for 10 million scores, we could ignore our rule of thumb of having 10 to 15 intervals; with so many scores we could make many more intervals. With 500 items, we could use intervals two units wide and have as many as 250 intervals. What would happen to our frequency polygon? The line connecting the points would be quite smooth. If, in fact, PSAS scores are normally distributed, the frequency polygon would look like a normal distribution such as that in Figure 3.4, and would indeed represent a mathematical function. In later chapters, we will represent "theoretical" normal distributions in exactly this way. A theoretical distribution is based on an infinite number of values for a variable. You can think of these theoretical distributions as frequency polygons with very tiny intervals.

GRAPHING NOMINAL DATA

The graphs presented so far have been used to display variables that have interval or ratio scale properties. (See Table 1.2 in Chapter 1.) Sometimes behavioral scientists are interested in how people identify with groups or categories, such as religious or ethnic identification, type of career, college major, and so forth. We often code nominal data (see Chapter 1) using numbers to identify and classify people or events. Although we use a numerical code, such as 1 for men and 2 for women, we cannot use those numbers like other numbers. Even if the code value is larger than another code value, there is no implication that someone classified in that category is faster, taller, smarter, or richer than someone in a different category. The hypothetical data about the mothers includes a nominal variable: racial/ethnic identification. Let's introduce a graphical technique to help inspect these data.

Figure 3.9 is a **bar chart** of racial/ethnic identity. Bar charts are a lot like histograms in that the people with the same value on a variable are grouped together in one column. Note, however, that the columns do not touch each other as the columns in the histogram did. Why not? Good question. The histogram is used for continuous data. Naturally, the columns of a histogram are in a particular order and could not be rearranged; rearranging them would be nonsensical, making it nearly impossible to visualize the shape of the distribution. In a bar chart, however, the order of the groups listed on the horizontal axis is arbitrarily defined; the categories have no quantitative relationship with each other. Consequently, we might place the bars in order, from the most frequently observed group to the least, or in any other convenient order.

Perhaps you noticed that the bar chart revealed an error in the coding of racial/ethnic identity because we did not have a category (33). An examination of the interviewer forms

FIGURE 3.9 ■ A frequency bar graph is made up of columns indicating the number of scores at each value of a variable used to categorize the observations. Bar graphs are also used to indicate the typical value of some variable describing the members of the categories. Note that the order of categories on the horizontal axis is arbitrary.

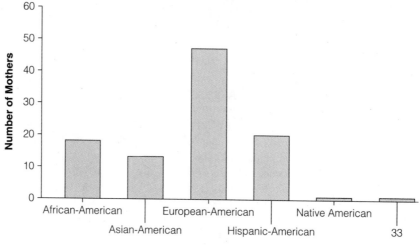

might reveal this had been really a 3, the code for European–American, suggesting that someone hit the computer key twice. To repeat the message of this chapter, we inspect data to catch errors, like that one, *before* we describe a sample or test a research hypothesis.

YOUR TURN 3-6

Suppose that you asked your classmates whether they lived in a college dorm (on campus), within one mile of campus (close to campus), or beyond one mile of campus (far from campus). Here are the returns: close, close, on, close, on, far, on, close, close, on, on, close, far, far, far, on, close, far, close, far, far, close, close, far, on, close, on, close, far, on, close, on, close. Prepare a bar chart to summarize your findings. ■

TRANSFORMING DATA

When we think about the arbitrary numerical codes that are used for nominal data, it is obvious that we can change those codes in any way we wish. Catholic could be coded "1" and Muslim "2" or Catholic could be "2000" and Muslim "153"; it makes no difference. It may be less obvious that we can reexpress any variable as long as we are consistent. Here is a reexpression you have used for years, probably without much thought. If you take a test with 75 possible points, scores might be transformed into percentages. A score of 70 becomes 93%. This transformation is made with a simple formula: % right = (number right/total possible) × 100. Students and teachers transform test scores in this manner to make it easier to interpret the test scores.

Sometimes it is useful to transform a variable by simply grouping several values together. For example, we might transform number of children in a family into categories such as No Children, One Child, Two Children, Three or Four Children, and Five or More. There is no single guideline for doing this: it may simply be helpful to have categories that contain approximately equal numbers of research participants. But at times there might be some theoretical reason for the categories chosen. With regard to family size, it is believed that having no children is very different from having some children. It is also believed that having one child is qualitatively different from having more than one. In industrialized countries, smaller families are generally the norm; consequently, families with more than two children might be grouped together. The suggested family size categories might not apply in all cultural settings. It is important to note that, when a ratio scale variable (such as number of children) has been transformed into categories, as illustrated here, the variable is now ordinal, not ratio or interval. If data are transformed from a ratio scale into an ordinal scale, the variable cannot be analyzed with most statistical procedures discussed in this textbook.

Another way in which researchers frequently transform observations is to group variables together. Social scientists seldom study the pattern of answers to single attitude statements or personality test items because they are usually interested in general concepts rather than the answers to one item. The hypothetical PSAS score is a transformation of the answers to the 75 items about parenting in the same way that the items of a classroom test are combined into one score (e.g., percentage correct). The SAT provides one score for mathematical aptitude rather than reporting whether each item was right or wrong. You have been taking tests so long that you might not have thought of a total score as a transformation. When you learn more about research methods and measurement, you will find out that combining the answers to a number of items about the same topic provides a variable that has greater reliability (or consistency) than do individual items. (Similarly, your knowledge of statistics is more reliably assessed by asking you to answer many different questions about the topic than by asking you to answer only a few questions.) The more reliable a variable is, the less random error it contains. The less random error, the more likely differences among scores reflect true differences among people and the more likely our hypotheses will be accurately tested. Before combining items into a total, however, it is necessary to inspect each item using the methods suggested in this and the previous chapters. After combining the scores, the total should also be inspected as well.

When a transformation involves adding, subtracting, multiplying, or dividing scores by constants, it is called a **linear transformation.** Figure 3.10 shows why the percentage transformation is called *linear*. The raw scores are plotted on the *x*-axis and the transformed scores, the percentages, on the *y*-axis. A straight line can connect the points. When we use a percentage transformation with a ratio scale (such as number right), all of the information in the original scores is retained. If Marjorie has twice as many correct answers as Jenny did, Marjorie's percentage will be twice Jenny's.

Linear transformations can be used with interval scales (such as intelligence, or PSAS scores, or introversion). After a linear transformation with such a variable, the transformed score is still an interval scale and the scores will retain all their relative values. For example, if Henry's original score was midway between Marjorie's and Jenny's, his linearly transformed score will also be midway between their transformed scores. *When we use a linear transformation, the pattern of the distribution of the variable does not change.* If a histogram were prepared for percentage correct, the pattern of the distribution would be exactly the same as for number right; the only difference would be in the labels

FIGURE 3.10 ■ Converting test scores into percentage correct is a linear transformation. When the data are joined, a straight line is formed. This means that equal interval scales remain equal interval scales after linear transformations.

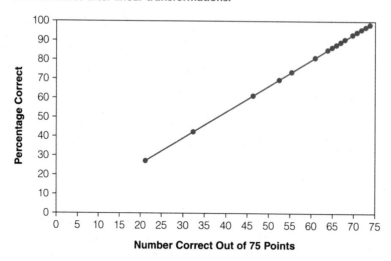

given on the *x*-axis. Of course, the value of the typical score would change, just as the average of test scores expressed as percentages is different from the average of the raw scores. But the interpretations of all statistical techniques covered in this text will be exactly the same whether the data are transformed with a linear transformation or not. Interpretations may change when nonlinear transformations are used; nonlinear transformations are a little more complicated, but they can sometimes save the day when variables are skewed markedly.

When data inspection reveals that we have skewed data, as in Figure 3.5, the extreme data points have a disproportionate effect on analyses compared to most of the data points. This disproportionate effect is undesirable because we want each data point to contribute its fair share. Prior to further analyses, it helps to reduce extreme skewness with a nonlinear transformation. A **nonlinear transformation** is one that retains the order of the values in the data but changes the scale of the data at different points in the range. It is not hard to see how a scale can shrink depending on which part of the range we are working with. Here is a nonlinear transformation: $Y = \sqrt{X}$. The square roots of the original values become the transformed values. Figure 3.11 is an illustration of the square root transformation; the figure shows three characteristics of nonlinear transformations. First, the line connecting the points is not a straight line; thus, the relationship between the original values, labeled *X*, and the transformed values, labeled *Y*, is nonlinear. Second, notice that the *ordinal* relationships among the points has been retained: K is bigger than H, which is bigger than B whether using the original values, *X*, or the transformed values, *Y*. Third, taking the square root reduces the size of the values of all of the data points; however, the larger values are reduced to a greater degree than are the smaller values. This can be seen by examining the dotted lines in Figure 3.11. Originally, child H exceeded B by four points on variable *X*, but after

FIGURE 3.11 ■ Taking the square root of scores is a nonlinear transformation. When the X, Y points are connected, a curved line is formed. This means that the relative sizes among the X scores are different from the relative sizes of the Y scores. An equal interval scale is no longer an equal interval scale after a nonlinear transformation. However, ordinal relationships among the values of X scores and among the values of the transformed scores are the same.

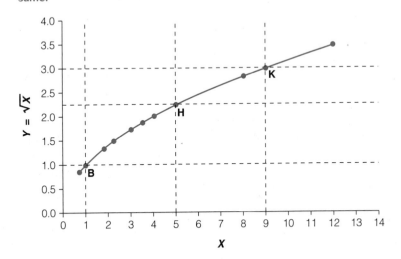

the transformation H exceeds B by only 1.24 points on *Y*. Compare that change to the relationship between K and H: originally, K exceeded H by four points on *X* also, but after the transformation K exceeds H by only 0.76 points on *Y*. These relationships are easier to see when the numbers are lined up:

Data points	Original difference on X	Difference on Y (i.e. $\sqrt{X}$) after transformation
H vs. B	$5 - 1 = 4$	$2.24 - 1.00 = 1.24$
K vs. H	$9 - 5 = 4$	$3.00 - 2.24 = 0.76$

Thus, differences among larger values of *X* are reduced proportionately more than are differences among smaller values of *X*. As we show in the next section, this feature of the square root transformation is useful in reducing positive skewness.

WHAT TO DO ABOUT SKEWED DISTRIBUTIONS

Skewed data can mislead us. The handful of very large sections at Maura's college (see Figure 3.2) would make it seem that the typical section is larger than it is. And highly skewed variables make many analyses inappropriate. However, sometimes skewed data can be transformed to eliminate skewness. It is important to emphasize that it would not matter that Maura's class size variable is skewed if she were simply trying to describe her results to college administrators; in fact, knowing that the data were skewed would be important to college administrators. However, if further analyses are planned, it may be necessary to worry about the positive skewness. Because additional analyses are often planned, it is important to learn about corrections for skewness at this point, when we are inspecting data and preparing it for further analyses.

Dealing with Positive Skewness

Figure 3.12 shows the positive skewness of the estimates that 85 students made of the number of thefts reported to campus security at a Midwestern university during a year. Note that estimates of theft is a variable that we might suspect would be positively skewed because, although there is a lower limit (zero), there is no upper limit on what students might estimate. Their estimates did range from 3 to 1,000. The stem-and-leaf plot shows that the most frequent estimates were between 10 and 40. Are you able to read the stem-and-leaf display? There were two estimates in the 80s; what were they? You should be able to see the estimates of 80 and 85. We also see that there were 9 estimates of 100 and 9 higher than 100.

FIGURE 3.12 ■ Stem-and-leaf plot for estimated thefts reported to campus security during a year.

Frequency	Stem	Leaf
2	0 .	36
11	1 .	00000225558
13	2 .	0000002555567
11	3 .	00000001555
10	4 .	0000005555
9	5 .	000000058
7	6 .	0000055
2	7 .	58
2	8 .	05
0	9 .	
9	10 .	000000001
0	11 .	
0	12 .	
0	13 .	
0	14 .	
2	15 .	00
0	16 .	
2	17 .	55
0	18 .	
0	19 .	
2	20 .	00
- - - - - - -*		
1	30 .	0
- - - - - - -*		
1	50 .	0
- - - - - - -*		
1	100 .	0

*Note that many stems have been omitted at these three points. The computer generated stem-and-leaf plot is not the best display technique when a variable is very skewed. A computer program may indicate the largest values as extremes and, consequently reduce the visual impact of the highly skewed data.

The bunching at 100 is not surprising because people often use round numbers when making estimates.

What is of concern in Figure 3.12 is the positive skewness and particularly the estimate of 1,000. One could argue that the 1,000 is an outlier and should be discarded. The 1,000 is twice as large as the next largest estimate and approximately 30 times larger than the most common of the estimates. But should the 500 be discarded also? The decision is getting harder. Instead of discarding outliers, there is another possibility when the scores trail out gradually toward the high end of a scale. Scores could be changed into a unit that reduces the skewness of the distribution. Our goal is to reduce the largest estimates relative to the smaller estimates. Clearly, we cannot simply reduce the large estimates. A nonlinear transformation might help us to change the distribution in a way necessary for subsequent analyses while preserving the essential information in the observations.

One way to reduce positive skewness is to use the nonlinear transformation that we previously discussed, that is, to take the square root of the scores. The formula is

$$\text{Transformed estimate of theft} = \sqrt{\text{raw estimate of theft}}$$

Taking square roots reduces positive skewness because, although 1,000 is a hundred times larger than 10, the square root of 1,000 (31.62) is only 10 times larger than the square root of 10 (3.16). Figure 3.13(a) shows a histogram of the untransformed estimates of the number of reported thefts. Figure 3.13(b) shows a histogram of the square root of the estimates of theft. Notice that there is less positive skewness in the second graph.

Finally, Figure 3.13(c) contains the histogram for theft estimates after another type of nonlinear transformation. This transformation was done by taking the log to the base 10. This transformation formula is

$$\text{Transformed estimate of theft} = \text{Log}_{10}\ (\text{raw estimate of theft})$$

Recall that the log of 10 is 1.0, the log of 100 is 2.0, and the log of 1,000 is 3.0. Logs are another systematic way to reduce the largest values relative to the smallest values. The histograms in Figure 3.13 make it easy to see that nonlinear transformations led to more-balanced distributions of estimates of theft. Transforming data is not laborious: the same computer programs that produce frequency distribution tables and histograms also transform data with a few clicks of a mouse.

We have introduced two transformations that may help reduce positive skewness in a set of observations. Which one should be used? We can't provide an answer to that question for you; you have to make the call. You should choose the transformation that creates the most bell-shaped distribution. Inspecting the shape of your distribution following both a square root and a log transformation is one way to proceed. As we have tried to emphasize, data analysis requires choices. Should you find yourself with a positively skewed data set, picking a transformation is one example of a choice that you will need to make.

Students are sometimes uneasy about transforming data. It seems that we are cheating in some way, but, as we have shown, you are quite familiar with some transformations. In fact, our brains transform stimuli all the time. Perception psychologists noticed long ago that people do not perceive the actual energy level in light but instead respond to the log of the energy. When the energy in a sound wave increases by a factor of 10, the perceived loudness of the sound increases by one unit (which is called a *sone*). When the energy increases by a factor of 100, the perceived loudness increases two sones. Our hearing system is carrying out a nonlinear transformation. This characteristic of hearing allows one to attend rock

FIGURE 3.13 ■ Notice how a positively skewed distribution can be transformed into a distribution that approximates a normal distribution by taking the log of each score.

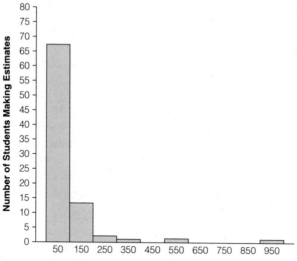

(a) **Estimated Number of Reported Thefts** (Interval Midpoints)

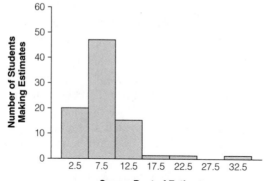

(b) **Square Root of Estimates of Number of Thefts** (Interval Midpoints)

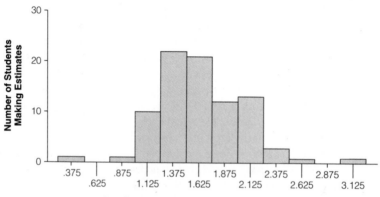

(c) **Log (base 10) of Estimates of Thefts** (Interval Midpoints)

concerts and hear sweet whispers in one's ear (well, maybe not immediately after the concert). The point is that there is nothing sacrosanct about a particular way of measuring a variable. We transform not only to get well-behaved statistics but to reflect psychological experience. In fact, a milestone in psychology was discovering the nonlinear relationships between the energy of physical stimuli and our perception of those stimuli. Introductory psychology texts often describe Fechner's Law. (See, for example, Atkinson, Atkinson, Smith, Bem, & Nolen-Hoeksema, 1996.) According to Fechner's Law, the *perceived* intensity of a stimulus equals the log of the *physical* intensity of the stimulus times a constant. Fechner's Law describes the perception of sound as well as other stimuli.

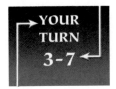

YOUR TURN 3-7 Why would you not transform negatively skewed grades on a course test using square root or log transformations, which worked well for the theft estimates in Figure 3.12? ■

Dealing with Negative Skewness

The examples of transformations of distributions we have discussed can correct positive skewness. Our experience is that positive skewness is a more frequent problem in data sets than is negative skewness; nevertheless, negatively skewed distributions do pop up now and then. Consider an example. Suppose that we are measuring the degree of extraversion among a large number of drama students at several universities. Suppose further that we discover that drama majors tend to be fairly extraverted on the whole, but yet there are some students whose scores are rather low, resulting in a negatively skewed distribution.

There are a number of ways to transform negatively skewed distributions into bell-shaped ones. Figure 3.14 shows a negatively skewed distribution of extraversion scores. The square

FIGURE 3.14 ■ Extraversion probably forms a negatively skewed distribution among drama majors. The top distribution shows the original distribution. The midsection shows the distribution after being reflected using the linear transformation, 50 minus extraversion score plus 1 equals introversion score. The lower distribution shows how a square root transformation has given a distribution that is close enough to normal to use in further analyses.

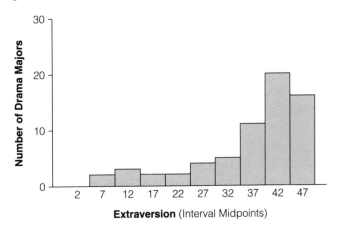

continues

FIGURE 3.14 ■ continued

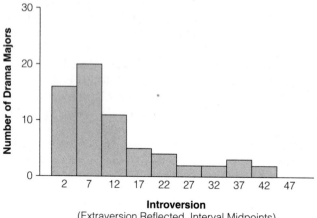

Introversion
(Extraversion Reflected, Interval Midpoints)

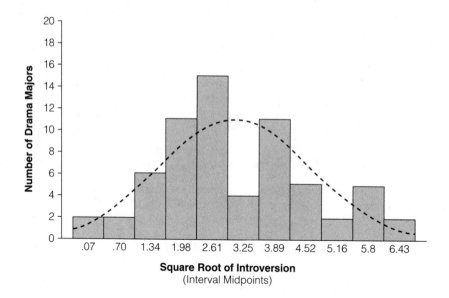

Square Root of Introversion
(Interval Midpoints)

root and log transformations would only make the distribution more negatively skewed. But consider what would happen to the distribution if we simply subtracted each score from the largest extraversion score and added 1 to each difference. This is the formula:

Transformed score = (Highest score − student's score) + 1

Such a transformation is called **reflecting scores.** Several examples are given in Table 3.3 showing how reflecting transforms a negatively skewed distribution into a positively skewed one. It is necessary, of course, to remember that, after the transformation, *higher*

TABLE 3.3 ■ Illustrations of the Reflection of Negatively Skewed Distributions Prior to Transforming to Reduce Skewness

Example values from negatively skewed original distributions	Reflection formulas	Positively skewed distribution after application of the reflection transformation
Test scores: 23, 85, 90, 97	Highest − test score + 1	$23 \rightarrow 97 - 23 + 1 = 75$ $85 \rightarrow 97 - 85 + 1 = 13$ $90 \rightarrow 97 - 90 + 1 = 8$ $97 \rightarrow 97 - 97 + 1 = 1$
Attendance at a stadium in which the crowds are large, but cold weather holds down attendance for some games: 4,328, 32,788, 34,761, 35,863	Highest − attendance + 1	$4{,}328 \rightarrow 35{,}863 - 4{,}328 + 1 = 31{,}536$ $32{,}863 \rightarrow 35{,}863 - 32{,}788 + 1 = 3{,}076$ $34{,}761 \rightarrow 35{,}863 - 34{,}761 + 1 = 1{,}103$ $35{,}863 \rightarrow 35{,}863 - 35{,}863 + 1 = 1$

Note: Once negatively skewed distributions are transformed into positively skewed distributions, the positively skewed distributions can then be transformed using the square root or log transformations.

scores would reflect higher levels of *introversion* (the opposite of extraversion). Once we have a positively skewed distribution, the square root or log transformations can be used. Kinney (1987) provides additional transformation procedures. In later chapters, more transformations—both linear and nonlinear—will be presented.

DISCARDING DATA

We gingerly skipped over a point: how do you defend discarding data? We bypassed the issue when we discovered that we could keep all the estimates of theft in the data set by taking the log of the students' estimates. But suppose we cannot handle this issue so deftly? Table 3.4 includes the estimates of the answer to two multiplication problems we mentioned earlier: $9 \times 8 \times 7 \times 6 \times 5 \times 4 \times 3 \times 2 \times 1$, and the reverse order. Recall that two groups of students were asked to quickly estimate the correct answer to learn how responses are affected by order of presentation. As you can see, there are some extreme values. Neither 560 million nor 8 million should be mixed in with answers ranging from 81 to 10,000. Summary statistics, such as the average of the numbers, would be seriously distorted. You will learn more about this problem in the next chapter. Suppose you did this experiment for a research methods class. Knowing that the presence of these extreme values is problematic when doing later analyses, what are you going to do?

It makes no sense to continue the analysis with these numbers in the data set, but it is unethical to discard data without justifying the decision. And, if data are discarded and then one does not mention discarding data, someone attempting to replicate the project would have no clue that outliers are likely to occur. What might you say in your report to justify discarding these values? For data such as that found in Table 3.4, we suggest phrasing something like this:

> One participant in each condition provided an estimate of the answer to the problem that was extremely different from the other estimates. In the ascending condition, the estimate of 8 million was 512 times larger than the total of the estimates of the other 11 participants. In the descending condition, the estimate of 560 million was almost 24,000 times larger than the total of the other 12 participants in that condition. It may be that these participants were indicating that the task was too hard or that they just refused to estimate the value. These data were not included in the final analysis.

We think that, given such an extreme situation, no one should object to discarding those values. Once you learn more about the normal curve and ways to describe distributions quantitatively, you will be able to use some additional approaches that apply when the outliers are not as extreme as those in Table 3.4.

TABLE 3.4 ■ Estimates for the Answer to a Multiplication Problem Presented in Two Ways; Discarded Outliers Indicated

$1 \times 2 \times 3 \times 4 \times 5 \times 6 \times 7 \times 8 \times 9 =$	$9 \times 8 \times 7 \times 6 \times 5 \times 4 \times 3 \times 2 \times 1 =$
81	24
100	150
100	190
130	200
172	250
256	350
306	500
1,200	987
3,645	1,250
4,125	2,898
5,500	6,761
✗8,000,000	10,000
	✗560,000,000

WHAT YOU HAVE LEARNED AND THE NEXT STEP

We would not be surprised if you felt that we have done a lot of work and no "real" statistics. That may seem true, but it is also true that it is necessary to do a lot of work when painting a room before opening the paint can. Preparation in data analysis as in house painting is very important. Painting over peeling paint is a bad idea; analyzing data containing errors or odd distributions is also a bad idea.

- The only way to find errors in data sets is to inspect carefully.

- Careful inspection, correction, and transformation of the data mean that, when the data are used in further analyses, one can be confident that the analyses will reflect the actual observations and will not have to be repeated because a problem was detected later and will not yield erroneous conclusions because problems were not detected.

- Distributions must be inspected as well as individual scores.

- Graphs are often useful in spotting deviations from a bell-shaped or normal distribution, as is found when distributions exhibit skewness or kurtosis.

- Graphical methods that are often used to inspect distributions of variables include
  - converting a frequency distribution into a histogram,
  - converting a grouped frequency distribution into a histogram or a frequency polygon,
  - using a bar chart for nominal variables.

- Nonlinear transformations can be used to reduce or eliminate skewness.

- Positive skewness can be handled by taking the square root or finding the log of the original scores.

- Negative skewness can be handled by reflecting the original scores (that is, subtracting the scores from the largest score and then adding 1 to the difference) and then treating the reflected scores as we would treat a positively skewed distribution.

- Other transformations can be used if it is not necessary to retain all the information in the original measurements.

Once the errors have been corrected, you are ready to describe your data. If your research mentor asked, "How did the people you tested do?", you can answer by handing your mentor a histogram, a frequency polygon, or a stem-and-leaf display. Any one of these is an improvement over a list of the scores. Presenting data this way is a bridge from the *Inspection* phase of analysis to the *Description* phase of the I-D-E-A model.

As you might guess, there are ways of describing a distribution of numbers besides using graphs. Sometimes people don't need the detail available in a graph. Indeed, once we know that a distribution meets the assumptions of the statistical technique we're planning to use, people often are properly satisfied with a handful of summary numbers to describe a distribution. Those summary indexes are the topics of the next chapter. But, remember, inspecting data comes first, not as an afterthought. If we wait until something in the analyses looks odd, we will discover only the errors and anomalies that are contrary to our expectations, not those that match our expectations. We need to avoid errors in the data whether they fit our expectations or challenge them. There have been some embarrassing instances in

TABLE 3.5 ■ Major Steps in Data Inspection

I. Examine carefully the original data records (pages, sheets, forms) *before* **coding and entering data into a computer file.**
What to look for: missing data; illegible or soiled sheets obscuring data; obviously impossible values; patterns of responses indicating intentional disregard for task; drawings or other marks suggesting lack of attention by respondents; any indications that respondents did not follow instructions.
What to do: clean data where necessary; discard inappropriate responses; deal with missing values appropriately; construct a verbal explanation (defense) of your actions at this stage.

II. Check the data file when coding and entering data into the computer.
What to look for: invalid data points (klinkers).
What to do: order the data; check original data records for possible reasons for unusual values; consult with researchers and data entry persons to find explanations for anomalies; correct or discard errors; construct a verbal commentary of your actions at this point.

III. Order the data in a frequency distribution or stem-and-leaf display.
What to look for: outliers and other anomalous values.
What to do: make decisions about outliers; discard if appropriate; write verbal commentary of nature of outliers and what you did with them.

IV. Examine shape of distribution using tabular or graphical methods.
What to look for: a data distribution that appears symmetrical and "normal" (bell shaped, that is, the scores are concentrated in the middle of the range and frequency drops off rapidly with few values in the tails); skewness and direction of skewness; problems of kurtosis.
What to do: if the distribution appears approximately normal, note that the data are appropriate for most analyses; if skewed, consider why the distribution is skewed and possible transformations. There is no simple way to correct for problems of kurtosis. When data are not or cannot be transformed, a note should be made of the possible problems and of the need for caution in later analysis and interpretation.

V. Examine data set as a whole.
What to look for: trends and patterns in the data.
What to do: make sure you have a good feel for your data; verbally describe to yourself "what happened." Begin to think about appropriate descriptive statistics that will summarize data numerically.

which errors favorable to a hypothesis were not detected by the original researcher, but by other people. (See Gould, 1978.) Careful inspection of the data will keep that from happening to you.

The purposes of data inspection are summarized in Table 3.5. Note how inspection begins with the original records containing data, continues through the data coding step, and involves the inspection of each data point. Then, the overall distribution is inspected. At that point, you are ready to describe your data more fully.

Key Concepts

histograms	kurtosis	bar chart
midpoint	platykurtic	linear transformation
normal distribution, or normal curve	leptokurtic	nonlinear transformation
	mesokurtic	reflecting scores
skewed distribution	frequency polygon	

Answers to *Your Turn* Questions

3-1. When an interval width is an even number (for example, 2, 4, or 10), the midpoint will be between two whole numbers, and, thus, the midpoint would be a decimal value. If the stated limits are 6 to 7, the real limits are 5.5 to 7.5 (a width of two points). The midpoint of that interval is 6.5.

On the other hand, when an interval width is an odd number (for example, 5), the interval midpoint will be a whole number. If the stated limits are 5 to 9, the real limits are 4.5 to 9.5 (a width of five points). The midpoint is then 7.0.

3-2. Football players can be safely assumed to be in favor of having a football team, so we would expect to see a ceiling effect in their attitudes.

3-3. Section sizes are positively skewed; the tail extends toward large numbers. This distribution is not artificially restricted; consequently, it is not affected by either floor or ceiling effects.

3-4. The distribution of heights is more platykurtic.

3-5. Here is the grouped frequency distribution:

0–19	1
20–39	3
40–59	4
60–79	1
80–99	3
100–119	1

Because the only state in the top interval had a murder rate of 100, many people might label the top interval as 80–100 and include Maryland in that interval. This little problem illustrates a reason why grouped frequency distributions and histograms are seldom used for so few data points. Because the variable is continuous, these statistical tools are appropriate.

3-6.

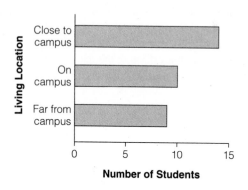

Some authors urge that bar charts be placed in order from most frequent to least frequent. A bar chart can be vertical or horizontal.

3-7. Taking the square root or the log is used for *positively* skewed data; those transformations will only make negatively skewed distributions worse. Further, class grades are seldom used for additional analyses. There is no need for test grades to form bell-shaped distributions.

Analyzing and Interpreting Data: Problems and Exercises

1. Consider the type (shape) of distribution for the data reported for the following variables. That is, would the distribution obtained be basically bell shaped (normal)? Positively or negatively skewed? Are there any that you suspect might be rather flat, that is, fairly evenly distributed across the range of scores?
   (a) ages of faculty members at your college
   (b) enrollments in all the sections in your college
   (c) scores on most classroom examinations
   (d) population of all cities in a state or province
   (e) weight of all students in the freshman class
   (f) scores on an IQ test

2. What is the shape of the distribution likely to be found for the data represented by the following variables? That is, would the distribution obtained be basically bell shaped (normal)? Positively or negatively skewed? Are there any that you suspect might be rather flat, that is, fairly evenly distributed across the range of scores?
   (a) the ages of students at your college or university
   (b) the SAT (or ACT) scores from the undergraduates of a college with a competitive admissions policy

   (c) the time in months from matriculation (first beginning classes) to graduation from college for all alumni of the last 20 years
   (d) the number of credit hours earned by the graduating seniors of a college
   (e) the heights of all students at your school
   (f) scores on a very easy classroom examination

3. Define the following terms:
   (a) histogram
   (b) frequency polygon
   (c) interval midpoint

4. A grouped frequency distribution for estimates of the percentage of male undergraduates who consume four or more alcoholic drinks each week follows. (These estimates were made by real students, but don't take the estimates that seriously because undergraduates predictably overestimate the drinking patterns of other students (Miller, 1999).)
   (a) Construct a grouped frequency histogram on the basis of this distribution.
   (b) Is the distribution skewed? If so, what is the nature of the skewness?

Interval	Frequency
0–9	1
10–19	1
20–29	8
30–39	13
40–49	12
50–59	15
60–69	30
70–79	31
80–89	35
90–99	18

5. As part of a study investigating cultural differences in religious beliefs, suppose you interview 50 college students. The number of students with self-reported religious affiliation was as follows: Protestant, 18; Catholic, 16; Muslim, 2; Jewish, 5; Buddhist, 2; Other, 7.

   Transform the data to show percentage affiliation of your total sample (50) and draw a graph showing the distribution of religious affiliation among the students.

6. A community decided that it wanted to eliminate dangerous high-speed driving on its streets. The city council passed an ordinance with the following six-category fine structure for people convicted of breaking the speed limits:

Category	Miles per hour over the speed limit	Fine
1	1–5	$15
2	6–10	$30
3	11–15	$60
4	16–20	$120
5	20–25	$240
6	25 or more	$480

Is the fine structure a linear or nonlinear transformation of the speeding category? Explain your answer.

7. Inspect the shape of the following set of numbers: 1, 1, 3, 1, 9, 7, 3, 5, 4, 2, 4, 3, 2, 3, 4, 3, 2, 3, 3, 3, 3.
   (a) Draw a simple histogram showing the shape of the distribution.
   (b) How would you characterize the shape of the distribution?

8. Use the data in problem #7.
   (a) Using an appropriate transformation, reexpress the data so that the distribution is more bell shaped.
   (b) Draw a simple (ungrouped) frequency distribution of the transformed scores to help show the shape of the distribution after transformation.

9. Consider the following set of numbers:
   9, 10, 8, 10, 7, 5, 10, 9, 9, 8, 3, 9, 2, 8, 7, 9, 9.
   (a) Is the distribution positively or negatively skewed?
   (b) Show how the data can be transformed to produce a more normal looking distribution.

10. Under what situations may you consider discarding data points from a data set?

11. (a) How does a platykurtic distribution differ from a normal distribution?
    (b) How does a leptokurtic distribution differ from a normal distribution?

12. How can a stem-and-leaf plot be made to look like a histogram?

13. Why are bar charts used when plotting variables such as numbers of people of various nationalities, rates of different types of crime, or numbers of people holding different kinds of jobs?

14. Assume that a variable is reflected. Then imagine that the original variable and the transformed variable are graphed in an X-Y plot (as in Figure 3.10). Why would a line connecting the points be a straight line?

15. Here are two transformations: (a) income transformed into taxes using a graduated income tax law, and (b) converting a test score from number correct into percentage correct. One of these is a nonlinear transformation and one is a linear transformation. Explain what kind of a transformation each one is.

16. If a clinical psychologist measured depression among a random sample of people in a city, what pattern would a stem-and-leaf plot (or a histogram) be likely to show if the instrument had been designed for use with hospitalized psychiatric patients?

17. (a) List the procedures that researchers use *before* considering discarding a discrepant data point.
    (b) Give an *inappropriate* reason for discarding a discrepant data point.

18. The stem-and-leaf plot to the right gives the sizes of 37 sections in a college.
    (a) How would you describe the distribution?
    (b) What transformations could be tried to handle the nonnormal distribution?

19. Consider the following data showing scores on a personality test given to 58 college freshmen (maximum score is 120): 92, 89, 78, 89, 88, 76, 56, 66, 67, 68, 69, 99, 101, 105, 91, 71, 87, 78, 77, 77, 89, 88, 83, 82, 82, 81, 71, 74, 75, 99, 105, 109, 103, 98, 91, 92, 85, 76, 76, 56, 85, 59, 69, 65, 64, 67, 79, 81, 89, 77, 89, 88, 88, 89, 91, 94, 95, 97.
    (a) Construct a grouped frequency distribution of these scores.
    (b) Construct a histogram from your grouped frequency distribution.
    (c) Describe the shape of the distribution in words.

20. Use the data and your answers to problem #19 to draw a frequency polygon for this set of numbers.

Frequency	Stem	Leaf
2	1	26
2	2	22
13	3	0004444445555
7	4	0125778
4	5	2566
2	6	56
0	7	
2	8	25
0	9	
0	10	
2	11	03
0	12	
0	13	
0	14	
1	15	0
0	16	
0	17	
1	18	0
0	19	
0	20	
1	21	1

Answers to Odd-Numbered Problems

1. (a) There might be different answers for this one. The distribution is most likely to be fairly even across ages. If the college underwent a rapid expansion, there might be a bulge at that point, but this would certainly not be a normal distribution.
   (b) Very likely positively skewed.
   (c) Very likely negatively skewed because the minimum passing score and the typical score are closer to 100% than to 0%.
   (d) Positively skewed; a small number would be very large.
   (e) Probably fairly normal.
   (f) Normal. IQ tests are designed to produce a normal distribution across the population.

3. (a) A histogram is a bar graph of a frequency distribution; the columns touch because it is used for continuous variables.
   (b) A frequency polygon is a line graph of a frequency distribution; the scores in intervals are treated as if they were all at the midpoints of the intervals and then these points are connected with straight lines.
   (c) The interval midpoint is a score that is halfway between the lower and upper limits of intervals.

5.

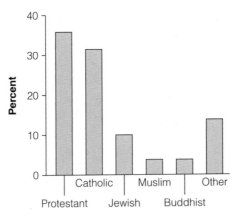

Religious Identification

7. (a)

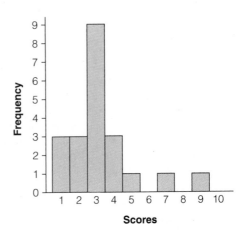

   (b) This distribution is positively skewed.

9. (a) The distribution is negatively skewed.
   (b) The first step is to reflect the scores. $10 -$ score $+ 1 =$ reflected score.
   The scores would now be 2, 1, 3, 1, 4, 6, 1, 2, 2, 3, 8, 2, 9, 3, 4, 2, 2.
   The square root transformation then yields a more symmetrical distribution 1.41, 1, 1.73, 1, 2, 2.45, 1, 1.41, 1.41, 1.73, 2.83, 1.41, 3, 1.73, 2, 1.41, 1.41.

11. (a) *Platykurtic:* fewer scores in the center and in the tails, and more scores that are moderately large or moderately small.
    (b) *Leptokurtic:* more scores in the center and more in the tails, and fewer in the moderate range.

13. Bar charts with the columns whose sides never touch the sides of another column are used when the variable being plotted is not a continuous variable and the categories being plotted are not required to be in a particular order.

15. (a) A graduated income tax means that the higher the income, the higher the percentage of income must be paid. People with large incomes pay more taxes, but they also pay proportionately more taxes than do people with lower incomes. Thus, this is a nonlinear transformation.
    (b) Converting a test score into a percentage is a linear transformation.

17. (a) A discrepant data point could be due to problems with lab equipment, a mistake in recording the data in the first place, or a mistake in handling the data as analysis begins. Once these possibilities have been dismissed, the analyst considers whether the participant is simply a very unusual person. Also, only after innocuous reasons are dismissed should the analyst consider possible problems due to participants who were uncooperative or who misunderstood directions.

(b) Inappropriate reasons include a person producing data that do not fit the experimenter's hypothesis. Remember that a data point must be quite discrepant before it can be discarded.

19. (a)

Stated Limits	Real Limits	Frequency	Midpoints
50–59	49.5–59.5	3	54.5
60–69	59.5–69.5	8	64.5
70–79	69.5–79.5	13	74.5
80–89	79.5–89.5	18	84.5
90–99	89.5–99.5	11	94.5
100–109	99.5–109.5	5	104.5

(b)

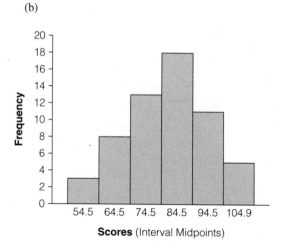

(c) The distribution is bell shaped (i.e., fairly normal).

 Go to http://psychology.wadsworth.com/courses/statistics/ and test your knowledge of this chapter by taking the online quiz. Another resource to check is the online workshops that provide a step-by-step guide through a number of topics at http://psychology.wadsworth.com/workshops/workshops.html.

CHAPTER 4

Describing Data From One Group

Data can be effectively summarized numerically, pictorially, or verbally.
Good descriptions of data frequently use all three modes.
    Shaughnessy et al. (2003, p. 369)

INTRODUCTION

Consider the following scenario.

Katie is a senior psychology major seeking a project for her honors thesis. Her adviser recommends her to a university administrator who has a question that Katie may be able to help answer. The administrator wants to know how "happy" students are at the university. Katie receives a small budget and a part-time work-study student to help her with data collection. With her knowledge of research methodology and through some hard work, Katie is able to design an appropriate, brief questionnaire and then obtain responses from what looks like a good random sample of students. Let's assume that her main measure of student happiness is a rating on a 7-point scale in answer to the question: "How happy are you attending this university?" The scale is anchored with the words "Not at All" next to the 1 on the scale, and the words "Extremely Happy" next to the 7. Students are asked to provide a number, 1 through 7, that indicates their level of happiness at this school. Data are obtained from 80 students.

The administrator who hired her telephones and asks that she present her findings to a meeting of upper administrators the following week. Katie cleans the data, looking for klinkers and outliers. In the process, she identifies two ratings of 8 that, on close inspection of the original data sheets, turn out to be poorly written 3s that had been mistakenly recorded by her assistant. A stem-and-leaf display suggested there were no outliers and that the distribution was somewhat negatively skewed. She decides that a histogram will be a good way to show the administrators what she found and uses a computer program to construct one, which she then prints on a transparency for group viewing.

Katie shows up for the meeting on time, is introduced, and then is asked to tell everyone what she did and found. She gives them information about her methodology and the kinds of questions she asked. Katie then tells them that her main measure was the response of students on a 7-point scale to a question about how happy they are attending this university. The administrators begin to come to the edge of their seats in anticipation of what she found. (After all, one of their jobs is to make sure students are satisfied with their college experience, and the data will, they believe, let them know if they are doing a good job.)

Katie begins her report by saying, "I surveyed 80 students and found this!" She throws up her histogram on the screen. (See Figure 4.1.) The college administrators look interested, but some seem a bit bewildered and confused. One comments, "This is looking good." But another chimes in with, "What are we to make of this drawing? What do we tell interested students?" Many were at a loss to know how they might use this picture to describe to current and prospective students the level of student satisfaction at their school. One administrator finally recovers enough to ask, "But can't you simply summarize what you found?" Another asks, "Exactly how would you describe student satisfaction?"

Of course, the histogram drawn by Katie is telling the administrators something important about the data (at least for those who can "read" a histogram). But the administrators are right to be concerned about how the data in this "picture" can be easily communicated to others. Thus, it is fair to ask Katie to do more when describing what was found. What else might she do?

FIGURE 4.1   ■   Frequency distribution (histogram) showing results of rating study.

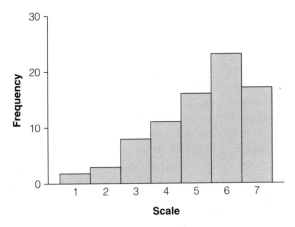

HOW DO WE DESCRIBE DATA?

Description begins with the inspection stage of data analysis. You saw in the last two chapters that we learn a great deal about our data as we check it for errors and outliers. When we have interval or ratio data, information about the shape of our data distribution is obtained by examining a stem-and-leaf display, frequency polygon, or histogram. We may already have made a decision to transform the data using another scale. However, the goal of data inspection is not the same as that of data description. At the description stage (i.e., the *D* in I-D-E-A), we seek to describe a data set using numbers (summary statistics) and graphs (figures) to more fully explain what it is that we found. The graphs we use may be the same ones we used to inspect the shape of our distribution, as Katie did; however, we will also want to describe our data set numerically.

Two characteristics of a data set always need to be summarized and described: *central tendency* and *variability* (dispersion). Measures of **central tendency** tell us what numbers our data tend to cluster around. As you will see, we usually look for a number that permits us to describe a "typical" score. For example, in our hypothetical happiness survey, the administrators would certainly want to know the typical level of student happiness. However, as you will see, a data set is not completely described unless we also provide information about the degree of dispersion or variability in the numbers. How different are the numbers in our data set? Do the numbers have similar values, or are many different values represented? Measures of central tendency, in other words, do not tell the whole story about a data set. In this chapter, we illustrate how both central tendency and variability can be described. We begin with a brief review of scales of measurement so that you can appreciate the relationship between the way that we measure behavior and the way we describe what we have found.

WHAT TYPE OF DATA ARE WE SEEKING TO DESCRIBE?

The way in which a research question is asked will often determine the scale of measurement. Our survey researcher simply could have requested a "yes" or "no" response to the question "Are you happy attending this university?" When *nominal data* are obtained (e.g., "yes" or "no" responses), data are simply described by reporting the proportion or percentage of scores in various categories. College administrators would learn something very important if they found out that 90% of a representative sample of respondents said "yes" they are happy at their university, whereas only 10% said "no." If the survey item had asked students to rank order activities in terms of what brings them the most happiness (e.g., attending this university, attending trade school, attending a corporate training program, attending another school across town, or attending Marine boot camp), then the data would be ordinal in nature. The description of *ordinal data* is usually done by reporting the most frequent rank given, or the proportion of people ranking a key item as 1st, 2nd, 3rd, and so forth. For example, we might find that 40% of the people surveyed report that, among these activities, attending this university ranked 1st, 20% ranked it 2nd, and so forth.

Our major focus will be on how to describe *interval* or *ratio data.* Thus, at this point, we must ask an important question: Are the data obtained from rating scales, such as the 7-point scale used by Katie, nominal, ordinal, interval, or ratio? (You may want to review the discussion of these types of data in Chapter 1.) Our experience teaching statistics tells us that many students initially say it is interval data. After all, there appear to be equal intervals (1, 2, 3, . . .) and no real absolute zero. Data obtained from rating scales appear frequently in the behavioral sciences, and knowing how to analyze such data is very important. But what kind of data are obtained from these scales? Consider Katie's "happiness" scale:

1	2	3	4	5	6	7
Not at all	Somewhat		Moderately	Very		Extremely happy

Strictly speaking, data obtained from rating scales reflects ordinal, not interval, measurement. Although the scale intervals look equal, one must question whether human beings can really use them in a way that they are equal. Consider your own happiness about something, for example, attending a university. How would you rate your experience on a 7-point scale? What is your degree of happiness? Got a number? Okay, now think about how you came up with that number. When you considered, for instance, a rating of 5 or 6, or perhaps a 7, do your believe that your "degree of happiness" is easily marked off in equal intervals? If you decided on a 6, is your degree of happiness that is represented by the 6 just as far from 5 as it is from 7? Do you believe that you can use the scale in such a way that your rated degree of happiness moves in "equal intervals" up and down the scale? It is highly unlikely that people can do this. Thus, if you report your happiness is a 6, you most likely are saying that it is more than what you might assign a 5, but less than a 7. That would be a rank order (ordinal) judgment.

But, having made this point, we can say that researchers generally treat rating scale data as if it were interval data. (This assumption is much safer when we use multiple scales and add scale values to create an index of some kind.) Working with interval data has important benefits, as you will see. We will proceed, therefore, under the assumption that ratings may be described as if they were from an interval scale (but realize that this is an assumption and that it may be worth questioning such an assumption in some situations).

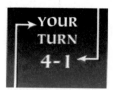

Although rating scales are often really ordinal in nature, they frequently are treated as if they were interval measures. One way to improve on this situation is to add results from multiple scales. However, if we must use one scale, can you suggest what a researcher might do to increase the likelihood that interval data are obtained? That is, what might you do to help the user to treat the intervals as equal?

MEASURES OF CENTRAL TENDENCY

Central tendency, as we noted, is usually described by reporting a score that other scores in the distribution tend to center around. Such a score can be thought of as a *typical* score. Ideally, it best represents the whole data set. There are several ways to describe the central tendency of a distribution, and each goes by a different name. These measures of central tendency are the *arithmetic mean* (or *average*), the *median,* and the *mode*. The characteristics of each are summarized in Table 4.1.

The **arithmetic mean** is the most important and most widely used measure of central tendency. It is defined as the sum of all the scores divided by the number of scores. In statistical symbols it is defined as:

$$\sum X/N$$

where Σ, the uppercase Greek sigma, means "sum of," X is a raw score value, and N = size of sample.

The sample mean is frequently expressed with the symbol $\overline{X}$ (read "X bar") when doing statistical procedures; when reporting a sample mean in a scientific manuscript, the symbol M is recommended (American Psychological Association, 2001). We will use M whenever we talk about a sample mean, but be aware that you will sometimes see $\overline{X}$ when the sample mean is discussed. The symbol for the population mean is the Greek letter μ (*mu;* pronounced *mew*).

Thus,

$$M = \sum X/N \qquad\qquad \text{Equation 4.1}$$

and, when we have all the data of interest, $\mu = \Sigma X/N$.

TABLE 4.1 ■ Measures of Central Tendency and Their Characteristics

Measure	Description/Characteristics
Mean	The sum of all the scores divided by the number of scores. What people mean usually when they talk about an "average." Is the most important measure of central tendency; it is a "balance point" in that the absolute value of the sum of the deviations of scores from the mean that are below the mean equals the sum of the deviations from the mean that are above the mean; the sum of the deviations from the mean is zero; it is affected by a change in any score in the distribution; is "pulled" toward extreme scores in the data set.
Median	The middle point of the distribution; separates the distribution in two halves with an equal number of scores in each half. Not affected by extreme scores; recommended measure of central tendency with skewed distributions.
Mode	The score value that appears with the greatest frequency. Can be misleading, especially with small data sets; informative when there is one or more distinctly most frequent scores.

BOX 4.1 ■ When to Use *N* and *n*

The *Publication Manual of the American Psychological Association* (2001) suggests that the capital letter *N* be used to designate the number of cases in a sample and that researchers use *n* to indicate a subset of a sample. Later in this book, we will need to use *n* as well as *N*. For now, we'll use *N* whenever we wish to symbolize the number of cases in a sample (but sometimes, too, in a population).

What is the mean of the following distribution: 3, 4, 6, 7? The mean, as you should be able to quickly calculate, is 5:

$$\sum X/N = (3 + 4 + 6 + 7)/4 = 20/4 = 5.$$

Note that the value of the mean in our example (5) does not appear in the distribution of numbers. The mean is often not exactly the same as any number in a data set.

Because the mean is based on the sum of all the numbers in a data set, the mean changes when any number in the distribution changes. But being sensitive to a change in any number in a distribution has its liabilities. In our example data set (3, 4, 6, 7), if the last number (7) were changed to 27, the mean would now be 10. The mean is pulled toward extreme scores in a skewed distribution. This is a major reason why outliers in a distribution pose problems for the researcher: the mean will be pulled in the direction of the outlier.

The *median* (symbolized as *Mdn*) is the middlemost position in the distribution when scores are ordered from lowest to highest. When there are no repetitions of scores near the middle of the distribution and there is an even number of scores, the median is halfway between the two middle numbers. (It is actually the mean of the middle two numbers.) For example, in the distribution 3, 4, 6, 7, the median is defined as $(4 + 6)/2 = 5$. If there is an odd number of numbers and no repetitions around the middle point, the median by convention is the middle number. Thus, in the distribution 3, 4, 6, 7, 10, the median would be 6. When the distribution has many numbers (as they often do) or there are repetitions of numbers around the middle of the distribution (as there often are), a statistical program will estimate the median for you. Keep in mind, however, that the median—no matter how it is calculated—represents the point in the distribution above which half the scores fall and below which half the scores fall.

BOX 4.2 ■ The Mean as a Balancing Point

The mean is a true "balance point" in the distribution in that the sum of deviations of scores from the mean that are below the mean equals (in absolute value) the sum of deviations of scores from the mean that are above the mean. *Another way to say this is that the sum of the deviations from the mean is zero.* Therefore, in our example set of numbers (3, 4, 6, 7), if we subtract the mean (5) from each score and add the deviations from the mean, we will find that: deviations of scores below the mean $= (3 - 5) + (4 - 5) = -3$ and, deviations of scores above the mean $= (6 - 5) + (7 - 5) = +3$.

FIGURE 4.2 ■ Two bimodal distributions.

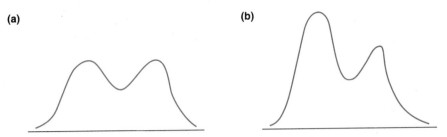

(a)   **(b)**

The **median,** unlike the mean, is not always affected by changes in scores, and this is its major advantage. If the last number (7) in the distribution 3, 4, 6, 7 were changed to 70 (or 7,000), the median would not change. Because the median is not affected by extreme scores, it is the preferred measure of the typical score when there are extreme values (e.g., outliers) or when the distribution is skewed. (See Chapter 3.)

The **mode** is simply the most frequent score and is thus a quick and easy way to get a measure of central tendency. The mode, however, often is not very useful as a measure of central tendency, particularly with small data sets, because it may not represent well the data set as a whole. Consider the following two distributions: (a) 2, 3, 4, 5, 6, 10, 10, and (b) 2, 2, 3, 4, 5, 6, 10. You can see that the mode in the first data set is 10 and the mode in the second is 2, but neither mode seems to represent well the typical score or the score that other scores in the distribution center around. On the other hand, many distributions contain an obvious value that is much more frequent than others, and this is worth noting when we describe the data set. The mode also turns out to be helpful when describing a distribution in which there is more than one frequent score. Figure 4.2 shows two examples of a **bimodal distribution.** When two numbers appear frequently but also differ substantially in the frequency with which they appear (as in distribution b), we speak of a bimodal distribution having a *major mode* and a *minor mode.* Consider a distribution of scores from a pro-am golf tournament. This is a contest wherein a professional golfer teams up with an amateur golfer. It seems reasonable to suggest that the final distribution of golf scores will be bimodal, with the professionals clustering around a low (good) score and the amateurs clustering around a slightly higher score. Bimodal distributions are likely to arise when a distribution contains scores from two different types of individuals.

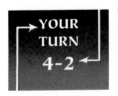

YOUR TURN 4-2

Which of the three measures of central tendency must change when even one number in the data set changes? Why?   ■

Choosing a measure of central tendency to represent the data should be made only after inspecting the distribution of scores. The relationship among the three measures of central tendency is shown in Figure 4.3 for both normal and skewed distributions. Note where the measures of central tendency fall in these distributions. In a bell-shaped, symmetrical distribution (i.e., a normal distribution), the mean, median, and mode all have the same value. Such is not the case when skewness is present. In Chapter 3, you learned that skewness is

FIGURE 4.3 ■ Normal and skewed distributions.

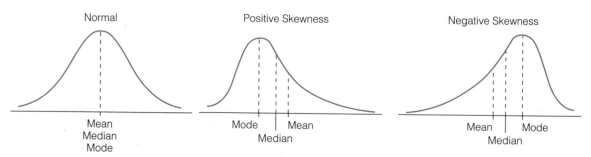

characterized as positive or negative depending on the direction of asymmetry. In a positively skewed distribution, scores are bunched up at the lower end of the scale and trail off to the upper end, in contrast, in a negatively skewed distribution, the bunching up occurs at the higher end of the scale and the frequency of scores trails off to the lower end of the scale. You may also remember that some types of data are inevitably skewed, such as the number of children in American families and scores on an easy class exam.

The mean is pulled toward the extreme scores in a skewed distribution. *As a general rule, when the data are skewed, report both the mean and median.* The relationship between the two will tell the astute observer the direction of skewness. (See Figure 4.3.) In a skewed data set, neither the mean nor the median is apt to exactly "fit" the set of numbers, but the median is likely to be closer to what we might consider a typical score.

Measures of central tendency for Katie's happiness data pictured in Figure 4.1 are: $M = 5.16$, $Mdn = 5.50$[1], and Mode $= 6$. Note that the mean is slightly lower than the median as would be expected when the distribution is negatively skewed.

If you were an admissions director at Katie's college, what measure of central tendency would you want to emphasize? How would you justify that choice? ■

HOW IS VARIABILITY (DISPERSION) MEASURED?

We have said that a measure of central tendency is not enough to describe fully a distribution of numbers. We need also to describe the degree of **variability** in the number set. A measure of central tendency, such as the mean, indicates the value that numbers in the data set tend to center around. But exactly how are the numbers dispersed around the mean? Are most numbers close to the mean or are they far from the mean? Measures of variability pro-

---

[1] For this particular data set where N or 80 is an even number, because there were exactly 40 scores 6 or higher and 40 scores 5 or lower, the median was calculated as the average of the two middle scores (i.e., 40th and 41st scores) which was $(5 + 6)/2$, or 5.50. If there had been many repetitions of a number (e.g., 5) around the middle, then the median would either be reported as that number or it could be calculated using what is called a *method of interpolation*. The method of interpolation is discussed by Gravetter and Wallnau (2000), among others.

vide us with descriptive indexes by which we can summarize variability (degree of dispersion) numerically. Let us illustrate with a concrete example why a measure of variability is needed to complement a measure of central tendency. Consider the following two distributions: (A) 2, 2, 3, 3, 6, 7, 8, 9, and (B) 4, 5, 5, 5, 5, 5, 5, 6.

The mean is 5 in both distributions. But clearly we will want to say more when describing these distributions. Numbers in distribution A are more spread out than in distribution B; numbers in B are bunched around the mean, but numbers in A do not cluster around the mean. The difference in dispersion or variability is obvious, but how should we communicate that? How do we describe variability?

As you have learned, one way in which we can describe the dispersion in data sets is by drawing graphs of the frequency distributions. The construction of frequency distributions and ways to picture (graph) a distribution were introduced in Chapter 2 and 3. We will assume that, for large data sets, a computer program will be used to generate graphs of the data set as we did for the 80 scores from the hypothetical happiness survey. (See Figure 4.1.)

Figure 4.4 shows several frequency polygons describing distributions that all have the same mean (and median and mode). Anyone looking at these three distributions can readily see that the degree of variability differs among them. In distribution A, the scores are much more tightly packed around the mean than in B or C. Two important statistical measures that tell us about variability (or dispersion) are the *range* and the *standard deviation*.

Most people think of the **range** as simply the difference between the lowest and highest value in the set of numbers. Given the data set 4, 6, 8, 8, 9, 14, 22, the range would be 18 (i.e., $22 - 4 = 18$). Some textbook writers will point out that the range is really 19 because there are actually 19 values between 4 and 22, not 18. Count them and you will see that they are correct. Following this logic, the range is defined as the difference between the lowest and highest value plus 1. Because we usually present the lower and upper limits of the distribution when identifying the range, the point is often moot; but, we suggest that you

FIGURE 4.4 ■ Distributions differing in variability.

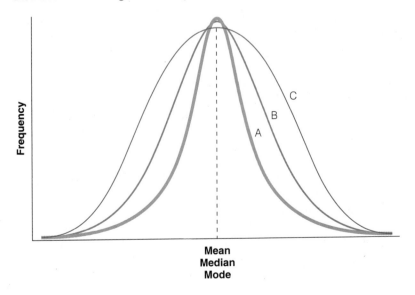

subtract the lowest from the highest value and then add 1 to obtain the true range. *It is generally good practice to begin a discussion of your data by mentioning the lowest (minimum) and highest (maximum) values (i.e., the range).*

Although often useful as a measure of dispersion, the range may be misleading at times. If, in the distribution 4, 6, 8, 8, 14, 22, we had a score of 42 rather than 22, the range would be 4 to 42, but we would not know based on the range that there was a large gap between 14 (the second highest) and 42. Or consider that all three distributions in Figure 4.4 would likely have approximately the same range, but yet they obviously differ in their degree of variability. The range is something like the mode in that it is a quick and easy way to begin to describe the data set, but not without problems.

The **standard deviation** is the most important measure of variability. Let's first provide a definition and then examine what it is that the sample standard deviation (symbolized as *s*) tells us about our data set. It is defined as:

$$s = \sqrt{\frac{\Sigma(X - M)^2}{N - 1}}$$

Equation 4.2

where *X* refers to an individual score, *M* is the sample mean, *N* represents sample size, and Σ is the symbol for summation

The "heart" of the standard deviation is the deviation of a score from the mean, that is, $(X - M)$. To obtain the standard deviation, we first find out how far each score is from the mean. Clearly, when scores are very close to the mean, the deviations from the mean will be small, and, when scores are far from the mean, the deviations will be large. This suggests that one way to describe variability in a data set would be to find the typical deviation from the mean. We could do this by summing all the deviations and then dividing by the number of deviations; in other words, we could find the mean of the deviations from the mean. However, you may recall that a characteristic of the mean is that the sum of the deviations from the mean is always zero. Dividing zero by the number of deviations won't work. We could consider using the absolute value of the deviations (i.e., ignoring the minus signs) and then find the average absolute deviation. In fact, this particular measure of variability was once regularly used in psychology.

Modern statistical procedures rely on a different technique to approximate the average deviation from the mean: the deviations are squared and then summed. We calculate the sum of the squared deviations from the mean $[\Sigma(X - M)^2]$ by subtracting the mean from each score, squaring that deviation, and then finding the total of the squared deviations. At this point, we calculate what is essentially the average of the squared deviations about the mean by dividing by 1 less than the sample size (i.e., $N - 1$). This particular value, the "mean" of the squared deviations, is called the *variance,* and, although it's not particularly helpful in the descriptive stage of analysis, you will find that the variance is important in later stages of analysis. Finally, to finish our calculation of the standard deviation, we take the square root of this variance so that our measure of variability is no longer expressed as squared deviations.

The standard deviation tells us approximately how far the scores vary from the mean on the average. In other words, the standard deviation is really a mean of sorts; it approximates the average distance of a score from the mean. If the standard deviation were 10, then the "typical" distance a score is from the mean is approximately 10. The smaller the standard

BOX 4.3 ■ Is it N or $N - 1$?

This average or mean squared deviation involves division by $N - 1$ rather than N so as to provide an unbiased estimate of the population variance based on a sample. The square root of the variance is the standard deviation. Remember, we use sample data to infer characteristics of the population. The standard deviation calculated with N in the denominator will (especially when sample size is small) underestimate the population standard deviation. Thus, to provide a better estimate of the population standard deviation, we subtract 1 from the sample size (N) before dividing into the sum of squared deviations. This raises slightly the mean squared deviation and results in a closer approximation to the population standard deviation than if N were used.

If we were describing a population of scores rather than a sample, there would be no need to correct for sampling bias and we would correctly divide the sum of the squared deviations by the total number of scores (N) before taking the square root. The symbol for the population standard deviation is the Greek letter (lower case) sigma, σ. Thus,

$$\sigma = \sqrt{[\Sigma(X - \mu)^2/N]}$$

where μ = population mean and N = total number of scores in population.

As you have learned, we most often work with samples and not populations. For this reason, most statistical computer programs provide by default a standard deviation based on $N - 1$ in the denominator. *We suggest that you simply use the formula for the sample standard deviation (i.e., based on $N - 1$) for describing variability of a data set unless you are sure that you have all the data of interest.* Moreover, with large data sets, as in most populations, it really doesn't make much difference whether all the scores or one less than all the scores are used in the calculation; thus, even here you are safe using $N - 1$.

deviation, the closer scores are to the mean of the distribution (on the average). Looking at Figure 4.4, we can correctly assume that the standard deviation of A is smaller than that of B, which is smaller than that of C. When comparing two distributions based on similar data, we know that a distribution with $s = 5$ is a "tighter" distribution than one with $s = 10$.

The standard deviation of a sample of scores is indicated as SD when appearing in research reports, but it is often symbolized as s in statistical formulas. The variance, a measure of dispersion that will be important later, in the estimation stage of analysis, is the square of the standard deviation, that is, s^2. In the next chapter, we will have more to say about variance as used in statistical inference.

Table 4.2 illustrates the calculation of the *standard deviation* based on sample data. You rarely will calculate a standard deviation from scratch; however, knowing how to do so will help remove the mystery that surrounds computer-generated statistics.

The range of happiness ratings in Katie's study was 1 through 7. The standard deviation was 1.55. We previously saw that $M = 5.16$, $Mdn = 5.50$, and Mode = 6. By combining numerical measures of central tendency and variability with the graph of the distribution seen in Figure 4.1, we can describe well what Katie found when she surveyed 80 university students.

TABLE 4.2 ■ Calculation of a Sample Standard Deviation

	X	$(X - M)$	$(X - M)^2$
$s = \sqrt{\dfrac{\Sigma(X - M)^2}{N - 1}}$	4	$4 - 5 = -1$	1
	9	$9 - 5 = 4$	16
$N = 5$	5	$5 - 5 = 0$	0
$M = \Sigma X/N = 25/5 = 5$	4	$4 - 5 = -1$	1
	3	$3 - 5 = -2$	4
$s = \sqrt{\dfrac{22}{4}} = \sqrt{5.5} = 2.35$	$\Sigma X = 25$		$\Sigma(X - M)^2 = 22$

THE STANDARD DEVIATION AND STANDARD SCORES

The standard deviation can be used to express a score's relative position in a distribution. This turns out to be particularly important when we wish to describe where someone stands in a distribution relative to his or her position in a different distribution. Consider an age-old question asked of students in their first statistics class: Are you taller than you are heavy? (Or, if you like, heavier than you are tall?) By using the standard deviation as a unit of measure, we can answer that question. Just watch.

Let's suppose that the mean weight of a large sample of adult Americans (both men and women) is 150 lbs. and the standard deviation is 15. And let us assume that the average adult height in this sample (again men and women are combined for our example) is 69 in. (5 ft. 9 in.) and the standard deviation of the height distribution is 4 in. Finally, let us assume that both distributions are bell shaped as shown in Figure 4.5.

Consider a student who weighs 160 lbs. and is 73 in. tall (6 ft., 1 in.). (Do you get the feeling we are talking about a rather tall, slender type?) Height and weight are like apples and oranges. How might we compare them?

A **z score** expresses a score's distance from the mean in standard deviation units. Specifically,

$z = (\text{score} - \text{mean})/\text{standard deviation}$ **Equation 4.3**

FIGURE 4.5 ■ Hypothetical distributions of height and weight.

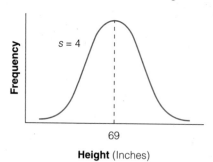

When calculating a *z* score, *N* may be used to find the standard deviation because we are not estimating the population standard deviation but are simply describing a score's distance from the mean of a distribution. As was noted previously, the standard deviation, when based on all the scores in the distribution, would be defined as

$$s = \sqrt{[\Sigma(X - M)^2/N]} \quad \text{or} \quad \sigma = \sqrt{[\Sigma(X - \mu)^2/N]}.$$

Therefore, the standard score, z, for a population would be defined as

$$(X - \mu)/\sigma$$

However, remember that the "default" standard deviation for many computer programs is that based on $N - 1$ because the assumption is made that typically we are using samples and are interested in making inferences about population characteristics. Moreover, *z* scores when calculated by popular computer programs (e.g., SPSS) are often based on a standard deviation using $N - 1$. For large data sets, a *z* score based on a sample standard deviation (i.e., when $N - 1$ is used) will closely approximate the *z* score obtained using *N*. Thus, once you have 50 or more scores, there is little difference between the two standard deviations or the *z* scores based on these standard deviations.

If the distance between the mean and a score equals the value of the standard deviation, a score's distance from the mean will be "1 standard deviation unit" or be equivalent to a *z* score of 1.00. Table 4.3 illustrates the transformation of a small set of data to *z* scores. Note that the sum of *z* scores is zero; this will always be true because a *z* score is based on deviations from the mean of a distribution. Recall that an important characteristic of the mean is that the sum of the deviations from the mean is zero. (See Table 4.1.)

As you can see in Figure 4.5, a student who weighs 160 lbs. is two-thirds of a standard deviation above the mean in the weight distribution, but someone who is 73 in. tall is one

TABLE 4.3 ■ Calculation of *z* scores for a Sample Data Set

$M = 3.33 \; s = 1.63$
z = (score − mean)/standard deviation, or $(X − M)/s$

X	$(X - M)/s$	= z
1	(1 − 3.33)/1.63	= −1.43
2	(2 − 3.33)/1.63	= −.82
3	(3 − 3.33)/1.63	= −.20
4	(4 − 3.33)/1.63	= .41
5	(5 − 3.33)/1.63	= 1.02
5	(5 − 3.33)/1.63	= 1.02
	$\Sigma z =$	0.0

BOX 4.5 ■ Questions (and Answers) about Rounding

About this time in a statistics course, questions about rounding numbers with decimal points become salient. After all, you need to report the results of your calculations, and decisions must be made about the number of decimal points to include in an answer. The *APA Publication Manual*, 5th edition (2001) states that *in general* (there are always exceptions!) *numbers should be reported with two decimal digits*. (See p. 129 of the *Manual*). But, to report numbers with two decimal digits, you must also decide how to round. The following conventions should be followed:

(a) Round up when the third decimal digit is 6 or greater. For example, round 5.6778 to 5.68, 24.3381 to 24.34.

(b) Do not round up when the third decimal digit is 4 or less. For example, report 5.6729 as 5.67, 24.3346 as 24.33.

(c) When the third decimal digit is 5 and *either there are no more digits or all other digits following 5 are zero,* round up when the second digit is odd and do not round up when the second digit is even. For example, round 8.775 to 8.78, 5.66500 to 5.66, and 8.7550 to 8.76.

(d) When the third decimal digit is 5 and *there are digits greater than zero following the 5,* always round up. For example, round 8.7751 to 8.78, 5.66523 to 5.67, 10.455004 to 10.46, and 8.74540 to 8.75.

Note: The *Manual* also has rules for reporting zero *before* the decimal point (p. 128). Specifically, use a zero before a decimal point when numbers are less than 1 (e.g., 0.45) *except* when the number cannot be greater than 1 (e.g., when reporting proportions or probabilities).

---

standard deviation above the mean of the height distribution. This difference in relative position within these distributions can be described using z scores:

z score (weight) $= (160 - 150)/15 = 10/15 = 0.67$

z score (height) $= (73 - 69)/4 = 4/4 = 1.00$

Because the student's z score for height is larger than that for weight, this particular student is taller than he or she is heavy.

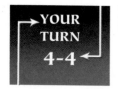

Your blind date is 6 ft. 6 in. and weighs 180 lbs. Relatively speaking, where does your date fall in each of the fictional height and weight distributions seen in Figure 4.5? ■

DATA DESCRIPTION AND THE NORMAL CURVE

Measures of central tendency and variability are related in important ways to normal distributions of scores. A normal curve is symmetrical in that one side is a mirror image of the other. However, other distributions may be symmetrical as well. The bimodal distribution seen in Figure 4.2(a) is one example of a symmetrical distribution that is not normal. Normal curves are bell shaped (and are able to be described mathematically), and many measures of interest to behavioral scientists have this form. Distributions of height, IQ scores, sizes of leaves, and numerous other naturally occurring variables have this form.

As noted previously, an important characteristic of the normal or bell-shaped distribution is that the measures of central tendency (mean, median, and mode) are all the same value. Think about what this tells you. For example, what proportion (percentage if you like) of the scores in a normal distribution fall above the mean? That is a question you are used to associating with the median, but remember that the mean and median (and mode) have the same value in a normal distribution. Therefore, half (.50 or 50%) of the scores in a normal distribution fall above (and below) the mean (and median or mode).

Measures of variability are also importantly related to normal distributions. For example, the range of a normal distribution is approximately six standard deviations. Thus, if you know the distribution is normal in form and you also know the standard deviation, you can easily estimate the range by multiplying the standard deviation by 6. (Note: This is only an approximation.) Given that it is a symmetrical distribution, it must be (approximately) three standard deviations in length on one side of the mean and three on the other side. Thus, you know that about half (.50 or 50%) of the scores fall between the mean and three standard deviations above the mean (or between the mean and three standard deviations below the mean).

The area under a normal curve is best represented in the form of a **relative frequency distribution.** A relative frequency distribution describes a data set by identifying the relative frequency or proportion of scores for each value or for each grouped frequency interval. Up to this point, we have described frequency distributions based on the number of actual scores in the distribution. In this case, the vertical axis of a frequency polygon tells us the number of times (actual frequencies) a particular value appears in the distribution. When there are very many scores in a distribution, constructing a simple frequency polygon or histogram often becomes impractical. This is particularly true when we need to talk about theoretical distributions based on an infinite number of scores. The vertical axis would need to range from zero to infinity! Moreover, when describing distributions in terms of the proportion of scores falling between any two specific values, it is often easier to use a relative frequency distribution. In this case, the vertical axis represents the relative frequency of each score.

Consider the following simple grouped frequency distribution of 20 scores:

Scores	Frequency
30–34	4
35–39	7
40–44	5
45–49	4
	Total = 20

Figure 4.6 is a histogram describing this distribution. The vertical axis shows the actual frequency of scores in each interval. Now consider what happens as we express each interval

FIGURE 4.6 ■ Histogram showing frequency of scores.

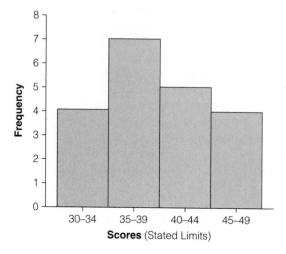

frequency in terms of its relative frequency in the distribution. We divide each frequency by the total number of scores to obtain a measure of relative frequency or proportion.

Scores	Frequency	Relative Frequency (Proportion)
30–34	4	4/20 = .20
35–39	7	7/20 = .35
40–44	5	5/20 = .25
45–49	4	4/20 = .20
Total = 20		Total = 1.00

Figure 4.7 is a histogram of the same set of scores but based on relative frequency. Note that the shapes of the distributions in Figure 4.6 and 4.7 are exactly the same.

In a normal distribution, the mean is (relative to the other scores) the most frequent score, as is the median and mode. Thus, a relative frequency distribution will show that the mean is the highest point in the distribution. Scores in the tails of a normal distribution are, relatively speaking, less frequent, and, therefore, the height of the relative frequency curve will be much lower in the tails. A polygon showing relative frequency retains exactly the same shape as a simple frequency polygon, but relative frequencies—not real frequencies—are described.

When a relative frequency polygon or histogram is constructed for very large sets of numbers, the label "Relative Frequency" will usually appear on the vertical axis but without any numbers on the axis. The vertical or y-axis may be thought of as relative frequency per unit of the horizontal or x-axis. The units of measure will vary from distribution to distribution (e.g., inches, pounds, IQ scores, etc.). When we plot relative frequency, we are choosing not to emphasize the actual frequency per unit; rather, a *relative frequency curve focuses*

FIGURE 4.7 ■ Histogram showing relative frequency of scores.

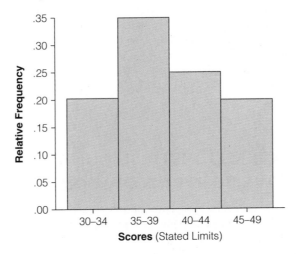

us on the shape of a distribution. One hundred percent (proportion = 1.00) of the scores fall under the curve.

Consider two normal distributions based on widely different numbers of scores and expressed in different units of measure. Relative frequency curves of both distributions will be bell shaped with 50% of the scores falling above and below the mean. When we don't need to know the actual frequencies but are simply interested in describing the overall characteristics of a distribution, a relative frequency distribution is often preferred.

Figure 4.8 is a relative frequency distribution of test scores from a very large sample of test takers. The relative frequency polygon describing this large sample is, as you can see,

FIGURE 4.8 ■ Relative frequency distribution of a large sample of test scores (dashed line shows that distribution resembles a normal curve).

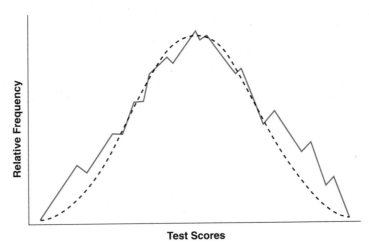

essentially symmetrical and looks like a normal or bell-shaped curve. You have learned something important about this distribution even though you do not know the actual number of test scores at any particular unit of measure. You know that you are dealing with a normal distribution of scores. As we will show in the next section, when a large number of scores are distributed normally, we are able to make decisions about a particular score's position in the distribution based on what we know about normal distributions in general. To help you understand how to make these decisions, we will need to refer to relative frequency distributions.

HOW DO WE USE A NORMAL DISTRIBUTION TO DESCRIBE THE RELATIVE POSITIONS OF SCORES?

Because of certain mathematical properties of a theoretical normal curve, the proportion of scores between any two points of the normal curve can be determined if we know the mean and standard deviation. Figure 4.9 is a theoretical normal curve with the proportion of scores falling between various points in the distribution marked off in standard deviation units. The relative frequency distribution in Figure 4.9 is a **theoretical distribution** and is thus assumed to be based on an infinite number of scores. On the other hand, the distribution of test scores in Figure 4.8 is called an **empirical distribution** because it is based on actual scores obtained from a large sample of test takers.

Consider first what we can learn about the proportion of scores falling between the mean and one standard deviation above or below the mean of a theoretical normal curve. As you can see in Figure 4.9, approximately one-third (exactly .3413) of the scores in a normal distribution fall between the mean and one standard deviation. Approximately 48% (exactly 47.72%) fall between the mean and two standard deviations. About 95% (exactly 95.44%) fall between plus two and minus two standard deviations from the mean.

FIGURE 4.9 ■ Theoretical normal curve.

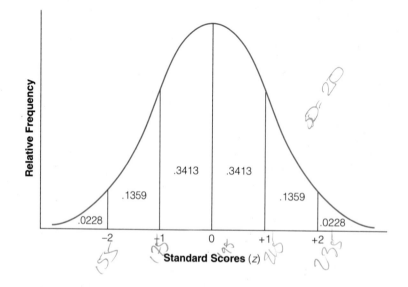

The concept of relative frequency is critical to understanding area within the normal curve. All (1.00 or 100%) of the scores are contained within the distribution. The proportion of scores (relative frequency) that fall between any two points in the distribution may be determined. This proportion is referred to as the *area* of the curve.

It is important to note that, as long as we are talking about a normal distribution, it does not matter what the specific mean and standard deviation are. That's the beauty of the normal curve. The area beneath the theoretical normal curve is described in terms of "standard deviation units" or "standard normal scores" (also called *z* scores) because these units measure the same thing no matter what the means and standard deviations are of the data plotted.

Look again at Figure 4.9 and consider the following questions. Assume a normal distribution of scores with a mean equal to 100 and a standard deviation equal to 10. (a) Approximately what proportion would fall above a score of 110? (b) Above a score of 120? (c) Below a score of 90? ∎

Now consider the following problem. You have just taken a standardized test along with thousands of other students across the country. The distribution of scores is normal with a mean of 100 and standard deviation of 20. Your score is 140. What percentage of the students taking the test scored below you? Closely examine Figure 4.9.

You should be able to see that your score was a very good one; you are two standard deviations above the mean. The *z* score equivalent is $(140 - 100)/20 = 2.00$.

Therefore, 97.72% of the people taking the test had scores lower than yours. Another way to state this is to say that your score is equivalent to a **percentile rank** of 97.72. A percentile rank indicates the proportion (percentage) of scores in a distribution falling at or below a particular score. The score associated with that percentile rank in the distribution is called a **percentile.** Thus, in our example, we may say that your score of 140 is approximately the 98th percentile (after rounding).

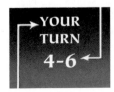

Assume that your performance on an exam earned you a percentile rank of 80, placing you at the 80th percentile. Explain what that means. ∎

We have been using scores that are always one or two standard deviation units from the mean. We did this so that you could answer questions using the information found in Figure 4.9 and get a feel for how relative distance from the mean can be described using a normal distribution. However, as we indicated, the proportion of scores falling between any two points can be determined. To do this, we first express a score in standard deviation units, that is, in terms of a *z* score. Once a *z* score is calculated, we need only to look at a standard normal table to find the proportion of scores falling between the mean and any *z* score. Such a table is found in Appendix A (Table A.1). It is the remarkable nature of the normal curve that only one table is needed to describe these proportions. The same values apply to any normal distribution. Because the distribution is symmetrical, we need to know the values in just one direction from the mean; the same proportion applies to scores in the other direction. We illustrate this procedure more completely in the next section.

COMPARING APPLES AND ORANGES
AGAIN (OR IQ AND HEIGHT)

As you have seen, when data from two distributions are converted (transformed) to z scores, we can compare an individual's performance across both distributions even when the scores refer to different variables. *Transforming all the scores in a distribution into z scores does not change the shape of the distribution* (as does a square root transformation discussed in Chapter 3). Converting scores into z scores is a linear transformation, and thus the distribution of z scores has the same shape as the original distribution. If the original distribution is normal in form, the distribution of z scores will be normal in form. If the original distribution is positively skewed, the z score distribution will be positively skewed. However, the mean and standard deviation of the transformed distribution are changed: the mean of a z score distribution is 0.0 and the standard deviation is 1.00.

We return now to the question we asked previously: Are you heavier than you are tall? In our previous example, we demonstrated that someone with a z score for height of 1.00 and a z score for weight of 0.67 would be considered to be taller, relatively speaking, than he or she is heavy. Just to make things interesting, let us ask if someone is smarter than he or she is tall. Of course, to answer that question, the same procedure and logic apply. If the z score corresponding to a student's height were 0.25 and the z score corresponding to that student's IQ were 1.75, we would know that this person is higher in the distribution of IQ scores than in the distribution of heights. Thus, this student would be judged smarter than he or she is tall.

Under the assumption that these are normal distributions, we can know even more about a person's relative position in these distributions. We can determine the proportion of people below someone in the IQ distribution and in the height distribution. In other words, we can find the percentile rank of these scores. To do this, we use a standard normal table, a portion of which is shown in Table 4.4.

To use the standard normal table, we need to know the z score corresponding to the value we are interested in. The standard normal table shows the proportion of scores falling between the mean and a particular z score *and* the proportion of scores falling between the z score and the end of the distribution. (See Table 4.4.) Because the normal curve is symmetrical, only the proportions for one side of the distribution need be given. What is on one side of the mean applies exactly to the other side; however, it is important to note whether we are looking at scores above or below the mean of the distribution. *A z score corresponding to a number below the mean will be negative; a z score of a number above the mean will be positive.* For example, a number that's exactly one standard deviation below the mean has a z score equivalent of −1.00, and a number that's exactly one standard deviation above the mean has a z score equivalent of 1.00. (By convention, we treat numbers without a minus sign as positive.)

To answer our question about the proportion of people below someone in the IQ distribution and in the height distribution, we use the z scores for the values of height and IQ as well as the information found in the standard normal table. For example, let's work with the example numbers we previously mentioned and assume that the z score corresponding to an individual's height is 0.25 and the z score equivalent of this person's IQ is 1.75. We next consult the standard normal table to determine the exact proportion of scores between the mean and each z score.

TABLE 4.4 ■ Portion of Standard Normal Table (see Table A-1 in Appendix)

z	0 z	0 z	z	0 z	0 z	z	0 z	0 z
0.00	.0000	.5000	0.55	.2088	.2912	1.10	.3643	.13S7
0.01	.0040	.4960	0.56	.2123	.2877	1.11	.3665	.1335
0.02	.0080	.4920	0.57	.2157	.2843	1.12	.3686	.1314
0.03	.0120	.4880	0.58	.2190	.2810	1.13	.3708	.1292
0.04	.0160	.4840	0.59	.2224	.2776	1.14	.3729	.1271
0.05	.0199	.4801	0.60	.2257	.2743	1.15	.3749	.1251
0.06	.0239	.4761	0.61	.2291	.2709	1.16	.3770	.1230
0.07	.0279	.4721	0.62	.2324	.2676	1.17	.3790	.1210
0.08	.0319	.4681	0.63	.2357	.2643	1.18	.3810	.1190
0.09	.0359	.4641	0.64	.2389	.2611	1.19	.3830	.1170
0.10	.0398	.4602	0.65	.2422	.2578	1.20	.3849	.1151
0.11	.0438	.4562	0.66	.2454	.2546	1.21	.3869	.1131
0.12	.0478	.4522	0.67	.2486	.2514	1.22	.3888	.1112
0.13	.0517	.4483	0.68	.2517	.2483	1.23	.3907	.1093
0.14	.0557	.4443	0.69	.2549	.2451	1.24	.3925	.1075
0.15	.0596	.4404	0.70	.2580	.2420	1.25	.3944	.1056
0.16	.0636	.4364	0.71	.2611	.2389	1.26	.3962	.1038
0.17	.0675	.4325	0.72	.2642	.2358	1.27	.3980	.1020
0.18	.0714	.4286	0.73	.2673	.2327	1.28	.3997	.1003
0.19	.0753	.4247	0.74	.2704	.2296	1.29	.4015	.0985
0.20	.0793	.4207	0.75	.2734	.2266	1.30	.4032	.0968
0.21	.0832	.4168	0.76	.2764	.2236	1.31	.4049	.0951
0.22	.0871	.4129	0.77	.2794	.2206	1.32	.4066	.0934
0.23	.0910	.4090	0.78	.2823	.2177	1.33	.4082	.0918
0.24	.0948	.4052	0.79	.2852	.2148	1.34	.4099	.0901
0.25	.0987	.4013	0.80	.2881	.2119	1.35	.4115	.0885
0.26	.1026	.3974	0.81	.2910	.2090	1.36	.4131	.0869
0.27	.1064	.3936	0.82	.2939	.2061	1.37	.4147	.0853
0.28	.1103	.3897	0.83	.2967	.2033	1.38	.4162	.0838
0.29	.1141	.3859	0.84	.2995	.2005	1.39	.4177	.0823
.	.	.	.	.	.	.	.	.
.	.	.	.	.	.	.	.	.
.	.	.	.	.	.	.	.	.
1.65	.4505	.0495	2.22	.4868	.0132	2.79	.4974	.0026
1.66	.4515	.0485	2 23	.4871	.0129	2.80	.4974	.0026
1.67	.4525	.0475	2 24	.4875	.0125	2.81	.4975	.0025
1.68	.4535	.0465	2.25	.4878	.0122	2.82	.4976	.0024
1.69	.4545	.0455	2.26	.4881	.0119	2.83	.4977	.0023
1.70	.4554	.0446	2 27	.4884	.0116	2.84	.4977	.0023
1.71	.4564	.0436	2 28	.4887	.0113	2.85	.4978	.0022
1.72	.4573	.0427	2.29	.4890	.0110	2.86	.4979	.0021
1.73	.4582	.0418	2.30	.4893	.0107	2.87	.4979	.0021
1.74	.4591	.0409	2.31	.4896	.0104	2.88	.4980	.0020
1.75	.4599	.0401	2.32	.4898	.0102	2.89	.4981	.0019
1.76	.4608	.0392	2.33	.4901	.0099	2.90	.4981	.0019
1.77	.4616	.0384	2.34	.4904	.0096	2.91	.4982	.0018
1.78	.4625	.0375	2.35	.4906	.0094	2.92	.4982	.0018
1.79	.4633	.0367	2.36	.4909	.0091	2.93	.4983	.0017
1.80	.4641	.0359	2.37	.4911	.0089	2.94	.4984	.0016
1.81	.4649	.0351	2.38	.4913	.0087	2.95	.4984	.0016
1.82	.4656	.0344	2.39	.4916	.0084	2.96	.4985	.0015
1.83	.4664	.0336	2.40	.4918	.0082	2.97	.4985	.0015
1.84	.4671	.0329	2.41	.4920	.0080	2.98	.4986	.0014
.	.	.	.	.	.	.	.	.
.	.	.	.	.	.	.	.	.
.	.	.	.	.	.	.	.	.

Consider first the proportion of scores falling between the mean and a *z* score of 0.25. We see in Table 4.4 that the proportion of scores between the mean and a *z* score of 0.25 is .0987. Because a positive *z* score indicates a value above the mean, we must add .50 to this proportion to find the proportion of people falling below this *z* score, that is, .50 + 0.0987 = .5987. Similarly, we can see that the proportion of scores between the mean and a *z* score of 1.75 is .4599. Again, we add .50 to this proportion so that we include those below the mean, that is, .50 + .4599 = .9599. These *z* scores and corresponding proportions below each *z* score (shaded areas) are shown in Figure 4.10.

FIGURE 4.10 ■ Normal distribution showing relative positions of height and IQ scores (example 1).

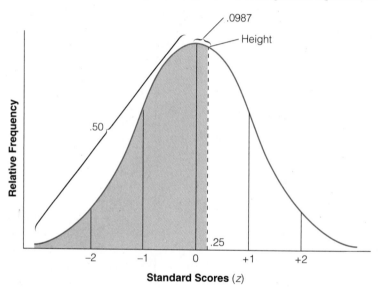

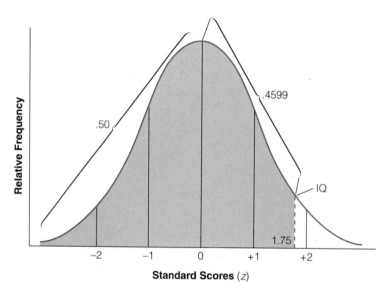

This individual's height is greater than approximately 60% of the people in this distribution, whereas this person's IQ is greater than about 96% of the people. To put this another way, the percentile rank associated with this individual's height is 60 and that of IQ is 96. (Although not too tall, this is a very smart person! His or her IQ is at nearly the 96th percentile.)

If a z score is negative (indicating that a score value is below the mean), the procedure changes slightly. Consider once again hypothetical z scores for a student's height and IQ. Assume that the z score equivalent for height is now -0.25 (and not 0.25 as before), and that this student also has a z score of 1.75 for IQ. We have indicated these values on the standard normal curve in Figure 4.11. It is easy to see looking at these distributions that the

FIGURE 4.11 ■ Normal distribution showing relative positions of height and IQ scores (example 2).

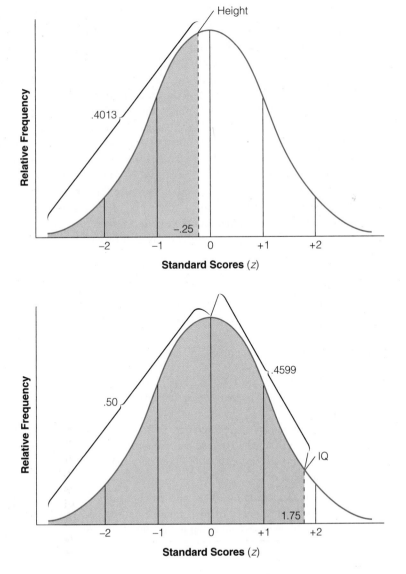

BOX 4.6 ■ HINT: Draw a Picture and Shade It (When Determining Proportions under the Normal Curve)

Look again at Figure 4.10 and 4.11. The areas of the curve we are interested in have been shaded. When seeking to determine the areas beneath the normal curve, it is helpful to draw a picture of a normal curve, indicate the mean (midpoint), mark off approximate areas (and proportions) corresponding to plus and minus one and two standard deviations, and then shade in the area of the curve that you are seeking. A picture helps! Try it when doing the standard normal problems at the end of this chapter.

---

z score for IQ places someone much higher in the distribution than does his or her z score for height. We consult the standard normal table as we did before to determine the exact relative frequency of people below these two z score values. Because we already did this for $z = 1.75$, let's look at the proportion of people below $z = -0.25$.

We look up the z score of 0.25 in the standard normal table as we did previously. The sign associated with the z score, plus or minus, is not important when consulting the standard normal table. It *is*, however, when calculating relative frequencies. The proportion of cases falling between the mean and a z score of 0.25 (either plus or minus) is .0987. Because in this case the z score is negative, one way to determine how many scores fall below this particular z score is to subtract that proportion from .50. Thus, $.50 - .0987 = .4013$. A simpler method is to use the other column in Table 4.4, the one showing the area between a z score and the end of the distribution. This area is shaded in Figure 4.11. You can see that a person with a z score of -0.25 is taller than 40.13% of the people in that distribution. We can say that this individual's height has a percentile rank of about 40.

Table 4.5 summarizes the steps taken to obtain information concerning relative standing in terms of percentiles and percentile ranks in a normal distribution.

TABLE 4.5 ■ Steps in Determining Percentiles and Percentile Ranks from Normal Curve

1. Calculate z score from raw score: $z = (\text{score} - \text{mean})/\text{standard deviation}$.
2. Use Table A.1 (Appendix A) to find proportion of scores between the mean and your z score.
   (a) If z score is positive, then add .50 to the proportion found in step #2;
   (b) If z score is negative then subtract proportion from .50 (or use the column showing the proportion of scores between your z-score and the end of the distribution).
3. Multiply proportion by 100 to give percentage.
   The result corresponds to the percentile rank of your raw score, or, stated slightly differently, your score is equal to this percentile point.

YOUR TURN 4-7

Follow the steps in Table 4.5 to answer the following question:

You are in a sociology class with a very large number of people. Two exams are given in the class, and scores are normally distributed. The mean on the first class exam is 79, the standard deviation is 12, and your score is 85. On the second exam, the mean is 84 with a standard deviation of 9, and you score 81. What is the percentile rank of your score on each of these two exams? ■

WHAT YOU HAVE LEARNED AND THE NEXT STEP

At this point, you should be able to describe both the central tendency and variability of a sample data set and, by using your knowledge of the normal curve, determine where an individual's score falls in a normal distribution of numbers. Major concepts we discussed in this chapter include the following:

- Both the central tendency (a "typical" score, the value our data tend to center around) and variability (dispersion) of a data set need to be calculated and described.

- The three major measures of central tendency are the arithmetic mean (or average), the median, and the mode.

- The choice of a measure of central tendency to represent the data should be made only after inspecting the distribution of scores. The relationships among the mean, median, and mode differ for normal and skewed distributions.

- We should begin a description of a data set by mentioning the lowest (minimum) and highest (maximum) values (i.e., the range).

- The standard deviation tells us approximately how far the scores vary from the mean on the average.

- A sample standard deviation calculated with N in the denominator tends to underestimate the population standard deviation (especially when sample size is small). Thus, to provide a better estimate of the population standard deviation, we subtract 1 from the sample size (N) before dividing into the sum of squared deviations (i.e., $N - 1$). This raises slightly the estimate of the true mean squared deviation and results in a closer approximation to the population standard deviation than if N were used.

- We can express a score's relative position in a distribution in the form of a z score, defined as (score − mean)/ standard deviation.

- A relative frequency distribution describes a data set by identifying the relative frequency or proportion of scores for each value or for each grouped frequency interval.

- Because of mathematical properties of a theoretical normal curve, the proportion of scores between any two points of the normal curve can be determined if we know the mean and standard deviation.

- A percentile rank indicates the proportion (percentage) of scores in a distribution falling at or below a particular score. The score associated with that percentile rank in the distribution is called a percentile.

In the next chapter, we show how your knowledge of descriptive statistics and the normal curve can be used to make inferences about population characteristics from sample data.

Specifically, you will learn how to determine the degree of confidence a researcher has that a sample mean represents the true population mean. In addition, we illustrate how the results of a study involving a single sample mean should be reported following the stylistic requirements of the American Psychological Association.

Key Concepts

central tendency	bimodal distribution	theoretical distribution
variability	range	empirical distribution
arithmetic mean	standard deviation	percentile rank
median	z score	percentile
mode	relative frequency distribution	

Answers to *Your Turn* Questions

4-1. One suggestion is to carefully instruct participants in the use of the scale and give specific examples of how the scale should be used. Another important suggestion is to clearly label the points of the scale so that participants can easily understand what each scale value represents.

4-2. Only the mean must change when the value of any number in a data set changes. This is because the mean is based on the sum of all the numbers; change any number and the sum (total) will change. The mode or median *may* change depending on what specific value in the data set was changed. Can you imagine a small data set where if we change a certain number the median and mode also will change? How about 1, 2, 2, 3, 4, 5, 6, 6, 6? What is the median and mode? Suppose a 6 was changed to a 2. Now what is the median? Mode?

4-3. Because the mean tends to be pulled toward extreme scores in a skewed distribution (e.g., a few low ratings), the median (which is not affected by extreme scores) is a better choice than the mean as a measure of central tendency for Katie's data set. The admissions director can safely say that half of the students expressed their degree of happiness as greater than 5.50. (Note, of course, that 5.50 was never an option on the 7-point scale; the median is a "midpoint" in the data.) Another way to describe these data is to say that the most frequent response (i.e., the mode) to the happiness question was 6 on a 7-point scale. Thus, we suspect that a clever college admissions director may tell prospective and current students that the "modal"

response was 6 on a 7-point scale. Your knowledge of descriptive statistics hopefully will make you cautious of accepting the mode as a "typical" response until you are made aware of the frequency distribution for the data set. Remember that the mode can be misleading at times. We believe you would want to know how more frequent is the modal score than other scores and whether the data are skewed, bell shaped, or even bimodal.

4-4. The following calculations reveal that your date is taller than he or she is heavy, but not by much, and both statistics are relatively high in these hypothetical distributions. Personal observation of people's heights and weights may have already told you this, but now you know how to speak "quantitatively."
z score (weight) = $(180 - 150)/15 = 30/15 = 2.00$
z score (height) = $(78 - 69)/4 = 9/4 = 2.25$

4-5. A glance at Figure 4.9 should reveal the answers. The answers are (a) about 16% (exactly 15.87%), (b) about 2.5% (exactly 2.28%), and (c) about 16% (exactly 15.87%), respectively.

4-6. A percentile is a number below which a certain percentage of the scores fall, whereas a percentile rank is a percentage identifying how many numbers are below a particular value. For example, we might say that your test score is the 80th percentile; or, we might say that your score has a percentile rank of 80.

4-7. Step 1. Calculate z score for your score [z = (score − mean)/standard deviation] on each exam: Exam 1, z score = $(85 - 79)/12 = 0.50$; Exam 2, z score =

$(81 - 84)/9 = -0.33$. Step 2. Use Table A.2 (Appendix A) to find proportion of scores between the mean and your z scores. From Table A.2, the proportion for Exam 1 (i.e., z score $= 0.50$) is .1915; for Exam 2, the proportion of scores between the mean and your z score of 0.33 is .1293. Step 3. Because the z score was positive in Exam 1, we add .50 to the proportion found in step #2, that is, $.50 + .1915 = .6915$. Because the Exam 2 z score was negative, we subtract

the proportion found in step #2 from .50, that is, $.50 - .1293 = .3707$, or, more simply, use the second column in Table A.2 to find the area between a z score of 0.33 and the end of the distribution. Step 3. Multiply each proportion by 100 to give percentage: .6915 $\times$ 100 $= 69.15$; $.3707 \times 100 = 37.07$. Step 4. The percentile rank of your raw score on Exam 1 was 69, whereas the percentile rank of your score on Exam 2 was 37.

Analyzing and Interpreting Data: Problems and Exercises

1. What two characteristics of a data set should always be summarized and described?

2. How does the description of interval or ratio data differ from that of nominal data?

3. Explain why the mode is always a score (value) in your data set, whereas the mean or median may not be actual scores in your data set.

4. A researcher examines a large data set and finds it to be symmetrical and bell shaped (normal). She calculates the mean to be 150. What are the most likely values of the mode and median?

5. Calculate measures of central tendency for the following sample data sets:
   (a) 1, 4, 5, 5, 6, 6, 6, 7
   (b) 16, 16, 22, 23, 24, 27, 28, 30, 31
   (c) 100, 145, 220, 245, 290, 301

6. Calculate measures of central tendency for the following sample data sets:
   (a) 2, 2, 2, 2, 3, 5, 6, 7, 9
   (b) 3, 4, 5, 6, 6, 6, 6, 8, 10, 21
   (c) 4, 5, 5, 5, 8, 8, 8, 11

7. (a) Discuss the advantages and disadvantages of each measure of central tendency for each of the distributions in problem #6.
   (b) For which of the data sets would the median be a better measure of central tendency than the mean? Why?
   (c) Which of the data sets is skewed?
   (d) Bimodal?

   (Jotting down a stem-and-leaf display will help make the characteristics of these data sets more apparent.)

8. Consider again the data sets in problem #6. Explain why the range as a measure of dispersion is severely limited in terms of the information that it provides.

9. Explain how the calculation of the standard deviation is based on an average or mean? What is this mean called?

10. Calculate the sample standard deviation for each of the data sets in problem #5.

11. Calculate the sample standard deviation for each of the data sets in problem #6. Which of the data sets shows the greatest variability as measured by the standard deviation?

12. Define a "z score."

13. Explain why a score that is one standard deviation above the mean in a distribution of scores must have a z score equal to 1.00.

14. Calculate z scores for raw scores of 22 and 28 in distribution problem #5(b).

15. (a) Calculate a z score for a raw score of 5 in each of the distributions in problem #6.
    (b) Find the mean and standard deviation for the following data set (assuming that the data represent all the data of interest): 12, 14, 15, 15, 16, 17, 20, 22, 25, 26, 29, 29, 30, 30, 31, 35, 35, 35, 40, 41, 42, 43, 44, 45, 46, 48, 48, 50
    (c) Calculate z scores for the raw scores of 20 and 42 in distribution (b).

16. The score 25 appears five times in a distribution of 50 scores. What is the relative frequency of 25?

17. How does a theoretical distribution differ from an empirical distribution?

18. Approximately what proportion of scores in a normal distribution fall between the mean and plus or minus one standard deviation? Between plus or minus two standard deviations?

19. Provide definitions for "percentile rank" and "percentile."

20. A large lecture class has 150 students. On the first exam in the class, you get 80 out of 100 correct. The instructor informs you that your score has a percentile rank of 75. What does that mean?

21. Look again at Figure 4.9. Assume a large normal distribution of scores with mean equal to 200 and standard deviation equal to 15.
    (a) Approximately what proportion of scores would fall above a score of 230?
    (b) Above a score of 190?
    (c) Below a score of 215?
    (d) What is the percentile rank of each of these scores (a, b, and c)?

22. Look again at Figure 4.9. Assume a large normal distribution of scores with mean equal to 195 and standard deviation equal to 20.
    (a) Approximately what proportion of scores would fall above a score of 200?

    (b) Above a score of 190?
    (c) Below a score of 185?
    (d) What is the percentile rank of each of these scores (a, b, and c)?

23. Can you, based on your knowledge of the normal curve (see, e.g., problem #18), answer the following questions *without consulting the standard normal table?*
    (a) Assume a large normally distributed set of scores. The mean is 100 and the standard deviation is 15. Approximately how many scores fall above a score of 115?
    (b) Above a score of 70?

24. You have taken a standardized exam of mathematical aptitude along with thousands of other college students. The exam scores are normally distributed with a mean of 100 and standard deviation of 15. Your score on the exam is 120. What is the percentile rank of your score?

25. Assume that you now take a verbal aptitude test with many other college students. The mean on this test is 500 and the standard deviation is 20. Your score is 520. Are you better at math (problem #24) or verbal tests?

Answers to Odd-Numbered Problems

1. Central tendency and variability (dispersion).

3. The mode identifies the score that appears most frequently, whereas the median represents the middle point in a data set and may or may not be an actual value (e.g., the median in the data set 4, 5, 6, 8, 9, 10 is 7, which does not appear in the data set.) Similarly, the mean is an average based on the sum of scores divided by the number of scores and often is not an actual value (e.g., the mean in the previous data set also is 7; 42/6 = 7).

5. (a) Mean = 5.00, mode = 6, median = 5.50
   (b) Mean = 24.11, mode = 16, median = 24
   (c) Mean = 216.83, mode = none, median = 232.50

7. (a) Only in distribution (c) are the mean and median similar. In the other distributions, it would be important to present both the mean and median when describing the data set.
   (b) In distribution (b), the median is a better "typical score" given the extreme score that is present.

   (c) Both data sets (a) and (b) are somewhat positively skewed.

   (d) The mode is actually helpful for these particular data sets. For example, in distribution (c), we can see two distinct modes, that is, that the distribution is bimodal.

9. The standard deviation is the square root of the "mean squared deviations." We first determine each score's deviation from a mean and then square each of these deviations, sum them, and divide by one less than the number of squared deviations ($N - 1$). This average (or mean) of these squared deviations is called the *variance*. The square root of the variance is the standard deviation.

11. The sample standard deviations (i.e., based on $N - 1$) for data sets from problem #6 are as follows: (a) 2.63, (b) 5.13, and (c) 2.38. Clearly, distribution (b) shows the greatest variability as assessed by the standard deviation.

13. Because a z score measures a score's distance from the mean in standard deviation units, any score that is exactly one standard deviation above the mean will have a z score equivalent of 1.00. For example, suppose the mean of a distribution is 100 and the standard deviation is 10. A score of 110, exactly one standard deviation above the mean, will have a z score equal to $(110 - 100)/10$ or 1.00.

15. (a) When calculating z scores for these small data sets, we recommend that you use a standard deviation based on N rather than $N - 1$ because we are describing position within a data set and not making inferences. The true standard deviations for these data sets are (a) 2.48, (b) 4.87, and (c) 2.11. The z scores corresponding to the number 5 in each of these distributions are (a) $(5.0 - 4.22)/2.48 = 0.31$, (b) $(5.0 - 7.5)/4.87 = -0.51$, and (c) $(5.0 - 6.75)/2.11 = -0.83$. (Note that z scores for (b) and (c) are negative.) Using the standard deviation based on $N - 1$, the z scores corresponding to the number 5 in each of these distributions are (a) $(5.0 - 4.22)/2.64 = 0.29$, (b) $(5.0 - 7.5)/5.13 = -0.49$, and (c) $(5.0 - 6.75)/2.37 = -0.74$. (Note again that z scores for (b) and (c) are negative.) (b) The mean is 31.54 and the standard deviation (based on N of 28) is 11.76. (c) The z score for a value of 20 in this distribution is $(20 - 31.54)/11.76$, or $-.98$; the z score equivalent of 42 is $(42 - 31.54)/11.76$, or $+0.89$.

17. A theoretical distribution is based on an infinite number of scores (i.e., "it is theoretical"), and, as a consequence, a theoretical relative frequency distribution will appear as smooth lines when drawn. An empirical distribution is based on actual observations of individuals or events. An empirical relative frequency distribution will not necessarily have smoothly drawn lines unless based on many, many scores.

19. A *percentile rank* indicates the proportion of scores in a distribution falling at or below a particular score. A *percentile* is the score associated with a particular percentile rank.

21. (a) .0228, (b) .7486, (c) .8413, (d) The percentile ranks for these numbers (230, 190, 215) in this distribution are 97.72, 25.14, and 84.13, respectively.

23. If you can keep in mind what you learned about the relationship between the standard deviation and area within the normal curve (e.g., that approximately .34 of the scores fall between the mean and one standard deviation and that approximately .48 fall between the mean and two standard deviations; see especially Figure 4.9), then you should be able to answer these questions without having to consult the standard normal table. Specifically, in (a) you should see that a score of 115 is one standard deviation above the mean. This means that .34 of the scores fall between the mean and this score, and thus there are approximately .16 (or 16%) that fall above this score. Similarly, in (b) you should see that a score of 70 is exactly two standard deviations below the mean. Thus, there are approximately .98 (or 98%) of the scores above a score of 70 because approximately .48 of the scores fall between the mean and a score that is two standard deviations from the mean. Adding .48 to .50 (because the question asks about the proportion of scores above this score), we have .98.

25. Your z score equivalent is $(520 - 500)/20 = 1.00$. You are better at math (problem #24; z score $= 1.33$) than verbal tests.

 Go to http://psychology.wadsworth.com/courses/statistics/ and test your knowledge of this chapter by taking the online quiz. Another resource to check is the online workshops that provide a step-by-step guide through a number of topics at http://psychology.wadsworth.com/workshops/workshops.html.

PART 2

I-D-E-A for a Study Involving
a Single Mean

CHAPTER 5

Estimating Confidence in a Mean

It is well known that a sample mean is the best estimator of a population mean, but it is desirable to accompany this estimate with a measure of its precision. The most commonly used measure is the CI, or confidence band. . . .

Estes (1997, p. 337)

INTRODUCTION

Think once again about Katie, the researcher we discussed in the last chapter. She had been asked to find out how happy students were at her university and to report her findings to a group of college administrators. Her initial approach was to display a frequency distribution (histogram) of the data. Although this is a good beginning, we hopefully convinced you that it was insufficient data description. We suggested that she should supplement this picture of the sample distribution with some descriptive statistics, that is, measures of central tendency and variability.

Assume that Katie, armed with these descriptive statistics (the *D* of I-D-E-A), prepares a new report for the college officials who hired her. She says that the mean happiness ratings, based on a 7-point scale from a random sample of 80 students, was 5.16, with a standard deviation of 1.54. She also points out that half the students in her sample had happiness ratings above 5.50 (the median) and that the modal rating was 6.0. Pointing to the histogram of the data (see Figure 4.1), she showed that the distribution was negatively skewed with the ratings somewhat "bunched" toward the higher end of the scale. All this made the college officials happy, at least until some of the officials began to worry if she were really right. As one put it in a telephone call, "How do we know that your results should be trusted? What kind of guarantee can you give us that the mean happiness rating you found really reflects the mean happiness of *all* the students? You only surveyed 80 students, and there are thousands on this campus!"

You should recognize that the concerns of the college officials are about differences between samples and populations. Remember, we aren't really interested in samples: the happiness ratings of 80 students at a university are not what the college administrators are concerned about. Sample data are important because they allow us to say (or infer) something about the characteristics of the population from which the sample was drawn. On the basis of the mean (and median and modal) ratings from her sample, Katie concluded that the students were generally happy. But the university officials have every right to ask her to justify that conclusion. Why should these results be trusted? How do we know that the mean happiness of all the students would be close to 5? How confident is she of her results?

A researcher might give two answers in this situation. One answer is that a relatively large random sample was drawn, and the probability is fairly high that a large sample taken randomly will be representative of the population from which it came. But, of course, there is no guarantee that the sample will be representative; it just happens that most of the time it will be. Therefore, one answer might be, "Just trust me. The sample was pretty big and random." But our researcher can do better than that. She can provide an answer that specifies the probability that her results do indeed reflect the attitudes of all students on campus. However, obtaining this second answer to the question of confidence posed by the college official is a bit more complicated than simply asking someone to trust a random sampling procedure to produce results that are representative of a population. In this chapter and the next, we examine how our researcher might answer the question of estimating confidence by assigning a specific probability to her findings (the *E* of I-D-E-A).

POINT ESTIMATES AND INTERVAL ESTIMATES

A single sample value is a **point estimate** of a population value. The sample mean, for example, is a point estimate of the population mean. The mean of a randomly obtained sample of scores is our best estimate of the population mean. Our survey researcher has suggested that her best (point) estimate of the mean happiness of *all* students (i.e., the population mean) is 5.16.

Another way to estimate a population value, however, is to determine an interval that we have some stated degree of confidence contains the population parameter. Whereas a point estimate of the mean says, "I think the mean is 12," an **interval estimate** says, "I think the interval 9 to 15 contains the population mean." Another name for an interval estimate is **confidence interval** because, when constructing the interval that we think contains the population value, we also will express our confidence that we are right. To construct confidence intervals for a population mean, we have to think about the variation that occurs among random samples, or what is called *sampling variability,* a topic that we first discussed in Chapter 1.

WHAT IS SAMPLING VARIABILITY?

In many ways, sampling variability is what makes a statistics course necessary. If each time we drew a random sample we were guaranteed to obtain a sample that exactly represented the characteristics of the population, there would be no need to go any further. The sample mean of a truly representative sample will be identical to the corresponding population mean. If random samples always produced truly representative samples, a researcher would need to report only the sample mean. End of analysis. (And we assume you wouldn't need a whole course to learn about the mean.)

However, as you know by now, random selection is a process based on chance, and chance produces some fluctuation in sample characteristics. Not every sample is going to be strictly representative of the population. (See, for example, the demonstration in *Your Turn* 1-6 in Chapter 1.) Sample values, such as the mean, will vary from sample to sample even when the same (random selection) procedures are followed each time. Sample means, therefore, frequently will be in "error." Sample variability occurs because a random (i.e., chance) selection procedure is followed, and chance events are going to vary. However, it turns out that when random sampling procedures are used, we can obtain estimates of the amount of sampling variability that will occur. In other words, we can estimate the degree of chance variation associated with our results.

If this idea of chance variation isn't clear to you, imagine taking a random sample of students from a college class. Suppose we take a random sample of 10 students from a class with 30 students. Let's assume that the 30 students are the only students of interest, that is, that the class of 30 students represents a population. Now, imagine asking the 10 students in your sample some questions, such as their height and weight, and how happy they are in this class and how much they like the instructor. For these latter two questions you provide rating scales for students to indicate their answers. Assume you write down the answers to these questions and find a mean for their responses to each question. Then, you take another random sample of 10 students from the same population of 30 students and repeat your questions with this sample. Again you calculate the sample means for their responses to your questions; then you do this several more times. The million-dollar question is: Do you expect a sample mean, let's say for height, to be exactly the same from sample to sample? Remember, means of random samples are all estimates of the same thing: the population mean. We believe that you will agree that, even though the sample means are all estimates of the same population mean (that is, the mean of all 30 students), there will be some variation among the means from one sample to another due to chance. The sample means won't all be the same. We call this sample-to-sample variation **sampling error.** Other names, as presented in Chapter 1, are **sampling variation** or **sampling variability.**

Now perhaps you can appreciate the concern expressed by the college official who asked our researcher whether her sample mean was really the same as the population mean. We can assume that the college administrator had at least some intuitive notion of sample variability. The official is asking: How do we know where the sample mean is likely to be relative to the population mean? Is it close? How close?

We might mention one thing before we go on: our survey researcher will never be able to know with absolute certainty the value of the population mean. Samples permit us to make inferences, guesses, estimates, but they do *not* provide certainty. Our researcher cannot prove what the population mean is (unless, of course, she was able to actually track down every student on campus and obtain a happiness rating). But, she can identify a specific interval that has a high probability of containing the population mean. Let's see how this is done.

In the introduction, we suggested that Katie might simply tell the school officials that her sample was "pretty big and random" and that they should trust the results. Although we suggested that she could do better than that, there is something to be said for large, random samples. Does it make intuitive sense that the bigger a random sample the more representative it is likely to be? Suppose you were asked to be a judge in a pie-baking contest, and you must assign a rating to each of several pies after sampling them. Can you suggest why a sample based on one spoonful of pie may not be as representative of the pie's taste as one based on five teaspoons? Can you also imagine a way that taking five spoonfuls of a pie would not be representative? Do you think that there is a point (perhaps after 10 spoonfuls!) that by eating more you won't really learn very much more about the pie's taste? ■

THE SAMPLING DISTRIBUTION OF THE MEAN

To construct a confidence interval for a population mean, we make use of a theoretical sampling distribution of sample means. A **sampling distribution** is a frequency distribution of a *sample statistic* based on many random samples of the same size. To appreciate a sampling distribution, you have to use your imagination again. Specifically, let us consider a **sampling distribution of means.** Imagine that, unlike our previous example, you don't stop with 4, 5, or even 20 random samples of a given size from a population, but that you continue to take random samples of the same size from a population forever. Well, okay, how about for 1,000 years? You get the point. You want to collect many, many, many random samples of the same size from the same population. For each of your samples, you calculate the sample mean. You can now construct a frequency distribution of all the sample means. Once that is done, to be able to describe this distribution, you will want to find measures of central tendency and variability for your distribution of sample means. You now have a sampling distribution of means based on nearly all possible sample means and, assuming you can divide by some very big numbers (!), you will know the mean and standard deviation of this sampling distribution. (Of course, computers could do all this for you very quickly.)

Well, it turns out that you and your descendants don't need to spend the next 1,000 years doing this. And the reason is not simply that a computer could do the job in seconds. The shape of this sampling distribution, as well as the mean and standard deviation, are already known. The properties of the sampling distribution of means have been worked out mathematically; the procedure assumes an infinite number of cases. Thus, the distribution is a theoretical sampling distribution (unlike the empirical distribution you actually would have obtained if you spent the next millennium doing this). We know the following three things about this theoretical sampling distribution:

a. The mean of the sampling distribution of means will be the same as the mean (μ) of the population from which the samples were drawn.

b. The standard deviation of the sampling distribution of means is related lawfully to the sample size (N) and population standard deviation (σ) as:

$$\sigma_{M} = \frac{\sigma}{\sqrt{N}} \qquad\qquad \textbf{Equation 5.1}$$

To distinguish this standard deviation from a standard deviation of the population of scores (σ), the standard deviation of a sampling distribution of means is called the **standard error of the mean (σ_M).**

c. The distribution of sample means will be normal if the population is normal or if the sample size is fairly large (e.g., > 30).

In truth, according to the **central limit theorem** (on which this last statement is based), the sampling distribution becomes more normal as sample size increases. In other words, as you construct sampling distributions with larger and larger samples (of the same size) from a population, the shape of the sampling distributions becomes more and more normal in form—no matter what the shape of the original distribution.

Because the sampling distribution of means will be normal for all sample sizes if the population is normally distributed, this is one important reason to inspect the shape of the sample distribution before beginning to do statistical analyses. And this is particularly important when the sample size is small. In the inspection stage, we want to examine the distribution of the sample to see if it tends to be bell shaped. This is not an exact test; we "eyeball" the distribution (after creating a stem-and-leaf display or graph). *If a random sample is generally normal in form, we can be fairly confident that the population from which it came also will be approximately normally distributed.*

Figure 5.1 illustrates one such theoretical sampling distribution of means. The figure is a relative frequency distribution of all possible sample means of a given size.

Consider that your mean must be one of those means in this theoretical distribution. Think about this. You know that (if certain conditions are met) the sampling distribution of means is approximately normal in form, and you know the standard deviation (called the *standard error*) of that distribution. Because it is a distribution of *all* possible means of a given size, your sample mean must be among the means in this population. But where?

FIGURE 5.1 ■ Sampling distribution of means.

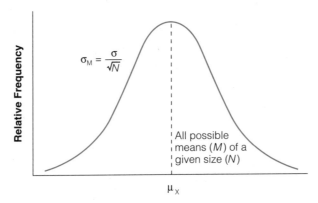

PROBABILITY AND NORMAL DISTRIBUTIONS

To obtain confidence intervals for a population mean, we need to make use of our knowledge of normal distributions and sampling distributions. Before proceeding, however, we must be certain that we understand both the notion of probability and its relationship to a normal distribution. First, let's review briefly the notion of probability.

You bring with you an intuitive notion of probability based on the many life experiences you have had. What are the odds that a coin, when fairly flipped, will land heads? (1 in 2, right?) What are the odds that, among three first-place winners in a contest, one name will be randomly drawn to get the prize? (1 in 3.) A typical deck of 52 playing cards contains 13 hearts, 13 spades, 13 clubs, and 13 diamonds. What is the probability that, when the cards are well shuffled, that a card with a heart on it will end up on top? (13/52, or 1 in 4.) Probabilities are typically expressed as proportions: 1/2 = .50, 1/3 = .33, 1/4 = .25.

Calculation of all these probabilities has something in common. Each expresses the following ratio:

$$\frac{\text{Number of Favorable Events}}{\text{Total Number of Events}}$$

What is considered a "favorable event" is up to you. When you are one of three finalists in a contest, your winning is the favorable event. When you are interested in knowing the probability of selecting randomly a spade from a deck of playing cards, the 13 spade cards are the favorable events. The total number of events will be defined by the situation. It is 52 when a normal deck of playing cards is used, but it would be 26 if only the black suits (spades and clubs) were present. When guessing randomly on a multiple-choice item with four alternatives, there typically is only one favorable event out of four possible events (probability = .25). Our odds of getting an answer correct "by chance" increase dramatically when an exam item is true or false (probability = .50), which no doubt explains some students' preference for this type of test.

Thus, when only chance is operating, **probability** is simply defined as the number of favorable events divided by the total number of equally possible events (Everitt, 1999). We think you likely had at least an intuitive notion of this already. There is certainly much more

FIGURE 5.2 ■ Theoretical normal curve revisited.

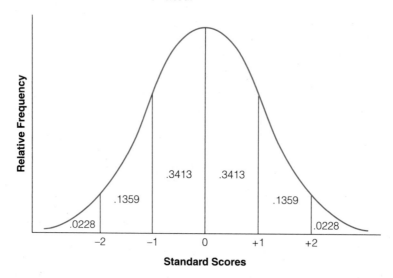

to this topic of probability (see, e.g., Thorndike & Dinnel, 2001), but we believe you can rely on this fundamental definition in what follows.

To apply this notion of probability to a normal distribution, we need to refer again to the area under the normal curve that was discussed in Chapter 4. Figure 5.2 again describes the proportion of cases associated with regions of the normal curve defined in standard deviation units (z scores). You learned in Chapter 4 that approximately 68% of the scores in a normal distribution fall between the mean and plus or minus one standard deviation (i.e., ± 1 z score). Now consider that the area underneath the normal curve defines the total number of possible scores (i.e., 1.00 or 100%). Given this fact, what is the probability of randomly drawing a score that falls within one standard deviation of the mean? Applying our definition of probability, you should see from Figure 5.2 that approximately 68 out of 100 cases (68.26%) are "favorable" or what we are interested in. Thus, the probability is .68 (approximately).

Just to be sure you are still with us, can you, by looking at Figure 5.2, answer the following questions?

a. What is the probability of reaching in randomly to a large normal distribution and selecting a score that is greater than one standard deviation from the mean?

b. What is the probability of randomly drawing a score that falls below a score that is one standard deviation above the mean?

c. What is the probability of randomly drawing a score that falls between a score that is one standard deviation below the mean and a score that is one standard deviation above the mean? ■

These questions about probability (see *Your Turn* 5-2) make use of your knowledge about the relative frequency of scores under the normal curve. As was noted in Chapter 4,

Table A.1 in Appendix A can be consulted to obtain specific proportions (or probabilities) under the normal curve once we have transformed a score into a z score. In what follows, we ask you to continue to use this knowledge to think about the probability of obtaining sample means of particular values when sampling randomly from a sampling distribution that is normal in form.

PROBABILITY AND THE SAMPLING DISTRIBUTION OF THE MEAN

It is time to put together what you know about normal distributions, sampling distributions, and probability.

You just saw that, under certain conditions, the sampling distribution of means is normal in form *and* we know its mean and standard deviation. Figure 5.3 illustrates a sampling distribution of means based on random samples of size 16 (i.e., $N = 16$) from a normal population with $\mu = 100$ and $\sigma = 20$. The shape of this sampling distribution will be normal in form because the population was normal in form. The standard deviation of this sampling distribution, or standard error of the mean ($\sigma/\sqrt{N}$) is $20/\sqrt{16}$, or 5.

Let's begin with a question about sample means based on this sampling distribution: What is the probability that a sample mean drawn randomly from this distribution will be greater than 100?

In some ways this is a trick question. We know the population mean is 100. Moreover, if the distribution is normal in form, then the mean and median (and mode) are the same value. Therefore, the median is also 100. And we know that the median separates the distribution into two equal halves. Thus *in any normal distribution 50% of the cases fall above the mean (and 50% fall below the mean)*. The probability is .50 that a mean selected at random from this sampling distribution will be greater than 100, the population mean.

Now consider a slightly more difficult question: What is the probability that a sample mean drawn randomly from this distribution of sample means when $N = 16$ will be greater than 105?

FIGURE 5.3 ■ Sampling distribution of means based on size $N = 16$.

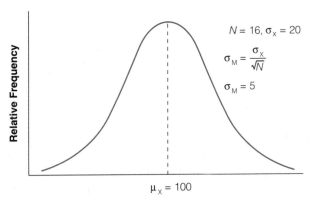

$$N = 16, \sigma_x = 20$$

$$\sigma_M = \frac{\sigma_x}{\sqrt{N}}$$

$$\sigma_M = 5$$

Relative Frequency

$$\mu_x = 100$$

Here is where your knowledge of z scores comes in. The standard error of the mean is 5. The standard error is the standard deviation of a sampling distribution of means. Thus, a sample mean with a value of 105 is exactly one standard deviation above the population mean. Thus, the z score corresponding to a sample mean of 105 is

$$\frac{105 - 100}{5} = 1.00$$

Looking at the relative frequency distribution in Figure 5.2, we see that approximately 16% of the scores (in this case, *scores* are *means*) will be greater than 105 (13.59% + 2.28% = 15.87%). Therefore, the probability that we will randomly draw a mean greater than 105 is .1587, or approximately .16.

Now consider another mean based on a random sample of size 16 taken from the population used in the last illustration ($\mu = 100$ and $\sigma = 20$). What if the mean we randomly drew from this population were 90? What is the probability of selecting at random a sample with mean equal to 90 *or less*? Converting 90 to a standard normal score produces:

$$z = (90 - 100)/5 = -2.00$$

An examination of Figure 5.2 reveals that .0228 of the scores in a normal distribution fall below a z score of -2.00. Therefore, we can say that the probability of obtaining a mean of 90 or less based on taking random samples of size 16 from a normal population with $\mu = 100$ and $\sigma = 20$ is .0228.

Of course, we don't need to rely on an examination of Figure 5.2 to obtain answers to these questions. The standard normal table in the appendix (see Table A.1) provides information about the relative frequency of scores between the mean and a particular z score and between a z score and the end of the distribution. Using the procedures described in Chapter 4, we can use Table A.1 to find the proportion of scores that fall between any two values in a normal distribution, or the proportion above or below a particular value.

YOUR TURN 5-3

The following two questions give you an opportunity to apply what you just learned. To answer them, you will need to use information found in the standard normal table (Table A.1 in Appendix A).

a. Assume that a random sample of size 25 was taken from a normal population with $\mu = 75$ and $\sigma = 10$. What is the probability that the value of the sample mean will be greater than 72?

b. Assume that you are sampling from the same population and wish to know the probability of randomly selecting a sample ($N = 25$) with mean greater than 80? (Recall the hint given in Chapter 4 (Box 4.4).) Draw a picture of a normal curve and shade in the area you are seeking. ■

Don't lose sight of the problem we began with. Katie, our happiness researcher, obtained a sample mean, and we are looking for a way to express confidence in this mean as an estimate of the population mean. The ideas presented thus far are critically important for this task. The problems and exercises at the end of this chapter give you additional opportunities to review probability and sampling distributions.

HOW DO WE USE A SAMPLING DISTRIBUTION TO ESTIMATE CONFIDENCE IN OUR FINDING?

Figure 5.4 shows theoretical sampling distributions of means based on sample sizes 5, 30, and 100, based on a normal population with $\mu = 50$. The relative frequency distributions in Figure 5.4 reveal that we know something else about the sampling distribution of means: *as sample size increases, the variability among sample means decreases.* If you think about this for a moment, you will realize why this is so. As the size of random samples gets larger, the sample mean becomes a better estimate of the population mean. Thus, as sample size increases, the sample means will more closely approximate the population mean.

This fact is also a simple deduction from the formula for the standard error of the mean. Look once again at the formula (Equation 5.1):

$$\sigma_M = \frac{\sigma}{\sqrt{N}}$$

What *has* to happen as N increases (and when the standard deviation remains constant)? You can see that dividing the population standard deviation by ever-increasing values of the square root of N will make for smaller and smaller standard errors.

Based on your knowledge of the normal curve, and the use of standard scores (z scores), we are in a position to answer some questions about the probability that a sample mean falls close to the actual population mean. As you might expect, we wish to transform the value of a sample mean to a z score to determine the probability of selecting a sample with a mean with a particular value. In other words, we wish to obtain answers to questions like those we posed previously (e.g., *Your Turn* 5-3). The problem is that one needs to know the population mean and standard deviation to calculate a standard normal score or z score for

FIGURE 5.4   ■   Sampling distributions of means based on different sample sizes from population with $\mu = 50$.

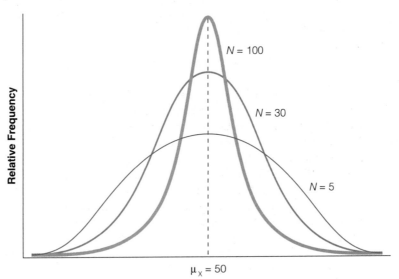

a sample mean [z = (sample mean − population mean)/population standard deviation]. In the preceding problems, you were given the values of the population mean and standard deviation. Armed with this information, and also knowing the sample size, you were able to calculate the standard error of the mean and then a z score for the value of the sample mean. (See, e.g., *Your Turn* 5-3.)

Our happiness researcher, Katie, knows neither the population mean nor the population standard deviation. She has a sample mean (and sample standard deviation) and wishes to know how close this sample mean is to an unknown population mean. We can help her do that; but first let us consider the rationale that underlies estimation procedures based on confidence intervals.

Just for the sake of argument, let's suppose that one did know the population standard deviation and thus could calculate the standard error of the mean. Although this may be the case in certain rare situations, more often than not, if you knew the population standard deviation, you would also know the population mean on which it is based. However, humor us for a minute, and assume that we possess a sample mean and the true standard error of the mean, but, alas, we do not know the population mean. The sample mean is a point estimate of the population mean. Not knowing anything else, the sample mean can be considered a good estimate of the population mean. But what if we want to know just how close the sample mean is to the true population mean? What if, for example, we wanted to find an interval that is likely to contain the population mean? We might proceed as follows.

We know that, if a population is normally distributed, 95% of the scores in the population fall between the mean ±1.96 standard scores. How do we know this? The value of 1.96 is obtained from the standard normal table by looking for the z score that contains .475 of the area (half of .95) under the normal curve between the mean and the z score of 1.96. Given that we are working with a symmetrical distribution, we know that .95 (.475 + .475) of the scores fall between −1.96 and +1.96. Because the theoretical sampling distribution of means contains *all* sample means, we know that the probability of any one mean falling 1.96 z scores, plus or minus, from the population mean is .95 (just as we know that the probability of any one mean falling plus or minus 1 z score from the mean is .6826). But, of course, we don't know the population mean.

However, consider this: assume we drew sample means randomly from the sampling distribution of all possible means, and every time we did this we calculated the following interval based on the sample mean:

$$M \pm 1.96 \, (\sigma_M)$$

If you think about this (really hard), you will realize that 95 times out of 100 we will actually capture the population mean within that interval no matter what the value of our sample mean. Let us explain why this must be the case.

Look carefully at the theoretical sampling distribution in Figure 5.5. Remember that this distribution contains all possible sample means. Imagine a sample mean falling somewhere in the distribution. Then consider an interval that extends 1.96 standard error units above your sample mean and 1.96 units below the sample mean. Now look to see if the population mean (μ) is in your interval. We have done this exercise in Figure 5.5 where we have plotted several intervals based on a sample mean ±1.96 times the standard error of the mean. Only when the sample mean happens to fall in the extreme tails of the distribution (where only 2 × 2.5% or 5% of the means fall) will an interval based on 1.96 *not* capture the true population mean. Therefore, there is a .95 probability that an interval that stretches ±1.96

FIGURE 5.5 ■ Determining 95% confidence interval for population mean when population standard deviation is known.

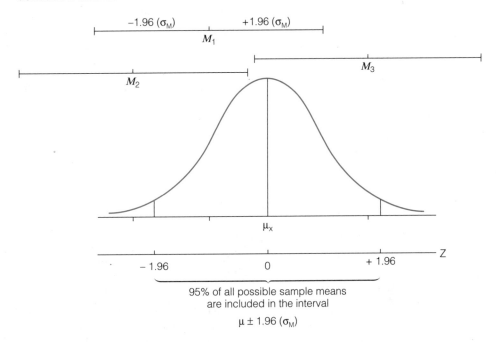

times the standard error of the mean *from any randomly selected sample mean* will capture the population mean. And 5% of the time an interval based on the sample mean will not contain the population mean. We refer to this interval $M \pm 1.96 \, (\sigma_M)$] as the **95% confidence interval** for the population mean.

The lower end of the interval is $M - 1.96 \, (\sigma_M)$

The upper end of the interval is $M + 1.96 \, (\sigma_M)$

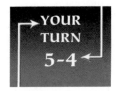

YOUR TURN 5-4 Suppose you wanted to find an interval that has a .90 probability of capturing the population mean. In other words, suppose you wanted the .90 confidence interval and not the .95 confidence interval. What is the z score that we would use to multiply by the standard error of the mean (σ_M) to form a .90 confidence interval? ■

WHAT YOU HAVE LEARNED AND WHAT IS THE NEXT STEP

In this chapter, we hopefully laid the groundwork that will allow us to determine a confidence interval for a population mean based on information obtained from a single sample. At this point, we have emphasized the following:

- A mean based on a random sample is a *point estimate* of the population mean. An *interval estimate,* also called a *confidence interval,* defines an interval that we can assign a probability that it contains the population value.

- Even though sample means based on random samples are all estimates of the same population mean, there will be variation among these means due to chance, which is called *sampling error* (also *sampling variation* or *sampling variability*).

- A sampling distribution of means is a theoretical relative frequency distribution of sample means based on an infinite number of random samples of the same size from the same population.

- The standard deviation from a sampling distribution of means is called the *standard error of the mean* (σ_M), and it equals $\sigma/\sqrt{N}$.

- The *central limit theorem* states that the sampling distribution approaches a normal distribution as sample size increases.

- Because the normal relative frequency distribution contains all the scores (i.e., a proportion of 1.00 or 100% of the scores), we can determine the probability of drawing randomly a score that falls between any two specified values.

- As sample size increases, the variability among sample means decreases. We know that, if a population is normally distributed, 95% of the scores in the population fall between the mean $\pm$ 1.96 z scores.

- Using information about the normal curve, we can construct an interval based on both the sample mean and the true standard error of the mean [$M \pm 1.96 (\sigma_M)$] that 95 times out of 100 will actually capture the population mean.

Our problem, of course, is that most of the time we don't know the population standard deviation and thus cannot calculate the true standard error of the mean. However, we can estimate it. And that is the topic of the next chapter. We will show how our survey researcher, Katie, can calculate a confidence interval for the population mean based on the information found in her sample.

Key Concepts

point estimate	sampling distribution	central limit theorem
interval estimate	sampling distribution of the mean	probability
confidence interval	standard error of the mean	95% confidence interval
sampling error (sampling variation or variability)		

Answers to *Your Turn* Questions

5-1. We believe that, if your pie recipe were being tasted, you likely would feel better if the judge ate five spoonfuls of your pie rather than just one, especially if the judge sampled from different places in the pie. Intuition, and perhaps personal experience, tells us that one small taste of something may not tell us everything about a dish we are eating. So it is with small samples: they may not be very representative of a large population (or pie). On the other hand, if the judge ate five teaspoons from the top of your pie, you might object because what is on top may not be representative of your pie. A random sampling procedure obviously would be better. Finally, we believe that you will recognize that, after eating many spoonfuls of your pie, the judge probably doesn't learn much more about your pie with each new tasting. So, too, is it with sample size: once we have a large random sample, adding more cases does not give us that much more information. You may remember that pollsters ask perhaps only 1,500 people in the United States their opinions and then infer what its whole adult population is thinking. Asking many more than 1,500 doesn't bring them that much more information.

5-2. The answers are (a) .1587, (b) .8413, and (c) .6826. Note that in (b) you must add .50 and .3413 to obtain your answer.

5-3. (a) We know that the standard error of the mean for a sampling distribution of samples of size 25 based on a normal population with $\mu = 75$ and $\sigma = 10$ is 2.00 [i.e., $\sigma_M = \sigma/\sqrt{N} = 10/\sqrt{25} = 10/5 = 2$]. We wish to know the probability of obtaining from that population a random sample with mean equal to or greater than 72. Because the population is normal in form, we can assume that the sampling distribution of the mean will be normal no matter what the sample size. The z score corresponding to a value of 72 is -1.5 [i.e., $(72-75)/2 = -1.5$]. In Table A.2, we find that .4332 of the scores in a normal distribution fall between the mean and a z score of -1.5. Because the z score is negative and

because we wish to know the proportion of scores falling above this value, we must add this proportion to .50, that is, $.50 + .4332 = .9332$. Therefore, the probability of randomly selecting a sample with mean equal to 72 or greater is .9332.

(b) To find the probability of selecting a random sample with mean equal to 80 or greater, we find the standard normal score for 80, which is 2.50 [i.e., $80 - 75/2 = 2.50$]. In Table A.1, we find that .0062 of the area beneath a normal curve is above a z score of 2.50. Thus, the probability of selecting at random from this population a sample with mean equal to or greater than 80 is .0062. Remember that, when attempting to answer questions such as these, it is important to draw a normal curve and identify, perhaps by shading, the area of the curve that relates to the question you are being asked.

5-4. Looking at Table A.1, we want to find the z score that contains .45 of the area (1/2 of .90) under the normal curve between the mean and the z score. This value is 1.65. Therefore, the 90% confidence interval for the mean is $M \pm 1.65\ (\sigma_M)$.

Analyzing and Interpreting Data: Problems and Exercises

1. Show that you know the difference between a *point estimate* and an *interval estimate* of a population value. What is another name for an *interval estimate*?

2. Explain why a random sampling procedure does not guarantee that the sample will be representative of the population from which it was taken.

3. Explain the relationship between a *sampling distribution of means* and the *central limit theorem*.

4. Assume that you have taken a random sample of size 20 from a large population of raw scores with population mean equal to 85. You want to know the probability that your sample mean will have a value greater than 90. What are two things you need to know before you can begin to answer this question?

5. What is the probability of the following:
   (a) selecting at random an Ace from a normal deck of playing cards?

   (b) getting a test answer right by chance when there are five alternatives to choose from?
   (c) selecting at random a score that is above the mean in a normal distribution of scores?

6. What is the probability of the following:
   (a) selecting at random a "red" card (heart or diamond) from a normal deck of playing cards?
   (b) winning a class lottery when there are 20 names in a hat and one name is drawn randomly?
   (c) selecting at random a score that is below the mean in a normal distribution of scores?

7. Two sampling distributions are created based on random samples from a population of scores that is normally distributed with $\mu = 88$ and $\sigma = 7$. The first sampling distribution (a) is based on samples of size 9, and the second sampling distribution (b) is based on samples of size 25. What are the standard deviations (standard errors) of the two sampling distributions (a) and (b)?

8. Use the information found in problem #7 to answer this question: In each distribution (a) and (b), what is the probability that a sample mean will be selected from the sampling distribution of means that is more than one standard error above 88? (This is a slightly tricky question.)

9. Use the information found in problem #7 to answer these questions:
   (a) In distribution (a), what is the probability of obtaining a random sample with mean equal to or greater than 90?
   (b) In distribution (b) what is the probability of obtaining a random sample with mean equal to or greater than 90?
   (c) Explain why the probabilities differ in question 9(b) and 9(c) when the sample mean (90) is the same and samples are selected from the same population.

10. (a) Assume that a random sample of size 36 was taken from a population with $\mu = 55$ and $\sigma = 12$. What is the probability that the value of the sample mean will be greater than 52?
    (b) Assume you are sampling randomly from the same population. What is the probability of randomly selecting a sample with mean greater than 56 when $n = 25$?

11. Why is the z score value of 1.96 so useful to researchers when constructing confidence intervals for a population mean?

12. What is a 95% confidence interval for a population mean?

13. Construct the 95% confidence interval for the population mean when:
    (a) $N = 9, M = 18, \sigma = 2$
    (b) $N = 20, M = 64, \sigma = 8$
    (c) $N = 36, M = 25, \sigma = 3$

14. Construct the 95% confidence interval for the population mean when:
    (a) $N = 25, M = 28, \sigma = 4$
    (b) $N = 16, M = 98, \sigma = 15$
    (c) $N = 22, M = 45, \sigma = 10$

15. Construct the .90 confidence interval for the population mean for the situations of problem #14(a), (b), and (c). Compare the confidence intervals that you obtained in problem #14 and #15 for each of the three situations, that is, compare the intervals for 14(a) and 15(a), for 14(b) and 15(b), and for 14(c) and 15(c). In which situations are the intervals wider? Why?

16. If the mean of a random sample is a point estimate of the population mean, what is the point estimate of the population standard deviation?

Answers to Odd-Numbered Problems

1. When a random sample is taken from a population, the sample mean is our best (point) estimate of the population mean. It is called a *point* estimate because we use a single point (i.e., the mean) to estimate the population mean. We can also estimate the population mean by constructing an interval that has a specific probability of containing the population mean. An interval estimate is also called a *confidence interval.*

3. A sampling distribution of means is a frequency distribution based on sample means obtained from random samples of the same size. This is generally a theoretical distribution that assumes an infinite process of random sampling and recording means.

   The central limit theorem states that, as sample size increases, the sampling distribution of means becomes more normal in form. Therefore, if we are sampling from a normal distribution *or* if the sample size is large, we may assume that the sampling distribution of means is approximately normally distributed.

5. (a) $4/52 = .077$
   (b) $1/5 = .20$
   (c) $.50$

7. The standard deviations of the sampling distributions, now called *standard errors,* are
   (a) $7/\sqrt{9} = 2.33$
   (b) $7/\sqrt{25} = 1.40$

9. (a) z score equivalent $= (90 - 88)/2.33 = .858$, and, using Table A.1, we find that there is .1949 of the area of the normal curve greater than $z = .86$. Therefore, the probability is .1949 that a sample mean of size 9 will have a value 90 or greater.

 (b) z score equivalent $= (90 - 88)/1.40 = 1.43$, and, using Table A.1, we find that there is .0764 of the area of the normal curve greater than $z = 1.43$. Therefore, the probability is .0764 that a sample mean of size 25 will have a value 90 or greater.

 (c) The difference in probabilities reflects the fact that, as sample size increases, the standard error decreases. Given the same distance from the mean (e.g., $90 - 88 = 2$), the z score will be greater when the standard error is smaller, and thus the z score will be farther away from the mean.

11. There is .475 of the area beneath a normal curve between the mean and a z score of $+1.96$. Of course, there is also .475 of the area between the mean and -1.96. That is, .95 of the area falls between the mean ± 1.96. There is, therefore, a .95 probability that a sample mean drawn randomly from a normal distribution of sample means will fall within this region. Researchers use this information to construct confidence intervals for a population mean that will "capture" the population mean with a probability of .95.

13. (a) $18 \pm 1.96 (0.67) = 16.69$ to 19.31
 (b) $64 \pm 1.96 (1.79) = 60.49$ to 67.51
 (c) $25 \pm 1.96 (0.50) = 24.02$ to 25.98

15. In a normal curve, .45 of the area (exactly .4495) falls between the mean and z of 1.64. (See Table A.1.) We can use ± 1.64 to define the .90 area under the normal curve. The calculations are the same as in problem #14 except that we now use 1.64 instead of 1.96. Therefore,
 (a) $28 \pm 1.64 (0.80) = 26.69$ to 29.31
 (b) $98 \pm 1.64 (3.75) = 91.85$ to 104.15
 (c) $45 \pm 1.64 (2.13) = 41.51$ to 48.49

 All the intervals are wider for the 95% confidence interval in problem #14 than for the 90% confidence interval because a larger standard normal value (1.96) is required to capture .95 of the area beneath the normal curve.

 Go to http://psychology.wadsworth.com/courses/statistics/ and test your knowledge of this chapter by taking the online quiz. Another resource to check is the online workshops that provide a step-by-step guide through a number of topics at http://psychology.wadsworth.com/workshops/workshops.html.

CHAPTER 6

Constructing a Confidence Interval and Announcing Results

Everyone knows that confidence intervals contain all the information to be found in significance tests and much more.
    Cohen (1994, p. 1002)

INTRODUCTION

We have been following Katie, our survey researcher, who seeks to provide evidence that the characteristics of the sample she collected are similar to those of the population from which the sample was taken. Specifically, she wishes to know how precisely her sample mean estimates the true population mean. Katie knows that the population mean is also the mean of the theoretical sampling distribution of means, and that her sample mean is in that sampling distribution. But where? The stumbling block to answering this question has been that she has information from only one sample and does not know the population standard deviation on which the standard deviation of the sampling distribution (called the standard error of the mean) is based.

This is a common problem in the behavioral sciences because, as we have noted, we generally don't have access to a population, but rather rely on samples to investigate the behavior of humans and animals. Consider the following research situations:

- Karla is working on her master's degree in clinical psychology. A grant from an agency sponsoring cross-cultural work in psychology has sent her to Africa where her thesis concerns the level of depression of men in several African villages. With the help of many local volunteers, she administers a culturally appropriate depression inventory to several dozen men in these villages.

- Paul is a research assistant at a major pharmaceutical firm. He has been asked to administer a newly developed sleeping pill to human volunteers in a sleep laboratory, measure the length of time it takes them to fall asleep, and note any reported side effects of the drug.

- An educational psychologist hired by the State of Illinois administers a "school-readiness" test to 50 children, 5 years of age, randomly selected from a rural community in the state. The data will be used as part of a grant proposal seeking funds for preschool programs in this rural community.

- A sociology major finds a job with the public relations department of a large hospital. She is asked to survey a sample of recently discharged patients concerning their satisfaction with the medical care they received and with hospital services in general. She obtains completed questionnaires from a random sample of 75 patients who were treated in the hospital during the first 6 months of the year.

- Of course, don't forget our happiness researcher, Katie, whom we have been following. She seeks to document the perceived happiness of students at her university by analyzing data obtained from a sample of students.

In each of these situations, the researcher has data from a sample and seeks to use that information to say something about a population: African village men, laboratory volunteers, 5-year-old children in a rural community, and patients treated at a hospital. The mean performance of the sample will be of interest to each investigator. Assuming that a random selection procedure was used, the sample mean will be a good estimate of the population mean. But how good? In this chapter, we show you how a researcher might construct a confidence interval (CI) for the population mean based on information obtained from a sample. We'll then be in a position to help Katie with her research study.

THE *t* DISTRIBUTION

Although the true population standard deviation is unknown, there is a way to estimate it. The *sample* standard deviation is a point estimate, our best guess, of the population standard deviation. Thus, we can substitute the sample standard deviation (*s*) into the formula for the standard error of the mean. The result is an **estimated standard error of the mean** because we are not using the true population standard deviation but are instead estimating it based on the sample standard deviation. Its symbol is: s_M. Therefore,

$$s_M = s/\sqrt{N}$$

Equation 6.1

We now possess a sample mean (*M*) from our research study and an estimate of the standard error of the mean (s_M). How can we use this information to construct confidence intervals for the mean of the population? You might suggest that we just continue where we were in Chapter 5 and multiply s_M by ±1.96 before adding the product to or subtracting it from the sample mean (i.e., $M \pm 1.96 [s_M]$). Recall that .475 of the area beneath a normal distribution lies between the mean and a *z* score of 1.96 and, thus, the population mean plus or minus this *z* score defines an area that contains 95% of all scores. This is not a bad suggestion, but a problem arises. Once we estimate the standard error of the mean, the *z* score transformation for sample means does not work exactly as it did when based on the true standard error. Let us explain.

The standard normal score or *z* score is a linear transformation of the data. The distribution of standard scores will be normally distributed as long as the population is normally distributed. Don't be misled into thinking that, because a *z* score is sometimes called a standard *normal* score, that using it produces a normal distribution; it doesn't. The *z* scores are normally distributed only when the population scores are normally distributed. When a distribution is normal in form and the scores are transformed into *z* scores, these *z* scores are called *standard normal scores*.

Do you remember what the necessary conditions are for a sampling distribution of means to be normal in form? ■

Consider again a theoretical sampling distribution of means based on an infinite number of random samples of the same size from a population. Let's assume that sample size is large or the population is normal so that the sampling distribution is normal in form. We know the mean of the sampling distribution will be the same as the population mean. But, not knowing the population standard deviation (σ), we will have to estimate the true standard error of the mean (σ_M) using the sample standard deviation ($s/\sqrt{N}$). The next step would be to perform a standard score transformation [$(M - \mu)/s_M$] for our mean. But, when we perform this transformation for sample means, we do not get another normal distribution. Using the estimated standard error of the mean for this transformation results in a different distribution, one that is not normal in form. We know this because a man by the name of William Gossett, an employee of the Guinness Brewing Company in the early part of the 20th century, figured it out. He published under the pseudonym, Student, and the new distribution he discovered is called *Student's t distribution,* or simply the **t distribution** (Howell, 2002). *The* *t distribution is appropriate when we don't know the population standard deviation and must estimate it from the sample standard deviation.*

This new distribution is based on the transformation: $(M - \mu)/s_M$. And, thanks to Gossett, we now think about *t scores* and not the value of *z* when we estimate the standard error of the mean. The *t* distribution, like the *z* distribution, has a mean of 0.0. The distribution of *t* values is mathematically predictable, as is the standard normal distribution, but it turns out there is more than one *t* distribution. Although the *t* distribution, like the normal distribution, is symmetrical, its exact shape varies systematically as a function of sample size. For relatively small sample sizes, the *t* distribution has more scores at the middle but also more scores in the tails than a normal distribution does. This makes it slightly leptokurtic (DeCarlo, 1997). As the sample size increases, the *t* distribution looks more and more like the normal distribution. These relationships are shown in an exaggerated form in Figure 6.1.

To use the theoretical *t* distribution, we need to know the sample size. Subtracting 1 from the sample size (*N*) gives what statisticians call **degrees of freedom (*df*)** for a single sample. In general, we can think of *df* as the number of scores that are free to vary when calculating a statistic. For example, suppose we know the mean of a sample of 10 scores (i.e., the sum divided by 10). Once we know the sum of nine scores, we can calculate the tenth because, if we know the overall sum, the last number is determined. In other words, the first nine scores are free to vary, but once the total of nine scores and the sum of all 10 are known, the tenth score can have only one value. For present purposes, just keep in mind that *the shape of the t distribution depends on the degrees of freedom associated with a sample, which for a single sample are always N − 1.* For example, if sample size is 24, then the degrees of freedom are 24 − 1, or 23.

We need to know one more thing: the shape of the distribution with which we are working. *The t transformation is appropriate only when a distribution is normal in form.* Therefore, it is important that we be assured the sampling distribution of means is normal in form. If we do not have a large sample (and thus can assume that the sampling distribution will be normal), it is important in the inspection and description stages of analysis to see if the distribution of

FIGURE 6.1 ■ Comparison of normal and *t* distributions.

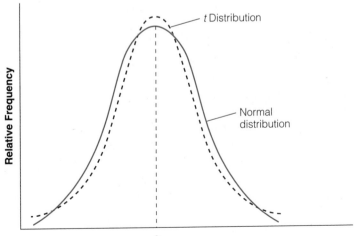

sample scores is generally bell shaped. If scores in a random sample are approximately normally distributed, the population also may be assumed to be generally normal in form (and the sampling distribution of means from this normal population will be normal even when sample size is small).

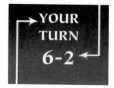

YOUR TURN 6-2

Our survey researcher, Katie, can be assured that the theoretical sampling distribution of means based on her sample size is normal in form. Why?   ■

Knowing both the sample size and assuming a normal distribution of sample means, we can now proceed as we did before to construct a 95% confidence interval for the population mean, but this time using the t distribution. Once we know the degrees of freedom for our sample, we can use a t table to obtain a value of t that separates the t distribution into two

FIGURE 6.2 ■ An abbreviated t table (see Appendix A for complete table).

Level of Significance For a Directional (One-Tailed) Test

	.10	.05	.025	.01	.005	.0005

Level of Significance for a Nondirectional (Two-Tailed) Test

df	.20	.10	.05	.02	.01	.001
1	3.078	6.314	12.706	31.821	63.657	636.619
2	1.886	2.920	4.303	6.965	9.925	31.598
3	1.638	2.353	3.182	4.541	5.841	12.941
4	1.533	2.132	2.776	3.747	4.604	8.610
5	1.476	2.015	2.571	3.365	4.032	6.859
6	1.440	1.943	2.447	3.143	3.707	5.959
7	1.415	1.895	2.365	2.998	3.499	5.405
8	1.397	1.860	2.306	2.896	3.355	5.041
9	1.383	1.833	2.262	2.821	3.250	4.781
10	1.372	1.812	2.228	2.764	3.169	4.587
.	.	.	.	.	.	.
.	.	.	.	.	.	.
.	.	.	.	.	.	.
26	1.315	1.706	2.056	2.479	2.779	3.707
27	1.314	1.703	2.052	2.473	2.771	3.690
28	1.313	1.701	2.048	2.467	2.763	3.674
29	1.311	1.699	2.045	2.462	2.756	3.659
30	1.310	1.697	2.042	2.457	2.750	3.646
40	1.303	1.684	2.021	2.423	2.704	3.551
60	1.296	1.671	2.000	2.390	2.660	3.460
120	1.289	1.658	1.980	2.358	2.617	3.373
∞	1.282	1.645	1.960	2.326	2.576	3.291

equal portions that, when combined, contain 0.95 of the area under the curve and that contain .025 in each of two tails. This *t* value, called *t* **critical,** will vary as sample size *(df)* varies. For large sample sizes, the *t* critical value becomes very close to 1.96 because, as sample size gets large, the *t* distribution becomes more normal. Therefore, we need to consult the table knowing the degrees of freedom for our sample. An abbreviated *t* table is shown in Figure 6.2. (The complete table is found in Appendix A.)

Before moving on, let's take a close look at the section of the *t* table illustrated in Figure 6.2. In the left-most column are degrees of freedom associated with our statistical procedure. The table columns are labeled both "Level of Significance for a Directional (one-tailed) Test" and "Level of Significance for a Nondirectional (two-tailed) Test." *Level of significance* is not something we have talked about thus far, but we will in a later chapter. For now, we want to look at the columns beneath the heading for a *non*directional test. We use the values of *t* for a nondirectional test because we are interested in the area between the two tails of the distribution. One column beneath the nondirectional heading is particularly important: that headed by .05. The numbers in this column are *t* values that separate the *t* distribution into two equal portions that together contain .95 of the area under the *t* distribution.

To construct the 95% confidence interval for a population mean, we want to find the *t* value in the .05 column associated with the degrees of freedom for our sample, which are $N - 1$. For example, assume we have taken a random sample of size 17. Therefore, the degrees of freedom for this single sample are $17 - 1$, or 16. Looking in the *t* table beneath the .05 column (under nondirectional test) across the row with 16 degrees of freedom, we find a *t* critical value of 2.12. Can you find it? The area between the mean and $t = 2.12$ in a *t* distribution based on samples with 16 degrees of freedom is .475. Note that, when using the *t* table, the column heading tells us what proportion of the area we are seeking. Therefore, in this *t* distribution, .95 of the area falls between plus and minus $t = 2.12$ from the mean with .025 in each of two tails. This is illustrated in Figure 6.3.

FIGURE 6.3 ■ Distribution of *t* with *df* = 16 showing the *t* value that separates the distribution with .025 in each tail (i.e., .05 in tails).

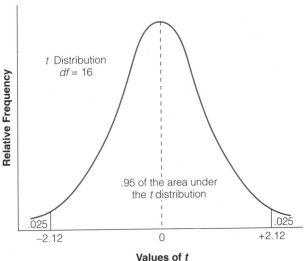

With 16 degrees of freedom, .95 of the area under the *t* distribution falls between a *t* equal to ±2.12 with .025 in each of two tails. In a standard normal or *z* distribution, a *z* value of ±1.96 separates the distribution into two equal parts that, when combined, contain .95 of the area under the normal curve with .025 in each of two tails. Based on your knowledge of the relationship between the *t* distribution and a normal distribution, explain why the *t* value that defines the same proportion (.95) of area is larger than 1.96.   ■

ESTABLISHING A CONFIDENCE INTERVAL FOR THE POPULATION MEAN BASED ON THE *t* DISTRIBUTION

We are ready to revisit Katie, our happiness researcher. She found a sample mean of 5.16 and sample standard deviation (*s*) of 1.55. She has been asked to estimate the confidence she has in her sample mean (the *E* in I-D-E-A). More specifically, she was asked to provide evidence that her sample mean is a good estimate of the population mean. How precise an estimate is this? We are now in a position to show how she might determine the precision of her estimate.

We can construct a confidence interval for the population mean using the following formula:

$$M \pm t_{\text{critical}} (s_M)$$

Equation 6.2

Because Katie sampled a relatively large number of students ($N = 80$), she can assume that the sampling distribution of means based on samples of this size will be normal in form. She can then refer to the *t* distribution associated with 79 degrees of freedom (i.e., $N - 1$). The most commonly used confidence interval is the 95% confidence interval. The critical *t* value associated with $df = 79$, which separates this distribution into two equal parts that when combined contain .95 of the sample means, is (approximately) 2.00. Let's be sure we know how the critical *t* value of 2.00 was obtained.

Consulting the *t* table for a sample with degrees of freedom equal to 79 immediately presents a problem. A value of 79 does not appear in the *df* column: there is a gap between 60 and 120 *df*. As you can see, *t* values decrease as degrees of freedom increase until reaching 1.96 with infinity *df*, which corresponds to the *z* value in a normal distribution. The *t* value we are looking for is in the .05 column (under nondirectional test) between the *t* values of 2.00 (60 *df*) and 1.98 (120 *df*). A general rule of thumb is to choose the *t* value associated with the *next lowest* degrees of freedom in the table.[1] Because 60 is the next value below 79 in the table, we estimate the *t* value to be 2.00. More often, you will be using a computer program to calculate confidence intervals, and the exact critical *t* value will be obtained automatically.

The estimated standard error of the mean for Katie's survey data is $s/\sqrt{N}$ or $1.55/\sqrt{80}$. This yields $s_M = 0.17$. Her sample mean is 5.16. To construct the 95% confidence interval based on Katie's sample of 80 students, we calculate the following:

upper limit = 5.16 + 2.00 (0.17) = 5.16 + 0.34 = 5.50

lower limit = 5.16 − 2.00 (0.17) = 5.16 − 0.34 = 4.82

---

[1] Since values of *t* decrease as degrees of freedom increase, a *t* value associated with the next lowest degrees of freedom is chosen so as not to use a smaller *t* value than is justified given the sample size (i.e., *df*). As we noted, computer software programs provide results based on exact *t* values so this issue is relevant only when determining *t* from the table.

> BOX 6.1 ■ Steps in Constructing a Confidence Interval for a Population Mean Using the *t* Distribution
>
> 1. Obtain mean (*M*) and standard deviation (*s*) from a sample randomly selected from a defined population.
> 2. Estimate standard error of the mean based on sample standard deviation and sample *N*, where $s_M = s/\sqrt{N}$.
> 3. Decide whether 95% or 99% confidence intervals are desired. (Although .95 is commonly calculated, .99 confidence may be preferred in some situations.)
> 4. Find the critical value of *t* associated with .95 (.05) (or .99 [.01]) in the *t* table. (See Appendix A.)
> 5. Multiply $t_{critical}$ by your estimated standard error: $t_{critical} (s_M)$.
> 6. Add your product from step #5 to the sample mean to obtain the upper limit of the interval; subtract the product from the sample mean to obtain the lower limit.
>
> $$CI = M \pm t_{critical} (s_M)$$
>
> **Note:** The range of scores specified by the interval calculated in step #6 is your confidence interval for the population mean. The population mean you are seeking is a constant; it does not change. However, intervals will vary because sample means and standard deviations vary. (Remember sampling variation.) Thus, the most appropriate interpretation of a confidence interval is that the interval contains the mean. It is *incorrect* to say that the probability is .95 that the population mean falls in the interval, the intervals fall around the population mean, not vice versa.

The 95% confidence interval for the population mean based on Katie's survey data is 4.82 to 5.50.

The steps in computing the confidence interval for the mean when we are estimating the standard error of the mean and must use the *t* distribution are reviewed in Box 6.1.

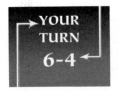

YOUR TURN 6-4

Assume that a researcher surveyed a random sample of 30 students at a large university concerning how much they liked the food served in a college cafeteria. The researcher summed the responses to three 7-point scales to obtain an index of satisfaction with the cafeteria food. The maximum score was, therefore, 21, indicating "extremely satisfied." The mean for the 30 students was 16.1, and the sample standard deviation was 3.7. What is the 95% confidence interval for the population mean? ■

INTERPRETING CONFIDENCE INTERVALS

Having calculated the 95% confidence interval for the population mean, what might our researcher conclude?

Confidence intervals are subject to sampling variation. This must be the case because confidence intervals are constructed from sample data (specifically the sample mean and standard deviation), and we know that these statistics will vary from sample to sample. On the other hand, a population mean—a parameter—is a constant; it does not change. Confidence intervals can be correctly interpreted if we keep these facts in mind. *The probability associated with a confidence interval (e.g., .95) refers to the probability that the population mean will be captured by the interval if we were to repeat the same procedure with repeated random samples of the same size from the population.* Howell (2002) suggests that we think of the population mean as a stake and confidence intervals as rings: "The confidence statement is a statement of the probability that the ring has been on target; it is not a statement of the probability that the target (parameter) landed in the ring" (Howell, 2002, p. 208). For example, having chosen to construct a 95% confidence interval, it is *not* strictly right to say that the probability is .95 that the population means falls in the interval. The population mean, like a stake, is fixed; it is the rings that do the falling. We are correct when we say that the probability is .95 that the confidence interval contains the population mean. Where exactly the rings land around the parameter stake depends on the particular values of the sample statistics (i.e., the mean and standard deviation), which will change from sample to sample due to sampling variation.

Katie can state with 95% confidence that the interval 4.82 to 5.50 contains the population mean representing the happiness level of students at her university. In other words, the probability is .95 that the interval has captured the mean. There is no certainty, just a high probability (.95), that this interval surrounds the mean. We cannot say with certainty that the sun will come up tomorrow, but that doesn't prevent us from making plans for tomorrow's lunch (because we usually assume with a high degree of confidence that the sun will come up). Similarly, knowing that an interval has a high likelihood of containing the population mean suggests that we should feel confident when making decisions based on this evidence.

The limits of the confidence interval provide information about **precision of estimation.** The narrower the interval, the more precise is our estimate of the population mean. Figure 6.4 is a bar graph showing hypothetical means obtained from a happiness survey at two different colleges. The 95% confidence interval for the population mean is plotted with each bar. A vertical line extends above and below each mean corresponding to the width of the confidence interval. You can see that the width of the intervals differs for the means from the two schools. In which case is the sample mean a more precise estimate of the population mean? Because the narrower the interval the more precise the estimate, the mean for College A is a

FIGURE 6.4 ■ Bar graphs showing hypothetical mean happiness ratings and 95% confidence intervals for two college surveys.

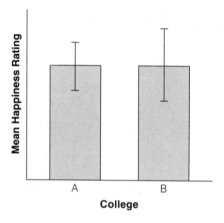

more precise estimate of the population mean than is the mean obtained for College B. In the next section, we will examine some of the factors that affect precision of interval estimation.

One should not think that all the values within the confidence interval are equally likely to be the population mean. The most likely values are those around the sample mean. Remember, the sample mean is our best estimate of the population mean. Thus, we might think of a confidence interval as something like a normal curve, with the most probable values in the middle of the interval, that is, near the sample mean, and with the less probable values away from the sample mean. Recall that a normal sampling distribution of means reveals that most sample means are close to the population mean. In a normal distribution, 68% of the values are within one standard deviation of the mean. Likewise, 68% of the sample means obtained through random selection will be no more than one standard error away from the population mean. When constructing confidence intervals based on sample means, therefore, most of the time the center of the interval (i.e., the sample mean) will be close to the population mean. In many repetitions of this procedure, the values near the middle of the confidence interval more likely represent the population mean.

Finally, and this is sure to be a bit frustrating, we have not learned exactly what we want to know when we have constructed a confidence interval. What we would like to know is the probability that our sample mean is the same or very close to (that is, no more than a trivial distance from) the population mean. What we know when we have constructed a confidence interval is the probability that the particular interval we constructed contains the population mean. Nevertheless, given a relatively high probability of that occurrence (e.g., .95), as well as a relatively narrow confidence interval, and armed with the realization that the sample mean is usually close to the population mean, we will have obtained a relatively precise estimate of the population value. Thus, at that point, based on this information we can confidently proceed to make practical decisions as well as to reasonably judge the truthfulness of psychological theories. Knowing that the mean happiness rating of students at Katie's school, for example, is highly likely to be within an interval defined by the mean plus or minus 0.34 units on a 7-point scale would seem to be sufficiently precise enough information for important decisions to be made.

On the other hand, if this result is not satisfactory (that is, we don't want to "live with" that much uncertainty), there are some ways to obtain increased confidence when estimating the true population mean.

INCREASING PRECISION AND CONFIDENCE IN OUR ESTIMATE

As we noted previously, the precision associated with our estimate is directly related to the width of the confidence interval. One way to increase precision in our estimate of the population mean is to increase sample size. Increasing sample size will, other things being constant, decrease the width of the confidence interval. The greater the sample size, the more precise is our estimate of the population mean, and this is reflected in narrower confidence limits. This may become apparent if you think about the formula for the estimated standard error: $s/\sqrt{N}$. *As sample size increases the standard error of the mean decreases.* (See Chapter 5.) A smaller standard error of the mean will translate into a smaller interval width. We hope that, conceptually, this makes sense. Recall that, as sample size increases, our sample mean better approximates the population mean. There is less variation around the population mean, and, consequently, the 95% confidence interval is narrower. One reason that the two confidence intervals differ in Figure 6.4 might be that the researchers used samples of widely different size.

If you consider once again the formula for the estimated standard error, you might see another way that increased precision can be obtained when calculating a confidence interval. The formula for the estimated standard error $(s/\sqrt{N})$ takes into account the amount of variability in the sample. Holding sample size constant, you can see that, as the measure of sample variation (the standard deviation, s), increases, the estimated standard error increases. In other words, other things being constant, *the more variability in the sample (and we assume the population), the less precise will be the estimate of the population mean.* Sampling from a relatively homogeneous population will produce a more precise estimate of the population mean than will sampling from a more heterogeneous population. Thus, another reason why the confidence intervals might differ for the two colleges represented in Figure 6.4 is that there is more variability in happiness ratings among students at College B than among those at College A.

Both increasing sample size and decreasing variability are ways to arrive at more precise estimates of the population mean. In both cases (other things being constant) the result will be a narrower confidence interval width. The narrower the confidence interval, the greater precision we have in estimating the population mean. By increasing the precision of our estimate of the population mean, we have every right to feel better about our estimation procedure. Which of the following would you rather hear: (a) there is a .95 probability that the interval 10–20 contains the population mean, or (b) there is a .95 probability that the interval 13–17 contains the population mean?

We believe you would prefer statement (b) over statement (a). *Increased precision leads to a more meaningful confidence statement* because the information is both more useful and more informative. We want to make decisions on the basis of the most precise information available.

Note that increasing sample size or decreasing variability does not change the probability associated with the confidence interval, but rather reduces the interval width, which we can state with confidence contains the population mean. Probability is determined by the critical t value we choose to multiply by the standard error, but we are still using the ".05 column." Another way to obtain increased confidence is to calculate confidence intervals based on .99 probability rather than .95. To do this, we look at the .01 column in the t table beneath the nondirectional heading. A larger area underneath the curve is needed to represent .99 rather than .95 of the scores. We must, in other words, "go farther out" in the tails of the distribution to find the critical t value. The obvious result is that the interval will be wider. That is why we can have greater confidence that our interval has captured the population mean: a larger interval will have a higher probability of containing the true population mean. The decision to use the .95 or .99 interval rests with the researcher. Although the .95 interval is most commonly used, there may be occasions when a researcher wishes to report a greater probability than .95 that the interval contains the population mean.

Figure 6.5 shows both the 95% confidence interval and the 99% confidence interval for the population mean based on Katie's survey data. As you can see, the width of the 99% interval is greater than that of the 95% interval and is why we can express a greater probability that this interval has captured the population mean. Increasing confidence by increasing the width of the confidence interval may or may not be a satisfactory solution.

FIGURE 6.5 ■ Both 95% and 99% confidence intervals for mean happiness ratings.

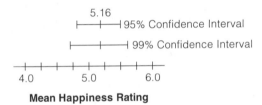

Perhaps the best way to increase confidence in our estimate of the population mean is to repeat (replicate) our sampling procedure and calculate new confidence intervals based on the new sample data. *Replication is the best way to increase confidence in a research finding.* And to repeat the procedure with an even bigger sample size yields even greater confidence.

A SLIGHT VARIATION WHEN THERE IS A HYPOTHESIZED POPULATION MEAN

The procedures we just described for estimating confidence in our estimate of a population mean based on sample information may also be applied to situations in which there is a hypothesized population mean and we wish to know how close our sample mean comes to the hypothesized population mean. In each of the example research scenarios that began this chapter, we could imagine a hypothesized mean. For example, Karla is seeking to estimate the mean level of depression of African men from several villages. Suppose that a similar inventory had been standardized on a large group of African men and that a particular score is associated with "normal" levels of functioning. Karla might want to ask if the mean depression score of these African villagers is different from that of African men in general.

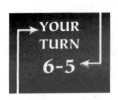

Look back to the introduction to this chapter and examine the research scenarios presented there. Consider the situation involving the laboratory scientist who is examining the time it takes people to fall asleep when administered a newly developed sleeping pill. Can you describe at least one hypothetical situation in which a hypothesized mean might be involved?   ■

Consider a slightly different situation at Katie's university than the one we have described thus far. Assume that college administrators claim in a recruiting brochure that the students at this university are "very happy." Assume further that we define "very happy" as a rating of 6 (or above) on a 7-point happiness scale. In other words, let's assume that the college administrators are claiming that ratings by students at their university would produce a mean of 6.00 or above if they were all asked to rate their happiness level on the 7-point scale described previously. How would you determine if the administration's claim is to be trusted? Is the mean happiness rating of *all* students at this university 6.00 (or higher)? (This is something you might like to know before enrolling.)

As you might suspect, the procedure for determining whether the administration's claim is accurate would be to obtain a random sample of students and measure their happiness. The mean of a random sample is always your best guess (point estimate) of the population mean. But you know that there is sample variation, and just because your sample mean is lower than 6.00 does not necessarily guarantee that the population mean is really lower than 6.00. Nor do you know for sure that the population mean is greater than 6.00 even if your sample mean rating is greater than 6.00. What you want to know is how likely it is that your sample mean comes from a population that has a mean of 6.00 or greater.

Confidence intervals can be constructed as before based on your estimate of the standard error of the mean. (See Box 6.1.) Once obtained, the interpretation of this interval proceeds from the same fact we reported previously: the odds are 95/100 (or 99/100 if using .99 limits) that the interval contains the true population mean.

This is not exactly what you wanted to know, though. You are trying to find out if the students are "very happy" at this school before you enroll. If they are, then students should average 6.00 (or higher) on the happiness scale if everyone was asked and everyone completed the rating task (that is, if we asked all the students). But the best that usually can be done is to sample randomly from the population (ask some students) and then make an inference about the true population parameter based on your sample information. What you have found out is, if 100 different random samples of a given size were taken and 100 sample means (and sample standard deviations) were obtained, then 95 of the 100 confidence limits based on that sample information would contain the population mean, which in this case is hypothesized to be 6.00.

As long as the obtained confidence interval contains the hypothesized mean, we should not reject the idea that the population mean equals 6.00. Even though the observed sample mean is not 6.00, an interval containing 6.00 shows that 6.00 could be the population mean. Thus, if the hypothesized mean (6.00 in this case) is within the obtained interval, our data cannot rule out the hypothesis that the population mean is the same as the hypothesized mean. On the other hand, if the hypothesized mean is not within the interval, we may want to reject the idea that the population mean equals the hypothesized mean.

As we said before, this isn't exactly what you wanted to find out. On the basis of your sample data, no matter whether the hypothesized mean is or is not within the interval, you cannot say for sure that the administration's claim is correct. Your results will tell you only whether the sample data are consistent with the administration's claim about the population mean (that it is at least 6.00). If the confidence interval contains the hypothesized population mean, you must admit that the claim cannot be ruled out given these data. Keep in mind, however, that it is important also to examine the width of the confidence interval when making a decision. As you learned, a wide interval may indicate that the estimation is lacking precision. Precision is directly related to sample size. We may view a wide confidence interval that contains the hypothesized mean as a weak test of the truthfulness of the claim, but we would not have evidence to reject the claim. It is important to obtain as precise an estimate as possible.

You should note this reasoning is only slightly different from that when there was no hypothesized value for the population mean. In both cases, when sampling randomly from a population, to estimate the population mean you can construct an interval that has a certain probability (e.g., .95) of capturing the population mean. If no population mean has been hypothesized, we interpret the confidence limits as a likely range of values for the population mean given this sample evidence. When a population mean has been hypothesized, we look to see if the confidence limits contain the hypothesized value. *If the hypothesized mean is within the obtained confidence limits, we do not have evidence to reject the hypothesized mean because, in all likelihood (e.g., .95), this interval contains the population mean.*

What would you want to say if the administrators at Katie's school had claimed in a brochure that students at their university were very happy (that is, would have an arithmetic mean of 6 on a 7-point happiness scale)? Remember, the 95% confidence interval she calculated based on a random sample of 80 students was 4.82 to 5.50. The value of 6.00 is not within these limits. We would, based on these results, have good reason to believe that the students at this school are *not* on the average "very happy" (at least when defined by a mean rating of 6 on a 7-point scale).

We noted in Chapter 4 that it would not be surprising if the university administrators chose to use the mode (which we saw was 6) as the typical score. The administrators truthfully may say that, when students were surveyed, the most frequent response provided was 6 on a 7-point happiness scale. Hopefully, your knowledge of statistics will lead you to be somewhat cautious about accepting the mode as a typical score, particularly until you know the mean and median as well.

Assume you are interested in attending Katie's university and decide to do your own survey of student's happiness at the school. Assume further that you just happen to use the same scale and are able to obtain results from 25 randomly selected students. (We realize these are somewhat unrealistic assumptions.) Suppose the 95% confidence interval for the population mean based on your survey of 25 students is 5.13 to 6.10. Explain why it is that your results are able to show that 6.00 is within the confidence interval when this was not the case for Katie's interval. Did someone make a mistake? ∎

ANNOUNCING RESULTS BASED ON A SINGLE-SAMPLE MEAN

It has taken us a while, but we are finally in a position to formally announce the results of our hypothetical study examining student happiness at a university. The convention we follow is recommended by the *Publication Manual of the American Psychological Association* (2001).

We can suggest that Katie might present her results in written form as follows:

A random sample of 80 students was surveyed to determine their level of happiness at this university. Students provided a number from a scale ranging from 1 *(not at all)* to 7 *(extremely happy)*. Figure 1 shows that the distribution of student ratings was slightly negatively skewed with a modal rating of 6, *Mdn* = 5.50, and *M* = 5.16 (*SD* = 1.55). There is a .95 probability that the interval 4.82 to 5.50 contains the true population mean.

Note that, because the distribution is somewhat skewed, both the mean and median are reported. A figure describing the shape of the distribution is recommended but is not required. A decision whether to use a figure will rest on such factors as the number of different results to be reported, how important the researcher believes it is for the reader to see the shape of the distribution, and possibly other concerns. The sample standard deviation (*s*) is abbreviated as *SD* in a research report, and the median and mean in a research report are abbreviated as *Mdn* and *M*, respectively. According to the *Publication Manual*, statistical abbreviations should appear in italics when preparing a manuscript for publication. The *Manual* also recommends that scale anchors (e.g., *not at all*) appear in italics.

WHAT YOU HAVE LEARNED AND THE NEXT STEP

Not all random samples will be representative of the population from which they were drawn. There is sampling error or variability. In this chapter, you learned how a researcher might communicate the degree to which the mean of a sample reflects the mean of a population. Interval estimates can be used to communicate precision of estimation more clearly than can the sample mean and standard deviation alone. By using the estimated standard error of the mean and the *t* table, a researcher can calculate a range of values and state with a particular degree of confidence (often 95%) that this interval contains the population mean. Furthermore, you now know how to use the 95% confidence interval as a tool to permit you to test whether an assertion about the value of a population mean is consistent with the sample data.

Major points we've made in this chapter include the following:

- The *estimated* standard error of the mean is an estimate of the true standard error of the mean based on the sample standard deviation. Its symbol is s_M.

- When we estimate the standard error of the mean of a normal distribution of means using the sample standard deviation and then perform the linear transformation $[(M - \mu)/s_M]$ for every mean, we obtain a *t* distribution.

- Subtracting 1 from the sample size (*N*) gives what statisticians call *degrees of freedom (df)* for a single sample. In general, we can think of *df* as the number of scores that are free to vary when the mean is known.

- The confidence interval for a population mean based on the estimated standard error of the mean is defined as $M \pm t_{\text{critical}} (s_M)$.

- Confidence intervals are subject to sampling variation.

- The probability associated with a confidence interval (e.g., .95) refers to the probability that the obtained interval has captured the population mean. For example, assuming that a 95% confidence interval is calculated, you can state that, if 100 different random samples of a given size were taken and 100 sample means (and sample standard deviations) were obtained, then 95 of 100 confidence limits based on that sample information would contain the population mean.

- The limits of the confidence interval provide information about the precision of estimation. The narrower the interval, the more precise is our estimate of the population mean.

- One should not think that all the values within the confidence interval are equally likely to be the population mean. The most likely values are those around the sample mean.

- Increasing sample size will, other things being constant, decrease the width of the confidence interval. That is, increasing sample size leads to a more precise estimate of the population mean and, therefore, less variability among sample means. Reducing variability increases precision of estimates because the standard error, on which the confidence interval is based, is now smaller.

- One way to obtain increased confidence is to calculate confidence intervals based on .99 probability rather than .95.
- Replication is the best way to increase confidence in a research finding.
- If the obtained confidence interval contains a hypothesized mean, we should not rule it out as a possible value of the population mean. If the interval does *not* contain the hypothesized value, then it is reasonable to reject the idea that the population mean is equal to the hypothesized mean.

At this point, you have moved through all four stages of data analysis and interpretation (I-D-E-A) when making decisions about a population mean using information obtained from a single sample. In Chapter 2 and 3, you saw how researchers inspect (the *I*) data before performing additional statistical analyses; in Chapter 4, we presented techniques for describing (*D*) data from a single sample. In this and the previous chapter, you learned to estimate (*E*) confidence in a finding and to announce (*A*) results in a manner that is recommended by the American Psychological Association.

Users of statistics—whether they be in medicine, education, marketing, or psychology—often work with means obtained from two samples rather than one. The question usually asked is whether the two means are sufficiently different to support the idea that they represent two different populations or whether they differ merely due to sampling error. Yes, once again, we must examine sample data in light of the possible sampling error that will always be present. Our next step is to take you through the I-D-E-A process when the question we are asking involves two means.

Key Concepts

estimated standard error of the mean (s_M)	*t* distribution	$t_{critical}$
degrees of freedom	*t* scores	precision of estimation

Answers to *Your Turn* Questions

6-1. The sampling distribution of means will be normal in form if the population of raw scores is normal or if sample size is large.

6-2. Katie's sample size was relatively large ($N = 80$), which means that the sampling distribution of means will be normal in form no matter what the shape of the original population.

6-3. An examination of Figure 6.1 reveals that the *t* distribution has more scores in the middle and more scores in the tails of the distribution. This means that one must go farther out in the *t* distribution than in the normal distribution to find the point that separates the distribution into two parts each equal to .475.

6-4. The estimated standard error of the mean is $s/\sqrt{N}$ or $3.7/\sqrt{30}$, which is 0.68. Because sample size was 30, the *df* for the single sample are 29. In Table A.2, we find that the critical value of *t* with 29 *df* is 2.045 (for $p = .05$, nondirectional, two-tailed, test). Thus, the 95% confidence interval for the population mean is $M \pm 2.045 (0.68)$. The confidence limits are 17.49 and 14.71. We can state that there is a .95 probability that the interval 14.71 to 17.49 contains the population mean.

6-5. We might assume that a rival pharmaceutical firm claims that its sleeping pill puts people to sleep in 14 minutes on the average. The researcher may wish to know whether the newly developed pill produces a mean time-to-sleep close to 14 minutes.

6-6. There is no need to assume that someone made a mistake (although of course that is always possible). Because confidence intervals are based on randomly selected samples, the mean and standard deviation will most likely vary from sample to sample (and hence the estimate of the standard error of the mean likely will vary). Thus, the confidence intervals constructed from sample data are expected to vary from sample to sample. The smaller sample size also will lead to less precision of estimation (i.e., a wider interval). Moreover, sometimes (actually five times out of 100 when a 95% confidence interval is constructed), the interval will be in "error" and not capture the population mean. On the other hand, on the basis of the data collected from two different random samples, we can see that the values 5.13 to 5.50 were included in both intervals. On this basis, we would infer that the population mean is closer to 5 than it is to 6.

Analyzing and Interpreting Data: Problems and Exercises

1. How specifically does the t distribution differ from a normal distribution?

2. In a normal distribution, a z score of 1.96 separates the distribution into two equal parts, each containing .45 of the area under the curve, with the mean as the midpoint. Where in the t table do we find a value of 1.96? Explain.

3. Assume that you have taken a random sample from a large population of raw scores. You want to know how precisely the sample mean estimates the population mean. What do you need to know before you can begin to answer this question?

4. What is the estimated standard error of the mean for the following samples:
   (a) $M = 14, s = 4, N = 16$
   (b) $M = 28, s = 3, N = 36$

5. What is the estimated standard error of the mean for the following samples:
   (a) $M = 24, s = 5, N = 25$
   (b) $M = 44, s = 12, N = 9$

6. Calculate the 95% confidence interval for the population mean using the sample data from problem #4(a) and #4(b).

7. Calculate the 95% confidence interval for the population mean using the sample data from problem #5(a) and #5(b).

8. Calculate the 99% confidence interval for the same sample data in problem #4(a) and #4(b).

9. Calculate the 99% confidence interval for the same sample data in problem #5(a) and #5(b).

10. A 95% confidence interval is determined to be 6.11 to 7.89 when a sample mean ($N = 20$) is 7.00. What may the researcher conclude?

11. When a 95% confidence interval has been calculated for the population mean, what exactly does "95% confidence" refer to?

12. Explain how the width of a confidence interval is related to precision of estimation.

13. What are three factors affecting the width of a confidence interval? For each factor, indicate how the interval width is affected (i.e., increased or decreased).

14. A researcher reports that the results of her study reveal that the population mean has a .95 chance of falling in the interval 14.5 to 16.5. What is wrong with this conclusion?

15. A study is done to determine the mean age of adult residents (18 and above) of a large community. The Chamber of Commerce advertises that the average age is 48.5. Based on a large random sample ($N = 100$), a 95% confidence interval is calculated as 55.4 to 69.6. What should one conclude regarding the hypothesized mean of 48.5?

16. A researcher is testing the effect of a drug that has been found to reduce tumor growth in rats. The drug was previously found to shrink tumors on the average 0.5 centimeter a day. The results of this more recent study found an average rate of shrinkage of 0.7 centimeter a day with a 95% confidence interval of 0.4 to 0.9. What should the researcher conclude regarding the effectiveness of the drug?

17. You work for a public relations firm that has been hired to obtain a measure of client satisfaction for an automobile service company. You obtain a random sample of 80 customers who have had their car serviced during the last year. You then design a brief questionnaire that can be administered on the telephone. Each member of your random sample is contacted and asked to respond. Several questions make use of a 10-point scale to assess customer satisfaction with courtesy of the service technicians, promptness of service, service completion (i.e., whether the problem was fixed), and cost. You decide to add together the customers' responses to these four scales to produce an index of overall satisfaction. Scores can range from 4 to 40 for each customer. The mean satisfaction index for your sample of customers was 34.5 with a standard deviation of 4.66. What is the 95% confidence interval for the population mean?

18. A newly designed intelligence test was given to a sample of 64 children, ages 6 to 7, who are developmentally delayed. The mean IQ was 88 ($s = 16$). Based on separate and independent psychological testing, the estimated mean for these children had been 85. Construct the 95% confidence interval to make a decision about the precision of estimation for the population mean. Are these data in agreement with the independently assessed mean of 85?

19. Write a summary of the results reported in problem #17 using the format suggested by the *Publication Manual of the American Psychological Association*.

20. Write a summary of the results reported in problem #19 using the format suggested by the *Publication Manual of the American Psychological Association*.

Answers to Odd-Numbered Problems

1. The t distribution is actually a family of distributions based on the sample size (or degrees of freedom). It is symmetrical with a mean of zero like the normal distribution. However, for small sample sizes, it is slightly more leptokurtic than the normal distribution, but it approaches a normal distribution as sample size increases. Like the theoretical normal distribution, the t distribution is a theoretical distribution with the area under the curve mathematically predictable.

3. In order to construct a confidence interval for the population mean, you will need to know, in addition to the sample mean:
   (a) sample size
   (b) sample standard deviation
   (c) the estimated standard error of the mean
   (d) the shape of the original distribution unless sample size is large
   (e) the critical t value associated with the degrees of freedom for your sample and with the desired confidence level (e.g., .95 or .99)

5. (a) 1.0 (b) 4.0

7. (5a) 21.94 to 26.06 (5b) 34.78 to 53.22

9. (5a) 21.20 to 26.80 (5b) 30.58 to 57.42

11. The 95% confidence interval refers to the probability that the interval contains the population mean. If you repeated this procedure 100 times with the same sample size (and same population), in 95 of the 100 confidence intervals you construct you will capture the population mean within your interval.

13. Factors affecting the width of the confidence interval include:
   (a) sample size, increasing sample size generally will decrease interval width
   (b) variability (i.e., standard deviation), reducing variability tends to decrease interval width
   (c) specific probability associated with the interval (e.g., .95 vs. .99), higher probabilities lead to wider interval widths

15. Because the obtained confidence interval of 55.4 to 69.6 does not contain the hypothesized mean of 48.5, we can be confident that the population mean is not 48.5. It is always possible that we can be wrong, but with the large sample size and relatively precise estimate provided by the confidence interval, it is very unlikely that the true population mean is as low as 48.5.

17. The 95% confidence interval is 33.47 to 35.53.

19. A summary of your analysis might look like this:

A random sample of 80 customers who have had their car serviced during the last year was administered a brief questionnaire. Several questions made use of a 10-point scale to assess customer satisfaction with courtesy of the service technicians, promptness of service, service completion (i.e., whether the problem was fixed), and cost. Customers' responses to these four scales were added to produce an index of overall satisfaction. Scores could range from 4 to 40 for each customer. The mean satisfaction index was 34.5 (SD = 4.66). There is a .95 probability that the interval 33.47 to 35.53 contains the mean satisfaction of all customers of this company during the past year. It appears the customers are generally satisfied with service.

(Note: The range as well as mode and median would likely be presented if available.)

 Go to http://psychology.wadsworth.com/courses/statistics/ and test your knowledge of this chapter by taking the online quiz. Another resource to check is the online workshops that provide a step-by-step guide through a number of topics at http://psychology.wadsworth.com/workshops/workshops.html.

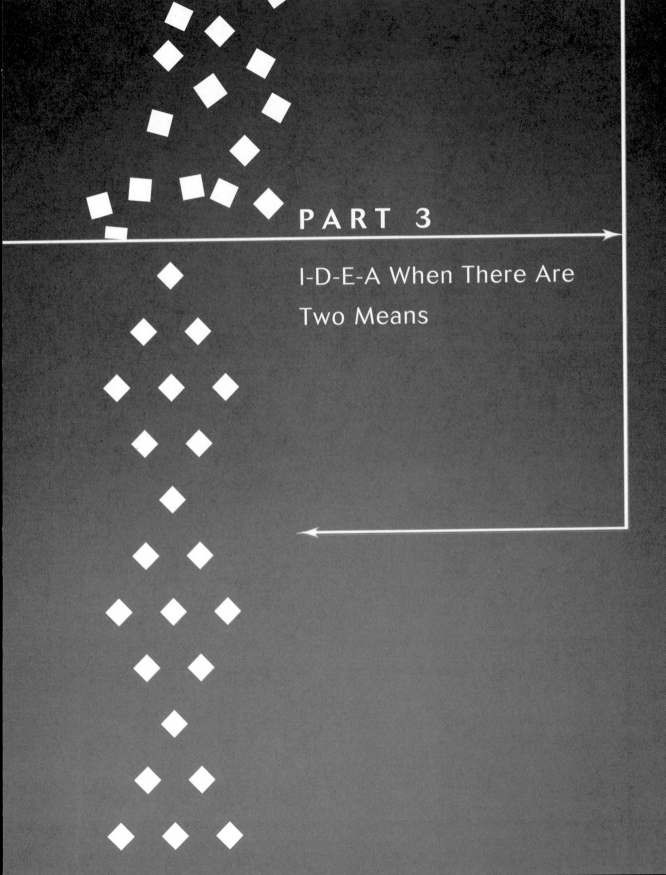

PART 3

I-D-E-A When There Are Two Means

CHAPTER 7

Inspecting and Describing Data from Two Groups

Basic to scientific evidence . . . is the process of comparison, recording differences or contrasts.
Campbell & Stanley (1963, p.6)

INTRODUCTION

The power of research is revealed when we compare observations that are made under different conditions. In fact, our senses make great use of contrasts. Imagine how easy it is to see a rabbit moving across a field compared to one sitting motionless. How many times have you entered a familiar room and known that something was different, but could identify the change only after a moment of thought? We are sensitive to differences. Beginning with this chapter, statistical methods to compare two sets of observations become the focus. We deal with methods to use when the variables observed and measured are continuous variables with the characteristics of interval or ratio scales of measurement. Questionnaire scores, measures of skills, number of points scored, and physical measurements are some examples of such variables; most behavioral research is based on the use of continuous variables. Here are three examples of researchers who are using continuous variables to make comparisons between two groups.

- The Director of Student Life at Bethlehem College wondered whether students living in college residence halls earned higher or lower grades relative to students living at home with their parents. She selected two random samples of students, one from campus residents and one from commuters. She was very persistent and obtained excellent cooperation from the student sample. After coding the answer sheets to remove names, the registrar provided her with the grade point averages.

- Janice read about errors made by eyewitnesses to crimes. She wondered if errors might be more likely when the crime involved violent crimes compared to nonviolent crimes. She decided to study this issue for her honors project relating psychology to criminal justice. She reasoned that watching a violent crime would create a greater emotional response than would watching a nonviolent crime. Janice hypothesized that this greater emotional arousal would interfere with the development of accurate memories. Because she may not ethically create violence for her research, she used a number of film clips of crimes. She picked two film clips, one of a violent crime and one of a nonviolent crime. They were carefully chosen so that the crimes were equally apparent and equally unanticipated by viewers. She had students watch both film clips as part of a larger set of short clips. After the students watched the films, Janice assessed the accuracy of the students' memory for details about the two types of crimes. She expected more errors when violence had been involved.

- Leonard noticed that students in his dorm listened to a wide variety of music while they studied. For his lab project, he decided to examine whether different types of music affected students' success in performing cognitive tasks. He randomly assigned students to listen to Mozart or Metallica while completing a complicated puzzle. He measured time to complete the puzzle as his dependent variable.

In Chapter 6, we described how Katie might compare a hypothesized happiness mean to the mean she had observed. Researchers are not often asked to compare an observed mean from one sample with a hypothesized mean. Instead, researchers usually compare the means of two samples. This is because we rarely know population values, and only infrequently does someone hypothesize a specific value. Most often, behavioral scientists obtain estimates of population values from two or more groups. In this chapter, we discuss statistical methods to compare two samples. We discuss statistical methods to use with more than two samples in the following unit.

GETTING TWO SETS OF DATA TO COMPARE

The three research projects just described illustrate the three primary ways in which researchers obtain two sets of data to compare. Janice wanted to learn if accuracy of memory was affected by the degree of violence involved in crimes seen in short film clips. She had just one group of people, but she had two sets of data to compare because she had a measure of accuracy of memory for a violent crime and for a nonviolent crime. When people in research studies are observed two or more times, psychologists speak of **repeated measures designs.**

When the participants form different groups, we speak of **independent groups designs,** of which there are two kinds. First, Leonard's project is an example of an experiment involving random assignment of participants to groups. He knew that it would be important to start with two comparable groups of students. If they were comparable to begin with, he could expect that they would be similarly skilled at completing the puzzles *prior* to the start of the experiment. The simplest way to obtain comparable groups is to assign research participants to conditions randomly. (See Chapter 1.) We call Leonard's experiment a **random groups design.** It is one type of independent groups design.

In contrast, the student life director used a second type of independent groups design, a **natural groups design.** Dorm students and commuter students are called natural groups, and natural groups are used whenever it is impossible to assign people to groups. Natural groups would be used to compare the political attitudes of men and women, or the personalities of first-born and second-born children. Natural groups are also used when it would be wrong (even unthinkable) to assign people to groups such as when we compare the quality of life of people with cancer and those with heart disease, or the work histories of alcoholics versus nonalcoholics. You can easily imagine many other possible pairs of natural groups. Note that in both random groups designs and natural groups designs different subjects form the groups of the experiment; thus the groups are independent of one another. For example, people are either first-born or later-born children. However, only when subjects have been assigned randomly may we make the assumption that the groups are comparable prior to beginning the study.

In each of these research designs, the two sets of data represent an independent variable. Degree of violence (violent vs. nonviolent crime), type of music (classical vs. heavy metal), and location of college residence (dormitory vs. homes) are the independent variables. These independent variables each have two "levels." (Levels are also called *conditions.*) Observing moving versus motionless rabbits can be described as observing under two conditions. A great many questions can be answered using two levels of independent variables.

We will follow the I-D-E-A approach to data analysis and interpretation as we examine data from two groups. In this chapter, we focus on inspection (the *I*) and description (the *D*). In the following two chapters, we will show how researchers in behavioral sciences and other fields estimate (*E*) the degree to which independent variables have affected behavior and thoughts and then how researchers test the idea that differences between groups are merely the results of sampling error. Last, we review how to use standard and informative ways to announce (A) findings to others.

INSPECTING TWO DISTRIBUTIONS

The reasons to inspect data, as Chapter 2 and 3 showed, include detecting data handling errors and anomalies in the data itself. The anomalies include outliers (extreme data points) and klinkers (invalid data points). Outliers sometimes are valid data points that represent very unusual people; however, outliers can mislead researchers because they can have surprisingly large effects on the statistics, especially when modestly sized samples are used. There is no way to confidently identify an outlier unless it is incredibly different from the other scores. The estimates given for the multiplication experiment discussed in Chapter 2 are shown in Table 7.1. These data included two estimates so much bigger than the other estimates that it seemed clear that these estimates were not part of the population of serious estimates. For less clear situations, there are several complicated ways to identify outliers, but let us introduce some simple ones. One approach is to calculate the 99% confidence interval and treat data points outside that interval as outliers. If we had reason to assume a normal curve, using the 99% confidence interval would mean that data points with z scores greater

TABLE 7.1 ■ **Estimates for the Answer to a Multiplication Problem Presented in Two Ways with the Discarded Outliers Indicated**

$1 \times 2 \times 3 \times 4 \times 5 \times 6 \times 7 \times 8 \times 9 =$	$9 \times 8 \times 7 \times 6 \times 5 \times 4 \times 3 \times 2 \times 1 =$
81	124
100	150
100	190
130	200
172	250
256	350
306	500
1,200	987
3,645	1,250
4,125	2,898
5,500	6,761
✕8,000,000	10,000
	✕560,000,000

than $+2.58$ or less than -2.58 would be called outliers. Some authors define outliers as values whose z scores are more extreme than ± 3.30 when N is greater than 100, but 2.58 when N is less than 100 (Tabachnick & Fidell, 2001). Yet another approach is simply to define outliers whose z scores are more extreme than ± 3.00 (or ± 4.00). Clearly, there is no single accepted definition of an outlier. It will be up to you, based on a close inspection of your data, and keeping in mind both the nature of the data and its eventual use, to decide which rule of thumb to employ and whether outliers once identified should be eliminated from further analysis.

Discarding outliers might suggest that the researcher was introducing a bias into the data. That is, the mean will change when an outlier is dropped, and one might reasonably ask what is then the "true" mean. To avoid appearing to bias the mean by discarding outliers, some researchers use **trimmed means.** Trimmed means refer to those means that are calculated after discarding the same number of the most extreme data points at both ends of the distribution. Following this approach with the data from the estimates of the products of multiplication problems in Table 7.1 would mean that we discard one incredibly large estimate in each group as well as the smallest estimate in each group. Sometimes a percentage of scores are discarded. One might, for instance, discard the most extreme 4%. If sample size were 100, this would mean the two highest and the two lowest scores would be deleted.

Before dropping scores, it is best to examine outliers to be sure that they are not in fact klinkers. As you recall, klinkers might reflect participants who did not want to be part of the research effort and who consequently provided invalid data. Klinkers also occur when something goes wrong with equipment or data collection procedures. At times, it might be impossible to distinguish an outlier score produced by an unusual subject from a klinker produced by an uncooperative participant. But distinguishing between them is less important than detecting them. Once it is certain that the suspicious data point is not a klinker, a transformation of skewed data should be tried as was illustrated with the estimates on the numbers of thefts in Chapter 3. If all efforts fail to correct or transform an outlier so that it fits into the distribution, Tabachnick and Fidell (2001) recommend replacing the outlier with a score that is one unit more extreme than the next-most-extreme score. Thus, for example, in Table 7.1, one would replace 8,000,000 with 5,501 (because 5,500 is the second largest estimate in the condition) and replace 560,000,000 with 10,001 (because 10,000 is the second largest in the condition). If the outliers had been very small numbers (rather than very large numbers), the outliers would have been replaced by scores one unit smaller than the next-to-smallest point. Abelson (1995) reminds us that, whatever approach a person decides to use, it is crucial to be consistent. Moreover, it is important to report exactly how outliers were treated. It would be unethical to examine the results of a study and then seek reasons to discard data so that the researcher's expectations are supported.

(a) Assume that a data set has a mean of 20 and standard deviation of 5. Treat the following numbers as a small portion of that data set. Find the outliers in the distribution using the rule of thumb that outliers are those scores with z scores more extreme than ± 3.00.

23, 19, 12, 27, 41, 20, 24, 18, 19, 17, 36, 18, 20, 21, 31, 22, 21, 4, 20, 19 . . .

(b) Suppose that a trimmed mean was to be used. Which scores are to be discarded?   ■

Look ahead to the data set in *Your Turn* 7-2. These data represent the scores of 18 students on an attitude inventory for which the maximum score is 100. In the hypothetical data set, there was an error in data entry for person #6. An impossible value of 139 was recorded.

Suppose that no one had detected that klinker; the mean of the total attitude score would then have been 82.83 and the standard deviation would have been 14.60. After correcting the data entry error that created the klinker, the mean dropped 3.30 points to 79.53 and the standard deviation dropped 10.39 points to 4.21. The mean was not greatly affected by this klinker, but note the effect of the klinker on the standard deviation: the klinker led to a standard deviation more than three times larger than the correct one. Such an undetected klinker would cause the confidence interval to be more than three times wider than the correct one. The moral here is that data inspection is the essential first step not only for descriptive accuracy (a terribly high priority for researchers), but also because the errors could have massive effects on some statistical values that we extract from the data.

YOUR TURN 7-2

Below are 18 attitude scores that may range from 0 to 100. Would a researcher using the simple "z equals ±3.00" rule for outlier detection have found the klinker (shown in bold)?

79, 83, 76, 74, 81, **139,** 76, 81, 88, 78, 80, 86, 75, 83, 76, 81, 82, 73

(The mean and standard deviation of the sample of 18 scores are 82.83 and 14.60, respectively.)

Using a Stem-and-Leaf Plot to Inspect Data from Two Small Samples

When samples are small, let's say less than 30, and the scores are no more than three digits long, stem-and-leaf plots are easy to construct. Constructing a stem-and-leaf plot forces the analyst to become very familiar with the data. For example, think of Leonard's 20 research participants who were randomly assigned to complete a complicated puzzle while listening to either Mozart or Metallica. Suppose that the dependent variable was time in seconds to complete the puzzle. Table 7.2 contains the original data for the two groups. Just glancing at the table suggests that it took the students who listened to Metallica longer to complete the puzzle. Stem-and-leaf plots for the two groups of participants are given in Figure 7.1. Because each group included only 10 people, quite simple stem-and-leaf plots were made. The tens digit was used as the stem (that is, 1 for 10 through 19, 2 for 20 through 29, etc.), and the units digits formed the leaves. For example, the person who took 40 sec. is represented at the top of the table by the 4 stem and a 0 leaf.

TABLE 7.2 ■ Time to Complete a Complicated Puzzle in Seconds While Listening to Mozart or Metallica

Mozart	Metallica
13	23
15	8
25	11
11	32
34	40
16	19
24	23
17	22
18	21
17	27

FIGURE. 7.1 ■ Back-to-back stem-and-leaf plot of time (sec.) to complete a simple puzzle while listening to one of two kinds of music.

Mozart Leaf	Stem	Metallica Leaf
8776531	1	189
54	2	12337
4	3	
	4	0

When the two stem-and-leaf plots are placed side by side, your eyes cannot fail to compare the two plots and notice how the groups differed. This plot is called a **back-to-back stem-and-leaf plot.** First, note that the left side is not what you might have expected from what you learned about stem-and-leaf plots for one group. We plotted the scores of the left side (the Mozart side) so that low scores are next to the stem. The scores on the left side need to be read from right to left. We can see that the data for both groups are positively skewed. As was pointed out in Chapter 3, finding positive skewness should be expected when a dependent variable has no upper limit, which is the case with time to complete a task. For our purposes, the plot tells us immediately that those students listening to Mozart tended to complete their puzzles slightly more quickly than those listening to Metallica. If we look a little more closely, we can find the medians in stem-and-leaf plots. There are 10 scores for each group, so the median falls between the lower five and the upper five scores. Count up (or down) five scores. The fifth and sixth data points for the Mozart group are 17 sec. When there is a repetition of a value at the median, we treat that value as the median. For the Metallica group, the median is between 22 and 23, or 22.5 sec. (the mean of the fifth and sixth scores). To repeat, constructing a stem-and-leaf plot by hand forces the researcher to pay close attention to the actual data points and makes it almost impossible to overlook critical differences between groups.

YOUR TURN 7-3

Construct a back-to-back stem-and-leaf plot to inspect the data from the following two-group experiment. Imagine that a taste test was conducted that contrasted a popular soft drink versus a drink with an experimental flavor. The dependent variable is a subjective liking rating ranging from 0 (Yuck!) to 20 (Great!) as rated on a 21-point scale.

0–1–2–3–4–5–6–7–8–9–10–11–12–13–14–15–16–17–18–19–20
Yuck   Great

The ratings for the popular drink were 18, 19, 19, 20, 19, 10, 17, 15, 19, and 18. The ratings for the experimental drink were 2, 6, 4, 4, 6, 20, 3, 2, 20, and 5. What can you learn from the plot? ■

Using Stem-and-Leaf Plots to Inspect Data from Large Samples

If we are using large samples, it becomes very time consuming to construct stem-and-leaf plots by hand. In such cases, we use computers. When we use computers, it is important to remember why we inspect data: we do so to spot outliers, klinkers, skewness, and other problems with distributions. To detect these problems, it is essential to examine data closely. Computers are valuable for efficient statistical analyses, but, when we do not deal with the data points ourselves, we are tempted to take short-cuts and, consequently, to do only a cursory inspection; we speak from personal experience. With that in mind, we move on to inspect data from two groups that most behavioral scientists would analyze using computers. A sample of 137 college students (91 women and 46 men) answered a questionnaire concerning how supportive and tolerant of others they believed their college peers are. The survey contained 15 items such as:

I can find students who will fill me in on class sessions that I have missed.

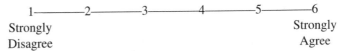

Strongly
Disagree
Strongly
Agree

The scores of women and men are given in Figure 7.2. The lowest possible score was 15, which would indicate that the respondent disagreed strongly with all 15 items. The highest score possible was 90, which would indicate that the student agreed strongly with every item. Figure 7.2 differs from Figure 7.1 in two ways: first, it is not a back-to-back stem-and-leaf because most computer programs don't produce them. Although it is easier to compare two samples with the back-to-back format, we thought it would be best for you to see the format from a widely used computer program. It is possible to line up the plots yourself.[1] Figure 7.2 differs from Figure 7.1 also because the larger samples permit more-detailed plots. Stem-and-leaf plots are quite flexible; in Figure 7.2 the scores are divided into five-value stems rather than one-value stems as in Figure 7.1.

What can we learn from inspecting Figure 7.2? By aligning the two plots side by side, it is easy to see that, in general, women were more positive about other students than were men. We see that women had the highest scores but men had the lowest. We can spot the modes of both distributions fairly easily: 51 for the men and 59 for the women. And with a little counting we can find the medians. For 91 women, we need to count up (or down) 46 scores to find the median. Several women in the middle of the distribution have the same score, 60; therefore, we treat 60 as the median. The median falls between two values for men, so we take the mean of 58 and 61 (59.5) as the median. The medians for men and women are almost equal. Also note that one man produced the lowest possible score (15). Overall, the distributions are not markedly asymmetrical although there is a slight negative skewness for the men; one guy on the very end of the distribution apparently did not find his college peers to be supportive.

Rotate Figure 7.2 so that the stems are horizontal and the leaves look like bars of a frequency histogram. Imagine superimposing normal curves onto these frequency distributions. You should note that the scores of women are clustered more closely in the middle of the distribution than are the scores for men. The distribution of the scores for men looks a little more like a normal curve than does the distribution for women. The distribution of women's scores is somewhat leptokurtic, and the distribution of men's scores is a bit negatively skewed. However, neither distribution differs enough from a normal distribution to be a concern.

---

[1] If the ranges of the groups were markedly different, the stems might be arranged differently. If that happens, a little work by hand might be needed to regroup the data to make the two stem-and-leaf plots more comparable.

FIGURE 7.2 ■ Stem-and-leaf plots from SPSS comparing male and female students in their attitudes toward the supportiveness of their college peers. (Note that each stem includes five values; for example, the women with scores of 80 through 84 are in one stem and those with scores of 85 through 89 are in another stem. Note also that some stems are empty.)

Female Undergraduate Students (n = 91)

Frequency	Stem	Leaf
	1 .	
	2 .	
	2 .	
3	3 .	1
3	3 .	577
3	4 .	334
5	4 .	78999
4	5 .	0134
26	5 .	55566677777777888999999999
14	6 .	00000112234444
16	6 .	5555566677888999
11	7 .	00001223344
3	7 .	699
2	8 .	04
3	8 .	678

Mode = 59 (points to the 5 . row, the 9999 values)

Median = 60

Male Undergraduate Students (n = 48)

Frequency	Stem	Leaf
1	1 .	5
	2 .	
1	2 .	7
	3 .	
1	3 .	8
3	4 .	244
1	4 .	8
7	5 .	1111114
10	5 .	5556677788
10	6 .	1122233334
9	6 .	555557778
3	7 .	134
1	7 .	5
1	8 .	0
	8 .	

Mode = 51

Median $\dfrac{58 + 61}{2} = 59.5$

In addition, our inspection has revealed that we do not have problems with ceiling or floor effects: only one person's score equaled either the minimum or maximum possible score. If several scores had matched either the highest possible score (90) or the lowest (15), the researcher might worry that the questionnaire was not able to measure the full range of attitudes because there would have been no way of knowing whether all the students with those scores hold equivalent views. There is no way to correct the data when floor or ceiling effects are found. When there are ceiling or floor effects, the values of the mean and standard deviation must be treated with caution. However, note that medians are not affected by floor and ceiling effects (unless more than half of a sample obtain scores that were equal to the maximum or equal to the minimum possible).

DESCRIBING TWO DISTRIBUTIONS

After becoming closely acquainted with the data points, researchers are ready for the second step in analysis following the I-D-E-A model: description. Basic summary statistics are used to describe the data concisely. The most common ways, as you learned in Chapter 4, are to calculate measures of central tendency and variation for both groups. Table 7.3 contains the descriptive information for the student attitude data just inspected. What can you learn from the numerical descriptions? On every index of central tendency (the mode, median, and mean), the scores for women are higher than for men. Furthermore, both the minimum and maximum scores for women were higher than those values are for men. It seems clear that women valued their peers a little more highly than men valued their peers. The advantage of the numerical indexes over the stem-and-leaf plots is that we can now say exactly how much the scores of women exceed those of men: we can say that the mean for women is 3.71 units higher than the mean for men. Is this difference big enough to be worth thinking about? It's a good question, and we'll come back to it later.

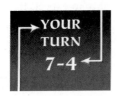

Look back to Figure 7.1. What can you learn about the differences between the measures of central tendency for the groups who worked puzzles while listening to Mozart or Metallica? ■

Table 7.3 also provides information on variation. Both the range and the standard deviation show that the scores for men differ more from each other than do the scores for women.

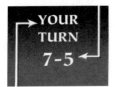

What do you learn in Figure 7.1 about the variation in the time to solve the puzzle for those working while listening to Mozart and those listening to Metallica? ■

TABLE 7.3 ■ Descriptive Indexes for the Data in Figure 5.2 on Student Attitudes

Descriptive Index	Women	Men
Number	91	48
Central Tendency:		
Mode	59	51
Median	60	59.5
Mean	61.48	57.77
Variation:		
Minimum Score	31	15
Maximum Score	88	80
Range	57	65
Standard Deviation	10.98	11.77
Standard Error of the Mean	1.15	1.70

Only after a thorough inspection of the individual data points and their distributions can we draw meaningful conclusions from numerical indexes such as means and standard deviations. Before rushing on to further analyses, it is important to follow this inspection and description procedure for both groups in all the studies that we do.

DESCRIBING THE DIFFERENCE BETWEEN TWO SAMPLES

Every sample mean is subject to sampling error. When we analyze the difference between the means of two samples, we need a way to estimate the sampling error of a *difference* between two means.

A single sample is described by a mean and standard deviation. In Chapter 5, we showed that means of samples cannot be expected to equal the population mean exactly because we will get different means from different random samples. Each of the means, of course, is a perfectly good (that is, unbiased) estimate of the population value, μ, but the means do not equal each other. It is important to have an index of how much variability to expect. Because we cannot spend the next year of our lives repeatedly drawing random samples in order to calculate the variation from sample to sample, it is fortunate that we have a way to estimate this variation. Instead of drawing sample after sample, we use the formula for the sampling error of a mean. As defined in Chapter 4:

$$s_M = s/\sqrt{N}$$

The formula reminds us that, the larger the sample, the smaller the standard error of the mean. The effect of sample size on the standard error is easy to see in Table 7.3. Even though the standard deviation of women's scores was larger than the standard deviation of men's scores, the standard error of the mean for men was larger than the standard error of the mean for women. This is true because fewer men than women were tested; with smaller samples, there would be more variation from sample to sample.

To describe the difference between the means of two groups, it is necessary to develop an additional statistical index, the **standard error of the difference between two means.** This index tells us how much variation in the difference between two means we should expect if we were to replicate a two-group study over and over again. The formula for the standard error of the difference between two group means contains the group sizes and standard deviations just as is the standard error of a single mean. If we replicated the attitude study with a new sample of men and a new sample of women drawn from the same population, we should expect to find a difference that is not exactly equal to 3.71. To estimate the variation from study to study that we should expect, we need the standard error of the difference between two means.

The standard error of the difference between two means is symbolized as $s_{M_1-M_2}$. The formula is

$$s_{M_1-M_2} = \sqrt{\left(\left[\frac{df s_1^2 + df_2 s_2^2}{df_1 + df_2} \right] \left[\frac{1}{n_1} + \frac{1}{n_2} \right] \right)} \qquad \textbf{Equation 7.1}$$

Did you read the formula? Carefully examine the terms in this formula. Note that n_1 and n_2 refer to the size of the two groups, respectively, and that the variances (the standard deviations squared) for each group are needed.

The left part under the radical (that is, under the square root sign) is called the **pooled variance.** That means that we have a type of average of the two group variances. The formula

TABLE 7.4 ■ Example Calculation of the Standard Error of the Difference Between Two Means

	Formula	Example calculations
Descriptors of the groups		$s_1 = 6.32, n_1 = 26$ $s_2 = 7.81, n_2 = 37$
Pooled standard deviation, s_{pooled}	$\sqrt{\left(\dfrac{df_1 s_1^2 + df_2 s_2^2}{df_1 + df_2}\right)}$	$\sqrt{\left(\dfrac{25\,(6.32^2) + 36\,(7.81^2)}{25 + 36}\right)} = 7.24$
Standard error of the difference between two means, $s_{M_1 - M_2}$	$s_{pooled}\sqrt{(1/n_1 + 1/n_2)}$	$7.24\sqrt{(1/26 + 1/37)} = 1.85$

provides the **weighted average** of the two variances. Many people have an intuitive notion of what is involved in a weighted average but have not thought about the issue in mathematical terms. Our goal throughout this text is to help you get a sense of the reasons behind the statistics. If you appreciate the reasons, statistical methods are a lot easier to understand, and you are more likely to be able to use your skills later in your laboratory classes or in a career. Consider the following example of a weighted average.

Imagine that you are interested in the mean SAT score of all fraternity members at a college that has two fraternities. Assume that you don't know the SAT scores of individuals, but that you do know the number of members and the mean SAT for each fraternity. You can calculate the mean SAT of all fraternity members by taking the weighted average of the means of the two fraternities. It is easier to illustrate this point with a few numbers than to describe it in words; here is the information for the two fraternities:

Fraternity	Mean SAT	Number of members
Gamma	532	28
Delta	488	17

To obtain the weighted average, the number of members in each fraternity is multiplied by its mean SAT, and the two products are added together. This sum is then divided by the total number of fraternity members:

$$\frac{28\,(532) + 17\,(488)}{28 + 17} = 515.4$$

You know that the overall mean must be between the two means we started with, and, because Gamma has more members, the overall mean must be closer to the mean for Gamma than to the mean for Delta. This weighted average procedure, by the way, applies regardless of how many groups we have.

This procedure is applied to obtain the left part of Equation 7.1, the pooled variance. Multiply the degrees of freedom by the variance for each group and add the two products together, that is, $df_1 s_1^2 + df_2 s_2^2$. Then that total is divided by the sum of the degrees of freedom for the two groups, $df_1 + df_2$. The result is the pooled variance. If we take the square root of the pooled variance, we have the **pooled standard deviation.** For the attitude data we have been using, the pooled standard deviation, s_{pooled}, is

$$s_{pooled} = \sqrt{\left[\frac{df_1 s_1^2 + df_2 s_2^2}{df_1 + df_2}\right]} = \sqrt{\left[\frac{(91-1)\,10.98^2 + (48-1)\,11.77^2}{(91-1)+(48-1)}\right]}$$

$$= \sqrt{\left[\frac{17361.48}{137}\right]} = \sqrt{126.73} = 11.26$$

Having followed the SAT example, you should not be surprised to see that the pooled standard deviation is closer to the standard deviation for women than the standard deviation for men because our sample had more women than men. (Table 7.4 has another example.)

The pooled standard deviation is used with two group sizes to calculate the standard error of a difference between two means. So that you can see the parallel between the formula for the standard error of the difference between two means and the formula for the standard error of a single mean, we have rearranged the formula for the standard error of a single mean. Recall that we calculated the standard error of the mean for one sample by dividing the standard deviation by the square root of the sample size (N). Dividing by a number is the same as multiplying by 1 over that number, the reciprocal. For example, dividing by 4 is the same as multiplying by 1/4. Thus, we can rewrite the formula for the standard error of one mean as follows:

$$s_M = s/\sqrt{N} = s\sqrt{\left[\frac{1}{N}\right]}$$

If we use the pooled standard deviation in place of s and two group sizes (n_1 and n_2) rather than the size of one sample, the formula for the standard error of the difference between *two* means is

$$s_{M_1-M_2} = s_{pooled}\sqrt{\left[\frac{1}{n_1} + \frac{1}{n_2}\right]} \qquad\qquad \textbf{Equation 7.2}$$

You should recognize that the square root of the reciprocal of the group size (i.e., $\sqrt{(1/n)}$) is used in the same way in both formulas; however, there are two groups involved in Equation 7.2. Consequently, the standard error of the difference between two means is larger than the standard error of a single mean. To find $s_{M_1-M_2}$ for the two groups in Table 7.3, we use the numbers of women and men and s_{pooled}:

$$s_{M_1-M_2} = 11.26\sqrt{\left[\frac{1}{91} + \frac{1}{48}\right]} = 2.01$$

Don't get lost in the numbers and forget the point. The final answer means that, if we were to replicate this student attitude study with thousands of randomly selected groups of 48 men and 91 women from the same college and calculate the differences of means across all the pairs of groups, our estimate of the standard deviation of those differences would be 2.01. Notice that the difference between the two means was 3.71, not quite two times larger

TABLE 7.5 ■ Illustration of the Calculation of the Standard Error of a Difference of Two Means

	Group 1	Group 2	Difference
Mean, M	23.23	18.48	4.75
Standard deviation, s	7.27	8.29	———
Group size, n	32	30	———
Pooled standard deviation, s_{pooled}	$\sqrt{\dfrac{31\,(7.27^2) + 29\,(8.29^2)}{31 + 29}} = \sqrt{60.52} = 7.78$		
Group size term	$\sqrt{\left[\dfrac{1}{32} + \dfrac{1}{30}\right]} = \sqrt{0.06458} = 0.2541$		
Standard error of difference between two means, $s_{M_1-M_2}$	$7.78\,(0.2541) = 1.98$		

than its estimated sampling error. This ratio will be used later. Table 7.5 provides an additional example of the calculation of $s_{M_1-M_2}$.

YOUR TURN 7-6

Suppose that 10 students (Group G) were randomly assigned to watch a movie on Gandhi and 15 (Group T) to watch Terminator II. After watching the movies, a measure of aggressiveness was obtained. Here are the standard deviations: Group G, 3.25; Group T, 3.74. What is the pooled standard deviation? What is the standard error of the difference between the two means of aggressiveness? (Note that you can calculate these values without knowing the means.)   ■

REPEATED MEASURES DESIGNS

Instead of testing two groups, sometimes behavioral scientists test one group twice. We noted earlier that using one sample with more than one observation is called *repeated measures design.* Janice tested one sample twice when she compared memory for different types of crimes. She wanted to learn whether accuracy of recall for facts was lower for violent crimes relative to nonviolent crimes. Clinical psychologists studying the effectiveness of therapy might test anxiety-plagued people prior to therapy and then again after therapy. The therapist would hope to observe that such psychotherapy clients were less anxious after treatment. Similarly, we would expect to find improved reading skills if we test children at the start of classes in the fall and then as classes are ending in the spring. The efforts of both teachers and psychotherapists are designed to bring about change. Testing one group of people twice at different times or under different conditions provides important advantages to statistical analyses that we will cover in a later chapter. At this point, we want to stress how to inspect and describe **difference scores.**

Inspecting Difference Scores

Even when difference scores are the focus of the research, both sets of measurements are to be inspected prior to calculating differences. We won't repeat everything we have already recommended regarding the inspection of a single set of measurements. When our interest is on difference scores, we want to be especially wary of how limitations in either or both of the two measurements might affect the difference between them. An undetected ceiling (or floor) effect might produce differences much smaller than had been hypothesized.

Suppose that one wanted to improve children's spelling, but a very easy spelling test was used. If many of the children received near perfect scores on a pre-test, the post-test cannot detect the effects of their work on spelling because the near perfect scores on the pre-test will mean that many difference scores would be very low if not zero. Their near perfect pre-test scores would mean that they would appear to have improved very little because their post-test scores could not be much higher than the pre-test scores. Such a ceiling effect would lead to the incorrect interpretation that children with average spelling skills made greater progress than did those with very good spelling skills. Inspecting difference scores serves as a check on the initial inspection of each variable separately.

Suppose that 20 students were given a visual discrimination task on a computer monitor. After this first measurement, they were retested on a monitor with an enhanced display. The differences between their accuracy with the enhanced screen and the standard monitor were found. Positive differences were expected. Inspect the following differences using a stem-and-leaf plot. Develop two possible reasons behind the problems you find.

Student	a	b	c	d	e	f	g	h	i	j	k	l	m	n	o	p	q	r	s	t
Difference	0	2	1	0	0	0	4	5	0	3	1	0	0	0	5	6	0	1	2	−1

■

Describing Differences

When there are two independent groups, the difference between two means is our focus. In contrast, when we have data from a repeated measures design, we first calculate a difference score for each participant and then focus on the mean of those difference scores. For example, if trainees took a pre-test on their skill in formatting a word processor document before beginning training and took a post-test after completing training, we would subtract the pre-test score from the post-test score to calculate an improvement score for each trainee. Here is a simple illustration:

Person	Pre-test	Post-test	Difference Score (Improvement)
1. Taylor	45	61	16
2. Sarah	27	37	10
3. Jim	12	29	17
4. Leslie	52	68	16
5. Lisa	32	47	15

When the trainees began, there were large differences among their skill levels, and these large differences remained when they completed the training. However, they improved to fairly similar degrees as the "Improvement" column shows. The mean of the "Difference Score" column (that is, the mean improvement) is 14.8; the standard deviation of the differences equals 2.77. It would be important, by the way, to use two equally difficult tests for the pre-test and the post-test rather than allow a trainee to use the same test twice. When people take a test for the second time, they usually do better because they have had some practice and may well remember the answers to some items. Using the same test for the pre-test and the post-test would make the training seem more effective than it is.

Janice's study is another example of the use of difference scores. The dependent variable is the percentage of facts about the crimes correctly recalled. A portion of her data on accuracy of recall might include these scores:

Person	Violent crime	Nonviolent crime	Difference
1. Paige	45%	67%	22
2. Jerry	23	36	13
3. Jan	78	82	4
4. Cary	51	62	11
Mean	49.25	61.75	12.50
s (of column)	22.63	19.16	7.42

If you wonder whether the mean of the second column minus the mean of the first column equals the mean of the differences, you are correct. But, even though the mean of the differences is exactly the same as the difference of the means, there is an advantage to focusing on the difference column. The advantage is the increased precision that was hinted at in the beginning of this chapter.

We can use Janice's accuracy of recall data to illustrate this point. The difference of the two means in Janice's study is indeed 12.50, but there are large differences among participants as shown by the large standard deviations—22.63 and 19.16—for the two types of crime. The pooled standard deviation, s_{pooled}, of accuracy is

$$s_{pooled} = \sqrt{\left[\frac{df_1 s_1^2 + df_2 s_2^2}{df_1 + df_2}\right]} = \sqrt{\left[\frac{3 (22.63^2) + 3 (19.16^2)}{3 + 3}\right]} = 20.97$$

In contrast, the standard deviation of the four differences—22, 13, 4, and 11—is only 7.42, less than half of the pooled standard deviation. This smaller value indicates that, although participants differed greatly from each other in their recall of facts related to either of the crimes, the independent variable (violent vs. nonviolent) seems to have had a relatively similar effect on each of the participants. In other words, all participants were more accurate in their recall of the facts concerning nonviolent crime compared to violent crime. You can see the result of this pattern in the following calculations.

The standard error of a difference between two means (as calculated in the way one would for independent groups, i.e., using Equation 7.2) would be

$$s_{M_1 - M_2} = s_{pooled}\sqrt{\left[\frac{1}{n_1} + \frac{1}{n_2}\right]} = 20.97\sqrt{\left[\frac{1}{4} + \frac{1}{4}\right]} = 14.83$$

In contrast, the **standard error of the mean of the differences** s_{MD} is smaller than the standard error of the difference between two means:

$$s_{MD} = s_D\sqrt{\frac{1}{N_{differences}}}$$

Equation 7.3

Note that N refers to sample size, or the number of different scores. If we substitute Janice's data into Equation 7.3, we have

$$s_{MD} = 7.42\sqrt{\frac{1}{4}} = 3.71$$

Using s_D results in a markedly smaller standard error. Remember what the standard errors tell us. If we were to use new samples to replicate data collection procedures precisely, we know that the results will differ due to sampling error; the findings will not be identical. The standard error tells us how much variation we should expect. If our design involves repeated measurements, as in these examples, then our data are more precise than when the data are obtained from independent samples. Why? In the first example, we are not surprised that the trainees began at quite different levels and finished at quite different levels. But their improvement levels were relatively similar. Likewise, in Janice's experiment, we are not surprised that some people are better at remembering details from film clips regardless of the content than are other people. The differences in both examples are less variable than either one of the original columns. Although these are hypothetical examples, it is a general principle that differences between repeated measurements show less variability among people than does either one of the two measurements of the dependent variable.

Matched Groups

There is another type of repeated measures design. Instead of measuring the same people twice, sometimes researchers begin by matching pairs of people who are similar to each other before the experiment begins. This approach is called a **matched groups design.** Imagine that you worked for a consumer research organization and wanted to know which of two SAT test preparation companies was more effective in raising scores on the verbal part of the SAT. It is clear that students begin the courses at different vocabulary levels. One way to decide which company is better would be to test all the students using a vocabulary test before they begin. Illustrative pre-test scores are given in Table 7.6. These pre-tests would be used to form pairs of students who have similar pre-test scores. This could be achieved by first placing their scores in order. One of the best two students would be randomly assigned to learn with the SAT preparation course from Company A and the other to learn from Company B. This procedure would be repeated for the next two best students and then the next two until one of each pair of students was assigned to one of the companies. The result is a matched group design.

Why would we match? Even before training begins we would expect the most-skilled students to end up with higher scores on the SAT than the less-skilled students regardless of

TABLE 7.6 ■ Illustration of Matching Prior to Assignment to Groups

Original vocabulary scores		Ordered vocabulary scores		Company assignment
Person	**Score**	**Person**	**Score**	
Albert	45	Carlos	68	A
Bianca	32	Howard	62	B
Carlos	68	Jeff	55	B
Dan	38	Esteban	51	A
Esteban	51	Kent	48	A
Freda	42	Albert	45	B
Genet	29	Freda	42	A
Howard	62	Dan	38	B
Izzey	35	Izzey	35	B
Jeff	55	Lester	34	A
Kerry	48	Bianca	32	B
Lester	34	Genet	29	A

which company's study program they use. This pattern is shown in Table 7.7. Instead of treating this experiment as an independent groups design, we would treat it as if we had repeated measures, and examine differences for each pair of students. We would then find the standard deviation of differences and the standard error of the mean of the differences. Difference scores would be used in exactly the same way as they are in a repeated measurement design as illustrated with Janice's data on accuracy.

TABLE 7.7 ■ The Arrangement of Post-test Data to Analyze a Matched Groups Design

Company A	Company B	Difference* (B minus A)
Carlos's SAT score = 540	Howard's SAT score = 610	70
Esteban's SAT score = 560	Jeff's SAT score = 580	20
Kent's SAT score = 520	Albert's SAT score = 540	20
Freda's SAT score = 520	Dan's SAT score = 500	−20
Lester's SAT score = 540	Izzey's SAT score = 560	20
Genet's SAT score = 460	Bianca's SAT score = 520	60

* It makes no difference which score is subtracted from the other, as long as you are consistent. Higher scores mean that Company B is more effective.

Greater precision in describing the differences between two means is usually provided by repeated measures and matched groups designs compared to independent groups designs. As we have shown, the standard error of the mean of the differences will usually be smaller than the standard error of the difference between two means. A smaller value means a more precise estimate of sampling error. As we will see in the next chapter, this increased precision pays important dividends when making decisions about the meaning of an observed difference between means. Thus, when appropriate, these types of designs are valuable tools for a researcher investigating the effect of an independent variable.

WHAT YOU HAVE LEARNED AND THE NEXT STEP

This chapter dealt with techniques to use to inspect and describe continuous data from two groups.

- There are three types of research designs in which the means of two groups are compared: natural groups, repeated measures (including matched groups), and random groups.

- There is no single accepted definition of an outlier. A researcher must decide, based on a close inspection of the data and keeping in mind both the nature of the data and its eventual use, which rule of thumb to employ and whether outliers once identified should be eliminated from further analysis. Whatever is decided must be reported when the results are presented to others.

- Trimmed means are means that are calculated after discarding the same number (or percentage) of scores at both ends of the distribution. Trimmed means may be appropriate when obvious outliers are present.

- Back-to-back stem-and-leaf plots provide an easy method to search for outliers and klinkers as well as to compare the shapes of two distributions.

- A poor choice of dependent variable (for example, one having floor and ceiling effects) can make it more difficult to detect differences between two means.

- Methods are available to describe the sampling distribution of differences between the means of two groups that are similar to those used to describe the sampling distribution of a single mean.

- The standard error of the difference between two means provides an estimate of the sampling error when comparing the means of two independent groups.

- When repeated measures designs are used, both the two original distributions *and* the difference scores should be inspected.

- The standard error of the mean of difference scores provides an estimate of the sampling error of difference scores for repeated measures and matched groups designs; these standard errors are smaller than if the data were treated in the same way as data from independent groups were treated.

- Greater precision in describing the differences between two means is provided by repeated measures and matched groups designs compared to independent groups designs. When appropriate, these designs are valuable alternatives to an independent groups design.

When we conduct research, we are interested in what we can conclude on the basis of the samples observed. In the next chapter, these descriptive indices are used to estimate parameters of populations.

Key Concepts

repeated measures designs

independent groups designs

random groups designs

natural groups designs

trimmed means

back-to-back stem-and-leaf plot

standard error of the difference between two means ($s_{M_1 - M_2}$)

pooled variance

weighted average

pooled standard deviation (s_{pooled})

difference scores

standard error of the mean of the differences (s_{MD})

matched groups design

Answers to *Your Turn* Questions

7-1. (a) Any value that differs from the mean by 5 times 3 is defined as an outlier by the ± 3.00 z score rule. Therefore, any value smaller than 5 (=20 − 15) or larger than 35 (=20 + 15) would be considered an outlier. Thus, 41, 36, and 4 would be treated as outliers.

(b) Once the data are ordered, it is apparent that 41 and 36 are the largest scores and 12 and 4 are the smallest. Either discard 41 and 4 or discard 41, 36, 12, and 4.

7-2. Using the sample standard deviation, any value differing from the mean by 43.8, that is, 3 times 14.60, would be considered an outlier. Thus, values larger than 82.83 + 43.8, or 126.63, or smaller than 82.83 − 43.8, or 39.03, are defined as outliers. Thus, yes, this rule would have detected the klinker of 139.

7-3. If you construct a back-to-back stem-and-leaf plot, it will become evident that people generally like the popular drink, but that there is a wide divergence of opinion about the experimental flavor. Note that 20% (2 out of 10) people who tasted the experimental flavor are wild about it. If the flavor is marketed correctly, there might be a part of the market in which this flavor will do quite well. Note that using a trimmed mean might lead us to miss this effect.

7-4. Table 7.1 reveals that the sample listening to Mozart generally solved the puzzle faster than the sample listening to Metallica.

7-5. The scores are more spread out for the Metallica sample.

7-6. The pooled standard deviation is

$$\sqrt{\left[\frac{9 \, (3.25^2) + 14 \, (3.74^2)}{9 + 14}\right]} = 3.56$$

The standard error of the difference between two means is 3.56 $\sqrt{(1/10 + 1/15)}$, or 3.56 (0.408) = 1.45.

7-7. Of the 20 differences, nine equal 0. This suggests either that the enhanced monitor is not particularly useful or that the measure of accuracy is too easy. (In other words, the better performance of the enhanced monitor cannot be detected with the images placed on the screens.) To check on this second interpretation, it would be necessary to examine the scores before calculating the differences. If there were ceiling effects, the images were too simple; if there were floor effects, the images were too complicated for these monitors or these participants. If there were neither floor nor ceiling effects, the enhanced monitor is not helpful at all for 50% of the people (that is, the nine people who did not better plus the one who did worse using the new monitor).

Analyzing and Interpreting Data: Problems and Exercises

1. Briefly describe the two major types of research designs that researchers use to compare two means, and identify two variations of each major type.

2. If, during an experiment on negotiation, research participants are randomly assigned to negotiate in teams of three or individually, how many conditions are there in the experiment? What is another name for research "conditions"?

3. (a) What is a "trimmed mean"?

(b) Why would a researcher use a trimmed mean?

4. What are two rules of thumb for identifying outliers in a distribution?

5. (a) After an outlier is discarded, does the mean get bigger or smaller relative to the mean prior to discarding the outlier? Explain your answer.

(b) After an outlier is discarded, is the standard deviation larger or smaller relative to what it would have been prior to discarding the outlier? Explain your answer.

6. How does one find the median in a stem-and-leaf plot?

7. Suppose that a back-to-back stem-and-leaf plot showed that the scores of research participants in one condition were highly positively skewed, whereas those in the other condition were not. Would it be wise to transform the scores in one condition while keeping the scores in the second condition unchanged? Explain your answer.

8. (a) How does the *pooled variance* compare to the *variances* of the two groups whose variances have been pooled?

   (b) How does the *pooled standard deviation* compare to the *pooled variance*?

9. Prepare a back-to-back stem-and-leaf plot of the ages of two groups of public school students:

   Sample A: 12, 12, 13, 11, 16, 12, 14, 9, 12, 13, 10, 11

   Sample B: 14, 12, 17, 15, 14, 15, 13, 16, 14, 13

10. (a) Find the median in the following set of numbers using a stem-and-leaf plot:

   12, 23, 23, 14, 13, 18, 22, 15, 16, 24, 12, 21, 22, 13, 26, 11, 12, 28, 14, 10, 11

   (b) Find the median in the following set of numbers using a stem-and-leaf plot:

   17, 28, 27, 13, 11, 10, 13, 15, 11, 19, 10, 29, 28, 33, 36, 19, 12, 32, 21, 18, 16, 15

11. Why might a comparison of the means of the following two samples be misleading? Both variables are answers to an attitude questionnaire having a possible range of scores from 0 to 20.

   Sample R: 3, 4, 5, 3, 6, 1, 2, 0, 0, 7, 11, 1, 0, 2, 15, 4, 0, 3, 1, 0, 2

   Sample Q: 13, 4, 15, 12, 16, 11, 7, 16, 12, 14, 15, 9, 8, 13, 3, 10, 20

   Hint: Create back-to-back stem-and-leaf plots to look for anything in the distributions that should concern the analyst.

12. (a) Calculate the mean height of a sample of 30 students who were measured in two groups:

Group A (n_1 = 20), M = 64.4 in.; Group B (n_2 = 10), M = 66.7 in.

   (b) Calculate the mean weight of a sample of 20 students who were measured in two groups: Group C (n_1 = 12), M = 145 lb.; Group D (n_2 = 8), M = 157 lb.

13. (a) Calculate the pooled standard deviation for two groups:

   s_1 = 23.33, n_1 = 20
   s_2 = 26.72, n_2 = 25

   (b) Calculate the pooled standard deviation for two groups:

   s_1 = 44.76, n_1 = 15
   s_2 = 52.87, n_2 = 21

14. Two groups of college students were asked to describe their satisfaction with courses in their majors using a 10-point scale (1 = Very dissatisfied, 10 = Very satisfied).

   Social Science majors (n = 21): 9, 3, 4, 6, 8, 3, 9, 10, 8, 3, 6, 7, 8, 6, 9, 6, 7, 8, 4, 8, 10
   Humanities majors (n = 19): 3, 6, 6, 3, 10, 8, 7, 4, 5, 4, 5, 7, 5, 3, 8, 9, 4, 5, 3

   (a) Inspect the data using back-to-back stem-and-leaf plots.

   (b) Describe the two groups using the means, standard deviations, the pooled standard deviation, the standard errors of the mean, and the standard error of the difference of two means.

15. In a random groups design, 14 children were asked to learn a list of names of either fruits or vegetables. They were randomly assigned to learn the fruits or the vegetables. The researcher wanted to learn whether the children were more successful (and thus more familiar) with fruits or with vegetables. Here are the number recalled out of the lists of 10 items:

Child	Fruit list	Child	Vegetable list
1	6	8	4
2	7	9	5
3	4	10	4
4	6	11	5
5	8	12	7
6	3	13	4
7	4	14	3

Calculate the following:

(a) the means and standard deviations of both groups

(b) the standard error of the mean of each group

(c) the pooled standard deviation

(d) the standard error of the difference between two means

16. Explain why it is important to inspect both the original distributions in a repeated measures design as well as the distribution of difference scores.

17. Fifteen pairs of twins were recruited from a college student body for a study of the effects of distraction on a coordination study. One twin of each pair was randomly assigned to complete tests of physical coordination administered by a physical therapist (e.g., walking on a 3 in. wide beam, keeping balance on one foot with eyes closed) while listening to random conversation played at 90 db. The other twin was tested for coordination while listening to white noise at 90 db. High scores indicated better coordination. Here are the data.

Twin Number	Conversation Condition	Noise Condition
1	45	49
2	12	17
3	37	41
4	50	49
5	25	26
6	35	33
7	42	52
8	25	31
9	28	22
10	45	47
11	32	37
12	45	42
13	38	41
14	49	51
15	19	23

(a) What is this design called?

(b) Calculate the standard error of the mean for both conditions. (To save some work, here are the standard deviations: $s_{conversation} = 11.42$, $s_{noise} = 11.52$.)

(c) Calculate the standard deviation of the difference scores and the standard error of the mean of the difference scores.

(d) Which of these standard errors is smaller? Why is that?

18. The accuracy of reading signs made out of blue or red neon lighting tubes (like those outside some stores) was tested. Names that were equally difficult to read were randomly assigned to be made out of red or blue neon tubing. Participants were tested at night. They were allowed to see each sign for an equally brief period of time; there were ten signs of each color. Participants could get scores from 0 to 10 correct for each color. The accuracy scores were as follows:

Participant	Red signs	Blue signs
WW	6	4
DE	7	8
HU	3	1
FE	6	5
OI	9	8
LW	5	4
RT	5	3
TH	6	5
KV	0	0
SJ	4	4

What do you think about KV's accuracy level? What might KV's scores represent? Is there any reason to discard KV's data?

Calculate the following:

(a) the mean of the differences

(b) the standard deviation of the differences

(c) the standard error of the mean of the difference

19. If the standard error of the difference of two means is 6.72 and if each of the two groups contained 20 participants, what is the pooled standard deviation?

20. If the pooled standard deviation in an independent group design was 23.75 and if the standard error of the difference between the two means was 4.75, how many research participants were in each group? Assume equal-sized groups.

Answers to Odd-Numbered Problems

1. Researchers use both independent groups designs and repeated measures designs. Independent designs include both random groups designs and natural groups designs. Repeated measures designs include those in which each participant is tested twice as well as matched groups designs in which pairs of participants are "matched" on a relevant variable and then assigned to one of two groups prior to experiencing one of two levels of an independent variable.

3. (a) A trimmed mean is a mean calculated after either replacing an outlier with a score that is one unit more extreme that the next-most-extreme score, or eliminating the most extreme scores on both the high and low ends of the distribution.
   (b) Trimmed means provide a standard way to handle outliers that avoids the appearance of bias when discarding outliers.

5. (a) It depends on whether the outlier was on the high or the low end of a distribution. The mean goes down if an extremely large score was omitted.
   (b) When outliers are discarded, standard deviations are reduced.

7. No, it would not be wise. Transformations (linear or nonlinear) change the mean and the standard deviation of transformed variables. The scores of both distributions are to be transformed or kept in the original units.

9.
B		A
	0	
	0*	9
444332	1	0112222334
7655	1*	6

11.
Q		R
43	0	0000011122233344
987	0*	567
4332210	1	1
6655	1*	5
0	2	

Distribution Q is roughly normal in shape, whereas Distribution R is positively skewed, possibly suggesting a floor effect.

13. (a) $[(20 - 1)(23.33^2) + (25 - 1)(26.72^2)]/[20 - 1 + 25 - 1] = 638.99 = s^2_{pooled}$; $25.28 = s_{pooled}$
    (b) $[(15 - 1)(44.76^2) + (21 - 1)(52.87^2)]/[15 - 1 + 21 - 1] = 2469.21 = s^2_{pooled}$; $49.69 = s_{pooled}$

15. Fruit list: $M = 5.43$, $s = 1.81$, $s_M = 0.685$
    Vegetable list: $M = 4.57$, $s = 1.27$, $s_M = 0.481$
    The pooled standard deviation is 1.57, and the standard error of the difference between two means is 0.837.

17. (a) This design is a matched groups design (a variation of the repeated measures design) because identical twins were tested.
    (b) The standard error of the mean for the conversation condition is 2.95, and that of the noise condition is 2.97.
    (c) The standard deviation of the difference scores is 4.01, and the standard error of the mean of the difference scores is 1.04.
    (d) The standard error of the mean of the differences scores, s_{MD}, is the smallest because the differences between individual coordination levels is greater than the difference in coordination due to listening to conversation versus noise. For example, compare the scores of the first set of twins who showed good coordination with the scores of the second set of twins who showed poor coordination *regardless* of experimental condition.

19. $6.72 = s_{pooled} (\sqrt{(1/n + 1/n)})$
    $6.72/\sqrt{(1/20 + 1/20)} = s_{pooled}$
    $6.72/0.316 = 21.25 = s_{pooled}$

Go to http://psychology.wadsworth.com/courses/statistics/ and test your knowledge of this chapter by taking the online quiz. Another resource to check is the online workshops that provide a step-by-step guide through a number of topics at http://psychology.wadsworth.com/workshops/workshops.html.

Estimating Using Confidence Intervals

Effect sizes . . . can help inform judgment regarding the practical or substantive significance of results.
Thompson (1999, p. 170)

INTRODUCTION

In previous chapters, you learned how to inspect (the *I* of the I-D-E-A model) and describe (the *D*) data obtained from two samples. In the last chapter, we showed how to describe the differences between the means of two independent samples (as well as the means of difference scores). Differences between sample means are the focus of the next several chapters. Differences between the means of samples selected randomly from a single population occur due to random or chance factors; sampling error cannot be avoided. In addition, differences might be found because experimental treatments effectively led to differences in the means of research groups beyond that expected by sampling error. To detect such nonrandom differences between means, we need a way to estimate the degree to which such differences are affected by sampling error. Ultimately, we use such estimates to decide whether there is enough evidence to conclude that nonrandom effects are present, but that's getting ahead of the story. In the present chapter, we show, first, how to estimate the effect of sampling error on differences between two means. Knowing the degree of sampling error means that we can estimate the precision of our findings. Second, we show how to standardize the difference between two means. Once standardized, the size of differences between groups can be compared to the differences found in other research. This allows one to test competing theories and to determine whether an observed difference is large enough to be helpful in practical settings, such as on the job or in a clinic.

The researchers introduced in Chapter 7 all face the question of estimating the impact of sampling error on their findings. Janice knows that some people will respond correctly and some incorrectly as they report what they remembered about the two crimes they witnessed. She knows that the mean of the differences between the recall of violent and nonviolent crime is affected by sampling error. Leonard knows that some of the students who were randomly assigned to listen to Metallica do indeed like heavy metal music and might be placed in a good mood by the music, but others do not and might find the music distracting. In addition, students will differ in how much experience they have in solving similar puzzles or in working while listening to music. Both Janice and Leonard need methods that permit them to estimate the effects of sampling error produced by these individual differences.

Consider another situation in which the effectiveness of a new procedure is examined by comparing two means. Adam was the assistant to Dr. Rickkets, a human factors psychologist, who was hired to find a way to reduce the number of mistakes made by power plant operators when warning lights indicated that a problem occurred. When the warning lights and buzzers came on, operators were slow to make the proper adjustments, and sometimes they initially made errors that made a problem worse. Dr. Rickkets concluded that more errors were made when warning lights were far away from the controls that the operator needed to adjust to correct the problems indicated by the warning lights. To test this idea, he designed two control panels to simulate power plant operation. In one panel, the lights were arranged together on the right side and the control knobs over on the left, like the standard control panel used by this utility company. In the other panel, each knob was placed beside the warning light that indicated an adjustment was needed. Dr. Rickkets randomly assigned operators to use one or the other control panel simulators. During the experiment, various warning lights would come on and the operators were to make the prescribed adjustments. His dependent variable was the total time it took to make the correct adjustments. He hoped that those using the new panel would require less time compared to those using the old panel. Indeed, he observed that the mean for the new panel was 6.4 sec. less than the one that simulated the control panels actually in use. He asked Adam to analyze the data from the two groups to learn how confident he could be about this finding.

All behavioral researchers need to decide whether their findings revealed useful information. Confidence intervals and effect sizes, the topics of this chapter, can help them to describe and interpret their findings.

CONSTRUCTING CONFIDENCE INTERVALS FOR THE DIFFERENCE BETWEEN TWO MEANS

Confidence intervals, as developed in Chapter 5 and 6, are very critical in understanding what we can and cannot say about a sample of observations. We could say that Katie's data permitted her to conclude that the students at her college reported being rather happy with their college. The college's administrators were interested in knowing that. For similar reasons, the managers of businesses and hospital executives are interested in how pleased customers or patients are with their experiences in making purchases or obtaining medical care.

Particular sets of individuals in random samples are unique, and thus there are differences among the means of samples. These differences are called *sampling error*. Nevertheless, when a sample is randomly selected from a population, the mean score on a dependent variable is an unbiased estimate of the population mean. *A statistic is unbiased if, in the long run, it neither consistently over- nor underestimates the parameter it describes.* We need to remember, however, that any given mean is affected by sampling error and, consequently, will not exactly equal the population mean. The standard error of the mean reflects that uncertainty. Or, to put that more positively: the standard error of the mean gives us information on the precision of our findings (Estes, 1997). This measure of precision can be used to construct a confidence interval that provides the likely boundaries for the estimate of the value of the population mean. Were the study to be repeated many times, 95% of such confidence intervals would contain the population mean, μ.

Let's review briefly the analysis and interpretation of Katie's survey described in Chapter 5 and 6. The standard error for the overall mean of Katie's happiness data was $1.55/\sqrt{80}$, or 0.17. The 95% confidence interval for Katie's whole sample was found by adding to and subtracting from the sample mean the product of t_{critical} times the standard error of the mean:

$$M \pm t_{\text{critical}} (s_{\text{M}})$$

The value of t is chosen so that it divides the most extreme 5% of the t distribution from the rest of the distribution for 79 degrees of freedom. (Half of the 5% lies in the high end of the distribution, and half in the low end.) The t table does not contain the values of t for 79 degrees of freedom; the most appropriate degrees of freedom in Table A-2 would be 60. To get the 95% confidence interval, the nondirectional α of .05 is used. These criteria give us a t of ± 2.00. Substituting into the equation, we have

$$5.16 \pm (2.00)\,(0.17), \text{ or } 4.82 \text{ to } 5.50$$

Because 95% of such confidence intervals contain the true population mean, Katie can feel confident that this interval contains the mean of all the students in her college. So far this has been review. Let us consider what else she might learn about student happiness.

Suppose that the Director of Residence Halls asserts that students are happier at college if they live in a campus residence hall rather than at home. Suppose that he asks Katie whether that advantage is reflected in her data. If Katie's data are coded for residence location, she can divide her sample into campus residents and commuters. Sometimes dividing a sample and comparing the different segments to each other can show important differences between people with different characteristics or experiences. Residence location would be likely to be part of a questionnaire on college life, so let's assume that Katie could present the happiness rating for dorm students and commuters separately. Assume further that her findings from the whole sample (N) as well as the two subgroups $(n_1$ and $n_2)$ were as follows:

Sample	Mean	s
All ($N = 80$)	5.16	1.55
Residence Hall ($n_1 = 51$)	5.27	1.58
Commuters ($n_2 = 29$)	4.97	1.50

When she displayed these means, the director argued that he was right because the mean happiness for campus residents exceeded that of commuters. The director appears to have concentrated on the difference in means, 5.27 versus 4.97, but ignored the standard deviations of the ratings of the groups. These standard deviations tell us that some commuters are very happy and some dorm students are rather unhappy. It is important that users of statistics not make the error of treating a mean as though it reflects every member of a group. When we report statistical findings, we should discourage people from making that mistake. The variation within each group can be displayed using several methods. First, we use stem-and-leaf plots for each group and later a confidence interval for the *difference* between the means of the two groups.

Figure 8.1 is a back-to-back stem-and-leaf plot that contrasts the happiness of ratings of residence hall students with those of commuters. A major reason to use graphs is to make it impossible to miss patterns in data. One important thing to note in the figure is that there are ratings at every level of the scale for both groups of students. The sample means differed, but the ratings of students in both samples varied from their group means with some ratings differing markedly from the means. This variation is impossible to detect if one simply examines the two means, but it is impossible to overlook this variation when one examines Figure 8.1. The stem-and-leaf plots also provide information on the central tendency of the two sets of ratings. For commuters, the fifteenth score from the top (or the bottom) divides the sample in half and, thus, 5 would be the median for commuters. Because there are 51 resident students, we count up (or down) 26 scores to find the median for residence hall students. In this case, the median equals 6.

FIGURE 8.1 ■ Back-to-back stem-and-leaf plot for the happiness with college rating for Residence Hall Students and Commuters separately. (Note that zeroes were used to indicate scores instead of the units digit because the data range from 1 to 7 only; there is no second digit to use for the leaves.)

Leaf for Residents (n = 51)	Stem	Leaf for Commuters (n = 29)
0	1	0
0	2	00
00000	3	000
0000000	4	0000
000000000	5	0000000
0000000000000	6	0000000000
00000000000000	7	000

YOUR
TURN
8-1

Would the 95% confidence intervals for residence hall students and commuter students be the same size as the 95% confidence interval of the whole 80-student sample?   ■

After using the stem-and-leaf plots to compare the distributions, Katie can focus on the question asked by the Director of Residence Halls: what is the difference between campus residents and commuters?

The difference between two means rather than the two means themselves is of interest. Figure 8.1 contains two distributions, but keep in mind that we are interested in the *difference* between the two distributions. Rather than working with two distributions and two means, let's focus on just the difference between the means. One goal of statistical analysis is to simplify the communication of the findings to others; focusing on the difference between the means helps us do that. The difference between the mean happiness ratings made by residence hall students and those made by commuters is 5.27 − 4.97, or 0.30. This is the estimate of the difference between the population means of residence hall students and commuter students at Katie's college. Like all estimates of population values based on samples, we know that the difference is affected by sampling error. If we replicated the study, the difference between the two sample means would not be the same. By calculating the precision with which we have estimated the difference between the two population means, we can reduce our uncertainty about the comparison between happiness ratings of residents and commuters. In Chapter 7, we developed the idea of the sampling error of a difference between two means:

$$s_{M_1 - M_2} = \sqrt{\left[\left(\frac{df_1 s_1^2 + df_2 s_2^2}{df_1 + df_2} \right) \left(\frac{1}{n_1} + \frac{1}{n_2} \right) \right]}$$

As mentioned before, this formula should be thought of as having two parts:

$$s_{pooled} \text{ and } \sqrt{(1/n_1 + 1/n_2)}$$

The first part is the best estimate we have for the standard deviation of the dependent variable; s_{pooled} is the square root of the weighted average of the variances of the two samples.[1] The second part incorporates the sample sizes.

We have all we need to estimate the value of the difference between the population means for residents versus commuters. The **confidence interval for a difference between two means** is found by

$$(M_1 - M_2) \pm t_{(df=n_1+n_2-2)}(s_{M_1-M_2}) \qquad \text{Equation 8.1}$$

If we seek to find the 95% confidence interval, we follow the same procedure that we followed when finding confidence intervals for one mean. The t will be the value that divides the upper 2.5% of the t distribution from the lower 97.5%. The t that divides the lowest 2.5% from the upper 97.5% has the same numerical value. The degrees of freedom for this t are found by adding the degrees of freedom associated with the two groups, $n_{residence\ hall} - 1$ and $n_{commuters} - 1$, or $(51 - 1)$ and $(29 - 1)$, or 78. (Note that the degrees of freedom for the whole sample equal 79, $N - 1$, but, when we work with two samples, the degrees of freedom are 78, $n_1 + n_2 - 2$.) We will use the t value associated with the next lowest degrees of freedom (60), namely 2.00, as we did before because the table does not include a value for 78 degrees of freedom. The confidence interval is

$$0.30 \pm 2.00 \sqrt{\left[\left(\frac{50\,(1.58^2) + 28\,(1.50^2)}{50 + 28}\right)\left(\frac{1}{51} + \frac{1}{29}\right)\right]}$$

$$0.30 \pm 2.00 \sqrt{[2.41(0.054]} = 0.30 \pm 2.00 \sqrt{0.13}$$

$$0.30 \pm 2.00\,(0.36) = 0.30 \pm 0.72 = -0.42 \text{ to } 1.02$$

Note what the confidence interval has told us: the difference between the happiness of resident hall students and commuters is 0.30 with a 95% confidence interval ranging from -0.42 to 1.02. If we could replicate this survey study over and over again with the same sample sizes drawn randomly from the same college, we would expect 95% of the confidence intervals to contain the true population mean. Because the confidence interval includes 0.0, Katie should report that her data do not provide sufficiently strong evidence that the two populations of students differed in their mean happiness ratings. The confidence interval tells us that not only is it possible that there is no difference in the mean happiness levels of the student groups, but that it is possible that the commuters are a little happier than are the residents. In the next chapter, we will develop the convention that we follow in deciding when a difference merits confidently concluding that the means are different from each other.

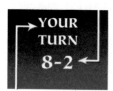

YOUR TURN 8-2 Find in the t table (see Appendix A-2) the t value used for estimating the difference between the population means of residents and commuters. Then, select the t for an 80% confidence interval and calculate the confidence interval. To find the 80% confidence interval, you will need to use the nondirectional t under the "alpha equals .20" column. Before making the calculation, predict whether the interval will be wider or narrower than the 95% interval. ∎

---

[1] When using the pooled standard deviation an assumption is that the variances of the two groups are similar, this assumption is called "homogeneity of variance." We discuss this assumption more fully in later chapters.

Table 8.1 summarizes the steps in the calculation of the 95% confidence interval for the difference between two means. The illustration refers to the hypothetical experiment that compares a more intuitively designed control panel with the one presently used in a power plant. The dependent variable was time (in seconds) to detect and correct simulated malfunctions in the plant. The descriptive information is as follows:

Sample	M	s	n
Control group using traditional panel	22.81 sec.	5.18 sec.	20
Experimental group using new panel	15.38 sec.	4.87 sec.	19
Difference between the two means	7.43 sec.		

The experiment was designed to lower the time to correct problems; that is what was found. Because the experimenter's expectation was supported, the difference between the two means is presented as a positive value. The mean of the experimental group was subtracted from the mean of the control group. As Table 8.1 shows, Adam's confidence interval, 4.37 to 10.49 sec., does not include 0.0. Thus, he is permitted to conclude that the experimental

TABLE 8.1 ■ Step-by-Step Summary of the Calculation of a 95% Confidence Interval for the Difference Between Two Means

Calculation Step	Formula	Substitution of Values into the Formula
Find the difference between the two means	$M_{control} - M_{experimental}$	$22.81 - 15.38 = 7.43$ sec.
Find the pooled standard deviation, s_{pooled}	$\sqrt{\left[\dfrac{df_{control}s^2_{control} + df_{experimental}s^2_{experimental}}{df_{control} + df_{experimental}}\right]}$	$\sqrt{\left[\dfrac{19\,(5.18^2) + 18\,(4.87^2)}{19 + 18}\right]}$ $= 5.03$ sec.
Find the standard error of the difference between two means, $s_{M_c - M_e}$	$s_{pooled}\sqrt{(1/n_{control} + 1/n_{experimental})}$	$5.03\,\sqrt{[1/29 + 1/19]} =$ $5.03\,(0.30) =$ 1.51 sec.
Find the appropriate t from the t table	$df = 20 + 19 - 2 = 37$ $\alpha = .05$, two-tailed test	2.028
Find the 95% confidence interval	$(M_{control} - M_{experimental}) \pm t(df = 37)(s_{M_c - M_e})$	$7.43 \pm 2.028\,(1.51) =$ $7.43 \pm 3.06 =$ 4.37 to 10.49 sec.
Draw a sound conclusion from the confidence interval	The 95% confidence interval does not include zero. It is highly likely that the experimental panel permitted more-rapid corrections of simulated power plant problems.	

control panel did facilitate the correction of simulated plant problems more rapidly than the current panel design permitted. Recall that, when examining differences between types of students, Katie's confidence interval included zero; thus, she was left in a state of uncertainty about whether the true mean difference was greater than zero. Adam and Dr. Rickkets, however, could report that the new control panel was more effective than the traditional one.

WHAT MAKES CONFIDENCE INTERVALS WIDE OR NARROW?

Another way of putting this question is: "what makes measurement of a difference between means precise?" Look carefully at Equation 8.1 as expanded here:

$$(M_1 - M_2) \pm t_{(df=n_1+n_2-2)} \sqrt{\left[\left(\frac{df_1 s_1^2 + df_2 s_2^2}{df_1 + df_2}\right)\left(\frac{1}{n_1} + \frac{1}{n_2}\right)\right]}$$

The smaller the standard error of the difference between two means, the narrower is the confidence interval. The standard error is smaller when the standard deviations of the scores in each group, s_1 and s_2, are small and when the group sizes, n_1 and n_2, are large. In Chapter 6, we discussed how these factors affected confidence intervals.

The standard deviations are larger when the participants in the research behave quite differently from each other. In other words, the more heterogeneous the people are in each group, the wider the confidence intervals are. Whatever serves to reduce the standard deviations reduces the width of confidence intervals. If the standard deviations can be reduced by more-consistent ways of treating the participants or more-reliable ways of making observations, confidence intervals will be found that are more narrow, indicating that greater precision has been achieved.

When group sizes are large, the pooled standard deviation is not affected because the group sizes (actually the degrees of freedom) appear in both the numerator and the denominator of s_{pooled}. Group sizes, however, appear only in the denominator of the formula for the standard error of the difference of two means. Consequently, the larger the group sizes, the smaller the standard error. Because the formula involves the square root of group sizes, raising the group sizes by a factor of four reduces the standard error by only one-half. You can see this relationship by looking at the group size part of the formula:

n_1	n_2	$\sqrt{(1/n_1 + 1/n_2)}$
100	100	$\sqrt{(1/100 + 1/100)} = \sqrt{(2/100)} = 1.414$
400	400	$\sqrt{(1/400 + 1/400)} = \sqrt{(2/400)} = 0.707$

The third effect on the width of the confidence interval is the size of t. You have noticed that the larger the degrees of freedom, the smaller t becomes. However, t changes little unless groups contain fewer than 10 people. Thus, unless groups are smaller than 10, the sizes of the groups have a much greater impact on the standard error than they have on t.

In summary, *estimates of the differences between groups are more precise when groups are large and when standard deviations are small.*

INTERPRETING DIFFERENCES BETWEEN MEANS

Katie found the difference in mean happiness ratings between residents and commuters and the confidence interval for that difference. But does a difference of 0.30 unit on a 7-point scale matter? Would this difference be big enough for anyone to care? This question is essential to ask; however, we cannot answer it for all comparisons because the answer depends on many aspects of the research being described. For instance, because rehabilitation from drug addictions is important, society should know about even small improvements in successful rehabilitation. On the other hand, finding differences in the degree to which New Yorkers and Texans like vanilla ice cream is important only to people who sell ice cream. In this chapter, we suggest some ways to go about thinking more clearly about how to answer the question whether a finding is important.

One difficulty when interpreting differences is that many dependent variables in the behavioral sciences refer to concepts, behavioral patterns, or traits. These variables cannot be placed on an examining table and measured with a ruler or a scale. Instead, indirect approaches are used. Psychologists, for example, measure the *effects* of psychological variables. We cannot, for example, see a memory, but we can record the number of words that people can remember after studying a list for 15 sec. Differences in memory are then inferred from differences in the number of words correctly recalled. Similarly, we cannot measure level of opposition to the death penalty, but we can measure the number of attitude statements against the death penalty with which people agree. Katie cannot measure happiness directly, but she did measure the degree to which students reported that they were happy using a 7-point scale.

The fact that we measure behavioral variables indirectly means that we cannot evaluate the importance of a finding simply by looking at the difference between two numbers. We have to ask "relative to what scale?" Common sense examples are easy to think of. For example, you never give your weight or height without referring to a scale. One answers "160 *pounds*" or "71 *inches.*" One way a society deals with the meaning of numbers is to standardize the units used. Pounds and inches are both precisely defined; governments and scientific panels define standards. There is a standard pound in the Bureau of Standards in Washington, DC, but, if you were to search in the Bureau of Standards, you will not find standards for extraversion, depression, happiness, or other behavioral variables.

Even though we lack standard units for the variables that behavioral scientists usually measure, there is a statistical standardization procedure. You have already learned about z scores (see Chapter 4). Original data points are converted into z scores by transforming the units of the scores into standard deviation units. We need such a standardization procedure because giving a person's score on an attitude test by reporting the numbers of attitude statements the person endorsed does not tell us whether the person holds a favorable or an unfavorable opinion about a political issue or a policy. But, if the number of attitude statements endorsed is converted into a z score, we have an idea of how that person compares to others in the group. As you learned, we find z scores by subtracting the mean of the sample from a person's score and dividing the difference by the standard deviation. Positive values of z mean that the score is above the mean. Besides telling us where a score falls in the distribution, z scores permit us to compare a person's relative position in *different* distributions. Thus, as you saw in Chapter 4, you can ask whether someone is taller than he or she is smart, and indeed you can decide whether you are doing better in French than in chemistry even when the distributions of scores are quite different.

Before we can decide whether a difference between two means is large or small, we first need a method of standardizing means and then we need some standard to use to evaluate our findings.

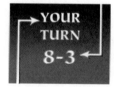

It would help to review the z transformation and its interpretation. Assume that variable M is normally distributed. Assume the mean is 20 and the population standard deviation is 5. Convert the following scores on variable M into z scores.

Maria   25
Jerome   15

Now imagine a second variable, Q, whose mean is 50 and population standard deviation is 10. Convert the following scores on Q into z scores.

Maria   45
Jerome   60

Did Maria get a higher z score on M or Q? What does the higher z score mean? How about Jerome? ∎

Standardizing Comparisons

The power of standardization helps us compare an individual's scores on two or more measures even though the scores are on very different scales. A similar standardization procedure can also be applied to differences between group means. This procedure will help us compare the results of different studies even if they used different dependent variables. The index that will help us is the **effect size.** Consider once again that Katie found a difference of 0.30 between the means for residents and commuters. We know that the size of this difference is partially determined by the number of steps on her rating scale. If she had used a rating scale 21 points long (rather than 7), the numerical difference in the group means would have been larger. Thus, we would like to have the difference between the two means expressed in some standard way that is independent of the original scale of measurement. The formula for the effect size called **Hedges' g** looks a little like the z transformation:

$$\text{Effect size} = \frac{M_{\text{experimental}} - M_{\text{control}}}{s_{\text{pooled}}} = g \qquad \textbf{Equation 8.2}$$

The pooled estimated standard deviation is the standardizing unit used in the effect size formula (Hedges, 1982). The best way to develop a sense of what an effect size tells us is to work through some examples.

Here again is the descriptive information that Adam was given regarding the time needed by the utility operators to detect and correct simulated problems:

Sample	M	s	n
Control group using traditional panel	22.81 sec.	5.18 sec.	20
Experimental group using new panel	15.38 sec.	4.87 sec.	19
Difference between the two means	7.43 sec.		

Note that the means are in accord with the intention to reduce the time required for operators to correct problems. Dr. Rickkets had hypothesized that the new control panel would lead to lower times compared to the traditional panel. It is standard practice to calculate effect sizes so that the sign of g is positive when the relative sizes of the group means match the experimenter's expectations. Because low times are desired, the numerator of the effect size, g, would be calculated by subtracting the mean of the experimental group from the mean of the control group.

The pooled standard deviation is the square root of the weighted average of the two variances. (Remember, standard deviation is the square root of the variance.) As shown in Table 8.1, for this experiment, s_{pooled} equals

$$\sqrt{\left[\frac{df_{control}s^2_{control} + df_{experimental}s^2_{experimental}}{df_{experimental} + df_{control}}\right]} = \sqrt{\left[\frac{19\,(5.18^2) + 18\,(4.87^2)}{19 + 18}\right]} = 5.03$$

The value of the pooled standard deviation lies between the two standard deviations we started with; if you ever get a value that is bigger (or smaller) than both, your s_{pooled} is wrong.

The effect size is

$$g = \frac{22.81 - 15.38}{5.03} = +1.48$$

The effect size reveals that the revised panel layout led the operators in the experimental group to correct simulated problems almost 1.5 standard deviations more quickly than those operators using the regular, old-style panel. The sign of the effect size is positive to indicate that the participants who were hypothesized to be faster, in fact, corrected the simulated malfunctions more quickly. We would use negative signs for effect sizes if a treatment that had been planned to help people made people worse (which sometimes happens). Converting the difference between the two means into units defined by the pooled standard deviation should remind you of the way in which the z transformation converted a person's score into standard deviation units. We have used Hedges' g for the effect size index; it is simple to use with the descriptive statistics that have been introduced. A second measure of effect size—Cohen's d—is widely used also. Box 8.1 describes the difference between g and d.

Effect sizes can be used with natural groups as well as with true experiments. An effect size can be calculated for Katie's data, for example, by considering that the effect size indicates the higher level of happiness with college reported by those living in a college residence hall relative to those living at home. Table 8.2 contains the calculation of g for Katie's data and provides a review of the formula. The effect size is 0.21. It is important to remember that her data are based on natural groups, so a causal interpretation is forbidden on the basis of the limited data she has. Further, don't forget that her 95% confidence interval did contain zero; she must be very tentative about drawing conclusions about the difference between commuters and residence hall students. In fact, as will be discussed in the next chapter, Katie should refrain from taking any stand on the question of whether commuters or resident students are happier.

To develop an intuitive sense for the effect size, it might help to examine several more pairs of distributions. Figure 8.2 contains the results of several hypothetical experiments. In Panel A, a distribution with a mean equal to 45 is compared to a distribution of scores from a group whose mean is 42. If the pooled standard deviation of the dependent variable is 4, then Hedges' g is

$$\frac{45 - 42}{4} = 0.75$$

BOX 8.1 ■ Hedges' g and Cohen's d

There is a close relationship between Hedges' g and another commonly used effect size measure, d, also called **Cohen's d.** Although these two effect size measures provide very similar values, they are not algebraically equivalent. The difference is due to how the standard deviation in the denominator is calculated. The formula for g is:

$$g = \frac{M_1 - M_2}{s_{\text{pooled}}}$$

The formula for d is:

$$d = \frac{M_1 - M_2}{\sigma_{\text{pooled}}}$$

The difference is in the denominator, s_{pooled} or σ_{pooled}. For g,

$$s_{\text{pooled}} = \sqrt{\frac{(n_1 - 1)s_1^2 + (n_2 - 1)s_2^2}{(n_1 + n_2 - 2)}}$$

For d,

$$\sigma_{\text{pooled}} = \sqrt{\frac{(n_1 - 1)s_1^2 + (n_2 - 1)s_2^2}{(n_1 + n_2)}}$$

Because the denominator of s_{pooled} (that is, $n_1 + n_2 - 2$) is slightly smaller than the denominator of σ_{pooled} (that is, $n_1 + n_2$), s_{pooled} will be a bit larger than σ_{pooled}. (Dividing by a smaller number leads to larger results.) That difference means that Hedges' g would be slightly smaller than Cohen's d for the same set of data. However, the difference is small. The difference is less than 2% when there are 30 people in each group; with larger sample sizes, the differences are even smaller. In fact, the differences are so small that some textbook authors do not distinguish between d and g. And, because the differences are so small, we have used Cohen's rules of thumb concerning the meaning of the size of d in our interpretations of g.

Normally, we reserve the Greek letter σ for the population standard deviation. Cohen used σ simply to indicate that degrees of freedom were not used to calculate d. Clearly, σ does not indicate that we have the population standard deviation in this formula.

TABLE 8.2 ■ Illustration of the Calculation of Effect Size for Commuters versus Resident Students

Calculation Step	Formula	Substitution of Values into the Formula
Find the difference between the means	$M_{\text{residents}} - M_{\text{commuters}}$	$5.27 - 4.97 = 0.30$
Obtain the pooled standard deviation, s_{pooled}	$\sqrt{\left(\dfrac{df_r(s_r^2) + df_c(s_c^2)}{df_r + df_c} \right)}$	$\sqrt{\left(\dfrac{53\,(1.37^2) + 30\,(1.56^2)}{53 + 30} \right)}$
Calculate effect size, g	$\dfrac{M_{\text{residents}} - M_{\text{commuters}}}{s_{\text{pooled}}}$	$\dfrac{0.30}{1.442} = 0.21$

In Panel B, a numerically larger difference between the means, 20, results in a smaller effect size, 0.40, because the pooled standard deviation of the dependent variable, 50, is much larger than in Panel A. In Panel C, an intervention that was planned to lead to an increase in a dependent variable, in fact, led to a decrease. The calculation of the effect size follows the convention of using a negative effect size when the means indicate an undesirable outcome or an outcome that's contrary to theoretical predictions. Imagine that the reading levels of children assigned to use an experimental reading curriculum did not increase to the same

FIGURE 8.2 ■ Illustrations of pairs of distributions showing various effect sizes.

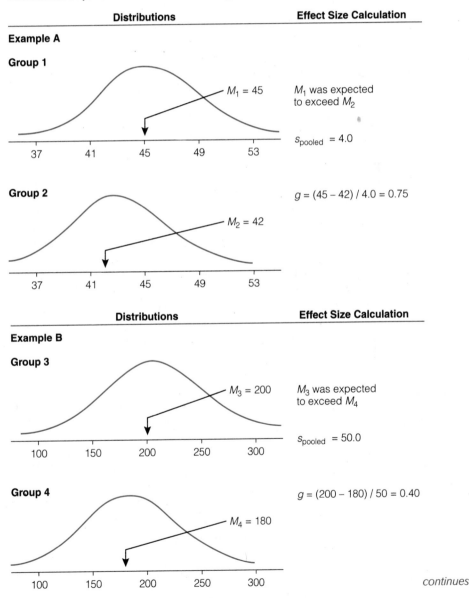

Distributions   **Effect Size Calculation**

Example A

Group 1

$M_1 = 45$

M_1 was expected to exceed M_2

$s_{pooled} = 4.0$

37   41   45   49   53

Group 2

$g = (45 - 42) / 4.0 = 0.75$

$M_2 = 42$

37   41   45   49   53

Distributions   **Effect Size Calculation**

Example B

Group 3

$M_3 = 200$

M_3 was expected to exceed M_4

$s_{pooled} = 50.0$

100   150   200   250   300

Group 4

$g = (200 - 180) / 50 = 0.40$

$M_4 = 180$

100   150   200   250   300

continues

FIGURE 8.2 ■ continued

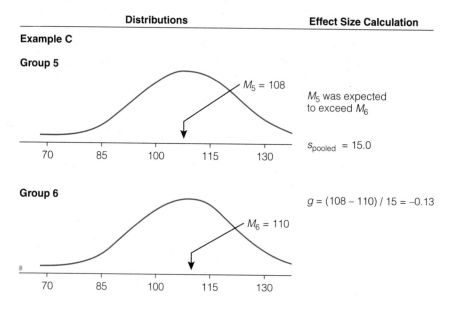

| Distributions | Effect Size Calculation |

Example C

Group 5

$M_5 = 108$

M_5 was expected to exceed M_6

$s_{pooled} = 15.0$

Group 6

$M_6 = 110$

$g = (108 - 110) / 15 = -0.13$

degree as those using the regular or control curriculum. The children using the standard curriculum averaged 110 on a reading test, but the experimental group averaged only 108. If the standard deviation of the reading test is 15, the effect size of the new reading curriculum would be a disappointing −0.13. We write *disappointing* because the developer of the innovation intended that those who used the new curriculum would do better. The findings are not disappointing, however, from the point of view that we have learned that the best course of action is for the school district to stick with the curriculum that the children have been using. The calculations are summarized in Table 8.3.

Did you notice that the three illustrations in Figure 8.2 did not refer to the sample sizes? Effect sizes for two-group experiments are standardized using the pooled standard devia-

TABLE 8.3 ■ Calculations on Which Figure 8.2 Was Based

| Example | Means and standard deviations of the two groups | | | | | Effect size |
	M	s	M	s	s_{pooled}	$g = (M_{large} - M_{small})/s_{pooled}$
A-Group 1 vs. 2	45.0	4.28	42.0	3.70	4.0	$(45 - 42)/4.0 = 0.75$
B-Group 3 vs. 4	155.0	52.85	135.0	48.00	50.0	$(155 - 135)/50.0 = 0.40$
C-Group 5 vs. 6	108.0	14.77	110.0	15.21	15.0	$(108 - 110)/15.0 = -0.13*$

* The negative effect size shows that the mean *expected* to be larger was, in fact, smaller.

tion. *Effect sizes are independent of sample size.* Each of the values of *g* found in Figure 8.2 would have been exactly the same whether the group means were based on 60 or 6,000 observations.[2]

Calculate the effect size, *g*, for the following results: the mean achievement of a tutored group was 29, the mean of an untutored group was 23, and the pooled standard deviation was 7.   ■

WHAT DOES THE MAGNITUDE OF AN EFFECT SIZE MEAN?

Table 8.2 shows how to calculate an effect size in the context of a research with two samples. But how is one to evaluate the value of the effect size? Does Katie's effect size of 0.21 indicate a strong, marginal, or weak effect? What about Adam's larger effect size, 1.48? The short answer is: it depends. But we have some guidelines. When Cohen (1988) examined the effect sizes of research published in major psychology journals, he found that the typical study reported an effect size of 0.50. Further, he called effect sizes of 0.20 and 0.80 *small* and *large,* respectively. If the effect size of Adam's hypothetical research on improved control panel design (*g* = 1.48) were placed in the context of psychological research, we would report that it was very large. Katie's (*g* = 0.21) would be small.

Lipsey (1990) examined the effect sizes of thousands of treatments such as drug rehabilitation, special school programs, and job training. He found that the median effect size of treatment programs described in published studies was 0.40. It appears that applied research, focused on practical concerns, has produced slightly smaller effect sizes than has basic research, focused on theoretical concerns. We mention Lipsey's work to make a point: the only way to decide whether a finding is large or small is to compare it with other findings in the same area of research.

Research on improving the rates at which people are cured of illnesses, the rehabilitation of drug addicts, the extent to which homeless people learn to hold jobs, and ways to help high school students remain in school are four critical issues (among many we can think of) in which even small effects are valuable. Success in these efforts is hard to achieve but socially important. In cases such as these, we would label numerically smaller effect sizes as more valuable than would be suggested by Cohen's categories. In other words, a *g* of 0.20 might be a terrific finding because these problems are serious and not easily resolved.

We don't want to confuse you, but neither do we want to imply that labeling an effect size *small* or *large* can be done mechanically. Our point is that, before one labels an effect size as large, one must take into consideration how valuable it would be to effect a change among the population studied (for example, to rehabilitate drug addicts). Or, in theoretical research, one must consider the degree to which a finding affects scientific understanding of some principle. For your immediate use, we suggest that you depend on Cohen's categories, as we do in the following chapters. As you become more familiar with effect sizes and as you use statistics in further classes or in a career, we hope that you reflect on the idea that the nature and context of the research determines what is a big effect, and that there is not a

---

[2] To be precise, *g* is affected by sample size when used with very small samples. We will mention this in a later chapter, but the effect is trivial for nearly all purposes.

single, general standard that can always be applied. Whenever you hear about an innovative medical, educational, or social science service, always look for some discussion of the strength of the innovation. You will probably discover that the strength of the innovation is rarely described. Consequently, popular reports seldom provide enough information to tell us whether it would be worthwhile to follow what the research suggests we should do.

Overwhelmed?

Perhaps you are ready to throw up your hands. Can we be perfectly sure of anything? Well, maybe not *perfectly* sure, but we can do a whole lot better than merely guessing or arguing about the possible differences between groups on the basis of little evidence. Effect sizes are part of the information that we use to improve our understanding of basic research as well as applied research. Can we label the findings of any single study "important"? Although we cannot provide an answer that applies at all times in all areas of research, behavioral scientists are coming to agree that reports of research findings should include measures of effect size so that people reading the reports can more easily compare findings from one study to another and, consequently, make their own judgments about importance (Schmidt, 1996; Thompson, 1999). In later chapters, we discuss standard ways of announcing (the *A* in I-D-E-A) findings that include effect sizes and confidence intervals.

CONFIDENCE INTERVALS FOR DIFFERENCE SCORES

The procedures used with two independent groups can also be applied to difference scores obtained in a repeated measures design (or matched groups design). As described in Chapter 7, it is often useful to measure a dependent variable twice under different conditions. An applied researcher might want to measure change or improvement. Thus, a client might be observed prior to treatment and then again after treatment. An experimental psychologist may want to measure differences on the dependent variable created by two levels of an independent variable. Each participant in the experiment would provide a score for each condition (level) of the independent variable and the difference would then be recorded.

The following discussion makes use of an example from Chapter 7. Imagine trainees taking a short course on formatting a manuscript using a computer program. Assume that they each took a test prior to beginning the course (the pre-test) and then an alternative form of the test after the course was over (the post-test). Our concern is to estimate the confidence interval for the difference scores. The mean of the differences, M_D, is 14.75, and the standard deviation of differences is 3.20. The standard error of the mean of the differences, s_{MD}, is $3.20/\sqrt{4}$, or 1.60.

Person	Pre-test	Post-test	Difference
1. Taylor	45	61	16
2. Sarah	27	37	10
3. Jim	12	29	17
4. Leslie	52	68	16

The **confidence interval of the mean of the differences** is

$$M_D \pm t_{(df=N-1)}\, s_{MD}$$

Equation 8.3

The t has three degrees of freedom in this example because it refers to the four difference scores ($4 - 1 = 3$). Even though there were eight data points, we are working with just four difference scores. Because df are so low, the t, 3.182, is a little larger than in other examples. This reminds us that small samples provide less precision than large samples do. Substituting into the formula, we have a 95% confidence interval of

$$14.75 \pm 3.182\,(1.60) =$$

$$14.75 \pm 5.09 =$$

$$9.66 \text{ to } 19.84$$

As long as samples of four people are randomly selected from the population of people who might take this training program, 95% of such confidence intervals will cover the population difference. Be sure you are getting comfortable interpreting confidence intervals. Our best estimate of the improvement due to the training program is 14.75 test points, the mean difference; however, we know that from replication to replication there would be a variety of mean differences. The confidence interval gives us a sense of the limits of those mean differences. When the standard error of M_D is small, the confidence interval is more narrow, indicating finer precision in our estimate of the mean of the differences. As you can see in this example, the confidence interval is quite wide; this is primarily due to the small sample size. Larger sample sizes make for greater precision of estimation.

YOUR TURN 8-5

Suppose that 16 participants were tested in a repeated measures design. If M_D equals 15.00, and s_D equals 8.00, what is the standard error of the mean of differences, s_{MD}? How many degrees of freedom would be used to look up the t needed to calculate the 95% confidence interval for M_D? ∎

Notice that the only difference between the confidence interval for difference scores and other confidence intervals is the standard error used in the formula and the definition of degrees of freedom. The standard error of the mean of the differences is not the same as the standard error of a difference between the means of two independent groups. The degrees of freedom for a repeated measures design are $N - 1$, where N refers to sample size or the number of difference scores.

EFFECT SIZES FOR DIFFERENCE SCORES

To use Cohen's categories to assess the size of g, the effect size of a repeated measures design must be calculated *as if* the experiment were an independent groups design. In other words, we must look for an effect size ignoring the fact that the experiment used a repeated measures design. We follow the calculations described previously for an independent groups design. The effect size g for the computer training course is

$$\text{Effect size} = \frac{M_{\text{post-test}} - M_{\text{pre-test}}}{s_{\text{pooled}}} = g$$

The pooled standard deviation for these four trainees is

$$s_{\text{pooled}} = \sqrt{\left[\frac{df_{\text{post-test}}s^2_{\text{post-test}} + df_{\text{pre-test}}s^2_{\text{pre-test}}}{df_{\text{post-test}} + df_{\text{pre-test}}}\right]} = \sqrt{\left[\frac{3\,(18.06^2) + 3\,(18.70^2)}{3 + 3}\right]} = 18.38$$

Thus, the effect size is

$$\frac{48.75 - 34.00}{18.38} = 0.80$$

This value corresponds to a large effect size according to Cohen's categorization.

WHAT YOU HAVE LEARNED AND THE NEXT STEP

This chapter focused on expressing the precision with which we can estimate the difference between the means of two populations and standardizing the difference to permit a comparison of the findings of one study to similar studies that perhaps made use of different dependent variables. The key points in this chapter are as follows:

- Most psychological research involves a comparison between two or more groups whose experiences differ in some known way.

- The difference between experiences of the groups may lead to different means on a dependent variable (in addition to the difference due to sampling error).

- Every statistical index used is affected by sampling error because behavioral scientists seldom observe every member of any population.

- Large sampling errors due to large standard deviations or small samples result in less precision, that is, wider confidence intervals. Large standard deviations may result when the population is very heterogeneous or measurement is unreliable.

- Small sampling errors due to small standard deviations or large samples result in greater precision, that is, narrower confidence intervals. Sampling from more-homogeneous populations, treating individuals more similarly, and using reliable measurement tools will reduce sampling error and lead to greater precision of estimation.

- When constructing confidence intervals for the difference between the means of two populations, we know that 95% of the time the interval will give us two values that bound the true difference between the means of the two populations.

- If the value of 0.0 is within the 95% confidence interval for the difference between two means, the data do not provide sufficient evidence to conclude that there is a difference between the two population means to meet scientific conventions.

- Effect size is a standardization procedure applied to group means that parallels the standard score (z) transformation for individual scores. Effect size measures are independent of sample size.

- Calculating an effect size permits one to compare the findings of a study with results of other research on similar topics regardless of the means and standard deviations of the specific dependent variables used in previous research.

- Unless there are reasons to do otherwise, one can consider effect sizes of 0.20 as small, 0.50 as medium, and 0.80 as large.

- Confidence intervals can be calculated for difference scores. The standard error of difference scores and a t based on $N - 1$ degrees of freedom are used. (The degrees of freedom for a repeated measures design are $N - 1$, in which N refers to the number of difference scores.)

- Effect sizes in repeated measures (and matched groups) designs are best calculated using the same procedure as with independent groups; when done in that way, they may be compared to the effect sizes of independent group designs.

In the next chapter, we use the sampling error of the difference between two means to test hypotheses regarding the difference between the means of two populations. At this time, we introduce a standard approach to discussing the results of research called *null hypothesis significance testing (NHST)*. The approach has been very important in the history of research in psychology, medicine, education, sociology, and other fields. Methods of dealing with data that are always affected by sampling error have been helpful in the development of scientific knowledge and in making choices in applied areas. NHST is used widely, but it has have often been misinterpreted (Nickerson, 2000; Wilkinsen et al., 1999). As we introduce you to this approach to analyzing data, we stress the proper use of NHST.

Key Concepts

confidence interval for a
   difference between two means

confidence interval for the mean
   of differences

effect size

Hedges' g

Cohen's d

Answers to *Your Turn* Questions

8-1. No. Confidence intervals are affected by the standard error of the mean, which is the standard deviation divided by the square root of the sample size. If we divide the original sample into parts, the sizes of the new samples are smaller than the whole sample; thus, both standard errors of the two means are typically larger than the standard error for the whole sample. These larger standard errors make the two 95% confidence intervals wider than for the whole 80-student sample.

8-2. The t for the 80% confidence interval would be 1.293 (that is, the t for .20 (two-tailed) or .10 (one-tailed) tests). Because the t is smaller, the 80% confidence interval would be more narrow than the 95% confi-

dence interval. The 80% confidence interval for the difference of the two means is 0.63 ± 1.293 (0.225), or 0.63 ± 0.29, or 0.34 to 0.92.

8-3. Maria: $z_M = (25 - 20)/5 = 1.0$
Jerome: $z_M = (15 - 20)/5 = -1.0$
Maria: $z_Q = (45 - 50)/10 = -0.5$
Jerome: $z_Q = (60 - 50)/10 = 1.0$

Maria had a larger z on M than on Q. The higher the z, the higher a score is relative to its distribution. Jerome in contrast, did better on Q than he did on M. Relative to Jerome, Maria did better on M, but worse on Q.

8-4. $g = (29 - 23)/7 = 6/7 = 0.86$

8-5. $s_{MD} = 8.00/\sqrt{16} = 2.00$; $df = 16 - 1 = 15$

Analyzing and Interpreting Data: Problems and Exercises

1. (a) Which of the following pairs of samples will have the wider 95% confidence interval for the difference between the two means? Explain your choice. (Hint: you don't need to calculate anything.)

Pair	M	s	n
R_1	12.91	4.81	25
R_2	10.45	4.35	25
Q_1	18.73	8.23	25
Q_2	16.95	8.56	25

(b) Select the pair of samples with the wider confidence interval from these two pairs of samples.

Pair	M	s	n
G_1	11.71	4.19	25
G_2	9.25	4.47	25
H_1	15.23	4.26	100
H_2	12.55	4.64	100

2. (a) Which of the following pairs of groups will have the wider 95% confidence interval for the difference between the two means? Explain your choice. (Hint: you don't need to calculate anything.)

Pair	M	s	n
F_1	−2.91	3.75	36
F_2	8.45	3.91	36
G_1	−8.73	1.23	36
G_2	−3.27	2.16	36

(b) Select the pair of samples with the wider confidence interval from these two pairs of samples.

Pair	M	s	n
D_1	−1.31	2.19	121
D_2	−4.25	2.47	121
W_1	12.53	2.26	49
W_2	11.45	2.64	49

3. When determining confidence in the estimate of the difference between two population means, what is indicated when the 95% confidence interval contains a zero difference? What conclusion should you reach?

4. What can be said about the difference between two means if the following 95% confidence intervals were found?
   (a) −4.25 to 16.75
   (b) 3.26 to 12.34
   (c) 4.84 to 5.61

5. For the confidence intervals in problem #4, which one comes from an experiment with the most precision?

6. Which of these two confidence intervals will be wider?
   (a) a 50% confidence interval
   (b) an 80% confidence interval
   Explain your choice.

7. Calculate the 95% confidence interval for the difference between two means using the following descriptive information. Group A is a control group, and Group B is a treatment group.

	M	s	n
Group A	23.4	7.8	21
Group B	32.1	8.4	21

8. Suppose that, instead of selecting only 42 participants in the previous problem, the researcher had selected 82 participants, 41 per group. If the means and standard deviations are the same, show how the confidence interval for the difference between these two means would differ from that using the smaller groups.

9. Compare the confidence intervals calculated for problem #7 and #8. In which case is the estimate of the difference between population means more precise? Why?

10. For these values, compare the 80% and 90% confidence intervals for the difference between two means. (Note: See *Your Turn* 8-2 to help you find

the critical t for the .80 interval.) Explain why the 90% confidence interval is wider than the 80% confidence interval.

	M	s	n
Group Q	45.9	10.7	30
Group P	52.1	12.8	32

11. For these values, compare the 80% and 95% confidence intervals for the difference between two means. (Note: See *Your Turn* 8-2 to help you find the critical t for the .80 interval.) Explain why the 95% CI is wider than the 80% CI.

	M	s	n
Group Z	−38.9	12.4	36
Group L	−45.2	13.5	49

12. What are three factors affecting the width of the confidence interval around the estimated difference between two population means?

13. Suppose that one found a difference of 25 points between two means. Does such a large difference mean that difference is important? Explain your answer.

14. (a) In your own words, explain what a measure of effect size tells you about the difference between two sample means? Be sure to explain why effect size measures are important to researchers when describing the outcome of a two-group experiment.
    (b) Explain how the calculation of effect size differs for an independent groups design and for a repeated measures design.

15. (a) Calculate the effect size for the two-group comparison in problem #7 and for the comparison in problem #8.
    (b) Explain why the effect size does not change even though group sizes doubled.
    (c) Based on Cohen's rule of thumb for effect sizes, is the effect size in these situations small, average, or large?

16. (a) Calculate and compare the effect sizes of the two pairs of mean in problem #1(a).

(b) Based on Cohen's rule of thumb for effect sizes, is the effect size in these situations small, average, or large?

17. As part of a psychology experiment conducted by a developmental psychologist, children were asked to play a game in which they win a prize of 20 nickels. Children played individually and all won. (Yes, the game was fixed.) After the game is over, they see someone (who is a confederate of the experimenter) place some money in a contribution container that is marked "Contributions to help poor children. Please give." Some children were randomly assigned to see *another child* make a contribution whereas others saw *an adult* (whom they did not know) make a contribution. It was hypothesized that the children who saw the child contribute would make larger contributions compared to those who saw the adult contribute. Below is a record of the number of nickels that each child donated after seeing one of the models make a donation and leave the room. The maximum possible donation is 20 nickels because that was the number that each child previously won.

Donation after seeing child model ($n = 15$): 0, 4, 3, 1, 5, 2, 6, 7, 0, 7, 5, 4, 3, 2, 3
Donations after seeing adult model ($n = 16$): 3, 0, 1, 1, 2, 5, 2, 2, 0, 1, 1, 4, 3, 2, 2, 4

(a) Does an inspection reveal any problems with the data? (Construct two simple frequency distributions to find out.)
(b) Describe the central tendency and variation for both groups.
(c) Estimate the 95% confidence interval for the difference between the two population means.
(d) Calculate g and evaluate its magnitude based on Cohen's rule of thumb.
(e) On the basis of these descriptions and estimates, does it appear that the researcher's expectation was supported?

18. In another experiment, the developmental psychologist asked children individually to play a game and then told them that they won a prize. Their prize was to take as many nickels from a basket as they thought would be "the right prize." They were shown a large basket containing 100

nickels. One-half of the children were randomly assigned to take their nickels immediately after seeing another child (who had been trained by the experimenter for this role) take her prize. The other half of the children did not see anyone take a prize before they took their prize. The child model audibly counted out 20 nickels as her prize. It was hypothesized that the children would take larger prizes after seeing a child model take 20 nickels compared to seeing no other person. Below is a record of the number of nickels each child took after seeing the model take her prize and leave the room and when there was no model.

Child model ($n = 17$): 20, 24, 23, 31, 25, 29, 16, 27, 20, 17, 25, 24, 23, 25, 31, 24, 30
No child model ($n = 16$): 23, 19, 21, 11, 12, 15, 12, 20, 10, 13, 14, 14, 23, 12, 12, 14

(a) Does an inspection reveal any problems with the data? (Construct back-to-back stem-and-leaf plots to find out.)
(b) Describe the central tendency and variation for both groups.
(c) Estimate the 95% confidence interval for the difference between the two means.
(d) Estimate the effect size, g, and evaluate its magnitude based on Cohen's rule of thumb.
(e) On the basis of these descriptions and estimates, does it appear that the researcher's expectation was observed?

19. A repeated measures design was used.
(a) Find the 95% confidence interval for the mean difference score.

Person	Condition 1	Condition 2
1	32	45
2	8	12
3	12	16
4	23	29
5	21	24
6	17	18

(b) Find the effect size for this finding. Compare to Cohen's criteria.

20. A matched groups measures design was used.
(a) Find the 95% confidence interval for mean difference score.

Person-Pair	Condition 1	Condition 2
1	17	12
2	28	12
3	15	16
4	19	15
5	21	16

(b) Find the effect size for this finding. Compare to Cohen's criteria.

Answers to Odd-Numbered Problems

1. (a) The means are not relevant to the answer. The standard deviations are larger for pair Q, but the sample sizes are the same for pair Q and pair R. Thus, the confidence interval for Pair Q would be wider.
1. (b) The standard deviations are about the same, but the sample sizes for Pair G are smaller than for Pair H; thus, the confidence interval for Pair G is wider.
3. If the 95% confidence interval for the difference between two population means contains zero, a researcher must conclude that the possibility that there is no difference between the two population means is too large to conclusively conclude that the means are different. The difference between the two sample means could simply represent error variation. The results do not prove the means are the same; of course, but, if zero is within the interval, the sample data do not provide sufficient evidence to conclude that the means are really different. Thus, the researcher must admit to being in a state of uncertainty regarding the true difference between the population means.
5. Precision is indicated by the narrowness of the confidence interval; thus, interval c indicates the most precise experiment.

7. $t_{(df=40,\alpha=0.5)} = 2.021$

$$s_{M_1-M_2} = \sqrt{\left[\left(\frac{20\,(7.8^2) + 20\,(8.4^2)}{20 + 20}\right)\left(\frac{1}{21} + \frac{1}{21}\right)\right]}$$

$$= 2.51$$

95% confidence interval $= (32.1 - 23.4) \pm 2.021$ (2.51) $= 3.64$ to 13.76

9. The confidence interval in problem #8 is more narrow because the group sizes are larger, thereby decreasing the standard error of the difference between two means.

11. The 95% confidence interval of the difference between the two means would be wider.

We have 35 plus 48, and thus 83 degrees of freedom. From the table, we use the value of t for the largest degrees of freedom less than 84. We will need to use 60, $t_{(df=60,\alpha=.05)} = 2.000$. Thus,

$$(-38.9 - (-45.2))$$

$$\pm 2.000 \sqrt{\left[\left(\frac{35\,(12.4^2) + 48\,(13.5^2)}{35 + 48}\right)\left(\frac{1}{36} + \frac{1}{49}\right)\right]}$$

$$= 6.3 \pm 2.000\,(9.06) = -11.82 \text{ to } 24.42.$$

For the 80% confidence interval of the difference between the two means we have:

$t_{(df=60,\alpha=.05)} = 1.296$, and

$6.3 \pm 1.296\,(9.06) = 6.3 \pm 11.74 = -5.44$ to 20.04.

The different widths of the confidence intervals arise because, the higher the confidence, the farther out in the distribution one must go to obtain the critical t value. It should be intuitively clear that, the wider the interval, the greater the confidence you can have that you have captured the true mean difference. If you are asked to judge the weight of someone who (unknown to you) weighs 120 lbs. and you are asked to guess by giving an interval that you believe contains this person's true weight, wouldn't you have greater confidence the wider the interval you are allowed to give? For example, it is likely you would have greater confidence in your estimate of the person's true weight if you guessed 100 to 140 lbs. than if you guessed 115 to 125.

13. The size of the difference between two means is related to the variables being measured. Imagine the difference in the mean weights of people in two weight loss programs. The difference between two means would be numerically greater if weights were measured in ounces than if they had been measured in pounds. And the difference would be greater if measured in pounds than if measured in kilograms. Thus, a 25 oz. difference might well be small, a 25 lb. difference quite respectable, and a 25 kg difference unbelievable large.

15. (a) The effect size for the means in problem #1 was $g = 1.07$ ($=8.7/8.1$); for the means in problem #2 (when sample size was much larger), the effect size remained the same (1.07) because the mean difference and variability remained the same while sample size changed. Because the effect size is standardized against the pooled standard deviation, it is not affected by sample size (the degrees of freedom are in both the numerator and denominator and thus cancel out) and is a major reason why the effect size measure is so important.

(b) Based on Cohen's rule of thumb, an effect size of 1.07 is considered large.

17. Simple frequency distributions for these two groups are

Value	Child	Adult
0	2	2
1	1	4
2	2	5
3	3	2
4	2	2
5	2	1
6	1	
7	2	

(a) The Child Model distribution is much more dispersed and somewhat platykurtic. The Adult Model distribution tends to be bell shaped but slightly positively skewed, although it is difficult to judge with such small numbers of scores. There do not seem to be serious problems at this stage. (Kurtosis has no easy remedies.)

(b) The mean and standard deviation for the Child group are 3.47 and 2.06, respectively, and 2.26 and 1.44, respectively, for the Adult group. These statistics confirm the impression one got from examining the frequency distributions.

(c) The difference between the sample means was 1.41, and the confidence interval for the difference between the two population means is 0.02 to 2.79.

(d) The effect size, g, is $1.41/1.88 = 0.75$.

(e) We can suggest that the researcher's expectations were confirmed because the 95% confidence interval does not contain zero and the effect size is close to large according to Cohen's rule of thumb. There is evidence that the true population mean difference is not zero and in the direction of the researcher's hypothesis. Our best estimate of the difference between the population means is 1.41.

Children who saw a child contribute made larger contributions (1.41 nickels larger) than those who saw an adult contribute.

19. (a) If we work with positive differences, we would take Condition 2 minus Condition 1. The differences are 13, 4, 4, 6, 3, 1. $M_D = 5.17$; $s_D = 4.17$; $s_{MD} = 4.17/\sqrt{6} = 1.702$.

$t_{(df=5, \alpha=.05)} = 2.571$

$5.17 \pm 2.571(1.702) = 5.17 \pm 4.40 = 0.77$ to 9.57 is the 95% confidence interval for the mean difference score.

(b) $\sqrt{\left[\dfrac{(5\,(8.52^2) + 5\,(11.92^2))}{5 + 5}\right]} = 10.36 = s_{pooled}$

$g = (24.00 - 18.83)/10.36 = 0.50$. This effect size is a medium effect.

Go to http://psychology.wadsworth.com/courses/statistics/ and test your knowledge of this chapter by taking the online quiz. Another resource to check is the online workshops that provide a step-by-step guide through a number of topics at http://psychology.wadsworth.com/workshops/workshops.html.

CHAPTER 9

Estimating Using Null Hypothesis Significance Testing

Significance tests fill an important need in answering some key research questions . . .
    Abelson (1997, p. 117)

INTRODUCTION

In the previous chapter, we demonstrated how to make estimates of effect size (*g*) (standardized estimates of the relationship between an independent variable and a dependent variable) and to estimate the precision (95% confidence interval) with which the difference between the two means has been measured. Research methodologists working in psychology, education, medicine, and related fields encourage the calculation and reporting of these estimates. Nearly all researchers in these fields use one additional common analytic technique: null hypothesis significance testing (NHST). NHST currently is the most frequently used procedure for statistical decision-making (and, of course, learned by students); however, even experienced researchers have not always used it correctly. It is important to understand both the advantages and limitations of NHST (Nickerson, 2000; Wilkinson et al., 1999). In the following three scenarios, a reasonable next step for the researcher is to complete a test of statistical significance.

Some people draw sweeping conclusions about their worth as persons after disappointments or failures. This tendency suggests that changing how those people think about problems would help them live more effectively; efforts to help people change how they think about themselves are central to cognitive therapy. Shelley conducted a study in the college counseling center for students who said that they were very stressed by class tests. Shelley reasoned that a major cause of their stress was fear of doing poorly, and that this was at least partially due to the students' tendency to concentrate on tests on which they did poorly in the past. The resulting stress made it difficult to remember concepts and facts or to reason logically during tests, regardless of how well students could work with the course material when not in a test setting. Shelley used a test anxiety measure with stressed students coming to the counseling center. With the students' agreement, they were randomly assigned to one of two approaches. One group was given traditional therapy sessions that focused on tracing the causes of stress back to early childhood experiences. The second group, using cognitive therapy, was helped to learn how their thinking patterns caused them to fail and to learn how to replace the negative thoughts with more-productive self-assessments. After the therapy, Shelley found that, relative to the traditional group, the cognitive therapy group became less anxious about tests and that the effect size was in the large range. She found the confidence interval for the difference between the two sample means. She wondered whether she was ready to communicate her findings to others.

Dr. Merton reviewed the standardized test scores of all 23,745 students in a very large school district. He was surprised to see that the two subareas of the district differed on some test scores. His statistical analyses revealed a difference in the average math achievement level for students from the north side of the district compared to those living in the south side of the district. He calculated the effect size and found *g* to equal 0.03. The confidence interval of the difference of the two means was very narrow, suggesting that his data provided rather precise estimates of the population means for the north and south sides of the district. He wondered whether the findings merited being presented to the local newspaper as a way of encouraging a governmental agency to work on finding the reasons for this difference in achievement levels.

Terri noticed that some of her classmates studied in utter silence while others seemed quite happy to study with dormitory conversations going on around them. She decided to examine study conditions for a psychology lab project. She taped several hours of dormitory conversation. From these tapes, she developed a 30 min. tape of conversation noise for her research. Students were asked to learn lists of words either in silence or with the tape playing. She used several lists of words that had been found to be equally difficult to recall. Each participant worked on four lists: two with conversations and two in silence. Some learned the first list in silence, the second with the conversation tape, the third in silence, and the fourth with the conversation tape. Others worked in the reverse order. (You should recognize this as a repeated measurement design.) The dependent variable was the accuracy of recall of lists learned either with conversation noise (the mean of the two conversation trials) or learned in silence (the mean of the two silent trials).

These scenarios represent three different research designs: an experimental design with random assignment to groups, a natural groups design, and a repeated measures design. For each design, g (the effect size) and the 95% confidence interval should be estimated. In this chapter, you will learn how to use NHST as the next step in analysis. The results of NHST complement the information provided by the effect size and confidence interval.

TESTING HYPOTHESES

Research is directed at testing the validity of tentative ideas. Ideas about behavior, learning, and rehabilitation are suggested and then tested. Because behavioral variables are not standardized (as are many physical variables such as time and distance), and because people do not behave as consistently as do chemical compounds, behavioral scientists usually examine the mean performance of a group. Furthermore, we can get more information when we compare two or more groups, as did the three hypothetical researchers described in the introduction. In the context of research using two groups, the tentative idea that is tested statistically is that the population means (as represented by the group means) are equal. This tentative belief is called the **null hypothesis.** The null hypothesis is tested; evidence against the null hypothesis may be used to support the **alternative hypothesis,** namely, that there is a difference between the population means. Such is the logic of NHST.

The null hypothesis in Shelley's case is that the two populations represented by the two groups of students have equivalent levels of stress due to being tested even after experiencing different approaches to therapy. If, in fact, the group means are different enough, Shelley can reject the null hypothesis. If she rejects the null hypothesis, she is permitted to conclude that one of the therapies was more successful. To be able to conclude that the cognitive approach is more effective, it is necessary, of course, to have observed that the cognitive group was less anxious than the traditional therapy group at the end of the treatment.

Before considering some numerical examples, we want to be sure that you recognize that the concept of a null hypothesis is not just a "statisticians' thing." Any time we test a tentative interpretation that is accepted until disproved, we have the equivalent of a refutable, null hypothesis. The American criminal justice system is founded on the presumption of innocence. People accused of crimes are presumed innocent until proven guilty: this presumption

FIGURE 9.1 ■ Testing a null hypothesis in statistical analysis is very similar to the decision process in a trial of a person accused of a crime in criminal justice systems in which a person is "presumed innocent" until proven guilty.

	The true situation of the person accused of a crime	
Decision	Did *not* commit the crime	Did commit the crime
Allow the null hypothesis ("Innocent until proven guilty") to stand.	A correct decision: an innocent person has not been falsely convicted.	An error: a person who has committed a crime is not punished.
Guilty; reject the null hypothesis concluding that the accused did commit the crime.	An error: an innocent person has been falsely convicted.	A correct decision: a guilty person has been found guilty.

means that guilt is not assigned until evidence is presented that jurors agree is sufficiently strong to merit rejecting the presumption of innocence. The null hypothesis is: the accused is innocent. Figure 9.1 displays the four possible outcomes from a trial. Note that two outcomes are valid and two are not.

We want to reject the presumption of innocence if the accused person did in fact commit the crime, and we do not want to reject the presumption of innocence if the person did not commit the crime; these would be the valid outcomes. The two possible errors are (a) convicting an innocent person and (b) failing to reject the presumption of innocence for a guilty person. Similarly, in a research situation, we want to reject the null hypothesis only when the population means are actually different and not reject the null hypothesis when the population means are the same. Similar to the courtroom analogy, researchers also can make two kinds of errors, as we demonstrate in the next chapter.

YOUR TURN 9-1

Are the errors in Figure 9.1 equally undesirable? Or is one of the errors worse than the other one?

■

Some of the standard ways of talking about null hypotheses often seem hard to follow, but, as we demonstrated, there is a logic here that is not limited solely to statistics. Later in this chapter and in the next one, some additional similarities between NHST and court trials will be mentioned.

REJECTION CRITERIA

When we set out to test the null hypothesis that the means of two populations are the same, we need to specify the evidence that we will use to reject this hypothesis. The evidence was hinted at in previous chapters: a 95% confidence interval for a difference between two sample means contains the most likely values of the true difference. If we knew the means for

FIGURE 9.2 ▪ The 95% confidence interval for the mean of Katie's whole sample.

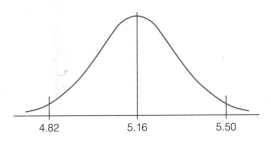

| 4.82 | 5.16 | 5.50 |

the two populations, we would know the true difference between the population means. What we have, instead, are two means based on *samples,* each drawn from one of the populations; thus, each is an estimate of a population mean. We can find the difference between the two sample means, and we can calculate the 95% confidence interval for the difference between the two population means. If we replicated the research with samples chosen in the same way, 95% of these confidence intervals would contain the true difference between the population means.

The null hypothesis posits that the difference between the two population means equals zero. If a 95% confidence interval does not contain zero, then zero is quite unlikely to be the actual difference between the population means. Thus, we can reject zero as a possible value of the difference between the two population means. When zero is outside the confidence interval, this is equivalent to saying that we are sure "beyond a reasonable doubt" that the defendant is guilty. Let's step back a bit and go through this strategy one step at a time.

Rejection Criteria With One Sample

Remember Katie, our happiness researcher? Figure 9.2 represents Katie's 95% confidence interval for the mean happiness of students at her college. As you know by now, 95% of such intervals will contain the population mean. You may recall that in one scenario an administrator suggested that the mean of the happiness ratings at the school was 6. Note that the mean of 6 suggested by the administrator is far larger than 5.50, the high end of her confidence interval. It seems quite safe to say that the mean happiness of the population does not equal or exceed 6; it is most likely lower than 6.

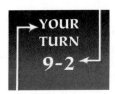
YOUR TURN 9-2

Suppose a cranky member of the administration at Katie's college said that he thought students were much less happy than in previous years. He asked if, on the basis of her data, it was possible that the true mean was 4, the middle of the 7-point scale. On the basis of Figure 9.2, what should Katie say?   ▪

Let us formalize a procedure for dealing with a hypothesized value of a population mean and show how Katie might make a decision about such hypothesized values. In other words, let us construct a rule for deciding whether a hypothesized population mean is so different from the sample mean that the hypothesized value should not be considered a reasonable estimate of the real population mean. Note, first, that there is no definite, objective way to decide what is "not reasonable" that everyone would agree on. Over the decades, users of statistics have decided that, if a hypothesized value does not lie in a 95% confidence interval, then we can safely say that the hypothesized value is not the population mean. That convention would mean that Katie can confidently say that any mean greater than 5.50 or less than 4.82 is unlikely to represent the students at her college. We call the areas in Figure 9.2 below 4.82 and above 5.50 **rejection regions.** All hypothesized population means in these regions are quite unlikely to equal the true population mean. By using the 95% confidence interval as the criterion of rejection or nonrejection of a hypothesized mean, we have decided that, when the chances of a value being the population mean are 5% or less, we may refuse to treat that value as a reasonable estimate of the population value. If a hypothesized value does lie inside the confidence interval, one should conclude that the value *may* equal the population mean, but one should not conclude that the hypothesized value really equals the population mean.

A college administrator may or may not propose different hypotheses about the value of the real population mean. We suggested that one might do that to introduce the idea of testing hypotheses about a population using a sample from that population. But do think carefully about the strategy we have been illustrating. Mathematically, there is only a small probability that the true population mean could be less than 4 or more than 6 because those values are beyond the limits of the 95% confidence interval. When the probability of a hypothesis being true gets to some small level, we decide that it is just not worth treating that hypothesis seriously. By convention, a probability of .05 has been defined as unlikely. If a million tickets to a lottery are sold, you will not plan your life around winning the prize. Even though it is possible that you will win, it is highly unlikely. Likewise, it is highly unlikely that Katie's sample of 80 students was so atypical that the actual mean of the student body is 4 or 6. This decision-making strategy is summarized in Box 9.1.

There is no objective reason for selecting a probability of .05 as being unlikely enough to permit rejecting a hypothesized value. The probability is low because scientists prefer to be conservative in what they assert to be true or not true. Most would rather leave a question unanswered than to answer it prematurely with the wrong answer. Consequently, the values within a 95% confidence interval based on a sample are treated as possible values of the population mean. We know that values toward the middle of a confidence interval are more likely to be true than those toward the ends, but, without better information, scientists would rather not take a stand. This convention provides some protection against claiming too much; however, it also has led to some misunderstandings, which we take up later.

Rejection Criteria When Comparing Two Groups

When we have two groups, we follow a strategy very similar to that outlined in Box 9.1. Imagine two groups of research participants having different experiences: the point of the research is to learn if these different experiences (the levels of the independent variable) are related to the scores on the dependent variable. For example, is an experimental beverage flavor rated more favorably than an older flavor? The two flavors form the levels of the independent variable, and rated taste quality is the dependent variable. We begin with the tentative belief that, as a group, people would show no preferences for one flavor over the other. In other words, the mean ratings from the two groups would be equal.

In an experimental setting, one would say that a treatment did not make the mean of the experimental group different from the mean of the control group at the end of the experiment. Think back to the therapy experiment on test anxiety mentioned at the beginning of

BOX 9.1 ■ Summary of the Strategy Underlying NHST of Means Using One Sample

- Information is available for one sample drawn from a population.
- The sample provides our only (and thus best) information about the population from which the sample was drawn.
- The data from the sample are used to estimate characteristics of the population (such as the mean).
- Such estimates do not perfectly match the mean of the population μ because samples vary due to which members of the population happen to have been selected for any particular sample; this is called *sampling error.*
- Using sampling error for samples of a given size drawn from the population, it is possible to calculate confidence intervals indicating the precision to which the population mean has been estimated.
- Often the 95% confidence interval is used; 95% of such intervals from independent samples (replications) will contain the true population mean.
- If a value for the population mean is hypothesized, it can be compared to the 95% confidence interval.
- This comparison can have only two outcomes: the value of the hypothesized mean is (a) within the interval (that is, larger than the lower limit, but smaller than the upper limit) or (b) outside the interval (that is, either smaller than the lower limit or larger than the upper limit).
- If the hypothesized value of the mean is outside the interval, we may reject that value as a reasonable estimate of the population mean. We treat a hypothesized value outside the interval as sufficiently different from the sample mean to feel safe in concluding that that value cannot equal the mean of the population.
- If the hypothesized mean is within the interval, we remain uncertain about the value of the population mean. The hypothesized value is not sufficiently different from the sample mean to feel safe saying that it cannot equal the population value. The hypothesized mean could be the population mean.
- It is incorrect to conclude that a hypothesized value for the mean falling within the 95% confidence interval equals the population value; after all, there are many values within every 95% confidence interval. At best, only one equals the population mean.
- What is "sufficiently different" has been defined in terms of probability. A correct hypothesized mean is expected to be within 95% of the confidence intervals calculated for samples drawn from the population.

this chapter. Shelley expected that the types of therapy would differ in effectiveness. If not, why do the research? In fact, she expected that cognitive therapy was particularly appropriate to this group; consequently, Shelley expected mean anxiety to be lower for the students who were treated using cognitive psychotherapy compared to those who received traditional therapy. However, finding that the cognitive therapy group shows less anxiety after therapy is not enough evidence for her to conclude that cognitive therapy is the method to use. Differences between two means in one experiment could be due to only sampling error and not to any differences in the effectiveness of types of therapy.

When we do research, we are cautious. We do not want to make a claim (such as "cognitive therapy is better than traditional techniques for these students") without sufficient evidence. Consequently, the logic of NHST requires that we start out tentatively expecting that the treatment techniques are equally effective. As stated previously, this tentative initial belief is the null hypothesis. In Shelley's case, the null hypothesis would be: students treated with traditional therapy end up no more and no less anxious than those treated with cognitive therapy. Because we are interested in the populations that the groups represent, the null hypothesis is stated with the regard to the populations of "test-anxious" people treated with cognitive therapy and those treated with traditional therapy. The null hypothesis states that the population means are equal; if the null hypothesis is true, the sample means would be equal *except* as they are affected by sampling error. Shelley's experiment tests whether this null hypothesis can be rejected.

The standard symbol for the null hypothesis is H_0. We will use μ_c to refer to the mean of students treated with cognitive therapy and μ_t to refer to the mean of students treated with traditional therapy. The null hypothesis says that these two means are equal. We can write the null hypothesis as

H_0: $\mu_c = \mu_t$

Note that we speak as though we are comparing population values, μ_c and μ_t, even though we have only sample values. We do this because the sample means are estimates of the population values. If the null hypothesis were really true, the means of two samples would likely differ, but only because both are affected by sampling error. In other words, the null hypothesis could be true even though the sample means are literally different. We seek evidence using NHST to discriminate between two possibilities: (a) the difference between sample means reflects sampling error only, and (b) the difference reflects actual population differences as well as sampling error.

Rejecting the null hypothesis means that we have evidence that the population means are not equal. What is the alternative to H_0? What would we then conclude? This question has a couple answers, but let's take the simpler one for a moment. If we begin an experiment not feeling very sure whether the experimental group will produce higher scores or lower scores compared to a second group, we should use a **nondirectional alternative hypothesis,** an alternative hypothesis that says that the two population means have different values. The alternative hypothesis is symbolized as H_1 and, when the hypothesis is nondirectional, is written as

H_1: $\mu_c \neq \mu_t$

If the null hypothesis is true, the difference between the two sample means will equal 0.0 on the average; that is, 0.0 is the "typical" value, although sampling error will produce differences greater than and smaller than 0.0 in any single experiment. When 0.0 does not lie in the confidence interval, but instead lies in one of the tails (that is, the areas outside the confidence interval), we say that 0.0 lies in the rejection region. We can reject the null hypothesis (i.e., that the difference is 0.0) and accept the alternative hypothesis (i.e., that the difference is not 0.0). The probability associated with the rejection regions is called the **alpha level.** The symbol for alpha is α. As noted, investigators generally employ an alpha of .05, that is, $\alpha = .05$.

An Illustrative Analysis

There is a close relationship between the mind and the body. Some psychologists have learned that physical fitness has a positive influence on mood. Suppose that Serena, an advanced graduate student in clinical psychology, developed an exercise program as part of group therapy for mildly depressed college students. Suppose, further, that 44 students seeking counseling for mild depression agree to be randomly assigned to one of two versions of counseling: one with exercise and one without. They did not know what the versions were except that Serena assured them that both forms were recommended for mild depression. The dependent variable was self-reported positive affect with higher numbers indicating that people have more-positive feelings. After three months of treatment, the means and standard deviations of the two groups of students were as follows:

Group	M	s	n
Regular therapy (controls)	17.95	3.63	21
Regular therapy + aerobic exercise	22.13	3.32	23

The pooled standard deviation is

$$s_{pooled} = \sqrt{\left[\frac{df_{control}(s^2_{control}) + df_{exercise}(s^2_{exercise})}{df_{control} + df_{exercise}}\right]}$$

$$= \sqrt{\left[\frac{20\,(3.63^2) + 22\,(3.32^2)}{20 + 22}\right]} = 3.470$$

The standard error of the difference between two means is

$$s_{M_e - M_c} = s_{pooled} \sqrt{\left[\frac{1}{n_{control}} + \frac{1}{n_{exercise}}\right]} = 3.470 \sqrt{\left[\frac{1}{21} + \frac{1}{23}\right]} = 1.047$$

To calculate the 95% confidence interval, we need a t value. The critical t, or t_{crit}, is found in Table A.2 for an alpha level of .05 (two-tailed) with 42 degrees of freedom. Because 42 is not in the table, she uses the critical values for the next lowest value, 40 degrees of freedom, which is 2.021. Therefore, the 95% confidence interval for the difference between the two population means is

$$(M_{exercise} - M_{control}) \pm t_{crit}\,(s_{M_e - M_c}) = (21.13 - 17.95) \pm 2.021\,(1.047) =$$
$$4.178 \pm 2.116 = 2.062 \text{ to } 6.294, \text{ or, rounding to two decimal places, 2.06 to 6.29}$$

Figure 9.3 displays this confidence interval. This interval does not contain 0.0; thus, Serena may reject the null hypothesis. Assuming that the research study was conducted in an appropriate way, she is permitted to conclude that the addition of exercise led to greater levels of positive affect among mildly depressed college students.

FIGURE 9.3 ■ The 95% confidence interval for the difference between two means for the therapy experiment.

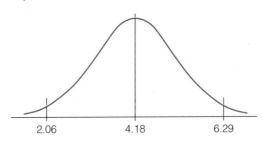

| 2.06 | 4.18 | 6.29 |

THE *t* TEST FOR INDEPENDENT GROUPS

Testing hypotheses as just shown with confidence intervals is a perfectly acceptable way to decide whether the null hypothesis (that is, the tentative assertion that the difference between population means is zero) can be rejected. We introduced testing the null hypothesis in this way because we believe it is easier to understand the criterion for rejecting null hypotheses if presented in the context of confidence intervals. However, there is a more standard way to test a null hypothesis involving two independent samples that (a) is more widely used than the confidence interval approach, and (b) provides additional information that isn't readily available from the confidence interval approach to testing null hypotheses. This method is called the *t* **test for independent groups.**

When we test null hypotheses using the 95% confidence interval, the confidence interval is centered around the difference between the sample means. Then, we determine if zero is contained in the interval or is outside of it. If zero is not within the interval, we may reject the null hypothesis stating that difference between the means is zero. We can test the null hypothesis in a closely related way that provides more information than the method using confidence intervals. This alternative method is the widely used *t* test for independent groups. We develop the rationale and present an example in a step-by-step fashion.

Step 1: If the Null Hypothesis Were True, What Would the Sampling Distribution of the Difference Between Two Means Be?

The null hypothesis states that the population means are equal.

$$H_0: \mu_1 = \mu_2$$

The difference of the two population means according to the null hypothesis must, therefore, be zero.

$$H_0: \mu_1 - \mu_2 = 0.0$$

If the null hypothesis is true, the means of specific pairs of samples drawn from the populations would, on the average, equal each other. However, due to sampling error, the actual difference between sample means would vary: sometimes M_1 would be larger than M_2 (creating positive differences) and sometimes M_2 would be larger than M_1 (creating negative differences). In addition, assuming the scores in the populations are normally distributed, the sampling distribution will be normal in form. The following distribution illustrates the form of the sampling distribution of the differences between two group means if H_0 is true.

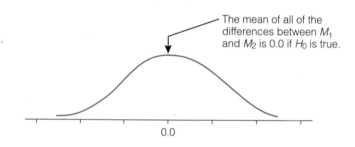

The mean of all of the differences between M_1 and M_2 is 0.0 if H_0 is true.

0.0

Step 2: What Is the Standard Deviation of the Sampling Distribution If the Null Hypothesis Is True?

To know the standard deviation of the sampling distribution, we would need to know the population standard deviation, σ, of the variable measured. We seldom know σ, but we have two estimates of σ, the standard deviations of the two groups, s_1 and s_2. As we have done before, we use these estimates of σ and the sample sizes to estimate the standard error of a difference between two means, $s_{M_1-M_2}$. With the mean of zero and the estimated standard deviation (the standard error), we can specify the sampling distribution if the null hypothesis is true as in the preceding distribution. As an example, let's use Serena's data; the standard error in her experiment was 1.047. The sampling distribution is as follows:

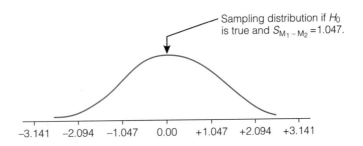

Sampling distribution if H_0 is true and $S_{M_1-M_2} = 1.047$.

-3.141   -2.094   -1.047   0.00   +1.047   +2.094   +3.141

As explained in Chapter 6, because we used estimates of σ, this sampling distribution is not exactly normal; it is distributed as a t. Although the t does not look markedly different from a normal distribution, the fact that it is a t distribution is important; we will come back to it in a moment.

Step 3: Where Is the Actual Difference Between the Two Group Means Located in the Sampling Distribution Based on the Null Hypothesis?

Serena found that the difference between the means of the two therapy groups was +4.18. This actual difference is toward the right tail of the sampling distribution. In fact, as shown next, the actual difference of +4.18 is even more extreme than three standard errors above the mean, 0.0.

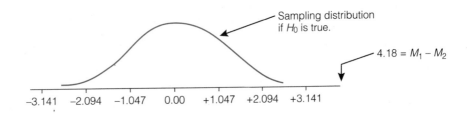

Sampling distribution if H_0 is true.

$4.18 = M_1 - M_2$

-3.141   -2.094   -1.047   0.00   +1.047   +2.094   +3.141

Step 4: How Do We Calculate the t of $M_1 - M_2$ with Respect to the Sampling Distribution Based on the Null Hypothesis?

The same approach used to calculate the value of z for a specific score in a distribution of one variable permits us to calculate the t corresponding to $M_1 - M_2$ in the sampling distribution defined by the null hypothesis; we call this the t **observed**, or t_{obs}.

$$t_{obs} = \frac{\left(\begin{array}{c} \text{Observed difference} \\ \text{between } M_1 \text{ and } M_2 \end{array}\right) - \left(\begin{array}{c} \text{Mean of the sampling} \\ \text{distribution of } M_1 - M_2 \text{ if } H_0 \text{ is true} \end{array}\right)}{s_{M_1-M_2}}$$

Specifically,

$$t_{obs} = \frac{(M_1 - M_2) - (\mu_1 - \mu_2)}{s_{M_1-M_2}}$$

Equation 9.1

Because the difference between the population values, $\mu_1 - \mu_2$, is zero according to the null hypothesis, the formula reduces to

$$t_{obs} = \frac{(M_1 - M_2)}{s_{M_1-M_2}}$$

For Serena's data, we have

$$t_{obs} = \frac{4.18}{1.047} = 3.99$$

This value is compared to t **critical** (t_{crit}) in Table A.2. Critical t values are the edges of the rejection regions and are associated with the alpha selected for the experiment. The degrees of freedom for t_{obs} equal the sum of the two group sizes minus 2. In Serena's case, the degrees of freedom were 42. Because 42 is not in the table, she uses the critical values for the next lowest value (40 degrees of freedom). Serena finds these critical t's for various levels of alpha: 2.021 ($\alpha = .05$); 2.423 ($\alpha = .02$); 2.704 ($\alpha = .01$); 3.307 ($\alpha = .002$). Because her t_{obs} exceeds the t_{crit} value associated with α equals .05, Serena can reject the null hypothesis. (See Figure 9.4.) Her results are said to be **statistically significant**. She may conclude that

FIGURE 9.4 ■ Null hypothesis rejection regions for α equals .05 for a t distribution with 43 degrees of freedom.

The difference posited by the null hypothesis is 0.0. If the observed difference is quite different from 0.0, it seems logical to conclude that the null is to be rejected.

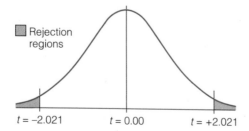

■ Rejection regions

$t = -2.021$ $t = 0.00$ $t = +2.021$

students in the aerobic exercise plus therapy group displayed a greater sense of positive affect compared to those in the traditional therapy alone group. Although the groups were initially drawn from the same population, the independent variable (therapy alone or therapy plus exercise) has made these groups different, and she now has evidence to say that after therapy they represent two populations. *"Statistically significant" means that we have enough evidence to reject the null hypothesis, the tentative belief that the means are equal. Statistically significant does* not *mean that the findings are important or valuable; it merely indicates that the difference observed is unlikely to be a random result.*

If Serena limits herself to concluding that she may reject the null hypothesis, she has learned nothing from the *t* test that she did not know from a 95% confidence interval. However, her observed *t* exceeded the critical *t* for .002, a probability much smaller than .05. Thus, Serena has obtained more information than she gained using the confidence interval alone; her data are very unlikely to reflect sampling error alone. Her findings allow her to be more confident that a replication will be statistically significant than if her observed *t* had barely exceeded the critical value of *t* at an alpha level of .05. Cohen (1994) suggested that "confidence intervals contain all the information to be found in significance tests and much more" (p. 1002; see also quote at beginning of Chapter 6 in this text). We believe that NHST does provide a view of the data that confidence intervals do not provide.

In the next chapter, we introduce a graph that, when using NHST, allows one to be more specific about the probability that an exact replication would be statistically significant. This information is typically not available when only confidence intervals are used.

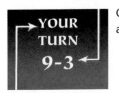

YOUR TURN 9-3

Calculate an observed *t* given the following values: $M_1 = 31.64$, $M_2 = 20.00$, $s_{pooled} = 5$, $n_1 = 15$, and $n_2 = 15$. ∎

Assumptions Underlying *t* Tests

All statistical tests are based on some assumptions. If these assumptions are markedly violated, the results will not be valid. It should be emphasized that these assumptions are relevant both when doing NHST based on the *t* distribution as well as when constructing confidence intervals using the *t* distribution. One assumption is that the distribution of the dependent variable is normal for both populations. We usually cannot verify this assumption because we don't, in fact, know the shape of the population distribution. However, we do know the shape of the sample distributions (assuming, of course, that we have carefully inspected our data). If the samples approximate a bell-shaped distribution, we can assume that the population is bell shaped, and we can apply the *t* test to the data. If there is obvious skewness, it is best to use the transformations given in Chapter 3 before using the *t* distribution. (Of course, the same transformation must be applied to both groups even if only one is skewed.) Even if the samples are rather skewed, using samples larger than 30 will generally permit using *t* (Hays, 1994) because sampling distributions of means approach a normal distribution with large sample sizes (as was discussed in Chapter 6). Of course, distributions showing floor or ceiling effects are going to reduce the validity of any experiment. When such effects are found, the dependent variable must be refined and additional data gathered.

The second assumption is that the standard deviations (i.e., variability) of the populations are equal. As with the shape of the distributions, we can examine only the standard deviations of the groups. Hays (1994) suggests that the t test works rather well even when this assumption is violated. However, if there are sizable differences between the two standard deviations, Hays recommends using groups of the same size. This is yet another reason that data should be inspected before testing null hypotheses with t tests. If the distributions are more-or-less bell shaped and if the standard deviations differ little, one can assume that the assumptions have been met. As a rule of thumb, we suggest that, if the standard deviations of the groups do not differ by more than 3 to 1 (i.e., the larger one is no more than three times larger than the smaller one), one can safely apply the independent groups t test. Inspecting the data will reveal if a difference in variability is due to skewness in one group; in such cases, a transformation of the data in both groups may reduce the difference in variability.

Directional and Nondirectional t Tests

When behavioral scientists conduct exploratory research, they are uncertain which sample will have the larger mean. This situation requires a nondirectional test with two rejection regions, one favoring the first group and one favoring the second group. This approach is, in effect, what we do when we use a 95% confidence interval for the difference between two means and reject the null hypothesis if 0.0 does not lie in the interval. As we showed previously, the null hypothesis and alternative hypothesis for a nondirectional test are written as

H_0: $\mu_1 = \mu_2$

and

H_1: $\mu_1 \neq \mu_2$

In contrast to exploratory research in which any statistically significant difference would be of interest, most researchers have some idea of which of two groups are expected to get higher scores on a dependent variable (Nickerson, 2000). This is true whether the research is theoretical or applied. Serena began her experiment expecting that the sample with therapy plus exercise would show more positive affect after counseling than would the sample with traditional therapy only. She was making what is known as a **directional alternative hypothesis.** She did not do the research to learn if there was *any* difference between the groups, as she might have done had she entertained no hypothesis about what difference to expect. In other words, she is conducting the experiment to test her idea that exercise helps mildly depressed college students as a supplement to therapy. She is really not interested in a difference favoring the control group and does not expect one. Her statement of the null and alternate hypotheses would look like this:

H_0: $\mu_{\text{exercise}} \geq \mu_{\text{regular}}$

and

H_1: $\mu_{\text{exercise}} < \mu_{\text{regular}}$

Note that both the statement of the null hypothesis and the alternative hypothesis change when a directional test is performed. The null hypothesis is that a population of individuals who received therapy plus exercise is on average equally depressed as (or more depressed than) the group receiving regular therapy. Thus, the null hypothesis states that the difference between the two populations after therapy is really zero (i.e., $\mu_{\text{exercise}} = \mu_{\text{regular}}$) or the differ-

TABLE 9.1 ■ Contrast Between Nondirectional and Directional Tests for Independent Groups t Tests

	Nondirectional Test	Directional Test
Null hypothesis	$\mu_1 = \mu_2$	$\mu_1 \leq \mu_2$
Alternative hypothesis	$\mu_1 \neq \mu_2$	$\mu_1 > \mu_2$
Degrees of freedom	$n_1 + n_2 - 2$	$n_1 + n_2 - 2$
Number of rejection regions	2	1
Critical t for $df = 20$, $p = .05$	± 2.086	$+1.725$
When to reject the null hypothesis	If $t_{observed}$ is $+2.086$ or larger, or if $t_{observed}$ is -2.086 or smaller.	If $t_{observed}$ is $+1.725$ or larger. (Be sure to use $M_1 - M_2$ when calculating t.)
Example 1: $t_{observed} = +2.328$	Reject null. (The difference between the means is statistically significant.)	Reject null. (The difference between the means is statistically significant in the expected direction.)
Example 2: $t_{observed} = -2.892$	Reject null. (The difference between the means is statistically significant.)	Do not reject null. (The relative sizes of the means are reversed from what was expected.)
Example 3: $t_{observed} = +1.828$	Do not reject null. (The t does not get into either rejection region.)	Reject null. (The difference between the means is statistically significant.)

ence is in the direction opposite to that which was predicted (i.e., $\mu_{exercise} > \mu_{regular}$). Note that the null hypothesis might be true even if both groups improve after therapy; if they improve the same amount, the null hypothesis would be true. The alternative hypothesis is that the population means are in the predicted direction (i.e., $\mu_{exercise} < \mu_{regular}$). In this case, only an observed t that is positive would permit Serena to reject the null hypothesis. *A directional t test would be used when one is interested only in a difference in one direction.*

Table 9.1 contrasts the application of directional and nondirectional t tests for an independent groups experiment. Note that the formula for the observed t is the same regardless of the alternative hypothesis; the difference lies only in the critical value of t which is used to test the null hypothesis and in the number of rejection regions. Figure 9.5 illustrates the rejection regions for directional and nondirectional tests. Notice that the critical values for the t value are smaller for directional tests than for nondirectional tests. This indicates that a smaller difference between the two means would be accepted as statistically significant compared to what is needed for a two-tailed test. This advantage is balanced by the fact that,

FIGURE 9.5 ■ Rejection regions for directional and nondirectional statistical significance tests.

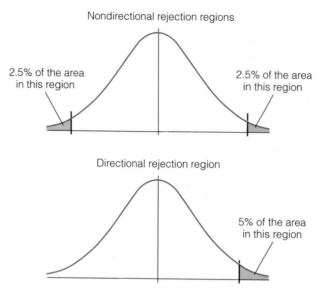

Nondirectional rejection regions

2.5% of the area
in this region

2.5% of the area
in this region

Directional rejection region

5% of the area
in this region

to use a nondirectional t test, one must begin with a definite idea of which group is expected to score higher on the dependent variable.

A nondirectional t test would be used when one is interested in a difference regardless of whether the first or the second group gets the higher score. For example, recalling the scenarios that began this chapter, Dr. Merton should not use directional tests in his comparisons of the north and south halves of this school district. He did not begin with a hypothesis that the scores of the children on the north side would exceed the scores of those on the south side.

It is important to remember that using a *non*directional, alternative test means that one can reject the null hypothesis regardless of which of the two means is the larger (as long as t_{obs} exceeds t_{crit}, of course). If one uses a directional alternative hypothesis, the t test may be done only if the group mean that was expected to be larger is, in fact, larger than the other mean. If the mean expected to be larger is smaller, it is wrong to calculate a t. Furthermore, it is also wrong to choose to use a directional t test after looking to see which mean was larger. That approach would be similar to the marksman who shot a bullet into the side of a barn and then drew the bull's eye around his bullet hole. Table 9.1 contains three illustrations that should help to appreciate this tradeoff.

EFFECT OF SAMPLE SIZE

The more observations we make about any phenomenon, the more sure we feel about the conclusions we draw. The more witnesses who say that Dirty Dirk pulled the trigger in the Dusty Gully Saloon, the more confidence we have that Dirty Dirk is the guilty party. One refinement of this common sense belief needs to be made, however: the witnesses are more compelling if they are *independent* of each other. If the witnesses were all standing in roughly the same place and talked with one another about the crime, their reports should be taken less seriously than if they were strangers to each other and viewed the murder from different vantage points. With that caveat in mind, we want to point out that the formula for the observed t reflects the common sense idea that, the more observations we make, the more confidence we have in our conclusions. Look back at Serena's calculation of the t. Suppose that she had worked with samples of 41 and 43 students instead of 21 and 23. If the means and standard deviations were the same, the standard error of the difference of the means would not be 1.047 as it was with 21 and 23 students, but would instead be

$$3.47 \, (\sqrt{(1/41 \ 1 \ 1/43)}) = 0.76$$

With larger sample sizes, the standard error is reduced. And, when the standard error is reduced, the observed t becomes larger. Using Serena's means and standard deviations, we would have

$$t_{obs} = \frac{22.13 - 17.95}{0.76} = 5.519$$

This observed t has 82 degrees of freedom (that is, $n_1 + n_2 - 2$). With a larger observed t the chance of rejecting the null hypothesis increases. This is just the same as saying that the more witnesses there are to a crime, the more likely there will be a conviction—a rejection of the legal null hypothesis of "innocent until proven guilty."

In contrast, let's consider what Serena's t would be if she had had only four clients in each group (assuming the means and standard deviations remain the same). The observed t would be

$$t_{obs} = \frac{22.13 - 17.95}{3.47 \, (\sqrt{(1/4 + 1/4)})} = \frac{4.18}{2.45} = 1.70$$

For a one-tailed test, the critical t (6) is 1.943. Thus, with only four clients per sample (eight in all), Serena's results would not have been statistically significant, and she would not have rejected the null hypothesis.

The point we are making is that statistical significance is closely related to sample size (as is the width of the confidence interval). A specific difference between sample means could be statistically significant for large samples, but not for smaller samples. If a t is based on small samples, the sampling error of the difference of two means will be larger and the t lower. Table 9.2 provides some additional examples of how t is affected by sample sizes.

TABLE 9.2 ■ Illustration of the Effect of Sample Size on the Pooled Standard Deviation, Standard Error of the Difference of Two Means, and t_{obs}. (For each example, $M_1 = 25$, $M_2 = 22$, $s_1 = 5.00$, and $s_2 = 5.00$.)

Example	n_1 & n_2	df	s_p	$s_{M_1 - M_2}$	t_{obs}	Nondirectional t_{crit}	Decision	Effect size, g
1	6 & 6	10	5.00	3.16	0.949	2.228	Don't reject H_0	0.60
2	11 & 11	20	5.00	2.13	1.407	2.086	Don't reject H_0	0.60
3	21 & 21	40	5.00	1.54	1.944	2.021	Don't reject H_0	0.60
4	41 & 41	80	5.00	1.04	2.717	1.990	Reject H_0	0.60

While examining Table 9.2, note that sample size does not change the effect size. The idea of effect sizes was developed to provide an index of the strength of the relationship between the independent variable and the dependent variable that was independent of sample size. Effect size calculations use s_{pooled}, which is unaffected by sample sizes. It is the standard error that gets smaller and smaller with larger samples, which leads to larger values of the observed t.

This relationship between statistical significance and sample size tells us that experiments differ in their power to reject false null hypotheses. This important topic is discussed in the next chapter.

THE t TEST FOR REPEATED MEASUREMENTS AND MATCHED GROUPS DESIGNS

Just as the confidence interval for independent groups designs was easy to adapt to a confidence interval for repeated measures and matched groups designs, the independent groups t test is easily adapted to a t test applicable to these alternative designs. The focus of attention in these designs is the difference between the repeated measurements or the matched pairs of participants. The **t test for repeated measures** is found by dividing the mean of the differences (M_D) by the standard error of differences. The standard error of the differences (s_{MD}) is the standard deviation of differences divided by the square root of the number of difference scores (N). Thus, the formula for observed t for designs focusing on differences is

$$t_{obs} = \frac{M_D}{s_D/\sqrt{N}}$$

Equation 9.2

Chapter 8 contained an example of a repeated measures design for a training workshop on formatting a document. The hypothetical data were

Person	Pre-test	Post-test	Difference
1. Taylor	45	61	16
2. Sarah	27	37	10
3. Jim	12	29	17
4. Leslie	52	68	16

It is clear that we would expect the post-test to exceed the pre-test because the people are being trained on the skills measured by the tests. Consequently, we would use a directional test. The null hypothesis says that the pre-test exceeds or is greater than the post-test:

H_0: $\mu_{pre\text{-}test} \geq \mu_{post\text{-}test}$

The alternative hypothesis says that the mean of the pre-test is less than the mean of the post-test:

H_1: $\mu_{pre\text{-}test} < \mu_{post\text{-}test}$

The confidence interval of the mean of the differences was 9.66 to 19.84. Because 0.0 is not between these two values, 0.0 is not included in the confidence interval, and we can thus reject the null hypothesis. The *t* test often allows us to say more than that.

We can test the null hypothesis by finding the observed *t* using Equation 9.2:

$$t_{obs} = \frac{1.75}{3.20/\sqrt{4}} = 9.22$$

This *t* has three degrees of freedom because only four differences are being examined; thus, the critical one-tailed *t* ($\alpha = .05$) is 2.353. (See Table A.2.) Clearly, the null hypothesis can be rejected because t_{obs} exceeds t_{crit} for the .05 level. The other critical values of *t* in the table show that we can reject the null hypothesis at the .005 level because 9.22 exceeds critical *t* for the .005 level, 5.841. When analyses are done on a computer, an exact probability is given. For this value of observed *t*, the exact probability to three decimal places is .003. Which probability should be reported? It is correct to report $p < .05$, but researchers are now encouraged to report the exact probability when available. Thus, in the announcement of findings, it would be better to report $p < .005$ if using table A.2 in the appendix, or $p \leq .003$ if a computer result is available.

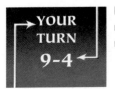

YOUR TURN 9-4

In the hypothetical example we have been using, people are given a training workshop on formatting a document. Why would a directional test be appropriate for a study of the effectiveness of training people to format a document?   ■

THE CONTRIBUTION OF THE *t* TEST

At this point, you might well be asking "What do we learn from the *t* test that we did not already learn from the 95% confidence interval?" Let's see if we can answer that. There are two aspects to the contribution of the *t* test. First, many researchers use directional hypotheses when they use *t* tests. It is very easy to compare the observed *t* to the directional *t* critical given in the *t* table. Although this can be done with confidence intervals, it is a little awkward because confidence intervals are easier to use with *non*directional hypothesis tests. The second contribution of the *t* test is that we can easily compare oberved *t* to a variety of values of *t* critical. Using the last example, the t_{obs} equaled 9.22, which clearly exceeded the t_{crit} of 2.353 at the .05 level. It also exceeded *t* critical at the .01 level. In fact, if the null hypothesis is true, the probability of a t_{obs} of 9.22 or more with three degrees of freedom is less than .003. If one stopped the analysis with the estimate of the 95% confidence interval, one could reject the null hypothesis, but it would not be easy to calculate the exact probability. The smaller this probability, the more sure we can be that we would be able to reject the null hypothesis if we replicated the research. We return to this point in the next chapter, but we wanted to reassure you that the *t* test does provide information that is not readily available from the confidence interval or the effect size. Investigators are beginning to use confidence intervals and effect size indices more and more, but these approaches to presenting the findings of research have not replaced NHST. We hope that you will come to see them as complementary ways to understand the results of experiments.

WHAT YOU HAVE LEARNED AND THE NEXT STEP

This chapter has presented null hypothesis significance testing as applied when two means are expected to differ. NHST is a key statistical tool that is used widely in many disciplines.

- The strategy underlying NHST is to posit tentatively that there is no difference between two population means, what is called the *null hypothesis.*

- When the null hypothesis can be rejected, researchers can announce that the difference between the two means is statistically significant.

- Behavioral researchers do not want to reject null hypotheses without sufficient justification. Thus, the null hypothesis is rejected only when the observed difference in means is so large that it would be quite unlikely to have occurred only by chance (i.e., by sampling error). The value of .05 (i.e., alpha = .05) is by convention typically used to define an unlikely probability of a difference if only chance is operating and assuming the null hypothesis is true.

- When using the 95% confidence interval for the difference between two means, we can reject H_0 if 0.0 is not within the interval. If 0.0 is within the interval, we are left in a state of uncertainty about the difference between the population means.

- Compared to using the 95% confidence interval, a null hypothesis can be tested in a more direct and more informative method using a *t* test for two means.

- If t_{obs} is larger than t_{crit} one can reject the null hypothesis and announce that the difference between the two means is statistically significant. Rejecting the null hypothesis does not mean that we know for certain that the null hypothesis is false; we do know that, if it were true, the observed results are quite improbable.

- A directional alternative hypothesis is more appropriate than a nondirectional one when we have a definite expectation (prediction) about the difference between the two means.

- The larger *t* observed is compared to the critical values of *t,* the more confidence we have that an exact replication of the study would provide data that would permit rejecting the null hypothesis. Or, in other words, the *t* test permits us to learn how far outside the 95% confidence interval the observed difference lies.

- The *t* test is based on two assumptions: that the population distributions are normal and that the standard deviations are equal. However, experience has shown that, even when these assumptions are violated, the results of the *t* test can be trusted. Severe violations of the assumptions may suggest that transformations ought to be considered before conducting a *t* test.

- The use of the *t* for repeated measures and matched groups designs was adapted from the *t* test for independent groups.

Null hypothesis significance testing has been misinterpreted in a number of ways. In Chapter 10, we discuss correct interpretations, statistical issues in planning research, and how to present confidence intervals, effect sizes, and null hypothesis tests when announcing findings (the *A* in the I-D-E-A model).

Key Concepts

null hypothesis	nondirectional alternative hypothesis	t critical, t_{crit}
alternative hypothesis	H_0 versus H_1	statistically significant
rejection regions	t test for independent groups	directional alternative hypothesis
alpha level	t observed, t_{obs}	t test for repeated measures

Answers to *Your Turn* Questions

9-1. In criminal trials, the U.S. legal system treats convicting innocent parties as more serious than letting a guilty person go unpunished.

9-2. Katie should point out that 4 lies outside the 95% confidence interval and thus is very unlikely to reflect the population value.

9-3. The t_{obs} (28) = 6.36, t_{crit} = 2.048 (.05), 2.467 (.02), 2.763 (.01), and 3.674 (.001). Thus, we can reject the null hypothesis, $p < .001$.

9-4. In this case, we expect that training will improve skill level.

Analyzing and Interpreting Data: Problems and Exercises

1. State in words the null and alternative hypotheses for Terri's study of learning in silence or with conversations going on.

2. NHST is said to be analogous to the legal process that the American judicial system uses to try criminals. Explain.

3. If we start with the presumption of innocence in U.S. criminal trials, the burden of proof lies on the prosecution who must prove guilt; the accused need not speak. In the context of science, if the researcher starts with the null hypothesis, who has the burden of proof? (Hint: recall the parallels between NHST and criminal trials.)

4. Draw a sampling distribution of the difference between the means of two samples. Indicate where the rejection regions would be for a nondirectional test of the null hypothesis.

5. Explain the difference between a directional alternative hypothesis and a nondirectional test of the null hypothesis. In your answer, show examples of both null and alternative hypotheses in terms of population means for these situations.

6. Show the relative sizes of two sampling distributions for means of samples randomly selected from the same population when sample K is four times larger than sample Q.

7. Why are the null and alternative hypotheses written in terms of population means when researchers never know population means?

8. What is the effect of sample size on the t test for independent groups?

9. What are two major assumptions underlying t tests?

10. If the assumptions for the t test are not clearly met, under what conditions would a researcher feel confident to proceed to use t tests anyway?

11. Could one analyze a repeated measures design (such as that of Terri in the introduction of this chapter) using the independent groups t test? What is the problem with using the independent groups t test with repeated measurements?

12. Choose the two experiments that violate an assumption of the t test. For each experiment, the dependent variable could be as low as 10 and as high as 50.

		M	s	n
A.	Group one	34.78	18.92	26
	Group two	45.20	4.82	13
B.	Group one	49.50	3.54	50
	Group two	38.99	5.34	50
C.	Group one	12.75	5.91	10
	Group two	15.62	7.28	11

If you cannot find two experiments that violate an assumption, here is a hint: don't forget *inspection*. Also, try finding the 95% confidence interval of the mean of each group; do they all make sense?

13. Test the null hypothesis that the population means are the same using an independent groups t test. Use a nondirectional alternative hypothesis.
    (a) Begin by stating clearly the null and alternative hypotheses in terms of population means.
    (b) Show work and state the outcome of your test in terms of rejecting or not rejecting the null hypothesis at the .05 level.

	Experimental	Control
M	15.67	12.87
s	6.00	5.50
n	24	24

14. (a) For the data in problem #13, calculate the 95% confidence interval for the difference between two means.
    (b) Based on your calculations, should the null hypothesis be rejected? (Be sure to explain your reasoning.)
    (c) Is your conclusion the same or different than that which is reached when conducting an independent t test for the same data? (See problem #13.)

15. Attitudes toward abolishing the death penalty were examined for a sample of economics majors and a sample of English majors; higher scores indicated a greater level of opposition. The scores could range from 5 through 25.
    (a) Test the null hypothesis that the two groups of majors have the same attitudes.
    (b) Calculate the effect size.
    (c) List the assumptions of the t test and comment on why you think that the assumptions were met.
    Economics: 10, 12, 6, 7, 20, 24, 11, 15, 11, 9, 12, 9, 11, 14, 8
    English: 13, 16, 18, 12, 24, 18, 20, 19, 22, 21

16. It was hypothesized that behavioral science majors who had studied statistics and research methods would be more skilled at detecting methodology errors in research reported in newspapers. The researcher found 10 reports on faddish topics, all of which described research that contained clear errors in how the data were handled. He developed a multiple choice test (five items per story, 50 items total). He then had students read the reports and answer five questions on each report. Higher scores meant more errors were spotted. He tested senior behavioral science majors and senior history majors. He found the following means and standard deviations:

	M	s	n
Behavioral science	34.32	10.23	52
History	28.67	12.35	38

(a) Should the researcher use a directional or nondirectional alternative hypothesis?
(b) Perform the appropriate t test and state your conclusion.
(c) What is the effect size?

17. An educational psychologist was investigating a self-paced Internet course. The idea was that the responses of the students would determine how fast the course would go. For those students who were getting questions correct, the program would automatically skip sections. The researcher in-

tended to randomly assign students to take either the self-paced course or a more traditional Internet style. The material to be learned was the same. He decided to match participants before randomly assigning them to course type. He matched participants in sex and experience with Internet learning. His data are as follows. (Note that each "pair" refers to two individuals with the same sex and same level of experience. The scores for the traditional Internet course and self-paced course are for the two individual's performance, respectively.)

	Sex	Experience	Score on Final Internet	Self-Paced
Pair 1	F	Very High	92	94
Pair 2	M	Very High	95	96
Pair 3	M	Moderate	87	88
Pair 4	F	Moderate	91	90
Pair 5	F	Slight	85	89
Pair 6	M	Slight	88	89
Pair 7	M	Slight	90	89
Pair 8	F	None	80	85
Pair 9	F	None	82	87

(a) What type of t test is appropriate?
(b) Is a nondirectional or directional alternative hypothesis appropriate?
(c) Perform the appropriate t test and state your conclusion based on a rejection level of .05.

18. What do you learn when performing a t test that is not learned easily when calculating confidence intervals for the difference between two means?

19. Rose hypothesized that 11- and 12-year-old boys acted out in school because they were socially insecure. She developed a social skills training program on the assumption that, if the boys ($N = 46$) were more skilled socially, they would be more at ease, act out less, and do better in their studies. She then randomly assigned half ($n = 23$) of the boys to the standard punishment (detention after school) and half ($n = 23$) to training by an assis-

tant coach on basic courtesy. Rose used two dependent variables: the boys' reaction (high ratings were more favorable) to the punishment (detention versus social skills training) and the boys' grades in the next grading period (A = 4). Her data were as follows:

	Rating of the Punishment		Grades in Next Grade Period	
	M	s	M	s
Social skills training	8.4	2.7	2.1	0.4
Detention	4.3	2.3	2.2	0.5

(a) Should Rose make directional or nondirectional hypotheses?
(b) Test the null hypotheses.
(c) Find and evaluate the effect sizes.

20. Sarah developed memory exercises to help maintain memory skills that could be used with elderly people by those who provide care for nursing home residents. She developed a procedure using either new material or material based on the residents' personal lives. Then, they were all tested on new material relevant to their current nursing home. Sarah hypothesized that memory exercises based on new material would help the residents learn new material faster. Residents were randomly assigned to one of the two types of memory exercises. Their scores on the memory test were as follows:

Memory Exercise Type
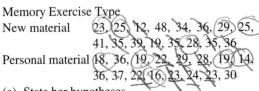
New material   23, 25, 12, 48, 34, 36, 29, 25, 41, 35, 39, 19, 35, 28, 35, 36
Personal material 18, 36, 19, 22, 29, 28, 19, 14, 36, 37, 22, 16, 23, 24, 23, 30

(a) State her hypotheses.
(b) Inspect the data.
(c) Complete the analysis. A complete analysis includes a 95% confidence interval for the difference of the two means, an effect size, and NHST.

Answers to Odd-Numbered Problems

1. The null hypothesis would state that learning is the same whether students study with conversations or silence. The alternative hypothesis states that learning is better under one of the conditions.

3. The burden of proof lies on the researcher. The researcher must produce sufficient evidence to support rejecting the null hypothesis, which stands until proven wrong.

5. A nondirectional test is conducted when the researcher has no definite hypothesis about the direction of the difference between the population means, and a difference in either direction is meaningful. The null and alternative hypotheses for a nondirectional test are: H_0: $\mu_1 = \mu_2$; H_1: $\mu_1 \neq \mu_2$. To conduct a directional test, the researcher must have a definite hypothesis about the direction of the difference between the two means. Both the null hypothesis and the alternative hypothesis are expressed differently than when a nondirectional test is conducted. For example, if the researcher hypothesizes that the first mean is greater than the second mean, the null and alternative hypotheses would be: H_0: $\mu_1 \leq \mu_2$; H_1: $\mu_1 > \mu_2$. If an examination of the sample means reveals that the difference is in the opposite direction than what was hypothesized, then a t test should not be conducted; the results clearly do not support the hypothesis.

7. Even though we do not know the population values, we are interested in samples because they provide estimates of population values. Thus, although we work with sample means, we are able to say something about population values as long as the samples represent the populations in which we are interested.

9. Two major assumptions underlying t tests are (a) the distribution of score values is normal for both populations, and (b) the standard deviations (i.e., variability) of the two populations are similar.

11. Yes, one could use the independent groups t test with repeated measures. However, it would be unwise. Compared to using the independent groups approach, the repeated measures approach using difference scores provides a way to examine the effect of the independent variable with more precision. The standard deviation of difference scores is smaller than the standard deviation of the dependent variable taking the conditions of the experiment separately. The higher the standard deviation, the less precise the estimate of the mean.

13. (a) H_0: $\mu_e = \mu_c$; H_1: $\mu_e \neq \mu_c$

(b) $s_{\text{pooled}} = \sqrt{[23\,(36.00) + 23\,(30.25)]/46]} = 5.755$

$\sqrt{[1/24 + 1/24]} = 0.289$

$t_{\text{obs}} = \dfrac{15.67 - 12.87}{5.755\,(0.289)} = 1.6.86$; which is compared to t_{crit} $(df = 46) = 2.02$

Therefore, do not reject null hypothesis, $p > .05$

15. (a) $t\,(23) = 3.51, p = .002$. Reject the null hypothesis that the population means are equal.

(b) $g = 1.45$

(c) Major assumptions of the t test are that the two populations are normally distributed and that the variability in the two populations is similar. Stem-and-leaf plots show that the scores of the economic majors are slightly positively skewed; however, the standard deviations of the samples are not all that different (4.80 vs. 3.80). The t test is robust in that it will still work well given these minor deviations from these assumptions.

17. (a) A t test for matched groups (repeated measures) is appropriate.

(b) A directional hypothesis is appropriate because the researcher hypothesizes that the newly designed self-paced course will be superior to the traditional course (and a finding in the opposite direction would not be of interest).

(c) $t\,(8) = 2.45, p < .025$. Reject the null hypothesis. The critical value of t for a one-tailed test with eight degrees of freedom is 1.86 (.05) and 2.306 (.025).

19. (a) Rose should make directional hypotheses because the new procedure is supposed to improve the students' reaction to the discipline and help them do better in school.

(b) Reactions to the discipline:

$s_{\text{pooled}} = \sqrt{[22\,(2.7^2) + 22\,(2.3^2)]/44]} = 2.508$

The sample size term $= \sqrt{[1/23 + 1/23]} = 0.295$

$t_{\text{obs}} = \dfrac{8.4 - 4.3}{2.508\,(0.295)} = 5.54$; which is compared to t_{crit} $(df = 40) = 3.551$ $(\alpha = .0005)$

Reject the null hypothesis, $p < .0005$, or to three decimal places, $p < .001$. We use t critical for 40 degrees of freedom because the t table does not include the value for 44 degrees of freedom. We use the directional value because the alternative hypothesis was directional.

School grades: Note that the children in the old approach did better than the children in the innovative approach. Because Rose found the reverse of what she hypothesized, using a directional alternative hypothesis suggests that she should not calculate the value of t for school grades. That is, if one uses a directional alternative hypothesis, the t test is done only if the group mean that was expected to be larger is, in fact, larger than the other mean. (See page 204.)

(c) $g = 4.1/2.508 = 1.64$. This is very large.

She would not calculate g for the school grades variable because what was observed was the reverse of what was desired. But here is the value anyway: $g = -0.1/0.453 = -0.22$. The minus sign indicates that the reverse of what was expected was observed.

 Go to http://psychology.wadsworth.com/courses/statistics/ and test your knowledge of this chapter by taking the online quiz. Another resource to check is the online workshops that provide a step-by-step guide through a number of topics at http://psychology.wadsworth.com/workshops/workshops.html.

CHAPTER 10

Interpreting and Announcing Results

NHST [null hypothesis significance testing] is easily misunderstood and misused.

Nickerson (2000, p. 241)

INTRODUCTION

Null hypothesis significance testing (NHST) is an important tool to use with data that are affected by sampling error. Data used in psychological, medical, educational, management, and marketing research must be analyzed with sampling error in mind. We have argued that NHST helps us to remain aware of sampling error and protects us from claiming too much for our data. However, NHST has been misunderstood by many who have used it (e.g., Nickerson, 2000). Here are several examples of the misuse of NHST.

- Twila was serving an internship in an advertising firm. Sam, another intern, claimed that male and female users of an Internet service rated the quality of service equally favorably. Clients had been asked to provide ratings on a 10-point scale. Twila said that she thought men and women were not equally satisfied with the service. Sam pulled 20 surveys at random from those returned to the firm (12 men and 8 women). He said, "Look, I don't have time to analyze all of the surveys. This random sample can be used to see if I am right." Twila calculated a t based on an independent groups design. The mean user rating for men ($n = 12$) was 7.9 with a standard deviation of 2.02; the women ($n = 8$) in the sample rated the service 7.0 with a standard deviation of 2.00. She found a 95% confidence interval for the difference between two means; it was -1.13 to $+2.93$ and included zero. She found a t_{obs} of 0.942. The t_{crit} for 18 degrees of freedom with alpha = .05 (two-tailed) is ±2.101. She could not reject the hypothesis that the population means represented by these groups were the same. Sam insisted that the results of Twila's analysis indicated that men and women were equally as satisfied with the service. Is this conclusion valid?

- Marcia is a graduate student in a health psychology program. She conducted a study for her master's thesis that compared knowledge of drug facts after participating in two different behavioral programs to reduce the symptoms of migraine headaches. Working with a physician at a large teaching hospital that also had a pain management clinic, volunteer patients were randomly assigned to the two different programs. (Patients were informed of the exploratory nature of the research, and all gave their consent to be randomly assigned.) The dependent variable was a measure of symptom frequency over a six-week period during and after program participation. Because of the size of the hospital, she was able to obtain data from many patients. The results of her independent t test produced a t_{obs} of 2.33. The probability of her observed t, assuming the null hypothesis was true, was less than .001. She concluded that this statistically significant finding showed that the difference between mean scores was important enough for her to recommend to the hospital administrators that they adopt the program with the lower mean symptom frequency. Does Marcia have enough information to make such a recommendation?

- Vince read a report describing how writing about stressful or fearful experiences helps people to cope with such negative experiences and to live happier and more productive lives. He found a report by a famous psychologist that was based on a study with 80 people who had been randomly assigned to write about problems ($n = 40$) or to write about their career goals (n = 40). Six months later, the group that wrote about problems was on the average less depressed and happier than the group that wrote about careers. The researcher reported that the null hypothesis was rejected, *p* = .04. Vince was intrigued, but thought he should replicate the study before beginning his honor's thesis on a related topic. Working with a counseling center, he found 15 people who would participate in a replication of the study on the effects of writing. Vince randomly assigned them to write about career goals (n = 8) or about stressful and fearful experiences (n = 7) using the same directions used in the original study. Six months later, he also used the same measures as those used in the original study. Vince found that the independent groups t for his two means was rather small, *t*(13) = 1.35. His observed *t* was less than the critical value. He concluded that the published study must have been a statistical fluke because he could not replicate it. Which study is correct?

Completing the statistical calculations given in Chapters 8 and 9 does not end our work. After finding a confidence interval, an effect size, and the probability associated with the value of the observed *t*, it is critical to make correct interpretations of the findings. This chapter draws a number of threads together with the goal of helping you make appropriate interpretations of your work. Several common misinterpretations of NHST have hampered the development of the behavioral sciences (Meehl, 1978; Rossi, 1997; Schmidt, 1996), and we discuss these misinterpretations. We also provide an illustration of a complete report announcing (the *A* in the I-D-E-A model) research findings from a study comparing two means. We show the complementarity of the three key tools we have introduced: confidence intervals, effect size, and NHST.

CORRECTLY INTERPRETING NULL HYPOTHESIS SIGNIFICANCE TESTING

"Statistically significant" means that the pattern of data found is unlikely to be due to chance. In the context of this chapter, we say that a result is *statistically significant* when two means differ enough that we feel confident in concluding that the difference is bigger than we would have expected if the reason for the difference was only chance. In a real sense, statistical significance is about the numbers, not the interpretation of the numbers. The following sections address some of the most common misinterpretations of NHST.

Statistically Significant Does Not Mean Causal

A statistically significant finding does not mean that the cause of the difference is understood. Inferring that an independent variable caused a dependent variable is an issue of research design, not an issue of statistical analysis. Poorly designed studies can easily produce significant results (in fact, maybe even more easily than well designed ones). Moreover, studies comparing natural groups do not allow causal claims.

Suppose that we were to discover that students who live in dormitories get higher grades than do those who live off campus. Even if the difference between the two means is statistically significant, the finding should not be interpreted as implying that grades will improve if all students live in campus housing. These two natural groups of students will differ in many ways: students decide on the basis of their finances, desired lifestyle, and convenience whether to live in a college residence hall or to live at home.

Using natural groups is often necessary because it is not always possible to assign individuals randomly to groups—for example, to live in a residence hall or at home, or to be male or female, or to be married or unmarried. This means that, even if one group does better (or worse) compared to the other group, we cannot conclude that it is the known difference between the groups that explains the finding.

On the other hand, in many research situations, participants can be randomly assigned to groups. In the previous chapter, we discussed Serena who had permission to randomly assign students to two forms of therapy. Recall that random assignment has the goal of establishing essentially equivalent groups prior to the introduction of an independent variable. (See Chapter 1.) The students in Serena's experiment began as one population; after the treatment, they are now members of two populations because they have been treated with different forms of therapy. If they have different levels of test anxiety after therapy, and the experiment was properly conducted, it is fair to conclude that the different forms of therapy are responsible. Serena may draw a causal conclusion if the only way in which the samples differ (at the end of the experiment) is in terms of what form of therapy they had, that is, if all other differences have been controlled. A random groups design is quite different from a natural groups design, such as our dormitory versus residents example. Only after carefully examining the methods used to test a difference between two means do we dare draw a casual conclusion, and even then we do so cautiously because a research study can go wrong in many ways.

Statistically Significant Does Not Mean Important

Just because a finding is statistically significant does not mean that the finding is important. In the previous chapter, we discussed Dr. Merton's study comparing the north and south sides of a large school district. His samples were huge. Large samples make the standard error very small and, consequently, the value of t observed large. Recall, however, that his effect size, g, was tiny (0.03). The school board probably has more pressing issues to think about than to discuss Dr. Merton's finding. Because the very word *significant* seems to mean *important,* some journal editors urge researchers to always write *statistically significant,* not just *significant* (Nickerson, 2000).

Of course, Dr. Merton also used natural groups. As we have seen, one may validly draw causal connections between an independent variable and a dependent variable only when all other possible causes have been controlled. Other causes were not controlled in Dr. Merton's research. If there had been an important difference between the two sections of his district, he could not be sure of what caused it because any number of differences might be responsible. Some methodologists remind us that almost any two groups will differ on most variables to some small degree (Meehl, 1978). When two-tailed (nondirectional) tests are used and many variables are examined with huge sample sizes, statistically significant differences will inevitably appear. However, the effect sizes can be trivially small; Dr. Merton should not call a news conference about the difference between the north and south sides of the school district he manages. *Given a large enough sample size, statistically significant results are easily obtained even for very small effects.* These small effects may not be important.

Because Marcia found a statistically significant difference in mean reported symptoms between programs aimed at alleviating migraine headaches does not mean that the difference is important. We will want to see the effect size associated with her difference. Moreover, a decision about what makes for an important difference rests on such factors as cost and the availability of resources, as well as risk and inconvenience to the subjects. If Marcia's experiment yielded a small effect size and the cost of the superior program was greater and produced greater discomfort to the patients, then the difference may not be judged to be important. *Statistically significant* does not necessarily mean *important*.

Statistically Significant Does Not Mean the Results Can Be Generalized

Even if we conduct a careful experiment, we cannot assume that the findings will apply to other groups of people or to other situations. A finding applies to only the population from which the samples were selected and to the conditions of testing. Our point is not that every finding must be replicated in every state of the United States, in every country in the world, and with all racial groups before we believe it. But we do need to think about group differences before claiming how widely the findings apply. Here are three examples from the field of clinical psychology to illustrate the point.

- Cognitive therapy may work well among college students because they are more reflective than a less-educated sector of society; less reflective individuals may not respond as well to this type of therapy.

- Psychotherapy in the United States is usually focused on individuals; however, in some cultures, family ties may be seen as superseding individual rights. Counseling techniques that assume an individual focus may be ineffective in a family-focused culture.

- Group therapy may be an efficient approach in a society whose members talk freely about feelings, even feelings that are not socially desirable. In contrast, in a society that highly values personal privacy and control, group therapy might not be appropriate.

The degree to which results can be applied to people not in the populations from which the samples were drawn—or the degree to which similar (but different) treatments may work to produce a change—is a question of **external validity.** Before concluding that a statistically significant finding is meaningful for the population or situation that you are interested in, there must be some evidence for the external validity of a finding. External validity cannot be assumed.

Statistically Significant Does Not Mean Replication Is Assured

This caution is a tough one to understand, so let's introduce a concrete example.

Imagine that we have a t observed that is just barely larger than the critical t. Here is such a calculation:

$$t_{\text{obs}} = \frac{M_t - M_c}{s_{\text{pooled}} \sqrt{(1/n_t + 1/n_c)}} = \frac{22.69 - 20.95}{3.32 \sqrt{(1/22 + 1/20)}} = \frac{1.74}{1.026} = 1.696$$

For 40 degrees of freedom and alpha equals .05, t_{crit} is 1.684 (one-tailed). In this case, the researcher may correctly reject the null hypothesis and announce that the sample means differ ($p < .05$). The results are statistically significant; although note that the observed t just barely exceeded the critical value.

Now imagine that the experiments were replicated exactly with two additional groups drawn from the same population as the initial experiment. Would the difference between the two means be (a) bigger than, (b) exactly the same size as, or (c) smaller than the difference observed in the original experiment?

Well, due to sampling error, (b) is very unlikely; we know that the differences will vary from study to study. However, there is no reason to chose option (a) over (c) or vice versa because options (a) and (c) are equally likely. (Yes, it was a trick question.) Let's examine why this must the case.

We know after the first experiment that the difference between the means was 1.74. Let's assume for a moment that 1.74 is the actual difference between the two populations, one treated and one untreated (the control). Given this assumption, we should expect that, if many more pairs of samples were drawn, each the same size as in the original study, the overall mean of the differences between two sample means would be 1.74. This must be true if the real difference between the population means is 1.74. The distribution of differences between means based on randomly selected samples will center around the true mean population difference.

In this case, we know that a difference of 1.74 is just barely statistically significant according to the previous calculation. (Remember that we are assuming that 1.74 is the real difference between the population means.) We also know that, due to random sampling, half the differences would be greater than 1.74 and half would be smaller than 1.74. That is, we expect a normal distribution of differences between means centered around 1.74. The half smaller than 1.74 would yield findings that were not statistically significant (assuming our estimate of error remains the same). Therefore, a replication of this experiment is just as likely to produce a smaller difference between the two means as it is to produce a larger difference compared to the original finding.

We cannot say that half of all replications of *each* two-sample study that was just barely statistically significant (that is, $p = .05$) will be nonsignificant. In other words, we are not predicting what will happen for a particular study. Any specific original study could have produced an underestimate of the true difference between the two populations; if so, replications will tend to produce larger differences and, thus, be statistically significant more than half the time. On the other hand, the finding of a specific first study might have been an overestimate of the true difference; if so, replications will tend to produce smaller differences and, thus, not be statistically significant. What we can say is that, over many different studies each of which produced a t observed that equaled the t critical ($p = .05$) value, only half of the replications will yield a t observed that is statistically significant.

We raise this point because students often leave statistics courses believing that, if a finding is statistically significant ($p < .05$), the chances of an exact replication being statistically significant are roughly .95. Instead, over the long run, if t observed is very close to t critical (that is, $p = .05$), the chances are only .50 that the finding will replicate. Note that, when we read a report in which the probability of t_{obs} was given simply as less than .05 (that is, $p < .05$), we do not know (at least without closer examination) how close t_{obs} was to t_{crit}. It could be that t_{obs} was just barely larger than t_{crit}.

The .50 figure is based on the assumption that the replications are exact replications of the original study. If a smaller number of participants were used in the replication compared to the original study, there will be an even smaller chance of rejecting the null hypotheses. It seems likely that Vince was fooled by his smaller samples when he sought to replicate the coping effect of writing about unpleasant experiences.

In general, statistical significance does not assure us that a replication will be statistically significant. If in the original study an observed difference is just barely within the critical region, the odds of replicating may be only .50. If smaller samples are used in the replication, the likelihood of a statistically significant replication is even smaller. If a larger number of participants are used compared to the original study, the chances of being able to reject a false null hypothesis increase.

Our findings do permit us to say something more specific about the chances of a statistically significant replication than what we may have implied thus far. *The larger the value of t observed the more likely it is that replications will permit rejecting the null hypothesis.* When we say that the larger is *t* observed the more likely the null hypothesis will be rejected, we are referring to what happens across many replications of experiments yielding findings with a specific probability (Greenwald, Gonzalez, Harris, & Guthrie, 1996; Posavac, 2002). We are unable to know what will happen with replications of a particular experiment. (We will return to this difficult point.)

Figure 10.1 shows the relationship between the probability of a t_{obs} being found when testing a null hypothesis and the probability that an exact replication will permit rejecting the null hypothesis at the .05 level. To use the graph, first find the probability of t_{obs} from a *t* test on the x (horizontal) axis and then read the probability that a replication will be statistically significant on the y (vertical) axis. For example, a t_{obs} of 2.62 (*df* = 120) is statistically significant at the .01 level. The likelihood of replicating such findings and being able to reject the null hypothesis at the .05 level is 0.74, roughly three-fourths of the time.

FIGURE 10.1 ■ The probability that a *t* test of an exact replication of an independent groups experiment would be statistically significant (*p* ≤ .05) as a function of the probability of the observed *t* found in the initial study.

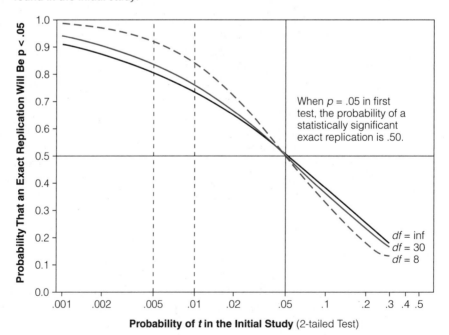

Probability That an Exact Replication Will Be p < .05

When *p* = .05 in first test, the probability of a statistically significant exact replication is .50.

df = inf
df = 30
df = 8

Probability of *t* in the Initial Study (2-tailed Test)

Let us emphasize again an important, but difficult, point. Figure 10.1 provides information about findings in general, not about every experiment. We can say that, across all two-group experiments that were statistically significant at the .01 level, exact replications of about three-quarters of them will be statistically significant in the same direction at the .05 level. The focus of Figure 10.1 is on many studies with a specific probability of t_{obs}, not on many replications of a specific study.

Use Figure 10.1 to estimate the probability that an exact replication of a *t* test with 30 degrees of freedom that led to a probability of .01 would produce a *t* observed that would exceed the critical value of *t* at the .05 alpha level. ∎

Not Significant Does Not Mean Zero Difference

We have showed that large sample sizes can lead to rejecting a null hypothesis even when the effect size is small. On the other hand, small samples may mean that the null hypothesis cannot be rejected. Thus, even when a difference between two means does not lead to a statistically significant finding, we cannot conclude that the experiment led to *no* differences between the groups. Small samples could mean that we don't have a sufficiently large sample (i.e., not enough independent witnesses) to detect the difference that does exist between the populations.

For a correct understanding of statistical significance, it is essential to appreciate the inverse relationship between sample size and the value of the standard error of the difference between two means. In other words, for a particular dependent variable and population, as sample size goes up, standard errors go down. As standard errors go down, *t* observed increases. Please don't say to yourself, "I should remember this." Instead, look at the formula for *t* observed and see how the values are related; once you see the patterns, then you are less likely to forget this point. Consider again the formula for comparing two means from independent groups:

$$t_{obs} = \frac{M_1 - M_2}{s_{pooled} \sqrt{(1/n_1 + 1/n_2)}}$$

The larger the samples, the smaller the right side of the denominator $[\sqrt{(1/n_1 + 1/n_2)}]$. The smaller the denominator, the larger *t* observed will be. The larger the observed *t*, the more likely the null hypothesis will be rejected.

The implication of these relationships reveals an important truth about statistics: a *t* test of a difference between two means is affected by sampling error. If groups are small enough, any hypothesized effect will not be statistically significant *even when there is a real difference between the population means*. Researchers fool themselves if they believe that nonsignificance means no difference. It could simply be that an actual effect of the experiment was obscured by sampling error. When sampling error leads to nonsignificance, a **Type II error** has occurred. Type II errors occur when there is a real population difference, that is, the null hypothesis (H_0) is really false, but the analysis does not detect the actual difference. (Type II errors are discussed in greater detail later in this chapter.) Although we never know for sure when nonsignificance reflects a Type II error, after several replications, each showing small effect sizes, we become quite confident that H_0 is true or at least that the effect size is so small that H_0 might as well be true in a practical sense. It is very important to remember that *testing small samples raises the chances of making a Type II error.*

Without understanding the relationship between sample size and rejecting null hypotheses, Twila was unsure of how to handle Sam's claim that male and female customers were reporting equal satisfaction levels. Here was her analysis for an independent groups t test:

$$t_{obs} = \frac{M_1 - M_2}{s_{pooled} \sqrt{(1/n_1 + 1/n_2)}}$$

$$t_{obs} = \frac{7.9 - 7.0}{2.014 \sqrt{(1/10 + 1/8)}} = 0.942$$

If these small samples had accurately reflected the values of the population means (i.e., the difference between the two population means equals 0.90), larger sample sizes would probably have led to a larger observed t. Of course, any difference between sample means might be very different from the population mean difference. However, if Sam's sample sizes had been 50 and 50 for male and female clients, respectively, and had produced roughly the same means and standard deviations, the observed t would have been larger and statistically significant, $t(98) = 2.24, p < .05$. Twila could then have told Sam that in the population the mean of the ratings by men was very likely to be larger than the mean of the ratings by women. Note that the only thing that changed in these two situations was the sample size.

YOUR TURN 10-2

What would the value of t_{obs} have been if Sam had chosen 30 male clients and 30 female clients, assuming that these larger samples had the same means and standard deviations as had the initial small samples?   ∎

Sam made the error of thinking that, if a difference between two sample means based on small samples was not statistically significant, he could conclude that his assertion was true (that there really was no difference between the population means). This type of mistake is called "proving the null hypothesis." *When a statistical test is not statistically significant, the proper conclusion is that we remain uncertain.* Twila's analysis did not produce evidence that Sam was wrong, but she did not produce evidence that he was correct either.

The misinterpretations just discussed are related to an important issue that we have only touched on previously. When interpreting findings we need to remember the two kinds of errors that we can make in statistical analyses: (a) we could conclude that two means are different when they are not, and (b) we could conclude that we cannot reject the null hypothesis when the populations really do differ. Understanding these two kinds of errors is critical in avoiding misinterpretations. We turn to a discussion of these two kinds of errors now.

TYPE I AND TYPE II ERRORS

Testing a null hypothesis requires a dichotomous decision. With all decisions, one can make two kinds of errors. One could reject H_0 when it is true. Testing at alpha equal to .05 means that, even when H_0 is true, statistical conclusions will be wrong 5% of the time. The other error occurs when H_0 is truly false, but the t observed does not exceed the critical value of t at the .05 level (from Table A.2). An analogy might help to make these errors less abstract.

FIGURE 10.2 ■ Four possible outcomes when a person accused of a crime is brought to trial.

What Is Decided	True Behavior of the Defendant	
	Did the crime	Did not do the crime
Defendant is guilty	Correct decision	Incorrect decision
Defendant is not guilty	Incorrect decision	Correct decision

Consider the legal decision of guilty/not guilty that we introduced in a previous chapter. As shown in Figure 10.2, a person accused of a crime either did or did not do it. Notice that two types of errors are given in the figure. If the defendant did not commit the crime but is convicted of it anyway, an error has been made. On the other hand, if the defendant did commit the crime, but the decision is that the evidence was insufficient to convict, an error has been made.[1] We would rather not make either error, but, until we learn how to get perfect evidence and learn how to evaluate it flawlessly, these errors will plague us. Note that these two errors are not seen as equally harmful. Societies have differed in how these two legal errors are treated. Many authoritarian societies have viewed failing to convict criminals as the worse error, and prosecutors in those societies have less concern about jailing innocent people than do leaders in other societies. The tradition in Britain and the United States has been the reverse: it is believed to be worse to punish an innocent person than to fail to punish a guilty person. In the late 1700s, Sir William Blackstone said, "It is better that ten guilty persons escape than one innocent person suffer."

Testing the null hypothesis can be presented in a way that is quite similar to testing a person's innocence. Figure 10.3 contrasts the decisions made after a null hypothesis is

FIGURE 10.3 ■ Four possible outcomes when a *t* test is conducted.

What Is Decided	Actual Situation	
	Null is false	Null is true
Reject the null hypothesis	Correct decision (Power)	Incorrect decision (Type I error)
Do not reject the null hypothesis	Incorrect decision (Type II error)	Correct decision

[1] By the way, a variety of mitigating circumstances could mean that a person had a reasonable excuse for breaking a law (for example, "the One Way sign was covered with poison ivy and so I could not see it"). Mitigating circumstances affect the punishment for guilty parties; they do not affect whether a person did or did not commit a certain act. Figure 10.2 refers to whether the person did or did not commit a certain act.

tested with the actual truth of the null hypothesis. The columns refer to the actual truth of the null hypothesis. H_0 is either true or false. The rows refer to the conclusions we make about H_0. The value of t_{obs} either exceeds or does not exceed t_{crit}, so H_0 is rejected or not rejected.

Now look at the cells of Figure 10.3. If the null hypothesis is true (see the right column), then an error is made if it is rejected. This is the error we make when we find that the probability of t_{obs} is less than .05 leading us to reject the null hypothesis, even though, if we had complete information, we would learn that the samples were indeed drawn from the same population and were not affected differently by the independent variable. This error is called a **Type I error**, symbolized as **α (alpha)**. Remember that alpha corresponds to the level of probability defining the region of rejection. (Note that Type I errors can occur only when the null hypothesis correctly reflects reality. The legal analogy is that the accused did not commit the crime, yet is found to be guilty.) The lower cell of the right column refers to correct decisions; H_0 is true and the statistical decision is that H_0 should not be rejected. The legal analogy is that the accused did not commit the crime and the decision is to allow the presumption of innocence to stand. The easiest way to reduce Type 1 errors is to lower the alpha level of a test, for example, from .05 to .01. However, reducing Type 1 errors in this way increases the chances of another error.

A *Type II error,* as initially mentioned, occurs when the independent variable has affected groups of people differently, yet the *t* does not exceed the critical value from the *t* table and one must refrain from rejecting the null hypothesis. A Type II error can occur only when the null hypothesis is indeed false. See the left column. If H_0 is rejected when it is false, this is a correct decision. Legally, this is similar to a guilty verdict when the accused had, in fact, committed the crime. The lower left cell refers to studies in which H_0 is not rejected, yet it really is false. This is similar to a truly guilty party not being declared guilty because insufficient evidence was found to justify rejecting the presumption of innocence. Using a small sample size (i.e., not enough independent witnesses) can lead to Type II errors. Type II errors are symbolized as **β (beta)**.

Just as in the legal setting, we cannot avoid these errors unless we have perfect information. Of course, our data are always flawed or limited. Which error is less acceptable? Researchers in all fields have decided that they do not want to claim that an independent variable is effective when it is not. The idea is that, when a theoretical understanding of some behavioral principle is investigated, we want to use only those findings that we believe are indeed true. If someone misses finding an effect (i.e., makes a Type II error), researchers expect that the finding will be discovered later. Type II errors are much more frequent than Type I errors (e.g., Rosnow & Rosenthal, 1989); however, delay is viewed as less important than cluttering up the research literature with false conclusions. This caution is similar to Blackstone's view that failure to punish ten guilty parties is less important than punishing one innocent person. The easiest way to lower Type II errors is to use larger samples.

Cohen (1988) has shown how to select sample sizes to reduce the probability of making a Type II error if the null is indeed false. Correctly rejecting a false null hypothesis, the lower cell of the left column of Figure 10.3, is called **power**. Power is symbolized as $1 - \beta$ (i.e., 1 minus the probability of a Type II error). The appendix to this textbook contains a fuller discussion of power and the selection of sample sizes to reduce Type II errors.

On the basis of the information given in the stories at the beginning of this chapter, which error seems to be affecting the analyses of Twila and Vince?   ■

It is impossible to know whether we have made a Type I or Type II error in any single analysis. As research is completed, expanded, replicated, and refined, it gradually becomes apparent when sampling error has misled us. We wish we could assure you that there are flawless procedures that we can follow to find the truth about behavioral processes. Seldom does a single study provide final answers. But we believe that better understandings of behavior and mental processes, effective medical treatments, and educational strategies emerge as various studies are conducted. Every study is flawed in some way; however, through dialog among researchers and replications (or near replications) of experiments, these flaws are detected, corrections are made, and knowledge is advanced.

We want to add one point about a difference between theoretical research and applied research. In some cases, it is just as undesirable to miss a potentially beneficial finding (Type II error) as it is to conclude that a real effect was observed when H_0 is true (Type I error). Missing the effect of a new medication (which would be a Type II error) means that some ill people will not be helped. This is an error we would not want to make. Sometimes data are gathered to help in making a choice between action A or B. For example, if a school board must choose a specific reading curriculum, the members must simply take the best evidence they have. It is not possible to withhold judgment until more research is done. In such situations, the relative importance of Type I and Type II errors may change, and researchers may wish to alter the alpha level to change these probabilities. Our emphasis in this book is on the use of statistics in basic research. When doing basic research, it is possible to withhold judgment because Type II errors are not disastrous. If you find yourself being asked to conduct research in an applied agency where an action must be taken, you would be wise to reconsider the cost of making a Type II error. (See Posavac, 1998.)

PULLING IT ALL TOGETHER AND ANNOUNCING RESULTS

Mastering this unit is very crucial in the development of your statistical skills. Several ideas have been introduced that are essential to understanding and using statistics and to understanding the development of additional statistical analyses in the balance of this book. An analysis of a hypothetical experiment is used to pull these ideas together and to provide a model to follow when comparing two means and when announcing results to others.

A Two-Group Experiment on Therapy

Shelley randomly assigned highly test-anxious students to one of two therapy treatments. One was a traditional counseling approach that sought to find developmental problems that led to severe test anxiety The other treatment used a cognitive approach based on the assumption that thoughts and beliefs influence our emotions and that treatment should focus on correcting automatic, but destructive, thinking patterns (Beck, Emery, & Greenberg, 1996). Let's assume that the students all participated in 10 group counseling sessions with experienced leaders who preferred either the cognitive or traditional approach that they were using. Further assume that Shelley used four dependent variables all gathered at the end of treatment: a 50-item test anxiety scale, a self-rating of anxiety that students completed just as they began an actual classroom test, a measure of the level of anxiety that students felt as they began work on a major written assignment, and a questionnaire on the extent to which the students liked their group leader. Because the therapy focused on test anxiety, the first two dependent variables were expected to differ between the two groups. Anxiety about writing papers was not the focus of the therapy, but Shelley reasoned that the effect of therapy for test anxiety might also reduce worry about writing papers. (Note that, for each of these three variables, low scores are better than high scores because low scores indicate less anxiety.) Last, she wanted to be sure that the students in both groups liked their therapists; of course, she wanted the two sets of therapists to be equally well liked.

What is the first step in Shelley's analysis?   ■

Inspecting

That's right: she needs to inspect her data (the *I* in the I-D-E-A model). Figure 10.4 provides a back-to-back stem-and-leaf plot of the primary dependent variable: test anxiety measured at the end of the 10 therapy sessions. What are we looking for? Outliers and klinkers. There do not seem to be any of either. Second, we look for odd distributions. In this case, the data from both groups seem well behaved. Because none of the dependent variables is open ended, we don't have badly skewed distributions. (See Chapter 3.) One would inspect each dependent variable in a similar way as shown in the lower part of Figure 10.4. (Keep in mind that low values on the first three dependent variables indicate less anxiety.) At this point, Shelley would note that the students in the cognitive therapy group seem to be reporting less test anxiety than those in the traditional therapy group.

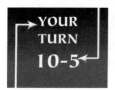

Examine carefully the stem-and-leaf plots in Figure 10.4. What suggests there are differences in the effectiveness of the two forms of therapy?   ■

Describing

With the assurance that the distributions are fairly normal and that no odd scores need attention, Shelley can turn to the next step: description (the *D* in the I-D-E-A model). The medians for test anxiety can be found in Figure 10.4. The median for the cognitive group was 22;

FIGURE 10.4 ■ Back-to-back stem-and-leaf plots for the four dependent variables in the study of therapy for test anxiety.

Test Anxiety Scores

Cognitive Leaf	Stem	Traditional Leaf
	1	
986555	1	57
4433222220	2	124
987	2	6666789
21	3	0022334
	3	7

Rating prior to a test

Cognitive Leaf	Stem	Traditional Leaf
20	6	
75	6	
4200	7	00
88	7	5
4200	8	004
877555	8	57888
0	9	0001
	9	5558

Anxiety when writing a paper

	1	4
9886	1	69
44444333211	2	02444
97	2	556779
2300	3	011124

Liking for the group leader

2	5	226
8888660	6	000268
8888420	7	068
4422	8	002246
00	9	00

in contrast, it was 26 for the traditional approach. In this example, the modes equal the medians. Table 10.1 contains the means and standard deviations for the four dependent variables for both types of treatments. One can see that those treated with cognitive therapy were less anxious than were those treated with a traditional approach. The students who received traditional therapy seem to have liked their therapists a little better than those who received cognitive therapy; however, the standard deviations were rather large compared to the difference between the means.

TABLE 10.1 ■ Description Statistics for the Two Therapy Groups After 10 Sessions of Group Counseling

Measure	Cognitive Therapy Group ($n = 21$)		Traditional Therapy Group ($n = 20$)	
	Mean	Standard Deviation	Mean	Standard Deviation
Test anxiety	22.33	5.05	27.40	5.66
Rating of anxiety	77.57	9.11	85.95	8.01
Anxiety about papers	24.05	4.67	25.55	5.41
Liking for group therapist	70.52	14.29	73.18	10.69

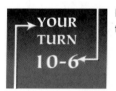

YOUR TURN 10-6

How can Shelley use Table 10.1 to verify that her data do not violate one of the two assumptions on which t tests are based? ■

Estimating

With the descriptive information in Table 10.1, one can calculate all of the statistical indices that we have introduced so far; these terms are needed for the third step: estimating (the *E* in the I-D-E-A model). We would be misleading you if we tried to convince you that researchers first calculate the effect size and confidence intervals before calculating the independent groups *t*. Most researchers would probably find the level of statistical significance first and then examine the effect size and the confidence interval. We presented *g* and the 95% confidence interval before introducing the *t* test to be sure that you get into the habit of paying attention to these tools. Simply finding four values of *t* is *not* a complete analysis; we hope that you will use all the information that a proper statistical analyses can provide.

Table 10.2 includes the three subvalues that we need to make the estimates of the confidence interval and effect size, and to calculate *t*. Note that for convenience the differences between the two group means were calculated so that the differences would be positive when Shelley's expectations about test anxiety were fulfilled. Many researchers use positive signs to indicate support for a hypothesis. (There is no reason why one could not find the differences by subtracting in the reverse order. What is critical is that one be consistent.) The differences do tell Shelley that, for all three anxiety measures, the cognitive group shows the more favorable values. The first three show that students felt less anxious after cognitive therapy compared to the traditional, insight-oriented approach. The last dependent variable is more favorable to traditional therapists; however, Shelley had no reason to hypothesize that either set of therapists would be better liked.

Table 10.3 contains the 95% confidence interval, *g*, and observed *t* for the four dependent variables. Each of these indices is important because they provide different views of the data. Let's look at the estimates for the primary dependent variable: the measure of test anx-

TABLE 10.2 ■ Key Subvalues Needed to Calculate Estimates for Shelley's Experiment

Measure	$M_{trad} - M_{cog}$	s_{pooled}	$s_{M_1-M_2}$
Test anxiety	5.07	5.36	1.67
Rating of anxiety	8.38	8.59	2.68
Anxiety about papers	1.50	5.04	1.57
Liking for group therapist	2.66	12.66	3.96

iety. On the basis of the experiment, the best information we have is that there is a 5.07-point advantage for the cognitive therapy approach. Remember that Shelley randomly assigned the students to receive one or the other therapy; consequently, we may assume that the students comprising the two groups were, on the average, equally distressed about taking tests when the experiment began. Because she used random assignment, it is not fair to dismiss her findings by saying, "Maybe the students in the cognitive group were less anxious to begin with."

For the first variable, the test anxiety measure, her best information is that cognitive therapy is 5.07 units better than insight therapy, but, because she knows means are affected by sampling error, she calculates the 95% confidence interval. The interval given in Table 10.3 extends from less than two units to more than eight units. Because the interval does not contain zero, she may assume that she has evidence for the superiority of cognitive therapy for reducing test anxiety in a college setting. The effect size, 0.95, is large for psychological

TABLE 10.3 ■ Three Estimates Calculated for the Cognitive Therapy Experiment

Measure	95% Confidence Interval of the Difference Between the Two Means	Effect size, g	t Test for Two Independent Groups
Test anxiety	$5.07 \pm 2.023 (1.67) =$ 1.68 to 8.45	$5.07/5.36 = 0.95$	$\dfrac{5.07}{5.36 (\sqrt{1/21 + 1/20})} = 3.027$
Rating of anxiety	$8.38 \pm 2.023 (2.68) =$ 2.96 to 13.80	$8.38/8.59 = 0.98$	$\dfrac{8.38}{8.59 (\sqrt{1/21 + 1/20})} = 3.127$
Anxiety about papers	$1.50 \pm 2.023 (1.57) =$ 1.68 to 4.68	$1.50/5.04 = 0.30$	$\dfrac{1.50}{5.04 (\sqrt{1/21 + 1/20})} = 0.955$
Liking for group therapist	$2.66 \pm 2.023 (3.96) =$ -5.35 to 10.67	$2.66/12.66 = 0.21$	$\dfrac{2.66}{12.66 (\sqrt{1/21 + 1/20})} = 0.672$

research. Last, the value of t_{obs}, 3.027, is to be compared to the critical value for 39 degrees of freedom. Because Shelley had a clear directional hypothesis when she began the research, she should use the critical values for a one-tailed test with 39 degrees of freedom. Table A.2 in Appendix A gives values for 30 and 40 degrees of freedom. If we adopt the conservative option, we would initially use the larger values of t_{crit} associated with 30 degrees of freedom. The table contains the following critical t values:

1.310 ($p = .10$)
1.697 ($p = .05$)
2.457 ($p = .01$)
2.750 ($p = .005$)
3.646 ($p = .0005$)

Shelley's t_{obs} exceeds four of these values of t_{crit}, but not the largest one. She can conclude that her results are statistically significant (i.e., they are unlikely to be due solely to sampling error), and the null hypothesis in unlikely to be true. Shelley can reject the null hypothesis at the .005 level.

Take a moment and reflect on the point of each of these three indices. The confidence interval provides two values that enclose the differences between the two population means in 95% of experiments. The effect size permits comparing the strength of the finding to other research findings on counseling, and the t test permits us to reject the null hypothesis using the appropriate rejection region. Further, using Figure 10.1, Shelley could expect that roughly 80% of exact replications would be statistically significant at the .05 level. Recommended practice is to utilize all of these approaches to statistical analyses; reporting whether the finding was statistically significant or not does not exhaust the information that is available (Nickerson, 2000; Wilkinson et al., 1999).

YOUR TURN 10-7

The findings for the second dependent variable follow the same pattern as for the first. However, the third variable does not. Interpret the three estimates (i.e., the confidence interval, g, and t) of the relative effect of the two types of therapy on anxiety about writing papers. ■

Note that Shelley did not have a specific hypothesis for the variable regarding how much the groups liked their therapists. One could think of this variable as affecting the interpretability of the results. If the students receiving one of the therapies found the group leaders particularly likeable, the results might reflect differences among the group leaders, not differences between the effectiveness of the therapies. Shelley would be interested if either set of therapists was more likeable. Thus, she should use a nondirectional t critical with the last t test. The t_{obs} is rather small. The nondirectional t_{crit} for 30 degrees of freedom (using the .05 level) is ± 2.042. If the t_{obs} is smaller than -2.042 or larger than $+2.042$, Shelley would reject the null hypothesis, and no doubt would be distressed because she would not be sure how to interpret the effects of her experiment. Rejecting the null hypothesis could mean that a possible interpretation of the findings is that the cognitive therapists were more likeable and the students simply said that they were less anxious to please their group leaders.

In the present case, she does not reject the null hypothesis; failing to reject the null hypothesis is what she wanted to do. *However, she has not proven that the two sets of thera-*

pists are equally likeable. But, by examining the effect size, *g,* she has shown that, even if the therapists did differ in how likeable they were, the difference would probably be in the small range according to Cohen's categories.

Announcing

What should Shelley say when she tells others about her findings? She should touch on all three steps that she followed: inspecting, describing, and estimating. Here is a condensed, but acceptable way for her to announce (the *A* in I-D-E-A) her findings:

> An inspection of the data for the four dependent variables showed that the data for both groups of students were not markedly skewed and did not contain any suspicious data points. There was no bunching of scores at the extremes suggesting floor or ceiling effects. Table 10.1 contains the means and standard deviations for the four dependent variables for both therapy groups. The two measures of test anxiety were expected to be the most strongly affected by the cognitive therapy. As shown in Table 10.1, these measures were lower for those who received cognitive therapy compared to insight therapy. The effect sizes, g, for these dependent variables were greater than 0.80, which Cohen (1988) called "large." In addition, there may have been some carryover positive benefit to reducing anxiety about writing papers even though that was not the focus of the treatment. This effect, 0.30, was small according to Cohen's criteria.
>
> With these relatively small samples, the 95% confidence intervals of the difference between the means of the two therapy groups are fairly wide: for test anxiety, the 95% confidence interval was 1.68 to 8.45 and, for the rating just before a test, the 95% confidence interval was 2.96 to 13.80. Neither of these confidence intervals includes zero; consequently, it seems clear that the students who participated in cognitive group therapy reported less test anxiety than did those in the traditional insight therapy. Although anxiety about writing papers was also lower, the 95% confidence interval includes zero: -1.68 to $+4.68$.
>
> The difference between the levels of test anxiety was statistically significant for test anxiety, $t(39) = 3.03, p < .005$ (one-tailed test), as well as for anxiety just prior to a test, $t(39) = 3.13, p < .005$ (one-tailed test). The difference for anxiety about writing papers was not statistically significant, $t(39) = 0.96, p < .25$.
>
> Liking for the two sets of group leaders was not expected to be different. Although the students did indicate somewhat higher liking for the traditional therapy leaders, this difference was quite small: 2.66 units on a 1 to 100 unit scale, with $g = .21$. Furthermore, the 95% confidence interval of the difference between the means included zero. The interval was -5.35 (showing more liking for cognitive-oriented therapists) to 10.67 (more liking for the traditional insight therapists). The t failed to reach statistical significance: $t(39) = 0.69, p < .25$.

Notice that Shelley rounded the values of *t* to two decimal places. Because the values of *t* listed in the tables are given to three places, researchers often use three decimal places during analyses even though they report just two. Shelley could have chosen to gather her data in additional ways, and she could have performed additional analyses with the data she gathered. Our focus here is on showing how the statistical analyses of data from two groups can be applied and discussed appropriately, not to exhaust all approaches to analysis.

PRESENTING EXACT PROBABILITIES

We need to mention one more detail when announcing findings. When one computes observed t values and compares them to the critical values found in the t tables, it is recommended that researchers report the lowest probability merited by the t_{obs} that was found. When Shelley looked up $t(39) = 3.027$, she found that her t_{obs} exceeded the t_{crit} for the .005 level, consequently, she reported "$p < .005$." It would have been correct for her to have reported "$p < .05$" because .005 is indeed smaller than .05. However, reporting .05 would not have been as informative as reporting .005. Recall that a t_{obs} that only exceeds the t_{crit} at the .05 level suggests a 50:50 chance for a statistically significant replication. In contrast, a t_{obs} that exceeds the .005 critical value suggests that 80% of exact replications will lead to statistically significant findings. (See Figure 10.1.) Reporting the smallest probability that t_{obs} justifies is more informative than reporting only that the results are "statistically significant."

When statistical analyses are done on a computer, t's are accompanied by an exact probability. If Shelley had found the 3.027 value with a computer, she might have found that p equaled .00218. Or, because many programs round the probability to three decimal points, her computer might have reported "$p = .002$." If she used such a program, she should report the value listed. A problem of rounding to three decimal points is seen when the exact probability is less than .0005 because the program output would read $p = .000$, which cannot be literally true. If a computer output reads $p = .000$, we can be assured that the probability is indeed very small. When faced with a reported probability given as .000, Nickerson (2000) suggests that the researcher report "$p < .001$." More accurately, one could also report $p \leq .0005$ because we know that any value greater than .0005 would have been rounded to .001 by the computer.

There are also some complicated reasons for presenting the exact probabilities rather than just saying *statistically significant, $p < .05$.* But we want to suggest that there is a very practical reason. The 95% confidence interval will tell us that a 0.00 difference is outside the interval and thus that the null hypothesis can be rejected at the .05 level. However, sometimes 0.00 is barely outside, and sometimes it is far outside. Calculating t_{obs} and reporting the exact probability of these findings if the null hypothesis were true gives more information than is given by reporting only that the null hypothesis may be rejected because 0.00 lies outside the interval. The lower the probability of t_{obs}, the higher the probability that an exact replication would permit rejecting the null hypothesis, as Figure 10.1 shows. This information is the unique contribution of the test of the null hypothesis using a t test.

WHAT YOU HAVE LEARNED AND THE NEXT STEP

This chapter completes the set of four chapters on data from two groups (or two observations on one group). The major points covered in this chapter include the following:

- *Statistical significance* does not mean that a causal relationship has been found. For example, natural groups could differ for a variety of reasons in addition to the way used to define the different levels of the independent variable. Even when subjects have been randomly assigned, an experiment can go wrong in many ways. Researchers are always cautious about making causal conclusions, and especially so until they have carefully examined the methodology used to produce the difference between means.

- Statistically significant findings in one population or situation may not apply to other populations or situations. This is a question of external validity and cannot be solved by NHST.

- *Not statistically significant* does not mean that the null hypothesis is true; it means that we have insufficient evidence to claim that the dependent variable was affected by the independent variable. We are left in a state of uncertainty regarding the difference between the means.

- Statistically significant findings are not necessarily important; importance is related to the nature of the dependent variable measured and the samples studied. Effect size measures, which are independent of sample size, are one form of evidence regarding the importance of a finding.

- *Statistical significance* does not necessarily mean that a finding can be replicated. The probability of a t_{obs} can be converted into the probability that a replication will permit rejecting the null hypothesis. The smaller the probability of a t_{obs}, the more likely it is that replications will permit rejecting the null hypothesis.

- A Type I error refers to rejecting the null hypothesis when it is true. The probability of a Type I error is the level of statistical significance, or alpha (α).

- A Type II error refers to failing to reject the null hypothesis when it is false. Testing small samples raises the chances of making a Type II error. The probability of a Type II error is symbolized as β.

- Statistical power, $1 - \beta$, refers to the probability of rejecting the null hypothesis when it is false.

- Announcing the findings of the statistical analysis of research is done most effectively when three statistical tools are used (confidence intervals, effect size, and results of NHST) rather than just one.

- Statistical significance has often been misunderstood within behavioral sciences. Using all three tools can improve understanding of statistically significant findings and non-statistically significant findings.

The principles discussed in this chapter apply to all forms of NHST that are described in the balance of this book. Next, we turn to the analysis of research in which three or more means are compared.

Key Concepts

external validity	Type I error	β (beta)
Type II error	α (alpha)	power $(1 - \beta)$

Answers to *Your Turn* Questions

10-1. 0.84

10-2. $t(58) = 1.73$.

10-3. Clearly both researchers were at a high risk of making Type II errors. Vince tried to replicate a finding with markedly smaller samples, and Twila analyzed data from the small samples that Sam gave her.

10-4. She should inspect the data before beginning.

10-5. It is easy to see that anxiety is lower for the cognitive therapy group relative to the insight therapy group for all three measures. The stem-and-leaf plot for liking is not so readily interpreted; whatever differences there are must be smaller than differences in levels of anxiety.

10-6. She can show that both groups have equivalent standard deviations for the difference measures; we have

adopted a rule of thumb that means should not be compared in a t test if the standard deviation of one group is three times that of the other group.

10-7. Shelley was not definite about how anxiety about writing would be affected by the therapy focused on test anxiety. She learned that if there were generalized effects on more than just test situations, such effects were not large.

Analyzing and Interpreting Data: Problems and Exercises

1. Identify why a result that is statistically significant might not be all that interesting (or important).

2. If a statistically significant t has been attained ($p < .05$), this finding *might* indicate that an exact replication would also be statistically significant, but it is possible that the chances of a statistically significant replication might be only 50:50. Explain.

3. Why is it equally as likely that a replication of a two-group experiment would find a bigger difference between the groups as it is to find a smaller difference?

4. Define Type II error. Give an example of a Type II error in the context of medical diagnosis. Is it like thinking a person has disease X when she does not, or is it like overlooking disease X when a person does have it?

5. In the following scenario, the researcher has not acknowledged the possibility of a Type I or a Type II error. Identify which error is a potential problem, and explain your choice.

   A large chemical manufacturer tested a sample of 50 people for cancer and several other diseases in a community near one of its plants. All these people had lived near the plant for at least 20 years. A random sample of 50 people from the same community but not living near the plant served as a comparison group. The data did not permit rejecting the null hypotheses for the five variables that the company examined (p > .05). The public relations office announced that the tests proved that the company was doing no harm.

6. Assume that a t test for independent groups was performed with the data from three different experiments. Assume further that the experiments were well done and that the sample sizes were similar and large. In the three different experiments, the probability of the observed t was .04, .01, and .001. Without knowing anything else about the experiments, what two important pieces of information do these p values communicate?

7. How can one decrease the chances of making a Type I error? How can a researcher decrease the chances of making a Type II error while not changing the chances of making a Type I error?

8. What information does a t test provide in addition to the information provided by using a 95% confidence interval?

9. (a) What is wrong with the interpretation in each of the following scenarios? (b) What would be the appropriate interpretation?

   (1) John is a residence assistant at a large university. He compared the dorm rooms of engineering, math, and physics majors with those of history, English, and literature majors. He observed that the rooms of the humanities majors were less clean and contained more clothing strewn about than were the rooms of the science-oriented students. Jim reasoned that the more formal and organized nature of the science-oriented majors caused these differences.

   (2) Molly, a nurse in a large university health center, was concerned that students follow good health practices. She administered a survey at freshman orientation dur-

ing the last six years at her large university. She compared those who said they were in excellent health with those who said they were in good health. She discovered that those who had rated their health as "Excellent" said that they watched less TV per day (M = 2.08 hr/day, n = 44,116) than those who described their health as "Good" (M = 2.15 hr/day, n = 5,212), t (49,326) = 2.41, p < 0.02. Molly concluded that a reduction in TV viewing would lead to improved health.

10. Under what circumstances would a researcher be especially concerned to lower the chances of making a Type II error?

11. What would you want to say to the PR department depicted in the following scenario?

    An experiment was conducted with all the nurses in a large nursing organization (N = 54,749). Half were randomly assigned to take an aspirin each day and half to take a look-alike pill with no medical effect (a placebo). When a researcher completed the analysis, she learned that the group with the aspirin had a mean diastolic blood pressure of 74.32 in. of Hg and the placebo group had a mean of 74.45 in. The t was statistically significant. The organization PR department wanted to announce that the study showed that everyone should take an aspirin a day to lower blood pressure (as long as one's personal physician said it was okay).

12. Read carefully the following description of an applied research project. Identify two major errors in the researcher's thinking about his results:

    Trent was an industrial psychologist with a large human resources department. He and the staff believed that physical coordination was an important element in successful work in several positions in the company. Trent tested 20 workers who were considered very successful in one of these positions and 20 more who were not as successful. When he compared the coordination

means of these two samples, he discovered that the null hypothesis could not be rejected: t(38) = 0.71, p = .48 (two-tailed test). Trent said that there was a 48% chance that the null hypothesis was true. Thus, he said that coordination was not related to success in these positions and that it thus should no longer be used as part of the tests to select which applicants to hire when openings in these jobs occur.

13. It is suggested that information obtained from all three stages of data analysis (inspection, description, and estimation) be presented when announcing results of a t test for two means. Explain.

14. When announcing results of a statistical test, such as a t test comparing two means, the American Psychological Association asks researchers to report exact probabilities for their obtained statistics rather than simply p < .05. What is one important reason for doing this?

15. Suppose that your cousin was ill and a physician had to choose one of two available medications. The efficacy of each medication had been studied in equally valid experiments. Study 1 showed a t_{obs} of 4.88, p < .001. The study involved about 2,000 patients. The effect size, g, of the first medication was 0.33. Study 2 showed a t_{obs} of 2.21, p = .042. Study 2 involved only 150 patients. The effect size was 0.91. The second medication cost 10% more than the first one. Which medication should your cousin get?

16. What do you see as wrong with Wendell's conclusion in the following scenario? (Hint: there's more than one error.)

    Wendell investigated two methods of training employees how to use dangerous metal stamping equipment. His experiment had two conditions: a traditional training method based on foremen's instructions, and an experimental method based on computer simulations of mistakes that workers have made and lessons on how to correct these mistakes. Each group contained five employees. He used a test of knowledge of safe procedures as his dependent variable.

Those trained by the foremen did worse (M = 67%) than those using the simulation (M = 93%); however, using a two-tailed test, the t was not statistically significant: t(8) = 1.95, p = .08. Wendell concluded that, because the null hypothesis could not be rejected, the training methods were equally effective.

17. Natalie believed that making eye contact was an important aspect of good interpersonal relations. In an experiment, she provided research participants with positive feedback given either while making eye contact or not making eye contact. The experiment was set up in such a way that an experimenter (who was actually an actress) gave the feedback report to a participant through a glass partition. However, the actress did not know that, for a random half, the glass was set to distort her image so that to these participants it appeared that she was avoiding eye contact. As the participants were leaving, an assistant who did not know what type of glass had been used asked the participants to fill out a short "evaluation" form which included a rating of how friendly the (apparent) experimenter (actually, the actress) was. Natalie hypothesized that eye contact would lead to a higher rating of experimenter friendliness. Here are the ratings:

Regular glass	Distorted glass
9, 6, 7, 7, 7,	5, 6, 4, 7, 3,
8, 6, 5, 10, 10,	5, 4, 6, 5, 5,
8, 8, 7, 9, 8,	7, 8, 6, 4, 7,
9, 10, 9, 7, 8	9, 6, 7, 5, 6

What analyses should she conduct? Follow the I-D-E-A model to analyze and interpret these data. Identify the analyses that Natalie should perform

at each step. Perform these analyses and state what you (and she) learned at each step.

18. What is the correct interpretation of a research finding that leads to "p > .05"?

19. Arrange the following symbols into the three essential formulas used in independent groups designs. Use these symbols in the formulas for (a) the 95% confidence interval for the difference of two means, (b) the effect size, and (c) t_{obs}.

$$M_1 - M_2, s_{pooled}, n_1, n_2$$
$$t_{crit(df=n_1+n_2-2)}(two-tailed, \alpha = .05)$$

20. Stan became interested in how people interpret political speeches. He obtained a speech from a senator on a general topic. He had students read the speech, but he randomly attributed the speech to a liberal senator or to a conservative senator. Stan hypothesized that students would view the speech as advocating a more conservative point of view if attributed to a conservation politician or a more liberal point of view if attributed to a liberal politician. The rating scale he used was scored in such a way so that large numbers indicated a more conservative interpretation of the speech. Apply the I-D-E-A model to analyzing Stan's data. Identify the analyses that he should do at each step. Perform these analyses and state what you (and he) learned at each step. The ratings are as follows:

Speaker said to be liberal:

16, 29, 26, 2, 3, 25, 55, 27, 25, 25, 13, 51, 17, 23, 27, 45, 41, 39, 30, 17, 53, 26, 30

Speaker said to be conservative:

57, 34, 32, 47, 22, 37, 53, 16, 33, 25, 32, 20, 54, 57, 19, 36, 43, 37, 43, 39, 32, 49, 38, 38, 42

Answers to Odd-Numbered Problems

1. Statistical significance does not guarantee that a result is important (or even interesting). First, a badly conducted research study can easily produce statistical significance. The results associated with a bad experiment would not be important. Also, even when a study has been done well, a statistically significant result may not

be important if the difference between means were very small. That is, if the "effect" of the independent variable is trivial, then the study may not be telling us anything practically important about the independent variable. Of course, there are other reasons why a statistically significant finding may not be important. For example, the independent variable chosen for study may not be important, at least in the sense that it does not tell us anything interesting that we do not know already. Hitting people over the head with a rubber mallet in one condition and not hitting them in another condition would (eventually) produce a statistically significant difference in terms of self-reported pain. Such a study would be silly to do (and clearly unethical).

3. The differences between the two means in the replications should be, on the average, expected to vary around the value observed in the initial study. When t_{obs} is just barely larger than t_{crit}, those differences that are smaller than the difference in the initial study would not be statistically significant, and those that are larger would be statistically significant. On the other hand, the degree to which the probability of t_{obs} is lower than .05, our confidence that a replication would be statistically significant increases. But remember that we start from a 50:50 level of confidence in the statistical significance of replications, whenever t_{obs} is nearly equal to t_{crit}.

5. A Type II error is always possible when a result is not statistically significant. A result that is not statistically significant does not mean that there is no difference, and it certainly does not prove that there is no difference present. A larger sample size may show a statistically significant outcome. The effects of environmental problems are usually numerically small even though important. (The numerical small effects are what makes it hard to identify the effects of pollutants even when they are present.)

7. One can decrease the chances of making a Type I error quite easily; simply use critical t values associated with small probability levels of such as .01, or .001. Unfortunately, this strategy leads to larger levels of Type II errors. One can reduce Type II errors by including greater numbers of people in the study groups, thus, increasing precision.

9. Scenario 1: (a) John inappropriately suggests a causal explanation for the difference (which of course also was not tested statistically). Because these students represent different natural groups, we cannot on the basis of an obtained difference conclude that their major was the cause of the difference. There may be many reasons why students majoring in science and those majoring in the humanities differ in orderliness other than because of the way these groups approach their studies. As one example, let us suggest that science majors were raised by stricter parents than were humanities majors. John may be right in his thinking, but he is not justified in making a causal claim on the

basis of this evidence alone. (b) The correct interpretation is that there is an observed relationship (correlation) between major and orderliness of dorm rooms.

Scenario 2: (a) We can see that the effect size for this independent variable will be very small, and that the result is no doubt statistically significant due to the very large sample sizes that were used. A difference this small (i.e., 0.07 hr/day, or 4.2 min/day) is not likely to be practically important. Moreover, these are "natural" groups that no doubt differ in many other ways. For example, those who rate themselves in excellent health may indeed watch TV less, but perhaps they also exercise more. Exercise—and not watching TV less—may be what contributes to better health. If people who watch a lot of TV are convinced to watch less TV, this does not mean that they will exercise more. It is inappropriate to draw a causal connection between rated health and TV watching. (The results also are obtained for college students who reported their own health and amount of teaching watching. There is no independent validation of these measures and no guarantee that these measures will generalize to other populations.) (b) The appropriate interpretation is that there is an observed relationship (correlation) between self-reported health and TV watching. This relationship is likely not worth further investigation given such a small difference between the means.

11. Although statistically significant, the difference between the means is very small. (An effect size measure should be reported to help interpret the difference.) It is unlikely that this very small difference has practical importance. Moreover, because the results were obtained with nurses, we do not know that this difference, especially because it is a small one, will generalize to other populations of people who may be of different age and health.

13. Information about errors or outliers, as well as about the shape of the distribution (to see if statistical assumptions are met), should be mentioned (*inspection*). Measures of central tendency and variability should also be reported to identify patterns and trends in the data (*description*). Finally, results of statistical procedures such as calculating effect size, confidence intervals, and results of NHST should be reported (*announce*) to provide information about how well the sample data estimate the population parameters.

15. Both studies were done well, and both permitted the rejection of the null hypothesis. The null hypothesis would have been that the medication was no better than no treatment. The decision should focus on the effect size. The second medication is much more effective

than the first one. The low probability of study 1 was due to the large samples, not the greater effectiveness. The difference in cost is rather small compared to the difference in effectiveness.

17. A step-by-step *I-D-E-A* answer for the study on eye contact and ratings of friendliness.

Step 1: Inspect the data.

Regular glass			Distorted glass		
Freq	Stem	Leaf	Freq	Stem	Leaf
			1	3	0
			3	4	000
1	5	0	5	5	00000
2	6	00	5	6	00000
5	7	00000	4	7	0000
5	8	00000	1	8	0
4	9	0000	1	9	0
3	10	000			

Natalie can conclude that the dependent variable is relatively normally distributed with no marked floor or ceiling effects (although there are three ratings at the highest value in the regular glass condition).

Step 2: Describe the data.

Variable	n	M	s
Regular glass	20	7.90	1.41
Distorted glass	20	5.75	1.48

Difference between means = 2.15

Conclude: the means are in the direction in which she hypothesized. She also notes that the standard deviations in the two groups are nearly equal, thereby meeting an assumption of *t* tests.

Step 3: Estimate the precision, effect size, and likelihood of replication.

(a) 95% confidence interval: $2.15 \pm t(df = 38)$ times standard error of the difference between two means
$2.15 \pm 2.024 (0.458) = 1.224$ to 3.076.
Note that 0.00 lies outside the confidence interval. Conclude: she can reject the null hypothesis.

(b) The effect size: $g = 2.15/ (\sqrt{((1.41^2 + 1.482^2)/2)}$
$= 2.15 / 1.446 = 1.49$
Conclude: the effect size is very large compared to Cohen's categories.

(c) Find the probability that an exact replication will be statistically significant at the .05 level.
$t = 2.15 / 0.458 = 4.70$. The test was directional; a computer program would give $p = .000$, so she can report $p < .0005$ (or $p < .001$ if she reports to three decimal places).
Using the figure in Chapter 10, she may conclude that the probability of a statistically significant replication is above .95.

Step 4: Announce the findings.
This is a way in which Natalie could announce her findings. This example is written in a concise fashion; however, it refers to the inspection, description, and estimation steps of the I-D-E-A model. It is important that statistical analyses be summarized in words with specific interpretations provided. If a researcher were to present the calculations or probability value without interpreting the analysis, the researcher is, in effect, expecting readers to complete the analysis.

   An inspection of the distribution of the dependent variable for both experimental conditions showed that the variable was normal in form with nearly equal standard deviations. The means were in the hypothesized direction, that is, the actress making eye contact was rated as more friendly ($M = 7.90$, $SD = 1.41$) compared to the same actress who could not make eye contact because her image was directed elsewhere by the distorting glass ($M = 5.75$, $SD = 1.48$). The difference between the means was 2.15 with a 95% confidence interval of 1.22 to 3.08. Because 0.00 was not in the confidence interval, the null hypothesis (that the means are the same, in other words, that eye contact makes no difference on rated friendliness) was rejected. The effect size, g, was 1.49, which is larger than Cohen's large category. The difference between the means was statistically significant: $t(38) = 4.70$, $p < .0005$ (one-tailed test).

19. (a) $g = \dfrac{(M_1 - M_2)}{s_{pooled}}$

(b) 95% confidence interval =
$(M_1 - M_2) \pm t_{crit(df=n_1+n_2-2)} (s_{pooled})(\sqrt{(1/n_1 + 1/n_2)})$

(c) $t_{obs} = \dfrac{(M_1 - M_2)}{s_{pooled}(\sqrt{(1/n_1 + 1/n_2)})}$

Go to http://psychology.wadsworth.com/courses/statistics/ and test your knowledge of this chapter by taking the online quiz. Another resource to check is the online workshops that provide a step-by-step guide through a number of topics at http://psychology.wadsworth.com/workshops/workshops.html.

PART 4

I-D-E-A When There Are
More Than Two Means

CHAPTER 11

Inspecting, Describing, and Estimating Using Confidence Intervals

. . . put confidence intervals around all sample statistics that are important for making conclusions.

Loftus (1996, p. 166)

INTRODUCTION

In Chapter 1, we briefly introduced you to Brandon, whom you might remember was conducting an experiment to investigate the effect of type of multimedia presentation on students' retention. The independent variable, or factor, in his experiment had three levels. Information was to be presented (a) using videos, (b) using slides, and (c) without videos or slides in what might be called a standard lecture format. Some suggested measures of students' memory (the dependent variable) were short-answer recall tests and multiple-choice recognition tests over the content of the presentation.

The goal of this hypothetical experiment was to determine if the independent variable (type of presentation) has an effect on the dependent variable (scores on a test of retention). To meet that goal, Brandon must control all those factors that might influence the dependent variable, except one (the independent variable). Therefore, the length of the presentation, the particular content, and so on must be held constant. Moreover, in order to begin the experiment with groups of students who are essentially equivalent in terms of their natural memory ability, interest, and motivation, as well as other individual differences factors, Brandon will need to assign participants randomly to the conditions of his experiment. (See Chapter 1.)

Let us assume that Brandon was able to carry out the control procedures necessary for his experiment (not an easy task) and obtain access to volunteer student participants through his psychology department's participant pool. He assigns 90 students randomly to the three conditions representing the levels of his independent variable (videos, slides, and standard lecture). There are 30 students in each of the three groups. Brandon chooses as his dependent measure the number correct on a 20-item recall test that he carefully constructed for his project. When students attend the presentation, they are informed that there will be a memory test following the presentation but they are not allowed to take notes. The presentation in all conditions lasts 30 min. Immediately after the presentation, the 20-item recall test is distributed. Tests are scored (possible range is 0–20 correct) and the data recorded.

In this chapter, we take a look at how a researcher might analyze and interpret the data from such an experiment: three or more independent groups are formed by random assignment, and the effect of one independent variable (or factor) is assessed. In previous chapters, we discussed how to apply the I-D-E-A model when we had data from two groups. These methods form the basis for analysis when there are more than two groups, but they cannot be applied without some modification. In this chapter, we discuss how the methods you learned previously may be applied when an independent variable has three or more levels.

INSPECTING DATA FROM AN INDEPENDENT GROUPS DESIGN WITH ONE INDEPENDENT VARIABLE THAT HAS THREE OR MORE LEVELS

What is the question that Brandon is asking? One thing Brandon wants to know, of course, is how students' retention was affected by the type of presentation they experienced. Given the description of his dependent variable, we know that the mean recall in each condition will be used to help make a decision about the effect of the independent variable. Scores on a 20-point test can be assumed to be at least an interval level of measurement. Of particular interest is the *pattern of means* and associated measures of variability across the conditions of our experiment (Loftus, 1993). In the description phase of analysis, the researcher examines the pattern of means to see if there is covariation between the independent and dependent variables. Specifically, is there evidence that behavior differs across levels of the independent variable?

Brandon will want to know more than just whether his independent variable "had an effect" on students' retention. If you were Brandon, wouldn't you also want to know whether the two presentations using multimedia led to better retention than the standard condition? And whether the two multimedia groups differed? Researchers usually want to know more than simply whether their variable had an overall effect, and we will introduce you to procedures in this chapter and the next to help you learn just that.

Independent groups also may be formed by selecting levels of an independent variable. As you have seen in previous chapters, groups may be formed "naturally" as, for example, would happen if we wished to compare the performance of fourth, sixth, and eighth graders on a cognitive task. We can't possibly randomly assign children to different grades. Nor could we assign people randomly to be in married, divorced, or single (never married) groups. People just come that way. Nevertheless, a researcher may wish to know the "effect" of grade level on children's performance, or the "effect" of marital status on emotional well-being. Data analysis for these natural groups designs proceeds essentially in the same way as it does for random groups designs, but, as you have seen, the interpretation of differences obtained in a natural groups design differs from that when differences are observed in a random groups design. Because natural groups designs do not satisfy the conditions of a true experiment, we are not able to draw cause-and-effect conclusions when we observe an effect of a natural groups variable.

Because data analysis proceeds similarly for the random groups and natural groups designs, we will focus on just one type of independent groups design: that in which subjects have been randomly assigned to the levels of a single independent variable. Thus, let us turn our attention to an analysis of Brandon's experiment. What effect did the type of presentation have on students' recall?

By now, we hope you are familiar with the first step in data analysis: inspection. Remember that data inspection begins by carefully examining the raw data sheets, for example, as each response sheet is scored. Is there any evidence that participants did not follow instructions or did not take the task seriously? Are there marks or notes on the response sheets to suggest that a participant was just "fooling around" and not trying to answer the questions? We'll assume that this initial inspection was made as Brandon's data were scored and recorded.

The procedure for inspecting data from a **single-factor independent groups design** with three or more levels is simply an extension of the inspection procedures that are used when an independent groups design has one independent variable with only two levels (which were described in earlier chapters). In addition to looking for errors and outliers, it is important to examine the shape of the distribution and the degree of variability in each group, as well as to determine whether there are floor or ceiling effects. Assumptions of normality and homogeneity of variance (of the various distributions), which we saw are important for statistical tests of the difference between two means, are also important for tests involving more than two means. Although the assumptions underlying various statistical tests refer to the populations from which the samples were obtained, an examination of the sample distributions gives us insight into the population distributions. For example, you have learned that, if the scores in a random sample are normally distributed, it is safe to assume that scores in the population are also.

Examining a stem-and-leaf display for each of the groups in an independent groups design is always a good way to start. By inspecting the stem-and-leaf displays, we cannot only spot klinkers and outliers in each group, we can also gain an impression of the shape of the distribution in each group, and even begin to learn (in general terms at least) what happened in our experiment as a function of the independent variable. Do scores on the dependent variable vary across experimental conditions? There is no easy way to join three or more groups of data with a stem-and-leaf plot as we did with two groups. Because a statistical software program will present a stem-and-leaf display for each group on a separate computer screen, it is a good idea to print each display and then examine the data in each condition while also looking across the displays. The software program may create stem-and-leaf displays using different numbers of stems for the various conditions depending on the degree of dispersion present in each sample. As a consequence, it may be important to re-create a stem-and-leaf display by hand to match the stems in each display to make clearer comparisons across conditions of the experiment. By lining up stem-and-leaf displays with similar stem structure, one quickly gains an impression of within-group variability and central tendency among the conditions of the experiment.

Figure 11.1 shows three stem-and-leaf displays for the data in Brandon's experiment.

Inspect carefully the three stem-and-leaf plots in Figure 11.1 and then answer the following five questions:

(a) Do any of the groups contain obvious klinkers (invalid data points)? (Hint: What is the largest acceptable score in Brandon's experiment?)

(b) Are there outliers in any of the groups?

(c) What is the general shape of the distribution in each group? (Roughly normal? Skewed? Platykurtic?)

(d) Is there similar variability (dispersion) among the scores in each of the groups?

(e) What is your impression regarding the "effect" of the independent variable (type of presentation) in this experiment?   ■

FIGURE 11.1. ■ Stem-and-leaf plots for Brandon's data

Video

Frequency	Stem	Leaf
0	0	
1	1	1
3	1	223
5	1	44555
10	1	6666677777
8	1	88888999
3	2	000

Slide

Frequency	Stem	Leaf
0	0	
2	1	01
2	1	33
7	1	4444455
8	1	66666777
8	1	88889999
3	2	001

Lecture

Frequency	Stem	Leaf
2	0	99
4	1	0001
6	1	222333
10	1	4444555555
6	1	667777
1	1	9
1	2	0

DESCRIBING THE DATA: MEASURES OF CENTRAL TENDENCY AND VARIABILITY

Inspection of the data from Brandon's experiment revealed a klinker, which turned out to be a score coded incorrectly. In the slide group, a 21 was really a 12. There were no obvious outliers, and examination of the distributions of scores does not indicate a ceiling effect in any condition. Scores in the three groups are generally bell shaped (close enough at least). (Remember that a stem-and-leaf display rotated so that the leaves are on top is analogous to a histogram. We can superimpose a normal curve on it to judge the distribution's symmetry and kurtosis.) There appears to be similar variability among the three conditions. Finally, one gets the impression from examining the stem-and-leaf plots that students generally remembered more of the presentation in the slide and video conditions than they did in the standard lecture condition. Numerical measures of central tendency and variability are important to translate these impressions into meaningful summary statistics.

Table 11.1 shows descriptive statistics for each of the three conditions in Brandon's experiment after correcting the one invalid data point.

TABLE 11.1 ■ Descriptive Statistics for Brandon's Experiment

	n	Mean	SD	Range
Video	30	16.43	2.43	11–20
Slide	30	15.93	2.65	10–20
Lecture	30	13.97	2.83	9–20

YOUR TURN 11-2

Consider carefully the descriptive statistics in Table 11.1. Do the impressions gained from an examination of the stem-and-leafs displays in Figure 11.1 appear to be confirmed by the descriptive statistics?   ■

LOOKING FOR COVARIATION

We do research to see if there is a relationship between conditions (levels) of our independent variable and the dependent variable. Do group means differ across levels of the independent variable? We are looking, in other words, for covariation between the two variables. If the dependent variable does vary across levels of the independent variable, we want to determine "how much" variation there is and whether that variation can reasonably be said to be due to the effect of the independent variable, or whether the differences we see are more reasonably suggested to be due to error (chance) variation.

During the description phase, we want to document the degree of covariation that is present between the independent and dependent variable. Thus, we look for trends and patterns among the group means. At this point in Brandon's experiment, we can see that the means do indeed vary with the conditions of the independent variable. Just as we used measures of central tendency and variability to confirm our impressions gained from an examination of the stem-and-leaf displays, we now turn to statistical techniques to help with decisions regarding the impression gained through an examination of the covariation between the independent and dependent variable.

CONSTRUCTING CONFIDENCE INTERVALS FOR AN INDEPENDENT GROUPS EXPERIMENT

Each of the group means in an independent groups experiment is a point estimate of the population mean represented by the treatment condition. We wish to know whether these group means represent the same or different population means. In other words, do the values of these several group means differ simply because of sampling error, *or* do these group means differ because of sampling error (which is always present) *and* because they represent populations with different means? Our inspection of the data, as well as the calculation of measures of central tendency and variability, can help us with this decision, but, very importantly, so too can the construction of confidence intervals. Judgments about differences among population means can be made on the basis of confidence intervals plotted around sample means (Loftus & Masson, 1994).

Remember that a confidence interval informs us about the precision with which we have estimated the population mean. By constructing a confidence interval, we can say with some degree of confidence (e.g., .95) that the confidence interval has captured the population mean. Admittedly, the range of possibilities for a population mean can be fairly large, but knowing this is important, too. When we calculate confidence intervals for each of the conditions of a multi-group experiment, we want to look at the pattern of sample means as well as the width of the confidence intervals (Loftus, 1996; Loftus & Masson, 1994). The interval width tells us "the degree to which the observed pattern of sample means should be taken seriously as a reflection of the underlying pattern of population means" (Loftus & Masson, 1994, p. 478). Moreover, when intervals overlap, *given these data,* we cannot reject the idea that the population means for the groups represented by the overlapping intervals have the same or similar values. We just don't know; in a real sense, the results are inconclusive. On the other hand, non-overlapping intervals provide evidence that the population means estimated by the sample means are not the same. In the context of a multi-group experiment, the construction of confidence intervals around sample means tells us first about the likely overall pattern of means. It is recommended that decisions about differences between specific pairs of means be made only after additional analyses (Loftus & Masson, 1994). We will take up this issue later.

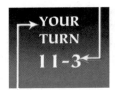

YOUR TURN 11-3

When examining confidence intervals, we must be sure we understand exactly what the interval is telling us (a topic dealt with in Chapter 6 and 8). Which of the following statements about a 95% confidence interval is most appropriate? Explain your answer.

(a) There is a .95 probability that the population mean falls in this interval.

(b) There is a .95 probability that the interval contains the population mean.

(c) There is a .95 probability that a replication will produce a sample mean in this interval. ∎

The calculation of confidence intervals for a single-factor, multi-group experiment is similar to that for a single-group study (Chapter 6) or for that of the difference between two means (Chapter 8). The standard error of the mean describes the degree of variation in the sampling distribution of the means. It is simply the standard deviation of the sampling distribution of means. Recall that the standard error of the mean (s_M) based on a single sample is estimated by dividing the sample standard deviation by the square root of the sample size: $s/\sqrt{N}$.

Because each group mean in an independent groups experiment potentially represents a different population mean, it would appear that we need to estimate the standard error of the mean for each condition in our experiment. However, rather than make separate estimates of the population variability for each group (the numerator in the formula), we can take advantage of the fact that the variances of scores in the different groups generally are assumed to be similar (homogeneous).[1] Therefore, as we did in Chapter 9 when calculating the standard error of the dif-

---

[1] Whether variances are sufficiently homogeneous should be determined during the inspection and description stages of analysis. It is generally acknowledged that specific statistical tests of homogeneity of variance are more sensitive than they need to be because relatively wide differences in group variability can be tolerated. In Chapter 9, we suggested that variability as measured by the standard deviation may differ among groups by as much as a factor of three before this assumption needs to be questioned. Of course, variability because of skewness sometimes may be reduced by an appropriate transformation of the data. (See Chapter 3.) Should variability among groups be very different, one solution is to construct separate confidence intervals for individual means based on estimates of the population variance for each group. (See Loftus & Masson, 1994.)

ference between two means, we can pool the variances of the different groups in our experiment to calculate one estimate of error due to individual differences. This pooled variance estimate generally will be a better approximation of the true variability of the dependent variable than is any one estimate based on a single sample.[2] The formula for the pooled *variance* estimate is

$$s_{pooled}^2 = \frac{(df_1)(s_1^2) + (df_2)(s_2^2) + (df_3)(s_3^2) + \dots}{df_1 + df_2 + df_3 + \dots}.$$

where df = group size minus 1 (i.e., $n - 1$).

Taking the square root of the pooled variance estimate yields an estimate of the pooled standard deviation: $s_{pooled} = \sqrt{s_{pooled}^2}$. Dividing the pooled estimate of the standard deviation by the square root of the group size (assuming sizes of groups are equal) produces the *estimated standard error of the mean* based on the pooled measure of error variation:

$$\text{pooled estimated standard error } (s_M) = \frac{s_{pooled}}{\sqrt{n}}$$

Note: If group sizes are not equal, we must obtain a different estimated standard error for each group by dividing the pooled estimate of the standard deviation by the square root of the appropriate group size (n).

Once we have the estimated standard error of the mean based on the pooled variability in our experiment, we can proceed pretty much as usual to construct confidence intervals for each of the conditions in our experiment. The formula for computing the confidence interval around a sample mean in an independent groups design based on the pooled variance estimate is $M \pm t_{crit} (s_M)$.

The critical t is obtained from Table A.2 as we have done previously. However, the degrees of freedom for the critical t are based on the sum of the degrees of freedom for all the groups. For each group, the degrees of freedom are one less than the group size (i.e., $n - 1$). Because we pooled our variance estimate we can use the critical value of t associated with degrees of freedom equal to $k(n - 1)$, where k equals the number of groups in our experiment.

Note: If the group sizes differ for the conditions in our experiment then we must sum the degrees of freedom for the individual groups [i.e., $(n_1 - 1) + (n_2 - 1) + (n_3 - 1)$, etc.] and not simply multiply $(n - 1)$ by the number of groups (k).

Assume that you have carried out a single-factor, multi-group experiment with four independent groups. The group n's are 13, 9, 10, and 12. What is the critical value of t associated with the 95% confidence interval for the means in this experiment? ■

For Brandon's data, we can compute the pooled estimate of the standard error of the mean as follows:

(1) $s_{pooled}^2 = \dfrac{[(29)(2.43)^2] + [(29)(2.65)^2] + [(29)(2.83)^2]}{29 + 29 + 29} = 6.99$

(2) $s_{pooled} = \sqrt{6.99} = 2.64$

(3) pooled estimate of $s_M = \dfrac{2.64}{\sqrt{30}} = 0.48$

---

[2]As will be seen in Chapter 12, the pooled estimate of error variation is used for inferential tests of multi-group designs involving independent groups.

BOX 11.1 ■ Using Computers to Construct Confidence Intervals for a Multi-Group Study

Statistical software packages do not necessarily pool the variance estimates when computing confidence intervals. When confidence intervals are based on the pooled estimate of the standard error (and group size is equal), the width of the confidence interval will be the same for each mean. Note that, for Brandon's data, the width of each interval is 1.92 (e.g., $17.39 - 15.47 = 1.92$). This is because the estimated standard error (0.48) is the same for each interval estimate. When variances are not pooled, or group sizes differ, the width of the confidence interval will vary from mean to mean. Thus, you need to examine carefully the confidence interval widths when examining the computer output; if they differ, then the program did not pool (or group sizes differed).

A 95% confidence interval is calculated for each group using the sample means from the respective groups. There were three groups ($k = 3$) in Brandon's experiment; n in each group was 30. Thus, the degrees of freedom for the critical t value are k times ($n - 1$) or 3 times 29, or 87. Because 87 is not in Table A.2, we use the value associated with 60, the next lowest degrees of freedom, a t value with $p = .05$ (two-tailed) of 2.00. The 95% confidence intervals for the three population means based on the data of each of the three groups in Brandon's experiment can be calculated as follows:

Video: $16.43 \pm 2.00\,(0.48) = 15.47$ to 17.39

Slide: $15.93 \pm 2.00\,(0.48) = 14.97$ to 16.89

Lecture: $13.97 \pm 2.00\,(0.48) = 13.01$ to 14.93

Table 11.2 summarizes the steps associated with calculating confidence intervals for an independent groups experiment with more than two groups *based on a pooled estimate of variability.*

Figure 11.2 shows the three confidence intervals from Brandon's experiment superimposed on a bar graph of the means. The sample mean is the best estimate of the population mean, and the width of the confidence interval provides information about the precision of that estimate. When constructing confidence intervals, the central portion of the interval (that immediately around the sample mean) most likely contains the population mean. Thus, when comparing confidence intervals across groups, although we look to see if they overlap, one should not consider each value within the interval as equally likely. But, the width of the confidence intervals does indicate probable values for the population mean given these data. The narrower the interval, the more precise is the estimate of the population mean.

We can suggest a general rule of thumb for interpreting the pattern of confidence intervals in a multi-group experiment: *if the intervals do not overlap, we have evidence that the population means differ. If the intervals overlap such that the mean of one group lies within the interval of another group, we can be confident that the means do not differ to a statistically significant degree.* If the intervals overlap slightly, we should postpone judgment about the difference between the means. When intervals overlap slightly, we need to look more carefully at the differences between pairs of means. We will discuss ways to do that later in this chapter.

TABLE 11.2 ■ Steps in Calculating Confidence Intervals in a Multi-Group Experiment Based on the Pooled Standard Deviation of the Difference between Means

1. First pool the variances of the different groups in the experiment to calculate one estimate of error due to individual differences. The formula for the pooled *variance* estimate is

$$s^2_{pooled} = \frac{(df_1)(s_1^2) + (df_2)(s_2^2) + (df_3)(s_3^2) + \dots}{df_1 + df_2 + df_3 + \dots}$$

   where df = group size minus 1 (i.e., $n - 1$).

2. Find the square root of the pooled variance estimate to yield an estimate of the pooled standard deviation:

$$s_{pooled} = \sqrt{s^2_{pooled}}$$

3. Divide the pooled estimate of the standard deviation by the square root of group size (assuming sizes of groups are equal) to obtain the estimated standard error of the mean based on the pooled measure of error variation:

$$\text{pooled estimated standard error } (s_M) = \frac{s_{pooled}}{\sqrt{n}}$$

   Note: If group sizes are not equal, we must obtain a different estimated standard error for each group by dividing the pooled estimate of the standard deviation by the square root of the appropriate group size (n).

4. The formula for computing the confidence interval around a population mean in an independent groups design based on the pooled variance estimate is $M \pm t_{crit} (s_M)$ The critical t is obtained from Table A.2 based on the sum of the degrees of freedom for all the groups. For each group, the degrees of freedom are one less than the group size (i.e., $n - 1$). Thus, we find the critical value of t associated with degrees of freedom equal to $k(n - 1)$, where k equals the number of groups in our experiment.

   Note: If the group sizes differ for the conditions in our experiment, we must sum the degrees of freedom for the individual groups [i.e., $(n_1 - 1) + (n_2 - 1) + (n_3 - 1)$, etc.] and not simply multiply $(n - 1)$ by the number of groups (k).

FIGURE 11.2. ■ 95% confidence intervals for Brandon's experiment

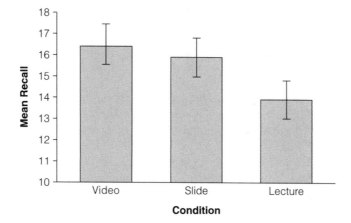

What have we learned? Keep in mind the question that Brandon (or for that matter any-one conducting a single-factor, multi-group experiment) is asking: what is the probable pat-tern of *population* means for the conditions of the experiment? The value of constructing confidence intervals around the sample means is that this question is directly addressed (Loftus & Masson, 1994). There is a natural tendency to want to know exactly what the pop-ulation means are or whether two or more population means are *really* different. But re-member the lesson you learned way back in Chapter 1: the evidence we obtain through sta-tistical analysis does not offer certainty; the evidence is in the form of probabilities that are less than 1.00. Thus, we cannot say for sure exactly what the population values are, but the analyses summarized in Figure 11.2 do provide information to help us with those decisions.

The confidence intervals for the two population means associated with the video and slide conditions overlap such that both means are within the two intervals. (See Figure 11.2.) We can be confident that the effect of video versus slide presentation would not be statistically significant if tested by null hypothesis significance testing (NHST). On the other hand, the fact that the interval associated with the standard lecture condition does not over-lap with that of either the slide or video conditions is evidence that the population means represented by the standard condition and those of the other groups do differ. These results support the impression obtained from the inspection and description stages of data analysis. At this point, we can be confident that we understand the overall pattern of population means estimated in Brandon's experiment.

The conclusions we reach by examining the patterns of confidence intervals are, as seen in Chapter 6, related importantly to the width of the confidence interval. The narrower the interval, the greater is the experiment's statistical power (Loftus & Masson, 1994). As you saw in Chapter 10, statistical power is related to sample size. The greater the sample size, the greater the power of the analysis to detect real differences. The greater the power, the narrower the confidence intervals around the mean and, consequently, the greater precision of our estimates of the population means. Low power, on the other hand, would produce wide and overlapping intervals among all the conditions of Brandon's experiment and leave us uncertain about how retention was affected by the different types of presentation. The topic of statistical power is discussed more completely in Appendix B.

It is perhaps important to review what we have said thus far about the interpretation of confidence intervals in a multi-group experiment. Consider the hypothetical data summa-rized in the three panels of Figure 11.3. The means from an independent groups experiment with four groups are shown in the figure. In Panel A, the confidence intervals surrounding the sample means are wide and overlapping. In Panel B, the interval width for each group is much narrower and not all intervals overlap (Condition D does not overlap with Condition B; Condition C does not overlap with A or B; but A and B overlap, as do C and D.) Finally, in Panel C, the interval width is even narrower, and no interval overlaps another. Note that the group means do not change across the three panels.

The width of the interval reveals the precision of our estimate in the population mean. One reasonable assumption is that sample size increases across Panel A, B, and C because larger sample sizes lead to narrower intervals. (It is unreasonable to assume that the sample means would remain exactly the same when sample sizes change; the means are the same in each panel to make a point about interval width and precision of estimation.) Looking at the result in Panel A, we cannot reject the idea that the sample means reflect population means that have the same or similar values. Given these data, we just don't know. Panel B provides evi-dence that not all the population means are equal. You should note that we gained confidence

FIGURE 11.3. ■ Changes in confidence interval width when means are the same

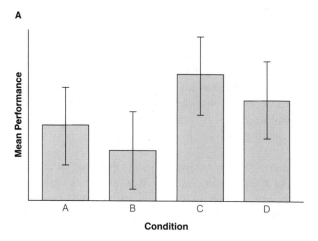

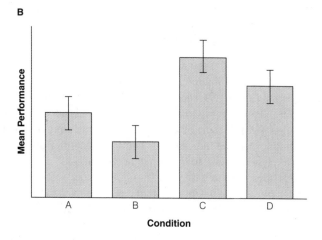

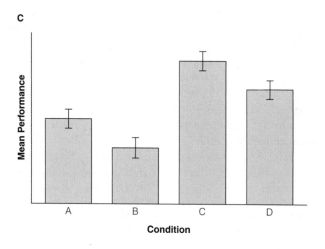

because of the increased precision of our estimates as reflected by narrower confidence intervals. We should be careful, however, about concluding that population means represented by the overlapping intervals (e.g., Condition A and B or C and D) do not differ; again we are left in a state of uncertainty about these differences. Finally, in the third panel, the data provide evidence that the pattern of population means matches that of the four sample means. The narrow confidence intervals reveal a high degree of precision in our estimates of the population means. We can be confident that the pattern of sample means (i.e., the relative differences among means) reflects the pattern of population means. The lesson to be drawn is that constructing confidence intervals around sample means improves our understanding of population differences among means.

Suppose you conducted an experiment with three independent groups. The size of each of the three groups was 10. The construction of confidence intervals for each of the three groups reveals that all of the intervals overlap. The experiment is then repeated with larger size groups. Specifically, group size is now 40 in each of the three conditions. Construction of confidence intervals for this second experiment now reveals that no intervals overlap. What lesson does this teach you about interpreting confidence intervals for a multi-group experiment? ■

ERROR BARS VERSUS CONFIDENCE INTERVALS

The larger the standard error of the mean, the greater is the variability among the means in the theoretical sampling distribution of means. A small standard error of the mean tells us that our sample mean is a pretty good estimate of the population mean. That is, the standard error of the mean tells us (approximately) the average distance that the sample means are from the population mean. If most of the means in the sampling distribution fall close to the population mean (as would be indicated by a small standard error), we can assume that our sample mean is likely to be close to the population mean.

Also recall that approximately two-thirds (.6826) of the "scores" forming a normal population fall between plus or minus one standard deviation from the population mean. Furthermore, approximately 95% (95.44%) fall within plus or minus two standard deviations. These relationships can be used to describe how well the sample mean approximates the population mean. For example, if the standard error equals 1.75, we can infer that approximately two-thirds of all sample means would fall within plus or minus 1.75 units from the population mean. A larger standard error—for example, 2.50—would indicate that two-thirds of the sample means would be found within a greater area (±2.50), assuming a normal distribution. In this latter case, therefore, our estimate of the population mean would not be as good as it was when the standard error was 1.75.

Frequently, a researcher will plot the error associated with a sample mean by indicating in a graph either the interval plus or minus one or two standard errors around the sample mean. These intervals are called **error bars,** and this general approach is called the **plot-plus-error-bar technique** (Loftus, 1993). Figure 11.4 shows error bars for Brandon's data based on the interval plus or minus two standard errors. Error bars were calculated in the same way we did when constructing confidence intervals—that is, by pooling the variance associated with within-groups differences. That is, as seen before,

$$\text{pooled estimated standard error} = \frac{s_{\text{pooled}}}{\sqrt{n}} = \frac{2.64}{\sqrt{30}} = \frac{2.64}{6.99} = 0.48$$

FIGURE 11.4. ■ Error bars (plus/minus two standard errors of the mean) for Brandon's experiment

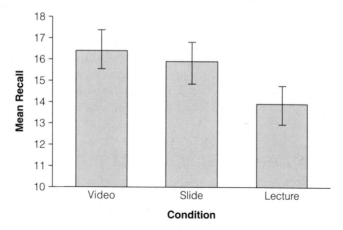

Error bars (plus or minus two standard errors) around the three sample means in Brandon's experiment are as follows:

Video: $16.43 \pm 2.00 \, (0.48) = 15.47$ to 17.39

Slide: $15.93 \pm 2.00 \, (0.48) = 14.97$ to 16.89

Lecture: $13.97 \pm 2.00 \, (0.48) = 13.01$ to 14.93

Except for small samples, a t_{crit} of 2.00 comes close to the value used to construct a 95% confidence interval. Therefore, *error bars based on plus or minus two standard errors will approximate a 95% confidence interval.* Comparing Figure 11.4 with Figure 11.2, you can see that the intervals represented by the error bars (± 2.00) are identical to the intervals produced when 95% confidence intervals were constructed. Remember that the confidence intervals for the means in Figure 11.2 were based on t_{crit} of 2.00, which of course is the same as 2.00 times the standard error. Note the t_{crit} of 2.00 was that associated with 60 degrees of freedom. Of course, critical values of t associated with degrees of freedom lower than 60 become larger as the degrees of freedom decrease (see Table A.2), and critical values of t associated with degrees of freedom above 60 degrees of freedom become slightly smaller. However, except for small samples, the result of multiplying the standard error by 2.00 is a close approximation to a 95% confidence interval (and is exactly the same with 60 df).

When looking at bars surrounding sample means in a graph, one must be sure what the bars represent. Unfortunately, not all researchers (nor all statistical software programs) are careful to identify the exact source of the bars surrounding their sample means. Are they error bars, or are they confidence intervals? If they are error bars, are they based on one standard error or two? How were they calculated? As we noted, statistical software programs do not necessarily pool the error variance when constructing either confidence intervals or error bars. *When using a computer, it is important to verify how error bars or confidence intervals were calculated before continuing with the analysis and interpreting the data.*

It is recommended that you display confidence limits rather than standard error bars when describing the precision of estimation (Estes, 1997). In this way, you will be consistent in your interpretation of the results no matter what the sample size. As Estes (1997)

points out, interpretation of error bars is not the same as that of confidence intervals. The interpretation of confidence intervals associated with a particular probability is straightforward: we know the probability that the interval has captured the population mean. Moreover, as you have seen, by examining the width of the confidence intervals among the various groups in our experiment, we can determine how precise our estimates are of the population means and whether the population means most likely differ. (See Loftus & Masson, 1994.) The interpretation of error bars is not as simply stated and frequently is stated incorrectly even by experienced researchers. (See, e.g., Estes, 1997.)

OBTAINING A MEASURE OF EFFECT SIZE FOR AN INDEPENDENT GROUPS EXPERIMENT WITH ONE INDEPENDENT VARIABLE

Measures of effect size describe the strength of the relationship between the independent and dependent variable in a manner that is independent of sample size. Effect size measures permit us to compare the effect of an independent variable across different studies. A popular measure of the overall effect of a single independent variable is *eta squared* (η^2). Because this measure is more easily understood once you have been introduced to the logic and procedures associated with the inferential test known as *analysis of variance (ANOVA)*, we will postpone discussion of this effect size measure until Chapter 12, following our presentation of ANOVA for an experiment with one factor.

In Chapter 8, you were introduced to Hedges' *g,* which is one way to assess effect size when two means are contrasted. Hedges' *g* expresses the difference between two means in terms of standard deviation units. There are various measures of effect size that may be used when results from two samples are compared as well as when results from more than two samples are compared. (See, e.g., Kirk, 1996.) We discussed *g* as a measure of effect size because it is one of the more important measures of effect size for two groups. The effect size *g* is important, too, when an independent variable has more than two levels but the investigator decides to focus on comparisons between particular pairs of levels. (See especially the next section.) We mentioned, for example, that Brandon might want to know about the differences between specific conditions of his multimedia experiment, such as the difference between a slide presentation and the standard lecture presentation. If such a comparison were of interest, *g* would be important when describing the effect size associated with these two levels of the independent variable. In the next section, we show how *g* might be used to describe effect size between two groups of a multi-group experiment.

DECISIONS ABOUT DIFFERENCES BETWEEN TWO MEANS IN A SINGLE-FACTOR EXPERIMENT

We mentioned that a researcher conducting a single-factor, multi-group experiment generally will want to know more than whether the independent variable had an overall effect on the dependent variable. *An overall effect is revealed when we can state with confidence that relative differences observed among sample means reflect actual relative differences in the pattern of population means.* Such was the outcome of the analysis up to this point for Brandon's multimedia experiment. Suppose, however, that Brandon wishes to analyze further the difference between the standard lecture condition and the slide or video condition. Knowing about these effects may be important in making a decision about which kind of multimedia presentation to use with students. Or suppose that Brandon wishes to examine further the difference between the two multimedia conditions (slide and video). What might be done?

We offer two suggestions for analyzing the difference between two means in the context of a multi-group experiment following the examination of confidence intervals based on the sample means. The first is to obtain a measure of effect size for the two-group comparison using an appropriate effect size measure such as g. The calculation of effect sizes allow us to compare our results with previous findings with the same or similar independent variables and also permits us to gauge the overall size of an effect based on accepted rules of thumb for effect sizes. (The procedures for calculating g for two independent means and the interpretation of g were detailed in Chapter 8.)

For example, Brandon may wish to obtain an effect size for the video condition versus the standard lecture condition, and an effect size for the slide condition and the standard lecture condition. If previous studies made these comparisons, Brandon can judge whether his effect size for these conditions is similar to previous findings. Because effect sizes will vary from study to study, Brandon may wish to average the effect sizes based on his findings and those of previous findings to estimate the true effect of multimedia presentation of this kind. Recall that

$$g = \frac{M_1 - M_2}{s_{\text{pooled}}}$$

When calculating g for a two-group comparison within a multi-group experiment, we may reasonably use the pooled variance estimate obtained across all groups. Therefore, s_{pooled} in the formula for g is the same estimate of within group variability that we used when obtaining the 95% confidence interval for each of the groups. For example, the effect size, g, for the contrast between mean retention in the video condition and mean retention in the standard lecture condition is

$$g = \frac{M_1 - M_2}{s_{\text{pooled}}} = \frac{16.43 - 13.97}{2.64} = \frac{2.46}{2.64} = 0.93$$

This would be a large effect according to Cohen's (1988) rule of thumb.

Another suggestion for analyzing the difference between two means is to construct a confidence interval for the difference between two means. (See Loftus & Masson, 1994.) The procedures and interpretation of confidence intervals for the difference between two independent means were discussed in Chapter 8. Note, however, that again we may reasonably use the pooled variance estimate based on all groups (k) in a multi-group experiment when constructing the confidence interval for a difference between two means. Specifically, when estimating the standard error of the difference between two independent means ($s_{M_1 - M_2}$), we find

$$\text{pooled estimate of } s_{M_1 - M_2} = (s_{\text{pooled}}) \sqrt{\left(\frac{1}{n_1} + \frac{1}{n_2}\right)}$$

The estimated standard error of the difference between two means (s_{M-M}) is multiplied by the critical t based on df associated with the pooled variance estimate [i.e., $k(n - 1)$] for the desired level of confidence, usually .95. Adding and subtracting the product to and from the difference between two means yields the confidence interval for the difference between the population means (see Chapter 8): $(M_1 - M_2) \pm t_{\text{crit}} (s_{M_1 - M_2})$

BOX 11.2 ■ Ilustration of Steps to Obtain the 95% Confidence Interval for Difference Between Two Means in a Multi-Group Experiment

The calculation of the 95% confidence interval for the difference between the means of the video and slide conditions in Brandon's experiment is as follows.

(1) Obtain pooled estimate of standard error of the difference between means:

$$\text{pooled estimate of } s_{M_1-M_2} = s_{\text{pooled}} \sqrt{\left(\frac{1}{n_1} + \frac{1}{n_2}\right)} =$$

$$(2.64) \sqrt{(1/30 + 1/30)} = 2.64 \sqrt{.067} = (2.64)(.258) = 0.68$$

(2) Calculate interval based on

$$(M_1 - M_2) \pm t_{\text{crit}} (s_{M_1-M_2})$$

where t_{crit} is based on df equal to $k(n-1)$ or, in this case, 3(29), or 87.

An examination of Table A.2 reveals that a critical value for 87 degrees of freedom is not in the table. As we saw before, the next lowest value, that associated with 60 degrees of freedom, may be used. This value of 2.00 may be judged to approximate the critical value of t for the .05 level (nondirectional). Thus,

95% confidence interval: $(16.43 - 15.93) \pm 2.00 (0.68) = 0.50 \pm 1.36$
$= -0.86$ to 1.86

As was suggested by the results seen in Figure 11.2, the value of zero (0.0) appears within the interval. Brandon would not be able to reject the idea that the population means for these two conditions are the same. Precision of estimation for this difference is indexed by the interval width.

By focusing on the specific two-mean comparison of interest, the researcher obtains information about probable differences between the two population means. For example, Brandon might wish to construct the 95% confidence interval for the difference between the means represented by the video and slide conditions of his experiment. An examination of Figure 11.2 suggests that the outcome of this procedure will show that 0.0 is within the confidence interval. If this were the case, Brandon would not be able to reject the idea that the population means for these two conditions are the same. Nevertheless, he would be able to judge the precision of estimation for his comparison based on the interval width.

WHAT YOU HAVE LEARNED AND THE NEXT STEP

In this chapter, you learned how to inspect and describe the data from a study involving more than two independent sample means. Moreover, as Loftus (1996) suggested, you learned that confidence intervals should always be placed around sample statistics that are used to make decisions about population values. We discussed how to interpret confidence intervals in a single-factor independent groups design, paying attention to the overall pattern of means and the associated confidence interval width. The pattern of population means indicated by confidence intervals around the experimental means gives us a good idea how scores on the dependent variable were affected by our independent variable. We obtain evidence regarding the covariation observed in the description stage of our analysis. Specifically, we estimate how confident we are that the overall pattern of means reflects true population mean differences.

Major concepts and ideas discussed in this chapter were as follows:

- When constructing confidence intervals for population means in a multi-group experiment, of particular interest is the *pattern of means* and associated measures of variability across the conditions of our experiment.

- The interpretation of differences obtained in a natural groups design differs from that when differences are observed in a random groups design. Because natural groups designs do not satisfy the conditions of a true experiment, we are not able to draw cause-and-effect conclusions when we observe differences between means that are associated with a natural groups variable.

- Assumptions of normality and homogeneity of variance, which we saw are important for statistical tests of the difference between two means, are also important for tests involving more than two means.

- By comparing stem-and-leaf displays with the same stem structure, one quickly gains an impression of within-group variability and central tendency among the conditions of an experiment with one independent variable.

- In the description phase of a multi-group experiment, we begin to look for evidence of covariation between the independent and dependent variables.

- Judgments about differences among population means can be made on the basis of confidence intervals plotted around sample means.

- We pay attention to interval width because it tells us how well the observed pattern of sample means is likely to reflect the underlying pattern of population means.

- The value of constructing confidence intervals around sample means in a multi-group experiment is that they directly address the question: What are the relative values of population means for the conditions of the experiment?

- The larger the sample size, the greater is the power of the analysis to detect real differences and the narrower the confidence intervals around the mean.

- Constructing a graph showing the error associated with sample means is called the *plot-plus-error-bar technique.*

- When using a computer software program, it is important to verify how error bars or confidence intervals were calculated before continuing with the analysis and interpretation of the data.

- Confidence limits rather than standard error bars are recommended when assessing the precision of your mean estimates.

- An overall effect of an independent variable is revealed when we can state with confidence that relative differences observed among sample means reflect actual differences among population means.

- Suggestions for analyzing the difference between two means in the context of a multi-group experiment following the examination of confidence intervals based on the sample means include obtaining a measure of effect size for the two-group comparison and constructing a confidence interval for the difference between two means.

We have tried to show that, by calculating descriptive statistics and confidence intervals for the population means, you are in a good position to infer what happened in your experiment. Why do more?

In some situations, there may be no need to do anything more to explain what happened in an experiment. This may be particularly true when your major interest is in the overall pattern of mean differences associated with the independent variable. At other times, however, you may want to know more. For example, it may be important to determine the size of the overall effect of the independent variable. In the next chapter, when we look at null hypothesis significance testing (NHST) for a multi-group experiment, we will show you how to do this. We may also wish to be able to state (based on probabilities, of course) that the independent variable did produce an overall effect. NHST tells us the probability that the pattern of sample mean differences is due to chance variation assuming that the population means are in fact the same. When the probability is low that chance may explain our results, we have increased confidence that our independent variable worked to produce a difference among means. We may wish to report this information with confidence intervals that show the likely pattern among the population means.

What you have learned so far should be seen as complementary to analyses of a multi-group experiment based on NHST. In the next chapter, we show how NHST procedures can complement these analyses. Whether one begins the estimation phase of multi-group data analysis by constructing confidence intervals around sample means or by performing NHST is partly a matter of individual preference. We have introduced confidence intervals first to focus your attention on the pattern of observed means in your data set. Presumably one conducts an experiment to learn if there is meaningful variation among the population means represented by the conditions of the experiment. By constructing confidence intervals around the experimental means, you can readily assess the precision of your estimation of population mean differences.

When conducting a multi-group experiment, we also may wish to make specific decisions about particular mean differences that are represented by our data. Measures of effect size for two-group comparisons are useful in this regard. So, too, may be the construction of confidence intervals for the difference between two means. In the next chapter, we will illustrate yet another approach to making decisions about the differences between two groups in the context of a multi-group experiment when using NHST.

Key Concepts

single-factor independent groups design

error bar

plot-plus-error-bar technique

Answers to *Your Turn* Questions

11-1. (a) Careful inspection reveals an invalid data point in the slide condition. The maximum number correct is 20, but a score of 21 appears in this condition. Brandon must examine the original data sheets and computer file to try to find the error.

(b) There are no outliers in any of the groups.

(c) The general shape of the distributions in each case is roughly normal.

(d) There is similar variability (dispersion) among the scores in each of the groups. Given that the maximum score is 20, the range is essentially the same in each group: 11–20, 10–20, 9–20.

(e) One can see that the scores in the lecture group tend to be centered around lower numbers than do scores in the video or slide conditions.

11-2. The means confirm the visual impression obtained from the stem-and-leaf displays. The standard deviations are similar among the groups; the mean in the standard lecture condition is two points lower than that of the slide condition and about 2.5 points lower than the video condition mean.

11-3. The correct interpretation is that there is a .95 probability that the interval contains the population mean. Intervals vary from sample to sample while the population mean remains constant. Thus, intervals "fall" around the population mean. It is *not* correct to say that there is a .95 probability that the population mean falls in this interval. The 95% confidence interval tells us that, if we were to repeat this procedure 100 times, we would capture the population mean within the intervals we calculated in 95 of those 100 replications. Thus, there is a .95 probability that a replication will produce an interval that contains the population mean. Probabilities refer to population values and not sample values, as suggested in the incorrect alternative (c).

11-4. The degrees of freedom ($n - 1$) for each of the four groups are 12, 8, 9, and 11. That is, a total of 40. The critical t for the 95% confidence interval is 2.021.

11-5. Our conclusions about the "real" differences between population means rests on the evidence (data) we have collected. When confidence intervals overlap, we have *not* proved that the population means are the same. On the other hand, given these data and this outcome, we also cannot conclude that the means differ. We are left in a state of uncertainty about the real difference between the means. However, we can examine the width of the confidence intervals to assess how precise is our estimate of the population mean. With larger sample sizes, we will have smaller interval widths (and greater precision). Thus, given small sample sizes, we may be left in a state of uncertainty about the difference between the means (due to wider, overlapping intervals), but with larger sample sizes we may (given greater precision of estimation) be able to conclude that a real difference is most likely present between the means.

Analyzing and Interpreting Data: Problems and Exercises

1. When analyzing results of a single-factor, independent groups experiment, a researcher typically wants to know more than simply whether the independent variable had "an effect." Explain.

2. How does a single-factor, independent groups experiment based on random groups differ from one based on natural groups? Provide an example of each.

3. What two major assumptions about the characteristics of populations under investigation are important for statistical analyses comparing differences among means?

4. What is a good way to begin data inspection of results from a single-factor independent groups study?

5. In the description phase of analysis of a single-factor experiment, a researcher looks for "covariation" between the independent and dependent variables. Identify what the researcher is looking for.

6. By constructing confidence intervals around sample means in a multi-group experiment, the researcher directly addresses what important question?

7. What is the general rule of thumb for interpreting the pattern of confidence intervals in a single-factor, independent groups experiment?

8. (a) An examination of confidence intervals for a single-factor, independent groups experiment with three levels of the independent variable reveals that none of the intervals overlap. What should the researcher conclude?

   (b) An examination of confidence intervals for a single-factor, independent groups experiment with four levels of the independent variable reveals that two of the intervals overlap and two do not overlap with each other or with any other interval. What should the researcher conclude?

9. Confidence intervals are constructed in a multi-group experiment using a "pooled estimate of the standard error of the mean." Explain.

10. You are examining the computer output from an analysis of a single-factor, independent groups design with groups of the same size. You note that the width of the confidence intervals around the sample means differs from one mean to another. What is the likely explanation for the fact that the confidence interval widths differ?

11. Explain how the concept of statistical power is related to the construction and examination of confidence intervals.

12. What generally is the most important factor affecting the width of a confidence interval?

13. What are the degrees of freedom for the critical t value used when constructing confidence intervals in a multi-group experiment?

14. Kathie conducts an experiment comparing three different types of persuasive messages intended to affect people's attitudes toward a new cola beverage. Random groups of 21 students each taste the beverage after listening to one of three different messages about the product. The mean "liking" rating (based on a 10-point scale where 1 = "not at all" and 10 = "very much") for the three groups, and measures of variability are:

Message	A	B	C
M	7.12	6.42	5.14
s	1.64	1.87	1.50

(a) Construct confidence intervals around the sample means using the pooled estimate of the standard error of the mean.

(b) State a conclusion about the effect of the three messages based on your examination of the pattern of means and associated confidence intervals for the population means.

15. Puja lands a job with a pharmaceutical firm. One of her jobs is to help with data analysis of experiments testing various drugs with animal subjects.

In one study, three different groups of rats ($n = 25$) are given variations of a new tranquilizer. In addition to looking for side effects of the drugs, the researchers measure activity level during the hour following drug administration. The floors of the animal cages are marked off in small squares, and the activity measure is the number of squares touched by a rat as it moves around the cage. The mean activity levels for the three groups (and standard deviations) for this experiment are

Drug	A	B	C
M	14.6	15.7	12.2
s	3.8	4.5	3.8
n	25	25	25

(a) Construct confidence intervals around the sample means using the pooled estimate of the standard error of the mean.

(b) State a conclusion about the differences among the drug groups based on your examination of the pattern of means and associated confidence intervals for the population means.

16. Jorge is taking a developmental psychology laboratory course at his school. He is asked to conduct an experiment testing children's cognitive abilities at four different age levels. He goes to the elementary school that he once attended and asks permission of the principal to test children at the school. She agrees only if he also gets permission from the parents and is willing to talk to children at the school about his university experience and the major of psychology. Jorge readily agrees to do both. The test takes only a few minutes, and, with the cooperation of the teachers at the school, he is able to test 34 children in four age groups during several recess periods in one week. Scores on the test vary from 0 to 30. The group size (n), mean performance, and standard deviation for each group are

Age Group (Years)	7	8	9	10
M	20.4	22.0	24.1	26.8
s	4.8	5.1	3.9	6.2
n	8	9	9	8

(a) Construct confidence intervals around the sample means using the pooled estimate of the standard error of the mean.

(b) State a conclusion about the differences among the age groups based on your examination of the pattern of means and associated confidence intervals for the population means.

(c) Comment on the width of the confidence intervals and what you believe is responsible for the relatively wide and overlapping intervals.

17. Josephine works for an advertising firm and is asked to conduct a study examining people's reactions to four different movie trailers for a new movie. Random groups of 30 people each at a local shopping mall are offered $2 to view one of the four short video features and respond to a brief list of questions about the video clip. An important question was "How likely are you to see this movie?" People responded using a 7-point scale where 1 = "not at all" and 7 = "very likely." The mean likelihood ratings for the four groups and measures of variability are:

Video	A	B	C	D
M	3.12	5.77	4.19	2.91
s	1.32	1.43	1.66	1.10

(a) Construct confidence intervals around the sample means using the pooled estimate of the standard error of the mean.

(b) State a conclusion about people's likelihood ratings of the four videos based on your examination of the pattern of means and associated confidence intervals for the population means.

18. (a) How does the interpretation of error bars around sample means differ from that of confidence intervals?

(b) Which measure is recommended when displaying sample means?

19. Explain how Hedges' g, a measure of effect size that is appropriate when comparing two means, may be important in a single-factor study with three or more groups.

20. Suppose that Kathie (problem #14) was particularly interested in the difference between the two means associated with Message A and B because these two messages had been used previously in related research. What would you recommend for her to do in addition to constructing the confidence interval for the difference between the individual means?

Answers to Odd-Numbered Problems

1. To find that an independent variable "had an effect" on the dependent variable is frequently insufficient information when there are three or more levels of the independent variable. A researcher chooses the levels of the independent variable for a reason. One reason might be to compare and contrast specific levels of the independent variable. Finding an "overall" effect of the independent variable would not, in this case, tell the researcher about specific differences between pairs of means.

3. Assumptions of normality and homogeneity of variance are important for many statistical tests. Whether these assumptions have been met is judged by carefully inspecting the shape of the sample distributions and obtaining measures of variability. If the samples meet these assumptions, we assume that the populations will also.

5. It is important in the description phase of data analysis to look for trends and patterns among the group

means. Do the means differ? How? As we look across levels of the independent variable, do group means change (i.e., covary with levels of the independent variable)? After all, a major reason for conducting an experiment is to see if the groups differ; if they do, we may state that (descriptively) means vary with changes in the levels of the independent variable.

7. A general rule of thumb for interpreting the pattern of confidence intervals in a multi-group experiment is: if the intervals do not overlap, we have evidence that the population means differ. If the intervals overlap such that the mean of one group lies within the interval of another group, we can be confident that the means do not differ to a statistically significant degree. If the intervals overlap slightly, we should postpone judgment about the difference between the means.

9. We first pool our estimate of the variance by including the variability from all the conditions of the experiment

in our calculation. Then, we take the square root of the pooled variance estimate to find the estimated pooled standard deviation. The pooled estimate of the standard error equals the estimated pooled standard deviation divided by the square root of the group size.

11. The greater the power of a statistical analysis, the more likely the analysis is to reveal real differences between means. The greater the power, the narrower the confidence interval and, consequently, the greater the precision associated with the interval estimate of the population mean. Sample size has a direct effect on precision of estimation: as the sample size increases, power increases and the confidence interval width decreases. See also the appendix chapter on power analysis.

13. The degrees of freedom (df) for the critical t when constructing confidence intervals in a multi-group experiment are $k(n - 1)$, where k equals the number of groups and n equals the sample size of each group. This assumes that there is the same n for all the groups. When group size differs, the degrees of freedom for the critical t are calculated by summing the degrees of freedom for the individual groups, or simply $N - k$, where N is the size of the data set.

15. (a) The 95% confidence intervals are, for Drug A, 12.98 to 16.22; for Drug B, 14.08 to 17.32; and, for Drug C, 10.58 to 13.82. (The degrees of freedom (df) for this experiment are 72, but, because 72 is not found in the table of critical t values, the value associated with $df = 60$ is used. The t_{crit} with 60 df is 2.00. The estimated standard error of the mean is 0.81.)

(b) The interval for Drug C does not overlap the Drug B interval, and we may thus suggest that the population mean estimated by Group C differs from that of Group B. The intervals for Drug A and B overlap substantially; the interval for A includes the group B sample mean. Given these data, we would not want to conclude that population means A and B differ. It appears that Drug C is the most effective in this situation in terms of measured activity.

17. (a) The 95% confidence intervals are, for Video A, 2.68 to 3.56; for Video B, 5.33 to 6.21; and, for Video C, 3.75 to 4.63. (The degrees of freedom (df) for this experiment are 156, but, because 156 is not found in the table of critical t values, the value associated with $df = 120$ is used. The t_{crit} with 120 df is 1.98. The estimated standard error of the mean is 0.22.)

(b) The intervals for Video A and D overlap substantially (the group mean of A is within the interval of D), but neither interval overlaps with those of B and C. Intervals for B and C do not overlap, and we may thus suggest that the population means estimated by Group B and C differ from each other and from that of the other two groups. In terms of rated likelihood of viewing the movie after seeing the trailer, it appears that Video B is most effective.

19. It is frequently important to focus an analysis on the difference between two means in an experiment involving three or more means. The effect size measure, Hedges' g, may be usefully employed to determine the size of an effect when two means are compared.

 Go to http://psychology.wadsworth.com/courses/statistics/ and test your knowledge of this chapter by taking the online quiz. Another resource to check is the online workshops that provide a step-by-step guide through a number of topics at http://psychology.wadsworth.com/workshops/workshops.html.

Estimating Confidence Using Null Hypothesis Significance Testing and Announcing Results

. . . significance tests . . . provide us with the criteria by which provisionally to distinguish results due to chance variation from results that represent systematic effects in data available to us.

Mulaik, Raju, & Harshman (1997, p. 81)

INTRODUCTION

Try to put yourself in the following research situations.

- Juan works for a pharmaceutical firm that is testing the effect of a tumor-reducing drug on rats with cancer. There are 120 rats randomly assigned to four conditions ($n = 30$) of his experiment. One group is left untreated. The other three groups are given various combinations of the tumor-reducing drug and a second drug that is expected to interact with the cancer drug to enhance its effect. For our purposes, we can simply think of these four conditions as A, B, C, and D, with A being the untreated group. Measures of tumor growth in the rats constitute the dependent variable. Juan knows how to do a t test, but he is concerned that doing t tests for all pairs of groups might not be right.

- Melissa is a clinical psychologist doing therapy outcome research on treatments for depression. She works at a large mental health clinic serving poor clients in the inner city of a large metropolitan area. Because the number of clients is large, Melissa is able to set up an experiment testing the effects of two different therapies with an untreated (waiting list) control group. Appropriate measures of therapy outcome are available, and 30 clients are assigned randomly to the three conditions ($n = 10$) of her experiment.

- Between his junior and senior years at college, Dalton found a summer job working for an educational psychologist who has collected data summarizing the reading skills of fourth-grade children in five different schools in the area. The psychologist asks Dalton to find out if there are meaningful differences in the reading level of the children sampled from these schools.

- For her honors thesis in a criminal justice program, Shona is interested in comparing the effect of three different kinds of persuasive messages on students' attitude change. She randomly assigns 66 female students to three experimental groups ($n = 22$) that differ in the type of message they receive about the need for a self-defense training course offered at the university. The messages are similar except for the number of examples of recent attacks on women in the vicinity of the university. The messages contain one, three, or five examples. The dependent variable is a sum of several 7-point scales that, after reading a message, students used to indicate their likelihood of taking a self-defense training course when it is next offered.

In each of these situations, a multi-group experiment was performed. The researcher is interested in what happens as a consequence of subjects participating in different levels of a single independent variable. In three of these scenarios, subjects are randomly assigned to the conditions of the experiment; in the third example, the participants are selected from natural groups (i.e., children attending a particular elementary school). In this chapter, we continue to examine how a researcher might analyze and interpret data from such independent groups experiments. You will recall that we began this discussion in the previous chapter when we examined the use of confidence intervals in a multi-group experiment examining the effect of multimedia presentation on students' memory. We will continue this discussion where we left off.

THE ROLE OF NHST IN AN INDEPENDENT GROUPS EXPERIMENT WITH ONE INDEPENDENT VARIABLE (THE *E* IN I-D-E-A)

We saw in the last chapter that our graduate student, Brandon, obtained evidence that his manipulated independent variable (type of multimedia presentation) produced differences in students' recall of the presented material. Mean performance on a test of retention varied with the levels of the independent variable.

In this chapter, we introduce a procedure based on null hypothesis significance testing (NHST), called **analysis of variance** (abbreviated *ANOVA*), which will permit Brandon to claim with a particular degree of certainty that there was indeed an effect of his independent variable. Traditionally, researchers have used NHST in the context of a multi-group experiment to determine whether there is something of interest in their data, that is, whether the observed differences among means might represent something other than simply chance variation (e.g., Abelson, 1997). One might argue that Brandon already knows this. After all, the pattern of confidence intervals seen in his experiment, given the degree of precision of estimation accompanying these intervals, strongly suggested that the population means are not all the same. We must agree. However, although the value of confidence intervals is that they directly address the question of the relative sizes of the population means (e.g., Loftus, 1993), the value of NHST is that it focuses us on the likelihood of making an error when concluding that there are real differences among population means. (See, e.g., Harris, 1997.)

Recall that a Type I error tells us the probability that we have mistakenly concluded that a real difference exists when in fact only chance is operating. Knowing that the probability of a Type I error is low provides assurance that there are systematic effects in our data and that the observed differences among sample means are meaningful. Moreover, as you saw in Chapter 10, the probability level associated with the outcome of a NHST procedure provides information regarding the likelihood that an exact replication will produce statistically significant results. In other words, the outcome of NHST gives us information about the degree of reliability of our finding.

Although some researchers may prefer to perform NHST first in order *"provisionally* to distinguish results due to chance variation from results that represent systematic effects" (Mulaik, Raju, & Harshman, 1997, p. 81), unfortunately, too often the analysis stops there. We began our discussion of the analysis of multi-group experiments by showing how confidence intervals can be used to examine precision of estimation and the probable pattern of population means (Chapter 11). Beginning this way calls attention to the value of the information obtained from an analysis of a multi-group study based on confidence intervals. This information may be supplemented with that obtained by NHST or, if one prefers, NHST may be supplemented by the use of confidence intervals. In either case, it is important to see how these approaches complement one another and how both contribute to a complete understanding of the data. *The result of NHST rarely is of value by itself.*

Brandon will likely want to learn more about what happened in his experiment by directly comparing pairs of sample means from among those obtained in his experiment. As we saw in Chapter 11, this will permit Brandon to say more than simply that his independent variable had "an effect." Rather, he will be in a position to state exactly what is the nature of that effect. In most situations, a researcher conducting a multi-group experiment will want to focus on differences between two means. As you will see, these means may include more than simply comparing two experimental conditions. NHST and confidence intervals also play complementary roles in this analysis.

The general logic of ANOVA is similar for both types of independent groups designs: natural groups and random groups. Because we assume that you will perform an ANOVA on a computer, our emphasis will be on understanding the logic of ANOVA and interpreting the computer output from this type of analysis.

In this chapter, we also show how to calculate measures of effect size for an experiment involving more than two groups, what are more generally called *measures of strength of association.* The "association," or covariation, is that between the independent and dependent variables. We had postponed this discussion from Chapter 11 until the logic of ANOVA was presented because measures of strength of association are closely related to the outcome of ANOVA. These measures, when used in combination with the descriptive statistics and confidence intervals, as well as the outcome of an inferential test such as ANOVA, will help determine the level of confidence you can have in your results (the *E* in the I-D-E-A model).

Finally, you will learn how to announce (the *A* in I-D-E-A) the results of an analysis involving more than two independent groups so that your results will be clearly understood by others and conform to the stylistic requirements of the American Psychological Association. As we show, the results of both NHST and the construction of confidence intervals play a role in this announcement.

THE LOGIC OF ANOVA

In the context of ANOVA, an independent variable usually is called a **factor.** The levels defining a factor may be manipulated or selected. A study with one independent variable is called a *single-factor design.* (See Chapter 11.) Such studies may represent independent groups or repeated measures designs. Our focus here will be on the ANOVA for independent groups designs. The question that a researcher using ANOVA seeks to answer is: Did the factor have an effect on the dependent variable? (Are the population means different?) Evidence for an answer to this question can be obtained using the null hypothesis significance test known as *ANOVA.*

The hypothesis to be tested, specifically the null hypothesis, is that the population means estimated by the sample means in the experiment are the same. In other words, the null hypothesis states that there is no effect of the independent variable on the dependent variable. You should be familiar with the statement of a null hypothesis from our discussion of NHST for comparing two means. (See Chapter 9 and 10.) It is important to emphasize that the null hypothesis is the *only* hypothesis that can be tested using NHST. The alternative hypothesis—that the treatment did have an effect—is not directly tested. The logic of NHST is indirect, as we will review for you.

The null hypothesis (H_0) for a single-factor design is symbolized as

H_0: $\mu_1 = \mu_2 = \mu_3 = \mu_4 =$ etc.

The alternative hypothesis (H_1) is simply NOT H_0. *Any difference among the means satisfies the alternative hypothesis.*

ANOVA is an inferential test to help researchers decide whether there is sufficient evidence to make a decision that a difference is present. When decision-making based on NHST was introduced in earlier chapters, we identified some of the problems with NHST (see especially Chapter 10), for example, the kinds of decision-making errors that are present (i.e., Type I vs. Type II). NHST is the most common method of statistical decision-making in psychology, and ANOVA is the most common statistical test for studies involving more than two means.

In addition to the requirement that the dependent variable be measured on at least an interval scale, the researcher using ANOVA assumes that the distributions in the populations corresponding to the conditions (levels) of the study are (a) normal in form and (b) have similar variances (i.e., homogeneity of variance).

A goal of the inspection and description stages of data analysis is to determine whether these assumptions are met. We saw in Chapter 11, for example, that Brandon's experimental results appeared to satisfy both the normality and homogeneity assumptions. Although ANOVA is known to be a robust test and not always affected even by substantial deviations in these assumptions (see, e.g., Rosenthal & Rosnow, 1991), it is important in the early stages of data analysis to decide whether the data at least approximate these assumptions.

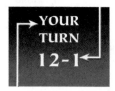

Just to remind you, when making statistical decisions using null hypothesis testing, we are capable of making one of two types of errors: Type I and Type II. Are you clear about the meaning of these two types of errors? Define each and check your answer. ■

What is interesting about ANOVA is that it is used to make a decision about differences among means by examining differences between variances. ANOVA is literally an analysis of *variance*. It involves separating the total variance (called *partitioning* the variability) according to the source of the variance. The end result of ANOVA is the calculation of a ratio between two variances that potentially express two different kinds of variability. Let's see how this works.

The total variability in a data set is first defined. We first talked briefly about variance in Chapter 4 when we discussed how to describe variability in a data set. Recall that the square root of the variance is called the *standard deviation.* When describing the degree of dispersal of numbers in a data set, the standard deviation is much more helpful than is the variance because the standard deviation is expressed in the same unit of measure as the original data. The variance is defined as the sum of squared deviations of scores from a mean $[\Sigma (X - M)^2]$ divided by the degrees of freedom, which for a single sample are $N - 1$. The sum of the squared deviations from a mean $[\Sigma (X - M)^2]$ is frequently abbreviated as SS (meaning "sum of squares"). A variance is essentially the mean or average of the squared deviations, that is, $SS/df.$ Consequently, another name for variance in the context of ANOVA is *mean square.*

We divide SS by the degrees of freedom (df) to produce the variance or mean square for a single sample (i.e., SS/df). Degrees of freedom typically are one less than the number of squared deviations in the numerator. Thus, if we have 20 scores, SS will be based on 20 squared deviations from the overall mean and degrees of freedom will be $20 - 1$, or 19. Technically speaking, therefore, a "mean" square is not strictly a mean because a mean is a sum divided by the total number (i.e., N) of values contributing to the sum and not $N - 1$. Do you remember why, when calculating a sample variance for purposes of statistical decision-making, the SS is divided by $N - 1$ rather than by N? ■

In previous chapters, you learned to use what is called the *pooled variance estimate* when calculating the estimated standard error of the mean as well as the estimated standard error of the difference between means. This pooled estimate also is important in ANOVA. Thus, before moving on, let us look more closely at the pooled variance estimate. Recall that it is defined as

$$s^2_{pooled} = \frac{(df_1)(s_1^2) + (df_2)(s_2^2) + (df_3)(s_3^2) + \ldots}{df_1 + df_2 + df_3 + \ldots}$$

Each *df* equals sample (group) size minus 1 (i.e., $n - 1$). Taking the square root of the pooled variance estimate yields an estimate of the pooled standard deviation that, as we reviewed, is then used to calculate the estimated standard error of the mean. (See Chapter 11.) However, look closely at the numerator of the formula for the pooled variance estimate.

For each group, we multiply *df* by the variance (s^2) of each. Variance, we repeat, is equal to the sum of the squared deviations from the group mean (SS) divided by the *df*; that is, $s^2 = SS/df$. Therefore, multiplying the variance by *df*, as we do in the previous pooled estimate formula, yields $(df)(s^2) = (df)(SS/df) = SS$.

In other words, the numerator of the formula for the pooled variance estimate is the sum of the squared deviations within each group; this total within-group variation is then divided by the sum of the degrees of freedom for the various groups, or

$$s^2_{pooled} = \frac{SS_1 + SS_2 + SS_3 + \ldots}{df_1 + df_2 + df_3 + \ldots}$$

As you will see, this same pooled variance estimate plays an important role in ANOVA.

We begin ANOVA by defining the total variability in the data set. We first find the squared deviation of each score (*X*) from the grand mean (*GM*) and sum these squared deviations. Note that this is exactly what we would do if we wished to calculate the variance for the complete set of numbers because the numerator of the variance is the sum of squared deviations from the overall mean. We aren't really interested in the overall variance or mean square of the data set, but we do need the sum of the squared deviations from the grand mean. This value is called the **SS total** (abbreviated SS_{tot}). It represents the sum of squared deviations from the grand mean of the data set: $SS \text{ total} = \Sigma(X - GM)^2$.

The overall variability expressed as *SS* total is partitioned into two types of variability. To better understand this partitioning of variability, consider the deviation of a single score from the grand mean of a data set with multiple groups. A score's deviation from the grand mean (*GM*) of the data set can be conceptualized as the sum of two separate deviations: the first is the deviation of a score from its group mean; the second is the deviation of a group mean from the grand mean. This is simply stated as follows:

$(X - GM) = (X - \text{GROUP MEAN}) + (\text{GROUP MEAN} - GM)$

Careful inspection of this equation shows that we are really saying in effect that the distance between A and C is equal to the distance between A and B plus the distance between B and C. In other words, we have taken the total distance of a score from the grand mean and expressed it as equal to two distances that when added together make up the total distance, [e.g., $14 - 17 = (14 - 16) + (16 - 17)$]. Figure 12.1 illustrates these deviations for an experiment involving three groups. This is more than simply a way to think about the deviation of a score from a grand mean of the data. The two different "distances" (i.e., deviations) represent different sources of variation.

FIGURE 12.1 ■ Illustration of deviation between individual score and group mean $(X - M_A)$ and deviation between group mean and grand mean $(M - GM)$ in a multi-group experiment with three groups.

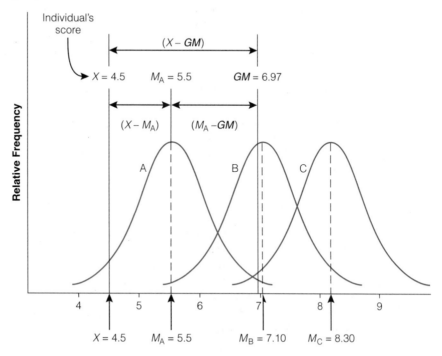

The first deviation—that between a score and its group mean $(X - M_A)$—represents what is called **within-group variability.** The second deviation—that between the group mean and the grand mean $(M_A - GM)$—is called **between-group variability.**

Overall variability or SS_{tot} (based on individual scores' deviations from a grand mean) is thus composed of two separate sources of variability. Each can be expressed in terms of sums of squared deviations from a mean. The SS between groups (abbreviated SS_{bg}) is based on squared deviations from the grand mean. Note that in this case the squared deviations represent differences between group means and the grand mean. This is something you have not seen before. The SS_{bg} represents variability among the means of your experiment. Are the group means similar or very different? The greater the differences, the greater the SS_{bg}.

The SS within groups (abbreviated SS_{wg}) is based on sums of squared deviations of scores from individual group means. Note that in this case the deviations represent differences between individual scores and a group mean, something with which you should be familiar by now. Everyone in a group does not behave similarly. It can be shown that:

$$SS_{tot} = SS_{bg} + SS_{wg}$$ **Equation 12.1**

A **mean square** (or variance) can be calculated by dividing a SS by the appropriate degrees of freedom (df):

$$MS_{bg} = \frac{SS_{bg}}{df_{bg}} \qquad MS_{wg} = \frac{SS_{wg}}{df_{wg}}$$

The df_{bg} for MS_{bg} are $k - 1$, one less than the number of means (k) being compared. The df_{wg} for MS_{wg} are the sum of the degrees of freedom for the individual groups: $(n_1 - 1) + (n_2 - 1) + \ldots (n_k - 1)$, or, when n is the same for each group, $k(n - 1)$. This formula should look familiar as it is the same one used to calculate df to find the critical t that you used to calculate confidence intervals around sample means in a multi-group experiment. (See Chapter 10.)

The critical question from the standpoint of ANOVA is: What are these sources of variability? What contributes to the variance of individual scores around a group mean (MS_{wg}) and what contributes to the variance of group means around the grand mean (MS_{bg})?

You are already familiar with one source of variance, MS_{wg}, or the variability of individual scores around a group mean. *The MS_{wg} is an estimate of population variability based on individual differences.* Why doesn't everyone in a condition respond the same way to the treatment? Scores vary because people vary. Within-group variation is simply a measure of error variation based on differences of individual scores from a group mean. Therefore, part of the total variability in a data set may be conceptualized as error due to individual differences as measured by deviations of scores from their respective group means. Because of the role it plays in ANOVA, MS_{wg} is also called **mean square error,** and abbreviated *MSE.*

The within-group variance estimate is the same pooled variance estimate as that used when performing a t test for independent groups (see Chapter 6) or when constructing confidence intervals in a multi-group experiment (see Chapter 11). The computational formula for MS_{wg} should look familiar as it is simply an extension of the pooled variance formula used for an independent groups t test (see Chapter 8), and is exactly the same as that used to construct confidence intervals for a multi-group experiment (Chapter 11). As we just reviewed, it can be expressed as follows:

$$s^2_{pooled} = MS_{wg} = \frac{SS_{wg}}{df_{wg}} = \frac{SS_1 + SS_2 + SS_3 + \ldots}{df_1 + df_2 + df_3 + \ldots}$$

The second source of variability in the data set, MS_{bg}, is based on differences between the group means and the grand mean, or, more simply, differences among the group means. Why are the group means different? There are two possible answers. The first is that the group means are different because of sampling error. Even if the samples all came from the same population, we would not expect the sample means to be the same. (See especially Chapter 5.) We expect chance variation among sample means due to sampling error just as we expect individual participants sampled from a population to differ. Therefore, the first answer to the question is that the differences among the means are due to **sampling error** based on random variation between means. Just like the within-group variance, the differences between group means are an estimate of the population variance.

In fact, error variation will *always* be present. You can't escape variation due to chance or sampling error; it will always be with you. But is there another reason why the group means are different? The answer, of course, is that they will be different *if* the independent variable had an effect on the dependent variable. In this case, the groups would differ because the subjects in the various conditions of the experiment were affected differently by the independent variable. Unlike sampling variability, which we know to be present, we don't know whether there was a treatment effect, that is, whether the various levels of the independent variable worked to pull apart the sample means. That is what we want to find out.

The effect of the independent variable, if any, is called *systematic variation* to differentiate this type of variation from chance variation that is due to sampling error. The formula for the between-groups variance estimate is

$$MS_{bg} = \frac{\Sigma\, n(M - GM)^2}{df_{bg}}$$ Equation 12.3

Because every individual (X) in a particular group is treated as being at the same distance from the grand mean (GM), the sum of squared deviations of the group mean from the grand mean ($M - GM$)^2 is weighted by the number of individuals (n) in each group. Thus, the numerator of the MS_{bg} estimate is $\Sigma\, n(M - GM)^2$ [and not simply $\Sigma\,(M - GM)^2$].

We now have two estimates of the population variance: one based on within-group differences and one based on between-group differences. Let's stop for a second and put these estimates of error variation in context.

Assume for a moment that you were a participant in Brandon's experiment investigating the effect of type of presentation on students' recall. Assume further that you were in the video condition and that your score on the recall test was 18. The logic behind partitioning variability in the data set suggests that your score, 18, is based on (a) the fact that you are not like anyone else in your group (individual differences; $X - M_{video}$) and (b) that you are in the video group (group differences; $M_{video} - GM$). (See again Figure 12.1.) If, by watching videos, students remembered more of the material presented than they did after listening to a standard lecture, then we can expect the mean of the video group (your group) to be greater than that of the standard lecture group. Therefore, your group mean will be greater than that of at least one other mean. On the other hand, if watching videos had no more effect on recall than did listening to a lecture, any difference between the video mean and the standard lecture mean will be due to chance (sampling error). How might we choose between these two possibilities?

To make a decision, we construct a ratio between two variances, called an **F ratio** after the statistician R.A. Fisher who first worked out the logic of ANOVA. It is calculated by dividing the MS_{bg} (between-group variance) by the MS_{wg} (within-group variance):

$$F = \frac{MS_{bg}}{MS_{wg}}$$ Equation 12.4

We want to think of this F ratio conceptually as

$$F = \frac{\text{error} + \text{systematic variation (if any)}}{\text{error}}$$

If the null hypothesis is true (i.e., the independent variable did not have an effect on the dependent variable), the differences among group means are simply due to sampling error. That is, if there were no systematic variation, we simply have sampling error divided by error. In this case, MS_{wg} and MS_{bg} are estimates of the same thing: error variation. The expected value of F in this case is 1.00. *A value of 1.00 is the expected value of F under the null hypothesis.*

If H_0: $F = \frac{\text{error}}{\text{error}} = 1.00$

Because of sampling error, we must acknowledge that there will be differences between these two variance estimates due to chance, but on the average, when H_0 is true, we expect the ratio to be 1.00.

FIGURE 12.2 ■ Illustration of variation between groups when within-group variation does not change appreciably.

```
                                    10 xx
                                     9 xxxxxxxx
                          8 xxxx     8 xxxxx
                          7 xxxxxxx  7 xxx
                          6 xxxx     6 xxxx
         5 xx             5 xxxx
         4 xxxx           4 xx
         3 xxxxxxx
         2 xxxxxx
         1 xxx
```

To the extent that the independent variable had an effect and the population means represented by the experimental means are not the same, the numerator of the ratio (MS_{bg}) contains more than simply an estimate of population variance error. For example, if, by watching videos, students learned more than they did by listening to a standard lecture, we would expect these two means to differ due to chance variation (i.e., sampling error) *and* to the type of presentation the students received (i.e., systematic variation). The numerator in this case would include both systematic variation and variation due to chance (error). We assume that within-group variation (MS_{wg})—that is, error variation based on individual differences—does not change when there is a treatment effect. (See Figure 12.2.) Therefore, when systematic variation is present in the numerator, the expected F value will be greater than 1.00. Support for the alternative hypothesis—that there is a difference among the means due to the independent variable—is obtained when the F ratio is appreciably larger than 1.00:

$$\text{If } H_1: F = \frac{\text{error} + \text{systematic variation}}{\text{error}} > 1.00$$

How much larger than 1.00 must the F ratio be in order to decide that the independent variable had an effect? Using NHST, we apply the same criterion when making a decision about F as we do when deciding about t (and other test statistics). Specifically, we compare our test result (the obtained F) with the degree of chance variation expected under the null hypothesis. Assuming that only chance is operating, we look to see if the test statistic (in this case the obtained F) is a likely event under the assumption of no difference among the population means, or if it is an unlikely event given this assumption. As you have seen, behavioral scientists traditionally treat a result that occurs fewer than five times out of 100 (i.e., $p < .05$), assuming the null hypothesis to be true, as one that is unlikely. That is, a test statistic falling in the critical region when only chance variation is assumed is an unlikely or rare event. We call that event *statistically significant.* Following the logic of NHST, if the obtained F is judged to be rare (i.e., unlikely to occur) when only chance is assumed to be operating, then we may wish to question this assumption and suggest that there is something in addition to chance that is producing variation among the sample means—that is, that there really is a difference among the population means. This form of reasoning illustrates the indirect logic of NHST.

Table 12.1 summarizes the steps in performing ANOVA for an independent groups design.

TABLE 12.1 ■ Summary of ANOVA for a Single-Factor, Independent Groups Design

1. State the null and alternative hypotheses:

   $H_0: \mu_1 = \mu_2 = \mu_3 = \mu_4 =$ etc. H_1: NOT H_0.

2. Partition overall variability as

   $SS_{tot} = SS_{bg} + SS_{wg}$

   Overall variability or SS_{tot} (based on individual scores' deviations from a grand mean) is composed of two separate sources of variability: between-group variability, or that between the group mean and the grand mean $(M - GM)$, and within-group variability, or that between a score and its group mean $(X - M)$.

3. Calculate a mean square (or variance) by dividing SS_{bg} and SS_{wg} by the appropriate degrees of freedom (df):

   $MS_{bg} = SS_{bg}/df_{bg}$ and $MS_{wg} = SS_{wg}/df_{wg}$.

   The df_{bg} for MS_{bg} are $k - 1$, one less than the number of means (k) being compared. The df_{wg} for MS_{wg} are the sum of the degrees of freedom for the individual groups: $(n_1 - 1) + (n_2 - 1) + \ldots (n_k - 1)$, or, when n is the same for each group, $k(n - 1)$.

4. Calculate an F ratio as

   $$F = \frac{MS_{bg}}{MS_{wg}}$$

5. Compare the obtained F ratio with F_{crit} based on the degrees of freedom for both the numerator and the denominator. (See Table A.3.)

If the obtained F ratio is larger than F_{crit} at the .05 level, we may reject the null hypothesis that the population means are equal and suggest that the independent variable had an overall effect on the dependent variable.

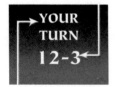

YOUR TURN 12-3

As you have no doubt come to appreciate, the logic of NHST is a bit confusing. In fact, even experienced researchers over the years have sometimes interpreted NHST results incorrectly. Let us assume that you have performed an ANOVA and the F ratio is statistically significant at the .05 level. Which of the following statements is most appropriate?

(a) The null hypothesis has less than a .05 probability of being true.

(b) Repeating this study with the same number of participants will produce a statistically significant result 95 out of 100 times.

(c) The alternative or research hypothesis has a .95 probability of being correct.

(d) Given the null hypothesis, the obtained F ratio has a less than .05 probability of occurring due to sampling error (i.e., chance variation). ■

Like the t distribution, there is not one F distribution but many depending on the degrees of freedom associated with the test. Unlike the t distribution, however, the F distribution depends on two different degrees of freedom and is a skewed distribution rather than symmetrical, as is the t distribution. The theoretical sampling distribution of F varies with the degrees of freedom associated with both the numerator (MS_{bg}) and the denominator (MS_{wg}). The distribution is skewed because MS_{bg} is always placed in the numerator; hence, F *can vary from 0.0 to very large positive values.* (An F ratio of 0.0 would occur if the group means were identical and thus there was zero variability in the numerator.)

Unlike the t distribution, there are no negative F values; the F ratio is always positive. Remember that we are dealing with squared deviations from means, and therefore no negative values may occur (as long as the calculations are done correctly). The specific value defining the .05 alpha level will vary from distribution to distribution. Values of **F critical** (abbreviated F_{crit}) associated with the .05 and .01 levels of significance for various distributions are found in Table A.3. The F_{crit} value is found by locating in Table A.3 the intersection of the column df (numerator, or MS_{bg}) and row df (denominator, or MS_{wg}). The obtained F ratio in an ANOVA comparing group means representing a single-factor is called the **omnibus F.** The omnibus F is compared to F_{crit} with the appropriate degrees of freedom. *If the obtained (omnibus) F ratio is larger than the tabled value for a particular alpha level (usually .05), then we are led to reject the null hypothesis.*

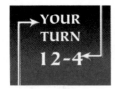

YOUR TURN 12-4

Consider the experiment conducted by Juan that was mentioned in the introduction to this chapter. He randomly assigned 120 rats in equal numbers ($n = 30$) to each of four different conditions of an experiment testing the effects of various combinations of tumor-reducing drugs. At this point, you should be able to answer the following questions about this experiment:

(a) What are the degrees of freedom for the MS_{bg}?

(b) For the MS_{wg}?

(c) What is the critical (table) F value (.05 level) for this experiment? (You'll need to consult Table A.3.) ∎

Despite differences between the distributions of t and F, these test statistics are closely related when two means are being compared. Although F is typically used to make decisions about more than two means, an F ratio obtained with two means will lead to the same decision regarding the null hypothesis as will a nondirectional t test for two independent groups. When there are two sample means, there is only one degree of freedom associated with the numerator (MS_{bg}) of the F ratio. In this case, the F and t test statistics are related in the following manner: $F = t^2$.

Thus, when means from two independent groups are compared, the F ratio is simply the square of the t ratio. Although an ANOVA, or F test, is appropriate when comparing two sample means, traditionally psychologists use the t test statistic when comparing two means and employ the F test when comparing more than two means.

AN ILLUSTRATION OF ANOVA: DOES TYPE OF PRESENTATION AFFECT RECALL?

Table 12.2 presents the ANOVA results for Brandon's data. These summary values make up what is called an **ANOVA summary table.** In the first column, two sources of the overall or total variability are identified: Between Group and Within Group. The SS associated with each source of variability and the overall SS are in the next column. Note that $SS_{bg} + SS_{wg} = SS_{tot}$. The degrees of freedom for each source of variability and for SS_{tot} are in the third column. The degrees of freedom for SS_{tot} are 89, or one less than the number of

TABLE 12.2 ■ ANOVA Summary Table for Brandon's Multimedia Experiment

Source	SS	df	MS	F	Probability
Between groups	102.022	2	51.011	7.297	.001
Within groups	608.200	87	6.991		
Total	710.222	89			

participants in Brandon's experiment (i.e., $N - 1 = 90 - 1$). Degrees of freedom for SS_{bg} are $k - 1$, or 2, one less than the number of groups $(3 - 1)$. The degrees of freedom for SS_{wg} are $k(n - 1)$, that is, $3(30 - 1)$, or 87. (Note: If group sizes are not equal, then the df for SS_{wg} must be obtained by adding the df for the respective groups $[(n_1 - 1) + (n_2 - 1) + \ldots]$. The Between Group df and Within Group df add up to the Total df. This must always be the case and is a check on the correct calculation of degrees of freedom.

Our major interest is in the *mean square estimates* for the Between Group and Within Group sources of variability. Dividing each SS by the appropriate df yields the respective mean squares. The ratio of these two mean squares yields the omnibus F value for this analysis:

$$F = \frac{MS_{bg}}{MS_{wg}} = \frac{51.01}{6.99} = 7.297$$

In the final column of the ANOVA summary table, we find the probability associated with this obtained F assuming the null hypothesis to be true, which is .001. Most computer software programs provide the exact probability of the obtained F ratio under the null hypothesis. Thus, there is often no need to consult a table to determine values of F_{crit}. As we saw in previous chapters, when carrying out NHST it is recommended that this exact probability be reported with the results of an analysis. It should be pointed out, however, that exact probabilities less than .001 are frequently not given. When probabilities are very low, the computer output will usually read $p = .000$. In these cases, one may correctly assume that the exact probability is something equal to or less than .0005 and should be reported as $p < .001$ or $p \leq .0005$.

Because the observed probability of the F ratio (i.e., .001) in Brandon's experiment is less than the conventional p level (alpha) of .05 that defines a rare event, we can say this F ratio is statistically significant and that we reject the null hypothesis. We have reason to believe that the null hypothesis is not true: the population means estimated by the sample means in Brandon's experiment are judged not to be the same. We can suggest that the type of presentation had an effect on students' retention of information. Moreover, the very low p value associated with this effect attests to the reliability of this finding. As you saw in Chapter 10, the lower the probability, the more likely an exact replication of the study will produce a statistically significant result at the .05 level (e.g., Harris, 1997). This information is not readily available from an examination of confidence intervals.

YOUR TURN 12-5

Suppose that all you knew of the results of Brandon's experiment is the information found in the ANOVA summary table (Table 12.2). (a) What would you know about "what happened" in his experiment? (b) What wouldn't you know? ■

BOX 12.1 ■ Repeated Measures ANOVA

Our emphasis in this chapter has been the analysis of a single-factor, independent groups design. However, the logic of ANOVA is easily extended to single-factor designs with repeated measures. Considerations of both efficiency (e.g., fewer subjects need to be tested) and sensitivity may lead a researcher to consider a repeated measures design. *A repeated measures design is usually more sensitive to the effect of an independent variable than is an independent groups design.*

As we have seen, when analyzing an independent groups experiment, we construct an *F* ratio based on two sources of variance. The population variance estimate in the numerator includes chance or population variation and any systematic variation associated with the effect of the independent variable. The denominator is an estimate of population variation only. An ANOVA for repeated measures proceeds similarly, except that the estimate of error variation in the denominator of the *F* ratio is not obtained in the same way. In this case, the estimate of error variation only is called *residual variation.* (See, e.g., Howell, 2002, for discussion of error estimates in a repeated measues design.) The interpretation of the *F* ratio is the same as that in an independent groups design.

Consider an experiment examining people's ability to find a "hidden figure" (as in the child's game "Where's Waldo?") in three different stimulus arrays. Time to identify the hidden figure is the dependent measure. If eight people are in the experiment, and each person is tested on each stimulus display (A, B, C), we might imagine obtaining time scores in seconds such as the following:

Subject	A	B	C
1	12	15	9
2	8	19	10
3	14	15	6
4	10	18	7
5	12	24	15
6	17	26	20
7	21	22	19
8	14	25	14
Means	13.5	20.5	12.5

The ANOVA summary table for this experiment based on a computer analysis looks like this:

Source of Variation	SS	df	MS	F	p
Subjects	346.67	7	49.52	—	—
Display (A, B, C)	304.00	2	152.00	21.00	.000
Residual (Error)	101.33	14	7.24		

In your research report, the results would be reported as $F(2, 14) = 21.00, p \leq .0005$.

Note: The computer output (display) for a repeated measures design generally will not be as simple as seen in this ANOVA summary table, and you may want to ask for guidance in identifying the important components of the analysis from the output.

MEASURES OF STRENGTH OF ASSOCIATION FOR INDEPENDENT GROUPS DESIGNS

A significant result associated with an omnibus F test is usually treated as good news by a researcher. Statistical significance suggests something interesting is going on (i.e., something other than simply chance variation). Given that we have conducted a methodologically sound experiment, a statistically significant result provides evidence that the independent variable had an effect on the dependent variable. Of course, there is always some small probability that the independent variable did *not* have an effect (that is, that a Type I error was made). The results of NHST, as we said previously, help to identify the probability of such an error in statistical decision-making.

The task of data analysis is not usually finished when we obtain an omnibus F. A problem arises when we try to interpret exactly what it means to say that a variable had a statistically significant effect on the dependent variable. The questions posed in *Your Turn* 12-5 are meant to emphasize that we do not really know all that we need to know following an ANOVA unless we also look closely at the pattern of sample means. The goals of the inspection and description stages of data analysis are to point out the direction and size of differences among the means. Confidence intervals suggest probable values for the population means represented by the various conditions. Without knowledge of these prior analyses, the meaning of a significant F is unclear. *The interpretation of a significant F can only be made following a careful examination of the means and measures of variability associated with the conditions of the experiment.* The F value by itself does not tell us about the direction of the differences among the means; inspection and description do that.

Furthermore, *neither the size of the F value, nor the probability of an obtained F under the null hypothesis, speaks directly to the effect size.* In other words, we cannot say that a treatment effect was large because the obtained F was large; nor can we claim a large effect size just because the probability of an obtained F is very small (e.g., $p = .001$). *Both the value of F and its probability under the null hypothesis are influenced by sample size.* A large F value may be obtained in a study using a large number of participants even though the size of the effect is small. Clearly, simply knowing that we have a statistically significant omnibus F ratio does not tell us all that happened in the experiment.

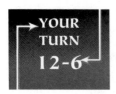

You have conducted an ANOVA for an independent groups experiment with four random groups. The results of your statistical analysis yields an omnibus F ratio of 3.08 with a probability of .06. You decide to repeat the experiment with a larger number of subjects in each condition and now find that the obtained F ratio is 4.28 with probability of .001.

(a) In which experiment (first or second) would the result be said to be statistically significant at the .05 level?

(b) How is it possible that a significant effect appears in one experiment but not the other?

(c) If we assume that the independent variable really did have an effect on the dependent variable, what type of decision error probably was made in the first experiment?

An important piece of information that complements an ANOVA is a measure of the effect size associated with the independent variable. This information should accompany an F ratio whether the ratio is statistically significant or not. Meaningful effect sizes may be present even when a statistically significant result is not found. Recall that effect sizes are important when comparing results with those of previous experiments using similar independent variables. A measure of effect size that is independent of sample size, and which is appropriate when the comparison involves two or more means, is **eta squared (η^2).** Eta squared is formally a measure of the strength of association between the independent and dependent variables (e.g., Kirk, 1996). Specifically, eta squared is a measure of the proportion of variance in the dependent variable accounted for by the independent variable. It is easily calculated once an ANOVA is completed.

Eta squared (η^2) in a single-factor, independent groups design, is defined as

$$\eta^2 = \frac{SS_{bg}}{SS_{tot}}$$

Because the amount of variability associated with the differences among means, expressed as SS_{bg}, is divided by the total variability in the data set (SS_{tot}), eta squared represents the proportion of total variability in the data set that is associated with between group differences. As a proportion, therefore, eta squared can vary from .00 to 1.00.[1] Eta squared for the factor, type of presentation, in Brandon's experiment is

$$\frac{102.02}{710.22} = .14$$

We can conclude that type of presentation accounted for 14% of the total variance in the dependent variable. The concept "variance accounted for" will be discussed at greater length later in this book when we discuss relationships between two variables. (See Chapters 14, 15, and 16.) At this point, let us emphasize that the more variance accounted for by an independent variable, the greater is our ability to explain statistically what happened. Importantly, eta squared, or a measure of proportion of variance accounted for, can be used to compare the effect of an independent variable with that obtained by others doing similar experiments.

Unfortunately, eta squared has some of the same drawbacks as does a statistically significant omnibus F ratio in that its interpretation is unclear when there are more than two groups. (See Rosenthal & Rosnow, 1991.) In other words, what exactly is indicated by this strength of association measure is not obvious because differences among means can arise in various ways. Thus, what exactly makes eta squared large is not necessarily clear if this is the only information we have. Careful examination of the sample means is necessary to describe what specific differences contributed to eta squared. Because this is not always done when eta squared is being compared across experiments, one must not assume that the reasons for a particular value of eta squared are known. Nevertheless, recognizing this limitation, we may use eta squared as an index of the strength of association between the independent and dependent variable, with the knowledge that the interpretation of eta squared requires careful data description.

The interpretation of a statistically significant omnibus F can be dramatically improved by focusing on comparisons involving two means.

---

[1]Some researchers prefer to report eta (η), the square root of eta squared. When there are only two groups, eta is equivalent to r (see Rosenthal & Rosnow, 1991), which is discussed in later chapters in this book.

TWO-GROUP COMPARISONS IN A MULTI-GROUP EXPERIMENT

A question that students sometimes raise when first introduced to ANOVA for a single-factor design is "Why not just do t tests?" Why not use a t test to test all possible two-group differences? The answer is that doing multiple t tests increases the risk of a Type I error. The probability of a Type I error is equivalent to alpha, the level of significance. For most tests, this probability is .05. However, this probability applies to a single, independent test. Consider an experiment with four means: A, B, C, D. If all possible two-group comparisons were made (AB, AC, AD, BC, BD, CD), six t tests would be required. (Note that each of the four means is part of three two-mean comparisons.) As a consequence, the **experimentwise error rate** (that is, the error rate across all comparisons) will be much greater than .05. Because an ANOVA for a single-factor design tests just one null hypothesis no matter how many means are involved, the Type I error rate remains at .05.

Although conducting as many t tests as it takes to make all possible two-group comparisons is a no-no, carrying out the equivalent of a t test for at most a few two-group comparisons has much to recommend it under certain situations. What are these situations? We can identify two. Both situations make the reasonable assumption that there are some comparisons that are more important to the researcher than others and that the researcher is not simply "fishing" for a significant difference.

Two-Group Comparisons Following a Significant Omnibus F

The first situation that merits consideration of two-group comparisons is when a significant omnibus F has been obtained. In this situation, a researcher is given a certain license to conduct tests to explore the effect of the independent variable. These tests frequently are called *post hoc* or *a posteriori* tests because they are conducted after the omnibus test results are examined. Because the overall effect of the independent variable was significant, the investigator is said to be "protected" against excessive error rates. (See, e.g., Rosenthal & Rosnow, 1991.) These two-group comparisons are called **multiple comparisons** or **contrasts** (e.g., Howell, 2002) or **analytical comparisons** (e.g., Keppel & Zedeck, 1989).

Consider the outcome of Brandon's experiment once again. Having obtained a significant overall or omnibus F, it may be important to use NHST to analyze this effect further. For example, a reasonable question might be whether the difference between the video group and standard lecture groups is statistically significant. Examination of the confidence intervals (see Figure 11.2) gives us every indication that such will be the case; however, a statement based on NHST may be important when reporting these results.[2] Moreover, it might also be important to be able to report an effect size for the video group relative to the standard group. By focusing on a specific two-group comparison, we can provide an effect size that is more easily interpreted than is one based on multiple groups. You learned about one such effect size measure, Hedges' g, in previous chapters.

The procedure for performing an analytical comparison between the standard lecture and video groups is equivalent to performing an independent groups t test for these two means,

---

[2]We also know that this difference will yield statistical significance because, when the null hypothesis is rejected following an omnibus F test, the difference between the largest and smallest means will be statistically significant. However, unless we perform the specific two-group comparison, we do not know at what level of significance the means differ.

with one exception. The exception is that the pooled variance estimate for an analytical comparison makes use of the MS_{wg} associated with the overall ANOVA rather than simply pooling the variance associated with the two groups of interest. Under the homogeneity of variance assumption, within-group variance is similar in all of the groups of the experiment. Thus, pooling a variance estimate using within-group variation from all groups should provide a truer variance estimate than would any one estimate alone. You may recall that this same assumption was made doing NHST with two means when we calculated a *t* test for independent groups. Thus, *carrying out a specific test of the difference between two means in the context of a multi-group ANOVA is the same as performing an independent groups t test for these two means with the exception that we now use a pooled variance estimate based on all within-group variation.* We call this contrast "*t* comparison" (also referred to as $t_{comparison}$).

The computational formula for $t_{comparison}$ can be written as

$$t_{comparison} = \frac{M_1 - M_2}{\sqrt{[MS_{wg}(1/n_1 + 1/n_2)]}}$$

For Brandon's data, the contrast between the video and lecture condition yields

$$t_{comparison} = \frac{16.43 - 13.97}{\sqrt{[6.991(1/30 + 1/30)]}} = 3.62$$

Convention permits one to compare the obtained contrast effect with a critical (table) value of *t* with degrees of freedom associated with the MS_{wg} from the ANOVA. Because the critical *t* for 87 *df* is not found in Table A.2, we use the next lowest value, which is 2.00, associated with 60 *df*. The obtained $t_{comparison}$ of 3.62 is greater than t_{crit} with 87 *df* at the .05 level; but it is also greater than the critical value at the .001 level. (See Table A.2.) Therefore, an obtained $t_{comparison}$ of 3.62 has a probability of occurring less than .001 by chance under the null hypothesis. Thus, the difference between the video and standard lecture conditions is statistically significant (as we already surmised it would be). The steps for making a two-group analytical comparison using *t* comparison following a significant omnibus *F* are summarized in Table 12.3.

A researcher can then proceed to obtain a measure of effect size,

$$g = \frac{M_1 - M_2}{\sqrt{MS_{wg}}}$$

As we did when calculating $t_{comparison}$, we may reasonably use the pooled variance estimate obtained across all groups when calculating *g* for a two-group comparison within a multi-group experiment. In the context of a multi-group experiment, as we have seen, the MS_{wg} in the omnibus *F* ratio serves as this pooled variance estimate. The effect size measure *g* can be obtained for the two-group comparison associated with the video and standard lecture conditions in Brandon's experiment, as follows:

$$g = \frac{16.43 - 13.97}{\sqrt{6.991}} = \frac{2.46}{2.64} = 0.93$$

Based on Cohen's rule of thumb (.20 = small, .50 = medium, .80 = large), an effect size of 0.93 can viewed as a large effect size. Importantly, one can now compare this effect size with others obtained when a multimedia presentation using videos is compared with a standard lecture condition and the dependent variable is student retention. Science is built on the

TABLE 12.3 ■ Summary of Steps for Comparing Two Means Based on MS_{wg}

Calculate $t_{comparison}$ as:

$$t_{comparison} = \frac{M_1 - M_2}{\sqrt{[MS_{wg}\,(1/n_1 + 1/n_2)]}}$$

1. Find difference between the two means that are to be compared.

   $M_1 - M_2$

2. Obtain MS_{wg} from results of omnibus F test.

3. Multiply MS_{wg} by $(1/n_1 + 1/n_2)$, where n_1 and n_2 represent the size of the two groups, respectively, being compared.

4. Take the square root of $[MS_{wg}\,(1/n_1 + 1/n_2)]$ to obtain the pooled estimated standard error of the difference between two means: $\sqrt{[MS_{wg}\,(1/n_1 + 1/n_2)]}$

5. Divide the difference between two means $(M_1 - M_2)$ by the answer to step #4 to find $t_{comparison}$.

6. Compare the obtained $t_{comparison}$ with t_{crit} at the .05 level with df equal to MS_{wg}, that is, $N - k$ for the omnibus F test.

If the obtained $t_{comparison}$ is greater than t_{crit} at the .05 level, we may reject the null hypothesis that the two population means are equal and suggest that the independent variable led to M_1 exceeding M_2.

cumulative results of independent experiments. Effect size measures allow us to assess the effect of an independent variable across many different studies.

The same steps may be taken to make additional comparisons if the situation warrants them. Imagine that you are Brandon and that you have been asked to report the results of your experiment to a group of interested college teachers. It is one thing to say that both the slide and video groups did better than a standard lecture, but it also will be important to say something about how much better these multimedia groups did relative to the standard lecture. By calculating effect sizes, Brandon can report how much of an effect both the slide and video groups had relative to the control. This will better inform people about the bang they can expect for their bucks when using the slide and video presentations. Such information will be important if a decision is needed about which type of presentation to implement in the classroom.

The contrast for the slide and lecture conditions yields the following:

$$t_{comparison} = \frac{15.93 - 13.97}{\sqrt{6.991\,(1/30 + 1/30)}} = \frac{1.96}{.68} = 2.88$$

The $t_{comparison}$ with 87 degrees of freedom is statistically significant at $p < .01$. (See Table A.2.) We are able to reject the null hypothesis. There was an effect of type of presentation when only the slide and video condition are contrasted. The effect size, g, for this comparison is

$$\frac{15.93 - 13.97}{\sqrt{6.991}} = \frac{1.96}{2.64} = .74$$

When slide and lecture conditions were compared, an effect size of 0.74 may be viewed as large (close to .80), although a somewhat smaller effect than that associated with the video condition (0.93). It appears that one may obtain a large effect over that of a standard lecture condition using either video or slide presentations. Should resources not be available to permit video presentations, it appears that a large effect on students' retention can still be obtained by substituting a slide presentation for a standard lecture.

Consider what we have learned about the effect of type of presentation on student retention. Inspection and description of the data provided strong evidence that the video condition was superior to the standard lecture condition and perhaps better than the slide condition. Although the overall effect of this factor was significant when tested in an omnibus ANOVA, you can see how this result did not really tell us what we wanted to know. Contrast tests between the video and lecture conditions and between slide and lecture conditions revealed that, although both two-mean contrasts were statistically significant, the effect size was slightly greater for the video than it was for the slide comparison. These combined analyses present a good picture of what happened as a function of type of presentation.

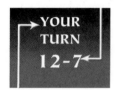

Given the preceding outcomes in Brandon's experiment, do you think it would be important to contrast the video and slide conditions using NHST?   ■

We should mention that analytical comparisons are not limited to the groups represented by the individual levels of the independent variable. A two-group comparison may be made between groups representing the average of two or more other groups. For example, suppose Brandon wished to test whether the two multimedia groups taken together did better than a standard lecture. An analytical comparison can be made comparing the mean of the standard lecture group with the combined mean of the two multimedia conditions. (See, e.g., Rosenthal & Rosnow, 1991, for information about conducting these comparisons.)

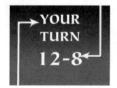

In the introduction you met Melissa, a clinical psychologist doing therapy outcome research on treatments for depression. She set up an experiment testing the effects of two different therapies with an untreated (waiting list) control group. Can you think of a reason why Melissa might wish to compare the combined treatment means with the mean for the waiting list control?   ■

Planned Two-Group Comparisons in a Multi-Group Experiment

Another situation that might legitimately involve specific two-group comparisons between levels of a single-factor design is one that does not rely on a significant omnibus F; in fact, it need not rely on even obtaining an F ratio. (See Howell, 2002, and Rosenthal & Rosnow, 1991.) *An important requirement, however, is that the specific two-group comparisons be limited in number and be planned before the experimental results are obtained.* These tests frequently are called *a priori* tests because they are planned before the results of the experiment are examined. If only two comparisons are made, for instance, there will be little effect on the experimentwise error rate (e.g., Howell, 2002). The ANOVA is carried out solely to obtain the MS_{wg} for the overall experiment, which is then used in the denominator of the two-group tests, as was done previously. The only differences between the prior situation and this one are that (a) specific two-group comparisons are planned prior to seeing the results based on the applied or theoretical considerations of the study and (b) the omnibus F ratio is not calculated (although the MS_{wg} is calculated).

Use of the MS_{wg} based on all the experimental groups provides a more stable estimate of the within-group variability (assuming that the homogeneity of variance assumption has been met). In addition, by making use of the MS_{wg} from the omnibus analysis, the researcher obtains a more powerful test of the two-group difference than would be obtained if the error associated with only these two groups were used. A more powerful test is produced because the degrees of freedom associated with MS_{wg} (i.e., $N - k$) are used to obtain a critical test statistic. The df for MS_{wg} are those associated with the denominator of the F ratio. When there are more than two groups, the df for the contrast will necessarily be greater than when there are only two groups and, hence, the critical value will be smaller. Statistical significance is more likely to be obtained when the critical (table) value is small.

A major advantage of this approach is that the researcher focuses only on those comparisons that are of interest and obtains specific information about the differences between two means that are not available when an omnibus F is calculated. Consider that Brandon might decide before the experiment was conducted that his major interest was in knowing whether the multimedia groups (slides and video) did better than the standard lecture group, and, of course, knowing how much better each was than the standard condition. Brandon can legitimately make these two specific comparisons (slides vs. standard and video vs. standard) without calculating an overall F ratio. These particular two-group comparisons using NHST, along with the descriptive statistics, including confidence intervals, may be all that he needs to make his case for the effect of type of presentation on students' recall. As you just saw, when results of these two contrasts are known, knowing also that there was a statistically significant overall F for type of presentation may not be all that important when making decisions about the effectiveness of multimedia presentations.

It is important for researchers to consider before beginning their analyses what exactly they want to know from their data. As we stated in Chapter 1, a researcher needs to clearly identify what questions are being asked. With this information, the researcher can then plan the appropriate analyses to answer these questions. Simpler analyses are always preferred to more-complex ones. (See Wilkinson et al., 1999.) *Carefully planning a limited number of specific two-group comparisons prior to conducting a multi-group experiment may lead not only to simpler data analyses but a clearer explanation for the outcome for the experiment.*

YOUR TURN 12-9

Consider again Melissa's experiment looking at the effects of psychotherapy. There were two treatment groups and a waiting list control.

(a) What are two questions that Melissa likely is asking as she plans her experiment?

(b) Describe how she might answer these questions without obtaining an omnibus F ratio. ■

ASSESSING POWER IN AN INDEPENDENT GROUPS EXPERIMENT

Recall that power is the probability that a false null hypothesis is rejected. (See Chapter 10.) Estimating the power of a statistical test of the effect of one independent variable with three or more levels is somewhat more complicated than is estimating power for a test between two means and is discussed in Appendix B.

Keep in mind, however, that you already have learned one way to obtain important information regarding the power of your analysis. Confidence intervals reveal the precision of your estimates of a population mean. Power is related to the width of the interval. (See Chapter 11.) Recall that wide intervals indicate low precision in the mean estimates; that is, wide intervals indicate low power. Greater sample size brings greater power.

You should also be aware that, once you focus on a comparison between two means within the context of a multi-group experiment, power can be estimated using the same procedures as that for a comparison between two means. (See Chapter 10 and the appendix chapter.)

ANNOUNCING RESULTS (THE *A* IN I-D-E-A)

We are now in a position to announce results of Brandon's independent groups experiment investigating the effect of type of presentation on student retention. The exact format for such an announcement will depend on which particular analyses have been conducted, on whether the results are statistically significant, and on other aspects of the research situation (e.g., whether a figure is used to describe the data). In the following example, we make use of the information obtained from inspection and description of the data, as well as from both confidence interval estimates (Chapter 11) and NHST (the present chapter). The analysis and interpretation of the results of this experiment may be announced as follows:

> The effect of type of multimedia presentation on student retention was investigated. The type of presentation factor had three levels: video, slide, and standard lecture. A 20-point recall test was used to assess student retention. Inspection of the data indicated there were no ceiling or floor effects, and the distributions did not depart markedly from a normal distribution. Mean recall was 16.44 (SD = 2.43), 15.93 (SD = 2.65), and 13.97 (SD = 2.83), in the video, slide, and standard lecture conditions, respectively. Figure 1 shows the 95% confidence intervals drawn around these sample means. As can be seen in the figure, intervals around the video and slide means overlap substantially, but neither interval overlaps with that of the standard lecture condition.
>
> An ANOVA for independent groups revealed that there was an overall effect for type of presentation, $F(2, 87) = 7.30$, $MSE = 6.99$, $p = .001$, $\eta^2 = .14$. Two analytical comparisons were made to determine the source of this effect. The first revealed that the video condition differed significantly from the standard lecture condition, $t(87) = 3.62$, $p \leq .0005$, effect size $g = 0.93$. A second comparison made between the slide and lecture conditions also reached statistical significance, $t(87) = 2.88$, $p = .005$, effect size $g = 0.74$. Thus, both video and slide presentations produced an effect on students' recall that were significantly greater than that of the lecture condition. In each case, the effect size was large, although a slightly greater effect size was obtained for the video condition relative to the standard lecture condition than was found for the slide condition.

Some commentary on the form of this announcement is in order. First, note that the results are presented in the past tense. The experiment has been done, and the obtained results are being reported. The first three sentences succinctly describe the independent and dependent variables, as well as the goal of the study. The summary of results combines information obtained from the construction of confidence intervals as well as that found with NHST.

Abbreviations of statistical terms, such as *t, F,* and *SD,* are italicized when they appear in a research report. (See *Publication Manual of the American Psychological Association,* 2001.) You may remember that the abbreviation for standard deviation of a sample is *s* when appearing in a formula, but is *SD* when appearing in a research manuscript.

It is also recommended that the mean square error (*MSE*) be presented with the results of an omnibus *F.* The *MSE* is the same as MS_{wg}. This term informs a reader about the overall variability in the data and permits the calculation of additional statistics if desired. The *APA Manual* (2001) recommends that the exact probabilities associated with results of statistical tests be reported (and not simply whether *p* is less than or greater than .05). Finally, measures of effect size are strongly recommend by the *APA Manual,* and have been reported here as eta squared (η^2) for the overall analysis and as *g* for the two-group comparisons. A verbal description of the meaning of these analyses accompanies these statistics. Students should refer to the *APA Manual* for further information about reporting results in a research manuscript.

WHAT YOU HAVE LEARNED AND THE NEXT STEP

In this chapter, you learned that NHST may be used as part of the I-D-E-A model in the context of a multi-group experiment. In particular, we focused on how to use NHST for results of a single-factor independent groups experiment. ANOVA also may be used with a repeated measures design, but we will leave details of this analysis for other texts (but see Box 12.1).

The goal of NHST is to tell researchers whether there is something of interest in their data. That is, researchers use NHST to help decide whether the observed differences among sample means represent something more than just chance variation (the *E* in I-D-E-A). The construction of confidence intervals can be seen as complementary to making this decision. Although confidence intervals focus the researcher on the precision of a mean estimate (and consequently provide information about the pattern among population means), NHST focuses the researcher on the probability of making an error when concluding that there are real differences among population means. That is, NHST provides important information about the probability of a Type I error. Although in most situations a researcher will want to know more than whether an independent variable had an overall effect on the dependent variable, researchers have traditionally first conducted an overall ANOVA for the results of a multi-group experiment. In this chapter, you have learned the following facts about this important null hypothesis significance test:

- In the context of ANOVA, an independent variable is called a *factor.*

- Although used to help make decisions about mean differences, the ANOVA is literally an analysis of variance.

- A *mean square* is another name for *variance.*

- The null hypothesis (H_0) for a single-factor ANOVA is that the population means represented by the sample means are equal. The alternative hypothesis (H_1) is that two or more means differ from one another.

- A decision about differences among means is based on the size of the ratio between the mean square between groups and the mean square within groups, which is called an *F ratio.*

- Within-group variability estimates the population variance (error variation) based on individual differences.

- Between-group variability represents sampling variability (error variation) plus any effect of the treatment (systematic variation).

- If the null hypothesis is true, the mean square between groups (MS_{bg}) and mean square within groups (MS_{wg}) are both estimates of the population variance (error variation). Under the null hypothesis, the expected value of the F ratio is 1.00.

- To the extent that the independent variable (treatment) led to differences among the means, the mean square between groups is also affected by systematic variation and the F ratio will be greater than 1.00.

- NHST relies on a determination of chance variation under the null hypothesis. In an ANOVA, this determination is made by examining a theoretical distribution of F based on appropriate degrees of freedom for both the numerator (MS_{bg}) and denominator (MS_{wg}) of the F ratio.

- A statistically significant F value is one that occurs only rarely in a sampling distribution when the null hypothesis is true.

- A measure of the strength of association between the independent and dependent variable, called *eta squared* (η^2), can be calculated to give information about the amount of variance in the dependent variable accounted for by the independent variable.

- Generally, researchers will focus on specific comparisons between two means when a multi-group experiment has been conducted. These comparisons are called *multiple contrasts* or *analytical comparisons*.

- One contrast typically used in a multi-group experiment is the $t_{comparison}$.

- The construction of confidence intervals complements the information obtained from ANOVA by providing information about the likely pattern of population means and the precision (power) of estimates of population means.

Research is frequently performed to look at the possible effects of more than one factor at the same time. A *complex design* is a study that includes two or more independent variables. In the next chapter, we examine how the construction of confidence intervals and NHST based on ANOVA are used to make decisions about each of the variables in a complex design, as well as the effect of the combination of these variables. The I-D-E-A for a complex design is an extension of what you have learned thus far about ANOVA for one factor.

Key Concepts

analysis of variance (ANOVA)	mean square error (MSE)	ANOVA summary table
factor	sampling error	eta squared (η^2)
SS total (SS_{tot})	systematic variation	experimentwise error rate
between-group variability (SS_{bg})	F ratio	multiple comparisons (contrasts)
within-group variability (SS_{wg})	F critical (F_{crit})	or analytical comparisons
mean square	omnibus F	$t_{comparison}$

Answers to *Your Turn* Questions

12-1. A Type I error results when we reject a true null hypothesis. That is, we conclude that more than chance is operating when really only sampling variation (chance) is present. A Type II error results when we fail to reject a false null hypothesis. In a sense, we "missed" a true effect: systematic variation is present, and we failed to detect it with our statistical test.

12-2. We typically want to say something about a population based on what we know about a sample taken from that population. For example, the mean of a random sample is our best estimate of the population mean. Similarly, we use a sample variance to infer the population variance. However, it has been shown that the variance calculated from relatively small samples tends to systematically underestimate the population variance. It is a *biased* estimate. This bias can be corrected to some degree by subtracting 1 from the sample size before dividing into the sum of squared deviations (i.e., $SS/[N - 1]$). This yields a slightly larger variance estimate that conforms more closely to the actual population variance. Therefore, we have an unbiased estimate of the population variance when we use $N - 1$.

12-3. Only (d) is correct. NHST tells us the probability of our results (i.e., the obtained test statistic such as t or F) assuming only chance variation is present (i.e., assuming the null hypothesis is true). If we find that our results have a low probability of occurring when we assume there is no real difference between population means, then we are led to question that assumption. Because none of the other options is correct, we want to be sure that we do not make those conclusions when we obtain a statistically significant finding.

12-4. (a) The df for $MS_{bg} = (k - 1) = (4 - 1) = 3$.

(b) The df for $MS_{wg} = (N - k) = (120 - 4) = 116$.

(c) F critical (.05) with 3 and 116 df is (approximately) 2.70 (based on $df = 100$ because 116 does not appear in the table).

12-5. (a) All that you would know is that the null hypothesis can be rejected. There is evidence that the variation among the means (MS_{bg}) is due to more than simply sampling error; that is, the results suggest that systematic variation is present.

(b) Note that there is no information in the ANOVA summary table about the nature of the mean differences. We must rely on descriptive statistics (e.g., means and standard deviations) and the construction of confidence intervals to better understand what the results mean. Without additional computations, we also do not know about the "size" of the effect that the independent variable had on the dependent variable.

12-6. (a) Only results of the second experiment ($p = .001$) are statistically significant at the .05 level.

(b) Statistical significance is related to sample size; everything else being equal, the larger the sample size, the greater is the likelihood that a statistically significant difference will be obtained.

(c) Type II error. We can suggest that the first experiment did not have enough statistical power to detect the difference among the population means. If there is a real effect of the independent variable, the null hypothesis is false, but it was not rejected in the first experiment.

12-7. We know that the confidence intervals around the video and slide means overlap substantially even though the width of the intervals is relatively narrow, indicating good precision of estimation. On this basis, we cannot conclude that the population means differ. Statistical significance would not be obtained in this case. It does not seem worthwhile to pursue this difference.

12-8. Melissa may wish to demonstrate that "treatment" is better than no treatment. This may be particularly important if there is little difference on therapy outcome for the two treatment conditions.

12-9. (a) Melissa, like Brandon, likely would be interested in examining the difference between each of the two treatment conditions and the control condition. After all, what does she really learn if she finds that there is an overall effect of her independent variable based on an omnibus F ratio?

(b) Melissa may decide before she conducts her experiment to make only two two-group comparisons in her data. In this case, there would be no need to conduct an omnibus F test.

Analyzing and Interpreting Data: Problems and Exercises

1. How do the construction of confidence intervals and findings from NHST complement one another in the interpretation of experimental results?

2. What are the null and alternative hypotheses for an omnibus F test of the differences among means in a single-factor, independent groups experiment?

3. What assumptions about the data does a researcher make when performing an ANOVA for independent groups?

4. What is "variance" called in the context of ANOVA and how is it calculated?

5. In your own words, explain these three sources of variability in a multi-group experiment: SS_{tot}, SS_{bg}, SS_{wg}.

6. Why might group means differ in an experiment with one independent variable?

7. (a) Conceptually, we should think of the F ratio as_____divided by_____.
   (b) Explain.

8. What do researchers mean when they state that a finding is "statistically significant"?

9. Tom tests three groups of rats ($n = 10$) in a maze after they have been injected with one of three memory-enhancing drugs (A, B, and C). Number of errors while learning the maze is the dependent variable. The results of his experiment for 30 rats are as follows:

   Drug A: 4, 6, 8, 3, 8, 4, 5, 6, 7, 5

   Drug B: 10, 11, 12, 6, 7, 9, 9, 9, 15, 12

   Drug C: 2, 6, 5, 5, 5, 4, 7, 8, 9, 11

   (a) Describe the mean performance in each condition and describe the covariation (if any) between the independent and dependent variable.
   (b) Perform an ANOVA on these data and report the F ratio and its probability given the null hypothesis.
   (c) State your conclusion regarding the effect of the independent variable.

10. Julie is investigating ways that children read and how this influences their later recall of the reading material. She randomly assigns 32 third-grade children to one of four different reading groups ($n = 8$): Group 1 reads silently; Group 2 reads aloud; Group 3 reads silently and answers silently (i.e., to themselves) simple questions inserted in the text; Group 4 reads aloud and answers aloud questions inserted in the text. The dependent variable is the number correct on a 10-point test of retention over the contents of the passages that were read.

Her results for the four reading groups are:

Group 1: 6, 7, 8, 9, 7, 8, 4, 5

Group 2: 5, 6, 4, 3, 4, 4, 5, 7

Group 3: 8, 5, 8, 9, 10, 10, 7, 8

Group 4: 10, 9, 8, 10, 9, 10, 10, 10

(a) Inspection of the data reveals what problem?

(b) Explain how this problem would confuse the results if an ANOVA were performed on these data.

11. David repeats Julie's experiment (see problem #6) but uses a 20-item test of retention. He randomly assigns the same number of children in each group (after making sure that the children were not previously in Julie's experiment). The results for David's experiment are:

Group 1: 7, 7, 8, 9, 7, 8, 4, 6,

Group 2: 6, 6, 5, 3, 10, 4, 5, 7

Group 3: 9, 6, 8, 9, 10, 10, 11, 8

Group 4: 14, 9, 12, 10, 13, 12, 15, 11

(a) Describe the covariation (if any) that is present between the levels of the independent variable and the dependent variable.

(b) Perform an ANOVA on these data and report the F ratio and its probability given the null hypothesis.

(c) State your conclusion regarding the effect of the independent variable.

12. The following is an ANOVA summary table for a single-factor, independent groups experiment. Examine the table carefully and then answer the following questions based on information obtained from the table.

Source	SS	df	MS	F	Probability
Between groups	82.23	4	20.558	4.78	.02
Within groups	408.32	95	4.298		
Total	490.55	99			

(a) How many groups (conditions) were in this experiment?

(b) What was the total number of subjects in this experiment?

(c) Were the results "statistically significant" at the .05 level?

(d) What will a researcher likely conclude about the differences among means in this experiment?

13. The following is an ANOVA summary table for a single-factor, independent groups experiment. Examine the table carefully and then answer the following questions based on information obtained from the table.

Source	SS	df	MS	F	Probability
Between groups	32.14	5	6.43	2.31	.07
Within groups	183.30	66	2.78		
Total	215.44	71			

(a) How many groups (conditions) were in this experiment?

(b) What was the total number of subjects in this experiment?

(c) Were the results "statistically significant" at the .05 level?

(d) What will a researcher likely conclude about the differences among means in this experiment?

14. How are t and F related?

15. (a) Calculate eta squared for the results of the experiment described in problem #11.

(b) What does eta squared tell you about these results?

16. (a) Calculate eta squared for the results of the experiment described in problem #12.

(b) What does eta squared tell you about these results?

17. Why not just do a bunch of t tests when comparing means in an independent groups experiment with three or more levels?

18. Under what conditions might a researcher carry out two-group comparisons in a single-factor independent groups study without calculating the omnibus F?

19. Assume that Tom (problem #9) decided, based on theoretical reasons and past results reported in the literature, that it was important to compare directly the results of Conditions B and C.

(a) Perform a contrast of the means in these two conditions and report your findings.

(b) Determine the effect size, g, for this comparison.

20. Assume that David (problem #11) decided, based on theoretical reasons and past results reported in the literature, that it is was important to compare directly the results of Conditions 2 and 4.

(a) Perform a contrast of the means in these two conditions and report your findings.

(b) Determine the effect size, g, for this comparison.

Answers to Odd-Numbered Problems

1. The construction of confidence intervals calls our attention to the probable pattern of population means, whereas NHST focuses us on the probability of making an error when deciding that there are real differences among population means. Moreover, the probability associated with the outcome of NHST gives information about the likelihood of an exact replication producing statistically significant results (i.e., $p < .05$).

3. The ANOVA requires that the data be of at least an interval level and that the populations corresponding to the conditions (groups) of the study are normal in form and have similar variances (i.e., homogeneity of variance).

5. Overall variability, or SS_{tot}, is based on individual scores' deviations from a grand mean. To calculate SS_{tot}, one would subtract the grand mean of the data set from each score, then square that deviation, and sum the squared deviations. The SS_{bg} is based on squared deviations of group means from the grand mean. The grand mean is subtracted from each group mean, the difference is squared, and then all squared deviations are summed. The SS_{wg} is based on sums of squared deviations of individual scores from the respective group means. It can be shown that $SS_{tot} = SS_{bg} + SS_{wg}$.

7. (a) Conceptually, the F ratio can be expressed as

$$\frac{\text{error} + \text{systematic variation (if any)}}{\text{error}}$$

(b) If the null hypothesis is true, there is no systematic variation, and the F ratio represents an error estimate divided by an error estimate. The expected value of F given the null hypothesis is 1.00. To the extent that systematic variation is present, the F ratio will be greater than 1.00.

9. (a) The means do vary with the levels of the independent variable: (A) 5.60, (B) 10.00, (C) 6.20.

(b) $F (2, 27) = 10.25, p < .001$.

(c) The null hypothesis may be rejected; given these data, there is evidence that the independent variable (type of drug) produced a difference in learning among the experimental conditions.

11. (a) An examination of mean performance revealed co-variation between the levels of the independent variable (type of reading) and the dependent variable (retention): (1) 7.00, (2) 5.75, (3) 8.88, (4) 12.00.

(b) $F (3, 28) = 17.92, p < .001$.

(c) Given these data, there is evidence that the independent variable (type of reading) produced a difference in retention among the experimental conditions.

13. (a) 6

(b) 72

(c) no

(d) There is not sufficient evidence to conclude that the differences among group means were the result of the independent variable (i.e., systematic variation) in addition to chance variation.

15. Eta squared (η^2) is a measure of the proportion of variance in the dependent variable accounted for by the independent variable. Eta squared (η^2) $= SS_{bg}/SS_{tot}$. We therefore need to obtain both the SS_{bg} and SS_{tot} from the results of problem #11. These are $SS_{bg} = 177.34$; $SS_{tot} = 269.72$. Thus, (η^2) $= 177.34/269.72 = .66$. We may say that the independent variable accounted for about 66% of the total variance in the scores.

17. Performing multiple two-group comparisons with three or more group means using t tests raises the experimentwise error rate above .05.

19. (a) The contrast can be made by calculating $t_{comparison}$ $= (M_1 - M_2)$ divided by $\sqrt{MS_{wg} (1/n_1 + 1/n_2)}$. For this experiment (#9), the comparison between Condition B and C yields $t_{comparison} = (10.00 - 6.20)/\sqrt{5.556 (1/10 + 1/10)}$ $= 3.8/\sqrt{1.11} = 3.8/1.05 = 3.62$. The t_{crit} with df $= 27$ is 2.052 (.05), 2.472 (.02), 2.771 (.01), 3.69 (.001). Thus, the obtained $t_{comparison}$ is significant at $p < .02$. There is a statistically significant difference between mean performance of Condition B and C.

(b) The effect size, g, for this comparison is $(M_1 - M_2)/ MS_{wg} = 3.8/2.36 = 1.61$. According to Cohen's rule of thumb, this is a very large effect.

Go to http://psychology.wadsworth.com/courses/statistics/ and test your knowledge of this chapter by taking the online quiz. Another resource to check is the online workshops that provide a step-by-step guide through a number of topics at http://psychology.wadsworth.com/workshops/workshops.html.

CHAPTER 13

I-D-E-A for Complex Designs

Experiments involving only one independent variable are not, however, the most common type of experiment in current psychological research. Instead, researchers most often use complex designs, in which two or more independent variables are studied simultaneously in one experiment.

Zechmeister et al. (2001, p. 182)

INTRODUCTION

Liz is a clinical psychology graduate student who is completing an internship year at a prestigious hospital on the east coast. As required by the American Psychological Association and state licensing boards, she must acquire a certain number of supervised clinical hours to complete her doctoral program in clinical psychology. Liz is also interested in researching the effectiveness of clinical treatment and is lucky enough to be assigned during her internship to work with a well-known clinical psychologist who does research on therapy effectiveness. She is asked to supervise a research project investigating the relationship between type of therapy and gender of the clients. Male and female clients with similar histories of emotional disorders are selected for the research project. These men and women are randomly assigned to one of two different psychotherapies: interpersonal therapy (IP) and a cognitive-behavioral (CB) therapy. All clients receive a six-week treatment of individual psychotherapy and are then evaluated by psychotherapists who did not participate in the treatment phase and do not know which type of psychotherapy that the clients received. Details of these types of therapies, outcome measures, and other experimental procedures need not concern us. Suffice it to say that men and women seeking help for emotional disorders are treated by either interpersonal or cognitive-behavioral therapy and the outcome of these treatments is measured. The design of this experiment is outlined as follows:

	Gender of Client	
	Male	**Female**
Type of Therapy		
Interpersonal	(a)	(b)
Cognitive-Behavioral	(c)	(d)

What questions does this research seek to answer? Obviously, Liz will want to know if people are better off being treated by one therapy or another. That is, does the type of therapy have an effect on clients' psychological well-being? A similar question can be asked about the "effect" of being male or female. Unlike the variable type of therapy, gender of the client is an individual differences or natural groups variable because the levels of this variable (male or female) were selected, not manipulated. Nevertheless, we can ask the following question: Is being male or being female related to therapy outcome? Yet a third question involves the combination of the two factors (type of therapy and gender of the client). It can be stated as: Does the effect of type of therapy (on outcome) differ for men and women?

The beauty of Liz's design is that all three questions can be answered. In this chapter, we introduce you to data analysis and interpretation of complex designs like the one used by Liz.

COMPLEX (FACTORIAL) DESIGNS

A **complex design** is one that involves more than one independent variable. More specifically, a **factorial design** is a complex design that combines each level of one independent variable with every level of another independent variable. Liz is using a factorial design that combines type of therapy (two levels) and gender of the client (two levels). Each level of the therapy variable appears with each level of the gender variable. Thus, there are four combinations of levels of variables, that is, four conditions, in her experiment:

(a) male clients and IP therapy   (c) male clients and CB therapy

(b) female clients and IP therapy   (d) female clients and CB therapy

Liz's design is called a "2 × 2" (read "2 by 2") to indicate that it has two variables, with each having two levels. Each number signifies an independent variable, and the value of the number identifies the number of levels of that variable. In a factorial design, the number of conditions is always the product of the number of levels, that is, 2 × 2 = 4.

A 2 × 2 complex design is the simplest factorial design. Factorial designs more complex than a 2 × 2 can be created by increasing the number of levels of an independent variable, by increasing the number of variables, or both. For example, factorial designs with two independent variables may be 2 × 3, 3 × 5, 4 × 4, and so forth. Factorial designs with two independent variables are frequently called A × B (read "A by B") designs. Keep in mind that the number of conditions is the product of the number of levels of the variables, so that a 3 × 5 design, for example, would require 15 conditions. Factorial designs also may combine more than two independent variables. Thus, we may speak of A × B × C designs, or A × B × C × D designs, for which each letter represents an independent variable. For instance, an A × B × C design might take the form of a 2 × 4 × 3 design with two levels of the first independent variable, four levels of the second, and three levels of the third independent variable. Such a design would require 24 conditions (2 × 4 × 3 = 24). Although any combination of number of independent variables and number of levels is permissible, practical considerations—as well as difficulties of interpretation that are associated with the outcome of very complex designs—make designs with more than four independent variables a rarity. And so we will concentrate on the rationale and interpretation of complex factorial designs with just two independent variables.

Complex designs may involve only independent groups variables, only repeated measures variables, or a combination of both repeated measures and independent groups variables. In this chapter, we focus on complex designs with only independent groups variables. As you saw, Liz's experiment involves two independent groups variables: one random groups variable (type of therapy) and one natural groups variable (gender of client). This type of design is outlined as follows. (Lowercase letters indicate levels of the variables, and each cell represents a different group of people.)

INDEPENDENT GROUPS COMPLEX DESIGN

	Variable A	
	a1	**a2**
Variable B		
b1	a1b1	a2b1
b2	a1b2	a2b2

FIGURE 13.1 ■ Stem-and-leaf displays for the four conditions of Liz's therapy outcome study.

IP Therapy–Men	IP Therapy–Women	CB Therapy–Men	CB Therapy–Women
2 9	2	2	2
3 3599	3 99	3	3 7
4 046	4 04568	4 49	4 468899
5 1	5 26	5 02599	5 55
6	6	6 16	6

INSPECTING DATA FROM A COMPLEX (FACTORIAL) DESIGN

Data inspection for a complex design is initially performed just as we would for any multi-condition experiment. Each of the experimental groups is examined for outliers and klinkers, as well as for possible ceiling or floor effects. The shape of the distributions in the groups must also be inspected. When null hypothesis significance testing (NHST) is used, the most common inferential test of data from a complex design is the analysis of variance (ANOVA), just as it is for a single-factor design. As you saw in the previous chapter, a researcher using ANOVA assumes that the populations from which the samples have been drawn are normally distributed and that the variances of these populations are similar (homogeneous).

In a complex design, the experimental groups represent, as we have seen, combinations of levels of independent variables. The distribution of scores within each experimental group should be examined to determine whether it is reasonable to assume that the populations represented by these groups are normally distributed and that the assumption of homogeneity of variance is met. In addition, a researcher should look to see if any of the conditions have floor or ceiling effects.

Let's assume that the dependent variable in Liz's therapy effectiveness study is an index of mental health based on psychotherapists' ratings of the clients' symptoms following therapy. This index can vary between 0 and 70, although in practice scores for normal individuals usually range from 50 to 60. The higher the score, the better is a person's overall mental health judged to be. This outcome measure can be said to represent an interval scale of measurement. Recall that the ANOVA test is appropriate only when data are measured on interval or ratio scales. Liz's study had 36 participants, with nine in each of the four conditions of the experiment. Figure 13.1 shows stem-and-leaf displays for the four conditions of Liz's therapy effectiveness study.

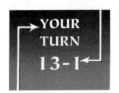

YOUR TURN 13-1

Based on your inspection of the stem-and-leaf plots for Liz's data, may we reasonably assume that the populations represented by these groups are normal in form? ■

DESCRIBING RESULTS OF A COMPLEX DESIGN: CELL MEANS, MAIN EFFECTS, AND INTERACTION

Cell Means

Table 13.1 displays the descriptive statistics for each of the four groups represented by the combination of levels of type of therapy and gender of client. The conditions of a factorial design are referred to as **cells** of the design. Cell means are estimates of the population

TABLE 13.1 ■ Descriptive Statistics for Liz's Therapy Outcome Study

	n	M	SD	Range
Men				
IP Therapy	9	39.56	6.78	29–51
CB Therapy	9	55.00	6.89	44–66
Women				
IP Therapy	9	45.44	5.88	39–56
CB Therapy	9	47.89	5.49	37–55

means corresponding to the various experimental conditions. If the conditions of the experiment represented levels of only one independent variable, as we discussed in Chapter 12, we would need only to examine the cell means and standard deviations to be able to describe how the independent variable affected the dependent variable. However, when there are two (or more) independent variables, additional descriptive statistics are needed.

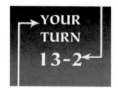

YOUR TURN 13-2

Does an examination of the standard deviations of the four groups (cells) in Liz's experiment suggest that the assumption of homogeneity of variance has been met? ■

Main Effects

As a clinical researcher, Liz is not simply interested in how the four groups in her experiment differed. We suggested that her research project sought answers to three different questions, two of which asked about the effect of each independent variable on the dependent variable. Did type of therapy make a difference? Did being male or female make a difference? These questions refer to the main effects of an independent variable. A **main effect** is the overall effect of an independent variable ignoring the other independent variable(s). A main effect is the effect of one independent variable collapsed across the levels of the other independent variable.

Main effects are also called *row and column effects* because, when cell means are presented in a matrix, as in Table 13.2, evidence of a main effect is seen in the row and column means. Table 13.2 shows the row and column means for Liz's therapy effectiveness study.

TABLE 13.2 ■ Design Matrix and Outcome Means for Liz's Experiment

	Gender		
	Male	**Female**	**Row Means**
Therapy			
IP	39.56	45.44	42.50
CB	55.00	47.89	51.44
Column Means	47.28	46.67	

When sample sizes are equal across the conditions of a factorial design, we can obtain row and column means simply by adding the cell means and dividing by the number of cells. Consider the row means associated with type of therapy. The mean for clients receiving IP therapy was 42.50, and that for clients receiving CB therapy was 51.44. To obtain these means, we simply added the means for male and female clients undergoing IP therapy (39.56 and 45.44) and divided by 2, and then added the means for male and female clients undergoing CB therapy (55.00 and 47.89) and divided by 2. Each row mean is the average of 18 clients (nine men and nine women). (If cells have unequal *n*'s, we would have to obtain a weighted mean taking into account the differences in cell size. [Weighted means were discussed in Chapter 7.])

We can see in Table 13.2 that the overall mean for CB therapy is greater than the overall mean for IP therapy. There is evidence of *covariation* between levels of therapy and the dependent variable. When only the variable type of therapy is considered, the overall mean outcome was better under CB therapy.

Column means in Table 13.2 represent the main effect of being male or female. As you can see, mean mental health scores are only slightly greater for men than for women. Therefore, we see only slight covariation between levels of the gender variable and the dependent variable. Note that the column means, like the row means, were obtained by collapsing across (ignoring) the other independent variable. Each column mean represents scores of 18 men or 18 women, half of whom were treated by IP therapy and half of whom were treated by CB therapy.

YOUR TURN 13-3

Consider a 2 × 2 experiment that involves people's judgments of honesty after looking at photographs of individuals who are either smiling or frowning (Variable A) and who either wear eyeglasses or don't (Variable B). Following are two different sets of hypothetical results from such an experiment. The mean judged level of honesty using a 10-point scale is shown for each of the four cells in the experiment. Assume that the experiment was an independent groups design with the same number of participants in each condition. Each cell mean is based on a different group of participants.

Data Set 1	Mean	Data Set 2	Mean
Smiling/eyeglasses	8.0	Smiling/eyeglasses	4.0
Smiling/no eyeglasses	6.0	Smiling/no eyeglasses	7.0
Frowning/eyeglasses	6.0	Frowning/eyeglasses	6.0
Frowning/no eyeglasses	4.0	Frowning/no eyeglasses	3.0

(a) Describe the main effects of facial expression and eyewear for each of these data sets.

(b) Is there evidence of covariation between levels of the independent variables and the dependent variable (judgments of honesty)? ∎

The means associated with the main effect of a variable are the same means we would obtain if that variable were the only independent variable in the experiment (that is, if the experiment involved just one factor). Thus, we may interpret differences among means representing the main effect of a variable in the same way in which we interpret mean differences for a single-factor study. We examine the differences between means to gain an impression about the effect of the independent variable. We are looking for covariation in the form of differences between levels of the independent variable and the dependent variable.

Interaction

The third question that may be asked about the results of a factorial design with two independent variables concerns the interaction of the two factors. An **interaction** occurs when the effect of one independent variable on the dependent variable varies with the setting (level) of another independent variable. We earlier posed a question about Liz's experiment in this way: Does the effect of type of therapy differ for men and women? If it does, the effect of therapy that we observe will depend on whether we are talking about men or women.

An interaction can be described in a couple of ways. Unlike when we describe main effects, when we describe an interaction we concentrate on the pattern of cell means. One way to look for an interaction is to examine differences between cell means at one level of an independent variable for each level of a second independent variable. For example, consider again the cell means for Liz's therapy effectiveness study:

	Gender	
Therapy	**Men**	**Women**
IP	39.56	45.44
CB	55.00	47.89

An interaction occurs when the effect of one independent variable differs across levels of another independent variable. We can consider an "effect" as a difference between two means just as we did when looking for main effects. Thus, we can ask, Is the difference between IP and CB therapy different for men and women? Looking at the means for IP and CB therapy for men, we can see that the difference is 15.44 (55.00 − 39.56). Looking at the means for IP and CB therapy for women, we see that the difference between IP and CB therapy is 2.45 (47.89 − 45.44). (It is important to subtract in the same direction when making these comparisons.) Therefore, descriptively at least, there appears to be an interaction. The effect of type of therapy depends on whether we are talking about men or women. For men, the difference between these two therapies was 15.44, whereas, for women, the difference was only 2.45. More specifically, for both men and women, mean therapy outcome was greater for CB therapy than IP therapy. When men were clients, however, the difference between the two types of therapy (15.44) was much greater than when women were clients (2.44). If the two differences were the same, there would *not* be evidence of an interaction.

Rather than looking at the difference between IP and CB therapies for men and women, we could just as well look at the difference between men and women for IP and CB therapies. The decision about what sets of means to compare depends on the rationale behind the study and the nature of the independent variables. In Liz's study, for instance, the investigators are clearly asking about whether type of therapy "worked" differently for men and women. Thus, it makes the most sense to look at differences between the two therapies for men and then for women and then compare those differences.

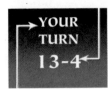

Examine the differences in mean outcome between men and women for IP therapy and for CB therapy.

(a) Do these differences suggest an interaction between the two independent variables? (Note: Be sure to subtract in the same direction for each level of therapy type.)

(b) How would you describe the interaction?   ■

Another way to describe an interaction is to draw a graph showing the relationship among the cell means. Figure 13.2 shows a plot of the cell means for Liz's experiment. Note carefully how the graph is drawn. The vertical axis represents the dependent variable. Inspection of the actual cell means tells us what range of mean values must appear on the vertical axis to describe the smallest and largest cell means. The dependent variable *always* appears on the vertical axis, and the horizontal axis is used to define one of the independent variables. Only one independent variable appears on the horizontal axis. The second independent variable is then plotted in the graph. Levels of the second independent variable are plotted separately. For each level, points are placed directly above the levels of the first independent variable. For example, in Figure 13.2, the gender variable appears on the horizontal axis and type of therapy is plotted in the graph. Cell means associated with IP therapy are indicated for male and female clients and are connected by a line to indicate that the means represent one level of the variable; cell means for CB therapy appear above both levels of the gender variable and again a line signifies that the means represent the same level of the second variable.

Once the results of a complex design are plotted, the researcher can easily decide whether there is evidence of an interaction between the independent variables. *Nonparallel lines in the graph suggest an interaction between the independent variables, whereas parallel lines indicate the absence of an interaction.* This must be the case if you think about it: when lines are parallel, the difference between means of levels of one independent variable is the same at both levels of the other independent variable. Nonparallel lines show that the difference in means depends on the level of the second independent variable. With just a little practice, you can learn to "read" a graph describing the results of a complex design.

FIGURE 13.2 ■ Graph showing mean rated psychological well-being for the four conditions of Liz's experiment representing the combination of type of therapy and gender of client.

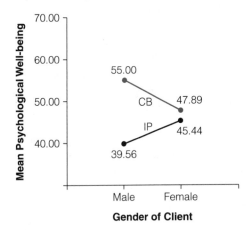

FIGURE 13.3 ■ Graph showing mean rated psychological well-being for the four conditions of Liz's experiment representing the combination of type of therapy and gender of client.

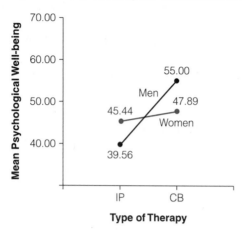

Type of Therapy

(a) Draw two figures to describe the two different sets of results reported in *Your Turn* 13-3.

(b) Is there evidence of an interaction between the two variables in your figures? ■

A researcher chooses the independent variable to be on the horizontal axis after considering the nature of the variables and how the results look when plotted. The actual results do not change, of course, depending on how the cell means are plotted, but the *appearance* of the results may change depending on which variable is chosen to be on the horizontal axis and which variable is put in the graph. Figure 13.3 shows how Liz's results look when the therapy variable is put on the horizontal axis and type of client is in the graph. Because the figure will be used to describe the pattern of means to others as well as to describe the effect of each of the independent variables, it is important to consider carefully the impression that the figure makes. A researcher should consider the questions that the study is asking and decide how the relationships among the means plotted in a graph might be best visualized so that the results are easily described.

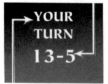

Which Figure, 13.2 or 13.3, do you believe best describes the results of Liz's experiment? Hint: There isn't an absolutely right answer to this question. ■

CONSTRUCTING CONFIDENCE INTERVALS FOR MEANS IN A COMPLEX DESIGN

Examining possible main effects and an interaction by describing row and column means, as well as cell means, in a table or figure does not tell us whether the differences we observe are due to sampling error or sampling error *plus* systematic variation due to the effect of

Variable A, Variable B, or the interaction between A and B. As you have learned, constructing confidence intervals around a sample mean is a good way to determine how precise our estimate of the population mean is. Confidence intervals can be meaningfully used in the context of a complex design.

One approach is to construct confidence intervals around all the cell means in a complex design. By now, you should be familiar with the procedure for constructing confidence intervals. Recall that the formula for the 95% confidence interval in a multi-group experiment is

$$M \pm t_{crit} (s_M)$$

where s_M, the pooled estimated standard error, is

$$\frac{s_{pooled}}{\sqrt{n}}$$

and

$$s_{pooled} = \sqrt{s^2_{pooled}}$$

and

$$s^2_{pooled} = \frac{(df_1)(s_1^2) + (df_2)(s_2^2) + (df_3)(s_3^2) + \ldots}{df_1 + df_2 + df_3 + \ldots} = MS_{wg}$$

The df = group (cell) size minus 1 (i.e., $n - 1$).

Recall from Chapter 11 and 12 that s^2_{pooled} is equivalent to MS_{wg} in an independent groups ANOVA and, therefore, s_{pooled} equals $\sqrt{MS_{wg}}$.

Once we have the estimated standard error of the mean based on the pooled variability in our experiment, we can construct confidence intervals for each of the cell means in our experiment. The critical t is obtained from Table A.2 with the degrees of freedom for the critical t based on the sum of the degrees of freedom for all the groups. For example, because there were four groups of size 9 ($N = 36$) in Liz's experiment, the degrees of freedom for t_{crit} would be $N - k$, or $36 - 4 = 32$. This sum is the same as the degrees of freedom for the MS_{wg} in ANOVA.

Confidence intervals for each of the cell means in Liz's experiment are shown next. Because cell sizes are the same, the pooled standard error of the mean ($\sqrt{MS_{wg}}/\sqrt{n}$) is the same for each mean and is equal to $\sqrt{39.54}/\sqrt{9} = 6.29/3 = 2.096$. Because Table A.2 does not have an entry for 32 df, the next lowest df, 30, was used. The t_{crit} for a two-tailed comparison at the .05 level with 30 df is 2.042. The 95% confidence intervals are as follows:

Men/IP = $M \pm 2.042$ (2.096) = 39.56 $\pm$ 4.28 = 35.28 to 43.84

Men/CB = $M \pm 2.042$ (2.096) = 55.00 $\pm$ 4.28 = 50.72 to 59.28

Women/IP = $M \pm 2.042$ (2.096) = 45.44 $\pm$ 4.28 = 41.16 to 49.72

Women/CB = $M \pm 2.042$ (2.096) = 47.89 $\pm$ 4.28 = 43.61 to 52.17

Figure 13.4 shows the confidence intervals around the four cell means in Liz's experiment. We can learn about the precision of our estimates by examining the interval width and the probable pattern of population means by examining whether the intervals around the sample means overlap, and, if so, to what degree. Recall that a rule of thumb for interpreting confidence intervals suggests that, if the interval around a mean includes the mean of another group, we can be confident that the two means would not be statistically significant if tested using NHST.

FIGURE 13.4 ■ Confidence intervals for the four conditions (cells) of Liz's study.

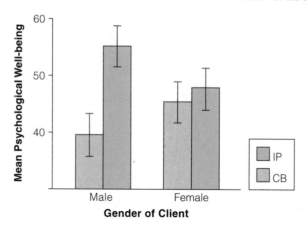

In the context of a complex design, our initial interest is usually on the main effects of each of the variables and the interaction between the variables, rather than on differences among cell means. As you have seen, main effects are described by differences between row or column means. Thus, another way to use confidence intervals is to create them both for the row means and for the column means.

Figure 13.5 shows 95% confidence intervals for the row means (that is, the means corresponding to the effect of the therapy variable) and for the column means (those corresponding to the effect of the gender variable).

The calculation of these intervals was as follows. The critical t value is obtained from Table A.2 based on the sum of the degrees of freedom for all the groups in the experiment ($N - k = 36 - 4 = 32$). As we did previously, because Table A.2 does not have an entry for 32 df, the next lowest df, 30, was used and therefore t_{crit} equals 2.042. The pooled standard error of the mean (s_M) is equivalent to $\sqrt{s^2_{pooled}}/\sqrt{n}$, which is the same as $\sqrt{MS_{wg}}/\sqrt{n}$, where n equals the number of participants at each level of the independent variable.

FIGURE 13.5 ■ Confidence intervals for row and column means (main effects) in Liz's study.

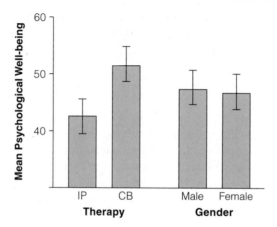

That is,

$$s_M = \sqrt{MS_{wg}}/\sqrt{n} = \sqrt{39.54}/\sqrt{18} = 1.48.$$

Row Means (Type of Therapy)

$$M \pm t_{crit}(s_M) = M \pm 2.042(1.48) = M \pm 3.022$$

The 95% confidence intervals for the two row means are

IP Therapy	$42.50 \pm 3.022 = 39.48$ to 45.52
CB Therapy	$51.44 \pm 3.022 = 48.42$ to 54.46

Column Means (Gender of Client)

The value of t_{crit} and the pooled standard error of the mean remain the same for this comparison.

$$M \pm t_{crit}(s_M) = M \pm (2.042)(1.48) = M \pm 3.022$$

Thus, 95% confidence intervals for the two column means are

Male clients: $47.28 \pm 3.022 = 44.26$ to 50.30

Female clients: $46.67 \pm 3.022 = 43.65$ to 49.69

Consider what we learn from these comparisons. The confidence intervals for the two therapy groups do not overlap. We can suggest that the population means for these two conditions are different. However, the confidence intervals for levels of the gender variable do overlap. To use the rule of thumb we previously introduced for examining confidence intervals, we look to see if the mean of one of the groups lies within the interval of another group. If it does, we do not have evidence to say that the difference between the two means is statistically significant. As seen in Figure 13.5, the mean outcome for male clients is well within the confidence interval for female clients. Given these data, we would not want to conclude that the population means corresponding to male and female clients' therapy outcomes differ.

We hopefully demonstrated that, when analyzing results of a complex design, it may be important to construct confidence intervals around the sample means in the same way we did when the study involved only one independent variable. It is also important to consider calculating a measure of strength of association for each independent variable in the study. When there are two levels (groups) of the independent variable, an effect size measure such as Hedges' g (see Chapter 8) may be used. When there are more than two levels, a measure of strength of association such as eta squared may be used (see Chapter 12). We will discuss effect size measures further later in this chapter.

BEYOND 2 × 2

Experimental designs more complex than 2 × 2 are easily created, and you will meet them regularly in the behavioral science literature. It is important that you be able to apply what you have learned about main effects and interactions in a 2 × 2 design to a design of slightly greater complexity. Let us briefly consider a 3 × 4 design, one in which there are three levels of Variable A and four levels of Variable B. The design matrix for such a design is as follows:

Variable A

	a1	a2	a3

Variable B

b1			
b2			
b3			
b4			

This factorial design has 12 cells or conditions. We might imagine a study with three age groups (e.g., 10, 12, and 14 years) and four reading tasks (A, B, C, and D), or three sets of instructions and four kinds of problems. Whatever the variables, this factorial design will have 12 combinations of levels, and, of course, the data in each condition would first need to be inspected carefully.

Description of main effects involves looking at row and column means just as it did for a 2 × 2 design. Of course, now there are either three means or four means represented in the main effect. Confidence intervals for the population means in each main effect can be constructed in the same manner as they were for a single factor design. (See Chapter 11.) If the experiment is an independent groups design, then the pooled standard error of the mean based on the ANOVA MS_{wg} is used to construct intervals just as it was for the 2 × 2 design.

The description of an interaction in a 3 × 4 complex design may be begun by drawing a graph showing the pattern of cell means for each of the levels of the variables. Such a graph is seen in Figure 13.6.

You know that, if the lines are not parallel, there is evidence of an interaction between the variables. Looking at Figure 13.6, we can suggest an interaction is present. When there are more than two levels, however, the differences between means that contribute to the interaction are not as simply described as they were in a 2 × 2 design.

FIGURE 13.6 ■ Mean performance in a 3 × 4 complex design.

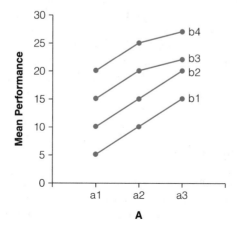

The cell means plotted in Figure 13.6 are as follows:

	Variable A		
Variable B	**a1**	**a 2**	**a3**
b1	5	10	15
b2	10	15	20
b3	15	20	22
b4	20	25	27

Remember that an interaction occurs when the effect of one variable differs across the levels of another independent variable, and that an effect is a difference between means. As perhaps you can see, both from Figure 13.6 and from the preceding table of means, the "effect' of Variable A is not the same at each level of Variable B. Specifically, the pattern of A means (a1, a2, a3) is not the same for each of the four levels of B. Let us walk through this result.

Consider first the effect of A at b1 and b2. That is, examine the relative differences among the A means for levels b1 and b2. The difference between a1 and a2 ($5 - 10 = -5$) and between a2 and a3 ($10 - 15 = -5$) is exactly the same for both b1 and b2.

Now look at the effect of A for levels b3 and b4. For both these levels of B, the difference between a1 and a2 is the same (b3: $15 - 20 = -5$; b4: $20 - 25 = -5$). And for both these levels, the difference between a2 and a3 is the same (b3: $20 - 22 = -2$; b4: $25 - 27 = -2$).

Notice that the effect of A seen at b1 and b2 is not the same as the effect of A seen at b3 and b4. That is, the pattern of A means for the first two levels of B (b1 and b2) does not match the pattern of A means observed for the third and fourth levels (b3 and b4) of B. The effect of A depends on the level of B. This is the definition of an interaction.

We selected only one example to illustrate an interaction in a 3 × 4 design. Keep in mind that evidence of an interaction is obtained whenever the effect of one variable differs across levels of the second variable. This can take many different forms.

In a complex design, differences between means representing one independent variable at a particular level of a second independent variable are called **simple main effects.** For example, look again at the relative differences between means for levels b2 and b3 in the preceding table. (Also see Figure 13.6.) In this example, the simple main effect of A at b2 is not the same as it is at b3. *Another way of describing an interaction is to say that the simple main effects in the research study are not the same.* Later in this chapter, we will discuss ways to analyze further the simple main effects of a complex design.

ANOVA FOR A COMPLEX DESIGN

The computation associated with an ANOVA for a complex design can be somewhat involved, especially when there are more than two independent variables. As a consequence, a multi-factor ANOVA is almost always performed using a computer. But that doesn't mean that you don't need to know what the computer is doing. In what follows, we describe the logic of an ANOVA for a complex design and show how information obtained from the computer output is used to assess the effect of the independent variables and their interaction.

Hypotheses

When conducting an A × B design, such as Liz's therapy effectiveness study, there are three *potential* sources of systematic variation: that due to Variable A, that due to Variable B, and that due to the interaction of Variable A and B. The goal of a complex ANOVA is to provide information for a researcher to be able to make a decision about each of these potential effects. The null and alternative hypotheses for each of the potential effects in an A × B design are as follows:

For Variable A:

H_0: $\mu_{a1} = \mu_{a2} = \mu_{a3}$ = etc.

The null hypothesis is that the population means represented by the means of the levels of Variable A are the same.

H_1: NOT H_0 (Any difference among means satisfies the alternative hypothesis.)

For Variable B:

H_0: $\mu_{b1} = \mu_{b2} = \mu_{b3}$ = etc.

The null hypothesis is that the population means represented by the means of the levels of Variable B are the same.

H_1: NOT H_0 (Any difference among means satisfies the alternative hypothesis.)

You should recognize that the null and alternative hypotheses for each of the main effects of the independent variables are equivalent to these hypotheses when there is only one independent variable present, that is, when a single-factor independent groups design is carried out and analyzed with ANOVA.

The null and alternative hypotheses for the interaction effect are deceptively simple. We'll state the obvious and then explain what these hypotheses mean:

For the Interaction between A and B:

H_0: There is no interaction.

H_1: There is an interaction.

To understand these hypotheses, we need to ask what it means to say that an interaction is or is not present. Remember that interaction effects are about differences between levels of a variable across the levels of another variable. Liz's data revealed evidence of an interaction because the difference in mean therapy outcome for the two levels of therapy (IP and CB) was not the same for the levels of the second variable (male and female clients). If, on the other hand, exactly the same difference between IP and CB therapy had been found for men and for women clients, then an interaction would not be present. But how is this tested in ANOVA?

An interaction is present when there is variability among the means that is not explained by the main effects and sampling error. In a real sense, an interaction reflects variability that is left over when the main effect of each of the variables is subtracted out. If there are differences among the means that cannot be explained by the differences seen in the main effect, then an interaction is present. Consider a different result for Liz's experiment:

	Gender		
	Men	**Women**	**Row Means**
Therapy			
IP	40	30	35
CB	60	50	55
Column Means	50	40	

Look carefully at the row means (35 vs. 55). The main effect (difference) of type of therapy is 20 (55 − 35 = 20). Now compare the effect of type of therapy for men and for women. Although both means are greater for men than for women, the difference between these means (IP and CB) is exactly the same for men and women (Men: 60 − 40 = 20; Women: 50 − 30 = 20). The effect of type of therapy was the same for men and women. Thus, the row means for type of therapy reflect the differences between the two therapies for both men and women. (Note again that it is important to subtract in the same direction when making these comparisons. If we subtract the row IP mean from the row CB mean, we must subtract the IP mean from the CP mean for each comparison within the matrix.)

Now examine the difference between the column means, that is, men and women clients as a main effect. The main effect (difference) of client gender is 10 (50 − 40 = 10). This is the same difference observed between men and women for IP therapy (40 − 30 = 10) and for CB therapy (60 − 50 = 10). Once again, the marginal means reflect the differences seen for this variable at each level of the second variable. Thus, *when an interaction is not present, the row or column mean difference describes completely the difference observed for each column or row of the matrix.* There is nothing left over.

Now consider another outcome of Liz's experiment:

	Gender		
	Men	**Women**	**Row Means**
Therapy			
IP	40	20	30
CB	60	50	55
Column Means	50	35	

As you can see, we changed only one cell mean—that for women who had IP therapy—and, of course, one row and column mean then changed. But a consequence is that the row and column mean differences are now unable to explain completely the differences seen within the matrix. The difference between column means (50 − 35 = 15) no longer equals the difference between men and women at either level of therapy. The difference between men and women for IP therapy is 20 (40 − 20), and for CB therapy it is 10 (60 − 50). Similarly, the row mean difference ($55 - 30 = 25$) does not reflect the difference between IP and CB therapy seen for men and women. There is something else going on, and this something else is the interaction. Thus, *when an interaction is present, the row or column mean difference does not completely describe the difference observed for each column or row of the matrix.* There is something left over.

Computation

To make a decision about each of the three sources of variability, the total variability in the data set is first partitioned in a manner similar to that when only one factor is present. (See Chapter 12.) In fact, the initial steps in a complex ANOVA are exactly the same first steps followed for a single-factor design. We begin by partitioning total variability into between-group variability and within-group variability. Recall that the total SS represents the sum of squared deviations from the grand mean of the data set:

$$SS_{tot} = \Sigma(X - GM)^2$$

The overall variability expressed as SS_{tot} is partitioned into two types of variability. The first deviation, that between a score and its group mean ($X - M$) represents *within-group variability.* The second deviation, that between the group mean and the grand mean ($M - GM$) represents *between-group variability.* In a complex design, these group means are the cells means of the design. Thus, just as we did when conducting a single-factor ANOVA, we define overall variability or SS_{tot} in terms of two separate and independent sources of variability:

$$SS_{tot} = SS_{bg} + SS_{wg}$$

Recall that SS_{wg} is a measure of error variation based on individual differences from a group mean. This part of the total variability in a data set may be conceptualized as error due to individual differences as measured by deviations of scores from their respective group or cell means. The SS_{wg} is the basis for calculating the mean square within groups (MS_{wg}). The computational formula for MS_{wg} is exactly the same as that for a single-factor ANOVA. The formula from Chapter 12 is

$$MS_{wg} = \frac{SS_{wg}}{df_{wg}} = \frac{SS_1 + SS_2 + SS_3 + \ldots}{df_1 + df_2 + df_3 + \ldots}$$

Each df equals group (cell) size minus 1 (i.e., $n - 1$) and $df_{wg} = N - k$ (where k = number of cells), or, when cell sizes are the same, $df_{wg} = k(n - 1)$.

The second source of variability in the data set, SS_{bg}, is based on differences between the group means (cells) and the grand mean, or, more simply, differences among the group means. As we did in Chapter 12, we can ask why the group means differ. Remember that one answer is that the means are different because of chance or sampling error. Sampling error will always be present. But the cell means also may differ because the subjects in the various conditions of the experiment were affected differently by systematic variation. When there is only one independent variable present, systematic variation logically is due only to that variable. When more than one independent variable is present, we must acknowledge that systematic variation may arise from any of three sources: Variable A, Variable B, and the interaction of A and B. In other words, variation among cell means is due to sampling error (which is always present) and *potentially* to the effect of Variable A, Variable B, and the interaction of A and B. How do we decide if systematic variation is present?

It is necessary to obtain estimates of variability for each of the three possible sources of systematic variation. This is accomplished by partitioning the SS_{bg} into variability due to each of the independent variables and their interaction. We partition between group variability as

$$SS_{bg} = \left\{ \begin{array}{l} SS_A \\ SS_B \\ SS_{A\times B} \end{array} \right.$$

Each of these sums of squared deviations represents an independent variance estimate and, consequently, $SS_A + SS_B + SS_{A\times B} = SS_{bg}$.

The sum of squared deviations for variables A and B correspond to the main effects of each of these variables. Keep in mind that a main effect is the effect of a variable on the dependent variable collapsing across the other variable. The calculation of a main effect is performed as if the variable were the only variable in the experiment (that is, exactly as is done for an experiment with one independent variable). Ignoring the second variable, sums of squared deviations of group means from the grand mean are obtained. In this case, however, the group means represent the mean scores from all those participants at the levels (groups) of the variable. These are the row and column means described previously.

The computation of SS_A and SS_B proceeds as follows:

$$SS_A = \Sigma n(M_a - GM)^2,$$

where M_a = mean of A levels and n = size of A-level groups, and

$$SS_B = \Sigma n(M_b - GM)^2,$$

where M_b = mean of B levels and n = size of B-level groups.

That is, to find SS_A, subtract the grand mean from each of the row means, square those deviations, multiply each squared deviation by the number of subjects in each row, and sum the products. To find SS_B, subtract the grand mean from each of the column means, square these deviations, multiply each by the number of subjects in each column, and sum the products. (It should be noted that it makes absolutely no difference whether we associate row and column means with "A" or "B.") The n for each of these comparisons represents the number of participants in each level of the independent variable and not the size of the cell means. In Liz's experiment, for example, there were 18 people at each level of Variable A and 18 people at each level of Variable B.

The df for each main effect equal the number of levels minus 1. Thus df_A = number of A levels − 1, or $2 - 1 = 1$; df_B = number of B levels − 1, or $2 - 1 = 1$.

The interaction sum of squares can be easily found because, as we have shown, $SS_{bg} = SS_A + SS_B + SS_{A\times B}$. Therefore, once we have obtained SS_A and SS_B, we know that

$$SS_{A\times B} = SS_{bg} - SS_A - SS_B$$

The df for the interaction effect equals df_A times df_B. A mean square is then calculated for each source of variability, as

$$MS_A = \frac{SS_A}{df_A} \qquad \text{where } df_A = \text{Number of A levels} - 1$$

$$MS_B = \frac{SS_B}{df_B} \qquad \text{where } df_B = \text{Number of B levels} - 1$$

$$MS_{A\times B} = \frac{SS_{A\times B}}{df_{A\times B}} \qquad \text{where } df_{A\times B} = (\#A \text{ levels} - 1)(\#B \text{ levels} - 1)$$

For each potential effect, an F ratio of mean squares is created. The MS_{wg} is the denominator for each ratio. Recall that it represents a variance estimate based on individual differences expressed as deviations of individual scores from their respective group means. Remember that another term for MS_{wg} is *mean square error (MSE)*.

The numerator of the F ratio will contain sampling error, and it *may* contain systematic variation. Under the null hypothesis, the F ratio represents error divided by error. That is, *under the null hypothesis, there is no systematic variation in the numerator. The alternative hypothesis holds that, in addition to sampling error, systematic variation is present in the numerator of the F ratio.*

$$F(\text{Variable A}) = \frac{MS_A}{MS_{wg}} = \frac{\text{error plus any systematic variation due to Var A}}{\text{error}}$$

$$F(\text{Variable A}) = \frac{MS_B}{MS_{wg}} = \frac{\text{error plus any systematic variation due to Var B}}{\text{error}}$$

$$F(\text{Variable A} \times \text{B}) = \frac{MS_{A \times B}}{MS_{wg}} = \frac{\text{error plus any systematic variation due to A} \times \text{B}}{\text{error}}$$

ANOVA Summary Table

Table 13.3 presents an ANOVA summary table for Liz's therapy effectiveness study. Major interest is in the F ratios obtained for the three potential sources of systematic variability. Based on the description of the mean performance in the conditions of the experiment, we already know something about the covariation between the factors and the means. The results of NHST determine the degree of chance variation in this covariation if the null hypothesis is true.

The ANOVA summary table is packed with information: it contains a description of the various sources of variability, the degrees of freedom for each source, the sums of squared deviations, mean squares, F ratios testing for the three potential sources of systematic variation in the experiment, and the exact probability associated with each F ratio assuming the null hypothesis is true.

First, look carefully at the probabilities for each effect. For variable A (type of therapy), the F ratio is 18.21 and the probability associated with this effect is .000. Recall that, when the probability is equal to or less than .0005, the computer output shows only .000. Therefore, the probability of this obtained F is very small ($p \le .0005$) assuming the null hypothesis is true. Because the probability was less than .05, we can say that type of therapy was

TABLE 13.3 ■ ANOVA Summary Table for Liz's Therapy Outcome Study

Source	SS	df	MS	F	p
Therapy	720.03	1	720.03	18.21	.000
Gender	3.36	1	3.36	.08	.773
T × G	380.25	1	380.25	9.62	.004
Error	1265.33	32	39.54		
Total	2368.97	35			

statistically significant as a main effect in this experiment. We must again emphasize that the ANOVA table provides no information about the size of the difference between the two therapies or about the direction of the difference. Which type of therapy produced overall better results? How large was the difference? Only through careful inspection and description of the data do we know the answer to these questions. The results of the ANOVA for Variable A confirm what we learned when we drew confidence intervals around the row means; however, NHST adds additional information. We know that, given this low probability, there is a good likelihood of replicating this result at the .05 level.

The probability of the F ratio for Variable B was .773. This is clearly an outcome that will occur frequently when the null hypothesis is true, that is, when only sampling error (chance) is responsible for the difference between means. Because the expected value of F is 1.00 under the null hypothesis, values under 1.0 would be expected half of the time when the null hypothesis is true. Because F is 0.08, which is considerably smaller than 1.0, the probability is much greater than .05, and, in fact, is .773. Given these data, there is no reason to conclude that systematic variation is also present—that the difference between mean outcomes for men and women is anything but chance variation. This does not mean that we have demonstrated conclusively that systematic variation is not present; rather, the results of NHST do not provide sufficient evidence for us to conclude that systematic variation is present. We are unable to reject the null hypothesis. Our description of therapy outcome for the two levels of the gender variable showed that there was little difference between the overall means for men and women and that the confidence intervals for this comparison overlap almost completely. The results of NHST do not allow us to conclude that this difference is due to systematic variation associated with being male or female.

Finally, the probability associated with the F ratio for the interaction between A and B was .004. The interaction effect was statistically significant ($p < .05$). We can reject the null hypothesis that states there is no interaction, that the differences between cell means at each level of an independent variable can be explained completely by the main effects of the variables. The statistically significant interaction effect suggests that there is something left over after the main effects of the independent variables are subtracted out. There is variability not explained by the differences observed between the row or column means. Of course, we must rely on descriptive statistics to describe the nature of this interaction.

YOUR TURN 13-7

The following summary table describes the results of an ANOVA for an independent groups design. Examine the table carefully and then answer the questions that follow.

Source	SS	df	MS	F	p
Var A	24	1	24	6.0	.03
Var B	12	2	6	1.5	.20
A × B	36	2	18	4.5	.02
Within (error)	216	54	4		
Total	288	59			

(a) How would you describe this A × B design? (That is, is it 2 × 2, 2 × 3, 2 × 4?). Explain how you arrived at your answer.

(b) If we assume that cell size is equal, how many participants were in each cell (condition)?

(c) Again, assuming cell size is equal, how many participants were at each level of Variable A? At each level of Variable B?

(d) Which effects were statistically significant? ■

Analytical Comparisons

When an independent variable has more than two levels and a statistically significant main effect has been found, it may be important to perform analytical comparisons in a manner similar to those for a single-factor experiment. (See Chapter 12.) Recall that analytical comparisons are "two-group" comparisons or contrasts. A researcher conducts analytical comparisons following NHST to learn about the specific differences between levels of an independent variable. Of course, when there are just two levels of an independent variable, there is no need for analytical comparisons.

Consider how an analytical comparison would be conducted following an ANOVA for a complex design. We assume that a statistically significant main effect was obtained and that the researcher seeks to contrast the means of two levels of that variable. In other words, we are looking for specific differences between row or column means. For example, if Variable A has four levels, an investigator may have an applied or theoretical reason to directly contrast two of these means. The procedure is similar to performing an independent groups t test of the difference between two means except that we use the MS_{wg} from the omnibus ANOVA as our pooled variance estimate. (See Chapter 12.) The formula from Chapter 12 is

$$t_{comparison} = \frac{M_1 - M_2}{\sqrt{[MS_{wg}\,(1/n_1 + 1/n_2)]}}$$

You should be familiar by now with all the terms in this formula. The means (M_1 and M_2) represent the two levels from the main effect of interest (e.g., a1 vs. a4). Recall that n_1 and n_2 refer to the size of the groups that you are comparing and not to cell sizes. That is, n_1 and n_2 refer to the number of subjects in either the columns or rows associated with the main effect of the variable. We compare the obtained contrast effect with a critical (table) value of t with degrees of freedom associated with the MS_{wg} from the ANOVA.

Analysis of Simple Main Effects

When evidence of an interaction is present, researchers often analyze the simple main effects of a variable. As we saw earlier, a simple main effect is the effect of a variable at only one level of the second variable. In Liz's experiment, for example, evidence of a simple main effect would be examined by comparing the difference between the means for the two types of therapies (IP and CB) for men only and then comparing the difference between IP and CB means for women only. We obtained information about these differences when we constructed confidence intervals for the cell means. (See Figure 13.4.) As you can see in Figure 13.4, confidence intervals do not overlap for means associated with male clients who had IP or CB therapy; on the other hand, intervals overlap to a great extent for means associated with female clients who had IP or CB therapy.

BOX 13.1   ■   Calculating Simple Main Effects When There Are Three or More Levels
of the Independent Variable

The procedure for calculating the simple main effect when there are three or more levels
makes use of ANOVA.

(1) One first calculates the sum of squares between groups for the groups represented by
the levels of the independent variable of interest. Consider, for example, the simple
main effect of A at b1 (b2, b3, etc.). First, compute

$SS_a = \Sigma n(M_a - GM)^2$, where M_a = mean of a levels at b1 (b2, b3, etc.) and n equals
size of a-level groups (cell size).

Note: This procedure is equivalent to obtaining the SS_{bg} for the groups (levels) of interest at one level of a second variable. Entering only the scores from these groups in
a single-factor, independent groups ANOVA will produce the desired SS.

(2) The sum of squared deviations is divided by degrees of freedom equal to number of
levels (groups) minus 1 to obtain a mean square. That is, divide SS_a by the number of
A levels minus 1 to find a mean square for the simple main effect.

(3) The mean square is then divided by the MS_{wg} from the overall analysis to find the F
ratio for the simple main effect.

(4) The significance of this F is tested by finding the critical F value in Table A.3 with df
equal to number of levels minus 1 and MS_{wg} df and comparing the F value found in
step #3.

An analogous pocedure would be used to find the simple main effect of B at a1 (a2, a3, etc.).

A statistically significant simple main effect for an independent variable with three or
more levels can be followed by two-group contrasts to more clearly define the source of
systematic variation. The procedure for a two-group comparison after finding a simple
main effect is similar to that for a two-group comparison for an overall main effect. The
differences are that the two means being compared are two levels of one independent
variable at one level of a second independent variable, and n_1 and n_2 are cell sizes.

A simple main effect may also be examined using NHST. (See Box 13.1) When there are
only two levels of an independent variable, a simple main effect may be calculated in a manner
analogous to performing a two-group comparison following a statistically significant main effect, except that the two means of interest are the cell means describing the effect of one variable at only one level of another variable. Let us illustrate this procedure by finding the simple
main effect of type of therapy (Var B) for both men and women (Var A) in Liz's experiment:

Simple Main Effect of Variable B (Type of Therapy) for Men (Level a1)

$$t_{comparison} = \frac{M_1 - M_2}{\sqrt{[MS_{wg}\,(1/n_1 + 1/n_2)]}}$$

$$t_{comparison} = \frac{55.00 - 39.56}{\sqrt{[39.54\,(1/9 + 1/9)]}} = \frac{15.44}{\sqrt{8.79}} = \frac{15.44}{2.96} = 5.22$$

We obtain MS_{wg} from the ANOVA summary table for Liz's experiment. (See Table 13.3.)
Note that n_1 and n_2 now refer to the cell sizes represented by the two means of interest. We
obtain t_{crit} by looking in Table A.2 for t with degrees of freedom associated with the MS_{wg},

which are 32. We can use the value associated with 30 *df* because the critical value for 32 *df* is not listed in Table A.2. This value is 2.042 for a two-tailed test at the .05 level, 2.75 at the .01 level, and 3.646 at the .001 level. The obtained $t_{comparison}$ is greater than t_{crit} at .001. Therefore, we can say that the simple main effect of type of therapy is statistically significant for male clients: $t(32) = 5.22, p < .001$.

Simple main effect of Variable B (type of therapy) for women (Level a2):

$$t_{comparison} = \frac{4.89 - 45.44}{\sqrt{39.54 \, (1/9 + 1/9)}} = \frac{2.45}{2.96} = 0.83$$

The simple main effect for variable B (type of therapy) is not statistically significant for female clients because the obtained $t_{comparison}$ is less than t_{crit} (2.042) for this comparison.

EFFECT SIZE MEASURES FOR COMPLEX DESIGNS

We may use the effect size measure, eta squared (η^2), to describe the results of a complex design just as we did for a single-factor design. (See Chapter 12.) Remember that eta squared indicates the proportion of variance accounted for by the independent variable. To calculate eta squared, we focus on each effect of interest (see Rosenthal & Rosnow, 1991). Eta squared expresses variability of an effect (in terms of SS) as a proportion of the total variability (in terms of SS) that would be present if the effect of interest was the only variable in the experiment. The denominator, therefore, is the sum of SS effect and SS_{wg}. Eta squared (η^2) is defined as

$$\text{eta squared} = \frac{SS \text{ effect of interest}}{SS \text{ effect of interest} + SS_{wg}}$$

As way of illustration, let us compute eta squared for the effect of type of therapy in Liz's experiment. The relevant sums of squares are from Table 13.3.

Variable A (Type of Therapy)

$$\text{eta squared} = \frac{720.028}{720.028 + 1265.33} = .36$$

We can say that the independent variable, type of therapy, accounted for 36% of the variance in the data.

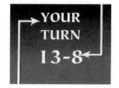

YOUR TURN 13-8

What is eta squared (η^2) for the interaction effect in Liz's experiment? ∎

When there are only two levels of an independent variable, as is the case for Liz's therapy outcome study, eta squared is easily interpreted (see Rosenthal & Rosnow, 1991).[1]

---

[1]When there are only two means, the effect is represented by the difference between the means, and, in this case, eta (or the square root of eta squared) is equal to *r*, a measure of linear relationship that will be discussed in the following chapters.

Nevertheless, when only two means are being compared, Hedges' g is a good estimate of effect size. (See Chapter 8.) We can calculate g for this same comparison as

$$\text{Hedges' } g = \frac{M_1 - M_2}{s_{\text{pooled}}} = \frac{M_1 - M_2}{\sqrt{s^2_{\text{pooled}}}} = \frac{M_1 - M_2}{\sqrt{MS_{\text{wg}}}}$$

Variable A (Type of Therapy)

$$\text{Hedges' } g = \frac{M_{\text{CB}} - M_{\text{IP}}}{\sqrt{39.54}} = \frac{51.44 - 42.5}{6.29} = 1.42$$

Based on Cohen's rule of thumb (in which .30, .50., and .80, correspond to small, medium, and large effect sizes, respectively), we can see that the independent variable—type of therapy—had a large effect on the outcome measure.

What is the effect size, g, for Variable B (gender of client) in Liz's experiment?   ■

When a complex design has more than two levels of an independent variable, eta squared has the same limitation that we saw when this measure was used in a single-factor design. Knowing that a multi-level variable accounts for a certain proportion of the variance is not always that informative because the specific differences between means that produced the effect are not necessarily clear. When there are only two means, there can be only one explanation for an effect. As we saw in Chapter 12, researchers often seek to make comparisons between two levels (means) to more fully describe the effect of a variable. Comparisons between two means can be made for an independent variable with three or more levels by using analytical comparisons or contrasts. (See preceding discussion.) A measure of effect size for the difference between two means, such as g, may then be calculated.

ANNOUNCING RESULTS OF A COMPLEX DESIGN

We are now in a position to formally announce the results of Liz's therapy outcome study. A general statement of her results is as follows:

> An experiment was conducted to investigate therapy outcome for men and women receiving two types of psychotherapy. Male ($n = 18$) and female ($n = 18$) clients with similar histories of emotional disorders were randomly assigned to one of two types of psychotherapy: interpersonal therapy (IP) and cognitive-behavioral (CB) therapy. Following a 6-week treatment of individual therapy, clients were evaluated by psychotherapists who were blind to the type of therapy that had been used. Ratings by the psychotherapists were combined to produce an index of mental health that ranged from 0 to 70, with normal individuals typically rated between 50 and 60. There were nine clients in each of the four conditions of this complex design.
>
> Inspection of the data in the four experimental conditions revealed that the distributions were generally normal in form with no outliers present. There also was

no evidence of ceiling or floor effects. Table 1 [see Table 13.1] shows the means and standard deviations for each of the four conditions of the experiment, as well as the overall means for men and women and for IP and CB therapies. Outcome scores for men were generally more variable than for women, but the standard deviations of the four conditions are similar enough to suggest that the assumption of homogeneity of variance has been met. As can be seen in Table 1, the overall mean outcome for CB therapy (51.44) was greater than that for IP therapy (42.5); overall mean outcome for men (47.28) and women (46.67) differed only slightly. Differences between cell means suggest an interaction between the two independent variables. This is more clearly seen in Figure 1.

Figure 1 [see Figure 13.4] plots mean outcome ratings for the four conditions of the experiment. A 95% confidence interval for the population mean is shown for each condition. As can be seen in the figure, mean therapy outcome was greater for CB therapy than IP therapy for both men and women. However, the difference between the two types of therapy was much greater for men (15.44) than for women (2.44). Confidence intervals overlap for women but not for men.

A 2 × 2 ANOVA for an independent groups design revealed a statistically significant main effect for type of therapy, $F(1, 32) = 18.21, p < .001, \eta^2 = .23$, as well as a statistically significant interaction, $F(1, 32) = 9.62, p = .004, \eta^2 = .36$ ($MSE = 39.54$). Simple main effects of the therapy variable were examined for male and female clients. As suggested by the pattern of confidence intervals seen in Figure 1, the simple main effect for type of therapy was statistically significant for men, $t(32) = 5.22, p \leq .0005$ but not for women, $t(32) = .83, p = .413$. The effect size, Hedges' g, for men was 2.45; for women, g was 0.39.

The results of this experiment demonstrate that the effectiveness of IP and CB therapy depends on the gender of the client. Although there was little difference in therapy outcome between IP and CB therapies for women, men showed a much better outcome with CB therapy than IP therapy.

A researcher chooses results of a various statistical analyses to help tell a coherent story about what happened in an experiment. This story may differ depending on what the researcher wishes to emphasize or what comparisons need to be made with results of previous studies. What is most important is that the researcher's audience obtains a good understanding of the nature of the experiment, the experimental results, and what the results mean. To accomplish this, a researcher must pay close attention to all aspects of the I-D-E-A model of data analysis and interpretation.

WHAT YOU HAVE LEARNED AND THE NEXT STEP

In this chapter, you saw how the I-D-E-A model of data analysis and interpretation is applied to a complex design. Although complex designs may take many forms, we focused on A × B designs in which experimental groups were independent. Participants are either assigned randomly to conditions or are selected to represent levels of a natural groups variable (e.g., men and women representing a gender variable). The value of complex designs is that they provide information both about main effects of independent variables and about the interaction of variables. Because so much information is obtained in one design, complex designs are the most common type of experimental design in the behavioral science literature. In this chapter, you learned the following concepts.

● A complex design is one that involves more than one independent variable.

● A factorial design is a complex design that combines all levels of one independent variable with all levels of another independent variable. The combinations of levels are called *cells* of the design.

● When null hypothesis significance testing (NHST) is used, analysis of variance (ANOVA) is the most common inferential test used to analyze complex designs.

● A main effect is the overall effect of an independent variable collapsed across levels of the other independent variable(s). Main effects are also called *row* and *column effects*.

● An interaction occurs when the effect of one independent variable on the dependent variable depends on the setting (level) of another independent variable. An effect is a difference between means. Interactions may be described by examining the effect of an independent variable across levels of another independent variable.

● When cell means of a complex design are described in a graph, nonparallel lines in the graph suggest an interaction between the independent variables. Parallel lines indicate the absence of an interaction.

● We can learn about the precision of our estimates of population means by examining the confidence interval width for each cell mean and about the probable pattern of population means by examining whether the intervals around the cell means overlap. Confidence intervals may also be created for row and column means.

● Differences between means representing one independent variable at a particular level of a second independent variable are called *simple main effects*. One way to describe an interaction in a complex design is to say that the simple main effects are not the same.

● ANOVA for complex designs is an extension of the ANOVA for a single-factor design. Overall variability (SS_{tot}) is partitioned into SS_{bg} and SS_{wg}. However, in a complex design, SS_{bg} is then partitioned into sums of squares for Variable A (SS_A), for Variable B (SS_B), and for the interaction ($SS_{A \times B}$).

● Three null hypotheses are tested in an A $\times$ B complex design. The null hypothesis for each main effect is that the population means represented by the means of the levels of the variable are the same. The null hypothesis for the interaction states that there is no interaction between the independent variables.

● An interaction is present when there is variability among the cell means that is not completely explained by the main effect of the independent variables.

● A mean square (variance) is calculated for each potential source of systematic variation: Variable A, Variable B, and the interaction of A and B. Each mean square is then divided by the MS_{wg} from the overall ANOVA to obtain an F ratio.

● Under the null hypothesis, the F ratio represents random variation (error) divided by random variation (error). That is, the null hypothesis states that there is no systematic variation in the numerator. The alternative hypothesis assumes that, in addition to sampling error, systematic variation is present in the numerator of the F ratio.

- Results of an ANOVA for a complex design typically are summarized in an ANOVA summary table.

- When an independent variable has more than two levels and a statistically significant main effect is obtained, a researcher may conduct analytical comparisons following NHST to learn about the specific differences between means of the levels of an independent variable.

- When evidence of an interaction is present, a researcher may analyze the simple main effects of a variable.

- The effect size measure eta squared (η^2) may be used to describe the results of a complex design. Eta squared indicates the proportion of variance accounted for by the independent variable.

- When only two means are being compared, Hedges' g may be used as a measure of effect size.

In the next few chapters, we look at the I-D-E-A model for research studies that emphasize the scientific goal of prediction. (See Chapter 1.) In these studies, researchers examine relationships among various measures of behavior and mental processes. When measures are found to be related, a value on one variable may be used to predict a value on a second variable. For example, researchers have shown a relationship between measures of how pessimistic people are and measures of overall health, especially in middle age. More-pessimistic people tend to experience more health-related problems. Thus, we may be able to predict a person's later overall health based on knowledge of their level of pessimism, or what psychologists call *explanatory style*. We turn in the next chapter to this important technique in behavioral research.

Key Concepts

complex design	main effect	SS_A
factorial design	interaction	SS_B
cells	simple main effect	$SS_{A \times B}$

Answers to *Your Turn* Questions

13-1. Although only based on nine values, an examination of the stem-and-leaf displays suggests that the population distributions are generally normal in form.

13-2. Outcome scores for men were generally more variable than for women, but the standard deviations of the four conditions are similar enough to assure one that the assumption of homogeneity of variance has been met.

13-3. (a) For data set #1, the main effect of facial expression (smiling vs. frowning) was 2 (7 − 5); that of eyeglasses (yes vs. no) was also 2 (7 − 5). (b) Thus, for each independent variable, there is evidence that mean honesty ratings varied with the levels of the independent variables. In general, honesty ratings were greater for people who were smiling, and when people wore eyeglasses.

(a) For data set #2, there was no evidence of a main effect for presence or absence of eyeglasses (5 − 5 = 0); however, there was a difference between mean honesty ratings of photographs of people smiling (5.5) and frowning (4.5).

(b) Only for the independent variable facial expression is their evidence of covariation between levels of the independent variable and the dependent variable.

13-4. The difference between men and women for IP therapy is 39.50 − 45.44 = −5.94; the difference between men and women for CB therapy is 55.00 − 47.89 = +7.11.

(a) The difference is not the same; in fact, it is in the opposite direction. This suggests an interaction between the two independent variables. Of course, we already knew that there would be evidence for an interaction because we previously saw that the mean differences were not the same for IP and CB therapy for men and between IP and CB therapy for women. An interaction may be described either way. If there are differences, they do not go away when we look at differences across levels of the second variable.

(b) The interaction may be described as showing that men exhibited poorer mean outcome than women when treated by IP therapy, but men showed better outcome than women when treated with CB therapy.

13-5. (a) Data Set 1

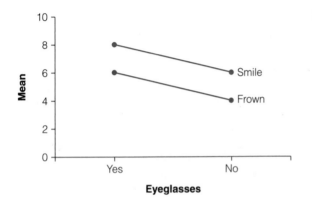

Data Set 2

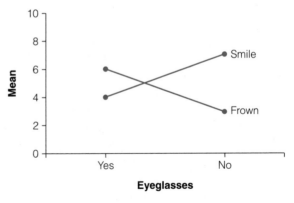

(b) Only in the second figure, data set #2, is there evidence of an interaction.

13-6. As we mentioned, the appearance of the results (not the results themselves) may change depending on which variable is chosen to be placed on the horizontal axis. This decision rests with the investigator. You may decide for yourself which figure best describes Liz's results. Our preference is Figure 13.2; however, as we mentioned in the *Your Turn*, there is no correct answer. The point of this exercise is to ask you to think about how the results will look to your audience before actually presenting them. You may find that a good strategy is to plot the results both ways and then decide which description of your results best fits your research story.

13-7. (a) The design is a 2 × 3 because there is one *df* for Variable A (# A levels − 1) and two *df* for Variable B (# B levels − 1).

(b) A 2 × 3 design has six conditions. The total *df* equals 59 ($N − 1$), and therefore we know that there are 60 participants, 10 in each of six cells.

(c) There will be 30 participants at each level of A and 20 participants at each level of B.

(d) The main effect of Variable A was statistically significant ($p < .05$), as was the interaction effect ($p < .05$). The main effect of Variable B was not statistically significant ($p > .05$).

13-8. Eta squared for the interaction effect is equal to 380.25/(380.25 + 1265.33), or .23.

13-9. The effect size, g, for the main effect of client gender is equal to $(47.28 - 46.67)/\sqrt{39.54}$, or 0.097 (a very small effect).

Analyzing and Interpreting Data: Problems and Exercises

1. Explain the difference between a factorial design that is described as 2 × 3 and one that is described as 4 × 4. Indicate for each design the number of experimental conditions or cells.

2. The results of a 2 × 2 design are as follows (cell means): a1b1, 5; a1b2, 20; a2b1, 10; a2b2, 15. Do the data suggest a main effect of A? How about of B? An interaction between A and B? Be sure to explain your answers.

3. The results of a 2 × 3 design are as follows (cell means): a1b1,15; a1b2, 22; a1b3, 20; a2b1, 10; a2b2, 15; a2b3, 20. Do the data suggest a main effect of A? How about of B? An interaction between A and B? Be sure to explain your answers.

4. Draw a graph describing the mean results in problem #2.

5. Draw a graph describing the mean results in problem #3.

6. The results of a 2 × 2, independent groups, complex design are as follows:

| | Variable A | | | |
| | a1 | | a2 | |
Variable B:	b1	b2	b1	b2
	12	16	22	14
	16	20	28	15
	11	21	19	11
	10	24	25	18
	9	19	30	17
	12	16	22	15
	15	23	27	13
	15	23	27	9
	13	25	26	11
	12	22	26	12

(a) Inspect the data.
(b) Provide the mean and standard deviation for each of the cells and find the row and column means.
(c) Use a computer to perform an ANOVA on the data and report results in an ANOVA summary table.
(d) Interpret the results of the ANOVA in light of the mean differences observed. (Hint: Draw a graph showing mean results to help with your interpretation of results.)

7. The results of a 2 × 2, independent groups, complex design are as follows:

| | Variable A | | | |
| | a1 | | a2 | |
Variable B:	b1	b2	b1	b2
	22	17	19	19
	26	20	18	19
	21	22	19	21
	20	19	12	18
	19	19	10	22
	19	16	12	15
	25	23	17	28

(a) Inspect the data.
(b) Provide the mean and standard deviation for each of the cells and find the row and column means.
(c) Use a computer to perform an ANOVA on the data and report results in an ANOVA summary table.
(d) Interpret the results of the ANOVA in light of the mean differences observed. (Hint: Draw a graph showing mean results to help with your interpretation of results.)

8. Complete the following ANOVA summary table by filling in the blanks with the appropriate values.

Source	SS	df	MS	F	p
Var A	24.0	1	_____	_____	.002
Var B	_____	_____	18.0	_____	.003
A × B	_____	2	_____	_____	.40
Error	168.00	_____	_____		
Total	240.00	47			

9. Complete the following ANOVA summary table by filling in the blanks with the appropriate values.

Source	SS	df	MS	F	p
Var A	_____	1	90.25	_____	.029
Var B	393.36	_____	_____	_____	.000
A × B	_____	1	_____	_____	.041
Error	552.00	_____			
Total	1113.64	35			

10. Examine carefully the following figure showing results of an A × B design.

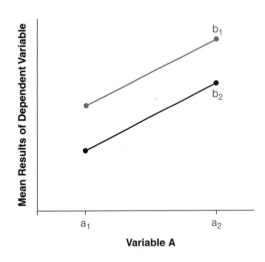

Variable A

(a) How many levels of A are there? of B?
(b) Does the pattern of means suggest a main effect of A? Of B?
(c) Does the pattern of means suggest an interaction between A and B?

11. Examine carefully the following figure showing results of an A × B design.

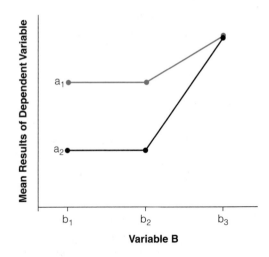

Variable B

(a) How many levels of A are there? of B?
(b) Does the pattern of means suggest a main effect of A? Of B?
(c) Does the pattern of means suggest an interaction between A and B?

12. Calculate 95% confidence intervals based on each of the cell means in problem #6. (Note: Use the MS_{wg} from the omnibus ANOVA as s^2_{pooled}.)

13. Calculate 95% confidence intervals based on each of the cell means in problem #7. (Note: Use the MS_{wg} from the omnibus ANOVA as s^2_{pooled}.)

14. Find eta squared for each of the potential sources of systematic variation in problem #6.

15. Find eta squared for each of the potential sources of systematic variation in problem #7.

16. Assume that Variable B in problem #6 actually had three levels and that results for Level b3 at a1 and a2 were as follows:

a1b3	a2b3
11	6
12	8
14	9
14	10
14	5
15	9
10	12
17	11
14	7
16	9

Combine these results with those of problem #6 to make a 2 × 3 design.
(a) Find the cell means and standard deviations, as well as the row and column means for this design.
(b) Use a computer to conduct an ANOVA for an independent groups design and report your results in an ANOVA summary table.
(c) Identify which effects are statistically significant.

17. Assume that Variable B in problem #7 actually had three levels and that results for Level b3 at a1 and a2 were as follows:

a1b3	a2b3
10	16
17	18
14	19
15	20
19	17
17	19
10	22

Combine these results with those of problem #7 to make a 2 × 3 design.

(a) Find the cell means and standard deviations, as well as the row and column means for this design.
(b) Use a computer to conduct an ANOVA for an independent groups design and report your results in an ANOVA summary table.
(c) Identify which effects are statistically significant.

18. Find the three simple main effects of Variable A (a1 vs. a2) for b1, b2, and b3, from the data of problem #16. Note that, to obtain a simple main effect, you begin by calculating the SS "between groups" for the groups of interest (e.g., SS_{bg} for variable A at b1).

19. Find the simple main effects of Variable B (i.e., among b1, b2, b3) for a1 and a2 from the data of problem #17. To obtain a simple main effect, you begin by calculating the SS "between groups" for the groups of interest (e.g., SS_{bg} for variable B at a1). See Box 13.1.

20. Calculate the effect size, Hedges' g, for each of the (two-group) simple main effects in problem #18.

Answers to Odd-Numbered Problems

1. A 2 × 3 complex, factorial design has two independent variables (A and B). One variable has two levels, and the second variable has three levels. A 2 × 3 design has six cells. A 4 × 4 complex factorial design also has two independent variables, but in this case each variable has four levels. A 4 × 4 design has 16 cells.

3. The means for a1 and a2 (assuming equal cell size and collapsing across b1, b2, and b3) are 57/3 or 19, and 45/3 or 15, respectively. This difference suggests a main effect of Variable A. The means for b1, b2, and b3 (ignoring Variable A) are 25/2 or 12, 37/2 or 18.5, and 40/2 or 20, respectively, providing evidence for a

main effect of Variable B. There is evidence of an interaction between A and B. The difference between a1 and a2 at b1 (15 − 10 = 5) is not the same as the difference between a1 and a2 at b2 (22 − 15 = +7), nor as the difference between a1 and a2 at b3 (20 − 20 = 0). Additional statistical analyses are needed to confirm these impressions gained from the descriptive stage of analysis.

5. A graph of the cell means from problem #3 is shown here. Variable B is on the horizontal or x axis, and Variable A is plotted in the graph. By placing Variable B on the x axis, only two lines need to be drawn in the figure to represent levels a1 and a2. The figure could

be drawn with Variable A on the x axis, but three lines would need to be drawn in the figure to represent the three levels of B. Either is correct.

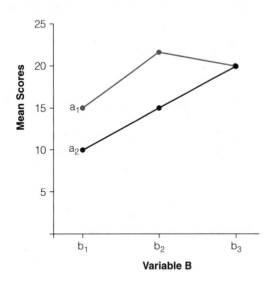

7. (a) Stem-and-leaf displays for the four cells are as follows:

a1b1			a2b1	
1	99		1	022
2	012		1	7899
2	56			

a1b2			a2b2	
1	6799		1	5899
2	023		2	128

Given the small sample size, it is difficult to judge the shape of the distributions in each cell; however, data do not appear to be skewed, and there are no outliers.

(b) Means and standard deviations (in parentheses) for this complex design are as follows:

	Variable A		
	a1	a2	B Means
Variable B			
b1	21.71 (2.81)	15.29 (3.81)	18.50 (b1)
b2	19.43 (2.51)	20.29 (4.07)	19.86 (b2)
A Means	20.57 (a1)	17.79 (a2)	

(c) The ANOVA summary table is as follows:

Source	SS	df	MS	F	p
Var A	54.32	1	54.32	4.49	.039
Var B	12.89	1	12.89	1.14	.297
Var A × B	92.89	1	92.89	8.20	.009
Within (error)	272.00	24	11.33		
Total	432.10	27			

(d) There was a main effect for Variable A: $F(1, 24)$ = 4.49, p = .039. The overall mean for Level a1 was 20.57 and that for a2 was 17.79. As this difference was statistically significant, there is evidence that systematic variation due to Variable A is present. The main effect of Variable B was not statistically significant ($p > .05$). The difference is not that unlikely simply by chance (i.e., due to sampling error). We may not conclude that systematic variation due to Variable B is present. The interaction between Variable A and B was statistically significant: $F(1,24)$ = 8.20, $p < .009$. The difference between a1 and a2 at b1 (21.71 − 15.29 = 6.42) was not the same as the difference between a1 and a2 at b2 (19.43 − 20.29 = −0.86).

9.

Source	SS	df	MS	F	p
Var A	**90.25**	1	90.25	**5.23**	.029
Var B	393.36	**1**	**393.36**	**22.80**	.000
A × B	**78.03**	1	**78.03**	**4.52**	.041
Within (error)	552.00	**32**	**17.25**		
Total	1113.64	35			

11. (a) There are two levels of A and three levels of B; that is, the design is a 2 × 3.

(b) The pattern of cell means in the figure suggests main effects of A and B. This is not easy to see in the graph, but if you look carefully you should be able to detect that the average of the a1 mean (i.e., averaging across b1, b2, and b3) will be higher than the average of a2. Also, although the average of b1 and b2 (across a1 and a2) will be similar, the average of b3 will be higher. Another way to "see" the possible main effects is to make up cell means for the six cells that correspond to the pattern seen in the figure, and then place them in a matrix. Calculate row and column means (assuming equal cell size) corresponding to the main effects of A and B. You will find that the overall mean for a1 differs from that of a2, and that there are differences among the means for b1, b2, and b3. Specifically, b1 and b2 means are identical, but both differ from b3.

(c) There is evidence of an interaction. Note that the lines are not parallel, which is a sure sign of an interaction. One way to state this is that the difference between a1 and a2 at b1 and b2 is the same, but this difference differs at b3, where there is no difference between a1 and a2. Of course, additional statistical analyses are needed to confirm these impressions gained from the descriptive stage of analysis. With practice, you can learn to "read" a figure and detect patterns suggestive of main effects and interactions.

13. The 95% confidence intervals surrounding the cell means for the data in problem #7 are as follows:

a1b1: $21.71 \pm (2.064) (1.27) = 19.09$ to 24.33
a1b2: $19.43 \pm (2.064) (1.27) = 16.81$ to 22.05
a2b1: $15.29 \pm (2.064) (1.27) = 12.67$ to 17.91
a2b2: $20.29 \pm (2.064) (1.27) = 17.67$ to 22.91

Note: Confidence intervals are based on $M \pm t_{crit} (s_M)$, where s_M is equal to $(\sqrt{MS_{wg}})/(\sqrt{n})$, and n equals cell size; that is, $(\sqrt{11.33})/(\sqrt{7}) = 3.37/2.65 = 1.27$. The value of t_{crit} is found in Table A.2 with 24 df (corresponding to the MS_{wg}) for a two-tailed comparison at the .05 level, which is 2.064.

15. Eta squared is calculated as $(SS$ of interest$)/(SS$ of interest $+ SS_{wg})$:

Variable A = $54.321/(54.321 + 272.00) = .17$
Variable B = $12.893/(12.893 + 272.00) = .05$
Int A $\times$ B = $92.893/(92.893 + 272.00) = .25$

17. (a) Means and standard deviations (in parentheses) for this complex design are as follows:

	Variable A		
	a1	**a2**	**Variable B**
Variable B			
b1	21.71 (2.81)	15.29 (3.82)	18.50 (b1)
b2	19.43 (2.51)	20.29 (4.07)	19.86 (b2)
b3	14.57 (4.15)	18.71 (1.98)	16.64 (b3)
Variable A	18.57 (a1)	18.10 (a2)	

(b) The ANOVA summary table is as follows:

Source	*SS*	*df*	*MS*	*F*	*p*
Var A	2.38	1	2.38	0.23	.633
Var B	72.90	2	36.45	3.56	.039
Var A $\times$ B	204.90	2	102.45	9.99	.000
Within (error)	369.14	36	10.25		
Total	649.33	41			

(c) There was no main effect for Variable A: $F(1, 36) = 0.23$, $p = .633$. The overall mean for Level a1 was 18.57, and that for a2 was 18.10. This small difference was not statistically significant; there is no evidence that systematic variation due to Variable A is present. The main effect of Variable B was statistically significant: $F(2, 36) = 3.56$, $p = .039$. The differences are unlikely to be due simply to chance (i.e., due to sampling error). We may conclude that systematic variation due to Variable B is present. The interaction between Variable A and B was statistically significant: $F(2, 36) = 9.99$, $p \le .0005$. The difference between a1 and a2 at b1 ($21.71 - 15.29 = 6.42$) was not the same as the difference between a1 and a2 at b2 ($19.43 - 20.29 = -0.86$), nor were either the same as the difference between a1 and a2 at b3 ($14.57 - 18.71 = -4.14$).

19. The procedure for calculating the simple main effect when there are more than two levels is outlined in Box 13.1.

(1) One first calculates the sum of squares between groups for the groups represented by the levels of the independent variable of interest.

For the simple main effect of B at a1, compute: $SS_b = \Sigma n(M_b - GM)^2$, where $M_b =$ mean of b levels at a1 and n equals size of b-level groups (cell size). This procedure is equivalent to obtaining the SS_{bg} for the groups (levels) of interest at one level of a second variable. Entering only the scores from these groups in a single-factor, independent groups ANOVA will produce the desired SS. For these data, the SS_{bg} at a1 equals 186.29.

For the simple main effect of B at a2 compute: $SS_b = \Sigma n(M_b - GM)^2$, where $M_b =$ mean of b levels at a2 and n equals size of b-level groups (cell size). This procedure is equivalent to obtaining the SS_{bg} for the groups (levels) of interest at one level of a second variable. Entering only the scores from these groups in a single-factor, independent groups ANOVA will produce the desired SS. For these data, the SS_{bg} at a2 equals 91.52.

(2) The sum of squared deviations is divided by degrees of freedom equal to number of levels (groups) minus 1 to obtain a mean square. That is, divide SS_{bg} for B at a1 by the number of B levels minus 1 to find a mean square for the simple main effect and SS_{bg} at a2 by number of B levels minus 1:

MS_{bg} for B at a1 = $186.29/2 = 93.14$
MS_{bg} for B at a2 = $91.52/2 = 45.76$

(3) The mean square is then divided by the MS_{wg} from the overall analysis to find the F ratio for the simple main effect:

F for simple main effect of B at a1 = 93.14/10.25 = 9.09

F for simple main effect of B at a2 = 45.76/10.25 = 4.46

(4) The significance of this F is tested by finding the critical F value in Table A.3 with df equal to number of levels minus 1 and MS_{wg} df from omnibus F and comparing the F value found in step #3. F_{crit} with 2 and 36 df is 2.86 (.05) and 5.25 (.01). Thus, both the simple main effects of B at a1 and a2 are statistically significant.

$F (2, 36) = 9.09, p < .01$

$F (2, 36) = 4.46, p < .05$

Go to http://psychology.wadsworth.com/courses/statistics/ and test your knowledge of this chapter by taking the online quiz. Another resource to check is the online workshops that provide a step-by-step guide through a number of topics at http://psychology.wadsworth.com/workshops/workshops.html.

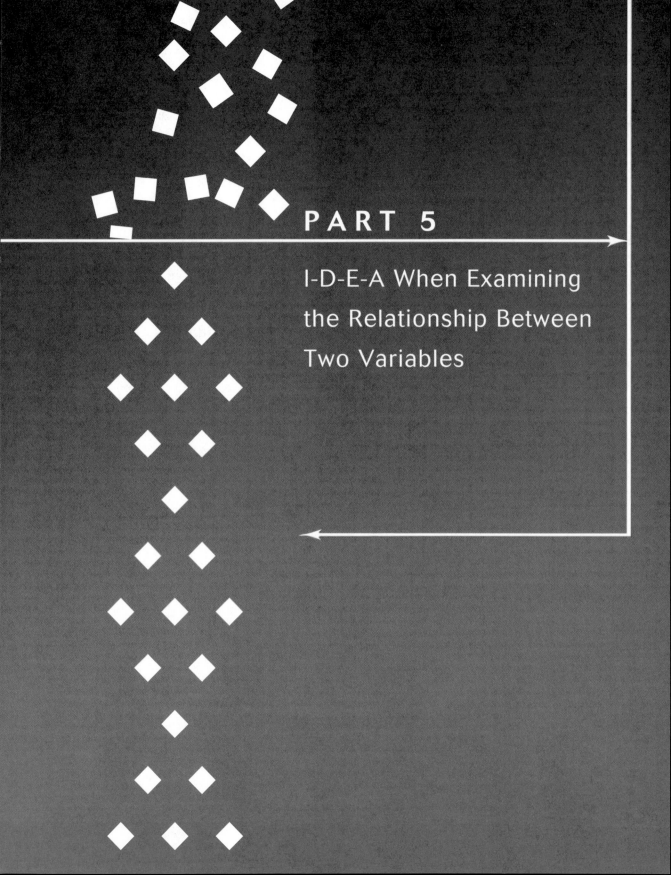

PART 5

I-D-E-A When Examining the Relationship Between Two Variables

CHAPTER 14

Inspecting and Describing Correlational Data

A sample has a distribution, a central tendency, and a variability. Each of these characteristics helps the researcher make sense out of the numbers. Although each reveals some important aspect of the data, none of them measures the relationship or association between two sets of numbers.

D. Kenny (1987, p. 90)

INTRODUCTION

Many questions we wish to answer cannot be treated with the techniques covered in previous chapters. Investigators often ask questions about the relationships between the characteristics of people and their behavior. Does the SAT measure the same competencies as the ACT does? Do two tests of extraversion measure the same characteristic of people? Do people with higher standard test scores earn higher grades, obtain better-paying jobs, and have children who score highly on standard tests? Other questions concern whether the activities of people permit us to predict what they would do in the future. Does the amount of TV watched relate to how fearful of crime people are? Does the amount of physical exercise predict level of self-confidence? It is very difficult to answer such questions by randomly assigning people to experimental conditions. And, although some of these questions may be addressed by examining the relationship between levels of a natural groups variable and mean scores on a dependent variable, there is, as you will see in this chapter, a better way to examine the degree of relationship.

Consider the following three scenarios that deal with important questions about relationships between variables.

- No doubt you suffered the three hours of agony known as the ACT or SAT as part of your application to college. Much criticism has been leveled at these examinations; however, a critical question is whether students with higher scores, in fact, do better in college than those with lower scores. In other words, is there some relationship between standard test scores and the grades students get after beginning college? If there is, then test scores could be used to predict college grades earned months after the tests were taken.

- Sally was interested in language development. She wondered whether the size of a child's vocabulary was related to the size of the parents' vocabularies. Sally administered a standard vocabulary test to 50 four-year-old children attending the same preschool. She tested their parents using an adult measure of vocabulary. Both variables were continuous. To analyze her data, she initially considered dividing the vocabulary scores of the parents into three categories (low, medium, and high) and then comparing mean performance of the children across the three groups. She told her adviser that she intended to use a three-group ANOVA to analyze the vocabulary levels of the three groups of children. She predicted that the children of parents with the largest vocabularies would show the largest mean vocabulary. Her adviser said that dividing the parents into three vocabulary groups would result in losing a lot of information. Her adviser said she should not use ANOVA.

- Two professors (actually the authors) wondered whether there was a relationship between number of psychology courses taken and accuracy in distinguishing between the names of prominent psychologists and non-psychologists. The expectation was that students who had completed more courses would be more accurate in recognizing the names of famous psychologists (e.g., Adler, Piaget). It is possible to divide students on the basis of courses completed; that is, one group made up of those students who had never taken a psychology course, a second group comprising those who had completed

Introductory Psychology only, and so forth. Then accuracy in recognizing names could be a dependent variable in an ANOVA that examines performance of many groups of students varying in the number of courses taken. This plan would have led to an independent groups ANOVA based on 14 or more natural groups defined by the number of previous psychology courses. There must be a better way. Indeed, there is.

The better approach is called *correlation*. The last chapters dealt with one continuous dependent variable used to examine differences among two or more samples of people. For example, the amount remembered was examined for students exposed to course material presented in lectures, on slides, or on videotape. Here, we are *reversing* the task: we are now concerned with analyzing data composed of *two* continuous variables from *one* sample of people, things, or events. When dependent variables are continuous and the research involves differences between groups, we use means and standard deviations to calculate confidence intervals, effect sizes (e.g., *g*), *t* tests, and *F* ratios. Some of these indices will appear in the next chapters, but they may look different because there is only one group. The focus in these next few chapters is on a way to quantify the degree to which one continuous variable is related to a second continuous variable. Sometimes behavioral scientists go a step further to develop a formula to make predictions of the value of the second variable; however, often learning how strongly the variables are related to one another is the goal of a correlational analysis—no predictions are actually made. Using correlations to make predictions is covered in Chapter 17.

THE ANALYSIS PROBLEM

When two continuous variables (such as vocabulary of children and vocabulary of parents) are to be analyzed, the means of samples do not tell us what we want to know. What is important is the degree to which the variables vary together. For example, we might inquire whether high values on one variable are associated with high values on a second variable, and whether low values on the first variable are associated with low values on the second variable, such as, the more TV watching, the more fear of crime. Or, we might ask if high scores on one variable are associated with low values on the second as we might expect when comparing the amount of time parents spend with their children and the seriousness of the trouble that children get into. When either of these patterns are observed, we say that the variables **covary,** that is, that scores are co-related. Knowing the value of one of the variables provides information about the value of the second variable. *Specifically, if two variables covary, we may use information obtained from the first variable to predict performance on the second variable.* You may remember that prediction is an important goal of the scientist. (See Chapter 1.) We might literally make predictions (see Chapter 17), or we might use correlations to increase understanding of the meaning of the variables we measure.

CONSTRUCTING SCATTERPLOTS

We can describe the association of two continuous variables using a **scatterplot,** a two-dimensional graph that shows the relationship between two continuous variables gathered from one sample of people, things, or events. A scatterplot shows whether knowing the value of one of the variables will allow us to predict the value of the second variable. Consider the following example.

Suppose that you are a manager of a beach park and are responsible for the lifeguards and the staff at the refreshment stand. Your job requires you to be sure that enough lifeguards are on duty and that the refreshment stand is adequately staffed to serve the people on the beach. You know that the more people on the beach, the more staff you need. And, you know that the warmer the temperature, the more people will be on the beach. You might be helped if you could see the relationship between daily temperature and the number of people on the beach. Here is information showing the daily high temperatures and number of people on the beach for several days:

	Day				
	a	**b**	**c**	**d**	**e**
High temperature (°Fahrenheit)	56	74	90	79	82
Number on beach	15	121	178	100	148

A graph of these variables can help you to use the expected high temperature to predict the number of people on the beach. *The convention is to plot the variable you want to predict on the y axis, the vertical one, and the one that gives the information needed to make the prediction on the x axis, the horizontal one.* Therefore, the x axis should be labeled "Daily High Temperature (°Fahrenheit)," and the y axis should be labeled "Number of People on the Beach."

To mark the scales on the axes, you must examine the range of values for each variable. The range of the daily high temperatures is 56 to 90. However, the temperature may well go to 100, and the coolest day during the season might be around 50. So, you might label the x axis 45 to 100 degrees. For each 5 degrees, that is, 45, 50, 55, and so on, you would mark off equivalent distances on the x axis. The number of people on the beach varies from 15 to 178 in the five-day data set, so the scale might simply be 0 to 200. This would be marked on the vertical axis (y) using equivalent distances between scale values. After the scales are labeled and the specific scale values determined, one is ready to place the data into the scatterplot.

To do this with our sample beach data, for day *a,* take the temperature, 56, find its place on the x axis. Then find the number of people on the beach for day *a,* which is 15. Place a dot on the graph at y equals 15 directly above 56. You will see this data point in the top portion of Figure 14.1. Each of the five data points are placed in the graph using the same convention: make a mark where the two values intersect. Once the graph is completed, the pattern in the scatterplot is obvious: the higher the temperature, the more people on the beach. Clearly, you will need to be sure that there are more lifeguards and more refreshment stand staff on duty when you expect the temperature to be in the 90s rather than in the 70s. The plot in the top of Figure 14.1 is said to show a **positive relationship** or a **positive correlation.** A positive correlation exists when high scores on one variable go with high scores on another variable and low scores on one variable go with low scores on the other.

The lower part of Figure 14.1 shows the general pattern of points in a scatterplot when two variables negatively covary, that is, when there is a **negative relationship** or a **negative correlation.** In a negative correlation, high scores on a variable go with low scores on another variable, and low scores on the variable go with high scores on the other. For example,

FIGURE 14.1 ■ There is a positive relationship between the number of people on a beach and the daily high temperature, but a negative relationship between the size of college class enrollments and the length of reading lists.

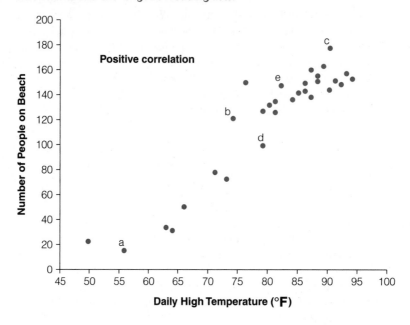

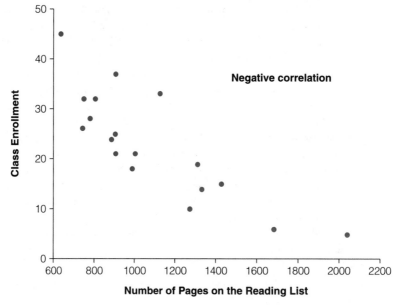

long reading lists for college courses might well be associated with fewer student enrollments. There are many reasons for this relationship: long reading lists are more likely in advanced courses that usually have smaller enrollments, and some students might avoid those courses with the most reading assignments. We do not need to know the reasons for the relationship to demonstrate that the relationship—the correlation—exists.

Some variables are not likely to covary. It is unlikely that the size of the vocabularies of college students covaries with their height. It is also unlikely for the friendliness of checkout staff in supermarkets to covary with how they feel about increased funding for space exploration. By the way, because behavioral scientists usually work with people, most of our examples deal with people. However, as we have shown, scatterplots can be used to summarize the relationship between two variables regardless of the focus of the research. That is why we said that correlation is about examining associations between people, things, or events. The points in the top portion of Figure 14.1 refer to different days. The bottom part of that figure refers to college courses. We could plot average vehicle speed and number of accidents per month for a number of different highways; in that case, each point in the scatterplot would be a particular highway. Or, one could examine relationship between the value of national product per capita and the literacy level of a number of countries. In that case, the points on the scatterplots would represent nations. We can construct scatterplots whenever there are two continuous variables for each person, event, thing, or location under study.

YOUR TURN 14-1

Think of a pair of continuous variables that would positively covary and a pair that would negatively covary. Describe these two kinds of relationships.   ■

So far, we have been using scatterplots to *describe* the relationship between the two variables, but we have not forgotten that the first step in the I-D-E-A model is *inspection.* We began with description so that you would understand the analysis problem and be in a better position to know what to look for in the inspection stage.

When we work with two continuous variables, one should inspect variables one by one before plotting relationships between pairs of variables. It is possible that errors have occurred in recording values, people have provided suspicious data, or outliers are present. Therefore, the inspection techniques you have learned, such as creating stem-and-leaf displays or histograms, should be used to examine each distribution of scores to examine the shape of the distributions and look for anomalous values. The degree of dispersion or variability present in each distribution should be noted because, as you will see, the range of scores on a variable can have important consequences for descriptive measures of the relationship between two variables.

When using two continuous variables, inspection also involves looking for suspicious data points in scatterplots; we will return to this point later in the chapter.

Some Things to Look for in a Scatterplot

Table 14.1 and Figure 14.2 contain scores that the students in a (real) class obtained on two exams. First, look at the axes in Figure 14.2. Some writers assert that graphs should always begin at zero if that is a possible value, but beginning scales at zero may mean that the data

TABLE 14.1 ■ Grades (Percentage Correct) for 16 Students on the First Two Tests in a Research Methods Course

Student	Test 1	Test 2
KA	69	72
SB	89	80
JG	85	76
SI	100	100
JJ	89	98
RJ	78	94
NK	84	58
KK	81	96
SO	73	66
MP	71	90
CR	95	88
CS	84	72
AS	85	48
PS	84	84
LT	89	86
RW	84	82

will be crowded into a small area. For example, classroom test scores (as in Figure 14.2) could be as low as zero, but, to be read more easily, the points in a graph need to be spread out as much as possible (Tufte, 1983). The scores on test #1 ranged from 69% to 100%, and the scores on test #2 ranged from 48% to 100%. After the values on the axes are determined in the light of the range of the scores on the examinations, the intersections of each student's two scores are plotted on the graph. Be sure that you can relate the scores in Table 14.1 to the points in the scatterplot. For example, student KA had a 69% on test #1 and a 72% on test #2; consequently, in Figure 14.2, KA appears above 69% and to the right of 72%. Continuing through the class produces the completed scatterplot.

Notice that, in general, the scatterplot in Figure 14.2 shows that those students who did well on the first exam tended to do well on the second exam. However, in spite of the overall positive relationship, not all high scores on the first exam are associated with high scores on the second exam and not all low first exam scores are associated with low second exam scores. For example, student AS was about average on test #1 but did the worst on test #2. On the other hand, student KA did least well on test #1, but toward the middle on #2. In other words, although the relationship is positive, the rank order of students compared in the class changed a lot between test #1 and test #2, except for one student, SI, who aced both tests.

Figure 14.3 is a scatterplot of the height and weight of 10 men who participated in a study of heart disease. Each point represents a different man. Figure 14.4 is a scatterplot of the weight and gas mileage of a sample of automobiles sold in the United States (*Consumer Reports*, 1999). Each point represents a car model. Figure 14.4 shows a negative relationship. Note how the variables were matched to the axes in these two figures. In Figure 14.3, height is on the x axis and weight on the y axis because, as most people grow taller, they

FIGURE 14.2 ■ A positive relationship between the scores on two tests in a research methods class is seen in this scatterplot. Note that although there is a clear positive relationship, a number of students made strikingly different scores on the two tests.

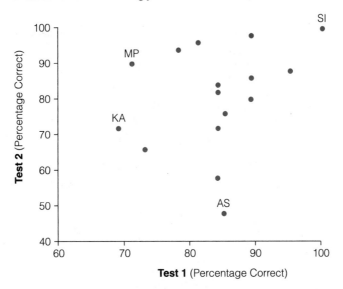

FIGURE 14.3 ■ A scatterplot of height and weight among men in a study of coronary health.

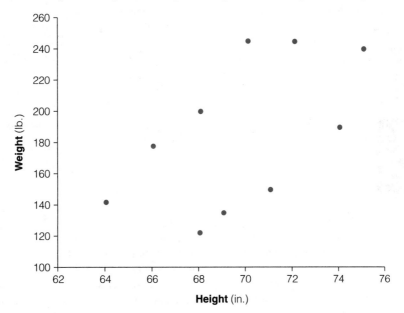

FIGURE 14.4 ■ A strong negative correlation between weight of 1999 automobiles and gasoline mileage. (Source: "Facts and Figures," 1999)

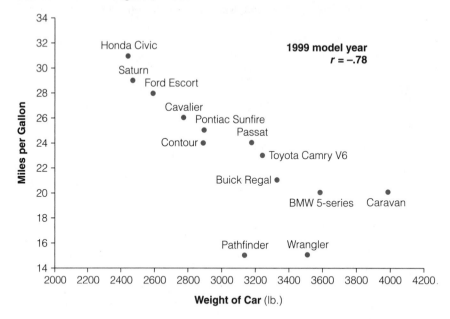

come to weigh more, but being heavier is not considered a precursor to growing taller. In Figure 14.4, making a car bigger, and thus heavier, will in general reduce the gas mileage, but raising gas mileage cannot lower the weight of a car; consequently, we would place weight on the x axis and mileage on the y axis. These choices in which variable to plot on which axis should not be taken as decisions about causal relations. However, finding positive or negative relationships means that information on the value of one variable makes it possible to anticipate the value of the second variable, or at least to reduce the range of the values of the second variable that one would expect. *In general, we put the variable we are using to predict, or that "came first," on the x axis, and the variable that we are predicting, or that "came later," on the y axis.*

If you were plotting SAT scores and the first semester freshman college grades of 500 students, which variable should you place on the x axis? ■

The preceding four figures ought to have given you a sense of what we mean by *covary* and how positive and negative relationships between variables look in scatterplots. At this point, you should be able to construct scatterplots of pairs of variables, such as height of basketball players and number of rebounds, hours studied and scores on a test, average time per day spent talking with a toddler and size of the toddler's vocabulary, or level of blood alcohol level and accuracy of hand-eye coordination. Often, when scatterplots are presented in textbooks, the general pattern of the points is summarized with egg-shaped forms (i.e., ellipses) drawn around the points, and sometimes the points themselves are not given at all, just the general shapes. Figure 14.5 provides several examples. We will use this convention in some figures later in this unit. Note that one of the shapes in Figure 14.5 is not egg shaped. Spotting this type of relationship is important in the inspection stage; we say more about this point later.

Plot the pairs of data points given here. These points represent the pattern that the authors found when they measured the number of psychology courses completed and the accuracy of the recognition of the names of psychologists. These data could be used to predict recognition from the number of courses taken; thus, number of courses would be plotted on the x axis. The first value is the number of psychology courses completed, and the second is the percentage of psychological concepts recognized. (Recognition was corrected for guessing.) Data: 2,40; 0,15; 4,45; 12,72; 10,68; 7,65; 1,35; 8,70; 5,50. Save this scatterplot for another *Your Turn* question later in this chapter.   ∎

Before continuing, we want to point out that, in making scatterplots, we have made an assumption about the variables plotted. For a scatterplot to make sense, the variables must have the properties of interval scales. (See Chapter 1.) When plotting temperatures at a beach, we used the same distance on the x axis to represent the five degrees between 50 degrees Fahrenheit and 55 degrees as between 85 and 90. In other words, we assumed that one degree Fahrenheit is the same regardless of the actual temperature. When we cannot make this assumption, we cannot use scatterplots because they would be misleading. Furthermore, if the variables do not have equal intervals throughout their range, it is misleading to use the standard correlational techniques we now introduce. We return to this point later.

DESCRIBING RELATIONSHIPS QUANTITATIVELY

We describe relationships between two continuous variables with a **correlation coefficient,** or *correlation* for short. The correlation, *r,* is the degree of **linear covariation,** in which the word *linear* means that a straight line could be used to summarize the relationship between the variables. One can draw a straight line on the scatterplot in the top half of Figure 14.1. Although the points (representing different days) fall above and below the straight line, there is a general trend for more people to be present as one moves up the temperature axis. A straight line could also be drawn on the bottom half of Figure 14.1 to summarize the overall negative relationship. Notice that it is not possible to place a straight line through the points that would make up the pattern shown in the upper right illustration included in Figure 14.5. This particular example illustrates a **nonlinear relationship.** For example, the phrase "law of diminishing returns" refers to a nonlinear relationship. Imagine preparing for a test: the first hours spent studying for it will repay you with the most correct test items per hour of studying. After some amount of studying, additional work will gain you only a point or two more. Figure 14.6 illustrates the law of diminishing returns. The graph suggests that less studying is needed to improve from a D to a C than is needed to improve from a B to an A. When there is a relationship as shown in Figure 14.6, knowing the value of one variable does permit us to make predictions about the value of the other variable; however, this process is harder because the relationship is not linear.

FIGURE 14.5 ■ The relationships between two continuous variables are often illustrated using ellipses that are tilted to indicate the signs of the relationships. The more consistent the relationship is between two variables, the more narrow the ellipse becomes.

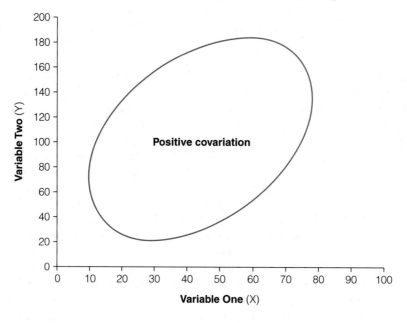

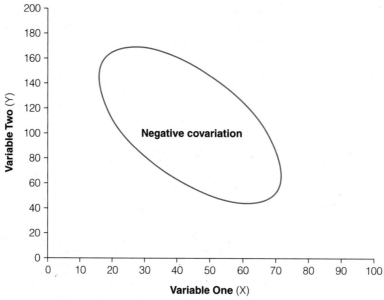

FIGURE 14.5 ■ (Continued)

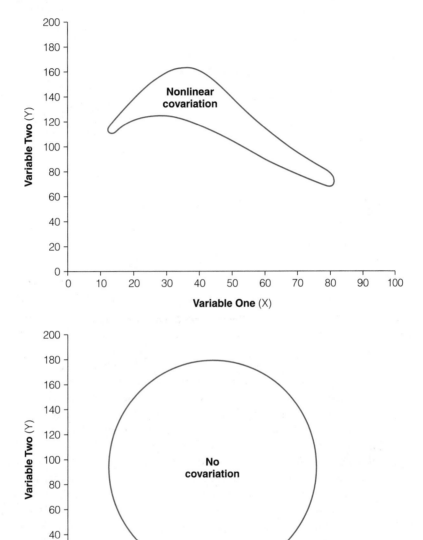

FIGURE 14.6 ■ Scatterplots can reveal nonlinear patterns such as the pattern we would expect if there were some students who studied far more than most students study. At some point additional study time does not result in as large an improvement in grade as the first hours of study do.

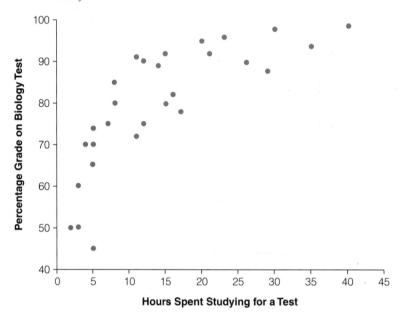

It is important to construct scatterplots prior to calculating correlations because there are many nonlinear relationships around us. In the inspection stage, we must be alert to the possibility that two variables may not be linearly related. Remember, *our description of the covariation between two continuous variables assumes that the best way to describe the degree of correlation is in terms of a straight-line or linear relationship.* As we show later in this chapter, *r* does not apply when the scatterplot shows that we are analyzing a nonlinear relationship. If, during the inspection stage, we detect a nonlinear relationship, we should not proceed to describe this relationship using the correlation, *r*. As Figure 14.1 to 14.5 show, when there is a linear relationship between two variables, the data points in a scatterplot are egg shaped (that is, form an ellipse or football shape). Whether this football shape points up or down reveals whether the relationship is positive or negative.

Correlation coefficients range from −1.00 to +1.00. The sign of the correlation tells whether the relationship is positive (i.e., high scores on variable *X* tend to be found with high scores on variable *Y*, and low scores on *X* with low scores on *Y*) or negative (i.e., high scores on variable *X* tend to be found with low scores on variable *Y*, and low scores on *X* with high scores on *Y*). Second, the value of the correlation tells us how predictable the relationship is. The absolute value of *r* can range from .00 through 1.0. An *r* of zero tells us that there is no linear relationship between the two variables. "No relationship" means that, for a specific score on variable *X*, one cannot predict scores on *Y* using a linear relationship (i.e., a straight line). Among adults there is probably no correlation between reading speed and body weight. In other words, regardless of how fast an adult reads, we cannot predict anything about his or her weight. In contrast, we expect a perfect correlation, an *r* of 1.0, between body weight measured in pounds and body weight measured in kilograms. Figure 14.7 illustrates these relationships. Note that a zero correlation usually corresponds to a

FIGURE 14.7 ■ A correlation of 1.00 is obtained when the scatterplot forms a straight line. A correlation of .00 would be found when the data points form a cluster whose axes parallel the x and y axes of the scatterplot.

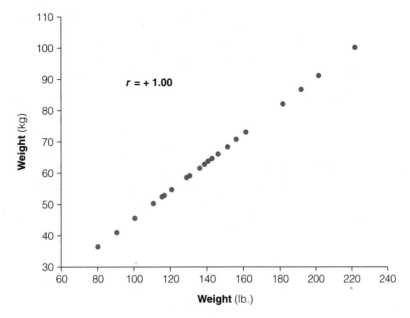

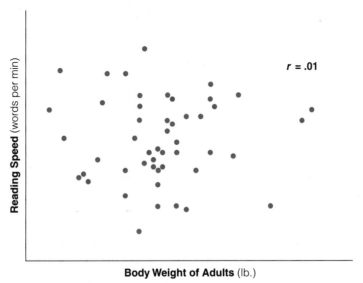

cluster of points where there is no obvious trend in the pattern; the scatterplot looks like a "blob" or at best an ellipse whose axes are parallel to the axes of the plot. On the other hand, a perfect correlation of 1.00 (plus or minus) produces a scatterplot in which every point is on a straight line. *The closer a correlation coefficient is to ±1.00, the more closely the scatterplot forms a straight line.*

THE ORIGINAL CORRELATION FORMULA

Karl Pearson developed the formula for the correlation coefficient. Francis Galton, Pearson's mentor, borrowed the word *correlation* from his cousin, Charles Darwin (Stigler, 1999). The full name of r is the *Pearson product-moment correlation.* We won't use the full name in this text, but the full name is important to distinguish r from other types of correlations.

Here is the definition of the correlation coefficient as Pearson presented it:

$$r = \Sigma z_x z_y / N \qquad \qquad \text{Equation 14.1}$$

where z_x and z_y are the z scores of the variables to be correlated and N is the number of people whose scores are being correlated. Recall that the formula for z, as we showed in Chapter 4, makes uses of either $(X - M)/\sigma$ when referring to a population or $(X - M)/s$ when dealing with a sample. That is, when psychologists report a standard deviation to describe a sample they refer to s, which is defined as $\sqrt{[\Sigma(X - M)^2/(N - 1)]}$. However, when working with all the data of interest, z scores may be calculated using the standard deviation based on

TABLE 14.2 ▪ Height and Vertical Jump for 17 Faculty Members

Faculty Member	Height (in.)	Jump (in.)
1	72	14
2	60	8
3	66	7
4	65	6
5	68	18
6	67	15
7	70	12
8	66	9
9	65	8
10	68	12
11	62	10
12	64	15
13	65	7
14	69	7
15	67	8
16	63	14
17	70	18

N rather than $N - 1$ and obtain the population standard deviation, or σ. For descriptive purposes, because z scores are typically used with large data sets, we suggested in Chapter 4 that it doesn't make much difference, practically speaking, which formula for z is used.[1] *However, Pearson used the z score formula for the population standard deviation, σ, $\sqrt{[\Sigma(X - M)^2/(N)]}$. To use Equation 14.1 to obtain r, you must, too.* We can rewrite the original formula in this way as an alternative way to calculate r without converting scores to z scores so as to emphasize which standard deviation formula is in the denominator:

$$r = \Sigma\,[(X - M_x)\,(Y - M_y)]/\sigma_x\,\sigma_y\,N$$

Let's work through an example. Pretend that someone managed to talk the faculty of the English department into letting someone measure their height as well as their vertical jump. The hypothetical data for these faculty members are seen in the columns of Table 14.2. Height is plotted on the x axis, and vertical jump is plotted on the y axis in Figure 14.8. The scatterplot tells us that the relationship is positive.

Pearson's original formula tells us to convert all the scores into standard scores, that is, z scores. (See Chapter 4 for a review.) For example, if the mean and standard deviation of a test are 50 and 10, respectively, a score of 55 can be converted into a z by subtracting the group mean from a score and dividing the difference by the standard deviation, or $(55 - 50)/10$ equals z of 0.5.

FIGURE 14.8 ■ A hypothetical scatterplot showing the heights and vertical jumps of the faculty of the English Department.

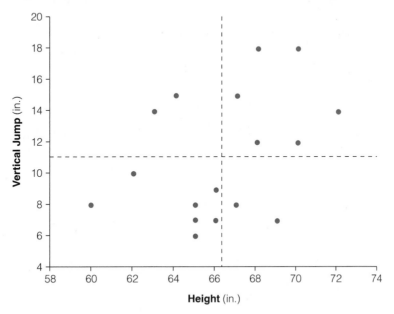

[1]That is, when N is relatively large, there is little difference in the obtained z scores when either σ or s is used. Moreover, some computer programs, such as SPSS, automatically calculate z scores based on the sample standard deviation.

Table 14.3 contains the same height and vertical jump data as Table 14.2 does, but, in addition, it contains the z scores for all the data points. You can see that tall heights convert into large positive values of z, whereas short heights become negative values of z. For example, faculty member #1 is 6 ft. tall and has a z of +1.90 for height; however, in contrast, faculty member #2 is 5 ft. and has a z for height equal to −2.09. In a similar fashion, the z scores for jump reflect the relative size of the jumps.

The last column of the table is the product of the two z scores for each person. We call such values ***cross-products***. When people are above the mean on height (i.e., the height z is positive) and above the mean on vertical jump (i.e., the jump z is positive), the cross-product will be positive. The product will also be positive when a person is below the mean on both variables. Notice that faculty member #2, who is the shortest in the department, has a below average jump and consequently a positive cross-product. On the other hand, faculty member #4 is a taller person whose jump is below the mean jump. (You can find those people in the lower right of Figure 14.8.) People such as faculty member #4 have negative cross-products. Last, some shorter people can jump higher than the mean; they also have negative cross-products.

Pearson realized that the total of the cross-products of z scores would be informative. If the variables covary positively, the sum of the cross-products will be positive. That is true because the signs for both z's for most people will be the same, that is, either both positive or both negative. In contrast, if there is a negative relationship, the sum of the cross-products

TABLE 14.3 ■ Calculation of the Correlation Between Height and Vertical Jump for 17 Faculty Members

Faculty Member	Height (in.)	Height (z_{ht})	Jump (in.)	Jump (z_j)	$z_{ht} z_j$
1	72	1.90	14	0.76	1.44
2	60	−2.09	8	−0.79	1.65
3	66	−0.10	7	−1.05	0.10
4	65	−0.43	6	−1.31	0.56
5	68	0.57	18	1.79	1.02
6	67	0.24	15	1.02	0.24
7	70	1.23	12	0.24	0.30
8	66	−0.10	9	−0.53	0.05
9	65	−0.43	8	−0.79	0.34
10	68	0.57	12	0.24	0.14
11	62	−1.43	10	−0.27	0.39
12	64	−0.76	15	1.02	−0.78
13	65	−0.43	7	−1.05	0.45
14	69	0.90	7	−1.05	−0.95
15	67	0.24	8	−0.79	−0.19
16	63	−1.09	14	0.76	−0.83
17	70	1.23	18	1.79	2.21

$$\Sigma_{ht} = 1127 \qquad \Sigma_{jump} = 188 \qquad \Sigma z_{ht} z_j = 6.16$$

The correlation is $\Sigma z_{ht} z_j / N = 6.16/17 = .36.$

will be negative because the signs of the pairs of *z* scores are more often opposite than they are the same. The sign associated with the sum provided Pearson with the sign of the correlation, positive or negative.

However, working with the *sum* of cross-products has a disadvantage in that the more people studied, the bigger the sum becomes. This is apparent if you simply imagine that the English department had twice as many faculty members; what would happen to the total of the cross-products in Table 14.3? That's right; it would roughly double. To make it possible to compare correlations from sample to sample even though the sample sizes differ, Pearson divided the sum by the number of people whose cross-products were added up. When we divide a sum by the number of items going into the sum, we have a mean unaffected by the number of items totaled. *The correlation coefficient, r, is, therefore, defined as the mean of the cross-products of z scores.*

Pearson showed that the mean of the cross-products of *z* scores is +1.00 when high scores on one variable are observed with high scores on a second variable *and* the points in the scatterplot form an exact straight line, such as that shown in Figure 14.7 relating weight in pounds to weight in kilograms. If the relationship is positive, but the points form a football and not a straight line, the sign of the mean of the products of the two scores will be positive, but the value of *r* will be less than +1.00.

When the relationship is negative, the sum of the cross-products and the mean of the cross-products of the *z*'s will be negative. Thus, the *r* will be negative. A hypothetical negative relationship is graphed in Figure 14.9. Often feelings of personal safety decline with age for older people. Imagine that we have measured feelings of safety on an 11-point scale, with zero indicating being terrified and 11 feeling perfectly safe. In this case, the correlation is very strong, but negative, −.91.

FIGURE 14.9 ■ A hypothetical negative relationship between the ages of several older residents and their feelings of safety in their neighborhood.

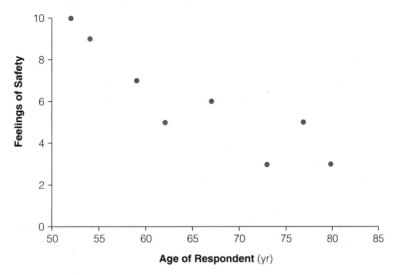

CHANGING SCALES

Would a correlation coefficient change if the scale of one or both variables changed? In the previous example, would it matter if we gave the elderly people a 21-point fear of crime scale rather than the 11-point scale? Would the correlation between weight of an automobile and gas mileage change if weight had been in kilograms rather than pounds and mileage had been given in kilometers/liter rather than miles/gallon? Suppose that you had a thermometer that read degrees Fahrenheit on one side and degrees Celsius on the other. Would you feel any differently on an August afternoon in Washington, D.C., if you read the temperature in Fahrenheit or in Celsius? Of course not, you say. Changing scales does not affect correlation coefficients either.

The formula for *r* based on *z* scores shows us why not. Converting original scores into *z* scores creates variables with common units regardless of the units of the original variables. After being converted to *z* scores, *all* variables have a mean of 0.00 and a standard deviation of 1.00. Consequently, a vehicle with a weight that is one standard deviation above the mean will have a *z* of +1.0 regardless of whether pounds or kilograms are used. Because the sum of the cross-products is based on *z* scores, the cross-products will be the same regardless of the scale used. *Changing measurement scales of one or both variables will not affect correlations.*

WHAT WE HAVE DONE SO FAR

Let's catch our breath. The first portion of this chapter showed you how to describe relationships between two continuous variables both graphically and quantitatively. A correlation coefficient, *r,* provides a standard numerical way of describing how closely two variables covary linearly. Constructing scatterplots is essential for developing a sense of the strength of the relationship indicated by an *r*. The next section of this chapter shows how to use scatterplots to inspect relationships between variables.

INSPECTING RELATIONSHIPS BETWEEN TWO VARIABLES

At this point in the course, you surely would remember to inspect each variable before calculating anything. Most assuredly! We won't review the inspection techniques for one variable. (See Table 3.4.) In this chapter, we stress inspecting *relationships*. Normally, this should be done before calculating correlations; however, we did not follow our own good advice in this chapter because you would not have known what to look for when inspecting scatterplots unless you knew what a correlation was. Now you are prepared. When inspecting a scatterplot summarizing the relationship between two continuous variables, we look for three things: the big picture, impossible combinations caused by klinkers, and two-dimensional outliers.

Because it is more efficient, most researchers prepare scatterplots using a computer. Before we discuss what to look for when inspecting scatterplots, we want to mention a possible confusion when examining scatterplots from computer programs. Some programs do not indicate when a single point on a scatterplot represents more than one data point. In Figure 14.10, the years of education of the mothers of 59 respondents are plotted against the years

FIGURE 14.10   ■   A scatterplot of the reported years of education for mothers and fathers of a group of older adults. For some common values, such as 12 years, there are several pairs of parents represented by one data point.

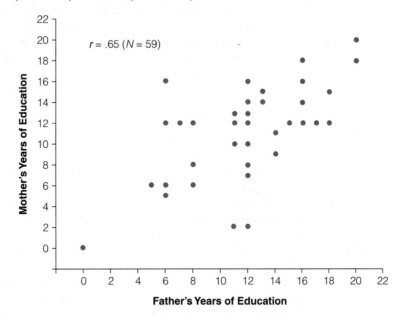

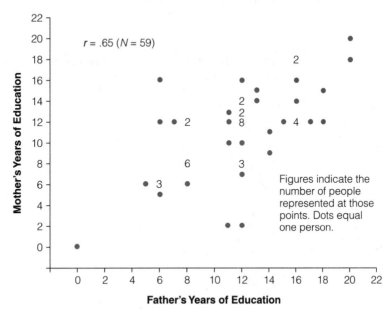

of education for their fathers. Even though there were 59 respondents, there are only 35 points in the upper part of Figure 14.10. The reason the points are missing lies in the fact that the parents of some respondents had equal amounts of education. For example, for several respondents, both parents completed high school; consequently, the point at 12 reflects more than one respondent. This duplication is taken into consideration in the lower portion of Figure 14.10 by replacing the points with the number of people represented when the point represents more than one person. If a scatterplot does not seem to contain enough points, consider the possibility that a number of people have identical sets of scores on the two variables.

The Big Picture

When looking at a scatterplot, first examine the overall trend. Is the relationship linear or is it more complicated than that? If the pattern of the relationship between the two variables does not follow a general linear pattern, the methods we have been presenting do not apply. Figure 14.6 displayed the diminishing returns as one studies longer and longer. There appears to be a systematic relationship between time studied and grade, but a straight line cannot represent this relationship accurately. The correlation formula will work; that is, Equation 14.1 can be applied and the statistical analysis program you use will do the analysis. Even if the value of the correlation coefficient is very large, the analysis would be misleading. If one does not inspect the data carefully, the nonlinear pattern might not be noticed.

Another form of nonlinear relationship is seen in the relationship between stress and success in a task as shown in Figure 14.11. If one has no stress at all, performance is often poor, but, if one has a great deal of stress, performance is not optimal either. It seems, that without

FIGURE 14.11 ■ The nonlinear relationship between performance level and stress means that a linear relationship cannot represent the graph accurately.

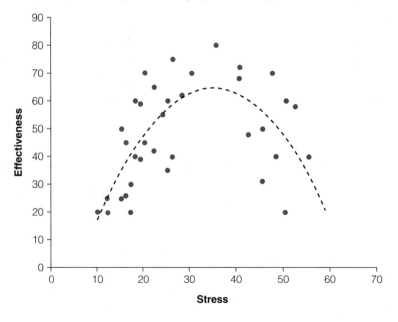

any stress, people don't put much effort into any task, taking a test, making a basketball shot, or driving a car. Without anything riding on our performance, we don't try very hard; some students, in fact, claim that they "work better under a time pressure." Stress improves performance up to a point; however, above that level, greater stress hurts performance. Different people flourish under different levels of stress, but in general the relationship between stress and performance is similar to an inverted U. A linear correlation does not apply to such relationships.

YOUR TURN 14-4

The correlation of hours studied and grades in Figure 14.6 was nonlinear, but the correlation would be positive. Figure 14.11 also displays a nonlinear relationship. Would you expect the correlation to also be positive? ■

Nonlinear relationships are quite common in the world around us. If you asked your physics teacher how long it would take a smooth stone dropped off the Empire State Building to hit the sidewalk, she may refer you to the formula, $d = 1/2gt^2$. You'll need to know how far the stone falls, d, to figure out how long the stone would be falling. (In this formula, g is the acceleration due to gravity, 32.2 ft./sec./sec. If the Empire State Building is 1,250 ft. high, the smooth stone you drop will hit the sidewalk 8.8 sec. later.) Figure 14.12 is a plot of the height of several buildings and the time it would take a stone to fall from the top to the ground. Note that it takes nearly a second for the stone to fall from Dad's garage (10 ft. high) but less than 9 sec. to fall from the Empire State Building, a distance 125 times higher than Dad's garage. If you use a ruler to connect the point for Dad's garage and the point for the hypothetical

FIGURE 14.12 ■ Obtaining a very large correlation using a formula based on a linear assumption does not prove that a relationship between two variables is linear.

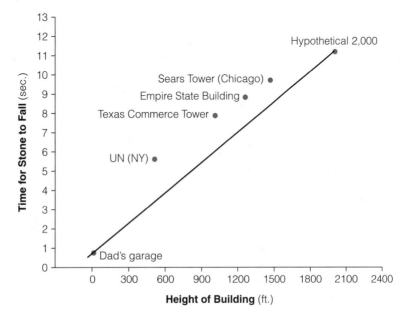

2,000 ft. building, you will see the nonlinear relationship. As you can guess, a *linear* correlation between height of building and time for a stone to fall will be very large. The points making up the graph lie quite close to the straight line, much closer than the points in Figure 14.10 would lie to a straight line drawn through them. To learn as much as possible from a set of data, it is necessary to continue to inspect data even when *r* is very large. *A very large correlation does not prove that the relationship between two variables is linear.*

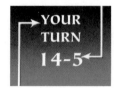

Look at the scatterplot from *Your Turn* 14-3. Was the relationship between number of completed psychology courses and accuracy in recognizing psychologists' names linear or nonlinear? ∎

The methods of this chapter cannot be applied to the relationship between test grade and time spent studying (Figure 14.6), stress and performance (Figure 14.11), height of a building and the time for a stone to fall (Figure 14.12), or other nonlinear relationships. Other correlational techniques may work just fine, but they are a little more complicated than the ones students learn in their first course.

Impossible Combinations

Sometimes the values of the two variables are related in a way that permits spotting an impossible combination of values. Wilkinson et al. (1999) described a study in which some elderly couples gave the length of their marriages as longer than their ages. Well, that simply can't be. Either they misunderstood the questions or they did not answer one of the questions accurately. Or, perhaps there were some data entry errors. The data about the mothers discussed in Chapter 2 (see Table 2.2) included two variables that are related in a way similar to the relationship between age and length of marriage. Figure 14.13 contains the ages of the mothers and the years of education they reported. Note, by the way, which variable is on which axis. Do you know why they were plotted that way? The variable, mother's age, is on the x axis because one must get older to get more education, but education cannot make someone older. Age comes before education. Consequently, we would graph education on the y axis.

The relation between age and education suggests an inspection strategy. Most children begin the first grade when they are five or six. Thus, an 18-year-old mother who reports a two-year Associate of Arts degree (i.e., 14 years of education) is mistaken, confused, or her answer was entered incorrectly. A more formal way of saying this is that age must be at least five years greater than years of education. Note that there is nothing unusual about someone who reports 14 years of education; 14 years of education would not arouse any suspicion when inspecting the values given for years of education. While inspecting variables one at a time, it would be impossible to detect the problem of the 18-year-old claiming 14 years of formal education. The problem can be detected only by examining the relationship between level of education and the age of the participant. A line has been placed on Figure 14.13 to show the mothers whose age and years of education are incompatible for the vast majority of people. Clearly, this approach cannot detect problems with reports of years of education once mothers are older than 24 or so.

Impossible or unlikely combinations can also be used to detect mistakes in data entry just as researchers inspect for anomalous values when inspecting single variables. An 18-year-

FIGURE 14.13 ■ A scatterplot sometimes permits the detection of impossible combinations of the values of two variables.

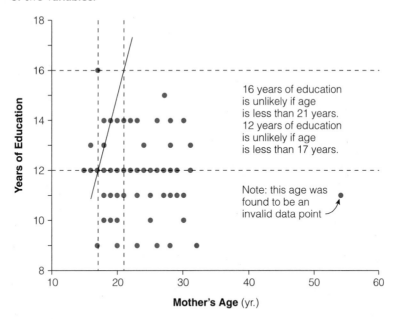

old with $100,000 annual income seems suspicious, a third-grade education does not seem compatible with subscribing to four newspapers, and so forth. A data entry error should be considered in these cases. For example, the $100,000 might be the result of missing a decimal point in $1,000.00.

If you were inspecting the ages of children and their mothers, what are some impossible combinations? ■

Two-Dimensional Outliers

You are already used to looking for outliers with respect to the scores in a single variable, but a different kind of outlier may occur when we deal with the relationship between two variables. When dealing with two continuous variables, the particular combination of values from two variables could be so unusual, or improbable, that it must be treated as an outlier. Look, for example, at Figure 14.3. Among men, a height of 5'-4" is not an outlier nor is a weight of 240 lb., but a 5'-4" tall man who weighed that much would be an outlier in the context of the sample represented in the figure. Recall the typical difference between klinkers and outliers. Klinkers result from researchers' mistakes or from the answers of uncooperative participants; they are invalid data points. In contrast, outliers are accurate reports from very unusual persons. For example, if 20 years of formal education is reported by a person who is 22, we can suspect that the data are not accurate. (Day care and preschool are

FIGURE 14.14 ■ A two-dimensional outlier detected using a scatterplot.

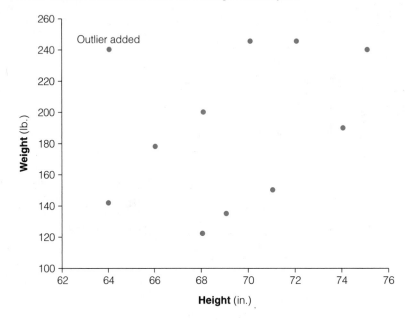

not considered formal education.) If you look back at Figure 14.10, there is a particularly suspicious point: someone is listed as having parents who failed to complete *any* years of formal education. A check of the data file, however, showed that this person was 77 years old. Consequently, this man's parents were probably born 100 years before the data were collected; thus, it is possible that they had no formal education. He may well be an outlier, not an uncooperative respondent. Outliers will not misrepresent relationships between two variables if the samples are very large. However, because many behavioral scientists usually work with modestly sized samples, the inclusion of an outlier can change a correlation so much that the analysis could be misleading.

Figure 14.14 contains the same heights and weights as Figure 14.3 did plus the hypothetical outlier we just mentioned. Note that the information about this man would not merit labeling him an outlier when inspecting one variable at a time, but this scatterplot reveals that he is an outlier. The correlation between height and weight for the information in Figure 14.3 was .56, but the inclusion of this one two-dimensional outlier reduces the correlation to .30. You might ask which correlation would be the right one. If data from a large representative sample of men were available, one would not discard such outliers. When using a sample of only 10 men, there is a possibility that someone with very unusual characteristics will appear in the sample who will distort the apparent relationship between the two variables being correlated. The better estimate of the correlation of height and weight in the population would be .56, the correlation without the outlier. Of course, dropping an outlier from an analysis requires that you provide an explanation to those who will use your findings.

Figure 14.15 includes a number of hypothetical data sets showing how one data point can change the correlation from negative to positive, positive to negative, and essentially zero to

FIGURE 14.15 ■ Adding outliers to scatterplots can reverse the sign of a correlation between two variables as well as turn zero correlations into either positive or negative correlations.

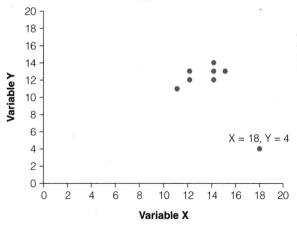

Adding a data point at X = 18, Y = 4 would make the correlation negative.

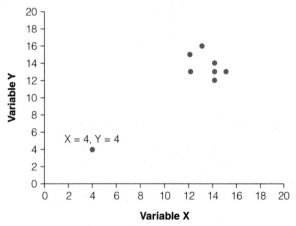

Adding a data point at X = 4, Y = 4 would make the correlation positive.

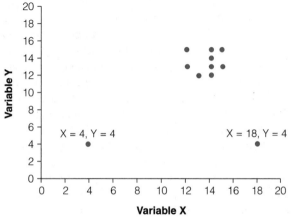

Adding a data point at X = 18, Y = 4 would change this near zero correlation, $r = 0.06$, to negative, but adding a data point at X = 4, Y = 4 would make the correlation positive.

positive or negative. Errors in transferring information from data collection forms or questionnaires into computer files can make the correlations change in those ways. When data that appear to be outliers are found, it is important to verify that no mistakes were made in compiling the data.

YOUR TURN 14-7

Examine the scatterplot for reading speed and body weight seen previously in Figure 14.7. Place an outlier on the plot in a location that would change the .00 correlation into a positive one. Now move that point to a location that would make the correlation negative.   ■

Much of the advance of medical treatments would not have occurred without statistical analyses, and many areas of psychology and education depend on correlational analyses to demonstrate test validity and reliability. Advanced correlational techniques permit the study of theoretical issues in natural settings that cannot be studied with controlled experiments. However, in our enthusiasm, we want to be sure that you appreciate and can spot the situations in which linear correlations are not appropriate and, even worse, would be misleading. Our discussion of nonlinear relationships, impossible combinations of scores, and two-dimensional outliers is intended to help you spot these situations. We now turn to a discussion of some limitations on what we may conclude from correlations between variables.

LIMITATIONS OF CORRELATIONAL ANALYSES

One limitation concerns the type of variables that we have. If the variables we seek to correlate do not meet the criteria of interval scales (see Table 1.2), we need to use a different technique. Box 14.1 deals with Spearman's rank-order correlation. We do not devote much attention to ordinal data because researchers frequently have reason to treat their data as being interval scales as explained in Chapter 1.

Other limitations involve misinterpretations of relationships. Noting relationships among variables is not just an aspect of formal research; people notice correlations as they make observations during their normal day-by-day lives. As the sun goes down (and it gets darker outside), we notice that more people turn on lights in their homes or cars. Students who do very well in one course often do well in other courses; students experiencing difficulty in one course frequently have difficulty in similar courses. It is incredibly tempting to think that a correlation implies some direct causal relationship between the two variables. It may be so tempting because causes are indeed correlated with the variables they effect. However, variables may be correlated when there are no direct causal relationships. Often, for example, there are third variables, sometimes called *lurking* variables, that can lead us to believe that there is something to be learned from a large correlation between two variables. In fact, a third variable might be responsible for the large correlation. Another limitation is seen when correlations disappear or are severely reduced even though there is a relationship between the variables in the populations from which our sample was drawn. Let us consider how correlations might appear or disappear and thereby fool the unwary researcher.

BOX 14.1 ■ Correlations When the Variables Are Ordinal, Not Interval

Suppose that you wanted to correlate the judgments of two teachers who have evaluated art projects. What they did was independently rank the projects: best, next best, etc. This sounds like a correlation problem, but there is a hitch: there is no reason to believe that the difference between first and second places is the same as the difference between second and third places. We have ordinal data (see Chapter 1), but the Pearson correlation, r, we have been using assumes that we have data whose units are the same whether the scores are high or low.

One can find the correlation coefficient between the judgments of the two teachers using the **Spearman rank-order correlation, r_S,** an adaptation of Pearson's formula. Suppose that we have the judgments that two teachers made of the quality of seven projects.

Child	Teacher A	Teacher B
MK	2nd	4th
LO	5th	6th
ER	1st (best)	3rd
JW	4th	2nd
OI	3rd	1st (best)
FG	6th	5th
HI	7th	7th

Our interest is in how similar their rankings are. The more the teachers agree, the smaller the differences will be between their ranks.

Here is the formula for the Spearman rank-order correlation:

$$r_S = 1 - \frac{6(\Sigma\, d^2)}{N^3 - N}$$

where d is the difference in the ranks given and N is the number of items ranked. In this case the calculation would look like this:

	Rank A	Rank B	d	d^2
MK	2	4	-2	4
LO	5	6	-1	1
ER	1	3	-2	4
JW	4	2	$+2$	4
OI	3	1	$+2$	4
FG	6	5	$+1$	1
HI	7	7	0	0

$$r_S = 1 - \frac{6(4 + 1 + 4 + 4 + 4 + 1 + 0)}{7^3 - 7} = 1 - .32 = .68$$

The rank-order correlation can also be used when a variable is very skewed and we cannot easily transform it. (See Chapter 3.) For example, when income data are very skewed, we might simply transform incomes into ranks. That is, the highest income is 1, the next highest is 2, and so forth. The variable that we wanted to correlate with income would also be transformed into ranks. Then, the Spearman procedure would be followed.

If two or more people have the same score (or if judges announce a tie), then the ranks are to be the same. If two people are said to be tied for best, then each would have a rank of 1.5 and the next person should be assigned a rank of 3. Or, if three people are tied for fourth place, each is to get a rank of 5 and the next rank is to be 7.

Of course, computer programs will do the transformation for you and calculate r_S if you just ask.

Third Variables

There is a positive correlation between mother's education and infant birth weight, a critical predictor of infant survival. Do more years of education lead mothers to have healthier babies? It is hard to imagine a direct process. However, education seems to be related to some variables that are more directly related to birth weight. One variable is the mother's smoking; people with less education smoke more than those with more education (*The World Almanac*, 1999). Smoking does lead to lower birth weights of babies. The positive correlation of birth weight with education is partially due to the greater rates of smoking among less-well-educated mothers. Figure 14.16 shows the pattern of mother's education and infant's birth weight for smoking and nonsmoking mothers separately (although in an exaggerated way to make the point more apparent). If the correlation is calculated for all of the mothers

FIGURE 14.16 ■ Combining two distinct populations into one correlational analysis can make it appear that two variables are related to each other when, in fact, there is no relationship.

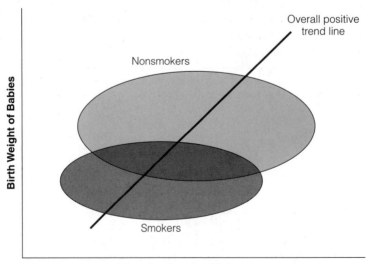

in the figure, the correlation between mothers' education and birth weight of infant is positive, but, if the correlation is calculated for smokers and nonsmokers separately, both correlations would be close to zero. In this situation, smoking is a **third variable** that is responsible for the obtained relationship between the other two variables: years of a mother's education and her infant's birth weight. It is smoking that causes lower infant birth weights, not fewer years of education. Third variables are also sometimes called *lurking variables* because they are hidden and perhaps unmeasured. Until one identifies the lurking variable, one could be misled by the correlation found.

Other third variables are causes of both variables and thus lead to those two variables being correlated. A study showed that men who retired were happier if, after retirement, they began another job, perhaps one requiring fewer hours. It could be that working makes older men happy, but it could also be that people in good health are happier than those in poor health and that those with good health are able to hold a new job. A naive interpretation of the positive correlation between happiness and holding a job might suggest that getting a job would make retirees more happy. However, if the real issue is quality of health, simply getting a job will not increase the life satisfaction of retirees; in fact, for those in poor health, the new job might make them less happy. Quality of health affects both life satisfaction and ability to hold a job.

The mother's education/infant birth weight and retirement/happiness examples show that *we simply must not infer causal relationships solely on the basis of a correlation.* Here is one more example. Many people have noted that school achievement and self-esteem are correlated; those children with higher self-esteem tend to perform better in school. It seems to follow that teachers should seek to raise the self-esteem of their students and thus help their students to perform better. But such a decision is based on the assumption that high self-esteem causes good performance. It might be the other way around. (See, Dawes, 1994.) If good performance causes higher self-esteem, one could suggest that careful and rigorous teaching might help students achieve, and then their self-esteem would increase. Or, both might be caused by something else, such as degree of parental support. Correlation does not prove causation.

Some advertisements have correctly pointed out that grade school children whose parents have supplied them with computers have gotten higher grades than those children whose parents have not gotten computers for their children. The ads implied that there was a causal connection: owning a computer produces better grades. List some lurking, unmentioned variables that might explain the positive correlation between grades and the degree of access to a computer. ■

Restriction of Range

Another limitation on the interpretation of correlations is observed when the range of one of the variables has been reduced. **Restriction of range** refers to limiting the range of one of the variables to be correlated with a second variable. *The effect of a restricted range is to reduce the size of the correlation coefficient.* Figure 14.17 provides a scatterplot that shows a strong positive correlation, $r_{xy} = .65$. Suppose that we simply divide the scores of the variable X at the median, thus making two groups. The lower part of Figure 14.17 shows these two groups and the correlations between X and Y for the two groups. The correlations between X

FIGURE 14.17 ■ Reducing the range of either the X or the Y variable will reduce a correlation between the variables. In the lower portion of the figure the correlations are given for the left and right halves of the original scatterplot.

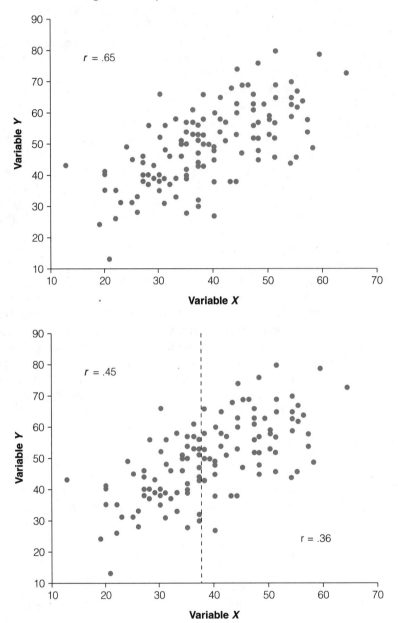

and Y for the left and right halves of the scatterplot are now .45 and .36, respectively. Of course, no one arbitrarily divides a scatterplot into two halves and calculates a correlation for each half. Instead, the possible sample may be divided for reasons unrelated to statistical analysis but which have the effect of restricting the range of one or both variables.

Range can be reduced when scores on one variable are used to select the people who will later get scores on a second variable. This is a subtle point, but let us consider an example. Critics of standardized testing correctly point out that, although SAT and ACT scores are correlated with college grades, the correlations are not very high (Murphy & Davidshofer, 1994). However, it is crucial to remember that college admissions decisions are partially based on standard test scores; those applicants with the lowest scores are not admitted, and those with the highest scores may well be accepted by many colleges but can, of course, attend only one. Thus, only a subset of applicants to a specific college ever take courses and earn grades there. Therefore, the range of the standardized test scores of the students at any single college is restricted. Given this restriction of range, the correlation between SAT or ACT scores and grades is smaller than it would be if applicants throughout the range of scores on the standard test actually attended. If students with a full range of scores attended any particular college, the correlation of test scores with grades would be much larger. (This again illustrates our point that a correlation could be drastically reduced even when there is an overall relationship.) The natural restriction of range makes it appear that standard test scores are weak predictors of college grades; this could have important practical implications if college administrators are unaware of the effect of calculating correlations after using the test scores to choose whom to admit to their college.

Another example of the effect of restriction in range can be found in pre-employment tests. The point of administrating such a test is to obtain information to use in predicting which applicants are most likely to do well on the job; these applicants are offered jobs. Again, once applicants are selected partially on the basis of the test, the test's range is narrowed. Correlations between the test scores and job performance will be lower than if *all* applicants had been hired, and then the test score was correlated with job performance among all applicants. Of course, no company is going to agree to accept every applicant just to learn what the value of the correlation between a selection test and performance would be without a restriction of range.

A special case of restriction of range is when all the values of one of the variables is a constant. Suppose that an admissions office of a large university searches through all the applications to find a sample of applicants who all have exactly the same admissions test score? The possible range of the ACT composite score is 1 to 36. Thus, among the applicants to a large state university, it would be possible to find hundreds of applicants with the same ACT score, such as 21. Among this sample of applicants, what would a scatterplot of ACT score versus any other variable look like? The scatterplot would be a straight line. See Figure 14.18. Although the scatterplot forms a straight line, the correlation is undefined. Consider the formula for r. What is the standard deviation of ACT scores in a sample whose members all have the same score? Zero. What are the values of X minus M_x when all the scores are the same? Zeros. What are the values of z when all the scores equal a constant? The z's are all equal to zero divided by zero. The answer is undefined. If one did not inspect data carefully and entered a variable with a standard deviation of zero into a computer program, no correlation will be calculated.

FIGURE 14.18 ■ Data and scatterplot for a hypothetical sample with same score on one of the variables. In such a situation the correlation is not defined.

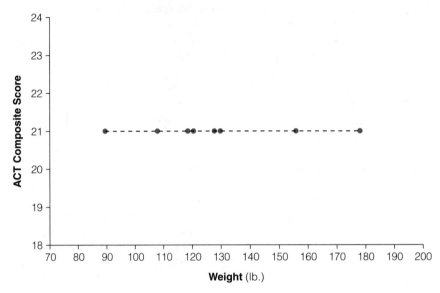

Applicant	ACT	Weight
1	21	90
2	21	156
3	21	121
4	21	119
5	21	156
6	21	178
7	21	108
8	21	130
9	21	128

WHAT QUESTIONS DO WE ASK THAT INVOLVE TWO VARIABLES?

Recall from Chapter 1, we gather data to *describe, understand, predict, and effect change.* Correlations are particularly useful in helping us to predict. The larger a correlation, the better we can predict the values of one variable from the values of another variable. For example, in general, the more time that one spends studying statistics, the better one does on statistics examinations—a positive correlation. The better one's health, the fewer days one is sick—a negative correlation. In a later chapter, we will show how one can develop a formula to use scores on a continuous variable to predict specific scores on a second continuous variable.

We can also use correlations to improve our interpretation of variables. If we discover that scores on a college admissions test are positively correlated with grades in engineering courses but not with grades in music courses, college admissions directors can use admissions test scores more validly if they omit them when considering music majors.

Relating two continuous variables to each other sometimes suggests how one might go about changing behavior. If people commit more driving mistakes after drinking alcoholic beverages, we might well conclude that accident rates would be lower if people did not drink before driving. Without controlled experiments, such suggestions would be just that: suggestions, not proof. It could be that an unmeasured variable—such as depression—is actually the cause of both drinking excessively and driving carelessly.

WHAT YOU HAVE LEARNED AND THE NEXT STEP

This chapter covered the concept of correlation between two continuous variables and demonstrated how to calculate r using Pearson's definitional formula and an alternative computational formula. You also learned the following concepts:

- When the data gathered consist of two continuous variables and we wish to determine the degree of covariation between the variables, correlation will be appropriate.

- Dividing a continuous variable into categories—such as low, medium, and high—wastes information; thus, a correlational analysis is more appropriate.

- The first step when doing a correlational analysis is to construct a scatterplot of the two variables.

- We put the variable we are using to predict, or that "came first," on the x axis, and the variable that we are predicting, or that "came later," on the y axis.

- Inspection of the scatterplot of the two variables is made to find two-dimensional klinkers and outliers.

- Examination of the scatterplot will provide the "big picture" to help us decide whether the relationship between the variables is roughly linear or whether the relationship is nonlinear. If the relationship is nonlinear, it would be inappropriate to calculate the linear correlation, r, illustrated in this chapter.

- Only when the data have been inspected and necessary corrections have been made and it is clear that the relationship is linear should a correlation, r, be calculated.

- A positive correlation exists when high scores on one variable go with high scores on another variable and low scores on one variable go with low scores on the other. A negative correlation exists when high values on one variable go with low values on the other variable and low scores go with high scores.

- The correlation coefficient is defined as the mean of the cross-products of the z scores of the two variables.

- The range of r is -1.00 to $+1.00$. The sign (plus or minus) shows the direction of the relationship; the value of r indicates the strength or degree of relationship.

- Across correlation coefficients ranging from .00 to $+1.00$, the form of the scatterplot approaches a straight line with an upward inclination.

- When the points on a scatterplot form a perfectly straight line rising from left to right, the correlation equals $+1.00$.

- If the points on the scatterplot form a perfectly straight line falling from left to right, the correlation equals -1.00.
- Changing measurement scales using linear transformations of one or both variables will not affect correlations.
- Third variables sometimes help explain the relationship between the two variables that are correlated. That is, the relationship between X and Y may be due to the fact that a third variable, Z, is causally related to one or both of the correlated variables.
- It is tempting to think of correlations as indicating some causal relationship between two variables, but a correlation alone cannot prove that a causal connection has been found.
- If the range of either or both of the variables to be correlated has been restricted (such as when those with the highest scores on a job skills test are hired), correlations of these variables with other variables will be smaller than if the full range were present.
- Correlations are particularly useful when the purpose of the research is to make predictions.
- It is possible for correlations to help us interpret the meaning of variables or to use them appropriately.
- If the values of the variables to be correlated reflect ordinal scales, not interval scales, then the Spearman rank-order correlation is to be used.

Our next step is to estimate how confident we can be of the correlations we calculate from our data. Correlations are based on sample information and, thus, are subject to sampling variability in the same way as are means and other sample characteristics. In the next chapter, we look at ways to estimate confidence in our estimation of population values of correlations. In a later chapter, we develop equations that permit using a score on one variable, such as SAT, to make a specific prediction of the value of a second variable, such as a grade point average that would not be earned until a year later.

Key Concepts

covary	correlation coefficient	cross-products
scatterplot	r	Spearman rank-order correlation, r_S
positive relationship (positive correlation)	linear covariation	third variable (lurking variable)
	nonlinear relationship	restriction of range
negative relationship (negative correlation)		

Answers to *Your Turn* Questions

14-1. Positive covariation: Amount of sugar in a recipe and ratings of sweetness, loudness of a voice and the degree people can understand what was said, size of shoes and height.

Negative covariation: Hours spent watching TV per week and college GPA, amount of alcohol in blood and length of time one can stand on one foot, the higher the temperature and the weight of clothes being worn.

14-2. Because SAT is measured before grades are available, SAT should be on the x axis.

14-3. 2,40; 0,15; 4,45; 12,72; 10,68; 7,65; 1,35; 8,70; 5,50

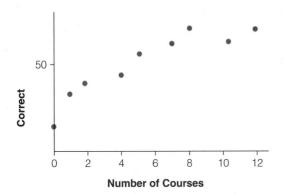

Number of Courses

14-4. The correlation would be roughly zero, yet there is a predictable pattern in the plot.

14-5. The relationship was nonlinear, accuracy increased more slowly as more courses had been completed.

14-6. We would normally expect biological parents to be at least 13 years older than their biological children.

14-7. By placing a point to the right and above the cluster of points, the correlation will become positive. The correlation would also become positive if a point were added to the left and below the cluster. By placing a point to the left and above the cluster, the correlation will be negative. A point to the right and below the cluster will also lead to a negative correlation.

14-8. The availability of a computer and higher grades may well be due to the lurking variable of family income or level of parental interest in the achievement of their children.

Analyzing and Interpreting Data: Problems and Exercises

1. (a) Prepare a scatterplot of the following data when 10 students provided SAT and GPA scores.
   (b) Decide which variable is to be plotted on the x axis and which on the y axis.
   (c) What do you observe in the scatterplot?

Variable	Student				
	A	**B**	**C**	**D**	**E**
SAT(Verbal)	400	500	600	480	560
GPA (1st term)	2.5	3.6	3.8	3.1	2.3

Variable	Student				
	F	**G**	**H**	**I**	**J**
SAT(Verbal)	680	420	540	580	560
GPA (1st term)	3.7	3.3	3.1	2.8	1.6

2. (a) Suppose that you were told that two variables were positively correlated. If you know that Jim's score was above the mean on one variable, would you predict his score on the second variable to be above or below the mean of the second variable?
   (b) Suppose that you were told that two variables were negatively correlated. If you know that Mary's score was above the mean on one variable, would you predict her score on the second variable to be above or below the mean of the second variable?

3. What are two things you might see in a scatterplot that would lead you to decide that you should not calculate a correlation between the two variables that are plotted?

4. What is the original mathematical definition of correlation provided by Pearson?

5. Imagine that the following data were gathered in a college advising center. Worry about grades was measured using a survey, with low scores indicating a little worry and high scores a great deal of worry.

Variable	Student					
	A	B	C	D	E	F
GPA (1st term)	3.1	2.3	1.8	1.5	2.1	2.3
Worry	25	30	10	12	28	16

Variable	Student					
	G	H	I	J	K	L
GPA (1st term)	1.7	1.5	2.4	2.5	2.1	1.4
Worry	35	38	21	24	26	40

(a) Construct a scatterplot of these variables.

(b) Is it appropriate to calculate a correlation between these two variables?

6. (a) In the following scatterplot, add *one* score that would change the correlation from a positive correlation to a negative one.

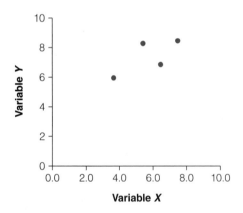

(b) In the following scatterplot, add *one* score that would change the value of the correlation from a negative to positive one.

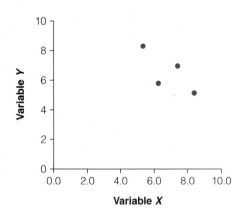

(c) In the following scatterplot, add *one* score that would change the correlation from essentially zero to positive.

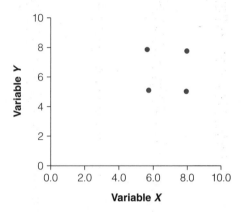

7. Explain how an outlier may appear in a scatterplot but not be identified during the inspection of the individual variables.

8. Comment on what you learn by inspecting the scatterplot of variables *M* and *Q*. Assume *M* comes before *Q* and is used to predict *Q*. Assume both variables are percentages.

Variable	Person						
	A	B	C	D	E	F	G
M	20	30	20	80	40	30	50
Q	30	50	40	90	60	50	80

Variable	Person					
	H	I	J	K	L	M
M	70	90	40	60	70	50
Q	95	95	70	90	95	90

9. Suppose that Juan was about to analyze the following data. What should he verify before calculating correlation coefficients? (Interest in graduate study was measured on a 7-point scale, 1 = no interest, 7 = high interest.)

Variable	Student				
	A	B	C	D	E
Interest in grad study	6	4	1	5	7
Hours of college work completed	70	30	12	45	90

Variable	Student			
	F	**G**	**H**	**I**
Interest in grad study	7	2	1	3
Hours of college work completed	3	30	16	40

10. What does it mean to say that correlation alone is not evidence for a causal relationship? Provide an example of a correlation between two variables that is likely produced because a third variable is causally related to both correlated variables. (You may use an example from the text or make one up.)

11. What third variables might help understand the following correlations?
    (a) A positive correlation between number of books owned and grade point average
    (b) A positive correlation between shoe size and size of vocabulary among grade school children
    (c) A negative correlation between height and interest in a career in counseling

12. Suppose that it seemed desirable to change the scale of variable Q in problem #8 by adding 100 to each score and dividing the result by 2.
    (a) Would it be necessary to recalculate the correlation with M after doing that? Explain.
    (b) Suppose that one first divided by 2 and then added 100; would you need to recalculate r then?

13. Imagine that the data in problem #5 reflect the pattern that we would find among a large sample of students. What should be the sign of the correlation between the worry and GPA if we used:
    (a) only the 33% of the students who were the least worried?
    (b) only the 33% who were the most worried?
    (c) only the 33% of the students with moderate levels of worry?
    Summarize what this pattern tells you about the effect of the restriction of range on correlations.

14. The relationship between mean happiness (subjective well-being) of citizens in different countries and gross domestic product per person follows roughly the pattern shown among these selection countries. (Higher values of happiness are more positive; GDP/person is given in $US. Source: Myers, 1992.)

Country	GDP/person	Happiness
Austria	19,800	63
Britain	15,000	75
Brazil	3,300	53
Estonia	3,200	23
Finland	23,500	76
India	200	27
Japan	27,200	56
Russia	3,200	1
S. Africa	2,899	29
S. Korea	6,300	51
Spain	11,300	65
Turkey	1,700	48

What is the sign of the correlation for those countries with GDP/person lower than $8,000? What is the sign of the correlation for those countries with GDP/person above $11,000? (Hint: Graph, don't calculate.)

15. Sarah wanted to learn how family income and level of interest in adopting mathematics as a major in college were related. Level of interest was measured using a seven-point scale (1 = not interested; 7 = highly interested). Family income was a self-report scale given in thousands of dollars per year.

Variable	Student								
	A	**B**	**C**	**D**	**E**	**F**	**G**	**H**	**I**
Interest in Math	2	3	1	4	2	4	2	1	5
Income	25	35	65	45	60	90	55	20	40

Variable	Student								
	J	**K**	**L**	**M**	**N**	**O**	**P**	**Q**	**R**
Interest in Math	6	2	3	1	1	7	4	2	7
Income	55	80	90	35	40	60	70	45	220

What can Sarah learn from the inspection of the scatterplot?

16. Suppose that you wanted to correlate family income with interest in earning an MBA after completing a bachelor's degree. Suppose the data are as follows with higher survey values indicating more interest.

	Student				
	FH	**KS**	**DF**	**PM**	**HJ**
Family Income ($1,000)	200	60	45	65	300
Interest in MBA	34	45	23	19	24

	Student				
	GB	**HA**	**OP**	**IS**	**VA**
Family Income ($1,000)	65	71	35	48	53
Interest in MBA	28	31	21	44	37

When you inspect the data, you will discover there is a problem. What is it?

One might find a correlation in spite of this problem; use Spearman's rank-order correlation to handle this problem.

17. (a) Which of the following variables are the most likely to be *positively* skewed and thus not appropriate for correlating with another variable? Explain.
    1. height of all *adults* in a community
    2. number of books read over the past 12 months
    3. length of index finger of adults
    4. age when first married
    5. height of all residents in a community
    6. ratings of satisfaction with medical care
   (b) Which of the variables are the most likely to be *negatively* skewed and thus not appropriate for correlating with another variable? Explain.

18. Prof. Smyth noticed that many students did not take all the allotted time on tests (50 min.), and he noted that many students received poor grades. He wondered if there were a correlation between test grade and how long students worked on a test. On the last test, he collected the tests as students handed them to him by placing them on a pile and carefully keeping them in the order in which they were handed in. Here is his data:

	Student Initials					
	AF	**BG**	**CD**	**EG**	**JJ**	**KU**
Order of handing test in (1 = first)	6	7	9	8	5	10
Test grade (%)	89	87	90	56	63	78

	Student Initials				
	MW	**PR**	**SO**	**TR**	**WT**
Order of handing test in (1 = first)	4	3	11	2	1
Test grade (%)	66	60	82	57	61

Why would a Spearman rank-order correlation be better than r? Calculate a correlation coefficient for Prof. Smyth.

For the next two problems, use the definitional formula for the correlation illustrated in Table 14.3. Remember that it is necessary to use the N, not $N - 1$, in the denominator of the standard deviation formula. If you are using a calculator, there may be two standard deviation keys. Use the one marked *sigma, σ, or N,* rather than the one marked, *s or $N - 1$.*

19. What is the correlation for the following data? (Be sure that you plot the data first so that you know what sign you should be expecting for the correlation.)

	Person				
Variable	**A**	**B**	**C**	**D**	**E**
Variable Y	18	16	10	12	15
Variable X	12	10	10	10	8

20. What is the correlation for the following data? (Be sure that you plot the data first so that you know what sign you should be expecting for the correlation.)

	Person				
Variable	**A**	**B**	**C**	**D**	**E**
Variable R	18	16	10	12	14
Variable T	8	10	10	10	12

Answers to Odd-Numbered Problems

1. (a) The scatterplot looks like this:

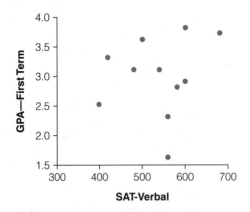

(b) SAT scores are plotted on the x axis because it is used to predict GPA.

(c) There is a slight positive correlation seen in the scatterplot showing the relationship between the two variables, SAT and GPA.

3. If the scatterplot showed a nonlinear relationship, we would not want to calculate a Pearson *r*. Also, if there were a clear two-dimensional outlier, we would want to drop it prior to calculating *r*. (We would, of course, need to explain when reporting our *r* that scores had been dropped prior to computing *r*.)

5. (a) The scatterplot showing the relationship between worry and GPA is as follows:

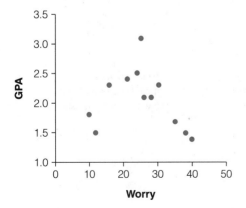

Note: It is difficult to decide which variables should be placed on the x and y axes. Worry could come before grades, but grades could also come before worry.

(b) No, we should not use a correlation coefficient, *r*, to describe this obvious nonlinear relationship.

7. Sometimes it is the combination of variables that produce an outlier. For example, we may not consider a 90 lb. female adult to be an outlier, nor would we perhaps consider a 6'-3" woman to be an outlier. But a 90 lb. woman who is 6'-3" may indeed be an outlier when plotted with other women in the sample and be easily identified in the scatterplot.

9. A scatterplot for Juan's data looks like this:

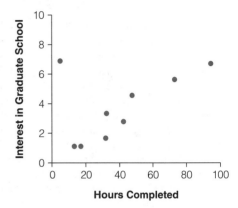

Juan would see that, in general, it appears that. as students approach graduation, they become more interested in graduate school. However, there is one student who is very definite about graduate school even though he or she is a long way from graduation with a bachelor's degree. Perhaps the student is that interested, but it also may be that a mistake was made when entering this individual's data or the individual misunderstood the instructions. Juan should verify the validity of this person's data before proceeding. (Including that individual in the correlation produces a correlation of .53; without that individual, *r* equals .92.)

11. (a) Interest in reading. GPA and number of books owned might be due to people who like to read, spending more time studying and reading books for recreation.

(b) Age. The older a child gets, the larger his or her feet and vocabulary.

(c) Gender. Somewhat more women than men are interested in counseling as a career, and women tend to be less tall than men. It might be useful to calculate the correlation separately for men and women.

13.

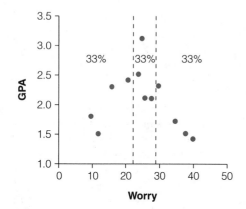

When drawn in this way and divided into thirds, the inverted U shape is apparent. The 33% least worried would produce a positive correlation, the 33% most worried would produce a negative correlation, and the middle third would produce a correlation close to zero. It should be clear that restricting the range of any variable (as would be the case if one decided to study only those with the most worry) leads to an unrepresentative correlation.

15. Sarah has an outlier in the family income variable. The point for student R would have a disproportional effect on the correlation. It appears that interest in math as a major is higher among students from families with higher incomes; however, the pattern is exaggerated by the student who looks like an outlier in this chart. Including R would make the correlation larger than it would be using only the other students. Special attention should be devoted to being sure that the data for R have been recorded accurately. If so, Sarah might want to use the Spearman rank-order correlation.

17. (a) *Positive skewness* means that the tail with the large numbers is longer than the other tail. The positively skewed variables are (#2) the number of books read over last year (unfortunately, the median is probably quite low, but there are some people who read many books each year), and (#4) age at time of first marriage (most first marriages occur when people are in their 20s, but some people first marry at much older ages).

(b) *Negatively skewed* means that the lower values string out more than the upper values. The negatively skewed variables are (#6) ratings of satisfaction with medical care (it is usually fairly positive, in fact, most scales show a ceiling effect); and all residents of a community include children, thus, (#5) the height of all residents is negatively skewed.

Note: Among adults, (#1) height and (#3) length of index finger are found to be normally distributed among people from a particular country, taking each sex separately.

19. Plotting the data should lead you to expect a positive correlation.

X	Y	X^2	Y^2	XY	z_x	z_y	$z_x z_y$
12	18	144	324	216	1.58	1.33	2.10
10	16	100	256	160	0.00	0.63	0.00
10	10	100	100	100	0.00	−1.47	0.00
10	12	100	144	120	0.00	−.77	0.00
8	15	64	225	120	−1.58	.28	−0.44
Sums	50	71	508	1049	716		1.66

$r = \Sigma z_x z_y / N = 1.66/5 = .33$

Go to http://psychology.wadsworth.com/courses/statistics/ and test your knowledge of this chapter by taking the online quiz. Another resource to check is the online workshops that provide a step-by-step guide through a number of topics at http://psychology.wadsworth.com/workshops/workshops.html.

CHAPTER 15

Estimating Confidence Using Confidence Intervals

Although we often hear that the data speak for themselves, their voices can be soft and sly.

Mosteller, Fienberg, & Rourke (1983, p. 234)

INTRODUCTION

In the previous chapter, we introduced you to the concept of linear correlation, illustrated the use of the formulas used to calculate r, and presented inspection methods to use when analyzing two continuous variables. The observed r is typically obtained from a sample, and—like the mean or variance, or other sample characteristic—it is subject to sampling variability. In other words, because of sampling error, the obtained r will vary from sample to sample. Thus, we need to consider techniques by which we can express confidence in the sample r as an estimation of the population correlation, symbolized by the Greek letter rho, ρ. The value of ρ corresponds to the correlation we would find if we tested everyone in the population. So, how precise is our estimate of this population value?

The concepts and procedures in the present chapter guide the interpretation of a correlation coefficient by showing how we determine the precision of our estimate of the correlation in a population and how we calculate effect sizes that can be compared with those found in other types of analyses. As in other chapters, we begin by presenting research scenarios that illustrate the need for the procedures introduced in this chapter:

- A radio talk show host asserted that taller men earn more money than shorter men do. Esteban realized that, to make such a statement, a correlation coefficient would be needed because both of the variables, height and amount of money earned, are continuous interval scales. He wondered what the value of the r was and what size of r really mattered. Esteban is 6'-3", but some of his cousins are 5'-6".

- The behavioral effects of genes relative to the effects of experience is an unresolved issue for psychology. One way to examine this issue is to compare the psychological similarities of parents and their biological children versus the similarities of adoptive parents and their children. *Authoritarianism* is defined as being inflexible, uncritical of authority figures, favoring toughness and power, and expressing general hostility. (See Funder, 2001, for a more detailed definition.) Suppose that Sandra had obtained the scores of parents and children on a personality scale that measured the tendency to be authoritarian. She found that the correlation between the scores from 100 parents and the scores of their biological adolescent-aged children was .40. She had a sample of 25 parents who had raised adopted adolescent-aged children from infancy; the correlation between the authoritarian scores of parents and children in this smaller sample was .10. This pattern of correlations matches the view that there is some biological component in the development of an authoritarian outlook. Sandra knew that both correlations were affected by sampling error; she thought she should estimate the sampling error before going any further with her analysis.

- While reading for her course in personnel selection, Indira noted that the text authors mentioned that a selection test for entry-level custodians of a large hotel chain was probably not worth using because it correlated only +.25 with success on the job. In a later chapter on the selection of management executives, the authors noted that one of the tests used to select people for promotion to executive positions correlated +.22 with later success. The authors seemed to imply that this was a useful assessment tool. Indria wondered why a selection test that correlated .25 with job success was seen as not worth using, yet a different one that correlated .22 was seen to be valuable.

In the previous chapter, we demonstrated how to inspect relationships between two continuous variables and how to calculate a correlation coefficient, r. We examined several pitfalls, including problems associated with two-dimensional outliers and nonlinear relationships. Researchers want to be sure that artifacts of the measurement process, unusual samples, or complicated relationships do not distort a correlation and thus produce misleading statistics. A linear correlation coefficient should be calculated only after careful inspection. But calculating correlation coefficients is one thing; knowing how to interpret them is quite another. Recall that, once a coefficient is calculated, it is tempting to conclude that a correlation between continuous variables implies a causal connection. In the previous chapter, we presented reasons why such a conclusion would be unfounded.

Interpreting the sizes of correlations has often been misunderstood. Correlations have been dismissed when they were important, while at other times correlations have been treated as informative even though they did not provide any new information. The current chapter provides several techniques that are widely used to evaluate the meaning of correlations. With these techniques, Esteban, Sandra, and Indira would be able to begin answering their questions about the correlations that interest them.

CONFIDENCE INTERVALS FOR CORRELATION COEFFICIENTS

Just as confidence intervals are important to help us interpret sample means, confidence intervals can help us evaluate correlations based on samples. As shown in earlier chapters, confidence intervals require an estimate of sampling error. In Chapter 6, you learned that the standard error of the mean ($s/\sqrt{N}$, or s_M) is an estimate of sampling variability. Recall that the standard error of the mean is used to calculate a confidence interval of a single mean. The lower value is the mean minus the standard error (s_M) times the value of t for $N - 1$ degrees of freedom (called t critical, or t_{crit}), and the upper value is the mean plus the standard error of the mean times t_{crit}. The critical values of t are chosen on the basis of the degrees of freedom for a single sample and in terms of the desired probability of the confidence interval (e.g., .95 or .99). In symbols, the confidence interval of a mean was defined in Chapter 6 as $M \pm t_{crit} (s_M)$. Confidence intervals for means are symmetrical; that is, the lower value is as much below the mean as the upper value is above the mean. The width of the confidence interval for means (that is, the larger end minus the smaller end) is based on the values of s and N, not on M, the statistic whose confidence interval is being found.

In contrast, **confidence intervals of correlations** are not usually symmetrical. Confidence intervals for correlations are symmetrical only when a correlation is zero—right in the middle of its possible range. This is true because the range of correlations is limited to -1.00 through $+1.00$. The closer the population correlation, ρ, is to -1.00 or $+1.00$, the more asymmetrical are the confidence intervals of r based on samples.

Consider an example. Let us suppose that ρ is $+.87$. Our sample r is an estimate of this population value. We expect the sampling distribution of r to vary around the population

FIGURE 15.1 ■ The sampling distribution of the values of *r* for samples randomly selected from a population in which two variables were highly correlated, $\rho = .90$. Note that the sampling distribution is negatively skewed.

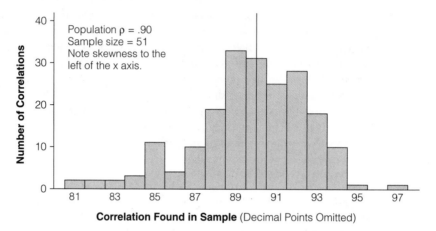

Correlation Found in Sample (Decimal Points Omitted)

value, ρ, just as we expect sample means to vary around the population mean, μ. If the population correlation, ρ, is positive, as in our example, then the sampling distribution of *r* will be negatively skewed. This must be the case because there are relatively fewer possible values of *r* above a correlation of $+.87$ relative to those below $+.87$. In other words, a sample *r* can range from $+.87$ to $+1.00$ on one side of ρ but can range from $+.87$ to -1.00 on the other. Values less than $+.87$ will form a longer tail than the values greater than $+.87$, as in Figure 15.1. In contrast, if ρ is negative, the sampling distribution of *r* will be positively skewed with a longer tail toward positive values than toward negative values. Of course, in the long run, half of sample correlations, *r*, would be greater than ρ and half would be less than ρ even though the distribution is skewed.

This might imply that it is hard to calculate confidence intervals for correlations; it isn't. The same Fisher who developed the ANOVA developed a procedure to make the calculation of confidence intervals for correlations very easy (Hays, 1994). Fisher showed that, if correlations are transformed before calculating the confidence interval, we can easily calculate the asymmetrical intervals. The transformation is called the Fisher ***r*-to-Z_r transformation.**[1] When samples are larger than 10 and the correlations not close to $+1.00$ or -1.00, the distribution of Z_r is approximately normal. Thus, we first convert *r* into Z_r and then find the confidence interval of Z_r. Then, we convert the confidence interval for Z_r back into a confidence interval for *r*. Keep in mind that the *z*, or standard score, introduced in Chapter 4 is not the same as the Z_r that Fisher defined; this is important because we use both symbols in this chapter. You can tell them apart because the standard score, *z*, is written in lowercase whereas Fisher's Z_r is written in uppercase with the subscript *r*.

---

[1] For the record, the formula to transform *r* to Z_r is $0.5 \log_e[(1 + r)/(1 - r)]$, but most people just use a conversion table.

An r-to-Z_r conversion table is found in the appendix.[2] (See Table A.4.) The other information needed to calculate a confidence interval of a correlation is the standard error of Z_r, or SE_{Z_r}. This equals $1/\sqrt{(N-3)}$. Therefore, the formula for the confidence interval of Z_r is

$$Z_r \pm z\,(SE_{Zr}) =$$
$$Z_r \pm z\,[1/\sqrt{(N-3)}] \qquad\qquad \text{Equation 15.1}$$

For a correlation of .45 based on a sample of $N = 103$ people, the 95% confidence interval would be found with these steps.[3]

(1) Z_r for $r = .45$ is 0.4847

(2) $SE_{Z_r} = 1/\sqrt{(103-3)} = 1/10 = .100$

(3) $0.4847 \pm 1.96\,(.100) = 0.2887$ to 0.6807

(4) We convert back to r by using the r-to-Z_r table in the reverse way from how we began. Now we look up a value of Z_r and find the equivalent r. The confidence interval in terms of r is .281 to .592, or .28 to .59.

The value of the standard normal score, z, is chosen on the basis of the confidence interval to be calculated. Although researchers usually use a 95% confidence interval, a variety of confidence intervals are presented in different contexts. Common confidence intervals and the appropriate values of z are 80% ($z = \pm 1.28$), 95% ($z = \pm 1.96$), and 99% ($z = \pm 2.16$).

When estimating the precision of our estimate of ρ, why is it critical to take into account the fact that the sampling distribution of r is not symmetrical (and thus not normally distributed)? Hint: Why, in other words, must we use the r-to-Z_r conversion? ■

The standard normal value of 1.96, which is associated with the 95% confidence interval, should be familiar to you. Recall from Chapter 4 that a z of 1.96 separates the right-hand half (and the left-hand half) of the normal distribution into two parts: the larger containing .475 of the scores, and the smaller (in the tail) containing .025 of the scores. (See also Table A.1 in the appendix.) Consequently, the portion of the normal curve between -1.96 and $+1.96$ contains .475 plus .475, or .95 of the scores in the normal distribution, or 95%.

The steps in the calculation of the confidence interval are reviewed in Table 15.1. The 95% confidence interval of a correlation of .30 based on a sample size of 87 is .096 to .480. The confidence interval of ρ in the table shows the asymmetry: the confidence interval extends .204 below .300, but only .180 above .30, the observed r. For correlations closer to ± 1.00, the asymmetry is even greater. Like confidence intervals for the mean, the 95% confidence interval based on a sample correlation coefficient refers to the precision with which we estimate a population parameter. In this case, if the samples are randomly selected from a population, 95% of the confidence intervals would include ρ. On the basis of this confi-

---

[2] As the r-to-Z_r table shows, when r approaches 1.00, Z_r approaches infinity. This is why the table cannot be used when r gets too close to ± 1.0, as mentioned. You do not need to worry about this because seldom do correlations in behavioral research get too close to ± 1.0.

[3] Recall that we follow the American Psychological Association *Publication Manual* (2001) in using the leading zero when a decimal value could be larger than 1.0, but omit the leading zero when a decimal value cannot be larger than 1.0.

TABLE 15.1 ■ Summary of the Steps in Calculating a 95% Confidence Interval for a Correlation

Step	Task	Illustration for $r = .30$ Based on 87 Observations
1	Convert r to a Z_r.	According to the r-to-Z Table, an r of .30 is equivalent to a Z of 0.3095.
2	Calculate the sampling error of Z_r, $1/\sqrt{(N-3)}$.	The sampling error is 1 divided by the positive square root of (87 minus 3), 0.1091.
3	Select the confidence interval desired and then the z needed.	If we wanted the 95% confidence interval, we would select ± 1.96.
4	Calculate the confidence interval for Z_r.	$0.3095 - 1.96\,(0.1091)$ and $0.3095 + 1.96\,(0.1091)$, or, 0.0957 to 0.5233
5	Convert the Z_r's back into r's to get a confidence interval for r.	Use the r-to-Z_r table in the reverse direction from step #1. A Z_r of 0.0957 is equivalent to an r of .096, and a Z_r of 0.5233 is equivalent to an r of .480.
6	Announce the conclusion.	For a sample of 87, the 95% confidence interval of a correlation of .300 is .096 to .480.

dence interval, we can conclude that it is quite unlikely for the correlation in the population, ρ, to be negative or to be over $+.50$. Thus, we have markedly narrowed down the range of possible values.

Table 15.2 contains several correlations from the previous chapter and the steps needed to calculate the confidence intervals. Be sure to review these examples before proceeding.

TABLE 15.2 ■ Calculation of 95% Confidence Intervals for Several Correlations

Variables	r	Z_r	N	Standard Error of Z_r $= 1/\sqrt{(N-3)}$	Confidence Interval in Terms of Z_r	Confidence Interval in Terms of r
Vertical jump and height of professors	.362	0.3792	17	$1/\sqrt{(17-3)}$ $= 0.267$	$0.3792 \pm 1.96\,(0.267) =$ -1.440 to 0.9030	$-.144$ to $.718$, or $-.14$ to $.72$
Mother's and father's years of education	.650	0.7753	59	$1/\sqrt{(59-3)}$ $= 0.1336$	$0.7753 \pm 1.96\,(0.1336) =$ 0.5134 to 1.0372	$.473$ to $.770$, or $.47$ to $.77$
Weight and gas mileage of cars	.780	1.0450	13	$1/\sqrt{(13-3)}$ $= 0.3162$	$1.0450 \pm 1.96\,(0.3162) =$ 0.4252 to 1.6648	$.426$ to $.926$, or $.43$ to $.93$

BOX 15.1 ■ Finding the 95% Confidence Interval for a Correlation: A Summary

Let's quickly summarize the strategy. We have calculated a correlation coefficient, r, based on a sample and wish to estimate confidence in our estimation of the population correlation, ρ. An observed r based on a random sample is the best estimate the researcher has of ρ, the correlation that we would find if we had tested every person or event in the population. But we know that all sample statistics are affected by sampling error. Moreover, in the case of correlation, we know that the sampling distribution of r will most likely be asymmetrical, that is, not normal in form. This raises problems when calculating a measure of sampling variability. However, Fisher's transformation permits correlations to be converted into a term, Z_r, that we can assume is normally distributed, thus permitting the use of the standard normal table. Thus, we take the following steps:

(1) Transform our observed r into Z_r using Fisher's transformation. (See Table A.4.)

(2) Select an appropriate standard normal score, z, for the desired confidence level (usually 1.96 to correspond to 95% confidence interval).

(3) Multiply this value by the standard error of Z_r, or SE_{Z_r}, defined as $1/\sqrt{(N-3)}$.

(4) Add this product to Z_r and subtract the product from Z_r to produce the upper and lower limits of the interval: $Z_r \pm z\,(SE_{Z_r})$ or $Z_r \pm z\,[1/\sqrt{(N-3)}]$.

(5) Reverse the procedure to obtain an interval based on r. That is, use Fisher's transformation to convert Z_r back to r for both the lower and upper values of r.

Assuming we found the 95% confidence interval, we may be confident that, if we replicated the research repeatedly, 95% of the confidence intervals would include ρ.

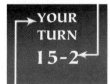

YOUR TURN 15-2

(a) Calculate the 95% confidence intervals for the two correlations between authoritarian scores for adolescents and parents found by Sandra that were mentioned in the introduction. For 100 parents and their biological children, the correlation was .40, and, for 25 parents and their adoptive children, the correlation was .10.

(b) What did you learn about the correlations? ■

INTERPRETING CONFIDENCE INTERVALS OF CORRELATION COEFFICIENTS

As with any evidence obtained from random samples, the larger the sample size the better is our estimate of a population parameter. Raising the sample size reduces uncertainty in estimation because correlations based on larger sample sizes have smaller sampling errors. Another way to reduce uncertainty is to improve measurement. The goal of improving measurement is to obtain a "purer" measure of what it is that we are seeking to measure. Measurement is improved to the extent that we remove the effects of random error. Error intrudes when we provide participants with vague or unclear instructions, test them in nonoptimal environments (e.g., in the presence of noise or distractions), or otherwise use measurements that do not yield consistent results. The less the measurements contain random error, the larger the correlation coefficients (Hunter & Schmidt, 1990). Improved measurement will lead to more-accurate correlations.

Confidence intervals are also more accurate when both variables are normally distributed. Therefore, *it is important in the inspection stage to verify that the distributions of scores are generally normal in form.* If the distributions are not precisely normal, then larger samples can reduce bias (Hays, 1994). When sample sizes are not large, a researcher may wish to consider a transformation of the data to make the distribution more bell shaped. (See Chapter 3.) Recall from the previous chapter that changing the measurement scale, as when performing a linear transformation, does not affect the correlation coefficient; however, using a square root or log transformation will affect the correlation.

If the sample is not randomly chosen, it is unlikely to be representative of the population; that is, it will be a biased sample. You have seen this important point before. To generalize the findings of an experiment, the people or events observed must represent the population of interest. For example, if we found no correlation between the amount of money spent on a car and yearly income, but our sample was chosen from people who are presidents of the 100 largest American companies, we would not have learned anything about Americans in general. *Unless correlations are obtained from random samples, we should be cautious about generalizing the results to the population of interest.*

In the previous chapter, we discussed Sally's research correlating the size of the vocabularies of children and their parents. Suppose that she had obtained her data in a daycare center organized by the faculty of a university. The range of vocabulary scores of the faculty would not represent the range of vocabulary scores among adults in general.

(a) What happens to correlations when the range of one of the variables is restricted?

(b) Comment critically on Sally's ability to generalize her findings. ■

In previous chapters, we provided some general guidelines for interpreting confidence intervals surrounding means. These guidelines may be used similarly when interpreting confidence intervals for sample correlations. The limits of the confidence interval provide information about the precision of estimate of the population correlation. The narrower the interval, the better is the estimate. You have seen that larger sample sizes and improved measurement lead to narrower intervals, that is, more-precise estimates of the population value, ρ.

Because confidence intervals surround probable values for ρ, when .00 is in a 95% confidence interval, we must remember that we have not found evidence for a linear relationship between the variables under investigation that meets the agreed-upon criterion for confidently announcing a finding. Of course, this does not mean that there isn't a relationship. A larger sample size or improved measurement may reveal one; however, *given these data, we should not speak as if a correlation has been found when .00 lies within the confidence interval.*

When comparing two or more confidence intervals, we may judge population correlations to be similar when intervals overlap considerably and different when there is no overlap. The confidence intervals for Sandra's two correlations overlap a great deal (see *Your Turn* 15-2). Given her sample sizes, she has not obtained sufficient evidence to conclude that the two correlations differ. Whenever the two intervals overlap substantially, a researcher may not claim to have found a difference. (Because larger sample sizes improve the precision of estimates of population values, obtaining larger samples might permit Sandra to support the theory she was examining.) When, on the other hand, non-overlapping intervals are found, the evidence would suggest that the population values do differ.

Constructing confidence intervals for the sample correlations permits us to examine precision and to begin to compare the relative sizes of two correlations. However, determining precision is only part of the task of interpretation. When should a correlation merit our attention? When is a correlation "big enough" to be important, either theoretically or practically? We take up this question next.

EFFECT SIZES OF CORRELATION COEFFICIENTS

What value of a correlation should catch our eye? When are researchers permitted to call a correlation "big" or "small"? The reason that we have not yet raised this issue is that, as you probably guessed, the answer is a little complicated.

Calling a correlation big or small solely on the basis of its size is not wise. It is absolutely false to think of a correlation of .12 as so small that it is not very interesting. A correlation of .87 is big relative to the possible range of r, but that fact does not make the correlation necessarily interesting or useful. It is possible that the large correlation simply reflects something already known quite well (or a correlation obtained from a biased sample). When is a correlation large enough to be interesting or useful? The answer is that it depends on (a) the size of correlations that are typically found in an area of research, (b) the nature of the variables themselves, and, as we have seen, (c) the nature of the sample. We have already noted that biased samples may give us misleading evidence about the population correlation. Thus, let us consider the first two points.

Effect Sizes When Comparing Two Means: A Review

We begin by reviewing the meaning of effect sizes for two means. When dealing with two groups, a control group and an experimental group, we typically measure the effect of an independent variable by finding the difference between the means of the dependent variable for the two groups, and then reporting that difference standardized by the variability of the dependent variable in the experiment. If a health psychologist developed a program to reduce smoking, one can think of its effect as the difference between the mean number of cigarettes smoked per day by members of the control group versus the mean number of cigarettes smoked by members of the treated sample. That difference would be an informative and useful measure of the effect of the program. However, not all health programs focus on reducing cigarette consumption. Others may focus on weight loss (or gain), hours of sleep, amount of exercise, and so forth. Thus, we standardize the effect of the program be dividing the difference of the two means by the variation of the dependent variable, s_{pooled}, giving us g. By now, you should be familiar with one such measure of effect size, Hedges' g, which is defined as

$$g = \frac{M_1 - M_2}{s_{pooled}}$$

In Chapter 7, s_{pooled} was defined as

$$s_{pooled} = \sqrt{\frac{(n_1 - 1)s_1^2 + (n_2 - 1)s_2^2}{(n_1 + n_2 - 2)}}$$

Health psychologists would then be able to compare this effect size with those of a variety of illness-prevention programs, including programs that are more complicated than getting people to stop smoking cigarettes. Some might be planned to change attitudes, and others to affect behaviors.

Using an effect size expressed in terms of the standard deviations allows researchers to compare effect sizes across a variety of dependent variables. Recall that Cohen (1989) suggested that, when the effect size is calculated by a difference between two means divided by a standard deviation of the dependent variable, effect sizes of 0.20, 0.50, and 0.80 may be called small, medium, and large, respectively.

r Is an Effect Size

But how do Cohen's observations apply to correlations? Because there is just one group and no means, the concept of effect size might not appear to apply to correlations. Effect sizes, however, can be found for correlations; in fact, *r* is an effect size.

When two variables, *X* and *Y,* are correlated, knowing the value of *X* for a person means that we have some information about the value of *Y* for that person. We can use *X* to reduce our uncertainty or to predict *Y*. Similarly, when the means of two samples are different, knowing whether a person was in the experimental or in the control group gives us some idea about that person's score on the dependent variable. For example, assume the mean of an experimental group is 20 and the mean of the control group is 10. If we know that a person is in the experimental group, we are likely to be much more accurate if we predict this person's score to be closer to 20 than to 10.

In neither case can we predict the value of a score without error, but we know more than we would have known without the correlation or without the information on group membership. Hedges' *g* is a measure of that increase in knowledge for research comparing two means; *r* is a measure of the increase in knowledge for research using two continuous variables. Thus, *both r and g are telling us the same thing, but for different designs,* and it turns out that we can learn something very important by comparing them.

Comparing *r* to Other Effects Size Statistics

We cannot compare *r* with *g* directly because *r* and *g* are not in the same units. The difficulty is compounded because the size of *r* is restricted to -1.00 to $+1.00$. Fortunately, there are fairly simple formulas for converting these measures into each other (e.g., Rosenthal & Rosnow, 1991). One way is as follows:

$$g = \frac{2r/\sqrt{(1-r^2)}}{\sqrt{(N/df)}} \quad \text{where } N = n_1 + n_2 \text{ and } df = n_1 + n_2 - 2 \qquad \textbf{Equation 15.2}$$

Suppose you conducted a study correlating two variables and found *r* equal to .40. The number (*N*) of subjects tested was 38. We can convert *r* to *g,* as follows:

$$g = \frac{2(.40)/\sqrt{(1-.40^2)}}{\sqrt{(38/36)}} = 0.84$$

Based on Cohen's (1988) guidelines for interpreting *g,* we can judge that an *r* of .40 based on 38 pairs of scores produced a large effect because a *g* of 0.84 exceeds Cohen's criterion for a large effect size, 0.80. Table 15.3 contains illustrations of various-sized correlations converted into *g* when the total group size (*N*) is 50 (i.e., $N = n_1 + n_2 = 50$). The table also

TABLE 15.3 ■ Illustrations of Converting Correlations into Hedges' *g* for Samples of 50 Participants

Correlation, *r*	*g**	Equivalent Cohen Categories of *g* as Found in the Psychological Research Literature
−.10	−0.196	small
.05	0.098	very small
.10	0.197	small
.20	0.400	low moderate
.25	0.506	moderate
.30	0.617	moderate
.37	0.781	large
.45	0.988	large

* Equation 15.2 was used to make these conversions, $g = \dfrac{2r/\sqrt{(1 - r^2)}}{\sqrt{(N/df)}}$.

includes Cohen's categories for interpreting the values of *g*. It is crucial to remember that the Cohen categories are just guidelines; they are not mathematically precise cutoffs as when we decide whether an observed value is significant at the .05 level by consulting a table of critical values. Cohen, in fact, rounded the values for effect size criteria to easily remembered magnitudes.

Note that the first correlation in Table 15.3 is a negative one. Converting a negative *r* into a *g* raises the question of whether a negative effect size makes any sense. One could argue that all effect sizes should be positive. When one finds a characteristic that correlates negatively with a behavior, the negative *r* is just as helpful for understanding the behavior as is a positive *r* (of the same numerical size). That is, the negative relationship would be just as "effective" as a positive one in explaining behavior because the absolute value of *r* indicates the strength of the relationship. The sign merely indicates the direction of the relationship. Therefore, it might seem that negative effect sizes for *r* should not be reported. On the other hand, if a negative *r* had been found with variables that had been positively correlated in previous research, the negative sign would be quite important. Or, to use an example with *g*, if therapy that was expected to help clients become better relative to a control group, in fact, led to the treated clients getting worse, dropping the negative sign of *g* would be highly misleading when it is compared to other research. Consequently, we recommend retaining the negative sign for effect size calculations of *r* and *g*. [See Rosenthal, Rosow, & Rubin (2000), as well as our discussion of effect sizes in Chapter 8.]

If the sample size is large, say 100, and if *r* is between −.30 and +.30, the conversion is very easy:

$$2r = g \hspace{4cm} \text{Equation 15.3}$$

This means that a correlation of .25 is approximately equal to an effect size, *g*, of 0.50, which is a medium size according to Cohen (1988). For smaller samples and larger correlations (i.e., less than −.30 or greater than +.30), use Equation 15.2. Box 15.2 provides additional details on these conversions.

BOX 15.2 ■ Hedges' *g*, Cohen's *d*, and *r*

In Chapter 8 (see Box 8.1), we briefly described the relationship between Hedges' *g* and Cohen's *d*, which is another commonly used effect size measure. Here we want to show you the relationship between these two measures of effect size and *r*.

Hedges' *g* and Cohen's *d* provide very similar values. You may recall that the difference is due to how the standard deviation in the denominator is calculated. As you are no doubt aware by now, the formula for *g* is

$$g = \frac{M_1 - M_2}{s_{\text{pooled}}}$$

The formula for *d* is

$$d = \frac{M_1 - M_2}{\sigma_{\text{pooled}}}$$

The difference is in the denominator, s_{pooled} or σ_{pooled}. For *g*,

$$s_{\text{pooled}} = \sqrt{\frac{(n_1 - 1)s_1^2 + (n_2 - 1)s_2^2}{(n_1 + n_2 - 2)}}$$

For *d*,

$$\sigma_{\text{pooled}} = \sqrt{\frac{(n_1 - 1)s_1^2 + (n_2 - 1)s_2^2}{(n_1 + n_2)}}$$

Because the denominator of s_{pooled} (that is, $n_1 + n_2 - 2$) is slightly smaller than the denominator of σ_{pooled} (that is, $n_1 + n_2$), s_{pooled} will be a bit larger than σ_{pooled}. (Dividing by a smaller number leads to larger results.) That difference means that Hedges' *g* would be slightly smaller than Cohen's *d* for the same set of data. However, the difference is small (less than 2% when there are 30 people in each group).

The relationship we presented between *r* and *g* that we have described is related to the relationship between *r* and *d*, which is

$$d = \frac{2r}{\sqrt{(1 - r^2)}}$$

The relationship between *d* and *g* is

$$g = \frac{d}{\sqrt{(N/df)}}$$

Therefore, the relationship between *g* and *r* can be stated as

$$g = \frac{2r/\sqrt{(1 - r^2)}}{\sqrt{(N/df)}}$$

If you look at this equation carefully, you can see the very simple relationship between *g* and *r* when correlations are between $-.3$ and $+.3$ and sample sizes are large. If *N* is 100, the denominator equals 1.0102, just slightly larger than 1.00. If *r* is .30, the numerator equals 0.63 and *g* is 0.62, which is just a little bigger than 2 times .30. When *r* is even closer to .00, the result of the conversion formula is even closer to 2*r*. Thus, *for correlations between $-.30$ and $+.30$ based on samples of 100 or more, g is always very close to 2r*. And, when the sample size is large, *g* and *d* are nearly equal. You can use this rule of thumb to easily convert correlations into effect size indices used with two means. See especially Rosenthal and Rosnow (1991) for more information about these and other effect-size relationships.

INTERPRETING THE EFFECT SIZE OF CORRELATIONS

Our purpose in discussing the conversion between correlations and effect sizes for the difference between two means is to be sure that you are not misled by the small numerical size of correlations. Our experience is that many students underestimate the value of correlations because frequently r is literally a small number. Cohen (1988) showed that—for differences between two means—effect sizes (i.e., d or g) of 0.20, 0.50, and 0.80 reflected small, medium, and large (respectively) findings in respected psychological journals. For correlations, Cohen observed that *values of r equal to .10, .30, and .50 reflect small, medium, and large relationships (respectively) in the psychological research literature.* Before he reported these values, no one had thought of doing this.

Cohen's information is helpful, but it does not fully answer our question as to what size correlation is important or big. Lipsey and Wilson (1993) summarized 302 review articles encompassing thousands of individual studies of education, corrections, and counseling. They found a median effect size of 0.47 for group comparisons; 0.47 is equivalent to an r of .23. The median effect size in applied research was remarkably close to Cohen's finding in theoretical research. Unfortunately, we still have not found a definitive answer to what exactly is a big correlation.

AVOIDING COMMON MISUNDERSTANDINGS OF CORRELATIONS

Some large correlations are not very informative, but some very small ones are. Suppose your roommate conducted a lab project and found a correlation of .75 between scores on the SAT verbal score and the ACT English score. And suppose that your roommate converted the r to an effect size of 2.27, a very large effect size. Are you going to be impressed? Probably not. Finding a large correlation between the scores of two well-developed, standardized tests that are supposed to measure many of the same skills is not at all surprising; it has been done many times. The immense effect size is neither interesting nor important. We have not learned anything new. *The central issue is the nature of the variables that are being correlated.* If the variables are well known and widely studied, probably any finding that replicates past research will not be very interesting even if the correlation is large. If the variables under study do not contribute to resolving an important theoretical puzzle or in meeting some applied purpose, few people will care about their correlation.

In contrast, Rosenthal (1990) pointed out that, in medical research, the dependent variables are often important in themselves—heart attack or not, survival or not. When researchers discover some treatment or preventive technique, the effect size can be quite small and yet be important simply because the dependent variable is really important. Medical experiments showing small effect sizes have been stopped because the results were seen as so strong that it was considered unethical to permit the control group to continue without the treatment or the preventive measure. Rosenthal described a decision to stop a medical study in which a relationship between a treatment and the dependent variable was equivalent to an effect size of 0.068 (or a correlation of .034). In a life-and-death context in which literally hundreds of thousands of people are involved, even numerically small correlations are useful and important to find.

Rosenthal's comments give us a clue as to how to resolve Indira's question about the comments made by the authors of her textbook on personnel selection. The explanation lies in the behavior to be predicted. Although custodial work is essential to hotel management, if it is not done well, problems can be readily detected, the work can be redone, and no permanent problems will occur. On the other hand, promoting the wrong person into an upper-management position could do major harm to an organization because poor decisions cannot be quickly discovered and they are expensive to correct. Thus, even rather small improvements to a selection process for executives could be valuable to obtain. Information permitting better predictions of variables that can have major effects on many people are valuable. In contrast, when mistakes are inexpensive to correct, we need not expend a great deal of effort making the most accurate predictions. Consequently, the .22 correlation used in selecting managers would be worth using even though a larger correlation, .25, might not be worth using for selecting employees for entry-level jobs.

Let's spend a moment on Esteban's question. Suppose that he discovered that the correlation between the height of men and income was +.05. Income is an important variable, but is this finding worth talking about? Figure 15.2 is a scatterplot of a positive correlation of .05. What do you see there? Would you have even known that it was a positive correlation? If you were one of Esteban's cousins, you have little reason to worry about tall Esteban earning much more money than you will. Furthermore, people cannot change their height; consequently, this weak finding cannot be put to practical use.

FIGURE 15.2 ■ This scatterplot illustrates the difficulty of visually detecting a small correlation. Rosenthal has discussed that a very small correlation is worth detecting if the relationship has some practical importance or affects many people. One purpose of statistical analyses is to detect patterns that cannot be easily detected in other ways. Whether the pattern is worth paying attention to depends on the nature of the variables.

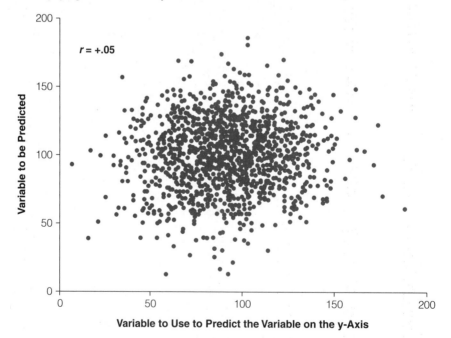

FIGURE 15.3 ■ Although the correlation between the height of buildings and the time it takes a stone to fall from the top to the ground is very large, the scatterplot shows that the relationships are not linear.

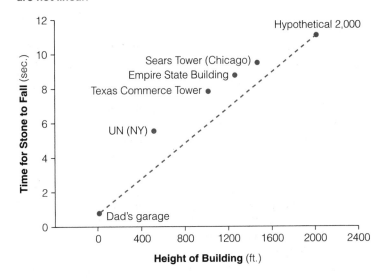

In contrast, sometimes small differences in correlations might tell us that someone has made a major improvement in the understanding of some phenomenon. For example, the linear correlation between the height of buildings and time for a stone to fall from the top of those buildings shown in Figure 15.3 is .9657. That coefficient is very close to +1.00, almost perfect. Yet, you can see that the scatterplot reflects a nonlinear relationship. Knowing what accounts for that tiny difference between .9657 and 1.0000 would be very important. Galileo experimented by dropping cannonballs, but Newton developed the formula relating time and distance fallen. Little research in education, public health, and other behavioral sciences is at a level of precision that merits our worrying about such small improvements; we are still working on the big stuff. And perhaps we will never get to that level of precision. Yet, the point is critical: *decisions about whether a correlation is meaningful cannot be based simply on the size of the coefficient or the precision with which we measure it.* Remember: statistics is an aid to thought, not a substitute.

Perhaps the best bottom line is this: *if the variables under study are interesting theoretically or have practical worth, a correlation of .20 or larger should be seen as respectable in the context of findings in both theoretical and applied psychology.* (See Table 15.3.)

Don't Underestimate the Meaning of r^2

It has been common to suggest that the strength of the relationship between two continuous variables be described using the square of the correlation between the two variables. *This index, r^2, tells us what proportion of the variance of one variable is explained by the second variable.* Proportion of variance accounted for is a concept you met when we discussed eta squared, η^2, which is used to assess the overall effect of an independent variable in the context of ANOVA. (See Chapter 12 and 13.)

Consider that if we want to predict college grades we look for variables that correlate with grades. Identifying variables that are correlated with grades would permit us to make more-accurate predictions of grades. Making "more-accurate predictions" means that we are able to predict who would earn relatively higher and who would earn relatively lower grades. In other words, we are *explaining* some of the variance among grades. The value of r^2 is called the **proportion of variance explained;** sometimes it is converted into percentage of variance explained by multiplying by 100. But how do we interpret r^2?

The error of underestimating the meaning of r^2 can be corrected by considering the amount of variance accounted for in terms of Cohen's rule of thumb for assessing the size of correlations. A correlation of .10, which is equivalent to a small effect in Cohen's terms, explains "only" 1% of the variance. A correlation of .30, equivalent to Cohen's medium effect size, explains "only" 9% of the variance.

The problem with r^2 is that many students (and behavioral scientists as well) have interpreted these small percentages as indicating relationships that are not strong enough to be taken seriously (Rosenthal et al., 2000). But, as you have just seen, to suggest that a correlation of .30 is not important because it accounts for "only" 9% of the variance is to say, in effect, that the average correlational study in psychology produces an effect size that is not to be taken seriously. The misunderstanding might be less prevalent in recent years because the use of effect size along with often-used t tests and ANOVAs has made it easier to compare the strength of findings based on correlations with the strength of findings based on an analysis of sample means. Interpretations of correlations will be more useful if one keeps in mind the importance of the variables themselves and Cohen's observation that correlations of .30 match the median of the correlations in the psychological research literature. Table 15.4 shows the relationship among Hedges' g, r, and r^2 for several different values of these measures based on a total sample size of 50 (i.e., $n_1 + n_2 = N = 50$).

At the same time, we are not suggesting that one be complacent when finding a correlation of .30. A correlation this size may merit respect in the context of psychological research, but it also conveys an important lesson. Knowing that the average effect size in psychological research is about 0.5 and that this effect size corresponds to an r of .30 explaining "only" 9% of the variance tells us that, in psychology, we have a lot left to study and to explain.

TABLE 15.4   ■   The Relationship Between Hedges' g, r, and Percentage of Variance Explained, r^2

Effect Size, g*	Correlation, r	% Variance Explained, r^2
0.10	.05	0.25%
0.20	.10	1.00%
0.50	.24	5.88%
0.80	.36	12.96%
1.00	.44	19.36%

* Hedges' g was based on the assumption of equal-sized groups: $n_1 + n_2 = N = 25 + 25 = 50$.

Don't Do a *t* Test When a Correlation Would Be Better

A common analysis strategy is to divide scores obtained from a variable, such as age or socioeconomic status, to form two natural groups based on a **median split.** Individuals above the median comprise one group, and individuals below the median comprise a second group. The groups are then treated as two levels of an independent variable, and a *t* test for independent groups is used to compare the means on a dependent variable. For example, to determine if there is a relationship between socioeconomic status (SES) and self-esteem, a researcher might obtain measures of both SES and self-esteem from a large sample of people, calculate the median SES score and then split the sample into high (above the median) and low (below the median) SES groups. A *t* test could then be conducted to see if self-esteem scores differ significantly for individuals in the high and low SES groups.

Although there is nothing absolutely wrong with this approach, the lessons we have presented in this chapter regarding effect sizes of correlations and the differences between means allow us to demonstrate that this is not a good idea because this strategy underestimates the strength of the finding. Our point is perhaps best made with a concrete example.

Kim was asked to examine the validity of a test of management skill being developed in her company. One way to assess validity of a test is to determine if it correlates with other measures supposedly tapping similar characteristics. Kim was asked to examine the degree to which the management skill test was related to a test measuring need for achievement *(nAch)*. She tested 208 middle-level managers in her company using the new scale and a standard *nAch* scale. Her boss suggested that Kim do a median split and divide the managers into two groups on the basis of *nAch* and then use a *t* test to compare the management skill means of the high and low *nAch* groups. Kim wondered if she shouldn't instead correlate scores on the two tests, but her boss insisted she split the groups. So Kim did as she was told.

The means and standard deviations of management skill (MS) for the high and low achievement groups following median split were as follows:

	M_{MS}	SD_{MS}	n
High *nAch* managers	40.33	12.15	104
Low *nAch* managers	31.38	13.87	104

These means reveal that high *nAch* managers show more management skill according to the new test: $t(206) = 4.95, p < .001$. Kim correctly continued her analysis. She calculated the effect size from the group means.

$$g = \frac{M_{high} - M_{low}}{S_{pooled}} = \frac{40.33 - 31.38}{\sqrt{[(12.15^2 + 13.87^2)/2]}} = \frac{8.95}{13.04} = 0.686$$

Kim then carried out the correlational analysis that she originally thought was more appropriate. She found that *nAch* and management skill were positively correlated, $r = .415$. Then she converted the correlation into an effect size, *g*:

$$g = \frac{2r/\sqrt{(1 - r^2)}}{\sqrt{(N/df)}} \quad \text{where } N = n_1 + n_2 \text{ and } df = n_1 + n_2 - 2$$

$$g = \frac{2(.415)/\sqrt{(1 - .415^2)}}{\sqrt{(208/206)}} = 0.90$$

Note that converting *r* to *g* produced a markedly larger effect size than the *g* found using the group means. Which one is right? We answer that question in what follows.

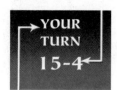

YOUR TURN 15-4 Use Cohen's guidelines to interpret the sizes of the two effect sizes Kim has calculated. ■

This example has an important lesson. The difference between these two effect sizes reveals an important lesson that demonstrates why doing a median split (or a three-way split, or four-way split, etc.) yields misleading results when analyzing two continuous variables. Although sometimes it seems useful to divide a continuous variable, such as *nAch,* into high and low scores and in that way produce two groups, the practice amounts to discarding information. The *nAch* scores range from low to high. Dividing the participants into high and low groups and reporting the means for the groups is equivalent to treating all those people above the median as if they showed the same level of *nAch* (i.e., the mean for high *nAch*) and treating those below the median as being the same as well (i.e., the mean for low *nAch*). The means, standard deviations, and maximum and minimum scores for the managers above and below the median of *nAch* in Kim's study were as follows:

Group	M_{nAch}	SD_{nAch}	Lowest	Highest
High *nAch*	110.63	8.96	98	135
Low *nAch*	85.67	8.85	58	97

Look at the scores for the first group. There is no reason to believe that a manager with an *nAch* score of 98 shows the same achievement-oriented behavior as a manager with a score of 135, although both would be in the high group, above the median. We think you can easily see how splitting research participants into two groups by dividing them at the median on a continuous variable means that information has been discarded. The effect of dichotomizing the *nAch* scores—that is, ignoring differences among the managers within the groups—lowers the apparent effect size.

The correct way to examine the relationships between continuous variables is to correlate them. It is poor practice to divide people into high and low groups so that one can conduct a *t* test. In general, *the result of dividing a distribution of scores in two halves is to reduce the apparent effect size.*

One way to emphasize the detrimental effect of dichotomizing is to code scores greater than the median as 2 and scores less than the median as 1, and then correlate scores on the dependent variable. For example, the management skill test with this reduced *nAch* scale would now have only two values: 1 and 2. The correlation for our example is .326, which is markedly lower than the .415 found using the original scores. In general, if a continuous variable is divided at the median to form two, equal-sized groups, correlations with the artificially dichotomized variable are on the average about 80% of what the correlations would have been had the full scale been used (Cohen, 1988; Hunter & Schmidt, 1990).[4] The proce-

---

[4] If the variables being correlated were normally distributed, the percentage is 79.8%. If a particular example is not distributed precisely normally, the ratio of the correlations will not be exactly 0.798. For Kim's data, the ratio was 0.756.

dures suggested by Kim's boss made the relationship between *nAch* and the management skills test look less strong than it is. Thus, we suggest that Kim's correlational analysis, and the corresponding effect size of .90, is the "right" one.

WHAT YOU HAVE LEARNED AND THE NEXT STEP

Some of the points in this chapter on interpreting correlations may have seemed abstract. Here are the major points we have made:

- Confidence intervals for correlations can be calculated in a way closely parallel to that for means.

- Information on the precision of the estimates of the population correlation provided by a confidence interval shows that uncertainty remains, but that the range of likely values of the correlation has been reduced.

- Converting *r* to *g* permits comparing the strength of findings in correlational analyses with findings in research on group means.

- Both *r* and *g* tell us the same thing, but for different ways of examining the data.

- Correlations in the range of .20 to .35 should be considered typical in behavioral research.

- For typical sized correlations in the behavioral sciences, $g = 2r$.

- Decisions about whether a correlation is meaningful cannot be based simply on the size of the coefficient or the precision with which we measure it. Concluding that a finding is important or of practical use depends on the nature of the variables used in the research, not just on the size of *r*.

- The concept of percentage variance accounted for, r^2, may be misleading as a way to decide whether a correlation is large enough to be worth finding; reference should also be made to Cohen's categories.

- Although performing a median split with a continuous variable to conduct a *t* test is a common analysis technique, it results in a loss of information and in a lower effect size than if the two continuous variables were correlated.

The next step is to examine the question of null hypothesis significance testing (NHST) in the context of correlations. There are parallels between these NHST procedures and those presented in previous chapters; moreover, the purpose is the same: we want a technique that permits us to conform to the convention of keeping Type I errors low, that is, not wanting to claim a finding that is not likely to be true. At that point, we will illustrate announcing the findings of a correlational study to others.

Key Concepts

confidence intervals of correlations	proportion of variance explained, r^2
r-to-Z_r transformation	median split

Answers to *Your Turn* Questions

15-1. The sampling distribution of r (whenever ρ does not equal 0.0) is asymmetrical and, thus, not normally distributed. One can use z to construct confidence intervals only if the sampling distribution is normal. Fisher's transformation produces a normal distribution.

15-2. (a) For the biological parents and children, the 95% confidence interval for Z_r would be 0.4236 ± 1.96 [$1/\sqrt{(100 - 3)}$], or 0.2247 to 0.6225. In terms of r, the 95% confidence interval is .22 to .55. Following the same procedure for the adoptive parents and children, the 95% confidence interval for r is −.31 to .48.

(b) Note how much wider the second 95% confidence interval is. The smaller sample size left Sandra with considerable uncertainty about the true population correlation.

15-3. (a) Restricting the range will reduce the size of the correlation coefficient.

(b) Sally will obtain smaller correlations based on this selective sample of parents and children than if a more varied group was studied; moreover, because the sample was not from the general population, she may only generalize her results to groups similar to that from which she selected her sample (e.g., other university faculty parents and their children).

15-4. When *nAch* was dichotomized, the effect size was smaller than large; however, when the correction (based on the original continuous variables) was transformed into g, the effect size was larger than Cohen's large category.

Analyzing and Interpreting Data: Problems and Exercises

1. A correlation found from a sample, r, just like a mean of a sample, M, is subject to sampling error. Whereas sample means vary around the population mean, μ, sample correlations vary around what population parameter?

2. Explain why confidence intervals for sample r's are not generally symmetrical.

3. Why are confidence intervals for a given value of a correlation coefficient smaller for large samples compared to the confidence intervals of small samples?

4. Calculate the 95% confidence intervals for the following correlations and sample sizes:

r	N
(a) +.80	19
(b) +.80	103
(c) −.40	52
(d) +.04	28
(e) −.32	39

5. Calculate the 95% confidence intervals for the following correlations and sample sizes:

r	N
(a) +.55	103
(b) +.19	103
(c) −.45	52
(d) +.83	19
(e) +.09	1000

6. A health psychologist interested in the value of anti-smoking programs and physical health wanted to choose a measure of the amount people smoked. She wanted to find the correlation between amount of smoking and lung capacity. Two ways of measuring smoking were examined: one measure was based on how much the family members of a sample of smokers thought the smoker smoked per day, and the second measure was a lab-based test that was based on nicotine

and tar in the blood of these smokers. If there really were a correlation between amount of smoking and lung capacity, which of these two measures is likely to produce a larger correlation with lung capacity?

7. At ACME Corp., an industrial psychologist found that a selection test correlated .38 with success on the job after three months ($N = 103$). Across town, another industrial psychologist working with a similar company, General Corp., found that the correlation of the same test with job success was only .21 ($N = 58$). At a conference, they discussed how differences in the companies might account for the difference in the size of the correlations. Use confidence intervals to explore whether the two industrial psychologists have reason to believe that the difference between the two correlations reflects anything other than sampling error. Explain your decision.

8. Sarah found that the correlation between height and GPA for 28 men was .16, but among 52 women it was .05. She concluded that physical strength leads to better GPA for men, but that physical strength does not affect women's grades. Using confidence intervals, discuss whether her findings merit explanation.

9. Convert each of the following correlations into an effect size, g. Use both the simple formula and the longer, more accurate formula (assume that $N = 102$):

	r	r^2	Cohen label for r	$2r = g$	g using the more accurate formula
(a)	.10				
(b)	.39				
(c)	−.68				
(d)	.76				
(e)	−.21				
(f)	−.33				

10. Convert each of the following correlations into an effect size, g. Use both the simple formula and the longer, more accurate formula (assume that $N = 123$):

	r	r^2	Cohen's label for r	$2r = g$	g using the more accurate formula
(a)	.30				
(b)	−.17				
(c)	−.22				
(d)	.50				
(e)	.37				

11. Suppose that one found the pairs of correlations and 95% confidence intervals given here. Use the confidence intervals to decide whether the difference between the correlations is large enough to provide the researcher assurance that the correlations differ by more than sampling error.
   (a) $r_1 = .32$, $N_1 = 63$, 95% confidence interval: .08 to .53
   $r_2 = .45$, $N_2 = 64$, 95% confidence interval: .23 to .63
   (b) $r_1 = +.12$, $N_1 = 63$, 95% confidence interval: −.13 to .36
   $r_2 = −.13$, $N_2 = 63$, 95% confidence interval: −.37 to .12
   (c) $r_1 = +.12$, $N_1 = 147$, 95% confidence interval: −.04 to .28
   $r_2 = +.38$, $N_2 = 148$, 95% confidence interval: .28 to .56

12. You hear a report that two variables are correlated .90. What do you need to know before concluding whether this large correlation is worth paying attention to?

13. The author of a college-level textbook for counseling courses called a correlation of −.34 a "weak negative correlation." In light of Cohen's categories of effect sizes, is that an appropriate comment?

14. A researcher is investigating the relationship between the personality trait of authoritarianism (A) and prejudice (P) toward minority groups. Let us assume that both these traits can also be measured in a valid and reliable manner. The investigator obtains responses for both the A and P scales from a sample of 100 adult males. Doing a median split, the researcher defines high A and low

A groups. A *t* test was then carried out to learn whether the means of the P scores of these two groups differ. Critically evaluate this approach to investigating the relationship between these measures of authoritarianism and prejudice.

15. Suppose Bill tests 15 randomly selected samples of 100 students each from the student body of a large university. With each sample, Bill measures how favorable the students are to heavy drinking and obtains the students' GPA (with their permission). He finds these correlations:

    $-.23, -.18, +.02, -.28, +.18, -.10, -.18,$
    $-.16, -.36, +.06, -.12, -.15, -.10, +.04, -.19$

    Bill selected his fifth sample and found the 95% confidence interval for a correlation of $+.18$ to be $-.02$ to $+.36$. He said that he was 95% sure that the true correlation was in this confidence interval, and, therefore, heavy drinking seems to be positively correlated with grade point average. How has Bill misused confidence intervals?

16. Suppose Jill found a correlation of .47 between an altruism scale and the amount of volunteer time that students devoted to community services. She used 139 students in the survey. She found the 95% confidence interval to be .33 to .59. Jill later obtained data from 13 additional students, among which Jill found a correlation of .29. She was confused. She thought the interval she had found would cover additional samples. "Why is this sample not in the confidence interval?" she asked. Give her two reasons why she should not be so surprised.

17. Robyn obtained a correlation of .64 based on the following data. He was sure that he found an important relationship. Did he?

Variable	A	B	C	D	E	F
X	10	10	10	16	10	10
Y	25	35	42	53	28	25

Variable	G	H	I	J	K
X	10	10	10	10	10
Y	38	41	36	31	29

18. Allen reported to his psychology lab class that there is "essentially no relationship" between subjective stress and performance. Allen found an *r* of .00005 among 11 students. Steve looked at Allen's data and told the class that Allen was wrong. Who is right? Discuss the reasons for your answer. Here is a list of Allen's data:

Variable	A	B	C	D	E	F
Stress	10	22	45	23	12	17
Performance	5	16	8	12	9	12

Variable	G	H	I	J	K
Stress	42	38	38	28	31
Performance	7	8	14	19	15

19. Suppose that an admissions director wondered if the correlation between the composite ACT score and GPA were the same for high ACT students as for low ACT students. He found the correlation for all students ($N = 10,000$) to be .33 with a 95% confidence interval of .31 to .35. He divided the students into two groups of 5,000 each on the basis of their ACT scores. Then he recalculated the correlation between ACT and GPA for the low ACT group. He found that the correlation for the lower ACT group to be .19 (confidence interval: .16 to .22). He was ready to announce that the ACT predicts less well for low ACT students than for students in general because the confidence intervals do not overlap at all. He hesitated and asked you if that interpretation was correct. Explain what is wrong. (Hint: In Chapter 14, the effect of reducing the range of a variable was discussed.)

20. Use *g* to compare the *strength* of these two findings:
    Study A: Kevin conducted an experiment comparing the means of two, equal-sized groups. He was able to reject the null hypothesis, $t_{obs} (174) = 2.02, p < .05$.
    Study B: Sarah correlated two variables, $r = .153$, accounting for 2.3% of the variance. Her sample included 175 people.
    Which finding is stronger?

Answers to Odd-Numbered Problems

1. Correlations obtained from random samples of a population are estimates of the population parameter rho, ρ, which is the correlation that would be found if all members of the population were tested.

3. The standard error of correlations equals $1/\sqrt{(1/N - 3)}$. The larger the sample size, the smaller the standard error becomes.

5. (a) $Z_r = 0.6184$; $\sqrt{(1/[103 - 3])} = 0.10$; 95% confidence interval of Z_r is: $0.6184 +/- 1.96(0.10) = 0.422$ to 0.814. Converting back to r's, we have .398 to .672.
   (b) 95% confidence interval of Z_r is -0.003 to 0.389. For r, it is $-.003$ to $.371$.
   (c) 95% confidence interval of Z_r is -0.765 to -0.205. For r, it is $-.644$ to $-.202$.
   (d) 95% confidence interval of Z_r is 0.698 to 1.678. For r, it is $.603$ to $.932$.
   (e) 95% confidence interval of Z_r is 0.028 to 0.152. For r, it is $.028$ to $.151$.

7. At Acme, 95% confidence interval of Z_r is 0.204 to 0.596. For r, it is $.201$ to $.534$. At General, 95% confidence interval of Z_r is -0.051 to 0.477. For r, it is $-.05$ to $.44$. The confidence intervals almost completely overlap; although the correlations are quite different, there is nothing that needs to be explained. If the results were replicated with bigger samples, the psychologists would have something to think about. At this stage of the research, however, there is not enough evidence to conclude that the companies are different.

9.

	r	r^2	$2r = g$	g	Effect size label
(a)	.10	.010	.20	0.20	low
(b)	.39	.152	.78	0.84	large
(c)	−.68	.462	−1.36	−1.84	very large
(d)	.76	.578	1.52	2.32	very large
(e)	−.21	.044	−.42	−0.43	low-medium
(f)	−.33	.109	−.66	−0.69	medium-large

(Note how closely the $2r = g$ formula approximates the more accurate formula when the correlation is between $-.3$ and $+.3$.)

11. (a) There is considerable overlap between these 95% confidence intervals; not sufficient evidence that the correlations differ.
    (b) There is considerable overlap between these 95% confidence intervals; not sufficient evidence that the correlations differ.
    (c) The upper edge of one interval just equals the lower edge of the other interval; this is sufficient evidence to conclude that these two correlations differ from each other.

13. Someone who called $-.34$ "weak" has not been converting correlations into effect sizes; .34 is clearly a medium sized effect.

15. Bill has chosen one of his correlations, the largest one. If one selects the most extreme finding among several, the meaning of the confidence interval changes. The idea was that 95% confidence intervals include the true correlation of the population (assuming the sample was randomly selected from the population) in 95 out of 100 studies. If one picks an extreme finding (and $+.18$ was the largest correlation he found), he cannot use the 95% confidence interval. His best estimate would be his median correlation, $-.12$.

17. Inspect Robyn's data. All the values of X are 10 except for person D's 16. That score is the only reason why there is a correlation. One cannot draw conclusions on the basis of one score.

19. The admissions director has divided his sample into two groups on the basis of ACT scores. As soon as that is done, he should expect that this reduction of the range of ACT should lead to smaller correlations of ACT with any other variable for both groups. The confidence interval is small because the sample is huge (5,000). His second error is that he compared the correlation of a subgroup (after reducing the range of ACT) to the correlation of the whole 10,000. Minimally, he should have calculated the correlation for the students with the higher ACT scores as well. If he had, he would have found that correlation to be less than the original .33 as well. Then, he might have recognized his error.

Go to http://psychology.wadsworth.com/courses/statistics/ and test your knowledge of this chapter by taking the online quiz. Another resource to check is the online workshops that provide a step-by-step guide through a number of topics at http://psychology.wadsworth.com/workshops/workshops.html.

Estimating Confidence Using Null Hypothesis Significance Testing and Announcing Results

The main purpose of a significance test is to inhibit the natural enthusiasm of the investigator.

Mosteller & Bush (1954, pp. 331–332)

INTRODUCTION

Correlations between two variables are calculated from samples to estimate the correlations between the variables in populations. Correlations are affected by sampling error just as are sample means. Calculating a confidence interval for a correlation, r, reveals the precision of estimates made of the population correlation, ρ. Finding a confidence interval for a correlation closely parallels the calculation of a confidence interval for a mean. When working with sample means, the larger the sample, the more precisely we can estimate the population value, μ, and, thus, the smaller the confidence interval. Likewise, the larger the sample, the more accurate estimates of ρ are and, consequently, the more narrow the confidence interval for ρ. The second statistical tool used in analyzing data is effect size. Rules of thumb for evaluating the size of the correlations have been developed that parallel the rules developed for comparisons between two means. The third tool we have for understanding our findings is null hypothesis significance testing (NHST). This chapter shows how researchers define and test null hypotheses involving correlations. We start with some research situations in which the techniques for testing the statistical significance of correlations are needed.

Recall Sandra's research from the last chapter. She found a correlation of .40 between the authoritarian scores of 100 adolescent children and their biological parents and a correlation of .10 between the authoritarian scores of 25 adolescent children and their adoptive parents. All children were raised by the parents included in the two samples. Sandra applied the techniques of the last chapter and found the 95% confidence intervals for the correlations obtained from the two samples:

For children and biological parents: .22 to .55

For adoptive children and adoptive parents: −.31 to .48

Sandra noted that the confidence interval for the larger sample was more narrow than the confidence for the smaller sample. She also considered the magnitude of the correlations. She noted that the correlation, .40, for biologically related parents and children was between Cohen's medium and large categories for correlations. Although the effect size for the smaller sample was in the small category, it was still in the range of the effect sizes of published behavioral research. Using the techniques in the present chapter, Sandra can test whether the difference between these two correlations is statistically significant.

After he earned his bachelor's degree, Kuan obtained a position as a researcher with a community agency helping former prisoners to learn job skills. The 10-week training program helped the 48 participants to learn skills needed for any job, such as finding possible jobs, interviewing effectively, understanding the rights and responsibilities of an employee, and negotiating about on-the-job disagreements. At the end of the training period, the trainees completed a lengthy test and simulated job interview. The test was scored, and the quality of the job interview was rated. The trainees agreed to be contacted three months after the training program. He correlated the test scores and the ratings of the simulated interview with their hourly pay rate after three months. He wanted to learn if the test score and the ratings predicted the pay rate of the trainees. He found the correlation between the test and pay rate to be .27 and the correlation between interview rating and pay rate to be .35. Kuan wondered whether these correlations were large enough to be more than random variation.

NULL HYPOTHESES INVOLVING CORRELATION COEFFICIENTS

Although the formulas used with means as discussed in the previous chapters are different from those to be presented in this chapter, exactly the same strategy is followed. In summary, the strategy is as follows:

(1) Posit a null hypothesis describing the population.

(2) Estimate the sampling distribution of the statistic (in this case *r*) if the null hypothesis is true.

(3) Determine how probable it is that the obtained statistic (r_{obs}) would have been found in a sampling distribution based on the null hypothesis, and either:

    (a) Reject the null hypothesis if the probability is sufficiently low (usually .05 or lower), or

    (b) Do not reject the null hypothesis.

This chapter shows how to apply this strategy to deal with a number of questions about correlations.

TESTING WHETHER *r* IS DIFFERENT FROM .00

The most common inferential test involving correlations is to test whether an observed correlation is *different from zero*. As with null hypotheses used with means, null hypotheses used with correlations refer to populations. Formally, we would state the null hypothesis as H_0: $\rho_{xy} = .00$. This null hypothesis says that the correlation between two variables, *X* and *Y*, in the entire population is zero. The alternative hypothesis says that the correlation coefficient is something other than zero, it is stated as H_1: $\rho_{xy} \neq .00$. Given that we normally test null hypotheses for alpha equals .05, if zero is not within the 95% confidence interval, we can use a confidence interval to test the null hypothesis. Sandra can confidently report that the correlation between authoritarian scores for adolescents and their biological parents is larger than .00 because her 95% confidence interval does not include zero; it extends from .22 to .55. Using the confidence interval for the null hypothesis tells us that a correlation of .40 is unlikely to be found if ρ, the population value, were indeed .00. The use of the 95% confidence interval cannot tell us *how* improbable .40 is. Nor can we learn how likely it is that a replication would yield a statistically significant finding. To achieve these purposes, we must test the null hypothesis in a different way. The null hypothesis can be tested using a form of the ***t* test for correlations.**

This is the familiar *t*, but it is calculated in a different way. The formula is

$$t_{obs} = \frac{r - \rho}{\sqrt{[(1 - r^2)/(N - 2)]}}$$

          Equation 16.1

In this formula, *r* is the observed correlation, ρ is the population value hypothesized in the null hypothesis, and *N* is the number of people who have been observed on the two variables.

This formula employs the common statistical procedure of dividing the difference between a statistic, r, in this case,) and the value specified in the null hypothesis ($\rho = 0.0$) by the sampling error. Equation 16.1 does not use the r-to-Z_r transformation used in the calculation of the confidence interval; however, Equation 16.1 can be used *only* when the null hypothesis is $\rho = .00$. When a population correlation equals .00, the correlations found from random samples from the population are distributed as a t with a sampling error of $\sqrt{[(1 - r^2)/(N - 2)]}$. As with all null hypothesis significance tests, we calculate how likely it would be to obtain our observation (or an observation even more different from .00) if the null hypothesis were true. In other words, we ask: How probable is it that r_{obs} is different from .00 just due to random sampling error? When that probability is very small, we reject the null hypothesis.

For Sandra's sample of children and their biological parents, her statistical significance test would be as follows:

$$t_{obs} = \frac{.40 - .00}{\sqrt{[(1 - .40^2)/(100 - 2)]}} = .40/.0926 = 4.320$$

The degrees of freedom for this t_{obs} (as well as for a correlation) equal N minus 2.

Sandra's sample size was 100; thus, her degrees of freedom equal 98. Most t tables will not include 98, so we use the *largest* value for df in the table that is *smaller* than the degrees of freedom we have. This is the same conservative procedure as you have followed for t and F in previous chapters; we follow this practice because using a critical value associated with greater degrees of freedom would increase the probability of Type I errors. In this case, we would use the critical values for 60 degrees of freedom. For a **nondirectional test for ρ,** the value of t_{crit} with 60 degrees of freedom from Table A.2 is ± 2.000 for the .05 level. The value Sandra found permits her to reject the null hypothesis, $\rho < .05$. However, she can say more because, for 60 degrees of freedom, the t_{obs} of 4.320 exceeds *all* of the t_{crit} values in Table A.2. Look at the row of t_{crit} values for 60 degrees of freedom for nondirectional hypotheses. We can reject the null hypothesis at a probability of p less than .001 because the observed value exceeds the critical value from the table of $+3.460$. The way to announce results of this hypothesis test is as follows:

> The correlation between the authoritarianism scores of 100 biological parents and their adolescent children (who were raised by their biological parents) was positive, $r(98) = .40, p < .001$.

(Although Sandra was able to use the t for 60 degrees of freedom, if she had wanted the approximate value for a t for 98 degrees of freedom she would have needed to interpolate. A review of interpolation is given in Box 16.1.)

If you wondered whether the t_{obs} of 4.320 is even less improbable than .001, you would be correct. When correlations are calculated using a computer program, the test of the null hypothesis test is carried out along with the calculation of r. If Sandra had used a computer program to calculate the correlation, she might have found the exact probability to be .00003. Many programs round such a probability to .000. Of course, the probability might be very small, but it will never be 0. Recall that, if .000 is given, we would report $p \le .0005$ because the computer program would have rounded anything larger than .0005 to .001.

The reason to test the null hypothesis even after noticing that .00 was not included in the 95% confidence interval is to learn how improbable it would be to observe an r of .40 or larger in a population in which ρ was .00. The t has told Sandra that it is quite improbable. Next, Sandra can use Figure 10.1 to estimate the probability that an exact replication would be statistically significant. She would locate the probability from using the t test, .001, on the x axis of Figure 10.1, then she would use the curve to learn what value on the y axis

BOX 16.1 ■ Review of Interpolation

Problem: a critical *t* for 98 degrees of freedom does not appear in the table. Here is the critical *t* for the entries with fewer degrees of freedom and with more degrees of freedom.

For 60 degrees of freedom, t_{crit} ($p = .001$) is 3.460.

For 120 degrees of freedom, t_{crit} ($p = .001$) is 3.373.

What is the approximate critical *t* for 98 degrees of freedom? It must be smaller than 3.460, but larger than 3.373.

$$\left(\frac{98 - 60}{120 - 60}\right)(3.460 - 3.373) = 0.055$$

Critical *t* for 98 degrees of freedom is $3.460 - 0.055 = 3.405$.

We would only interpolate if observed *t* had exceeded the value of critical *t* for 120 degrees of freedom, but had not exceeded the value of critical *t* for 60 degrees of freedom. In Sandra's situation, her observed *t* (4.320) exceeded both values of critical *t*, so there would have been no reason to worry about interpolation.

corresponds to a probability level of .001 in the initial study. She would find that the probability of exact replications being statistically significant ($\rho \le .05$) is greater than .92. In other words, of the studies that were statistically significant at less than the .001 level, more than 92% of their exact replications can be expected to be statistically significant at the .05 level. Thus, Sandra can be quite confident that she would find a statistically significant positive correlation if she were to replicate her study with another sample of the same size from the same population of adolescents and their biological parents.

Be sure to note the conditions given in the previous sentence. To be confident about the findings of a replication, it would be necessary to sample 100 adolescents and their parents from the same population as she used to find the first correlation. If the population from which a replication sample is taken differs, for example, in location, nationality, race, or income from the original population studied, she cannot be quite so sure. *Generalizing conclusions based on tests of null hypotheses involving correlations are subject to the same limitations as all other tests of null hypotheses.*

YOUR TURN 16-1

Test the correlation of Sandra's second sample against the null hypothesis of $\rho = .00$. The critical *t* table, Table A.2, permits one to test the statistical significance of t_{obs}. ■

To report a failure to reject a null hypothesis, follow this model taken from a hypothetical example in a previous chapter:

The correlation between height and vertical jump among 17 faculty members was .36; the null hypothesis that the population correlation was zero could not be rejected, $t(15) = 1.61$, $p > .10$.

We are going to repeat a point we have made several times before: not rejecting the null hypothesis does not mean that we have proved the null hypothesis. In fact, it seems quite likely that taller people in general can jump higher than shorter people. Our failure to reject the null hypothesis in our light-hearted, hypothetical study of faculty members is probably a Type II error. What are some of the reasons that might suggest a Type II error in this situation? First, the sample size is too small ($N = 17$) to provide a powerful statistical test. Second, there was no attempt to control for age; it is very likely that younger faculty members could jump higher than older faculty members of the same height. That is, the height of a jump is probably negatively correlated with age and weight. *When we fail to reject the null hypothesis, we should suspend judgment.* If researchers talk as though they have discovered that there is no relationship between two variables when the *only* evidence they have is that they were unable to reject a null hypothesis, they are making a mistake.

TESTING WHETHER *r* IS GREATER THAN .00

We can test whether r is greater than .00 using an approach that is very similar to the approach we just used for a nondirectional test. If the researcher was interested only in testing whether an observed correlation was *greater than zero,* the null and alternative hypotheses are stated differently and one-tailed t values are used as the critical values. The null hypothesis being tested and the alternative hypothesis are as follows:

H_0: $\rho \leq .00$

H_1: $\rho > .00$

The null hypothesis states that the correlation is less than or equal to zero. The directional alternative hypothesis states that the correlation is greater than zero.

Suppose that a correlation of .28 is found between the scores on the Graduate Record Examination (GRE) in psychology and the grades of 45 students in a master's program in psychology. We begin with the expectation that such scores are positively correlated with grades in a psychology program; the higher the GRE, the higher the expected grades. It is very hard to imagine how the correlation could be negative; a negative correlation would mean that higher psychology GRE scores are associated with lower graduate school grades. To test the statistical significance of this correlation we would use a **directional hypothesis for ρ**. We would calculate the t_{obs} just as before:

$$t_{obs} = \frac{.28}{\sqrt{[(1 - .28^2)/(45 - 2)]}} = 1.913$$

We compare this t with a critical value of t. Table A.2 does not include a t for 43 degrees of freedom. The conservative alternative is to use the value of t for the largest value of degrees of freedom in the table that is *less than* the degrees of freedom of the t we have. We should use 40; the critical values of t for 40 degrees of freedom using a directional null hypothesis are 1.303 ($p = .10$), 1.684 ($p = .05$), 2.021 ($p = .025$), and 2.423 ($p = .01$). Because 1.913 exceeds 1.684, we may reject the null hypothesis at the $p < .05$ level. We could announce this finding as follows:

The correlation between the GRE Psychology score and grades in the master's program was positive ($r = .28$) and statistically significant, $t(43) = 1.91$, $p < .05$, one-tailed.

If the correlation had been calculated using a computer, one could report an exact probability; the exact probability of this t with 43 degrees of freedom using a one-tailed (or directional) test is .031.

For a correlation of .28 with 43 degrees of freedom, one would not be able to reject a nondirectional null hypothesis. The phrasing of the null and alternative hypotheses makes a difference in being able to reject or not reject the null hypothesis in some studies because, for a given probability, the critical values for two-tailed t's are always larger. For 40 degrees of freedom, the two-tailed t_{crit} is 2.021. Our 1.913 does not exceed 2.021; consequently, if we had used a two-tailed null hypothesis, we would not have been able to reject the null hypothesis. But don't forget: we do *not* decide whether we will perform a directional or nondirectional test *after* looking at the data. *Making a directional hypothesis means that, even before gathering the data, one would be absolutely uninterested in a correlation with a sign opposite to what was hypothesized.*

FIGURE 16.1 ■ Applying nondirectional and directional alternative null hypotheses to statistical significance testing for positive and negative correlations. Take special note of the statement of the hypotheses and the criteria for rejecting H_0.

	Positive Correlations	Negative Correlations
Nondirectional alternative null hypothesis	H_0: ρ = .00 H_1: $\rho \neq$ .00 $r = +.43$ $N = 32$ $t_{obs} = \dfrac{r - \rho}{\sqrt{[(1 - r^2)/(N - 2)]}} =$ $\dfrac{.43 - .00}{\sqrt{[(1 - .43^2)/(32 - 2)]}} = 2.609$ Reject H_0 if $t_{obs} \geq t_{crit}$ **OR** if $t_{obs} \leq$ the negative value of t_{crit} for $df = 30$, $\alpha = .05$ (or lower), two-tailed. t_{crit} (30) = ± 2.042 ($\alpha = .05$) t_{crit} (30) = ± 2.457 ($\alpha = .01$) Reject H_0 at $p < .01$	H_0: ρ = .00 H_1: $\rho \neq$ .00 $r = -.41$ $N = 29$ $t_{obs} = \dfrac{r - \rho}{\sqrt{[(1 - r^2)/(N - 2)]}} =$ $\dfrac{-.41 - .00}{\sqrt{[(1 - [-.41]^2)/(29 - 2)]}} = -2.336$ Reject H_0 if $t_{obs} \geq t_{crit}$ **OR** if $t_{obs} \leq$ the negative value of t_{crit} for $df = 27$, $\alpha = .05$ (or lower), two-tailed. t_{crit} (27) = ± 2.052 ($\alpha = .05$) t_{crit} (27) = ± 2.473 ($\alpha = .01$) Reject H_0 at $p < .05$
Directional alternative null hypothesis	H_0: $\rho \leq$ .00 H_1: $\rho >$ .00 $r = +.48$ $N = 52$ $t_{obs} = \dfrac{r - \rho}{\sqrt{[(1 - r^2)/(N - 2)]}} =$ $\dfrac{.48 - .00}{\sqrt{[(1 - .48^2)/(52 - 2)]}} = +4.312$ Reject H_0 if $t_{obs} \geq t_{crit}$ for $df = 50$, $\alpha = .05$ (or lower), one-tailed. t_{crit} (40) = 1.684 ($\alpha = .05$) t_{crit} (40) = 3.307 ($\alpha = .001$) Reject H_0 at $p < .001$	H_0: $\rho \geq$ .00 H_1: $\rho <$ .00 $r = -.37$ $N = 74$ $t_{obs} = \dfrac{r - \rho}{\sqrt{[(1 - r^2)/(N - 2)]}} =$ $\dfrac{.37 - .00}{\sqrt{[(1 - [-.37]^2)/(74 - 2)]}} = -3.426$ Reject H_0 if $t_{obs} \leq$ the *negative* of t_{crit} for $df = 72$, $\alpha = .05$ (or lower), one-tailed. t_{crit} (60) = − 1.671 ($\alpha = .05$) t_{crit} (60) = − 3.232 ($\alpha = .001$) Reject H_0 at $p < .001$

The examples we have been presenting refer to positive correlations, but the same procedures can be used with negative correlations. In that case, the null and alternative hypotheses would be

H_0: $\rho \geq .00$

H_1: $\rho < .00$

The null hypothesis states that the correlation is greater than or equal to zero, and the alternative hypothesis states that the correlation is less than zero (that is, negative). Figure 16.1 contains a summary of the use of nondirectional and directional null hypotheses with both positive and negative correlations.

USING A TABLE INSTEAD OF THE *t* FORMULA

Testing whether a correlation is different from zero or greater than zero is the easiest procedure presented in this text. This is so because the test can be performed without actually calculating t_{obs}. Critical values of *r* corresponding to critical values of *t* can be calculated and placed into a table. Thus, the intermediate step of calculating a *t* might not be necessary. It is possible to make such a table because correlations have a limited and known range, -1.00 through $+1.00$, regardless of the variables used. Critical *r*'s that have been calculated for various sample sizes are given in the appendix (Table A.5). Table A.5 provides the values of *r* needed to reject both one- and two-tailed hypotheses for a range of degrees of freedom. For a sample of 92 (*df* = 90), the critical values of *r* for a directional null hypothesis are .173 (*p* = .05), .205 (*p* = .025), .242 (*p* = .01), and .267 (*p* = .005). If a calculated correlation (r_{obs}) exceeds any of these values, the null hypothesis may be rejected and the probability is reported as less than the probability given in the table. For example, if a correlation expected to be positive was found to be $+.25$ among data gathered from 92 people, one can reject the null hypothesis at the $p < .01$ (directional or one-tailed test) level because .25 exceeds .2422 (the value in Table A.5 for $p < .01$).

If one uses the Critical *r* Table, the results of the test of the null hypothesis would be reported as follows:

The correlation between X and Y was found to be positive and statistically significant, $r(90) = .25, p < .01$, one-tailed.

This description of findings is phrased in exactly the same way as when the *t* was used to test a null hypothesis involving a correlation. To repeat a point from before, if the correlation were found using a computer program, the exact probability would be given. Whenever the exact probability is available, it should be reported. For a correlation of $+.25$ (*df* = 90), the exact probability is .008 (for a one-tailed alternative hypothesis).

YOUR TURN 16-2

Suppose that during your internship you are told that a test of attitudes toward drug use predicts success in a rehabilitation program. When you ask what the correlation is, you learn that the correlation is .39 calculated from 20 program participants. Use Table A.5 to determine whether the correlation was statistically significant. ∎

TESTING WHETHER *r* DIFFERS FROM A KNOWN ρ

One can also test whether an *r* differs from a specified value other than .00. This initially appears a little more complicated than using the null hypothesis of ρ equals .00, but don't panic: this test simply uses the *r*-to-Z_r transformation we used in calculating the confidence intervals of correlations. Suppose that the correlation of .50 between two variables was found in a representative sample that was so large that it can be treated as a population. It might be of interest to test whether the correlation between these two variables among people living in a particular community was different from the value found in the population. In this case, the null and alternative hypotheses would be stated as

H_0: ρ = .50

H_1: ρ ≠ .50

As with all tests of null hypotheses, we ask what the sampling distribution of scores would be if the null were true. We set the rejection regions in relation to that theoretical sampling distribution. Then, we calculate where in that distribution the observed value is located. Last, we ask whether its location suggests that the observed value could well be from the distribution based on the null hypothesis or whether it is so extreme that the null can be rejected. Because the distribution of *r*'s is not normal when ρ does not equal .00, one cannot use the *t* formula (Equation 16.1). Instead, we use the *r*-to-Z_r transformation and the sampling error of Z_r to calculate a (lowercase) z.

This approach is simply an application of the general approach for testing null hypotheses that we have been using for testing null hypotheses about means and correlations; it can be summarized in this formula:

Observed value of a statistic (*M* or *r*) minus the population value
in the null hypothesis (μ or ρ)

Standard error of the statistic if the null hypothesis were true

This approach locates the observed value in the sampling distribution that we would expect if the null hypothesis were true. When testing an *r* against a specific value of ρ (rather than against .00), we need to use the *r*-to-Z_r transformation to find the sampling distribution of *r* when the population value, ρ, is the value given in the null hypothesis. To test whether an *r* is different from a specified population value, the formula is used as follows:

$$z = \frac{Z_r - Z_\rho}{\sqrt{1/(N-3)}}$$

Equation 16.2

The observed *r* and the specified population value are converted into Z_r values, and the difference between them is found. This difference is then divided by the sampling error of Z_r. The probability of the resulting z can be found using Table A.1, the standard normal table. An example will show that carrying out this test is not hard. Suppose we observe a correlation of .30 based on 134 people and wish to test whether it is different from a population value of .50. Follow these steps.

(1) Make the *r*-to-Z_r transformations.

ρ = .50; $Z_{r=.50}$ = 0.5493

r = .30; $Z_{r=.30}$ = 0.3095

(2) Substitute into Equation 16.2.

$$\frac{0.3095 - 0.5493}{\sqrt{1/(134 - 3)}} = -2.744 = z$$

(3) Estimate the probability of observing $r = .30$ by looking up the probability of z. The area under the normal curve cut off by a z of -2.744 or smaller (i.e., more extreme) is .0031. Because this was a nondirectional test, we need the area beyond z of $+2.744$ also; the probability associated with a nondirectional is, thus, .0062.

(4) Announce the findings. The difference between the correlation of X and Y, $r(132) = .30$, and the population correlation ($\rho = .50$) is statistically significant, $z = -2.744$, $p = .006$, nondirectional test.

Figure 16.2 on page 400 contains an additional example, a summary of the conceptual steps, and a reminder that drawing the sampling distribution is often helpful in understanding the meaning of the formula.

Follow the procedures just listed and those in Figure 16.2 to test whether the correlation between standard test scores and freshman grades for students choosing a particular major is different from the correlation for the entire freshman class (that is, the population). The correlation in the entire class is .35, and the correlation for the 45 students selecting the particular major is .27. (By the way, there is a possible problem with the research plan. What should the researcher verify before drawing conclusions from this NHST?)   ■

A slight alteration of the procedure just described can be used for directional alternative hypotheses. A directional alternative hypothesis would be used if one wanted to learn whether an *r exceeds* a particular value, perhaps a value from test norms based on a very large number of people. One might want to do this, for example, if it is necessary for an industrial psychologist to show that a revised job selection test correlates more strongly with a dependent variable of interest (such as, success in a job) than an older test does. A directional test would be appropriate because the question is whether the new test is *more predictive* than the old test, not whether the correlation of the new test is different from the correlation of the old test. Clearly, a firm would not adopt a new selection test if it correlated less strongly with success on the job than the old one did. Thus, the alternative hypothesis is directional. Assume that the norms say that the correlation of the older test with job success is .30. The correlation given in the norms is treated as the population value. In this case we would state the null and alternative hypotheses as

$H_0: \rho \leq .30$

$H_1: \rho > .30$

Suppose that the observed r between the scores on the new test and a measure of success on the job was .56 for 83 employees.

$$z = \frac{Z_{r = .56} - Z_{r = .30}}{\sqrt{(1/(N - 3))}} = \frac{0.6328 - 0.3095}{\sqrt{(1/(83 - 3))}} = \frac{0.3233}{0.1118} = 2.892$$

To find the probability of this z, we simply find the z in Table A.1. The table shows that a z of 2.89 divides the most extreme .0019 from the rest of the distribution. In other words,

FIGURE 16.2 ■ **Testing whether *r* is different from a known population value.**

	Conceptual statement	Example
1	The null hypothesis is that ρ equals .30. We will test it with a non-directional alternative hypothesis.	H_0: ρ = .30 H_1: ρ ≠ .30
2	Suppose that *r* among 52 people is found to be .42. If the null hypothesis is true, how likely is it to have observed the correlation found in the data?	If ρ equaled .30, how likely is it to observe an *r* of .42?
3	The sampling distribution of r is not normal when ρ does not equal .00; however, the sampling distribution of Z_r is close to normal. Thus it is necessary to convert ρ to Z_r and convert r to Z_r.	If ρ = .30; $Z_{r=.30}$ = 0.3095 r = .42; $Z_{r=.42}$ = 0.4477
4	Sketch the sampling distribution.	$Z_{r=.42}$ = 0.4477 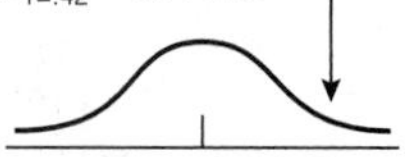 $Z_{r=.30}$ = 0.3095
5	Calculate the (lower case) z for a correlation of .42 in the sampling distribution centered around ρ for ρ equals .30.	$\dfrac{Z_{r=.42} - Z_{r=.30}}{\sqrt{1(N-3)}} = \dfrac{0.4477 - 0.3095}{\sqrt{1(52-3)}} =$ 0.967 = z
6	Use the Standard Normal Table (the z table) to learn how likely it is that a correlation of .42 would be observed if ρ equaled .30.	The area under the normal curve cut off by a z of 0.967 or larger (i.e., more extreme) is .165. Since we used a non-directional test (i.e. we would have been just as interested if *r* had been bigger or smaller than .30), we need to double that area, .310.
7	Decide whether to reject the null hypothesis or to fail to reject it.	Since .310 is larger than .05, we cannot reject the null hypothesis.
8	Announce the findings.	The difference between the correlation of *X* and *Y*, r(50) = .42, and the population correlation (ρ = .30) is not statistically significant, z = 0.967, p = .310.

the probability of a *z* of 2.89 or higher is .0019. We would announce the finding in this way:

> The correlation of the newer selection test with job performance was .56 (*N* = 83). This correlation exceeds the correlation of the older selection test (ρ = .30), z = 2.89, *p* = .002, directional test.

Figure 10.1 permits us to estimate the probability that replications of studies with this probability level would be statistically significant ($p \leq .05$) 85% of the time.

TESTING WHETHER TWO INDEPENDENT CORRELATIONS DIFFER FROM EACH OTHER

Suppose that you have been hired as a research assistant at a large state university. As part of your responsibilities, you are to check on the degree to which entrance tests correlate with first-year grades. Because some members of the state legislature question the relevance of standard tests such as the SAT, the admissions director wants to have up-to-date correlations between the variables used to make admission decisions and grades earned by students in the first term after admission. Because the courses taken by different majors require different skills, the director asked you to compare engineering students and humanities students in terms of how well first-term grades can be predicted from SAT scores. As part of this assignment you have been given the following correlations between SAT mathematical scores and first-term grades:

	r	n
Engineering majors	.34	859
Humanities majors	.23	491

The question is whether the correlation of the SAT mathematical (SAT-M) score with grades for engineering students differs from the correlation of SAT-M with grades for humanities majors. The admissions director would have been interested regardless of which correlation is higher, so you should conduct a two-tailed null hypothesis test. The hypotheses would be written as

H_0: $\rho_{\text{gpa, SAT-M-eng}} = \rho_{\text{gpa, SAT-M-hum}}$

H_1: $\rho_{\text{gpa, SAT-M-eng}} \neq \rho_{\text{gpa, SAT-M-hum}}$

To test the null hypothesis, we use the **z test of the difference between two independent correlations**:

$$z = \frac{Z_{r-\text{eng}} - Z_{r-\text{hum}}}{\sqrt{[1/(n_{\text{eng}} - 3) + 1/(n_{\text{hum}} - 3)]}}$$ Equation 16.3

The first step is to transform each correlation into Z_r using Table A.4. For example, .34 becomes 0.3541. Substituting into Equation 16.3, we have

$$z = \frac{0.3541 - 0.2342}{\sqrt{[1/(859 - 3) + 1/(491 - 3)]}} = \frac{0.199}{0.0567} = 3.51$$

Because this was to be a nondirectional test, the z could be statistically significant if it were large and positive or large and negative. In other words, there are two null hypothesis rejection regions. To test at the .05 level using a nondirectional test, these rejection regions are the areas under the normal curve containing the most extreme 2.5% of the scores in either of the two tails. Table A.1 shows that a z equal to 1.96 divides the most extreme 2.5% of the scores from the rest of the distribution. Because the normal curve is symmetrical, ± 1.96 are the critical values to use for a two-tailed statistical significance test. That is, if the null hypothesis were true, 5% (2.5% plus 2.5%) of the time, the values of z from Equation 16.3 would be greater than $+1.96$ *or* smaller than -1.96. The observed z is more extreme than the critical z; thus, we can reject the null hypothesis: $p < .05$.

As in the previous example, finding the exact probability requires finding the largest z in Table A.1 that the calculated z exceeds; there is an entry for 3.50 corresponding to a proportion in the tail of .0002. Because a nondirectional hypothesis was used, we would have rejected the null hypothesis regardless of which of the two rejection regions contained the calculated z. To reflect the nondirectional alternative hypothesis, the probability given in Table A.1 is doubled. The exact probability is, therefore, less than .0004. Because we are following the convention of reporting probability values to three decimal places, we convert .0004 to "less than .001." To announce this finding one could write:

> The difference between the correlation of SAT-M with first-term grades for 859 engineering students, $r = .34$, and the correlation observed for 491 humanities majors, $r = .23$, was statistically significant, $z = 3.51$, $p < .001$, nondirectional test.

Suppose that the admissions director also provided the correlations between SAT verbal (SAT-V) and first-term grades for the same two groups of students.

	r	n
Engineering majors	.29	859
Humanities majors	.31	491

Do these correlations differ from each other to a statistically significantly extent? ∎

PULLING IT ALL TOGETHER

Two tools of statistical analyses—confidence intervals and effect sizes—were applied to correlations in Chapter 15. The present chapter demonstrated the use of the third tool, testing null hypotheses involving correlations. Although the data being analyzed consist of two continuous variables rather than the one continuous variable obtained from two or more samples, we emphasized that there are conceptual parallels to the analyses of both types of data. No new concepts were introduced in this chapter.

At this point, we want to illustrate how we apply these correlational techniques to test a theoretical question in an experimental context. This illustration requires close reading; however, we think that it is worth the effort because it serves as a review of independent sample t tests, confidence intervals of correlations, effect sizes, as well as null hypothesis testing using correlations.

For his honors project, Jurgen decided to test an implication of Eysenck's theory about the extraversion-introversion dimension of personality. Eysenck suggests that the more introverted people are, the more they react to negative information from their environment (Funder, 2001). Jurgen gave the 200 students a set of personality measures including an introversion-extraversion scale. It was scored so that higher scores indicated greater introversion. For example, higher scores meant that people were more likely to report they were described by statements such as the following:

I would prefer to have a quiet conversation with one person than to attend a lively party.

Those with lower scores were people who reported that statements such as the previous one did *not* describe them, but that statements such as the following *did* describe them:

I take the initiative in making new friendships.

After completing the personality test, the students learned that they were individually to rate the quality of a set of educational video programs. Suppose that Jurgen randomly assigned 200 students to one of two groups. One set of programs, on illnesses, was chosen because these programs were rather threatening and caused many viewers to become somewhat anxious. The other set was on career development and seemed to be boring. Jurgen was not actually interested in the quality ratings; he had students make the ratings so that they would pay attention to the information that the videos contained. The ratings of quality were not relevant to the theory being tested. After viewing the programs and completing their quality ratings, the students answered several questionnaires including a standard mood survey to measure how anxious the students felt at that time. A summary of his design and his procedures is contained in Figure 16.3.

Jurgen hypothesized that there would be a positive correlation between introversion and anxiety scores among those who viewed and rated the illness videos because those videos

FIGURE 16.3 ■ A summary of Jurgen's design and procedure.

1. Students complete a personality test.

2. Students are randomly assigned to rate one of two sets of video programs.

3. Students view one of two sets of video programs and rate quality.

4. Students take a mood test to detect the effect of the programs (if any) on their current level of anxiety.

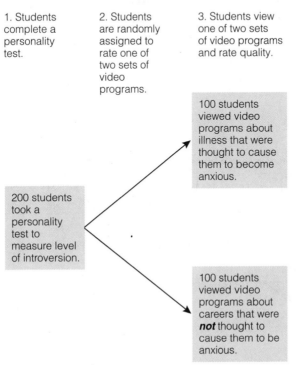

200 students took a personality test to measure level of introversion.

100 students viewed video programs about illness that were thought to cause them to become anxious.

100 students viewed video programs about careers that were **not** thought to cause them to be anxious.

contained threatening information. He made this hypothesis on the basis of Eysenck's theory, which predicts that introverts would be more influenced by negative experiences than extraverts would be. Thus, the more introverted a student was, the more likely the illness-related videos were expected to put him or her into an anxious mood. In contrast, Jurgen expected to find approximately a zero correlation among those who rated the career tapes because he believed that typically there is no correlation between introversion and anxiety in the absence of negative experiences.

The first step in an analysis based on the I-D-E-A model, *inspection,* is taken to be sure that the data have been coded correctly and that the distributions are relatively normal. The quickest way to check on distributions is by making stem-and-leaf plots of introversion and anxiety for both samples. Figure 16.4 contains plots for introversion and anxiety for both

FIGURE 16.4 ■ The stem-and-leaf plots of introversion show that the groups were equivalent on introversion before viewing any videos. Further there were no outliers or floor or ceiling effects. The stem-and-leaf plots of anxiety show that those who watched the illness videos were on the average in more anxious moods after viewing the videos compared to those who viewed the career videos. Again no outliers or floor or ceiling effects were found.

Scores on the Introversion Measure

Career videos group (n = 100)

Frequency	Stem	Leaf
1	2 .	5
7	3 *	1222344
7	3 .	5678899
16	4 *	0001111222223344
23	4 .	56666666777777778888899
19	5 *	0000001111233344444
12	5 .	566777778999
10	6 *	0000022334
4	6 .	5556
1	7 *	2

Illness videos group (n = 100)

Frequency	Stem	Leaf
2	2 .	99
2	3 *	34
13	3 .	5666777889999
10	4 *	0000133334
22	4 .	5555556666677788888999
20	5 *	00011112222233344444
16	5 .	5555666777889999
11	6 *	01123333444
2	6 .	78
2	7 *	01

Scores on the Measurement of Anxiety *After* Viewing the Videos

Career videos group (n = 100)

Frequency	Stem	Leaf
1	0 *	4
2	0 .	59
10	1 *	0123344555
10	1 .	6666679999
23	2 *	00001112233333334444444
31	2 .	5555566677777777788888888999999
16	3 *	0000011112222244
6	3 .	588889
0	4 *	
1	4 .	5

Illness videos group (n = 100)

Frequency	Stem	Leaf
2	1 *	03
8	1 .	55556779
15	2 *	000002222223344
18	2 .	566666666777888889
18	3 *	000001112222233344
14	3 .	55556678888899
14	4 *	00001112222344
9	4 .	556677888
1	5 *	3
1	5 .	6

groups. Those four plots looked acceptable with roughly normal distributions showing no outliers and no ceiling or floor effects. Second, it would be important to be sure that the scatterplots of the variables to be correlated did not show two-dimensional outliers. Such outliers, as mentioned in Chapter 14, are not detectable when examining one variable at a time. Figure 16.5 displays these scatterplots. A positive correlation between introversion and anxiety is evident in the plot for those who viewed illness videos, whereas the plot for those who viewed the career videos showed no obvious correlation. Furthermore, neither of the

FIGURE 16.5 ■ Scatterplots of both groups in the experiment on introversion and anxiety. No two-variable outliers were revealed.

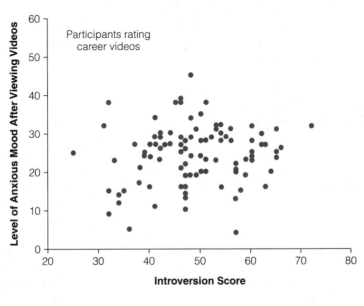

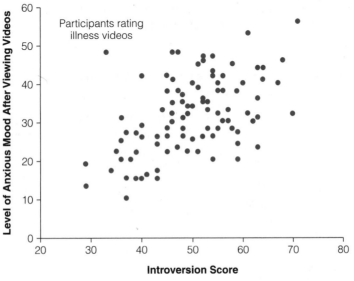

scatterplots shows any hint of a nonlinear relationship between anxiety and introversion nor two-dimensional outliers.

Next, Jurgen turned to the *description* phase of his analysis. First, if the random assignment procedure was effective, the mean introversion scores should be nearly equal for the two groups. Table 16.1 includes the means and standard deviations for both samples. The table shows that the means of introversion for the two groups were similar. This pattern was as expected because the students were randomly assigned to one of the two groups. The 95% confidence intervals for introversion showed a great deal of overlap as shown in Table 16.2 and here:

Illness video group: 47.87 to 51.59

Career video group: 46.97 to 50.69

Usually researchers do not have an opportunity to show that a random assignment procedure was effective. In fact, researchers nearly always trust the random assignment procedure to produce equivalent groups. In Jurgen's experiment, he could check that the introversion levels were essentially equivalent.

Next, Jurgen should verify that the illness-related videos did increase the mean anxiety level among those students who viewed those videos. These means are included in Table 16.1. This step of the analysis shows that the videos affected the participants as hypothesized. Examining the level of anxiety for the two groups is called a *manipulation check*. If the group making the ratings of the illness videos had not shown a higher mean level of anxiety after making the ratings, the critical comparison of the two correlation coefficients could not be made because the experimental task would have failed to affect the students' anxiety levels.

The correlations between introversion and anxiety for both samples (those who rated the career videos and those who rated the illness videos) were found; these correlations were the focus of Jurgen's research. He found that the correlation of introversion and anxiety scores among the illness video group to be .521, but the correlation of introversion and anxiety scores among the career video group was .115. He noted that the relative sizes of the correlations supported his predictions. In other words, as the theory predicted, introversion scores were a good predictor of anxiety scores among students who watched the illness videos, but a much weaker predictor of anxiety among those who watched the career videos. These steps are part of the description phase of his analysis.

TABLE 16.1 ■ Means and Standard Deviations from Jurgen's Experiment on the Effect of Stress on Introverts Compared to Extraverts

	Group That Viewed Illness-Related Video Programs ($n = 100$)	Group That Viewed Career-Related Video Programs ($n = 100$)
Introversion		
Mean	49.73	48.83
Standard deviation	9.35	9.31
Level of Anxious Mood		
Mean	31.58	24.56
Standard deviation	9.88	7.50

TABLE 16.2 ■ Confidence Intervals for Introversion and Anxious Mood in the Experiment on the Effect of Stress on Anxiety as Related to Introversion and Extraversion of Participants

	Group That Viewed Illness-Related Video Programs ($n = 100$)	Group That Viewed Career-Related Video Programs ($n = 100$)
Introversion Confidence Intervals of Means	$M \pm t\,(s_{pooled}/\sqrt{n}) =$ $49.73 \pm 1.99\,(9.33/\sqrt{100}) =$ 47.87 to 51.59	$M \pm t\,(s_{pooled}/\sqrt{n}) =$ $48.83 \pm 1.99\,(9.33/\sqrt{100}) =$ 46.97 to 50.69
Anxiety Confidence Intervals of Means	$M \pm t\,(s_{pooled}/\sqrt{n}) =$ $31.58 \pm 1.99\,(8.77/\sqrt{100}) =$ 29.83 to 33.33	$M \pm t\,(s_{pooled}/\sqrt{n}) =$ $24.56 \pm 1.99(8.77/\sqrt{100}) =$ 22.81 to 26.31

The next step in the I-D-E-A model is to *estimate* population values. As he examined the correlations, he once again used the three statistical tools at his disposal: the confidence interval to estimate precision, an estimate of effect size, and a test of the appropriate null hypothesis. Figure 16.6 provides the results of these analyses for his two correlations. The confidence intervals remind us of the level of precision that samples of 100 provide. Correlations themselves can be considered measures of effect size because they are not affected by sample size. Cohen (1988) suggested that correlations of .50 and greater may be considered large, whereas those in the area of .10 may be considered small; he suggested that .30 can be considered a medium correlation. The correlation between introversion and anxiety for the illness video group is equivalent to a large effect size using Cohen's conventions. For those students who rated the career videos, the correlation of .115 is in the small range.

Jurgen also compared his correlations with the null hypothesis of a zero correlation. Because .00 lay outside the confidence interval for the group that rated illness videos, he can conclude that the null hypothesis can be rejected, but he needs to conduct the t test to learn how unlikely his correlation of .521 would be. For the illness video group, the alternative hypothesis would be that his observed correlation is greater than zero. The probability of observing a t as large as he found if the null hypothesis were true was less than .001. This would be the probability level reported. On the other hand, the correlation between introversion and anxiety for the career video group was small. The confidence interval included zero, so he knew that the null hypothesis could not be rejected. The t for the correlation of .115 with 98 degrees of freedom was also small with a probability greater than .20.

For the career video group, the alternative hypothesis would have been nondirectional because the correlation was not hypothesized to be positive or negative. Because Jurgen hypothesized that the correlation would be trivial for the career video sample, he, of course, had not wanted to reject the null hypothesis for that group. We have pointed out that failing to reject the null hypothesis is not equivalent to proving the null hypothesis true. In this case, however, Jurgen can show that (a) .00 is well within the confidence interval, (b) the effect size was small, and (c) Figure 10.1 shows that the probability of the t indicated that replications would be very unlikely to be statistically significant. When variables do not

FIGURE 16.6 ■ Summary of Jurgen's findings.

	Group that Viewed Illness-Related Video Programs	Group That Viewed Career-Related Video Programs
Correlation found between Introversion and Anxiety	$r = .521$	$r = .115$
r to Z_r transformation	0.578	0.116
95% Confidence Interval for Z_r	$Z_r \pm t[\sqrt{(1/(N-3))}]$ $0.578 \pm 1.99[\sqrt{(1/(100-3))}]$ 0.375 to 0.779	$Z_r \pm t[\sqrt{(1/(N-3))}]$ $0.116 \pm 1.99[\sqrt{(1/(100-3))}]$ −0.086 to +0.318
95% Confidence Interval for r	.36 to .65	−.09 to .31
Effect size category	Large (r is greater than .50)	Small (r is close to .10)
Test of null hypothesis for each sample $\rho = .00$	$t = \dfrac{r}{\sqrt{[(1-r^2)/(N-2)]}} = 6.043$	$t = \dfrac{r}{\sqrt{[(1-r^2)/(N-2)]}} = 1.146$
Alternative hypothesis	$\rho > .00$ (directional)	$\rho \neq .00$ (nondirectional)
Decision	Reject Null Hypothesis, $\rho < .001$ (directional test)	Do Not Reject Null Hypothesis, $\rho > .20$ (nondirectional test)
95% confidence interval for the *difference* between the two correlations	In terms of Z_r: $(0.577 - 0.116) \pm 1.96 (\sqrt{[1/(N-3) + 1/(N-3)]}) =$ $(0.577 - 0.116) \pm 1.96 (0.1436) = 0.180$ to 0.743 In terms of r: $+.18$ to $+.63$	
Test of null hypothesis: $\rho_{illness} \leq \rho_{career}$	$z = \dfrac{0.577 - 0.116}{\sqrt{[(1/(N-3) + (1/(N-3))]}} = \dfrac{0.461}{0.1436} = 3.21$	
Alternative hypothesis	$\rho_{illness} > \rho_{career}$ (directional)	
Decision	Reject Null Hypothesis $p = .0007$ (directional test), or $p < .001$	

concern life-and-death matters and g is very small, a nonsignificant t often permits us to conclude that the correlation is too small to be of interest. We hope that you are feeling confident in applying the three tools of statistical analysis and seeing how they complement each other.

The last step for Jurgen is to analyze the difference between the two correlations. *Although this is the central focus of the research, he did not immediately perform this test because the initial analyses were necessary to demonstrate that the randomization was adequate and that the illness video did lead to higher levels of anxiety.* The 95% confidence interval for the *difference* of the two correlations was .18 to .63. Because .00 is outside of the 95% confidence interval, the null hypothesis that the two correlations are equal can be rejected. He went on to use Equation 16.3 to find the exact probability for this statistical significance test. The alternative hypothesis was directional because the correlation between introversion and anxiety for the participants viewing the illness videos was hypothesized to exceed the correlation found among those viewing the career videos. As shown in Figure 16.6, the calculated z, 3.219, greatly exceeded the critical, directional z of 1.67. According to Table A.1, the probability of finding a z as large or larger than 3.219 is less than .0007. Following our convention of reporting the exact probabilities to three decimal places, Jurgen may report that the difference between the correlations was in the hypothesized direction, $p < .001$.

At this point, Jurgen is ready to complete the final step in the I-D-E-A model—*announcing*. A highly condensed version of what Jurgen could report to his research adviser would follow this pattern:

Preliminary Analyses

The distributions of introversion and anxiety were reasonably close to normal with no marked outliers. The random assignment procedure resulted in two groups with very similar introversion scores, M(illness) = 49.74 and M(career) = 48.83, $t(198) = 0.69$, $p = .491$ (nondirectional test). An examination of the means for both samples showed that the illness videos did lead to greater anxiety ($M = 31.58$) compared to the career videos ($M = 24.56$), $t(198) = 5.56$, $p < .001$, directional test). Because the illness videos led to higher levels of anxiety, it was concluded that the manipulation was effective in raising anxiety levels as planned.

Correlations Between Introversion and Anxiety

Among research participants watching illness videos. Introversion and anxiety were positively correlated for research participants who watched the illness-related videos: $r = .52$. The 95% confidence interval was .36 to .65. The correlation was equivalent to large correlations according to Cohen's (1988) criteria. The correlation was hypothesized to be positive, and the null hypothesis could be rejected, $t(98) = 6.04$, $p < .001$ (directional test).

Among research participants watching career videos. Introversion and anxiety were positively correlated for research participants who watched career-related videos, $r = .12$. The correlation is small according to Cohen's categories. The 95% confidence interval was −.08 to +.30. The confidence interval included .00. The null hypothesis could not be rejected: $t(98) = 1.15$, $p = .255$ (nondirectional test).

The difference between the two correlation coefficients for the two experimental conditions. The major hypothesis of this research was that the correlation between introversion and anxiety would be greater among those students watching videos that aroused anxiety compared to the group of students who watched fairly dull videos. The 95% confidence interval of the difference between the two correlations was .18 to .63. The null hypothesis that the correlations came from the same population was rejected, $z = 3.22$, $p < .001$ (directional test). For an analysis comparing two correlations, Cohen suggested that, when the difference between the Z_r values of the two correlation coefficients being compared equaled or exceeded 0.50, the effect size could be considered large. The difference between the two Z_r values in this case was 0.46, nearly a large effect. It appears that situations that cause worry affect people who are introverted more strongly than they do those who are extraverted in accordance with Eysenck's theory. When faced with material causing them to think about the possibility of becoming seriously ill, the level of a student's introversion score predicts how anxious the student becomes. On the other hand, when caused to think about nonthreatening topics, level of introversion does not permit one to predict level of anxiety.

This example was designed to illustrate using NHST with correlations. Further, the example shows how correlational analyses can be combined with experimentation (that is, random assignment to groups) to examine theoretical questions about personality. Jurgen could also use Figure 10.1 to learn that the probability that replications of findings with this initial statistical probability will be statistically significant ($p \leq .05$) is approximately .95.

WHAT YOU HAVE LEARNED AND THE NEXT STEP

This chapter shows how to apply NHST, our third statistical tool, to correlations. Tests of null hypotheses involving correlations utilize formulas that appear quite different from those used with means; however, we have demonstrated that the very same principles are being used.

- As with other statistical significance tests, when using NHST with r, the null and alternative hypotheses refer to the population values, in this case, ρ.

- The degrees of freedom for a correlation are the size of the sample minus two ($N - 2$).

- To test whether a correlation is different from zero, one can use a formula to calculate the t associated with an r. The t that is calculated is used in exactly the same way as the t is used when the analysis involves comparing two means. When the t_{obs} exceeds the t_{crit}, the null hypothesis can be rejected.

- To test whether a correlation is different from zero, one can also use a table of critical r's (Table A.5). If the observed r exceeds the critical value given for r, the null hypothesis may be rejected.

- When a researcher is interested in testing a hypothesis that ρ differs from a specific value, it is necessary to transform r into Z_r so that the sampling distribution will approximate a normal distribution.

- When the r-to-Z_r transformation is used, a z is calculated that can be compared with the standard normal table (Table A.1).

- The difference between two independent correlations can also be tested using the r-to-Z_r transformation.

- Just as with t tests, both nondirectional and directional statistical significance tests can be done when testing correlations.

- Recommended practice is to report exact probabilities whenever available; for example, $p = .023$ would be reported rather than simply $p < .05$.

- Finding that a correlation is statistically significant does not provide sufficient evidence to conclude that there is a causal relationship between the two variables.

Correlations provide information on the accuracy of predictions of a variable made on the basis of knowing the value of a second variable. Knowing that one variable provides information to predict the values of a second variable is one thing, but knowing how to make those predictions is quite another. The next chapter introduces the techniques that are used to convert knowledge of a relationship between two variables into specific predictions of the values of a second variable. Sophisticated versions of these techniques are used in basic and applied research in many fields.

Key Concepts

t test for correlations

nondirectional hypothesis
  for ρ

directional hypothesis for ρ

z test of the difference between
  two independent correlations

Answers to *Your Turn* Questions

16-1. The correlation for the adopted children is not statistically significant, $t(23) = 0.482, p > .10$ (nondirectional test). (The exact probability would be .634.)

16-2. A directional test makes sense here; it seems highly unlikely that believing in the benefits of being drug free would lead to rehabilitation failure. The critical values of *r* for 18 degrees of freedom are .3783 ($p = .05$) and .4438 ($p = .025$). Thus, we can reject the null hypothesis ($p < .05$) because .39 exceeds .3783, but not .4438. Believing in the benefits of being drug free predicts success in a drug rehabilitation program.

16-3. This question is presented as a nondirectional test. The calculation after converting to Z_r is $z = (0.277 - 0.365)/\sqrt{1/(45 - 3)} = -0.570$; the proportion under the normal curve beyond a *z* of 0.570 is .2843. This proportion should be doubled because this is a nondirectional test, .5686. Thus, the probability of the data given the null hypothesis is .569, and the null hypothesis cannot be rejected. The re-searcher should verify that the standard deviations of the 45 students in the major are similar to the standard deviations of the whole class. If these 45 students have smaller standard deviations compared to the whole class, selecting students in a particular major might restrict the range and produce a smaller correlation.

16-4. This is presented as a nondirectional test. After converting to Z_r, Equation 16.3 would be

$$z = \frac{(0.299 - 0.321)}{\sqrt{[1/(859 - 3) + 1/(491 - 3)]}} = -0.388$$

A *z* of 0.39 or greater occurs 34.83% of the time; a *z* of −0.39 or less occurs 34.83% of the time. So the probability of the difference or a greater difference under the null hypothesis is .3483 + .3483, or .6966, or $p = .697$. Clearly, we do not have the evidence to conclude that the difference in the predictive power of SAT-V is different for students in engineering compared to students in humanities majors.

Analyzing and Interpreting Data: Problems and Exercises

1. Why do we test for the statistical significance of correlations?

2. What are the null and alternative hypotheses when a researcher wants to test whether a correlation is positive, i.e., greater than zero?

3. What are the degrees of freedom for a correlation calculated from two variables measured on 35 people?

4. What preliminary step is necessary when testing a null hypothesis that does not refer to .00, but to some specific value such as .45?

5. Test the following correlations against a null hypothesis that the population correlation is .00. Use a nondirectional alternative hypothesis.
   (a) $r = .30, N = 62$
   (b) $r = -.38, N = 23$

(c) $r = .025, N = 12,005$

(d) $r = .82, N = 32$

6. Which of the tests in problem #5 would lead to the greatest probability of a Type I error?

7. Suppose that a human resource manager was checking on the degree to which several selection tests correlated positively with measures of success on the job. Test the null hypothesis for each job type. Because only positive correlations were expected (or would be useful), the alternative hypothesis was $\rho > .00$.

(a) Clerical positions: $r = .41, N = 53$

(b) Bookkeeping positions: $r = .28, N = 41$

(c) Lab assistants: $r = .38, N = 16$

(d) Custodial positions: $r = .15, N = 123$

8. Which of the tests in problem #7 would lead to the greatest probability of a Type II error?

9. As implied in problem #7, tests are often validated using data from current employees. These correlations represent applicants who were hired; no one who was not hired could have gotten a rating for "success on the job." What problem do human resource researchers have with validation data from *current* employees when the intention is to use the selection tests with *future* applicants?

10. Suppose that several correlations were found relating an experimental personality inventory with an older one. All of the correlations were intended to be positive because the new measures were supposed to measure the same personality characteristics as the old ones did. However, it is not sufficient that the correlations be merely positive. The test developer wanted the new tests to correlate strongly with the older tests. Suppose that the developer wanted to be sure that the correlations between the new tests and the old tests exceed .50. The research sample included 157 people who took both old and new tests. Half of them took the older tests first and the newer one second; the other half took them in the reverse order.

(a) For introversion: $r = .63, N = 157$

(b) For depression: $r = .82, N = 157$

(c) For altruism: $r = .71, N = 157$

(d) For ascendancy: $r = .55, N = 157$

For which of these four tests may the test developer conclude that correlations exceed .50 to a statistically significant degree?

11. Use Equation 16.1 to verify these critical values in Table A.5.

(a) For a sample of 72 ($df = 70$), Table A.5 lists .2319 as the critical value for r in a nondirectional test at $p = .05$. Verify that .2319 is correct.

(b) For a sample of 32 ($df = 30$), Table A.5 lists .2960 as the critical value for r in a directional test at $p = .05$. Verify that .2960 is correct.

12. The alumni office of a college conducted a study of satisfaction with the college experience. The director asked for a correlation between GPA and satisfaction with attending the college. A student intern provided the director with two correlations: one from a random sample of 200 seniors and one for all the 64 seniors in honors sections. The intern and the director were not surprised that the correlation was positive, .41, among the random sample of seniors, but they were puzzled about the low correlation, .063, among the honors students.

(a) Calculate the 95% confidence intervals for both correlations.

(b) Test each correlation against a null hypothesis that ρ equals .00 using nondirectional tests.

(c) Test the null hypothesis that the correlations of the two populations are equal.

(d) Develop at least one interpretation of the data. What data would the intern need that would permit checking on the validity of the interpretation you suggest to explain the difference between the correlations for the seniors and the honors students?

13. Two psychologists (Schroeder & Dugal, 1995) wondered how materialism (a concern to have many possessions) was related to other personality characteristics. They measured materialism and envy (for the possessions and income of others), among 63 undergraduates along with a number of personality measures. The correlation between the measure of materialism and the measure of envy was .69.

(a) Find the confidence interval for their correlation

(b) Test the correlation's statistical significance.

(c) Would this finding permit the psychologists to conclude that materialism causes envy? Explain.

14. Some people carefully conform to social norms whereas others seek to be unique by flaunting social conventions. For a sample of American college students ($N = 63$), a measure of materialism was correlated with a need for uniqueness. The correlation was found to be $-.33$ (Schroeder & Dugal, 1995).
    (a) Find the confidence interval for the correlation.
    (b) Test the correlation's statistical significance.
    (c) Are the psychologists permitted to conclude that materialism is negatively correlated with need for uniqueness in an economically undeveloped country? Explain.

15. Why do the critical values of r (in Table A.5) become smaller as the size of the samples (and the associated degrees of freedom) become larger?

16. Assume that you know for sure that the correlation between R and Q in a population is .20. Suppose that you took many random samples from the population, measured R and Q each time, and calculated the r_{RQ} for each sample. What proportion of the correlations from these samples should be expected to exceed .20, and what proportion should be expected to be less than .20?

17. Prof. Stickler and Prof. Cloudy have argued for years over the value of a mathematics placement test used by their college. Stickler thinks it is a valid test, but Cloudy thinks it is invalid. With the support of Dean Placid, they agreed on an experiment. The experiment was conducted in the following manner:
    (1) Dean Placid randomly selected 56 students from the new first-year class.
    (2) The students all took the placement test. They were not given their scores.
    (3) Half of them ($n = 27$) were randomly assigned to take Math 101 from Stickler and the other half from Cloudy. Neither professor was given any information about the scores on the placement test.
    (4) At the end of the term, both professors submitted their grades to Dean Placid. The dean discovered that the correlation between the placement test scores and grades for Stickler was .39, but for Cloudy it was .07. Both Stickler and Cloudy claimed that the experiment vindi-

cated their own positions. The dean made sure that the correlations were correct. Then the dean turned to you to straighten this out. "They can't both be right," Dean Placid said. Be sure to answer the following questions:
    (a) Why did both professors claim vindication? (Carry out NHST tests.)
    (b) What should you examine in the two grade distributions of the two classes to explore this mystery? What might you discover about the grades that would explain these conflicting findings? (Hint: Don't forget what we look for in the description phase of analysis. What might you find in the description of the data that might resolve this impasse?)

18. Marvin obtained data from a large marketing firm that included household income and amount spent on food per month for 200 households in a community. Suppose that he found a correlation of .44. He was concerned about advertising aimed at different income levels, so he divided the sample into five groups (each $n = 40$) on the basis of income. When he calculated the correlation for income and amount spent of food for each of the subgroups, he found that the correlations for the five subgroups were .05, .12, .09, .11, and .06.
    (a) Test his correlations to see whether they differ from zero.
    (b) Explain why the correlations dropped in the second phase of his analysis.

19. If a researcher found that the correlation between two variables was not statistically significant, why is it incorrect to conclude that the variables are not intercorrelated?

20. (a) Explain the essential difference between directional and nondirectional statistical tests.
    (b) Imagine a researcher who decides which version of the two directional null hypotheses to test *only after* looking at his correlations. That is, if the correlation is positive, he sets his null hypothesis as $H_0: \rho \le .00$, but, if the correlation is negative, he chooses his null hypothesis to be $H_0: \rho \ge .00$. If someone does this, which increases: Type I error or Type II error? Explain.

Answers to Odd-Numbered Problems

1. We test for statistical significance for two reasons: (a) researchers are hesitant to treat findings as reliable unless the probability of the findings would be unusual if the null hypothesis is true, and (b) researchers want a guide as to how likely it would be that an exact replication would be statistically significant, $p < .05$.

3. $df = 33$

5. (a) $t(60) = 2.436, p < .02$ (two-tailed) (exact: $p = .018$)
   (b) $t(21) = -1.883, p < .01$ (two-tailed) (exact: $p = .736$)
   (c) $t(12,003) = 2.740, p < .01$ (two-tailed) (exact $p = .006$)
   (d) $t(30) = 7.847, p < .001$ (two-tailed) (exact: $p < .001$)

7. (a) $t(51) = 3.210, p < .005$ (one-tailed) (exact $p = .001$)
   (b) $t(39) = 1.821, p < .05$ (one-tailed) (exact $p = .038$)
   (c) $t(14) = 1.537, p < .10$ (one-tailed) (exact $p = .073$)
   (d) $t(121) = 1.669, p < .05$ (one-tailed) (exact $p = .049$)

9. The concern would be that those who have been hired in the past and are still on the job (current employees) are doing the job successfully. Not all of the applicants would be able to do the job successfully. Therefore, when the current employees are used to validate a selection test, there is a restriction of range problem.

11. (a) $$t = \frac{.2319}{\sqrt{[(1 - .2319^2)/(72 - 2)]}} = 1.995$$

   The critical value for $t(70)$ is between 1.98 ($df = 120$) and 2.00 ($df = 60$) for nondirectional tests. Thus, using the t formula, we find that $r = .2319$ would be statistically significant just as we would conclude if we had used Table A.5.

   (b) $$t = \frac{.2960}{\sqrt{[(1 - .2960^2)/(32 - 2)]}} = 1.697$$

   The critical value of $t(30)$ for a one-tailed test is 1.697.

13. (a) Confidence interval: $.8480 \pm 1.96 \, (1/\sqrt{(63 - 3)}) = .8480 \pm 1.96 \, (.129) = 0.595$ to 1.101; converting back to r, .534 to .801, or .53 to .80.
   (b) $t = .69/\sqrt{[(1 - .69^2)/(63 - 2)]} = 7.445, p < .001$
   (c) No, one cannot draw a causal conclusion; it is conceivable that either one could cause the other, or that some other characteristic causes both.

15. The formula to convert an r into a t has the sample size in the numerator. The larger the sample size (and the associated df), the larger t becomes for the same correlation. Therefore, with a large sample, a smaller correlation is more likely to yield a value of t that exceeds the critical value. (Note: In fact, sample size is in the denominator of the denominator of Equation 16.1, which is equivalent to being in the numerator. For example, $4/(1/x) = 4x$.)

17. (a) Both of the professors can claim vindication because Stickler's class showed that higher grades were found with higher placement test scores ($r(25) = .39, p < .025$ (directional test)), but Cloudy's correlation was not ($r(25) = .07, p > .05$). These probabilities are from Table A.5. If done on a computer, Cloudy's probability for a nondirectional test would have equaled .36, which is decidedly not statistically significant.
   (b) One needs to look at the grade distributions in the two classes. If Cloudy assigns students largely the same grades (e.g., all B's and A's) but Stickler gives a wide range of grades (F's through A's), the restriction of Cloudy's range would reduce the correlation.

19. When the correlation between variables is not statistically significant, it could be that a small sample was used and a Type II error occurred.

 Go to http://psychology.wadsworth.com/courses/statistics/ and test your knowledge of this chapter by taking the online quiz. Another resource to check is the online workshops that provide a step-by-step guide through a number of topics at http://psychology.wadsworth.com/workshops/workshops.html.

Making Predictions

The human being is on any view the most complex rational entity known to us.
  Carr (1962, p. 89)

Compared to predicting people, predicting the weather is easy.
  Myers and Jeeves (1987, p. 66)

INTRODUCTION

The previous chapter showed how to draw conclusions about the statistical significance of a correlation and the probability that an exact replication of a correlational study would be statistically significant. Correlations between two variables suggest that we might be able to use a person's relative position on one variable to predict his or her relative position on a second variable. How to calculate those predictions is the subject of this chapter. Consider the following research scenarios.

- Sarah was serving her internship with an industrial psychologist who developed tests of job skills. Sarah understood that scores on these tests were correlated with success on the job. Knowing that a test is positively correlated with job success would mean that people who score high on the test are likely to be better on the job than those who score low. She wondered whether the test scores permitted making predictions that were more precise than simply saying "those with high test scores are predicted to do better than those with low tests scores."

- While entering data for the records of the Board of Education, Franklin noticed that those students who did well on a standardized test in the third grade tended to do well on the fifth-grade version of the same test. Of course, there was a lot of variation. His supervisor told him that the correlation was +.52. Franklin wondered if it were possible to predict a child's score on the fifth-grade test if one knew the third-grade test score.

- Marshall was hired by a political action group to examine school records and school budgets. He focused his analysis on the financial support for schools and standardized test scores. Among 128 school districts, he found a strong positive correlation between dollars spent per student and mean student achievement. This is the pattern the group expected. Marshall's boss asked him if he could relate financial support to test points so that he could say that spending $500 more per student is related to so-and-so many additional points on the standardized test. The assignment reminded Marshall of regression analysis, and he reached for his statistics book.

Learning that variables correlate with each other can be helpful in describing people and organizations. Correlations also help to predict possible future values of variables. But if we have only correlations, such predictions are limited to being able to say things such as "because Stephan has high SAT scores, we expect he will get a better than average GPA in our freshman class," or, "Martina has high extroversion and social skills scores, so she probably will do well as a leader of a small discussion group." Clearly such conclusions are more accurate than guessing who will do well at a task or who would be better off trying something else. But often it would be helpful to make a more precise prediction. It would be more precise if, for example, we could say that on the basis of Stephan's SAT scores, he is predicted to earn a first year GPA of 3.45 at Downstate Tech. Of course, by this time in the course you would suspect that we cannot predict with perfect precision. But, even without absolute certainty, we would know that Stephan is not expected to earn all A's, but is expected to earn above a B average (on a 4-point scale).

The point of this chapter is to show you how to use a person's score on one variable to predict a specific score that the person will, in the future, get on a second variable. The precision of such predictions can be found. As you might suspect, such predictions will be more accurate when the correlation between the variables is large. The process of making specific predictions of the values of a continuous variable based on values of another continuous variable is called **regression** and makes use of what we call a *regression equation*. Before we can make predictions, it is necessary to review how equations can be plotted in two-dimensional graphs.

GRAPHING LINEAR EQUATIONS

Graphing linear equations is covered in introductory algebra courses. Although we are confident that you did master this skill, we are also aware that you may have forgotten the details. To understand regression, it is necessary to understand how to graph linear equations; this section provides a brief review. We start with calculating a charge for babysitting and then gradually move on to variables that are less objective.

Babysitters often charge per hour and also for coming to the home of the child. Regardless of how long they are asked to care for a child, it takes the same amount of time to travel to the home. Suppose a babysitter charges $5.00 per hour and $4.00 for showing up. Such a pay scale means that the first hour of babysitting costs $5 plus $4, or a total of $9. Two and a half hours would cost $4 plus 2.5 hours times $5 per hour, or $16.50. This relationship is graphed in Figure 17.1. The hours spent watching the child are plotted on the x axis and the total charge on the y axis. Three-and-a-half hours would cost $4 plus 3.5 hours times $5 per hour, or $21.50.

We can write an equation for the babysitter's charge in this way:

Charge for Babysitting = Base charge to show up + (Hours of work times Charge per hour)

FIGURE 17.1 ■ The relationship between hours of caring for a baby and the cost of babysitting can be written as a linear equation with an intercept and a slope and represented as a graph.

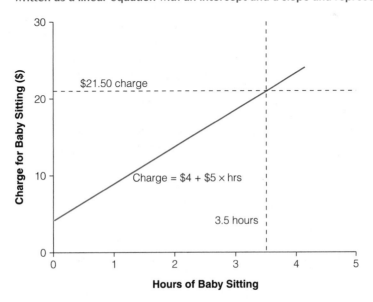

The base charge for showing up is the cost of no hours of babysitting and is plotted at time equals zero. The value of Y at the point where the line crosses the y axis is called the **intercept.** The rate at which Y changes per unit change in X is called the **slope.** Thus, we can rewrite the equation of the line as follows:

Y = intercept + (slope) (X)

Often, the intercept is called a, and the slope is called b. Thus, the equation becomes

$Y = a + bX$ **Equation 17.1**[1]

The way to determine the total charges is fixed very precisely. (What parents tip is another matter, of course.) All of the possible charges for the babysitter can be represented by a smooth straight line as in Figure 17.1. One does not need to calculate anything if one had Figure 17.1; simply find the time spent on the x axis, move vertically up to the line and then see what the total charge is on the y axis. An example is given in Figure 17.1 for a babysitter who has stayed 3.5 hours. Go up vertically to the line in the figure at 3.5 hours, then across horizontally to the y axis. You should find a total charge of $21.50.

The equation of a straight line can be thought of as linear transformation. The equation for the babysitting charge shows how to transform hours of babysitting into the cost of babysitting.

YOUR TURN 17-1

Write an equation summarizing a plumber's bill if he charges $40 for coming to your home and $70 for each hour worked. If he spends 45 minutes on your problem, what will your bill be? ■

The last idea to be reviewed regarding graphing equations involves turning the problem around, that is, going from points on the line to the formula. Assume that the food service department in your college delivers refreshments for meetings. And assume that a delivery charge is made and that each gallon of coffee costs a set fee with no volume discount. Suppose that one gallon costs $15 to be delivered and three gallons cost $35 to be delivered. On the basis of this information, we can figure out the delivery charge and the cost of each gallon. The formula can be found using algebra alone, but thinking of it graphically may help as well. The sizes of the urns and their costs are plotted in Figure 17.2. The slope of the line can be found by taking the difference between the two charges and dividing by the differences between the two amounts of coffee, as follows:

$$\frac{\$35 - \$15}{3 \text{ gallons} - 1 \text{ gallon}} = \$20/2 \text{ gallons} = \$10.00 \text{ per gallon}$$

Sometimes the slope is called the *rise* (the change in Y values) divided by the *run* (the change in X values). We can substitute the size and the cost of either order into the general formula for a straight line to find the intercept, which is the cost of delivery:

$35 = intercept + ($10.00/gallon) (3 gallons) = intercept + $30, or

$35 − $30 = intercept

$5 = intercept, or the cost of the delivery

[1]You may have learned a different set of symbols in algebra class. Some texts write the linear equation this way: $y = mx + b$. In the behavioral sciences we use a and b for the intercept and slope, respectively. Of course, the order in which the elements of the equation are written makes no difference.

FIGURE 17.2   ■   Illustration of the steps that permit finding the slope of a straight line from two points that are known to be on the line.

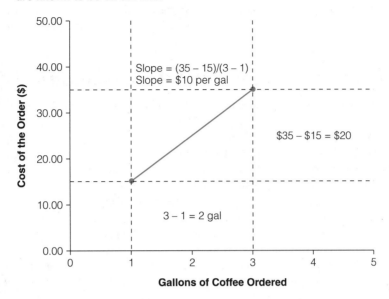

If one had constructed the graph very precisely, one could place a ruler on the points and draw a line "southwest" toward the origin and discover that line crosses the y axis at $5, the intercept. As long as we know that the data points form a straight line, this method permits us to calculate the formula underlying the two specific points in a graph. The intercept is often called the *constant* in statistical programs. You can easily see why using our coffee example: the cost of delivery is always the same, a constant, regardless of the number of gallons ordered.

YOUR TURN 17-2

In chemistry or physics class you learned how to convert degrees Fahrenheit into Celsius. You may have forgotten the formula, but you can derive it for yourself. The formula is a linear transformation and thus can be graphed as a straight line. You know two points that lie on the line: the freezing point of water ($0°$ C , $32°$ F) and the boiling point of water ($100°$ C, $212°$ F). Use the method just illustrated to find the conversion formula. Hint: Place degrees Fahrenheit on the x axis and Celsius on the y axis. If you think of the problem in this way, you can derive the formula to convert degrees Fahrenheit into Celsius.   ■

We have reviewed the algebra of a straight line. You should now be able to write a formula for a verbal description of how a variable is calculated (as, for example, the cost of a babysitter). And, you should be able to take two data points that you know are on a straight line and find the equation for that straight line.

If the values of two variables form a straight line when graphed, the relationship can be summarized in a linear equation. We can use the value of one variable to calculate the other one. Parents arriving home after an evening out check the time to calculate what they owe the babysitter. And, if the calculation is done according to the agreement they had with the babysitter, the sitter will accept the pay. Social scientists would love to use one variable to predict a second one as perfectly as parents can predict what a sitter will expect. Wouldn't it be helpful to find a job-selection test to predict job success with as much accuracy as we can predict a babysitter's charge? Alas, we can't do that because relationships between selection tests and job success are not as precise as between hours and a babysitter's pay.

GRAPHING VARIABLES USED IN THE BEHAVIORAL SCIENCES

Relationships between pairs of variables used in the behavioral sciences do not lead to correlations of ±1.00; hence, they do not plot as straight lines. Figure 17.3 displays a scatterplot of Franklin's data. Even though a plot of the third-grade scores and fifth-grade scores doesn't form a straight line, the graph does show a general linear pattern. The graph looks like a football (with rounded rather than pointed ends). When one end of this football is elevated higher than the other, we know that the correlation is something other than zero. In fact, the correlation is .52. A correlation that does not equal zero suggests that we ought to be able to make predictions of the value of one variable if we know the value of the other variable. In Franklin's case, he can use third-grade test scores to predict fifth-grade test scores more accurately than would be possible by just guessing randomly.

Finding an equation that summarizes the trend seen in a scatterplot is called **regression analysis.** The purpose of **linear regression** analysis is to define a *straight* line that best summarizes the pattern seen in the scatterplot. If Franklin has the equation of that straight line, he can use Jimmy's third-grade test score to predict what score Jimmy will get in the fifth-grade test. Figure 17.3, the scatterplot of Franklin's data, includes a straight line drawn through the scatterplot. The balance of this chapter shows how to find the **regression line** and the **regres-**

FIGURE 17.3 ■ The scatterplot of third- and fifth-grade tests shows the relationship between the tests which suggests that the earlier test could be used to predict students' scores on the test taken two years later.

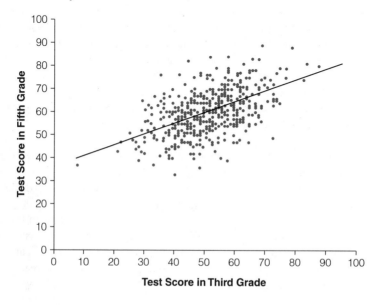

sion equation that defines the line and how to use them to make predictions in applied settings. Last, in keeping with our emphasis on examining the precision of statistical indexes, we describe how certain we can be about the predictions that are made using regression analyses.

CALCULATING A REGRESSION EQUATION

A general trend in a scatterplot can be summarized with a correlation coefficient, r. The correlation reveals the strength of the linear relationship between two continuous variables. However, r does not show how to use a person's score on one variable to estimate what that person's score would be on the second variable. When we seek to use one score to estimate a second, we call the first score the **predictor,** or the independent variable, and the estimated score the **criterion,** or the dependent variable. Although the use of the terms independent and dependent variables might sound as though a causal relation is assumed, using regression is not based on an assumption of a causal relationship between the variables. For example, doing well on a job skills test does not cause success on the job; both are caused by good work habits, appropriate levels of work skills, normal health, and so on. However, even though there may be no causal connection, human resource personnel can use job skill scores to predict level of job success using a regression equation.

A regression equation is the **best-fitting straight line** summarizing the relationship in a scatterplot. *Best fitting* has a precise meaning: a regression line is the prediction line that minimizes the sum of the squares of all of the prediction errors. We'll return to this point later.

Inspect Data

Without repeating all the steps in the inspection stage of data analysis (the *I* in I-D-E-A) covered in previous chapters, we remind you that it is necessary to inspect the data prior to developing a regression equation. All of the points from the earlier chapters apply. The variables must be continuous, not strongly skewed. Extreme outliers and overly skewed variables can distort the results; extreme outliers need to be discarded, and transformations may be used to correct highly skewed variables (such as income) before calculating a regression equation (or performing the other statistical analyses discussed in previous chapters). Furthermore, the scatterplot should demonstrate a general linear pattern as discussed in Chapter 14. The relationship can be negative or positive, but it must be linear. Inferential statistical techniques are based on the assumption that the variables are normally distributed; however, many inferential tests are fairly robust in that they provide quite accurate results with moderate violations of the normality assumption.

Find the Regression Equation

There is no reason to find a regression equation to use X to predict Y if the correlation between X and Y is zero. Once r_{xy} has been shown to be greater than .00, the correlation coefficient can be used to find the slope of the regression line and then to develop a regression equation. What we need is r and the means and standard deviations of each variable. Table 17.1 includes the values for six people on X and Y with the means and standard deviations for each variable. The correlation is .706. We can summarize the relationship between X and Y, as shown in Figure 17.4, with a straight line.

TABLE 17.1 ■ Data and Means and Standard Deviations of Two Variables for Illustrative Regression Calculation

Person	X	Y
1	2	2
2	3	4
3	4	3
4	4	6
5	5	4
6	6	6
Sum	24	25
M	4.00	4.17
s	1.41	1.60

The slope can be found using Equation 17.2:

$$b_{y \cdot x} = r_{xy} \frac{s_y}{s_x}$$

Equation 17.2

The standard deviation of the dependent variable, Y, is divided by the standard deviation of the independent variable, X, and the result is multiplied by the correlation to find the slope. The subscript of the slope is important; it is to be read as *"y given x."* The standard deviations of the variables in Table 17.1 have been substituted in this equation as follows:

$b_{y \cdot x} = 0.706 \, [1.602/1.414] = 0.7999$, or 0.80

FIGURE 17.4 ■ A scatterplot of the data for six people given in Table 17.1.

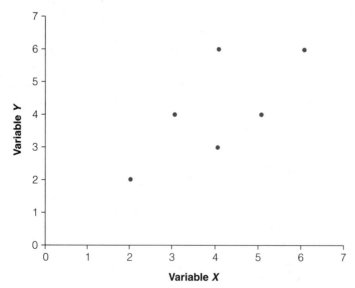

Once the slope, $b_{y \cdot x}$, is known, the intercept can be found because one point on the regression line is known—the point defined by the means of the two variables.

It should seem reasonable that the two means lie on the regression line. If a person's score on X is the mean of X, we would have no reason to predict that she would have a score on Y that exceeded M_y. Similarly, we would have no reason to predict that her score on Y would be less than M_y. Thus, we know that the point defined by M_x and M_y must lie on the linear regression line.

We enter M_x and M_y into Equation 17.1:

$$Y = a_{y \cdot x} + b_{y \cdot x} X$$

along with the slope found with Equation 17.2. Substituting the means into the equation, we have:

$$M_y = a_{y \cdot x} + b_{y \cdot x} M_x$$

We want to calculate the intercept, $a_{y \cdot x}$, so we can solve this equation for $a_{y \cdot x}$. The intercept is found using Equation 17.3:

$$a_{y \cdot x} = M_y - b_{y \cdot x} M_x \qquad\qquad \textbf{Equation 17.3}$$

Substituting values of the means from Table 17.1 into Equation 17.3, we can find the intercept as follows:

$$a_{y \cdot x} = 4.17 - [(0.80)(4.00)] = 4.17 - 3.20 = 0.97$$

The intercept is the value of Y when X equals zero; it is like the babysitter's charge for showing up. Combining our findings, the regression equation relating X to Y for the data in Table 17.1 is

$$Y' = 0.97 + 0.80 X$$

Notice that a prime symbol (′) has been added to distinguish a predicted Y from a value of the original data. The prime simply reminds us that the predicted Y score, Y' (read "Y prime" or "Y predicted"), is not from the original data for Y. Instead Y' is the value predicted for people with a particular score on X. To calculate a Y', we substitute a value for a person's score on X into the regression equation. For example, for someone with a score of 4 on X, we would calculate Y' as

$$Y' = 0.97 + 0.80 (4) = 4.27$$

Note that, in Table 17.1, two people had a score of 4 on X. The Y score for one was 3, and the Y score for the other was 6. When calculating Y', we use information from all the obtained scores on X and Y to arrive at a prediction of Y for someone who scores 4 on X.

The upper part of Figure 17.5 is a scatterplot of the data in Table 17.1 with the regression line added. Take a moment to examine this scatterplot. Note how the line reflects the trend seen in the scatterplot. The regression line minimizes the total of the *squared* errors in predicting Y. In Figure 17.5, the errors in prediction are marked. These errors are called **residuals.** Think of residuals as the variation in Y scores that cannot be predicted or reproduced by knowing the values of X. If the residuals (i.e., the errors for all predictions) are calculated and each one is squared, the sum of these squared errors would be smaller than the sum of squared errors for any other straight line that might be used to approximate the trend of the relationship. The formulas to find the regression equation make use of a strategy called the **method of least squares.** This phrase is short for minimizing the sum of squared residuals. In examining Figure 17.5, note that the errors illustrated are the *vertical* distances between

FIGURE 17.5 ■ The data in Table 17.1 have been plotted with the regression line in the upper portion of this figure. The errors of prediction have been added also. Note that the errors are the *vertical* distances between data points and the regression line. The middle portion shows errors from a prediction line that is *not* the one that minimizes the sum of the squared errors. The last portion shows the errors from a regression line when the correlation between the two variables is very small.

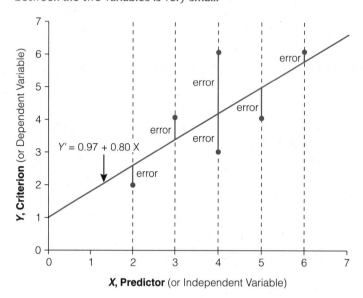

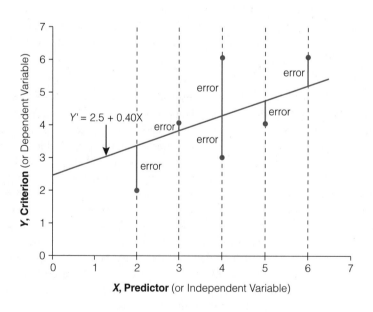

FIGURE 17.5 ■ (Continued)

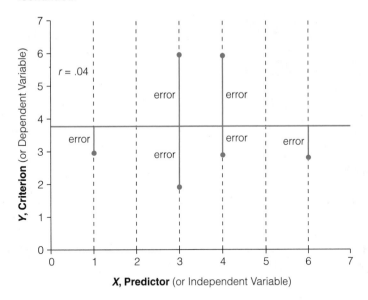

the regression line and the original data points. Errors of prediction refer to the difference between the predicted Y' values and the original Y values. Such differences appear in the graph as *vertical* distances.

The middle section of Figure 17.5 shows the errors in prediction from an equation that does not minimize the sum of the squared residuals for the same data points in the upper section. The last section of Figure 17.5 shows a scatterplot for two variables that are less strongly correlated than those in the other sections. It should be evident that the residuals are larger when a line other than the regression line is used and when the correlation is lower.

Figure 17.3 presented the hypothetical data from Franklin's data on tests of children in their third and fifth grades. The correlation is .52. Table 17.2 contains the values needed to find the regression line for Franklin's data. The slope is found using Equation 17.2 and then the intercept using Equation 17.3. The steps to find the regression line are reviewed in Figure 17.6. No other straight line can be found that better represents the relationship between these two variables given that the goal was to minimize the sum of the squared errors.

TABLE 17.2 ■ Means and Standard Deviations for Franklin's Test Data

	N	*M*	*s*
Test score in fifth grade	474	60.31	9.70
Test score in third grade	474	50.94	11.32

FIGURE 17.6 ■ Review of the steps to calculate a regression equation using Franklin's test scores.

Step	Formula	Answer
1. Find the slope using the correlation and the standard deviations	$b_{y \bullet x} = r_{xy}(s_y/s_x) =$ .52 (9.70/11.32)	$b_{y \bullet x} = 0.443$
2. Find the intercept using the slope and means of the two tests	$a_{y \bullet x} = M_y - b_{y \bullet x} M_x =$ 60.31 − 0.443 (50.94)	$a_{y \bullet x} = 37.74$
3. Write the regression equation	$Y' = 37.74 + 0.44\ X$, or in words, Predicted 5th-grade score = 37.74 + 0.44 (3rd-grade score)	

YOUR TURN 17–3

Find the regression equation for predicting variable C from P. The descriptive data are $r_{CP} = .41, M_P = 12.4, s_P = 3.1, M_C = 72.1, s_C = 24.9$. (Note: You are to predict the values of C using the values of P.) ■

The Relationship Between r_{xy} and $b_{y \cdot x}$

Although the correlation, r_{xy}, and the slope, $b_{y \cdot x}$, are related to each other, they are not identical. The correlation and the slope must have the same sign: both positive or both negative. They will equal each other only under limited conditions. Equation 17.2 reveals when r_{xy} and $b_{y \cdot x}$ will be equal:

$$b_{y \cdot x} = r_{xy} \frac{s_y}{s_x}$$

If s_y equals s_x, the ratio of s_y/s_x would be 1.0 which would make the correlation and the slope equal. Because the standard deviations are always positive, the slope will always have the same sign as the correlation. However, in actual data sets, when raw data are used, s_y will seldom equal s_x; consequently, r_{xy} and $b_{y \cdot x}$ will seldom have the same value. On the other hand, if both X and Y are converted to z scores, a transformation that sets the standard deviations of distributions to 1.00, then r_{xy} and $b_{y \cdot x}$ will have the same value. The only other situation in which the r_{xy} would equal $b_{y \cdot x}$ occurs in artificial data sets in which the correlation is exactly equal to zero. In such a situation the standard deviations could be anything, and yet r_{xy} and $b_{y \cdot x}$ would be the same, namely, zero.

YOUR TURN 17–4

The correlation coefficient, r, is limited to a range of −1.0 through +1.0 regardless of the variables that are correlated. Is the slope, $b_{y \cdot x}$, also limited to some range of values regardless of the variables in the regression equation? (Hint: Look at Equation 17.2 and imagine a variety of variables with various standard deviations being used in a regression equation.) ■

Plotting Regression Equations

Plotting a regression line onto a scatterplot is quite easy. To locate a straight line, we need two points that we know are on that line. Figure 17.7 illustrates the steps. The regression line for Franklin's data is as follows:

Predicted fifth-grade test score = 37.74 + 0.44 (third-grade test score)

Or, the equation in symbols is

$$Y' = 37.74 + 0.44 \, (X)$$

The figure shows that a score of 10 on the third-grade test is on the left end of the scatterplot. If we substitute 10 into the regression equation, we have

$$Y' = 37.74 + 0.44 \, (10) = 42.10$$

Remember what this means: for students scoring 10 on the third-grade test, the regression equation says that we should predict a score of 42.10 on the fifth-grade test taken two years later.

To define a straight line, two points are needed. For the second point, pick a large possible value of X, say 90, and substitute 90 in the regression formula:

$$Y' = 37.74 + 0.44 \, (90) = 77.34$$

The two points, ($X = 10$, $Y' = 42.10$) and ($X = 90$, $Y' = 77.34$), have been plotted on the figure. To draw the regression line, all we need to do is to connect these two points.

FIGURE 17.7 ■ Three steps in drawing a regression line once the equation is known.

Step 1: Use the regression equation, $Y' = 37.74 + 0.44X$, to find two points on the regression line and add them to the scatterplot.

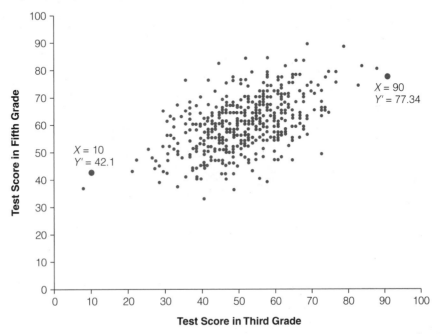

(continues)

FIGURE 17.7 ■ (continued)

Step 2: Connect the two points with a straight line.

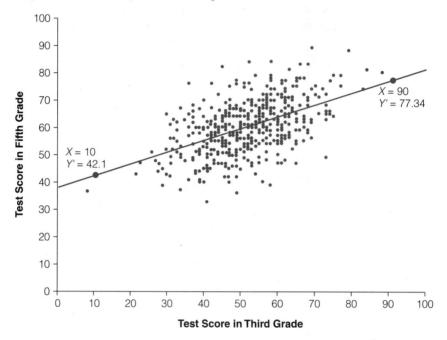

Step 3: Find the point defined by the means of the two variables; that point will fall on the regression just drawn if it is drawn correctly.

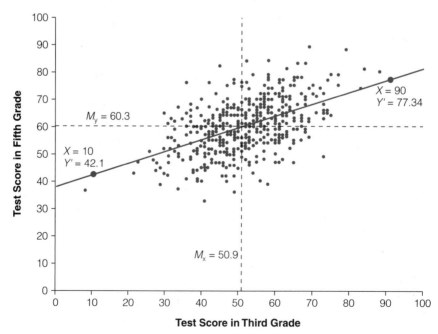

If one were extremely accurate, the regression line could be drawn using any two points that are found using the regression equation. However, using a point from the extreme left and one from the extreme right of the scatterplot minimizes the effects of small errors plotting those points. As a check on your work, you can find the means for X and Y (the means for Franklin's data are in Table 17.2) and verify that the point defined by M_x and M_y lies on the line you drew. Of course, computer programs also draw the regression lines through scatterplots.

YOUR TURN 17–5

Suppose that you know that the range of X is 200 through 800 and the range of Y is 10 through 100. Further, suppose that you have the regression formula that summarizes the relationship between X and Y, $Y' = 10 + 0.095X$. Find two points on the regression line that would be convenient to use to plot the regression line given the ranges of X and Y. (That is, choose appropriate values of X and then obtain the two Y' values you would use to plot the regression line.) ∎

USING REGRESSION PREDICTIONS

At several points, we have illustrated regression analysis showing how regression permits making predictions of the value of one variable on the basis of the value of another. For example, we have said that industrial psychologists use job skills tests to predict how well an applicant might do on the job if hired. A question might have come to mind as you have been working through this chapter: "If the values of both the independent variable, X, and the dependent variable, Y, are needed to calculate a regression equation, why do statisticians talk about 'predicted' values of Y? After all, we don't need to predict values that we already know." Good question.

There are two answers. First, the idea behind the development of regression equations is to make the most efficient use of information about the relationships between two variables to improve *future* decisions. If we notice or suspect that two variables are correlated and if one comes earlier in time than the second one does, we might improve the effectiveness of decisions by using the information from that first variable to predict values of the second variable. This process has two steps. First, use existing data (or gather new data) to find the regression equation. Second, use the regression equation to make predictions for people for whom only the first variable is available. These steps are different from each other. To make that difference more clear, we can use the terms *derivation* and *application* to distinguish these steps from each other. To develop a regression equation, we need the values of two variables, X and Y, from some large sample of people making up the **derivation sample.** Ideally, values on variable X will not have been used in decisions that might affect the values of variable Y. For example, in a job-selection context, the information provided by a job skills test should not have been used in any way that might affect which people had been hired and appear in the derivation sample. If the correlation between the test and job performance is statistically significant, a regression equation can be developed from the data. (Actually, one can calculate a regression equation whether the correlation is statistically significant or not. But if the correlation is not large enough to satisfy accepted standards for treating it as trustworthy, there is no point to planning to use the relationship to make practical decisions.)

Once the regression equation is available, the regression equation can be applied to people whose values on X are known, but who have not had the opportunity to have a value on Y. For example, Air Force enlistees take placement tests prior to being assigned to train for particular jobs such as pilot, mechanic, office manager, radar technician, and so on. It is a lot more economical to use placement tests to find the most promising enlistees for pilot training than simply to permit anyone to begin pilot training and depend on weeding out pilot-wannabes whose skills and aptitudes would have suggested that they would not have been able to complete the rigorous training successfully. Such a *laissez-faire* policy would waste effort and money, place unqualified enlistees in dangerous conditions, and lead to a morale problem. In applied settings, regression is useful if there is a derivation sample for whom both X and Y are known and an **application sample** composed of people for whom only X is known but for whom we would like to estimate what Y would be if they were to be hired for a job, enter a training program, or begin studies at a college.

A second answer to the question of why one would find a regression equation when X and Y are already known refers to research on theoretical questions. Psychologists, economists, sociologists, and others refer to model building (i.e., theory development). Social scientists try to summarize social or economic processes using regression analysis. Bandura (1997) hypothesized that people who have high scores on measures of self-efficacy (feeling capable) will volunteer for more challenging tasks than those with low scores. Merely calculating correlations just tells us "Yep, there is a strong relationship here." Regression equations give us more information on just what the relationship is. For example, a theorist might be able to say that people who differ by 5 points on their scores on a self-efficacy test, differ by 10 points in their willingness to choose the more challenging task when given a choice between two experimental tasks. *This specificity is the contribution of regression analyses beyond the information given by correlations.*

We have covered only introductory material on regression in this text. Limiting ourselves to linear regression with only one independent variable will not advance social science or lead to better economic planning by the Federal Reserve Bank. Far more complicated forms of regression analyses are used in both theoretical and applied research. You may have wondered how economists make projections of inflation, job growth, or federal budget surpluses or deficits. Economic projections are informed by estimates based on very complicated regression equations with many independent variables, not all of which are linear. Although the projections are never perfect, especially when projecting far into the future, economic forecasts are not simply guesses. Economic forecasts are the product of sophisticated regression analyses that cannot be covered in the first course. Many college admissions offices use regression equations that include both high school information and standard test scores to inform their admissions decisions. When two or more predictors are used, the analysis is called multiple regression. We cannot cover multiple regression in this introductory text, but Box 17.1 provides a peek.

How Certain Can We Be of These Predictions?

As you well know by now, we have emphasized that statistical analyses should include estimates of the precision of findings. When predictions are made, the precision of those predictions should be reported as well. Some of the computational illustrations used to this point in this chapter were based on a tiny sample of six observations; however, the sample of six is simply too small to yield statistically significant findings even though the correlation was large. On the other hand, the example of correlation between third- and fifth-grade test scores was based on 474 students. The correlation was large and statistically significant: $r(472) = .52$, $p < .001$. When the correlation is statistically significant, we are justified in finding a regression equation and making predictions. The prediction line was included in Figure 17.7, and it is easy to see that not all of the scores fall close to the regression line.

BOX 17.1 ■ Multiple Regression

Regression techniques are widely used in many behavioral sciences, such as education, psychology, sociology, economics, medicine, political science, and market research. Most of the applications make use of two or more predictor variables. When more than two predictors are used, we speak of multiple regression. Several predictors are used because all behaviors have multiple causes; combining several predictors into one regression equation has the potential to increase the precision of our predictions. For example, we could imagine trying to predict fifth-grade reading test scores using third-grade test scores, parents' educational level, percentage of school days attended, and reading level of classmates. We might use those variables because (a) parents' educational level is probably correlated with expectations for the child to do well in school, (b) percentage of school days attended is probably sensitive to the health of the child, and (c) reading level of classmates might be sensitive to quality of the school. The regression equation would then have four predictors:

fifth-grade score = $a + b_1$ (third-grade score) + b_2(parents' ed.) + b_3 (% days in school) + b_4 (mean reading score of classmates)

Or, in symbolic form, the equation is

$$Y' = a + b_1 (X_1) + b_2 (X_2) + b_3 (X_3) + b_4 (X_4)$$

Using four predictors instead of one usually leads to more-accurate predictions. Multiple regression analyses must be done with computers. The computer results tell how strong the overall prediction is and how much each of the predictors contributes to making accurate predictions of the dependent variable (fifth-grade test scores in our example). Sometimes that analysis shows that a particular predictor is not very useful in the context of the other predictors used.

Multiple regression can get tricky. It is best not to try to use it until one has carefully studied the topic and thoughtfully *inspected* and *described* the data to be used in an analysis.

There is a way to reflect the certainty, or uncertainty, of our predictions using a confidence interval. First, let's quickly review finding the confidence interval for the correlation itself. In Chapter 15, we showed how to transform the correlation into a Z_r, find the confidence interval of Z_r, and then transform back into a confidence interval for r. Here is a brief review:

Converting r to Z_r	$Z_{(r=0.52)} = 0.5763$
Calculating the standard error of Z_r	$\sqrt{(1/(474 - 3))} = 0.0461$
Calculating the 95% confidence interval of Z_r	$0.5763 \pm 1.96 \times 0.461 =$
	$0.5763 \pm 0.0903 = 0.4860$ to 0.6666
Converting the 95% confidence interval of Z_r, into the confidence interval of r	.451 to .584, or .45 to .58

Error in Predictions

The preceding paragraphs discuss precision in the overall analysis; with a correlation of .52, we can be sure that our predictions will be more accurate than random guessing overall. But when applying regression we are making predictions about individuals. It is fair to ask: How accurate are these predictions for individuals? To deal with this question, we need one more concept: the **standard error of the estimate.** The term *standard error* is used whenever a standard deviation is estimated. Figure 17.5 included the differences between the actual Y scores and the Y scores that would be predicted for people with the same values on X as those people. The sizes of these errors provide an overall estimate of accuracy of predictions. One way to find the standard error of estimate would be to find the standard deviation of all those errors. This standard deviation is symbolized as $s_{y \cdot x}$ which is read as "the standard error of Y given X." The formula is

$$s_{y \cdot x} = \sqrt{\frac{\Sigma(Y-Y')^2}{N-2}}$$

Equation 17.4

The numerator is the sum of the squares of the errors of prediction mentioned earlier and illustrated in Figure 17.5. The degrees of freedom $(N-2)$ reflect the fact that we used the data to find a and b (two pieces of information) in finding a regression equation. Equation 17.4 is almost identical to the formula for the sample standard deviation:

$$s_y = \sqrt{\frac{\Sigma(Y-M_y)^2}{N-1}}$$

In the standard deviation formula, M_y replaces Y' and only one degree of freedom is lost because the data were used to extract only one value, the mean, M_y. Each value of $(Y-Y')$ is the vertical distance between the regression line and a point in the scatterplot of X and Y. It is the sum of the squares of these differences that is minimized by the best-fitting line. Using Equation 17.4 would be laborious even with small samples. The standard error of the estimate is given by computer programs. When the sample is large, say 100 or more, there is a simple formula for the standard error:

$$s_{y \cdot x} = s_y \sqrt{(1 - r_{xy}^2)}$$

Equation 17.5

Using Franklin's data, we have

$$s_{y \cdot x} = 9.70 \sqrt{(1 - .52^2)} = 8.28$$

Equation 17.5 tells us that, as r_{xy} gets larger and larger, the $s_{y \cdot x}$ will get smaller and smaller relative to s_y. On the other hand, if r_{xy} equaled zero, $s_{y \cdot x}$ would equal s_y; if $s_{y \cdot x}$ equals s_y, that would mean that the use of the regression line does not lead to any improvement in predictions relative to simply predicting M_y for every child.

The meaning of $s_{y \cdot x}$ is important; it helps us with two aspects of the interpretation of predictions: it tells us how empty the glass is and how full it is. We should not forget that the glass is not full; prediction is not perfect. Prediction is not perfect as long as $s_{y \cdot x}$ is greater than zero. Yet, we must not forget that the glass is not empty either; the predictions are better than random guesses. The smaller the standard error of the estimate, the less error when predicting from the equation. The larger the correlation between variables, the smaller the standard error is relative to the standard deviation of Y.

YOUR TURN 17-6

(a) If a correlation of .38 were found between X and Y and if s_y equals 12.38, find $s_{y \cdot x}$.

(b) If X were correlated with K, $r_{xK} = .25$, and if s_K equals 1.72, find $s_{K \cdot x}$.

Which is a better indicator of the accuracy of the prediction, a large correlation coefficient or a small standard error of estimate? ∎

When predictions are made, we can place a confidence interval around them. Let's imagine Jessie who, as a third grader, earned a score of 62 on the examination. What would her predicted fifth-grade score be? We can use Franklin's prediction equation:

$$Y' = 37.74 + .44 (62) = 65.02$$

The scatterplot in Figure 17.3 shows that some students with a 62 in third grade earned a score higher than 65.02 in fifth grade and some earned lower scores. To find the expected range, we can find a confidence interval as we did for means and correlations. To do so, we need a nondirectional t_{crit} for N minus 2 degrees of freedom and α equals .05. The 95% confidence interval would be

$$Y' \pm t_{crit} (s_{y \cdot x}) \qquad \text{Equation 17.6}$$

For students with third-grade scores of 62, the 95% confidence interval would be

$$65.02 \pm 1.98 (8.28) =$$

$$65.02 \pm 16.39 = 48.63 \text{ to } 81.41$$

We would expect 95% of third-grade students with scores of 62 to earn fifth-grade scores between 49 and 81. The original range of all the fifth-grade scores was 33 to 89. Thus, using the regression equation has narrowed down our predictions.

To find the 50% confidence interval, we follow the same procedure using a nondirectional t with a probability of .50 rather than the t with a probability of .05. The calculation of the 50% confidence interval is

$$65.02 \pm 0.677 (8.28) =$$

$$65.02 \pm 5.61 =$$

$$59.41 \text{ to } 70.63$$

On the basis of this 50% confidence interval, we predict that 25% of the fifth graders with a score of 62 on the third-grade test will earn 71 or over in fifth grade, and 25% will earn 60 or lower in fifth grade.

What is the 80% confidence interval for predictions of fifth-grade scores for students who obtained a score of 65 in third grade? ∎

Reporting the confidence intervals for Jessie's predicted grade reminds us that, with a correlation of .52, predictions have a lot of uncertainty. But remember the glass is not empty. The correlation of .52 is large for psychological research according to Cohen's standards. (See Chapter 15.)

How precise may we expect predictions to be? When we think about predicting reading skills two years later, we need to consider influences on the development of reading skills. Some of the influences affecting reading development include: quality of school and teachers, parents' example and encouragement, health, family crises, and the child's own study habits, as well as how well they read in third grade. Children will differ in their exposure to these influences, and thus their rates of reading development will differ. *Any single influence will not permit one to make pinpoint predictions of the development of reading skills, but predictions will be better than guessing randomly.*

Notice that we are trying to predict how an *individual person* will do. Physicists work with much simpler variables than do behavioral scientists, yet a physicist cannot accurately predict the path that a particular sheet of paper will follow when it is dropped. We all agree that the sheet will fall, but the specific path is simply unpredictable. Behavioral scientists, like physicists, must be content with knowing the general pattern; improvements we can make in predictions for individuals are seldom large, but we can reduce uncertainty. The real issue is whether some other approach to making predictions about grades or job performance provides more accurate predictions. It has been repeatedly demonstrated that predictions of future scores or future success at a job based on subjective opinion is *not* on the average more valid than a statistical prediction. (See Dawes, 1994, and Meehl, 1954.) This is true even when the person who makes a subjective prediction is given the results of the regression formula.

AN IMPORTANT ADDITIONAL DETAIL ABOUT THE PRECISION OF PREDICTIONS

Finding the confidence intervals for predictions is actually a bit more complicated than how we calculated the interval for Jessie. For small samples and for values of X that are far from the mean of X, $s_{y \cdot x}$ must be corrected and predictions are less precise. It is necessary to multiply $s_{y \cdot x}$ by the following term:

$$\text{Correction for } s_{y \cdot x} = \sqrt{\left[1 + 1/N + \frac{(X - M_x)^2}{s_x^2(N-1)} \right]}$$

Equation 17.7

TABLE 17.3 ■ When Finding Confidence Intervals of the Predictions Made from Regression Equations, the Standard Error of Estimate, $s_{y \cdot x}$, is to Be Multiplied by These Correction Factors

	Value of the Predictor, X, Used in the Regression Formula		
N	**Mean**	**Mean $\pm$ 1*sd***	**Mean $\pm$ 2*sd***
5	1.0954	1.2042	1.4832
10	1.0488	1.1005	1.2428
20	1.0247	1.0501	1.1227
40	1.0124	1.0250	1.0619
80	1.0062	1.0125	1.0311
120	1.0042	1.0083	1.0208
200	1.0025	1.0050	1.0125
500	1.0010	1.0020	1.0050

Note: Once the size of the sample from which the regression equation was developed exceeds 120, the correction factor for someone with a predictor score (a value of X) that equals two standard deviations above (or below) the mean of X, the correction is at most only about 2%. For less extreme values of X, the correction is even smaller. This table shows that the correction of $s_{y \cdot x}$ is important when samples are small; once sample sizes equal or exceed the sizes that are recommended for regression analyses that are to be used to make predictions for individuals ($N > 100$), the size of the correction is so small that it would have little effect on the confidence intervals even for scores that are quite different from the mean of X.

Notice that this term must always be greater than 1.0. For large samples, $1/N$ will be small, and the whole term will not be very different from 1.0. For small samples, however, the correction is fairly sizeable. Table 17.3 provides the correction terms for several sample sizes. Note that, as sample size increases, the correction terms are closer and closer to 1.0. The table also shows the effect of making predictions for people whose X scores are far from the mean. Columns are given for making predictions for people whose X score (a) equaled the mean, (b) was one standard deviation above or below the mean, and (c) was two standard deviations above or below the mean. The correction terms in Table 17.3 can be used in place of calculating correction terms for all predictions to be made. For Jessie, whose third-grade score was near the mean of the 474 students, the correction term is approximately 1.0010.

ANNOUNCING THE RESULTS OF A REGRESSION ANALYSIS

If Franklin wanted to tell others about the regression equation relating third-grade scores to fifth-grade scores, he could say the following:

> Children ($N = 474$) took our school district's standard reading test in both third and fifth grades. The scores from these two administrations were positively correlated to a statistically significant degree, $r(472) = .52$, $p < .0005$. The correlation found is large and reveals that children reading poorly in the third grade are at risk of reading poorly in the fifth grade. The third-grade reading scores were used to predict the fifth-grade reading scores in a regression analysis. The regression formula was
>
> $$Y'_{\text{fifth}} = 37.74 + 0.44\,(X_{\text{third}})$$
>
> We know that the slope is statistically significant because the correlation is statistically significant. The standard deviation of fifth-grade scores is 9.70. The use of the regression formula improves accuracy of predictions; the standard error of estimate, $s_{y \cdot x}$, was 8.28.
>
> Poor third-grade readers are at greater risk of reading poorly in the fifth grade; consequently, those children reading at the lowest levels might benefit from special attention to increase their chance of reading at levels closer to those of their fifth-grade classmates. On the other hand, the large size of the standard error of estimate tells us that the reading levels of children change relative to each other. That is to say, some of our students get better compared to their classmates and some get worse as they mature during the two years from third to fifth grades. Because predictions of fifth-grade levels cannot be made with precision, perhaps improved or more intensive reading instruction for all might have favorable effects because the analysis tells us that reading levels are not fixed.

This possible announcement of the findings of a regression analysis has two messages: one focused on improved prediction, and the other focused on the remaining uncertainty. The uncertainty is important to remember because, in regression analysis, the goal is to predict the behavior of a specific individual—a very difficult task as Myers and Jeeves (1987) pointed out. In an organization with definite criteria of success, one might use the regression formula to simply predict, for example, whether a job applicant will succeed on the job or whether the applicant would not succeed. Further, don't forget that hire/don't hire decisions are seldom (if ever) made on the basis of only one predictor.

CAUTIONS IN USING REGRESSION EQUATIONS TO MAKE PREDICTIONS

Like all statistical techniques, one can misuse regression. First, the discussion in these chapters on correlation and regression concern linear relationships. These are not perfect, one-to-one relationships, but the scatterplots must show a general linear pattern. If a scatterplot looks like a banana or a boomerang, or a U (or an inverted U), as initially mentioned in Chapter 14, the regression formulas presented do not apply. Even though they don't apply, the formulas and statistical programs do not object when misused: the slope and intercept can be calculated even though the data are inappropriate for such an analysis. Inspection is always the necessary first step. Here are five more cautions about interpreting regression equations.

Don't Predict Beyond the Range of the Derivation Sample

One tempting misuse of regression equations is to attempt to predict beyond the range of the independent variable. In some cases, it may seem very likely for a linear relationship to hold for values of X that are smaller or larger than those observed in the derivation sample. But, unless observations are available, one cannot be certain that the linear pattern applies to values of X that are not represented in the derivation sample. We mentioned already that, for low levels of stress, stress is positively correlated with success on many tasks. It might seem that, for even higher levels of stress, performance would continue to increase, but, in fact, for high levels of stress, performance begins to fall.

Don't Try to Predict the Independent Variable Using the Dependent Variable

It might seem permissible to use a regression equation to predict either Y from X or X from Y. It might seem reasonable to ask: If I know a fifth-grade score, can we use the regression equation to estimate the child's third-grade score? The short answer is "No." First, it does not make practical sense to use a fifth-grade score to "predict" a third-grade score that was earned two years earlier. Nevertheless, such an equation can be found, but it is necessary to start over. In what follows, we will continue to use Y to refer to the fifth-grade score and X to refer to the third-grade score. What we need is the slope of the regression line for the third-grade score given the fifth-grade score (that is, X given Y, $b_{x \cdot y}$—note the order of the subscripts) and not the slope of Y given X, $b_{y \cdot x}$, which we have been using.

For Franklin's data, he would find the slope to predict third-grade scores using a variation of Equation 17.2. Notice that the standard deviations in the following equation are reversed compared to Equation 17.2.

$$b_{x \cdot y} = r_{xy} \frac{s_x}{s_y}$$

In this case, s_x is the standard deviation of the third-grade test, and s_y is the standard deviation of the fifth-grade test. Of course, the correlation is the same. Substituting into this equation, we have

$$.52 \, (11.32/9.70) = 0.61 = b_{x \cdot y}$$

We would then find the intercept by substituting the means into a variation of Equation 17.1:

$$M_{\text{third}} - b_{x \cdot y}(M_{\text{fifth}}) = 50.94 - 0.61\,(60.31) = 14.15 = a_{x \cdot y}$$

When we put $a_{x \cdot y}$ and $b_{x \cdot y}$ together, we have a regression equation to predict third-grade scores from fifth-grade scores:

$$Y'_{\text{third}} = 14.15 + 0.61\,(X_{\text{fifth}})$$

This equation is to be compared to the first one we found when we predicted fifth-grade scores from third-grade scores:

$$Y'_{\text{fifth}} = 37.74 + 0.44\,(X_{\text{third}})$$

We can solve this equation for X_{third} to make it easier to compare it to the previous equation (i.e., the one to predict third-grade scores from fifth-grade scores). Solving for X_{third}, we have

$$Y'_{\text{fifth}} - 37.74 = 0.44(X_{\text{third}})$$
$$(Y'_{\text{fifth}} - 37.74)/0.44 = X_{\text{third}}$$
$$Y'_{\text{fifth}}/0.44 - 37.74/0.44 = X_{\text{third}}$$
$$X_{\text{third}} = -85.77 + 2.27(Y'_{\text{fifth}})$$

Compare this rearranged equation to the one used originally to predict third-grade scores from fifth-grade scores. It is apparent that using the original formula (*incorrectly*) to make predictions of Y would lead to quite different predictions.

The differences in the formulas are due to the different criteria used to minimize squared errors. The errors that are minimized are different depending on which variable is considered the independent variable and which is considered the dependent variable. Figure 17.4 is redrawn in the top panel of Figure 17.8 showing the errors whose squares were minimized in the first illustration used in this chapter. Note that the errors are the differences between the predictions of the values of the dependent variable, Y', and the actual Y values. In the top panel, these differences are *vertical distances* between data points and the regression line. In the lower panel, the errors given are those that would be minimized if values plotted on the y axis were used to predict those on the x axis. Note that the errors in the lower panel of Figure 17.8 are *horizontal distances*. The point is that, for a particular regression line, the sum of the squares of the vertical errors does not equal the sum of the squares of the horizontal errors. *If one wants to reverse the independent and the dependent variables, that is, to predict in the opposite direction, one must start by calculating a new regression equation.*

Remain on Guard for Restriction of Range

It was shown in Chapter 14 that, when the range of variables has been restricted in some way, correlations are reduced. Similarly, restriction of range reduces the accuracy of predictions using regression equations. Suppose that a college wishes to develop a regression equation to use SAT scores to predict the GPA that students will earn in their classes during their first terms. One would develop such a regression equation from the college's files. However, if SAT scores had been used in the decisions of which students to admit into the college, then the range of SAT scores in the derivation sample would have been reduced. That reduction in range would reduce the correlation between SAT and GPA. And that means that the apparent effectiveness of the regression equation would have been reduced. An analyst working with the admissions director to develop a regression equation to predict

FIGURE 17.8 ■ If one wanted to predict X from Y, the errors to be minimized are different from the ones minimized when predictions are made of Y from X. The upper panel displays the errors in going from X to Y which is the usual procedure. The lower panel displays the errors in going from Y to X. Thus, the equation for Y' cannot be applied in the lower panel.

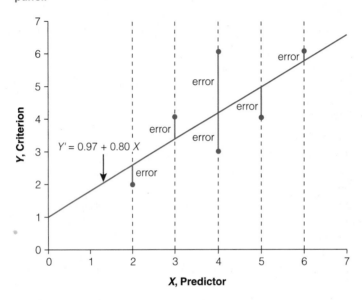

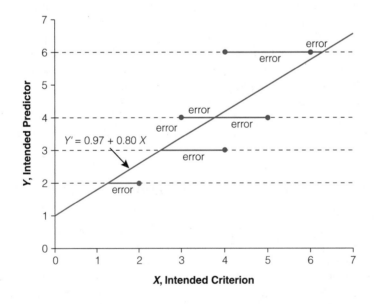

GPA among the following year's applicants cannot correct for a restriction of range. This caution simply reminds us that predictions will be less precise whenever the range of variables has been restricted in some way.

Rick obtained the mean number of rebounds per 10 minutes played for all the NBA players over 6'-9" tall. He calculated a regression equation for predicting number of rebounds from height. He found that the slope was essentially zero as was the correlation coefficient. He concluded that height was not related to number of rebounds among NBA players. How did Rick go wrong? ■

Make Predictions Only When the Derivation Sample Reflects the Population for Whom Predictions Are Being Made

It is important to remember that regression equations are derived from a particular sample to reflect a particular population. A regression equation developed to predict freshman grades in Midtown College may not be applicable at Prairie College. This point is obvious if one imagines that Midtown admits only 20% of its applicants whereas Prairie admits 80%. This is the same issue that comes up when comparing standardized test scores to norms in test manuals. If the sample described in a manual is quite different from the people being tested, the norms don't apply.

As part of her work for the career center at a university, Melissa obtained the GPA and salary of the first jobs of arts and sciences majors. She found a positive correlation between GPA and salary. She also found this regression equation:

Salary' = $25,000 + 500 times GPA

She intended to apply this formula to predict the starting salaries of the graduates of the engineering school. Because the students were from the same university and were drawn from the same geographical area, she felt justified in doing this. Was she right? ■

Verify That Predictions Would Be Equally Precise Throughout the Range of X

The final caution in using regression takes us back to inspecting scatterplots. Sometimes the scatterplots are not shaped like footballs, but are shaped like ice cream cones. Figure 17.9 displays the contrast between the types of scatterplots shown earlier and one shaped like an ice cream cone. Even though both scatterplots show positive linear relationships, there is a crucial difference between them. The top part of the figure illustrates *homogeneity of variance* for Y across the range of the X variable. The idea is that, for people who have a certain score on X, the standard deviations of their Y scores is about the same as the standard deviation of Y scores for people with different X scores. In contrast, in the lower portion of the figure, the variance of Y is much larger for people with high values of X compared to those with low values of X. *Regression analysis assumes homogeneity of variance across the range of X.* Severe violations of the assumptions would result in misleading conclusions about the standard error of estimate, $s_{y \cdot x}$. In the scatterplot in the lower portion of Figure

FIGURE 17.9 ■ The scatterplot in the upper half shows homogeneity of the variance for Y across the values of X. In contrast, the scatterplot in the lower half shows less variance in Y for low values of X than for high values of X scores.

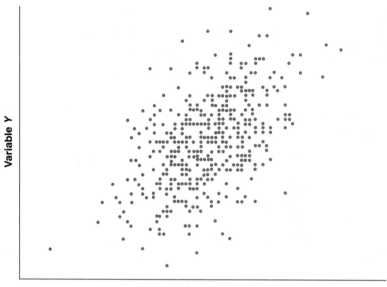

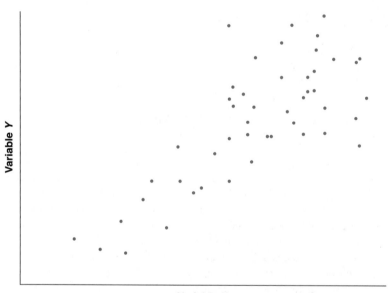

17.9, predictions for people with low values of X are much more precise than are the predictions for people with high values of X; however, using the standard error formula would not reveal that.

WHAT YOU HAVE LEARNED AND THE NEXT STEP

This chapter ends the unit on correlation and regression. The main points covered in this chapter demonstrate how to use simple (one predictor) regression analysis.

- Regression is a technique to provide specific predictions of the values of one continuous variable on the basis of the values of another continuous variable. The variable we use to predict is called the *predictor,* or *independent variable,* and the values we predict represent the *criterion,* or *dependent variable.*

- Regression as presented in this chapter is linear regression. The purpose of linear regression is to define a straight line that best summarizes the pattern of points relating X and Y seen in a scatterplot.

- The intercept, $a_{y \cdot x}$, of the line indicates where the line crosses the y (criterion) axis. The slope, $b_{y \cdot x}$, of the line indicates the rate of change in Y per unit change in X (predictor).

- To find the regression line, a regression equation for a straight line is used: $Y' = a_{y \cdot x} + b_{y \cdot x} X$. In the equation, Y' ("Y prime" or "Y predicted") is the predicted value of Y.

- The best-fitting line is one that minimizes the sum of the squares of all the prediction errors. Thus, regression analysis makes use of the method of least squares.

- Before calculating a regression equation, data inspection must be performed to detect outliers and klinkers. The distributions of the variables must not show extreme skewness or floor or ceiling effects.

- To plot a regression line, the regression equation is used to find Y' for two values of X, which are both within the range of X but are quite different from each other. After the points are plotted, they are connected with a straight line.

- It is important to distinguish between a derivation sample, which makes use of existing data for X and Y to obtain a regression equation, and an application sample, which provides only values of X but for which values of Y are predicted.

- Because we know that predictions will not be precise, it is important not only to calculate statistical significance, but also to find confidence intervals of predictions.

- Confidence intervals make use of the standard error of estimate, $s_{y \cdot x}$, which provides a measure of the overall accuracy of prediction.

- There are many contributing causes of any specific behavior; consequently, we should not be surprised that predictions we make will be imprecise, although useful nevertheless. The value of the predictions made from regression analyses depends on the nature of the variables involved; predictions of important variables that cannot be predicted in any other way are valuable even though not precise.

- Often the variable to be predicted is measured later in time compared to the other variable. At other times, the variables are gathered at the same time, in which case relating the variables to each other is done for theoretical reasons.

- Cautions regarding the use of regression equations include (a) don't predict beyond the range of X in the derivation sample, (b) don't try to predict X from Y using a regression equation obtained for predicting Y, (c) watch for restriction of range, (d) make predictions only when the derivation sample is similar to the application sample, (e) verify that there is homogeneity of variance in Y across the range of X.

Beginning in Chapter 4, we have covered variables for which means and standard deviations can be calculated. Such variables are continuous and can be considered to be interval (or ratio) scales. Sometimes, researchers do not measure a variable that possesses the characteristics of interval scales (as mentioned in Box 14.1 about Spearman's rank-order correlation). Some variables are identifications (such as Jewish, Catholic, Protestant, or Muslim) and other variables simply show order of magnitude (such as Maria studied longer than Juan who studied longer than Mark who studied longer than Tracey). Means cannot be taken when variables do not provide interval information. If the variables provide only information on category membership or relative order, the techniques we have presented cannot be used. There are statistical techniques to use with ordinal and categorical variables. We cover the analysis of categorical data in the next chapter.

Key Concepts

regression	regression line	residuals
intercept	regression equation	method of least squares
slope	predictor	derivation sample
regression analysis	criterion	application sample
linear regression	best-fitting straight line	standard error of the estimate

Answers to *Your Turn* Questions

17-1. Charge = $40 + $70 times hours worked = $92.50

17-2. Slope for converting degrees Fahrenheit to degrees Celsius = $(100 - 0)/(212 - 32) = 100/180 = 5/9$

Intercept: 100 = Intercept + 5/9 times 212; Intercept = $100 - 5/9$ times $212 = -17.8$.

°C = $-17.8 + 5/9$ times °F

(Note: You may have used a somewhat rearranged formula (°C = 5/9 (°F − 32)) in a chemistry class. It's the same formula: 5/9 times 32 is 17.8.)

17-3. $b_{C.P} = .41 (24.9/3.1) = 3.293$

$a_{C.P} = M_C - 3.293(M_P) = 72.1 - 3.293(12.4)$

$C' = 31.3 + 3.29(P)$

17-4. No, the slope is not limited. This can be seen in Equation 17.2. If the standard deviation of Y is very large (as you will find with Graduate Record Examination scores among a representative sample of college students) and the standard deviation of undergraduate grade averages is small (as it is when value of the grades range from 0 (F) through 4 (A)), the slope will be numerically small. If Y is income in dollars (a variable with a large standard deviation) predicted from grades (a variable with a small standard deviation), the slope will be numerically large.

17-5. The easiest two points to calculate would be for $X = 200$ (leading to $Y' = 10 + 19$) and $X = 800$ (leading to $Y' = 10 + 76$).

17-6. (a) $s_{y \cdot x} = 12.38 \sqrt{(1 - .38^2)} = 11.45$

(b) $s_{y \cdot x} = 1.72 \sqrt{(1 - .25^2)} = 1.66$

The size of the correlation is the better measure. Prediction accuracy in application (b) may seem better because $s_{y \cdot x}$ is smaller than in application (a), but the critical contrast is not how large $s_{y \cdot x}$ is, but how $s_{y \cdot x}$, the error, compares to how much variation there was to predict, s_y. Thus, the size of the correlation is the correct index of accuracy of prediction.

17-7. The predicted score is 88.5. For the 80% confidence interval, we need to use the nondirectional t for a probability of .20, $t(120) = 1.289$. (Note: We use the entry for 120 degrees of freedom because we do not have the actual value for 472 degrees of freedom; the error introduced by doing this is very small. The t for infinite degrees of freedom is 1.282, which is not very different from 1.289.) The confidence interval is $88.5 \pm 1.289 (8.31) = 77.8$ to 99.2.

17-8. Rick wanted to concentrate on those who are taller and would get the most rebounds, but that meant the range of height was restricted. Thus, he obscured the correlation that exists between the height of NBA basketball players and the number of rebounds they get.

17-9. Melissa tried to apply a regression equation derived from arts and sciences majors to engineering majors. Her derivation sample is inappropriate for the application she had in mind. Engineering majors get initially higher salaries than arts and sciences students get for their first jobs.

Analyzing and Interpreting Data: Problems and Exercises

1. What is the goal of regression analysis?

2. (a) What is the linear regression equation?
   (b) Identify and define each term in the equation.

3. Plot each of the following equations. Remember that a graph is not complete unless the axes are labeled.
   (a) $Y = 8 + 4X$
   (b) $Y = 10 - 5X$

4. Plot each of the following equations. Remember that a graph is not complete unless the axes are labeled.
   (a) $Y = -2 + 10X$
   (b) $Y = 3 + .50X$

5. Find the regression line (equation) that includes the following sets of two points for X and Y', respectively: Point 1, 100, 90; Point 2, 50, 60.

6. Find the regression line (equation) that includes the following sets of two points, X, Y': Point 1, 5, 10; Point 2, 10, 50.

7. Suppose that Conrad related the number of cookies a group of seven male students ate during an experiment with the number of hours since their last meal.
(Note: Because the size of the sample is so small, ignore concerns about normal distributions of the original variables. You should check on whether the data show a linear pattern.)

Student	Hours Since Last Meal	Number of Cookies
A	2.0	2
B	3.0	4
C	2.0	6
D	7.0	6
E	8.0	6
F	7.0	8
G	10.0	10
M	5.57	6.00
s	3.21	2.58

Conrad found the correlation to be .805. Find a regression equation predicting the number of cookies eaten from the number of hours since the last meal.

8. Jennifer replicated the study (in problem #7) relating number of cookies eaten and hours since last meal with eight women. Use her data to calculate a regression equation to predict number of cookies eaten from hours since last meal. (Note: Because the size of the sample is so small, ignore concerns about normal distributions of the original variables. You should check on whether the data show a linear pattern.)

Student	Hours Since Last Meal	Number of Cookies
H	0.5	1
I	2.0	2
J	2.0	1
K	4.0	5
L	2.0	1
M	0.5	2
N	1.0	3
O	2.0	4
M	1.75	2.38
s	1.13	1.51

Jennifer found the correlation to be .607. Find the regression equation to predict number of cookies eaten from hours since the last meal.

9. Suppose that an admissions director at Large State University had a regression equation prepared to predict first-semester grades on the basis of SAT_{comp}. The equation is $GPA' = -2.0 + 0.010$ (SAT_{comp}). The correlation (r) in the derivation sample of 200 students was .30.

(a) Use the equation to make predictions of GPA for the following students:

Student	SAT_{comp}
Jonathan	560
Paige	380

(b) Assume the standard deviation of $Y(s_y)$ equaled 0.40. Use Equation 17.6 to find the standard error of the estimate and then calcu-

late 95% confidence interval based on Equation 17.6 for each of your predictions.

10. Suppose that an admissions director at Large State University had a regression equation prepared to predict first-semester college grades (GPA_{Coll}) on the basis of high school grades (GPA_{HS}): $GPA_{Coll}' = 1.14 + 0.56 (GPA_{HS})$. The correlation (r) in the derivation sample of 250 students was .45.

(a) Use the equation to make predictions for the following students:

Student	GPA_{HS}
Jonathan	3.4
Paige	2.8

(b) Assume the standard deviation of Y, s_y, equaled 0.40. Use Equation 17.5 to find the standard error of the estimate and then calculate the 95% confidence interval based on Equation 17.6 for each of your predictions.

11. Acme Products, Inc., developed a selection test for use in deciding whom to hire for the loading docks. The test was used in a regression equation to link test scores to rated success on the job after six months. A new person in the Human Resources Department at Diamond Motors wanted to use the test and the regression equation to predict success on the job for the applicants for the file clerk positions whom she was interviewing for her company. She felt she could do this because the on-the-job rating form says nothing about the type of work, it refers simply to "successful work" on a scale of 0 to 100 as rated by a supervisor. Explain why she should not do that.

12. Klu Less began to work in a human services office of a large company that used a regression equation to predict on the job success from a test score. The measure of job success was the composite of several ratings of quality and volume of work products. Klu wondered if he could tell what the test scores of successful employees were likely to be if he had their rating on the job

success rating. He took the regression equation used in the office and entered the job success rating of a hypothetical employee and solved for the test score. He told his boss that, if an employee's performance is better than 80% of employees (the 80th percentile), then that employee probably earned score X. Explain what he did wrong.

13. Suppose that a researcher asked several students what they thought would predict the level of participation in extracurricular activities at college. One student suggested that extraversion scores could predict the amount of time devoted to those activities. But another student said that interest in building an impressive résumé was more important because the students who were most career oriented would probably be most active. Suppose that data were gathered, and the research team discovered that the correlation of extraversion and time on activities equaled .34 and the correlation of concern over building a good résumé also correlated with time spent on activities to the same extent, .34.
    (a) Is either student more right than the other?
    (b) Have they learned that extraversion is highly correlated with concern over building a good résumé?
    (c) What might Box 17.1 suggest would be the best approach to analyzing the data they gathered?

14. If the following observations were made, would regression be a good way to summarize the relationship between Variable A and Variable B? Explain your answer.

	Person								
	1	2	3	4	5	6	7	8	9
Variable A	3	6	7	2	8	7	5	4	5
Variable B	10	15	12	11	9	11	20	18	22

15. If the following observations were made, would regression be a good way to summarize the relationship between Variable A and Variable B? Explain your answer.

	Person								
	1	2	3	4	5	6	7	8	9
Variable A	3	6	6	2	8	7	9	4	5
Variable B	10	11	9	11	19	18	18	9	11

16. Given the following regression equation: $Y' = 23 + 0.50X$. (a) Is the r_{xy} positive or negative? (b) Is $b_{y.x}$ positive or negative? (c) Is $s_{y.x}$ positive or negative? (d) Is r_{xy} large or small?

17. Given $s_{y.x} = 10.0$, $N = 200$, and $Y' = 75$. Find the 90% confidence interval for the prediction.

18. Given $s_{y.x} = 12.0$, $N = 102$, and $Y' = 62$. Find the 99% confidence interval for the prediction.

19. Given $s_x = 10.0$, $M_x = 100.0$, and $Y' = 50.0 + 0.20 (X)$ based on a derivation sample of 200 people:
    (a) Calculate Y' for someone with an X score of 120. What correction would you apply to the standard error of estimate used to find the confidence interval for that prediction?
    (b) Calculate Y' for someone with an X score of 90. What correction to the standard error would you now use?

20. Imagine that the following data represent a larger data set.

	Person										
	1	2	3	4	5	6	7	8	9	10	11
Variable A	10	15	32	21	17	34	52	39	42	44	51
Variable B	10	16	25	22	13	85	68	90	72	78	80

Does this selection from the larger data set suggest that a regression analysis using A to predict B would be a good idea?

Answers to Odd-Numbered Problems

1. The goal of regression analysis is to obtain an equation to permit making specific predictions of the values of a continuous variable based on values of another continuous variable.

3. (a)

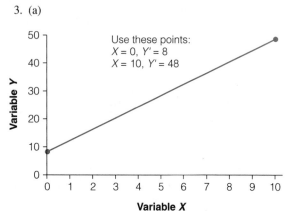

Use these points:
X = 0, Y' = 8
X = 10, Y' = 48

(b)

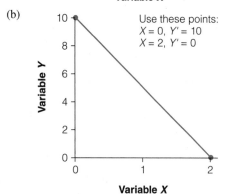

Use these points:
X = 0, Y' = 10
X = 2, Y' = 0

5. The regression equation that includes these sets of two points $(X, Y)'$, Point 1, 100, 90, and Point 2, 50, 60, is $Y' = 30 + 0.6\,X$.
Rise $= 90 - 60 = 30$; Run $= 100 - 50 = 50$; Slope $= 30/50 = .60$; Intercept $= 90 - .6(100)$

7. Slope $= 0.805\,[(2.58/3.21)] = 0.647$; Intercept $= 6.00 - [(0.647)\,(5.57)] = 2.396$
Cookies eaten predicted $= 2.40 + 0.65$ (hours since last meal)

9. Based on the equation, $GPA' = -2.0 + 0.010\,(SAT_{comp})$, and a correlation (r) in the derivation sample $(n = 200)$ of 0.50, we can make the following predictions for these students:

Student	SAT_{comp}	Y'
Jonathan	560	$-2 + 0.01\,(560) = 3.60$
Paige	380	$-2 + 0.01\,(380) = 1.80$

(b) The 95% confidence intervals for each of these predictions are based on Equation 17.6, $Y' \pm t_{(df = N-2,\ \text{two-tailed},\ \alpha=.05)}(s_{y\cdot x})$. The formula for the standard error of the estimate, based on Equation 17.5, is $s_{y\cdot x} = s_y = \sqrt{(1 - r_{xy}^2)}$, which, for these data becomes $0.40\sqrt{(1 - .30^2)}$, or 0.38. Because sample size was 200, degrees of freedom for t_{crit} $(N - 2)$ are 198, which is not in Table A.2. The next lowest value in Table A.2 is 120, and thus, the t_{crit} (.05) is 1.98. Therefore, the 95% confidence intervals for these predictions are:
Jonathan: $3.60 \pm 1.98\,(0.38) = 2.85$ to 4.35.
Paige: $1.80 \pm 1.98\,(0.38) = 1.05$ to 2.55.

11. Human Resources at Diamond Motors should not use the regression equation. The derivation sample comprised loading dock workers—outside people required to move heavy boxes and to work machinery—whereas Diamond intends to hire people for work in offices doing detailed filing. What predicts success for one group may not predict for the other group.

13. (a) Both students appear to be correct; both principles seem to be involved.
(b) It might be tempting to think the extraverted students are building their résumés, but that may not be true. These two variables might not be correlated at all.
(c) Box 17.1 suggests that, when more than one variable might predict a behavior, it would be best to use them together in one analysis. Unfortunately, we have not covered this technique in this text.

15. Construct a scatterplot. Regardless of whether you think of using A to predict B or vice versa, you will see that there are two sets of points. The values of B do not form a normal-like distribution. The scatterplot has two clusters. Regression (as well as correlation) would be misleading.

17. $75 \pm 1.645\,(10.0) = 58.55$ to 91.45

19. (a) $Y' = 74$. A score of 120 is two standard deviations above the mean of 100. Using 200 people, Table 17.3 shows that the correction should be 1.0125. In calculating a confidence interval, the standard error of estimate should be multiplied by 1.0125.
(b) $Y' = 78$. A score of 90 is one standard deviation below the mean; the correction factor is 1.0050.

Go to http://psychology.wadsworth.com/courses/statistics/ and test your knowledge of this chapter by taking the online quiz. Another resource to check is the online workshops that provide a step-by-step guide through a number of topics at http://psychology.wadsworth.com/workshops/workshops.html.

PART 6

I-D-E-A for Studies with Nominal Data

I-D-E-A with Nominal Data

Let us not forget that judgment is required in every analysis of scientific information.

Cortina & Dunlap (1997, p. 171)

INTRODUCTION

In this final chapter, we use the I-D-E-A model of data analysis to make decisions about nominal or categorical data. Nominal data involve the classification of people, events, or things into mutually exclusive categories; hence, researchers also use the term *categorical data* for this type of data. Consider, for example, a classic study in psychology carried out by Gibson and Walk (1960) to measure infants' perception of depth. Very young children were coaxed by their mothers to crawl across a "visual cliff" that appeared under a transparent surface. Children were placed on top of the transparent surface at a point where underneath a textured surface indicated little or no depth (the "shallow" side). The mother stood a few feet away. To reach the mother, the child had to crawl on the transparent surface into an area where greater depth was indicated (i.e., the "deep" side). Children at a very young age were clearly reluctant to do so, suggesting that depth perception may be innate. But note what Gibson and Walk recorded: children either crossed the visual cliff or did not cross the visual cliff (and more of them definitely did not!). The children were placed into two categories based on their behavior in the visual cliff apparatus.

Similarly, a school psychologist who asks middle-school students to identify their favorite sport, given the choice of football, hockey, basketball, and soccer, is collecting nominal data. Each child's response falls into one of four mutually exclusive categories. The number of responses in each category can be used to measure children's preferences among these sports.

Nominal or categorical data differ from the kind of data that we have been examining so far in this book in several important ways. For example, there is no mean or median to calculate, and the very nature of nominal data makes it inappropriate for statistical procedures that require interval or ratio data, such as t and F tests.

Perhaps the best way to get a feel for the issues confronting a researcher who conducts a study using nominal data is to provide, as we often have done in this book, some research examples to which we can refer as we show how to apply the I-D-E-A model to studies of this type. Consider the following scenarios:

- Tomas is a member of the Green Party in New Mexico and works for a candidate in the upcoming state election. The candidate asks Tomas to survey people in Santa Fe County to find out if they support logging of trees in the Santa Fe National Forest. Tomas obtains a random sample of 200 voters. Among the questions Tomas asks is: "Do you support the logging of trees in the Santa Fe National Forest?" Tomas records their opinion: yes or no. He then tallies the results for this question and finds that 84 said yes and 116 said no. Expressing the results as a percentage of the total number of people surveyed indicates that 58% (116/200) are opposed (and 42% in favor). The candidate asks Tomas how sure he is that this result applies to all the voters in the county.

- Kristen is hired after graduation by a marketing firm. Her first assignment is at a shopping mall where she is to ask shoppers to examine three different logos for a new computer company and to select the one they like best. The company logos are presented together in an array, but the order of the logos within the display is randomly varied across shoppers. Kristen gets 300 shoppers to make a judgment. Each shopper is tested individually. The preferences for logos A, B, and C were 80, 130, and 90, respectively. Upon showing these data to her department manager, her manager asks Kristen to provide evidence that the differences in observed frequencies reflect more than simply sampling error.

● Sally is a graduate student helping her faculty mentor investigate the roots of alcoholism. Together, they conducted a study to determine whether children have preferences for alcohol-related smells and whether their preferences differ depending on whether their mother drinks alcohol (based on an idea from a study by Minnella & Garcia, 2000). The researchers asked 250 three- to six-year-olds to smell a bottle scented with beer and a bottle scented with bubble gum. Of the 250 children, 164 had a mother who drank beer, and 86 children came from homes in which the mother did not drink beer. (Fathers were not considered in this study.) After smelling both bottles, the children were asked to place the bottle with the scent they liked better on a smiley face. The results revealed that the numbers of children from these two groups who liked these smells were as follows:

Group	Preferred Smell of Beer	Preferred Smell of Bubble Gum
Mother drinks beer	75	89
Mother doesn't drink beer	24	62

Sally's faculty mentor asked her to analyze and interpret the results.

WHAT QUESTION ARE YOU ASKING?

All of these research scenarios have some important things in common. First, each makes use of nominal data. Tomas classifies people as for or against a particular proposition, Kristen records the number of people who select a particular logo, and Sally determines whether children prefer the smell of beer or bubble gum in each of the two experimental groups. In each case, the researcher records the number of participants appearing in two or more categories. The research scenarios also have something else in common that may not be readily apparent: in each study, the classification of participants is into mutually exclusive categories. For example, Kristen recorded only each person's most preferred logo. The data analysis techniques that are discussed in this chapter apply only to those situations in which a person, event, or thing is placed in only one category. (More advanced statistics procedures are available to deal with nominal data that are generated from repeated measures designs.)

As way of review, consider the following dependent variables. Identify those that are measured on a nominal scale. (If necessary, consult Table 1.2 in Chapter 1, which summarizes characteristics of the four levels of measurement: nominal, ordinal, interval, and ratio).

(a) number correct on a class exam
(b) students classified according to major
(c) the amount of time (seconds) drivers stop at a stop sign
(d) number of drivers who stop, slow down, or do not slow down at a stop sign
(e) temperature (Fahrenheit)

These hypothetical research scenarios differ from one another in an important way: the researchers are asking somewhat different questions. Tomas has a single sample of people, and, based on their responses to his survey question, he determines the proportions (expressed as percentages) of people who say yes or no. Tomas's boss wants to know if he should have confidence that the results reflect the population as a whole. You may see this research scenario as very similar to the happiness study conducted by Katie that was discussed beginning in Chapter 4. Recall that Katie asked a random sample of students how happy they were at their university. However, Katie used a 7-point scale that was judged to represent interval data. Consider that Katie might have asked people at her school: "Are you happy here? Yes or no?" If she had, the data she obtained would have been nominal, not interval, and she would be interested, as is Tomas, in the proportion of people falling in one of two categories (yes and no).

Kristen, on the other hand, asks a sample of adults to choose a company logo that they like best. She has people choose from three different logos. She is interested in the relative frequency (proportion) of responses across the three types of logo. Is there evidence that people's preferences differ?

Finally, Sally is seeking to analyze a study that resembles the factorial design that Liz used in a previous chapter to investigate the effectiveness of two types of therapy on the mental health of male and female clients. Of course, Sally's dependent variable is measured on a nominal scale. Sally is primarily interested in whether children's frequency of choosing smells reveals a similar or different distribution for the two groups. One way of asking this is "Does the relative frequency (proportions) of responses depend on group membership?" This question is analogous to the question asked of an interaction effect in a factorial design when interval or ratio data are used.

We now look at how the I-D-E-A model may be applied to each of these types of designs.

THE I-D-E-A MODEL FOR A PROPORTION
FROM A SINGLE (LARGE) SAMPLE

To review, a sample is selected, and behavior is measured on a nominal scale having two categories. A proportion is calculated for each category by dividing the number of people, events, or things in the category by the total number in the data set. The question we wish to examine is how well the sample proportion approximates the proportion that would have been obtained if all members of the population had been included. We chose an example based on an election issue because it is likely that you have previously seen or heard the results of such election polling. Have you not heard media statements such as "50% of the people polled approve of the President's actions" or "67% of those polled support candidate X for governor"? It is also likely that, when hearing these news reports, you also heard a phrase such as "the margin of error in the poll is five [or some similar small number] percentage points." We will explain margin of error later. Of course, one need not deal only with election issues. A psychologist might ask, for example, what is the proportion of men over age 60 who suffer from depression. Or, as Gibson and Walk did, ask what proportion of infants are unwilling to cross the visual cliff.

Inspection

Inspection of data in a study involving two categories of responses is rather straightforward. The researcher wants to make sure that there are no missing scores, that data have been recorded and entered into a computer accurately, that responses are indeed coded as falling into either one of two categories (e.g., that there are no "maybe" responses), and that the total number of responses in the two categories equals the total number of participants. This last point is important because it serves as a check on the tabulations within each category. Remember, a participant may appear in only one category; thus, *the sum of the category frequencies should equal the total number of participants in the study.* Unlike when interval or ratio data are involved, there is no need to look for a normal distribution of responses.

Description

The description stage is quite simple when there are two categories. The number of participants falling into each of the categories is determined, and each of these numbers is divided by the total number of participants to provide a **sample proportion (P)**. A sample proportion is defined as

$$P = n_c/N \qquad \qquad \text{Equation 18.1}$$

In this formula, n_c is the number of participants in a particular category, and N is the total number of participants in the sample. Of course, the sum of the two proportions in a two-category study should equal 1.00.

Estimation

There are a couple of different ways to estimate confidence in a sample proportion. Perhaps the most useful technique is to construct confidence intervals for the population proportion in a manner analogous to constructing confidence intervals around a sample mean. We have used μ to indicate a population mean; we now use p to symbolize a **population proportion**. The value of p would (as would the value of μ) be known if all members of a population were included. Thus, when random samples are taken, P is an estimate of p (just as M is an estimate of μ when interval or ratio data are available).

When the total number of participants (N) is relatively large (say, 100 or greater), it can be assumed that the values of the sample proportion, P, are normally distributed across many samples (Hays, 1994). However, as we found when estimating the value of μ, we usually do not know the standard deviation of the population and thus cannot determine the standard error of the sampling distribution. Rather, we must estimate it. The **estimated standard error of a proportion** (based on large sample sizes) is

$$\sqrt{[P(1 - P)/(N - 1)]} \qquad \qquad \text{Equation 18.2}$$

A confidence interval for p, the population proportion, may be defined using the z value associated with the appropriate level of confidence. A z score of 1.96 leaves .025 in the tail of the distribution and is associated with an alpha level of .05 (two-tailed test). (See Table A.1.) Therefore, the **95% confidence interval for p** is defined as

$$P \pm (1.96) \sqrt{[P(1 - P)/(N - 1)]} \qquad \qquad \text{Equation 18.3}$$

As we noted previously, this formula is most reasonably used when sample size (N) is 100 or greater.

BOX 18.1 ■ A Word About Margin of Error

When reported percentages (proportions) from surveys appear in the media and are accompanied by a statement of the "margin of error," we unfortunately cannot always tell *exactly* what this means. Although plus or minus the margin of error is often the 95% confidence interval, it sometimes may be plus or minus 2 times the standard error. You may recall from Chapter 11 that researchers frequently approximate the 95% confidence interval by multiplying the standard error by 2. Although we strongly encourage the use of confidence intervals rather than intervals based on 2 times the standard error, in actual practice this makes little difference because the result, especially with large samples, is basically the same. When nominal data are collected from large samples and a proportion obtained, the margin of error is essentially the same whether based on a confidence interval or standard error bars. Multiplication of the standard error is either by 2.00 (when only the standard error is used) or 1.96 (when the value of z is used). We suggest that you think of plus or minus the "margin of error" as equivalent to a 95% confidence interval unless you have information to the contrary.

Let's use Tomas's results to illustrate these calculations. His sample size was 200. Tomas found that 116 people said "no" to his survey question and 84 said "yes." The proportion of people opposed is, therefore, .58 ($P = 116/200 = .58$); .42 of the people said "yes." The 95% confidence interval for the population proportion of "no" responses[1] is

$$P \pm (1.96) \sqrt{[P(1 - P)/(N - 1)]} = .58 \pm (1.96)\sqrt{[.58(.42)(/200 - 1)]}$$
$$= .58 \pm (1.96) \sqrt{.001224}$$
$$= .58 \pm (1.96)(0.035), \text{ or } .58 \pm .07$$

The 95% confidence interval for Tomas's data is .51 to .65.

Tomas can be confident that there is a .95 probability that the true population proportion has been captured by this interval. The **margin of error** in this example is .07 and, therefore, .58 $\pm$.07 represents the confidence interval for the population value. Tomas knows something else from an examination of this interval: because the value of .50 is not within the interval, Tomas may conclude that there is not equal preference for the two options (Hays, 1994); rather, more people opposed logging than were in favor of logging. (The value .50 would represent an equal split, that is, 50:50, of people saying "yes" and "no.")

As with all confidence intervals, we want to examine the width of the interval to assess the precision with which the population value is estimated. Tomas's interval width may be judged to be reasonable, but it is somewhat larger than the margin of error often reported in media polls. And the reason is simply that surveys conducted by polling firms typically rely on N's larger than 200. As you have come to appreciate, an increase in sample size serves to increase precision of estimation of parameters, as indicated by a narrower width for the confidence intervals.

[1]It should be apparent by examining the formula closely, that the width of the confidence interval for no responses will be exactly the same as that for yes responses. Note that the numerator under the radical sign would, for yes responses, simply change from [.58 (.42)] to [.42(.58)], which of course would lead to exactly same interval width (but of course surrounding a different value of P). The choice of which category proportion to report is up to the researcher; we chose the proportion of no responses because we think the Green Party in New Mexico would be more interested in "no" responses.

Let us assume that Tomas had surveyed 1,000 people rather than 200 and had obtained the same proportion of "yes" and "no" responses. Substituting 1,000 for 200 in Equation 18.3 yields a 95% confidence interval of

$$P \pm (1.96)\sqrt{[P(1 - P)/(N - 1)]} = .58 \pm (1.96) \sqrt{[.58(.42)/(1000 - 1)]} =$$
.58 ± .03, or 55% to 61%, and a margin of error of ±3 points

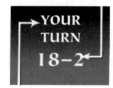

Assume that you are interested in the proportion of students at your school who have acrophobia (fear of heights). You design a questionnaire asking about various phobias and include acrophobia on your list. You randomly sample 150 students of which 24, or 0.16 (16%) indicate they have a fear of heights. What is the 95% confidence interval for the population proportion? ■

Just as we might wish to compare mean results from two different samples by inspecting the degree of overlap between confidence intervals based on interval or ratio data, we can also inspect the overlap between confidence intervals for proportions. Assume that, in an election campaign, 54% of the citizens of California favor candidate X and in New Jersey 49% favor this candidate. Knowing that there is variation due to sampling error, we might want to know if the difference in candidate preference for the two states is worth paying attention to. Suppose that in both states the margin of error is plus or minus three points? Thus, we have

California: .54 ± .03, or .51 to .57

New Jersey: .49 ± .03, or .46 to .52

What are you to make of this difference? As you can see, the intervals overlap slightly. The rule of thumb we have used is that, in such cases, we want to be cautious about assuming there is a significant difference between the two population parameters, in this case the population proportions, p. In other words, it is still too close to call.

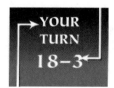

In a presidential election year, two candidates, Bore and Mush, are campaigning for the presidency. A media report states that a survey of a nationwide sample of voters shows that 56% favor Mush and 44% favor Bore. The margin of error is reported to be four percentage points. What would be a reasonable conclusion to make of this difference? ■

Announcing Results

The format for announcing results is similar to that when any confidence interval is created. Tomas's report to his boss might look like the following:

A random sample of 200 registered voters in Santa Fe County was surveyed. Each prospective voter was asked "Do you support the logging of trees in the Santa Fe National Forest?" Results revealed that 58% said "no" and 42% said "yes." The 95% confidence interval for the population proportion of "no" responses is .51 to .65. There is a .95 probability that this interval contains the population proportion. Because .50 is not within the interval, we may conclude that more people were opposed to logging than were in favor of logging.

There is yet another way to estimate confidence in the results of a study involving a two-category classification of responses and when sample size is less than 100. We will illustrate that approach following an introduction to null hypothesis significance testing (NHST) with nominal data.

NHST WITH NOMINAL DATA

We mentioned that NHST procedures based on t or F cannot be applied with nominal data. One reason is that these statistical procedures make assumptions about the distribution of scores, for example, that the scores come from a normal distribution or that the variances of two different populations are similar. Such assumptions are not always applicable when we have nominal data. Parameters are characteristics of populations (e.g., μ, σ), and techniques of nominal data analysis do not make assumptions about these population characteristics in the same way as do procedures associated with, for example, the t and F distributions. The statistical techniques used for NHST with nominal data are, therefore, frequently called **distribution-free** or **nonparametric tests**.

The most widely used nonparametric test is based on the distribution of **chi-square (χ^2)**. Like the t and F distributions, the chi-square distribution is mathematically determined and defined by its degrees of freedom. Unlike the t and F distributions, however, the degrees of freedom for a chi-square distribution vary not with the number of subjects, but with the number of independent categories. It is a positively skewed distribution that changes shape with the degrees of freedom. Figure 18.1 shows how the shape of a chi-square distribution changes as degrees of freedom increase.

FIGURE 18.1 ■ The shape of the chi-square distribution changes as the degrees of freedom (number of categories) increase. Because χ^2 is always positive, the region of rejection is always at the extreme positive end of the distribution.

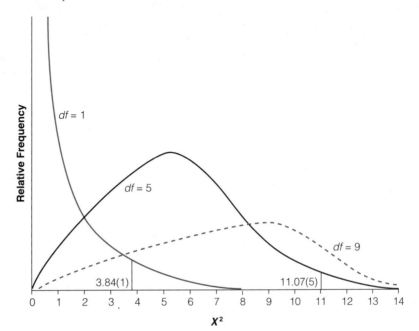

A chi-square test is applied in two general situations. The first is one wherein the investigator asks whether a distribution of observed frequencies matches the distribution of expected frequencies. The distribution of expected frequencies is generated on the basis of the question being asked. This particular application of chi-square is called a **goodness-of-fit test** because one is testing to see if the observed relative frequencies "fit" the distribution of relative frequencies expected on the basis of the research question. The second situation is one wherein the investigator seeks to determine whether the distribution of observed relative frequencies is independent of group membership. This application of chi-square is called a **test of independence**. We will now examine in detail these two chi-square tests.

CHI-SQUARE (χ^2) GOODNESS-OF-FIT TEST

Kristen tested 300 people individually. Each was shown three company logos and asked to identify the logo most preferred. The preferences of her participants for each of the logos were as follows:

Logo A	Logo B	Logo C
80	130	90

The frequencies she records in each condition of her experiment are the **observed frequencies**. These are what Kristen observed in her logo test.

Inspection and Description

Having found the observed frequencies for her study, Kristen should check the data to make sure that all responses have been recorded accurately and that the sum of the observed frequencies equals the number of participants in her study. As can be seen, the three frequencies sum to 300, the number of people who were in her sample (N). Data description should include calculating the proportion of responses for each of the categories. This is simply done by dividing each category frequency (n_c) by N (i.e., $n_c/N = P$). The proportions for her study are as follows:

Logo A	Logo B	Logo C
80/300 = .27	130/300 = .43	90/300 = .30

By calculating proportions, Kristen is able to easily summarize the relative frequency of responses across categories of her study.

Estimation

Kristen is asking whether the observed relative frequencies indicate definite differences in relative frequency of preferences or whether the distribution of observed frequencies is simply chance variation. As can be seen, Logo B was more preferred than A or C, which were about equally preferred. To decide how well the distribution of responses fits a distribution that represents chance, Kristen must determine what would be expected if only chance were operating. A reasonable expectation if only chance is operating is that the three logos would be equally preferred. This expectation becomes the null hypothesis for the study. Because 300 people were tested, the **expected frequencies** under the hypothesis of no difference, or chance, would be 100, 100, and 100 (or, in terms of proportions. 33, .33, .33). Thus, the observed and expected frequencies would look like this:

	Logo A	Logo B	Logo C
Observed frequency	80	130	90
Expected frequency (chance)	100	100	100

The formula for χ^2 makes use of the information in the preceding table. Specifically,

$$\chi^2 = \Sigma \left[\frac{(O - E)^2}{E} \right]$$

where O is an observed frequency, E is an expected frequency

Equation 18.4

The formula indicates that, for each category, the difference between the observed (O) and expected (E) frequencies is squared and then divided by the expected frequency. This is done for each category, and the results are then summed across all the categories.

Because chi-square depends on squared differences, the value of chi-square will never be negative. Let us illustrate with Kristen's data. For these data,

$$\chi^2 = \Sigma \left[\frac{(O - E)^2}{E} \right] = \frac{(80 - 100)^2}{100} + \frac{(130 - 100)^2}{100} + \frac{(90 - 100)^2}{100}$$

$$= \frac{(-20)^2}{100} + \frac{(30)^2}{100} + \frac{(-10)^2}{100}$$

$$= \frac{400}{100} + \frac{900}{100} + \frac{100}{100} = 4.00 + 9.00 + 1.00 = 14.00$$

$$\chi^2 = 14.00$$

The value of the obtained chi-square increases as the relative frequencies become more different from each other. Thus, for Kristen's data, if the differences among the observed relative frequencies had been smaller, the obtained chi-square would have been smaller (but never negative). Greater departures from chance variation yield a larger test statistic, as we saw with t, F, and r. And, as we have done with t, F, and r, the obtained value of our test statistic is compared with a critical value at the appropriate alpha level, usually .05.

The degrees of freedom (df) for a chi-square goodness-of-fit test are the number of categories minus 1. For Kristen's study, the degrees of freedom are 3−1, or 2. Table A.6 contains the critical values of χ^2 for various degrees of freedom and for both directional and nondirectional tests of significance. A nondirectional test is typically employed; however, see Box 18.2. The critical value of χ^2 with 2 df and alpha equal to .05 (nondirectional) is 5.99; the critical value at the .001 level is 13.82. (See Table A.6.)

Because Kristen's obtained χ^2 is larger than the critical χ^2 with alpha at .05, she may judge that her obtained value falls in the region of rejection and that her results are statistically significant. (See Figure 18.2.) As with t and F tests, the use of NHST with alpha equal to .05 protects the researcher against excessive Type I errors. The power of the chi-square

BOX 18.2 ■ Is the Chi-Square Test Always Nondirectional?

As Howell (2002) points out, the chi-square test is usually conducted as a nondirectional (i.e., two-tailed) test. Consider that the observed frequencies in Kristen's study were 80, 130, and 90, for the three logos A, B, and C, respectively. The expected frequencies were 100 for each category under the assumption of chance or equal preference. The chi-square test was statistically significant as a nondirectional test with alpha equal to .05. Now consider what would happen if the observed frequencies had been 130, 90, and 80, for the three categories, respectively. The three observed frequencies are the same, but the order is different; for example, logo A is now the most preferred. The expected frequencies remain the same, and therefore the observed chi-square will be the same. The point is that statistical significance is achieved no matter what the order of the observed frequencies (and there are six possible ways to order three things). Howell (2002) suggests that this really makes chi-square a "multi-tailed test."

As you have seen when the t test was discussed (see Chapter 9 and 10), a directional t test based on NHST requires the researcher to specify in advance how the two means will be ordered. Similarly, to perform a directional chi-square test, a researcher would need to (a) specify the relative order of the observed category frequencies, and (b) only consider testing the null hypothesis when this particular order appears in the data set. In this case, some adjustment may be made to the alpha level to compensate for the fact that only one order (or some selected orders) is tested. These issues take us beyond this book, and we suggest you consult a more advanced statistics text, such as Howell (2002), if you believe that a directional alternative hypothesis is more appropriate in your research situation.

Bottom line: As usually applied, chi-square is a nondirectional test.

test is primarily a function of sample size as we have already seen is the case with other tests such as t and F. (See the chapter on power analysis in the appendix.)

What exactly do her findings mean? Kristen may conclude that, given the expected category frequencies, the likelihood of obtaining this distribution of observed frequencies by chance is very low, that is, less than .05. Her results are unlikely, therefore, under the hypothesis of no difference or equal preference. As when reporting t, F, and r, it is important to present the exact probability when a computer is used or the lowest probability from the table of critical values. The lower the probability, the greater assurance we have about obtaining a statistically significant replication at the .05 level. (See Chapter 10.) We previously noted that Kristen's obtained χ^2 is larger than the critical χ^2 with alpha at .001 (nondirectional).

Like all statistical tests, the chi-square goodness-of-fit test comes with a set of assumptions that should be met if we are to have confidence in the results. *A major assumption is that the observed frequencies are independent of one another.* This assumption will be satisfied if each person, event, or thing contributes to only one category, and if any one classification does not influence that of another (e.g., by not allowing participants to see each other's choices). Another major assumption is related both to sample size and to the size of expected frequencies in a particular category, as both of these are related (e.g., Howell, 2002). *This second assumption is that expected frequencies in a particular category are not too*

FIGURE 18.2.   ■   With two degrees of freedom, Kristen's obtained χ^2 of 14.00 falls in the region of rejection with alpha equal to .05 level and also exceeds the .001 level.

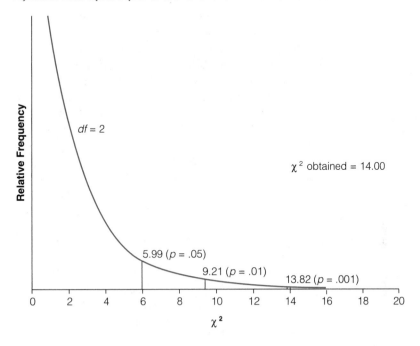

small. What is too small? A useful convention is that expected category frequencies should not be less than 5. Should you determine that an expected frequency is less than 5, it would be wise to increase the sample size before calculating χ^2.

A political scientist is testing a theory of human choice behavior. The scientist decides to test the theory in the context of choosing stocks in the stock market. Participants ($N = 88$) are provided with a written set of instructions and information about four different stocks. After reading the information, the participants are allowed to purchase shares in one or more of the stocks. As part of the analysis, the researcher identifies the stock each person preferred most. The theory states that the proportion of people preferring stocks A, B, C, and D, should be .20, .20, .40., and .20, respectively. Assume that the researcher wishes to conduct a chi-square goodness-of-fit test on these data. What would be the *expected frequencies* for this test?   ■

Announcement

An announcement of Kristen's marketing study completes the I-D-E-A model for a chi-square goodness-of fit test:

Adults at a shopping mall were individually shown three different logos for a new computer company and asked to select the one they most preferred. The percentage preferences were A, 27; B, 43; and C, 30. A chi-square goodness-of-fit test permitted rejection of a hypothesis of equal preference: χ^2 (2, $N = 300$) = 14.00, $p < .001$. Among the three logos, option B was most preferred.

BOX 18.3 ■ How Are Expected Frequencies for a Chi-Square (χ^2) Test Determined?

Expected frequencies are typically determined in one of two ways. First, as was illustrated by Kristen's study, expected frequencies are assumed to be the same for each category when a researcher is testing whether the relative frequencies (proportions) among the categories in the population are equal. Expected frequencies will be the same when the researcher assumes only chance to be operating and each category is equally likely to be chosen. A pollster may wish to determine if several candidates are equally preferred by the electorate, or a psychologist may wish to determine if several pathways to a goal are equally selected by animal subjects. The specific value of the expected frequencies will be based both on the number of subjects and number of categories. Of course, even if the frequencies in the population are the same for each category, there will be differences in observed frequencies due to sampling error. The researcher is testing whether the differences between the observed and expected frequencies are greater than would be expected by chance under the hypothesis of no difference among category frequencies.

A second way that expected frequencies may be determined is on the basis of prior research results or on normative values. Suppose a researcher wishes to know whether the proportions of political party affiliation by students at College X differ from the proportions reported nationally by students. The observed frequencies could be obtained from College X by taking a large sample and asking students their party affiliation. Because the researcher is testing whether the observed relative frequencies at College X are different from those expected on the basis of national samples, the expected frequencies would be determined by multiplying the sample size, N, by the proportion of national party affiliation. Assume that, in a national survey, college students were distributed as follows: .30 Republican, .35 Democrat, .05 Green, .25 Independent, .05 Other. Suppose further that, based on a random sample of 300 students at College X, the observed *frequencies* for party affiliation were Republican, 90; Democrat, 150; Green, 10; Independent, 30; Other, 20. Expected frequencies would be determined for each category by multiplying N (300) by the national proportions [e.g., Republican, (.30) (300) = 90]. The researcher is testing whether the differences between the observed and expected frequencies are greater than would be expected by chance under the hypothesis of no difference (i.e., null hypothesis) between frequency of affiliation at College X and that expected on the basis of the nationwide survey.

Note that the degrees of freedom for the chi-square test are placed in parentheses following χ^2 when the obtained value is presented. In addition, information is provided in the announcement regarding the observed frequencies for each category. Both the sample size (N) and the observed category frequencies should be presented. In this case, taking a percentage of N will identify the observed frequencies. Finally, the announcement should be written in a manner that clearly identifies the question being investigated. Kristen's announcement makes it clear that the hypothesis of equal preference was tested.

The chi-square goodness-of-fit test is appropriate when there are two or more categories. Therefore, this form of NHST may be used to help make decisions about the significance of a proportion based on a two-way classification of responses, as was the case in Tomas's sit-

BOX 18.4 ■ A Word of Caution About Interpreting Results of a Goodness-of-Fit Test

Look again at Kristen's results and conclusions in her announcement of results. She was able to reject the idea that there were equal preferences for the three logos, and she pointed out to the reader that, among the three options, logo B was most preferred. Note that she is simply reporting the fact that logo B was preferred by more people than was either A or C. It would seem that the company should choose option B for its logo because the other two options were noticeably less favored overall by the sample of people who were tested. But what if the observed percentages were not 27, 43, and 30, respectively, but were instead 42, 43, and 15? A goodness-of-fit test would yield a significant chi-square, and once again the null hypothesis can be rejected: the logos are not equally preferred. But which logo should the company choose? No one would want to claim that the difference between A and B (i.e., 42 and 43) is big enough to conclude that B is most preferred. In this case, the company might as well flip a coin to decide between options A and B.

The point is that we do not want to blindly accept the results of a goodness-of-fit test without carefully examining the data. Of course, that is what the inspection and description stages of data analysis are all about. As Cortina and Dunlap (1997) remind us, "judgment is required in every analysis of scientific information" (p. 171). Good judgment: don't leave home without it.

uation. We may test the hypothesis that the two propositions were equally preferred. Because 200 voters were questioned, the expected frequencies under the hypothesis of no difference would be 100 for each of the two categories, yes and no. Of course, having calculated confidence intervals for the proportion and finding that .50 is not within the interval, we know that they are not equally preferred. However, let us see how NHST may supplement an analysis of Tomas's study based on the construction of confidence intervals. The obtained chi-square for Tomas's data is as follows:

$$\chi^2 = \Sigma \left[\frac{(O - E)^2}{E} \right] = \frac{(84 - 100)^2}{100} + \frac{(116 - 100)^2}{100}$$

$$= \frac{(-16)^2}{100} + \frac{(16)^2}{100}$$

$$= \frac{256}{100} + \frac{256}{100} = 2.56 + 2.56 = 5.12$$

$$\chi^2 = 5.12$$

Because there are two categories, the degrees of freedom are 2 − 1 or, 1. The critical χ^2 for one degree of freedom with alpha set at .05 is 3.84. With alpha set at .02, the critical value is 5.41. (See Table A.6.) Thus, the obtained χ^2 is statistically significant at the .05 level, but not at the .02 level. The null hypothesis of equal preference for the two propositions may be rejected.

It appears that we have not learned anything more than we did from the construction of confidence intervals for a proportion. However, we did learn something that was not readily apparent from the construction of 95% confidence intervals. Specifically, the obtained chi-square provides information about the probability of successful replication. Given that the obtained value of chi-square is greater than the critical value with alpha at .05 but not

BOX 18.5 ■ The Chi-Square Goodness-of-Fit Test Summarized

Situation: On the basis of their responses, subjects are placed in two or more mutually exclusive categories and the relative category frequencies determined. For example, individuals are classified according to ethnic/racial background, and the relative frequency of each category is calculated.

Hypotheses:

H_0: The relative category frequencies in the population are equal (or are no different than those specified by the researcher on the basis of expected frequencies).

H_1: The distribution of relative frequencies in the population is different from that specified by the null hypothesis.

Assumptions: Observations are independent and a relatively large sample was taken, such that no expected category frequency is less than 5.

Calculation:

$$\chi^2 = \Sigma \left[\frac{(O - E)^2}{E} \right] \text{ where } O \text{ is an observed frequency, and } E \text{ is expected frequency}$$

Decision: If the obtained chi-square value is greater than the critical (tabled) value at the appropriate alpha level (usually .05), with degrees of freedom equal to the number of categories minus 1, then the result is statistically significant.

Conclusion: A statistically significant χ^2 allows the null hypothesis to be rejected. It may be concluded that the relative category frequencies in the population are not equal (or that the proportions are not the same as specified by the expected frequencies).

greater than alpha at .02, we have somewhat less confidence in a successful replication than if the obtained value had exceeded the critical value at .01 or .001. Moreover, consider what we would have learned if we had proceeded to conduct NHST first and stopped there. Yes, we would be able to reject the hypothesis of equal preference, and, yes, we would obtain information about the probability of successful replication, but, if only NHST were used, we would not have information about the precision of estimation (i.e., the margin of error). Therefore, as we have seen with other designs and types of data, the construction of confidence intervals and NHST supplement each other by providing different kinds of information about our data.

A revised announcement for Tomas's study based on both the construction of confidence intervals for a proportion and NHST using the chi-square goodness-of-fit test might look like this:

A random sample of registered voters in Santa Fe County was surveyed. Each prospective voter was asked "Do you support the logging of trees in the Santa Fe National Forest?" Results revealed that 58% said "no" and 42% said "yes." The 95% confidence interval for the population proportion of "no" responses is .58 to .61. There is a .95 probability that this interval contains the population proportion. A goodness-of-fit test resulted in χ^2 (1, $N = 200$) = 5.12, $p < .05$. Because .50 is not within the confidence interval, we may conclude that more people were opposed to logging than were in favor of logging.

CHI-SQUARE (χ^2) TEST OF INDEPENDENCE

The second major situation wherein NHST based on the chi-square distribution is used is when a researcher seeks to determine whether a distribution of observed relative frequencies is independent of group membership. Groups may be defined naturally (e.g., men vs. women, married vs. single) or on the basis of an experimental manipulation (e.g., students shown a small perceptual illusion vs. students shown a large perceptual illusion). The number of groups may vary, but in practice is most often two and usually no more than five. On the basis of their responses, subjects in each group are placed in one of two or more mutually exclusive categories. For example, men and women may be asked to identify their preference for one of three political candidates; their responses place them in one of three categories (i.e., the preferred candidate). Consider the scenario we introduced previously.

Sally is helping a faculty member investigate the roots of alcoholism. They seek to determine whether children have preferences for alcohol-related smells and whether their preferences differ depending on whether their mother drinks alcohol, specifically beer. The researchers asked 250 three- to six-year-old children to smell a bottle scented with beer and a bottle scented with bubble gum. Of the 250 children, 164 had a mother who drank beer, and 86 children came from homes in which the mother did not drink beer. After smelling both bottles, the children were asked to indicate which smell they liked better.

Inspection and Description

Having inspected the data obtained in her study and verifying that responses have been coded and summed correctly, the observed frequencies can then be summarized.

Group	Preference for Beer Smell	Preference for Bubble Gum Smell	Total
Mother drinks beer	75	89	164
Mother doesn't drink beer	24	62	86
Total	99	151	250

The combinations of group and response categories are called **cells**. Because there are two groups and two response categories, the table (design) is described as 2×2. It is important at this stage of analysis to describe the data in the table by calculating the proportion of responses in each of the four major cells of the table. Proportions must be determined for each group separately. For each group, frequencies in each cell are divided by the number of participants in the corresponding group. These totals are found in the row margins. For example, for children with mothers who drink beer, the proportion of children liking better the smell of beer was 75/164, or .46. *Note that the proportions are determined for each group (i.e., based on row totals because groups define the rows) and not for each column.* A summary of the proportions for each cell appears in the following table.

Group	Preference for Beer Smell	Preference for Bubble Gum Smell	Total
Mother drinks beer	75/164 = .46	89/164 = .54	164
Mother doesn't drink beer	24/86 = .28	62/86 = .72	86
Total	99	151	250

Estimation

The question that Sally and her mentor are asking is whether the relative frequencies of children selecting beer and bubble gum smells differ for the two groups. The proportions calculated on the basis of the observed frequencies (see previous) begin to answer that question. Although in each group more children liked the smell of bubble gum better (.54 and .72), the greatest proportion of children liking the bubble gum smell better was from the group with mothers who don't drink beer (.72). The difference between the preferences for beer or bubble gum smells was greater when mothers did not drink beer (i.e., .72 − .28 = .44 versus .54 − .46 = .08).

The data from the preceding table are used to generate the expected frequencies under the assumption that the relative frequencies (proportions) for both groups are the same; this is the null hypothesis. If the distribution of relative frequencies is independent of group membership, we would expect similar distributions for each group. If the distribution of relative frequencies is not independent, then the distributions *depend on* which group we are observing. Another way to express this is to ask whether the results are *contingent on* group membership. Thus, tables such as this one are frequently called **contingency tables**. Although Sally's data fall into a 2 × 2 contingency table, other tables may be 2 × 4, 3 × 3, and so forth, depending on the number of groups (rows) and categories (columns) under study. Earlier, we suggested that the question asked by a chi-square test of independence is analogous to that of an interaction effect. Do the results differ depending on the level (group) of a variable? Let's see how Sally might obtain evidence to answer that question.

Consider first the data from the bottom row in the preceding table. Of 250 children tested, 99/250, or 39.6%, liked the smell of beer better than that of bubble gum. If the same proportion of children *in both groups* behaved this way, we would expect 39.6% of children with mothers who drink beer and 39.6% of children with mothers who do not drink beer also to behave this way. Specifically, we would expect 39.6% of 164 children and 39.6% of 86 children to select beer over bubble gum. The expected frequencies then for these cells are (.396)(164) = 64.94 and (.396)(86) = 34.06. A similar logic may be applied to the percentage of children who selected bubble gum. Of 250 tested, 151/250, or 60.4%, favored the bubble gum smell. Finding 60.4% of 164 and 86 provides the expected frequencies for these cells: (.604)(164) = 99.06 and (.604)(86) = 51.94. In Box 18.6, we outline a simple procedure for calculating expected frequencies. The expected frequencies for Sally's study are entered in the following table.

Group	Preference for Beer Smell	Preference for Bubble Gum Smell	Total
Mother drinks beer	$O = 75$ $E = 64.94$	$O = 89$ $E = 99.06$	164
Mother doesn't drink beer	$O = 24$ $E = 34.06$	$O = 62$ $E = 51.94$	86
Total	99	151	250

Once the expected frequencies are determined, the calculation of χ^2 proceeds almost exactly has it did for the goodness-of-fit test. (See Equation 18.4.) The chi-square test of inde-

---

BOX 18.6 ■ Determining Expected Frequencies in a Contingency Table

There is a simple formula for calculating expected frequencies in a contingency table: *for any cell of the table, simply multiply the marginal total for the row that contains the cell and the marginal total for the column that contains the cell and then divide this product by the total number of responses.*

Let us illustrate with the cell showing the number of children observed to prefer beer smell in the group with a mother who drinks. The observed frequency is 75. The marginal *row* total for that cell is 164; the marginal *column* total is 99. Using the formula,

$$\frac{\text{(marginal row total) (marginal column total)}}{N} =$$

$$\frac{(164)(99)}{250} = 64.94$$

---

pendence makes the same assumptions about the data as does the goodness-of-fit test. If any expected cell frequency is less than 5, a larger sample is recommended.

For each cell, we obtain $(0 - E)^2/E$ and sum the results across all cells of the contingency table. Using the information from the preceding table, we find

$$\chi^2 = \Sigma \left[\frac{(0 - E)^2}{E} \right]$$

$$= \frac{(75 - 64.94)^2}{64.94} + \frac{(89 - 99.06)^2}{99.06} + \frac{(24 - 34.06)^2}{34.06} + \frac{(62 - 51.94)}{51.94}$$

$$= \frac{(10.06)^2}{64.94} + \frac{(-10.06)^2}{99.06} + \frac{(-10.06)^2}{34.06} + \frac{(10.06)^2}{51.94}$$

$$= 1.56 + 1.02 + 2.97 + 1.95 = 7.50$$

$$\chi^2 = 7.50$$

If r equals the number of rows and c equals the number of columns in the contingency table, then, the degrees of freedom for a chi-square test of independence are $(r - 1)$ times $(c - 1)$. In Sally's case, the degrees of freedom are $(2 - 1)(2 - 1)$, or 1. The critical χ^2 value from Table A.6 for one degree of freedom and alpha set at .05 is 3.84. For alpha at .01, the critical value is 6.64. Sally may state that her results are statistically significant at the .01 level.

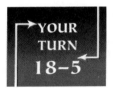

YOUR TURN 18-5

A university official wonders whether men and women at the university differ in their support of Greek organizations. The official surveys a random sample of 200 students (100 men and 100 women). Each student is asked "Are you in favor of maintaining the Greek system of fraternities and sororities at this school? (Yes or No?)" The observed frequencies for men are 80 yes, and 20 no; for women, the results are 65 yes and 35 no. Do these results suggest that support for the Greek system depends on the gender of the student? ■

CALCULATING AN EFFECT SIZE FOR A CHI-SQUARE TEST OF INDEPENDENCE

The results of NHST tell us whether we may confidently reject the null hypothesis given an acceptable level of Type I errors. But, as you have learned when t and F tests are performed, statistical significance (and the magnitude of the test statistic) does not tell us how strongly two variables are related. For that we need effect size measures or what are often called *measures of association*. (See Chapter 12.) *The value of calculating effect sizes is to permit a comparison with results of other studies looking at the same variables and to help us decide about the practical significance of our study.* A statistically significant chi-square value based on a test of independence tells us that we may confidently reject the idea that the data are independent of group membership, but it does not tell us the degree of association between the variables. There are measures of association that will do that for the chi-square test of independence.

A popular measure of the degree of association of two nominal variables *that is appropriate for 2 × 2 contingency tables* is the **phi (ϕ) coefficient**. It is defined as the square root of the obtained χ^2 divided by sample size. That is,

$$\phi = \sqrt{(\chi^2/N)}$$ **Equation 18.5**

Phi varies from .00 to 1.00. A phi value of .00 would be obtained if there were no relationship between the variables. A zero relationship exists when knowing what group subjects are in tells us nothing about their response; the data are completely independent of group membership. Phi is 1.00 when group membership and responses are perfectly correlated. This would mean that knowing what groups participants are in allows us always to predict their responses. For example, if all the children in Sally's study who had mothers who drink beer liked the beer smell better, and all the children with mothers who did not drink beer liked the bubble gum smell better, just knowing what group children belonged to would tell us their smell preference. Of course, most of the time the degree of association is something less than 1.00.

Let us calculate phi for Sally's study. The obtained chi-square was 7.50 and sample size (N) was 250. Thus,

$$\phi = \sqrt{(\chi^2/N)} = \sqrt{(7.50/250)} = \sqrt{0.03} = .17$$

How might we interpret phi? Once again, Cohen (1988) provides a rule of thumb for interpreting effect sizes. He suggests that a phi coefficient of .10 is a small effect size, .30 is medium, and .50 is a large effect size. Sally's study, therefore, resulted in an effect size somewhere between small and medium.

The phi coefficient is appropriately calculated only when the contingency table is 2 × 2. For larger contingency tables, Cramer's phi coefficient(ϕ_c) is recommended (e.g., Howell, 2002). It is defined as

$$\phi_c = \sqrt{\frac{\chi^2}{N(k - 1)}}$$ **Equation 18.6**

In this formula, N is the sample size and k is the smaller value of the rows and columns. For example, if a 2 × 3 contingency table is used, $k = 2$. Unfortunately, Cohen's rule of thumb for interpreting values of phi applies only to 2 × 2 tables (when $\phi_c = \phi$) and must be amended when Cramer's phi is used. (See Cohen, 1988.) Nevertheless, Cramer's phi coefficient allows a researcher to compare the strength of association obtained from two or more independent chi-square tests with more than one degree of freedom and different sample sizes. This information may be useful when assessing the effectiveness of a particular variable or when decisions are made about the practical significance of results from different studies.

ANNOUNCING RESULTS OF A CHI-SQUARE TEST OF INDEPENDENCE

We are now in a position to announce the results of Sally's study based on the format suggested by the American Psychological Association (2001).

What may Sally conclude? Recall the question she is asking: "Does the distribution of relative frequencies differ for the two groups in her study?" The null hypothesis states that they do not, that the distribution of relative frequencies in the population is the same for the two groups. In this case, responses would be independent of group membership. Given the obtained chi-square, Sally may conclude that her data indicate that the two groups do differ in the distribution of relative frequencies, that the pattern of relative frequencies is not the same and, rather, depend on the group to which the child belongs. This is something we first began to learn about in the description stage of analysis. Note that obtaining a statistically significant chi-square value does not tell Sally exactly how the distributions differ; she must rely on data description to determine just what happened in her study, and this information should be incorporated into her announcement of results. Such an announcement might look like this:

Children, ages 3 to 6 years, were asked to smell a bottle scented with beer and a bottle scented with bubble gum. Of the 250 children tested, 164 had a mother who drank beer, and 86 children came from homes in which the mother did not drink beer. (Fathers' drinking behavior was not considered in this study.) After smelling both bottles, the children were asked to indicate which smell they liked better. The proportions of children in each group who liked beer and bubble gum smells better are summarized in the following table.

Group	Preference for Beer Smell	Preference for Bubble Gum Smell
Mother drinks beer (164)	.46	.54
Mother doesn't drink beer (86)	.28	.72

As can be seen in the table, more children in each group liked the smell of bubble gum better than that of beer; however, the difference between proportions of children liking the smell of beer or bubble gum better was much less when the mother drinks beer. A chi-square test of independence revealed χ^2 (1, $N = 250$) = 7.50, $p < .01$. An effect size measure based on phi was .17, a somewhat greater than small effect size according to Cohen's (1988) guidelines. It may be concluded that childrens' relative frequency of preferences for beer and bubble gum smells depends on whether the mother drinks beer.

Once again note that the degrees of freedom for the chi-square test are placed in parentheses and the reader is informed about the overall sample size (N), the size of the groups, and the observed frequencies for each cell. This may be efficiently done using a table as was the case here. Proportions serve to summarize the relative frequencies in the cells of the table. The observed frequencies can be calculated given the proportions and the sample sizes for each group.

WHAT YOU HAVE LEARNED AND THE NEXT STEP

In this chapter, you learned about data analysis and interpretation when a study involves nominal data. Confidence intervals for a proportion as well as NHST for studies with nominal data were discussed. It is important to remember that the techniques discussed in this chapter apply only to situations in which responses are independent and may be placed into mutually exclusive categories (cells). That is, each person, event, or thing falls in only one category (cell). The major ideas discussed in this chapter include the following:

- Confidence intervals for a population proportion may be calculated and interpreted in a manner similar to that for a population mean.

- An important check on nominal data during the inspection stage is to verify that the sum of the category frequencies equals the total number of participants, events, or things.

- A sample proportion (P) is calculated by dividing the observed frequency in a category by the size of the sample (N).

- Plus or minus the margin of error is essentially the same as the 95% confidence interval for a proportion.

- NHST procedures with nominal data are called *distribution-free* or *nonparametric tests* because they do not assume that the distribution of scores is normal in form or that population parameters such as the variance are the same between groups.

- In a chi-square goodness-of-fit test, a researcher seeks to learn if the distribution of observed relative frequencies fits a distribution of frequencies expected on the basis of the research question.

- Expected frequencies for a goodness-of-fit test are based on the assumption that category frequencies will be equal (i.e., preference is the same) or on the basis of prior research results or on normative values.

- The assumptions for a chi-square goodness-of-fit test are that observations are independent and a relatively large sample was taken (so that no expected category frequency is less than 5).

- A chi-square test of independence determines whether the distribution of observed relative frequencies is independent of group membership.

- Before conducting a chi-square test of independence, data should be arranged in a contingency table and results summarized in terms of proportions.

- The chi-square test of independence depends on the same assumptions about the data as does the goodness-of-fit test.

- A measure of the degree of association or effect size for a chi-square test of independence based on a 2 × 2 contingency table is the phi coefficient.

This chapter concludes our introduction to data analysis and interpretation following the I-D-E-A model. It may be discomforting to know that we have just scratched the surface and that there is much more to learn about data analysis and interpretation should you pursue a research career in the behavioral sciences, in medicine, business, or in one of the many other disciplines that rely heavily on quantitative information. Nevertheless, you have come a long way and have learned much. A major goal in writing this book has been to introduce you to some important analytical tools, as well as a systematic way to approach data based on the I-D-E-A model. Hopefully, this knowledge will serve you in a variety of situations, both as a student and in your chosen career. More importantly, perhaps, we believe that this knowledge will put you in a better position to deal with the myriad numerical facts that face us as consumers of statistical information. Statistics often play an important role in the many claims and counterclaims of politicians, government officials, educators, business leaders, pressure groups, and advertisers. Your knowledge of data analysis and interpretation should help you to better critically evaluate these issues.

Key Concepts

sample proportion (*P*)	distribution-free tests	observed frequencies
population proportion (*p*)	nonparametric tests	expected frequencies
estimated standard error of a proportion	chi-square (χ^2)	cells
95% confidence interval for *p*	goodness-of-fit test	contingency tables
margin of error	test of independence	phi (ϕ) coefficient

Answers to *Your Turn* Questions

18-1. Only (b) and (d) may be considered nominal data. Do not be misled by the fact that in (d) the "number" of drivers is recorded. It should be clear that "number" represents the frequency of drivers observed in the three mutually exclusive categories. Both (a) and (e) may be judged to be at least interval data; (c) represents a ratio level of measurement.

18-2. $P \pm 1.96 \ [\sqrt{P(1 - P)/(N - 1)}] = .16 \pm 1.96 \ [\sqrt{.16(.84)/(150 - 1)}] = .16 \pm .06$

18-3. Given a margin of error of four percentage points, the 95% confidence intervals for Bore and Mush are 52 to 60, and 40 to 48, respectively. Because the intervals do not overlap, we may conclude that the population proportions differ for these two candidates. And, whereas Mush may be considered to be leading significantly in the polls, keep in mind that pre-election polls suffer from two serious weaknesses: (a) they are taken before the election and events may occur before the election to change people's minds, and (b) the survey is of registered voters, and, because all eligible voters don't actually vote, it is unclear as to whether more of one candidate's supporters will vote than will another's.

18-4. Expected frequencies would be calculated by multiplying the proportion of category responses expected on the basis of the theory by the sample size. That is, for A, (.20)(88) = 17.6. Similarly for B and D. For C, the expected frequency is (.40) (88) = 35.2. Thus, expected frequencies for the four stock choices, A thru D, are 17.6, 17. 6, 35.2, and 17.6, respectively.

18-5. The observed and expected frequencies for this study are as follows:

Group	Yes	No	Total
Men	$O = 80$ $E = (100)(145)/200$ $= 72.5$	$O = 20$ $E = (100)(55)/200$ $= 27.5$	100
Women	$O = 65$ $E = (100)(145)/200$ $= 72.5$	$O = 35$ $E = (100)(55)/200$ $= 27.5$	100
Total	145	55	200

$$\chi^2 = \Sigma \left[\frac{(O - E)^2}{E} \right] = .776 + 2.04 + .776 + 2.04 = 5.63$$

Degrees of freedom are $(r - 1)(c - 1) = (2 - 1)(2 - 1) = 1$. The critical value of χ^2 with one df and alpha at .05 is 3.84; with alpha at .02, the critical value is 5.41. The distribution of relative frequencies for men and women may be judged to differ, $\chi^2(1) = 5.62$, $p < .02$. Attitudes toward the Greek system do depend on the gender of the student. Note that the data must be described in terms of proportions to fully interpret the statistically significant χ^2. Because each sample of men and women included 100 respondents, the observed frequencies are easily converted to proportions. For both men and women, the majority favor maintaining the Greek system (i.e., .80 and .65); however, fewer women than men favor maintaining the system. (One should also not overlook the fact that, across all 200 students, 145/200, or .72 favor the system.)

Analyzing and Interpreting Data: Problems and Exercises

1. The data analysis techniques introduced in this chapter apply only to those situations in which a person, event, or thing is placed into mutually exclusive categories. Explain.

2. One type of design to be considered in this chapter is analogous to a factorial design discussed in Chapter 13. In fact, the question the researcher is asking in this situation is similar to that asked about an interaction effect in a factorial design. Suppose that a researcher seeks to determine whether the results obtained by Gibson and Walk in their study of infant depth perception vary with the gender of the child. Very young boys and girls are exposed to the visual cliff apparatus. What is the specific question that the researcher seeks to answer?

3 M is to μ as P is to p. Explain.

4. You ask 150 students whether they want to replace the current university mascot. Ninety-five say "yes" and 55 say "no." What is the estimated standard error of a proportion for these data?

5. For problem #4, what is the 95% confidence interval for the population proportion of students saying "yes" (that they want the current mascot replaced)?

6. A psychologist finds that 14% of the students in a random sample of 300 college students are suffering from academic "burnout." What is the 95% confidence interval for the population proportion?

7. A social psychologist interested in gun violence tests 135 six-year-old children in a laboratory setting. As part of the experiment, the children are asked to play a game alone for 10 minutes. The game is structured so that, during the course of the game, the children discover a gun in the room (a real gun but unable to fire). The psychologist reports that only 65 children later told the psychologist abut the gun. What is the 95% confidence interval for the population proportion of children reporting the gun?

8. A TV reporter states that 34% of those people polled favor the president's initiative to build a "Star Wars" missile defense system. The margin of error is three points. Explain what this means.

9. Why is a chi-square test called a "nonparametric" test?

10. What research question is addressed by a chi-square goodness-of-fit test?

11. A developmental psychologist presents 120 first-grade children with four pictures of male adults who obviously vary in age (young adult, older adult, middle-aged, elderly). The researcher asks each child to select the picture of the man they like the most. The observed frequencies of children who choose the four pictures are 25, 35, 20, 40 for the four pictures, respectively. Perform an appropriate test of whether the four pictures were chosen equally often.

12. An experimental psychologist tests 45 rats in a maze that has three possible paths to the goal. The observed frequencies of following the three paths are 12, 8, and 25, for paths (1), (2) and (3), respectively. Perform an appropriate test of whether the paths were chosen equally often.

13. What research question is addressed by a chi-square test of independence?

14. The 95% confidence interval for a proportion is found by a survey researcher who reports the proportion of people who favor marriage between same-sex individuals. A chi-square goodness-of-fit test is used to evaluate the same results. What additional information is gained by the results of NHST?

15. The admission rates at two mental hospitals are compared for schizophrenia and borderline personality disorders. At hospital A, in the past six months, 23 patients were admitted with a diagnosis of schizophrenia, and 14 patients were admitted with the classification of borderline personality disorder. For these same disorders, respectively, at hospital B, the frequencies over the past six months were 44 and 34. Do the hospitals differ significantly in the relative frequencies of admissions for these two types of disorder?

16. A sample of 240 people was asked to write a story about the time they seriously hurt someone socially or emotionally. The participants were also asked whether they went to religious services regularly. Of the 240, 180 said "no" and 60 said "yes." The stories were coded for the presence or absence of seeking forgiveness from the person they hurt. The researchers sought to determine if the presence or absence of forgiveness in the stories was contingent on whether the participants attended religious services regularly. Of the stories written by the 180 people who said they did not attend religious services regularly, 114 contained a forgiveness element. Of the 60 who said "yes," 35 stories contained a forgiveness theme. Perform a chi-square test of independence on these data.

17. Calculate phi as a measure of the degree of association between the variables in the study described in problem #16.

18. A researcher reports the results of a study examining the relationship between gender and type of aggression observed on a school playground (verbal, physical, or both). Thus, the study represents a 2 × 3 (gender by type of aggression) design. A total of 186 different aggressive episodes is observed at several schools. Boys and girls are placed in one of three categories according to the type of aggression observed. A chi-square test of independence yields $\chi^2 (2, N = 186) = 10.40$, $p < .01$. What is the degree of association of these two variables? Hint: Be sure you know what measure of association is appropriate in this case.

Answers to Odd-Numbered Problems

1. A person, event, or thing is placed in only one category. For example, in Kristen's study, shoppers are asked to select one, and only one, logo from among three that are presented to them. When mutually exclusive categories are used, the number of people (or events or things) in the study will equal the total number of people (or events or things) in all the categories. When Kristen's study is completed, the sum of the three categories will equal the total number of shoppers that she interviewed.

3. When random samples are taken, M is a point estimate of μ when interval or ratio data are available; so, too, P is an estimate of p when nominal data are obtained.

5. The estimated standard error of a proportion for these data is equal to: $\sqrt{[.63(1 - .63)/(150 - 1)]}$, or .039. (See answer to problem #4.) The 95% confidence interval for "yes" responses is equal to $.63 \pm 1.96 (.039) = .63 \pm .076$, or .55 to .71.

7. $P = 65/135 = .48; P \pm 1.96 \left[\sqrt{P(1-P)/(N-1)}\right] = .48 \pm 1.96 \left[\sqrt{.48(.52)/134}\right] = .48 \pm .08$, or .40 to .56.

9. Unlike t or F tests, which are called *parametric tests*, the chi-square test of statistical significance is a non-parametric test because it does not make the same assumptions about population characteristics (parameters) as do these tests. For example, recall that both the t test for independent groups and F test for random groups designs assumes that the variance (σ^2) in each of the populations is the same (i.e., homogeneity of variance assumption). The chi-square test does not require this assumption about population variances, nor does it assume that the shape of the distributions in the populations is normal.

11. The chi-square goodness-of-fit test is appropriate given the research question. The expected frequencies are assumed to be the same for each picture, that is, 30, 30, 30, and 30. The observed frequencies are 25, 35, 20, and 40. Chi-square may be calculated as

$$\chi^2 = \Sigma \left[\frac{(O-E)^2}{E}\right] = \frac{(25-30)^2}{30} + \frac{(35-30)^2}{30} + \frac{(20-30)^2}{30} + \frac{(40-30)^2}{30}$$

$$= 0.83 + 0.83 + 3.33 + 3.33 = 8.32$$

The critical value of χ^2 with 3 *df* and alpha at .05 is 7.815; the critical value is 11.345 at .01. (See Table A.6.) Therefore, χ^2 (3) = 8.532, $p < .05$. Given these data, we can confidently conclude that the distribution of relative frequency of children's choices is not the same for these four pictures.

13. A chi-square test of independence is used to determine whether the distribution of observed relative frequencies is independent of group membership.

15. The observed and expected frequencies for this study are as follows:

Group	Schizophrenic	Borderline	Total
Hospital A	$O = 23$ $E = (37)(67)/115$ $= 21.56$	$O = 14$ $E = (37)(48)/115$ $= 15.44$	37
Hospital B	$O = 44$ $E = (78)(67)/115$ $= 45.44$	$O = 34$ $E = (78)(48)/115$ $= 32.56$	78
Total	67	48	115

Chi-square may be calculated as

$$\chi^2 = \Sigma \left[\frac{(O-E)^2}{E}\right]$$

$$= \frac{(23-21.56)^2}{21.56} + \frac{(14-15.44)^2}{15.44}$$

$$+ \frac{(44-45.44)^2}{45.44} + \frac{(34-32.56)^2}{32.56}$$

$= 0.096 + 0.134 + 0.046 + 0.064 = 0.34$. Thus, χ^2 (1, $N = 115$) = 0.34, $p > .05$.

There is insufficient evidence that the relative frequencies of admission for patients with these two types of disorders differs for the two hospitals.

17. The degree of association as assessed by phi [$\phi = \sqrt{\chi^2/N}$] is $\sqrt{0.56/240}$, or .05. There is little if any association between these two variables.

Go to http://psychology.wadsworth.com/courses/statistics/ and test your knowledge of this chapter by taking the online quiz. Another resource to check is the online workshops that provide a step-by-step guide through a number of topics at http://psychology.wadsworth.com/workshops/workshops.html.

Statistical Tables

TABLE A.1 ■ Proportions of Area Under the Standard Normal Curve

z	0 z	0 z	z	0 z	0 z	z	0 z	0 z
0.00	.0000	.5000	0.55	.2088	.2912	1.10	.3643	.1357
0.01	.0040	.4960	0.56	.2123	.2877	1.11	.3665	.1335
0.02	.0080	.4920	0.57	.2157	.2843	1.12	.3686	.1314
0.03	.0120	.4880	0.58	.2190	.2810	1.13	.3708	.1292
0.04	.0160	.4840	0.59	.2224	.2776	1.14	.3729	.1271
0.05	.0199	.4801	0.60	.2257	.2743	1.15	.3749	.1251
0.06	.0239	.4761	0.61	.2291	.2709	1.16	.3770	.1230
0.07	.0279	.4721	0.62	.2324	.2676	1.17	.3790	.1210
0.08	.0319	.4681	0.63	.2357	.2643	1.18	.3810	.1190
0.09	.0359	.4641	0.64	.2389	.2611	1.19	.3830	.1170
0.10	.0398	.4602	0.65	.2422	.2578	1.20	.3849	.1151
0.11	.0438	.4562	0.66	.2454	.2546	1.21	.3869	.1131
0.12	.0478	.4522	0.67	.2486	.2514	1.22	.3888	.1112
0.13	.0517	.4483	0.68	.2517	.2483	1.23	.3907	.1093
0.14	.0557	.4443	0.69	.2549	.2451	1.24	.3925	.1075
0.15	.0596	.4404	0.70	.2580	.2420	1.25	.3944	.1056
0.16	.0636	.4364	0.71	.2611	.2389	1.26	.3962	.1038
0.17	.0675	.4325	0.72	.2642	.2358	1.27	.3980	.1020
0.18	.0714	.4286	0.73	.2673	.2327	1.28	.3997	.1003
0.19	.0753	.4247	0.74	.2704	.2296	1.29	.4015	.0985
0.20	.0793	.4207	0.75	.2734	.2266	1.30	.4032	.0968
0.21	.0832	.4168	0.76	.2764	.2236	1.31	.4049	.0951
0.22	.0871	.4129	0.77	.2794	.2206	1.32	.4066	.0934
0.23	.0910	.4090	0.78	.2823	.2177	1.33	.4082	.0918
0.24	.0948	.4052	0.79	.2852	.2148	1.34	.4099	.0901
0.25	.0987	.4013	0.80	.2881	.2119	1.35	.4115	.0885
0.26	.1026	.3974	0.81	.2910	.2090	1.36	.4131	.0869
0.27	.1064	.3936	0.82	.2939	.2061	1.37	.4147	.0853
0.28	.1103	.3897	0.83	.2967	.2033	1.38	.4162	.0838
0.29	.1141	.3859	0.84	.2995	.2005	1.39	.4177	.0823
0.30	.1179	.3821	0.85	.3023	.1977	1.40	.4192	.0808
0.31	.1217	.3783	0.86	.3051	.1949	1.41	.4207	.0793
0.32	.1255	.3745	0.87	.3078	.1922	1.42	.4222	.0778
0.33	.1293	.3707	0.88	.3106	.1894	1.43	.4236	.0764
0.34	.1331	.3669	0.89	.3133	.1867	1.44	.4251	.0749
0.35	.1368	.3632	0.90	.3159	.1841	1.45	.4265	.0735
0.36	.1406	.3594	0.91	.3186	.1814	1.46	.4279	.0721
0.37	.1443	.3557	0.92	.3212	.1788	1.47	.4292	.0708
0.38	.1480	.3520	0.93	.3238	.1762	1.48	.4306	.0694
0.39	.1517	.3483:	0.94	.3264	.1736	1.49	.4319	.0681
0.40	.1554	.3446	0.95	.3289	.1711	1.50	.4332	.0668
0.41	.1591	.3409	0.96	.3315	.1685	1.51	.4345	.0655
0.42	.1628	.3372	0.97	.3340	.1660	1.52	.4357	.0643
0.43	.1664	.3336	0.98	.3365	.1635	1.53	.4370	.0630
0.44	.1700	.3300	0.99	.3389	.1611	1.54	.4382	.0618
0.45	.1736	.3264	1.00	.3413	.1587	1.55	.4394	.0606
0.46	.1772	.3228	1.01	.3438	.1562	1.56	.4406	.0594
0.47	.1808	.3192	1.02	.3461	.1539	1.57	.4418	.0582
0.48	.1844	.3156	1.03	.3485	.1515	1.58	.4429	.0571
0.49	.1879	.3121	1.04	.3508	.1492	1.59	.4441	.0559
0.50	.1915	.3085	1.05	3531	.1469	1.60	.4452	.0548
0.51	.1950	.3050	1.06	3554	.1446	1.61	.4463	.0537
0.52	.1985	.3015	1.07	.3577	.1423	1.62	.4474	.0526
0.53	.2019	.2981	1.08	.3599	.1401	1.63	.4484	.0516
0.54	.2054	.2946	1.09	.3621	.1379	1.64	.4495	.0505

z	0 z	0 z	z	0 z	0 z	z	0 z	0 z
1.65	.4505	.0495	2.22	.4868	.0132	2.79	.4974	.0026
1.66	.4515	.0485	2 23	.4871	.0129	2.80	.4974	.0026
1.67	.4525	.0475	2 24	.4875	.0125	2.81	.4975	.0025
1.68	.4535	.0465	2.25	.4878	.0122	2.82	.4976	.0024
1.69	.4545	.0455	2.26	.4881	.0119	2.83	.4977	.0023
1.70	.4554	.0446	2 27	.4884	.0116	2.84	.4977	.0023
1.71	.4564	.0436	2 28	.4887	.0113	2.85	.4978	.0022
1.72	.4573	.0427	2.29	.4890	.0110	2.86	.4979	.0021
1.73	.4582	.0418	2.30	.4893	.0107	2.87	.4979	.0021
1.74	.4591	.0409	2.31	.4896	.0104	2.88	.4980	.0020
1.75	.4599	.0401	2.32	.4898	.0102	2.89	.4981	.0019
1.76	.4608	.0392	2.33	.4901	.0099	2.90	.4981	.0019
1.77	.4616	.0384	2.34	.4904	.0096	2.91	.4982	.0018
1.78	.4625	.0375	2.35	.4906	.0094	2.92	.4982	.0018
1.79	.4633	.0367	2.36	.4909	.0091	2.93	.4983	.0017
1.80	.4641	.0359	2.37	.4911	.0089	2.94	.4984	.0016
1.81	.4649	.0351	2.38	.4913	.0087	2.95	.4984	.0016
1.82	.4656	.0344	2.39	.4916	.0084	2.96	.4985	.0015
1.83	.4664	.0336	2.40	.4918	.0082	2.97	.4985	.0015
1.84	.4671	.0329	2.41	.4920	.0080	2.98	.4986	.0014
1.85	.4678	.0322	2.42	.4922	.0078	2.99	.4986	.0014
1.86	.4686	.0314	2.43	.4925	.0075	3.00	.4987	.0013
1.87	.4693	.0307	2.44	.4927	.0073	3.01	.4987	.0013
1.88	.4699	.0301	2.45	.4929	.0071	3.02	.4987	.0013
1.89	.4706	.0294	2.46	.4931	.0069	3.03	.4988	.0012
1.90	.4713	.0287	2.47	.4932	.0068	3.04	.4988	.0012
1.91	.4719	.0281	2.48	.4934	.0066	3.05	.4989	.0011
1.92	.4726	.0274	2.49	.4936	.0064	3.06	.4989	.0011
1.93	.4732	.0268	2.50	.4938	.0062	3.07	.4989	.0011
1.94	.4738	.0262	2.51	.4940	.0060	3.08	.4990	.0010
1.95	.4744	.0256	2.52	.4941	.0059	3.09	.4990	.0010
1.96	.4750	.0250	2.53	.4943	.0057	3.10	.4990	.0010
1.97	.4756	.0244	2.54	.4945	.0055	3.11	.4991	.0009
1.98	.4761	.0239	2.55	.4946	.0054	3.12	.4991	.0009
1.99	.4767	.0233	2.56	.4948	.0052	3.13	.4991	.0009
2.00	.4772	.0228	2.57	.4949	.0051	3.14	.4992	.0008
2.01	.4778	.0222	2.58	.4951	.0049	3.15	.4992	.0008
2.02	.4783	.0217	2.59	.4952	.0048	3.16	.4992	.0008
2.03	.4788	.0212	2.60	.4953	.0047	3.17	.4992	.0008
2.04	.4793	.0207	2.61	.4955	.0045	3.18	.4993	.0007
2.05	.4798	.0202	2.62	.4956	.0044	3.19	.4993	.0007
2.06	.4803	.0197	2.63	.4957	.0043	3.20	.4993	.0007
2.07	.4808	.0192	2.64	.4959	.0041	3.21	.4993	.0007
2.08	.4812	.0188	2.65	.4960	.0040	3.22	.4994	.0006
2.09	.4817	.0183	2.66	.4961	.0039	3.23	.4594	.0006
2.10	.4821	.0179	2.67	.4962	.0038	3.24	.4994	.0006
2.11	.4826	.0174	2.68	.4963	.0037	3.25	.4994	.0006
2.12	.4830	.0170	2.69	.4964	.0036	3.30	.4995	.0005
2.13	.4834	.0166	2.70	.4965	.0035	3.35	.4996	.0004
2.14	.4838	.0162	2.71	.4966	.0034	3.40	.4997	.0003
2.15	.4842	.0158	2.72	.4967	.0033	3.45	.4997	.0003
2.16	.4846	.0154	2.73	.4968	.0032	3.50	.4998	.0002
2.17	.4850	.0150	2.74	.4969	.0031	3.60	.4998	.0002
2.18	.4854	.0146	2.75	.4970	.0030	3.70	.4999	.0001
2.19	.4857	.0143	2.76	.4971	.0029	3.80	.4999	.0001
2.20	.4861	.0139	2.77	.4972	.0028	3.90	.49995	.00005
2.21	.4864	.0136	2.78	.4973	.0027	4.00	.49997	.00003

TABLE A.2 ■ Critical Values of t

<table>
<tr><th></th><th colspan="6">Level of Significance for a Directional (One-Tailed) Test</th></tr>
<tr><th></th><th>.10</th><th>.05</th><th>.025</th><th>.01</th><th>.005</th><th>.0005</th></tr>
<tr><th></th><th colspan="6">Level of Significance for a Nondirectional (Two-Tailed) Test</th></tr>
<tr><th>df</th><th>.20</th><th>.10</th><th>.05</th><th>.02</th><th>.01</th><th>.001</th></tr>
<tr><td>1</td><td>3.078</td><td>6.314</td><td>12.706</td><td>31.821</td><td>63.657</td><td>636.619</td></tr>
<tr><td>2</td><td>1.886</td><td>2.920</td><td>4.303</td><td>6.965</td><td>9.925</td><td>31.598</td></tr>
<tr><td>3</td><td>1.638</td><td>2.353</td><td>3.182</td><td>4.541</td><td>5.841</td><td>12.941</td></tr>
<tr><td>4</td><td>1.533</td><td>2.132</td><td>2.776</td><td>3.747</td><td>4.604</td><td>8.610</td></tr>
<tr><td>5</td><td>1.476</td><td>2.015</td><td>2.571</td><td>3.365</td><td>4.032</td><td>6.859</td></tr>
<tr><td>6</td><td>1.440</td><td>1.943</td><td>2.447</td><td>3.143</td><td>3.707</td><td>5.959</td></tr>
<tr><td>7</td><td>1.415</td><td>1.895</td><td>2.365</td><td>2.998</td><td>3.499</td><td>5.405</td></tr>
<tr><td>8</td><td>1.397</td><td>1.860</td><td>2.306</td><td>2.896</td><td>3.355</td><td>5.041</td></tr>
<tr><td>9</td><td>1.383</td><td>1.833</td><td>2.262</td><td>2.821</td><td>3.250</td><td>4.781</td></tr>
<tr><td>10</td><td>1.372</td><td>1.812</td><td>2.228</td><td>2.764</td><td>3.169</td><td>4.587</td></tr>
<tr><td>11</td><td>1.363</td><td>1.796</td><td>2.201</td><td>2.718</td><td>3.106</td><td>4.437</td></tr>
<tr><td>12</td><td>1.366</td><td>1.782</td><td>2.179</td><td>2.681</td><td>3.065</td><td>4.318</td></tr>
<tr><td>13</td><td>1.350</td><td>1.771</td><td>2.160</td><td>2.650</td><td>3.012</td><td>4.221</td></tr>
<tr><td>14</td><td>1.345</td><td>1.761</td><td>2.145</td><td>2.624</td><td>2.977</td><td>4.140</td></tr>
<tr><td>15</td><td>1.341</td><td>1.753</td><td>2.131</td><td>2.602</td><td>2.947</td><td>4.073</td></tr>
<tr><td>16</td><td>1.337</td><td>1.746</td><td>2.120</td><td>2.583</td><td>2.921</td><td>4.015</td></tr>
<tr><td>17</td><td>1.333</td><td>1.740</td><td>2.110</td><td>2.567</td><td>2.898</td><td>3.965</td></tr>
<tr><td>18</td><td>1.330</td><td>1.734</td><td>2.101</td><td>2.552</td><td>2.878</td><td>3.922</td></tr>
<tr><td>19</td><td>1.328</td><td>1.729</td><td>2.093</td><td>2.539</td><td>2.861</td><td>3.883</td></tr>
<tr><td>20</td><td>1.325</td><td>1.725</td><td>2.086</td><td>2.528</td><td>2.845</td><td>3.850</td></tr>
<tr><td>21</td><td>1.323</td><td>1.721</td><td>2.080</td><td>2.518</td><td>2.831</td><td>3.819</td></tr>
<tr><td>22</td><td>1.321</td><td>1.717</td><td>2.074</td><td>2.508</td><td>2.819</td><td>3.792</td></tr>
<tr><td>23</td><td>1.319</td><td>1.714</td><td>2.069</td><td>2.500</td><td>2.807</td><td>3.767</td></tr>
<tr><td>24</td><td>1.318</td><td>1.711</td><td>2.064</td><td>2.492</td><td>2.797</td><td>3.745</td></tr>
<tr><td>25</td><td>1.316</td><td>1.708</td><td>2.060</td><td>2.485</td><td>2.787</td><td>3.725</td></tr>
<tr><td>26</td><td>1.315</td><td>1.706</td><td>2.056</td><td>2.479</td><td>2.779</td><td>3.707</td></tr>
<tr><td>27</td><td>1.314</td><td>1.703</td><td>2.052</td><td>2.473</td><td>2.771</td><td>3.690</td></tr>
<tr><td>28</td><td>1.313</td><td>1.701</td><td>2.048</td><td>2.467</td><td>2.763</td><td>3.674</td></tr>
<tr><td>29</td><td>1.311</td><td>1.699</td><td>2.045</td><td>2.462</td><td>2.756</td><td>3.659</td></tr>
<tr><td>30</td><td>1.310</td><td>1.697</td><td>2.042</td><td>2.457</td><td>2.750</td><td>3.646</td></tr>
<tr><td>40</td><td>1.303</td><td>1.684</td><td>2.021</td><td>2.423</td><td>2.704</td><td>3.551</td></tr>
<tr><td>60</td><td>1.296</td><td>1.671</td><td>2.000</td><td>2.390</td><td>2.660</td><td>3.460</td></tr>
<tr><td>120</td><td>1.289</td><td>1.658</td><td>1.980</td><td>2.358</td><td>2.617</td><td>3.373</td></tr>
<tr><td>∞</td><td>1.282</td><td>1.645</td><td>1.960</td><td>2.326</td><td>2.576</td><td>3.291</td></tr>
</table>

The value listed in the table is the critical value of t for the number of degrees of freedom listed in the left column for a directional (one-tailed) or nondirectional (two-tailed) test at the significance level indicated at the top of each column. If the observed t is *greater than or equal to* the tabled value, reject H_0. Since the t distribution is symmetrical about $t = 0$, these critical values represent both $+$ and $-$ values for nondirectional tests.

© 1963 R. A. Fisher and F. Yates, reprinted by permission of Pearson Education Limited.

TABLE A.3 ■ Critical Values of F (.05 Level in Roman Type, .01 Level in Boldface)

Degrees of Freedom for the Numerator

The critical value for the .05 level of significance is presented first (roman type) followed by the critical value at the .01 level (boldface).

Denom. df	1	2	3	4	5	6	7	8	9	10	11	12	14	16	20	24	30	40	50	75	100	200	500	∞
1	161 / 4,052	200 / 4,999	216 / 5,403	225 / 5,625	230 / 5,764	234 / 5,859	237 / 5,928	239 / 5,981	241 / 6,022	242 / 6,056	243 / 6,082	244 / 6,106	245 / 6,142	246 / 6,169	248 / 6,208	249 / 6,234	250 / 6,261	251 / 6,286	252 / 6,302	253 / 6,323	253 / 6,334	254 / 6,352	254 / 6,361	254 / 6,366
2	18.51 / 98.49	19.00 / 99.00	19.16 / 99.17	19.25 / 99.25	19.30 / 99.30	19.33 / 99.33	19.36 / 99.36	19.37 / 99.37	19.38 / 99.39	19.39 / 99.40	19.40 / 99.41	19.41 / 99.42	19.42 / 99.43	19.43 / 99.44	19.44 / 99.45	19.45 / 99.46	19.46 / 99.47	19.47 / 99.48	19.47 / 99.48	19.48 / 99.49	19.49 / 99.49	19.49 / 99.49	19.50 / 99.50	19.50 / 99.50
3	10.13 / 34.12	9.55 / 30.82	9.28 / 29.46	9.12 / 28.71	9.01 / 28.24	8.94 / 27.91	8.88 / 27.67	8.84 / 27.49	8.81 / 27.34	8.78 / 27.23	8.76 / 27.13	8.74 / 27.05	8.71 / 26.92	8.69 / 26.83	8.66 / 26.69	8.64 / 26.60	8.62 / 26.50	8.60 / 26.41	8.58 / 26.35	8.57 / 26.27	8.56 / 26.23	8.54 / 26.18	8.54 / 26.14	8.53 / 26.12
4	7.71 / 21.20	6.94 / 18.00	6.59 / 16.69	6.39 / 15.98	6.26 / 15.52	6.16 / 15.21	6.09 / 14.98	6.04 / 14.80	6.00 / 14.66	5.96 / 14.54	5.93 / 14.45	5.91 / 14.37	5.87 / 14.24	5.84 / 14.15	5.80 / 14.02	5.77 / 13.93	5.74 / 13.83	5.71 / 13.74	5.70 / 13.69	5.68 / 13.61	5.66 / 13.57	5.65 / 13.52	5.64 / 13.48	5.63 / 13.46
5	6.61 / 16.26	5.79 / 13.27	5.41 / 12.06	5.19 / 11.39	5.05 / 10.97	4.95 / 10.67	4.88 / 10.45	4.82 / 10.29	4.78 / 10.15	4.74 / 10.05	4.70 / 9.96	4.68 / 9.89	4.64 / 9.77	4.60 / 9.68	4.56 / 9.55	4.53 / 9.47	4.50 / 9.38	4.46 / 9.29	4.44 / 9.24	4.42 / 9.17	4.40 / 9.13	4.38 / 9.07	4.37 / 9.04	4.36 / 9.02
6	5.99 / 13.74	5.14 / 10.92	4.76 / 9.78	4.53 / 9.15	4.39 / 8.75	4.28 / 8.47	4.21 / 8.26	4.15 / 8.10	4.10 / 7.98	4.06 / 7.87	4.03 / 7.79	4.00 / 7.72	3.96 / 7.60	3.92 / 7.52	3.87 / 7.39	3.84 / 7.31	3.81 / 7.23	3.77 / 7.14	3.75 / 7.09	3.72 / 7.02	3.71 / 6.99	3.69 / 6.94	3.68 / 6.90	3.67 / 6.88
7	5.59 / 12.25	4.74 / 9.55	4.35 / 8.45	4.12 / 7.87	3.97 / 7.46	3.87 / 7.19	3.79 / 7.00	3.73 / 6.84	3.68 / 6.71	3.63 / 6.62	3.60 / 6.54	3.57 / 6.47	3.52 / 6.35	3.49 / 6.27	3.44 / 6.15	3.41 / 6.07	3.38 / 5.98	3.34 / 5.90	3.32 / 5.85	3.29 / 5.78	3.28 / 5.75	3.25 / 5.70	3.24 / 5.67	3.23 / 5.65
8	5.32 / 11.26	4.46 / 8.65	4.07 / 7.59	3.84 / 7.01	3.69 / 6.63	3.58 / 6.37	3.50 / 6.19	3.44 / 6.03	3.39 / 5.91	3.34 / 5.82	3.31 / 5.74	3.28 / 5.67	3.23 / 5.56	3.20 / 5.48	3.15 / 5.36	3.12 / 5.28	3.08 / 5.20	3.05 / 5.11	3.03 / 5.06	3.00 / 5.00	2.98 / 4.96	2.96 / 4.91	2.94 / 4.88	2.93 / 4.86
9	5.12 / 10.56	4.26 / 8.02	3.86 / 6.99	3.63 / 6.42	3.48 / 6.06	3.37 / 5.80	3.29 / 5.62	3.23 / 5.47	3.18 / 5.35	3.13 / 5.26	3.10 / 5.18	3.07 / 5.11	3.02 / 5.00	2.98 / 4.92	2.93 / 4.80	2.90 / 4.73	2.86 / 4.64	2.82 / 4.56	2.80 / 4.51	2.77 / 4.45	2.76 / 4.41	2.73 / 4.36	2.72 / 4.33	2.71 / 4.31
10	4.96 / 10.04	4.10 / 7.56	3.71 / 6.55	3.48 / 5.99	3.33 / 5.64	3.22 / 5.39	3.14 / 5.21	3.07 / 5.06	3.02 / 4.95	2.97 / 4.85	2.94 / 4.78	2.91 / 4.71	2.86 / 4.60	2.82 / 4.52	2.77 / 4.41	2.74 / 4.33	2.70 / 4.25	2.67 / 4.17	2.64 / 4.12	2.61 / 4.05	2.59 / 4.01	2.56 / 3.96	2.55 / 3.93	2.54 / 3.91
11	4.84 / 9.65	3.98 / 7.20	3.59 / 6.22	3.36 / 5.67	3.20 / 5.32	3.09 / 5.07	3.01 / 4.88	2.95 / 4.74	2.90 / 4.63	2.86 / 4.54	2.82 / 4.46	2.79 / 4.40	2.74 / 4.29	2.70 / 4.21	2.65 / 4.10	2.61 / 4.02	2.57 / 3.94	2.53 / 3.86	2.50 / 3.80	2.47 / 3.74	2.45 / 3.70	2.42 / 3.66	2.41 / 3.62	2.40 / 3.60
12	4.75 / 9.33	3.88 / 6.93	3.49 / 5.95	3.26 / 5.41	3.11 / 5.06	3.00 / 4.82	2.92 / 4.65	2.85 / 4.50	2.80 / 4.39	2.76 / 4.30	2.72 / 4.22	2.69 / 4.16	2.64 / 4.05	2.60 / 3.98	2.54 / 3.86	2.50 / 3.78	2.46 / 3.70	2.42 / 3.61	2.40 / 3.56	2.36 / 3.49	2.35 / 3.46	2.32 / 3.41	2.31 / 3.38	2.30 / 3.36
13	4.67 / 9.07	3.80 / 6.70	3.41 / 5.74	3.18 / 5.20	3.02 / 4.86	2.92 / 4.62	2.84 / 4.44	2.77 / 4.30	2.72 / 4.19	2.67 / 4.10	2.63 / 4.02	2.60 / 3.96	2.55 / 3.85	2.51 / 3.78	2.46 / 3.67	2.42 / 3.59	2.38 / 3.51	2.34 / 3.42	2.32 / 3.37	2.28 / 3.30	2.26 / 3.27	2.24 / 3.21	2.22 / 3.18	2.21 / 3.16

Degrees of freedom for the denominator

The values in the table are the critical values of F for the degrees of freedom listed over the columns (the degrees of freedom for the numerator of the F ratio) and the degrees of freedom listed for the rows (the degrees of freedom for the denominator of the F ratio). The critical value for the .05 level of significance is presented first (roman type) followed by the critical value at the .01 level (boldface). If the observed value is *greater than or equal to* the tabled value, reject H_0. F values are always positive. The function, $F = e$ with exponent $2z$, is computed in part from Fisher's table VI. Additional entries are by interpolation, mostly graphical.

Statistical Methods, 6th Edition, by G. W. Snedecor and W. G. Cochran, © 1967 Iowa State University Press. Used with permission.

TABLE A.3 ■ (continued)

Degrees of Freedom for the Numerator (upper value = 0.05 level, lower bold value = 0.01 level). Rows indexed by Degrees of freedom for the denominator.

den. df	1	2	3	4	5	6	7	8	9	10	11	12	14	16	20	24	30	40	50	75	100	200	500	∞
14	4.60 / 8.86	3.74 / 6.51	3.34 / 5.56	3.11 / 5.03	2.96 / 4.69	2.85 / 4.46	2.77 / 4.28	2.70 / 4.14	2.65 / 4.03	2.60 / 3.94	2.56 / 3.86	2.53 / 3.80	2.48 / 3.70	2.44 / 3.62	2.39 / 3.51	2.35 / 3.43	2.31 / 3.34	2.27 / 3.26	2.24 / 3.21	2.21 / 3.14	2.19 / 3.11	2.16 / 3.06	2.14 / 3.02	2.13 / 3.00
15	4.54 / 8.68	3.68 / 6.36	3.29 / 5.42	3.06 / 4.89	2.90 / 4.56	2.79 / 4.32	2.70 / 4.14	2.64 / 4.00	2.59 / 3.89	2.55 / 3.80	2.51 / 3.73	2.48 / 3.67	2.43 / 3.56	2.39 / 3.48	2.33 / 3.36	2.29 / 3.29	2.25 / 3.20	2.21 / 3.12	2.18 / 3.07	2.15 / 3.00	2.12 / 2.97	2.10 / 2.92	2.08 / 2.89	2.07 / 2.87
16	4.49 / 8.53	3.63 / 6.23	3.24 / 5.29	3.01 / 4.77	2.85 / 4.44	2.74 / 4.20	2.66 / 4.03	2.59 / 3.89	2.54 / 3.78	2.49 / 3.69	2.45 / 3.61	2.42 / 3.55	2.37 / 3.45	2.33 / 3.37	2.28 / 3.25	2.24 / 3.18	2.20 / 3.10	2.16 / 3.01	2.13 / 2.96	2.09 / 2.89	2.07 / 2.86	2.04 / 2.80	2.02 / 2.77	2.01 / 2.75
17	4.45 / 8.40	3.59 / 6.11	3.20 / 5.18	2.96 / 4.67	2.81 / 4.34	2.70 / 4.10	2.62 / 3.93	2.55 / 3.79	2.50 / 3.68	2.45 / 3.59	2.41 / 3.52	2.38 / 3.45	2.33 / 3.35	2.29 / 3.27	2.23 / 3.16	2.19 / 3.08	2.15 / 3.00	2.11 / 2.92	2.08 / 2.86	2.04 / 2.79	2.02 / 2.76	1.99 / 2.70	1.97 / 2.67	1.97 / 2.65
18	4.41 / 8.28	3.55 / 6.01	3.16 / 5.09	2.93 / 4.58	2.77 / 4.25	2.66 / 4.01	2.58 / 3.85	2.51 / 3.71	2.46 / 3.60	2.41 / 3.51	2.37 / 3.44	2.34 / 3.37	2.29 / 3.27	2.25 / 3.19	2.19 / 3.07	2.15 / 3.00	2.11 / 2.91	2.07 / 2.83	2.04 / 2.78	2.00 / 2.71	1.98 / 2.68	1.95 / 2.62	1.93 / 2.59	1.92 / 2.57
19	4.38 / 8.18	3.52 / 5.93	3.13 / 5.01	2.90 / 4.50	2.74 / 4.17	2.63 / 3.94	2.55 / 3.77	2.48 / 3.63	2.43 / 3.52	2.38 / 3.43	2.34 / 3.36	2.31 / 3.30	2.26 / 3.19	2.21 / 3.12	2.15 / 3.00	2.11 / 2.92	2.07 / 2.84	2.02 / 2.76	2.00 / 2.70	1.96 / 2.63	1.94 / 2.60	1.91 / 2.54	1.90 / 2.51	1.88 / 2.49
20	4.35 / 8.10	3.49 / 5.85	3.10 / 4.94	2.87 / 4.43	2.71 / 4.10	2.60 / 3.87	2.52 / 3.71	2.45 / 3.56	2.40 / 3.45	2.35 / 3.37	2.31 / 3.30	2.28 / 3.23	2.23 / 3.13	2.18 / 3.05	2.12 / 2.94	2.08 / 2.86	2.04 / 2.77	1.99 / 2.69	1.96 / 2.63	1.92 / 2.56	1.90 / 2.53	1.87 / 2.47	1.85 / 2.44	1.84 / 2.42
21	4.32 / 8.02	3.47 / 5.78	3.07 / 4.87	2.84 / 4.37	2.68 / 4.04	2.57 / 3.81	2.49 / 3.65	2.42 / 3.51	2.37 / 3.40	2.32 / 3.31	2.28 / 3.24	2.25 / 3.17	2.20 / 3.07	2.15 / 2.99	2.09 / 2.88	2.05 / 2.80	2.00 / 2.72	1.96 / 2.63	1.93 / 2.58	1.89 / 2.51	1.87 / 2.47	1.84 / 2.42	1.82 / 2.38	1.81 / 2.36
22	4.30 / 7.94	3.44 / 5.72	3.05 / 4.82	2.82 / 4.31	2.66 / 3.99	2.55 / 3.76	2.47 / 3.59	2.40 / 3.45	2.35 / 3.35	2.30 / 3.26	2.26 / 3.18	2.23 / 3.12	2.18 / 3.02	2.13 / 2.94	2.07 / 2.83	2.03 / 2.75	1.98 / 2.67	1.93 / 2.58	1.91 / 2.53	1.87 / 2.46	1.85 / 2.42	1.81 / 2.37	1.80 / 2.33	1.78 / 2.31
23	4.28 / 7.88	3.42 / 5.66	3.03 / 4.76	2.80 / 4.26	2.64 / 3.94	2.53 / 3.71	2.45 / 3.54	2.38 / 3.41	2.32 / 3.30	2.28 / 3.21	2.24 / 3.14	2.20 / 3.07	2.14 / 2.97	2.10 / 2.89	2.04 / 2.78	2.00 / 2.70	1.96 / 2.62	1.91 / 2.53	1.88 / 2.48	1.84 / 2.41	1.82 / 2.37	1.79 / 2.32	1.77 / 2.28	1.76 / 2.26
24	4.26 / 7.82	3.40 / 5.61	3.01 / 4.72	2.78 / 4.22	2.62 / 3.90	2.51 / 3.67	2.43 / 3.50	2.36 / 3.36	2.30 / 3.25	2.26 / 3.17	2.22 / 3.09	2.18 / 3.03	2.13 / 2.93	2.09 / 2.85	2.02 / 2.74	1.98 / 2.66	1.94 / 2.58	1.89 / 2.49	1.86 / 2.44	1.82 / 2.36	1.80 / 2.33	1.76 / 2.27	1.74 / 2.23	1.73 / 2.21
25	4.24 / 7.77	3.38 / 5.57	2.99 / 4.68	2.76 / 4.18	2.60 / 3.86	2.49 / 3.63	2.41 / 3.46	2.34 / 3.32	2.28 / 3.21	2.24 / 3.13	2.20 / 3.05	2.16 / 2.99	2.11 / 2.89	2.06 / 2.81	2.00 / 2.70	1.96 / 2.62	1.92 / 2.54	1.87 / 2.45	1.84 / 2.40	1.80 / 2.32	1.77 / 2.29	1.74 / 2.23	1.72 / 2.19	1.71 / 2.17
26	4.22 / 7.72	3.37 / 5.53	2.98 / 4.64	2.74 / 4.14	2.59 / 3.82	2.47 / 3.59	2.39 / 3.42	2.32 / 3.29	2.27 / 3.17	2.22 / 3.09	2.18 / 3.02	2.15 / 2.96	2.10 / 2.86	2.05 / 2.77	1.99 / 2.66	1.95 / 2.58	1.90 / 2.50	1.85 / 2.41	1.82 / 2.36	1.78 / 2.28	1.76 / 2.25	1.72 / 2.19	1.70 / 2.15	1.69 / 2.13

479

Degrees of Freedom for the Numerator

Denominator df	1	2	3	4	5	6	7	8	9	10	11	12	14	16	20	24	30	40	50	75	100	200	500	∞
27	4.21 / 7.68	3.35 / 5.49	2.96 / 4.60	2.73 / 4.11	2.57 / 3.79	2.46 / 3.56	2.37 / 3.39	2.30 / 3.26	2.25 / 3.14	2.20 / 3.06	2.16 / 2.98	2.13 / 2.93	2.08 / 2.83	2.03 / 2.74	1.97 / 2.63	1.93 / 2.55	1.88 / 2.47	1.84 / 2.38	1.80 / 2.33	1.76 / 2.25	1.74 / 2.21	1.71 / 2.16	1.68 / 2.12	1.67 / 2.10
28	4.20 / 7.64	3.34 / 5.45	2.95 / 4.57	2.71 / 4.07	2.56 / 3.76	2.44 / 3.53	2.36 / 3.36	2.29 / 3.23	2.24 / 3.11	2.19 / 3.03	2.15 / 2.95	2.12 / 2.90	2.06 / 2.80	2.02 / 2.71	1.96 / 2.60	1.91 / 2.52	1.87 / 2.44	1.81 / 2.35	1.78 / 2.30	1.75 / 2.22	1.72 / 2.18	1.69 / 2.13	1.67 / 2.09	1.65 / 2.06
29	4.18 / 7.60	3.33 / 5.42	2.93 / 4.54	2.70 / 4.04	2.54 / 3.73	2.43 / 3.50	2.35 / 3.33	2.28 / 3.20	2.22 / 3.08	2.18 / 3.00	2.14 / 2.92	2.10 / 2.87	2.05 / 2.77	2.00 / 2.68	1.94 / 2.57	1.90 / 2.49	1.85 / 2.41	1.80 / 2.32	1.77 / 2.27	1.73 / 2.19	1.71 / 2.15	1.68 / 2.10	1.65 / 2.06	1.64 / 2.03
30	4.17 / 7.56	3.32 / 5.39	2.92 / 4.51	2.69 / 4.02	2.53 / 3.70	2.42 / 3.47	2.34 / 3.30	2.27 / 3.17	2.21 / 3.06	2.16 / 2.98	2.12 / 2.90	2.09 / 2.84	2.04 / 2.74	1.99 / 2.66	1.93 / 2.55	1.89 / 2.47	1.84 / 2.38	1.79 / 2.29	1.76 / 2.24	1.72 / 2.16	1.69 / 2.13	1.66 / 2.07	1.64 / 2.03	1.62 / 2.01
32	4.15 / 7.50	3.30 / 5.34	2.90 / 4.46	2.67 / 3.97	2.51 / 3.66	2.40 / 3.42	2.32 / 3.25	2.25 / 3.12	2.19 / 3.01	2.13 / 2.94	2.10 / 2.86	2.07 / 2.80	2.02 / 2.70	1.97 / 2.62	1.91 / 2.51	1.86 / 2.42	1.82 / 2.34	1.76 / 2.25	1.74 / 2.20	1.69 / 2.12	1.67 / 2.08	1.64 / 2.02	1.61 / 1.98	1.59 / 1.96
34	4.13 / 7.44	3.28 / 5.29	2.88 / 4.42	2.65 / 3.93	2.49 / 3.61	2.38 / 3.38	2.30 / 3.21	2.23 / 3.08	2.17 / 2.97	2.12 / 2.89	2.08 / 2.82	2.05 / 2.76	2.00 / 2.66	1.95 / 2.58	1.89 / 2.47	1.84 / 2.38	1.80 / 2.30	1.74 / 2.21	1.71 / 2.15	1.67 / 2.08	1.64 / 2.04	1.61 / 1.98	1.59 / 1.94	1.57 / 1.91
36	4.11 / 7.39	3.26 / 5.25	2.86 / 4.38	2.63 / 3.89	2.48 / 3.58	2.36 / 3.35	2.28 / 3.18	2.21 / 3.04	2.15 / 2.94	2.10 / 2.86	2.06 / 2.78	2.03 / 2.72	1.98 / 2.62	1.93 / 2.54	1.87 / 2.43	1.82 / 2.35	1.78 / 2.26	1.72 / 2.17	1.69 / 2.12	1.65 / 2.04	1.62 / 2.00	1.59 / 1.94	1.56 / 1.90	1.55 / 1.87
38	4.10 / 7.35	3.25 / 5.21	2.85 / 4.34	2.62 / 3.86	2.46 / 3.54	2.35 / 3.32	2.26 / 3.15	2.19 / 3.02	2.14 / 2.91	2.09 / 2.82	2.05 / 2.75	2.02 / 2.69	1.96 / 2.59	1.92 / 2.51	1.85 / 2.40	1.80 / 2.32	1.76 / 2.22	1.71 / 2.14	1.67 / 2.08	1.63 / 2.00	1.60 / 1.97	1.57 / 1.90	1.54 / 1.86	1.53 / 1.84
40	4.08 / 7.31	3.23 / 5.18	2.84 / 4.31	2.61 / 3.83	2.45 / 3.51	2.34 / 3.29	2.25 / 3.12	2.18 / 2.99	2.12 / 2.88	2.07 / 2.80	2.04 / 2.73	2.00 / 2.66	1.95 / 2.56	1.90 / 2.49	1.84 / 2.37	1.79 / 2.29	1.74 / 2.20	1.69 / 2.11	1.66 / 2.05	1.61 / 1.97	1.59 / 1.94	1.55 / 1.88	1.53 / 1.84	1.51 / 1.81
42	4.07 / 7.27	3.22 / 5.15	2.83 / 4.29	2.59 / 3.80	2.44 / 3.49	2.32 / 3.26	2.24 / 3.10	2.17 / 2.96	2.11 / 2.86	2.06 / 2.77	2.02 / 2.70	1.99 / 2.64	1.94 / 2.54	1.89 / 2.46	1.82 / 2.35	1.78 / 2.26	1.73 / 2.17	1.68 / 2.08	1.64 / 2.02	1.60 / 1.94	1.57 / 1.91	1.54 / 1.85	1.51 / 1.80	1.49 / 1.78
44	4.06 / 7.24	3.21 / 5.12	2.82 / 4.26	2.58 / 3.78	2.43 / 3.46	2.31 / 3.24	2.23 / 3.07	2.16 / 2.94	2.10 / 2.84	2.05 / 2.75	2.01 / 2.68	1.98 / 2.62	1.92 / 2.52	1.88 / 2.44	1.81 / 2.32	1.76 / 2.24	1.72 / 2.15	1.66 / 2.06	1.63 / 2.00	1.58 / 1.92	1.56 / 1.88	1.52 / 1.82	1.50 / 1.78	1.48 / 1.75
46	4.05 / 7.21	3.20 / 5.10	2.81 / 4.24	2.57 / 3.76	2.42 / 3.44	2.30 / 3.22	2.22 / 3.05	2.14 / 2.92	2.09 / 2.82	2.04 / 2.73	2.00 / 2.66	1.97 / 2.60	1.91 / 2.50	1.87 / 2.42	1.80 / 2.30	1.75 / 2.22	1.71 / 2.13	1.65 / 2.04	1.62 / 1.98	1.57 / 1.90	1.54 / 1.86	1.51 / 1.80	1.48 / 1.76	1.46 / 1.72
48	4.04 / 7.19	3.19 / 5.08	2.80 / 4.22	2.56 / 3.74	2.41 / 3.42	2.30 / 3.20	2.21 / 3.04	2.14 / 2.90	2.08 / 2.80	2.03 / 2.71	1.99 / 2.64	1.96 / 2.58	1.90 / 2.48	1.86 / 2.40	1.79 / 2.28	1.74 / 2.20	1.70 / 2.11	1.64 / 2.02	1.61 / 1.96	1.56 / 1.88	1.53 / 1.84	1.50 / 1.78	1.47 / 1.73	1.45 / 1.70

Degrees of freedom for the denominator

df											Degrees of Freedom for the Numerator												
	1	**2**	**3**	**4**	**5**	**6**	**7**	**8**	**9**	**10**	**11**	**12**	**14**	**16**	**20**	**24**	**30**	**40**	**50**	**75**	**100**	**200**	**500**	**∞**
50	4.03 / **7.17**	3.18 / **5.06**	2.79 / **4.20**	2.56 / **3.72**	2.40 / **3.41**	2.29 / **3.18**	2.20 / **3.02**	2.13 / **2.88**	2.07 / **2.78**	2.02 / **2.70**	1.98 / **2.62**	1.95 / **2.56**	1.90 / **2.46**	1.85 / **2.39**	1.78 / **2.26**	1.74 / **2.18**	1.69 / **2.10**	1.63 / **2.00**	1.60 / **1.94**	1.55 / **1.86**	1.52 / **1.82**	1.48 / **1.76**	1.46 / **1.71**	1.44 / **1.68**
55	4.02 / **7.12**	3.17 / **5.01**	2.78 / **4.16**	2.54 / **3.68**	2.38 / **3.37**	2.27 / **3.15**	2.18 / **2.98**	2.11 / **2.85**	2.05 / **2.75**	2.00 / **2.66**	1.97 / **2.59**	1.93 / **2.53**	1.88 / **2.43**	1.83 / **2.35**	1.76 / **2.23**	1.72 / **2.16**	1.67 / **2.06**	1.61 / **1.96**	1.58 / **1.90**	1.52 / **1.82**	1.50 / **1.78**	1.46 / **1.71**	1.43 / **1.66**	1.41 / **1.64**
60	4.00 / **7.08**	3.15 / **4.98**	2.76 / **4.13**	2.52 / **3.65**	2.37 / **3.34**	2.25 / **3.12**	2.17 / **2.95**	2.10 / **2.82**	2.04 / **2.72**	1.99 / **2.63**	1.95 / **2.56**	1.92 / **2.50**	1.86 / **2.40**	1.81 / **2.32**	1.75 / **2.20**	1.70 / **2.12**	1.65 / **2.03**	1.59 / **1.93**	1.56 / **1.87**	1.50 / **1.79**	1.48 / **1.74**	1.44 / **1.68**	1.41 / **1.63**	1.39 / **1.60**
65	3.99 / **7.04**	3.14 / **4.95**	2.75 / **4.10**	2.51 / **3.62**	2.36 / **3.31**	2.24 / **3.09**	2.15 / **2.93**	2.08 / **2.79**	2.02 / **2.70**	1.98 / **2.61**	1.94 / **2.54**	1.90 / **2.47**	1.85 / **2.37**	1.80 / **2.30**	1.73 / **2.18**	1.68 / **2.09**	1.63 / **2.00**	1.57 / **1.90**	1.54 / **1.84**	1.49 / **1.76**	1.46 / **1.71**	1.42 / **1.64**	1.39 / **1.60**	1.37 / **1.56**
70	3.98 / **7.01**	3.13 / **4.92**	2.74 / **4.08**	2.50 / **3.60**	2.34 / **3.29**	2.23 / **3.07**	2.14 / **2.91**	2.07 / **2.77**	2.01 / **2.67**	1.97 / **2.59**	1.93 / **2.51**	1.89 / **2.45**	1.84 / **2.35**	1.79 / **2.28**	1.72 / **2.15**	1.67 / **2.07**	1.62 / **1.98**	1.56 / **1.88**	1.53 / **1.82**	1.47 / **1.74**	1.45 / **1.69**	1.40 / **1.62**	1.37 / **1.56**	1.35 / **1.53**
80	3.96 / **6.96**	3.11 / **4.88**	2.72 / **4.04**	2.48 / **3.56**	2.33 / **3.25**	2.21 / **3.04**	2.12 / **2.87**	2.05 / **2.74**	1.99 / **2.64**	1.96 / **2.55**	1.91 / **2.48**	1.88 / **2.41**	1.82 / **2.32**	1.77 / **2.24**	1.70 / **2.11**	1.65 / **2.03**	1.60 / **1.94**	1.54 / **1.84**	1.51 / **1.78**	1.45 / **1.70**	1.42 / **1.65**	1.38 / **1.57**	1.35 / **1.52**	1.32 / **1.49**
100	3.94 / **6.90**	3.09 / **4.82**	2.70 / **3.98**	2.46 / **3.51**	2.30 / **3.20**	2.19 / **2.99**	2.10 / **2.82**	2.03 / **2.69**	1.97 / **2.59**	1.92 / **2.51**	1.88 / **2.43**	1.85 / **2.36**	1.79 / **2.26**	1.75 / **2.19**	1.68 / **2.06**	1.63 / **1.98**	1.57 / **1.89**	1.51 / **1.79**	1.48 / **1.73**	1.42 / **1.64**	1.39 / **1.59**	1.34 / **1.51**	1.30 / **1.46**	1.28 / **1.43**
125	3.92 / **6.84**	3.07 / **4.78**	2.68 / **3.94**	2.44 / **3.47**	2.29 / **3.17**	2.17 / **2.95**	2.08 / **2.79**	2.01 / **2.65**	1.95 / **2.56**	1.90 / **2.47**	1.86 / **2.40**	1.83 / **2.33**	1.77 / **2.23**	1.72 / **2.15**	1.65 / **2.03**	1.60 / **1.94**	1.55 / **1.85**	1.49 / **1.75**	1.45 / **1.68**	1.39 / **1.59**	1.36 / **1.54**	1.31 / **1.46**	1.27 / **1.40**	1.25 / **1.37**
150	3.91 / **6.81**	3.06 / **4.75**	2.67 / **3.91**	2.43 / **3.44**	2.27 / **3.14**	2.16 / **2.92**	2.07 / **2.76**	2.00 / **2.62**	1.94 / **2.53**	1.89 / **2.44**	1.85 / **2.37**	1.82 / **2.30**	1.76 / **2.20**	1.71 / **2.12**	1.64 / **2.00**	1.59 / **1.91**	1.54 / **1.83**	1.47 / **1.72**	1.44 / **1.66**	1.37 / **1.56**	1.34 / **1.51**	1.29 / **1.43**	1.25 / **1.37**	1.22 / **1.33**
200	3.89 / **6.76**	3.04 / **4.71**	2.65 / **3.88**	2.41 / **3.41**	2.26 / **3.11**	2.14 / **2.90**	2.05 / **2.73**	1.98 / **2.60**	1.92 / **2.50**	1.87 / **2.41**	1.83 / **2.34**	1.80 / **2.28**	1.74 / **2.17**	1.69 / **2.09**	1.62 / **1.97**	1.57 / **1.88**	1.52 / **1.79**	1.45 / **1.69**	1.42 / **1.62**	1.35 / **1.53**	1.32 / **1.48**	1.26 / **1.39**	1.22 / **1.33**	1.19 / **1.28**
400	3.86 / **6.70**	3.02 / **4.66**	2.62 / **3.83**	2.39 / **3.36**	2.23 / **3.06**	2.12 / **2.85**	2.03 / **2.69**	1.96 / **2.55**	1.90 / **2.46**	1.85 / **2.37**	1.81 / **2.29**	1.78 / **2.23**	1.72 / **2.12**	1.67 / **2.04**	1.60 / **1.92**	1.54 / **1.84**	1.49 / **1.74**	1.42 / **1.64**	1.38 / **1.57**	1.32 / **1.47**	1.28 / **1.42**	1.22 / **1.32**	1.16 / **1.24**	1.13 / **1.19**
1000	3.85 / **6.66**	3.00 / **4.62**	2.61 / **3.80**	2.38 / **3.34**	2.22 / **3.04**	2.10 / **2.82**	2.02 / **2.66**	1.95 / **2.53**	1.89 / **2.43**	1.84 / **2.34**	1.80 / **2.26**	1.76 / **2.20**	1.70 / **2.09**	1.65 / **2.01**	1.58 / **1.89**	1.53 / **1.81**	1.47 / **1.71**	1.41 / **1.61**	1.36 / **1.54**	1.30 / **1.44**	1.26 / **1.38**	1.19 / **1.28**	1.13 / **1.19**	1.08 / **1.11**
∞	3.84 / **6.64**	2.99 / **4.60**	2.60 / **3.78**	2.37 / **3.32**	2.21 / **3.02**	2.09 / **2.80**	2.01 / **2.64**	1.94 / **2.51**	1.88 / **2.41**	1.83 / **2.32**	1.79 / **2.24**	1.75 / **2.18**	1.69 / **2.07**	1.64 / **1.99**	1.57 / **1.87**	1.52 / **1.79**	1.46 / **1.69**	1.40 / **1.59**	1.35 / **1.52**	1.28 / **1.41**	1.24 / **1.36**	1.17 / **1.25**	1.11 / **1.15**	1.00 / **1.00**

Degrees of freedom for the denominator

TABLE A.4 ■ Transformation of r to z_r

r	z_r	r	z_r	r	z_r	r	z_r	r	z_r
.000	.000	.200	.203	.400	.424	.600	.693	.800	1.099
.005	.005	.205	.208	.405	.430	.605	.701	.805	1.113
.010	.010	.210	.213	.410	.436	.610	.709	.810	1.127
.015	.015	.215	.218	.415	.442	.615	.717	.815	1.142
.020	.020	.220	.224	.420	.448	.620	.725	.820	1.157
.025	.025	.225	.229	.425	.454	.625	.733	.825	1.172
.030	.030	.230	.234	.430	.460	.630	.741	.830	1.188
.035	.035	.235	.239	.435	.466	.635	.750	.835	1.204
.040	.040	.240	.245	.440	.472	.640	.758	.840	1.221
.045	.045	.245	.250	.445	.478	.645	.767	.845	1.238
.050	.050	.250	.255	.450	.485	.650	.775	.850	1.256
.055	.055	.255	.261	.455	.491	.655	.784	.855	1.274
.060	.060	.260	.266	.460	.497	.660	.793	.860	1.293
.065	.065	.265	.271	.465	.504	.665	.802	.865	1.313
.070	.070	.270	.277	.470	.510	.670	.811	.870	1.333
.075	.075	.275	.282	.475	.517	.675	.820	.875	1.354
.080	.080	.280	.288	.480	.523	.680	.829	.880	1.376
.085	.085	.285	.293	.485	.530	.685	.838	.885	1.398
.090	.090	.290	.299	.490	.536	.690	.848	.890	1.422
.095	.095	.295	.304	.495	.543	.695	.858	.895	1.447
.100	.100	.300	.310	.500	.549	.700	.867	.900	1.472
.105	.105	.305	.315	.505	.556	.705	.877	.905	1.499
.110	.110	.310	.321	.510	.563	.710	.887	.910	1.528
.115	.116	.315	.326	.515	.570	.715	.897	.915	1.557
.120	.121	.320	.332	.520	.576	.720	.908	.920	1.589
.125	.126	.325	.337	.525	.583	.725	.918	.925	1.623
.130	.131	.330	.343	.530	.590	.730	.929	.930	1.658
.135	.136	.335	.348	.535	.597	.735	.940	.935	1.697
.140	.141	.340	.354	.540	.604	.740	.950	.940	1.738
.145	.146	.345	.360	.545	.611	.745	.962	.945	1.783
.150	.151	.350	.365	.550	.618	.750	.973	.950	1.832
.155	.156	.355	.371	.555	.626	.755	.984	.955	1.886
.160	.161	.360	.377	.560	.633	.760	.996	.960	1.946
.165	.167	.365	.383	.565	.640	.765	1.008	.965	2.014
.170	.172	.370	.388	.570	.648	.770	1.020	.970	2.092
.175	.177	.375	.394	.575	.655	.775	1.033	.975	2.188
.180	.182	.380	.400	.580	.662	.780	1.045	.980	2.298
.185	.187	.385	.406	.585	.670	.785	1.058	.985	2.443
.190	.192	.390	.412	.590	.678	.790	1.071	.990	2.647
.195	.198	.395	.418	.595	.685	.795	1.085	.995	2.994

From *Statistical Methods* by A. L. Edwards © 1967. Reprinted with permission of Brooks/Cole.

TABLE A.5 ■ Critical Values of the Pearson Product-Moment Correlation Coefficient, *r*

	Level of Significance for a Directional (One-Tailed) Test				
	.05	**.025**	**.01**	**.005**	**.0005**
	Level of Significance for a Nondirectional (Two-Tailed) Test				
df = N − 2	**.10**	**.05**	**.02**	**.01**	**.001**
1	.9877	.9969	.9995	.9999	1.0000
2	.9000	.9600	.9800	.9900	.9990
3	.8054	.8783	.9343	.9587	.9912
4	.7293	.8114	.8822	.9172	.9741
5	.6694	.7545	.8329	.8745	.9507
6	.6215	.7067	.7887	.8343	.9249
7	.5822	.6664	.7498	.7977	.8982
8	.5494	.6319	.7155	.7646	.8721
9	.5214	.6021	.6851	.7348	.8471
10	.4973	.6760	.6581	.7079	.8233
11	.4762	.5529	.6339	.6835	.8010
12	.4575	.5324	.6120	.6614	.7800
13	.4409	.5139	.6923	.6411	.7603
14	.4259	.4973	.5742	.6226	.7420
15	.4124	.4821	.5577	.6065	.7246
16	.4000	.4683	.5425	.5897	.7084
17	.3887	.4555	.5285	.5751	.6932
18	.3783	.4438	.5155	.5614	.6787
19	.3687	.4329	.5034	.5487	.6652
20	.3598	.4227	.4921	.5368	.6524
25	.3233	.3809	.4451	.4869	.5974
30	.2960	.3494	.4093	.4487	.5541
35	.2746	.3246	.3810	.4182	.5189
40	.2573	.3044	.3578	.3932	.4896
45	.2428	.2875	.3384	.3721	.4648
50	.2306	.2732	.3218	.3541	.4433
60	.2108	.2500	.2948	.3248	.4078
70	.1954	.2319	.2737	.3017	.3799
80	.1829	.2172	.2565	.2830	.3568
90	.1726	.2050	.2422	.2673	.3375
100	.1638	.1946	.2301	.2540	.3211

If the observed value of *r* is *greater than or equal to* the tabled value for the appropriate level of significance (columns) and degrees of freedom (rows), reject H_0. The degrees of freedom are the number of pairs of scores minus two, or N − 2. The critical values in the table are both + and − for nondirectional (two-tailed) tests.

TABLE A.6 ■ Critical Values of Chi Square, χ^2

	Level of Significance for a Directional Test					
	.10	**.05**	**.025**	**.01**	**.005**	**.0005**
	Level of Significance for a Nondirectional Test					
df	**.20**	**.10**	**.05**	**.02**	**.01**	**.001**
1	1.64	2.71	3.84	5.41	6.64	10.83
2	3.22	4.60	5.99	7.82	9.21	13.82
3	4.64	6.25	7.82	9.84	11.34	16.27
4	5.99	7.78	9.49	11.67	13.28	18.46
5	7.29	9.24	11.07	13.39	15.09	20.52
6	8.56	10.64	12.59	15.03	16.81	22.46
7	9.80	12.02	14.07	16.62	18.48	24.32
8	11.03	13.36	15.51	18.17	20.09	26.12
9	12.24	14.68	16.92	19.68	21.67	27.88
10	13.44	15.99	18.31	21.16	23.21	29.59
11	14.63	17.28	19.68	22.62	24.72	31.26
12	15.81	18.55	21.03	24.05	26.22	32.91
13	16.98	19.81	22.36	25.47	27.69	34.53
14	18.15	21.06	23.68	26.87	29.14	36.12
15	19.31	22.31	25.00	28.26	30.58	37.70
16	20.46	23.54	26.30	29.63	32.00	39.29
17	21.62	24.77	27.59	31.00	33.41	40.75
18	22.76	25.99	28.87	32.35	34.80	42.31
19	23.90	27.20	30.14	33.69	36.19	43.82
20	25.04	28.41	31.41	35.02	37.57	45.32
21	26.17	29.62	32.67	36.34	38.93	46.80
22	27.30	30.81	33.92	37.66	40.29	48.27
23	28.43	32.01	35.17	38.97	41.64	49.73
24	29.55	33.20	36.42	40.27	42.98	51.18
25	30.68	34.38	37.65	41.57	44.31	52.62
26	31.80	35.56	38.88	42.86	45.64	54.05
27	32.91	36.74	40.11	44.14	46.96	55.48
28	34.03	37.92	41.34	45.42	48.28	56.89
29	35.14	39.09	42.69	46.69	49.59	58.30
30	36.25	40.26	43.77	47.96	50.89	59.70
32	38.47	42.59	46.19	50.49	53.49	62.49
34	40.68	44.90	48.60	53.00	56.06	65.25
36	42.88	47.21	51.00	55.49	58.62	67.99
38	45.08	49.51	53.38	57.97	61.16	70.70
40	47.27	51.81	56.76	60.44	63.69	73.40
44	51.64	56.37	60.48	65.34	68.71	78.75
48	55.99	60.91	65.17	70.20	73.68	84.04
52	60.33	65.42	69.83	75.02	78.62	89.27
56	64.66	69.92	74.47	79.82	83.51	94.46
60	68.97	74.40	79.08	84.58	88.38	99.61

The table lists the critical values of chi square for the degrees of freedom shown at the left for tests corresponding to those significance levels which head each column If the observed value of χ^2_{obs} is *greater than or equal to* the tabled value, reject H_0. All chi squares are positive.

A Brief Introduction to Power Analysis

INTRODUCTION

Data analysis and interpretation in the sciences are about probabilities. Any time researchers study something that is not directly observable (even electrons), there is error in measurement. Sampling errors occur in medicine and the life sciences just as they do in the behavioral sciences. Projections of reactions to medications and prognosis in medicine (e.g., there is a 1 in 200 chance that you will die from this surgery) are always probabilistic.

When constructing confidence intervals, we specify the probability that our interval contains the parameter of interest, for example a population mean or proportion. In the context of null hypothesis significance testing (NHST), we state a null hypothesis and then determine the probability of a test statistic, such as t or F, under the assumption that the null hypothesis is true. Low probabilities associated with our test statistic define rare events and under the rules of NHST lead us to lose confidence in the truth of the null hypothesis. The **power** of a statistical test is the probability that a false null hypothesis will be rejected. Power refers to the probability of making a correct decision (rejecting the null hypothesis when it is false). However, the concept of statistical power is best understood in the context of yet other probabilities: those associated both with correct and incorrect statistical decisions.

TYPE I AND TYPE II ERRORS

Because the probabilities we deal with in statistical decision-making are less than 1.00, there is always some probability that our conclusions are wrong. Figure B.1 summarizes errors and correct decisions that can be made using NHST. (See also Figure 10.3.) Rejecting the null hypothesis when the null hypothesis should not be rejected is a **Type I error,** and the probability of this error is equivalent to **α (alpha).** With alpha equal to the .05 level, we have some assurance that we will make this mistake relatively rarely. Researchers traditionally set alpha at .05 to keep the number of false claims for effective variables low. A Type I error is the equivalent of "crying wolf" (i.e., yelling *wolf!* when a wolf is not there), or, as suggested in Chapter 10, it's analogous to convicting someone who did not commit a crime. (See Table 10.2.) Scientists are (or should be) generally hesitant to claim an effect is present until sufficient evidence has been accumulated. Keeping alpha low is one way to prevent too many false cries of *wolf* or too many innocent people from being found guilty. Researchers traditionally have been most concerned about Type I errors.

Of course, another error can be made when using NHST. Refer again to Figure B.1. In this case, we decide (again based on the probability of our test statistic) that the null hypothesis should not be rejected when, in fact, it is false. We missed a real difference. The independent variable has an effect, but we failed to detect it. Making this kind of mistake is a **Type II error** and is symbolized as **β (beta).** Staying with a legal analogy, this is similar to a truly guilty party not being declared guilty because insufficient evidence was found to justify rejecting the presumption of innocence. (See Table 10.2.) (Or, if you like, the wolf is there but we didn't see it; in other words, we should have called *wolf.*) Researchers generally have not given Type II errors the same attention they have given to Type I errors.

FIGURE B.1   ■   Four possible outcomes when a null hypothesis has been tested.

Decision	The True Situation	
	Null hypothesis is true	Null hypothesis is false
Allow the null hypothesis to stand; do not reject the null hypothesis.	A correct decision; one has not rejected a true null hypothesis.	An error; the population means differ, but the null hypothesis has not been rejected (Type II Error).
Reject the null hypothesis and conclude that the two means are indeed different.	An error; a true null hypothesis has been rejected (Type I Error).	A correct decision; a false null hypothesis has been validly rejected (Power).

In Chapter 10, we pointed out that Type II errors are often of particular concern to applied researchers. In some cases, it is just as undesirable to miss a potentially beneficial finding (a Type II error) as it is to conclude that a variable was effective when it is not (a Type I error). Missing the real effect of a new medication (which would be a Type II error) means that some ill people will not be helped. This is an error we would not want to make. The point is that the cost of making a Type II error may not be the same in all research situations. (See Posavac, 1998.)

As we also discussed in Chapter 10, one reason researchers over the years have focused more on Type I than Type II errors is that it was generally believed that making false claims for an effective treatment is worse than missing an effective treatment. This is coupled with a general belief among scientists that science is self-correcting. That is, if an effect occurred, although not recognized at this point, it will be found eventually. Although this takes time, the delay was perhaps seen as better than making false claims for the effectiveness of a treatment (Type I error.) But, as we just noted, this type of thinking was probably more prevalent among basic researchers than applied researchers. In applied research, time is often of the essence.

TYPE II ERRORS AND POWER

Scientific complacency regarding Type II errors began to disappear when two facts about such errors became evident:

(a) The probability of a Type II error is, in most psychological studies, greater than that of a Type I error (e.g., Cohen, 1990; Rosnow & Rosenthal, 1989; Schmidt & Hunter, 1997). (Simply put, Type II errors occur more frequently than do Type I errors.)

(b) At least in the abstract, Type II errors may actually be the only kind of error possible (e.g., Schmidt & Hunter, 1997).

The latter point is based on the obvious logic that, for a Type I error to occur, it must be possible for the null hypothesis to be true. A Type I error occurs when a null hypothesis is said to be false when it isn't. But what if the null hypothesis as the "hypothesis of no difference" were always false (or nearly always)? That is, what if there were always *some* difference, at least to some decimal point? If the null hypothesis were always false, it would not be possible to *mistakenly* claim that the null hypothesis is false. Critics of the application of NHST (e.g., Cohen, 1994; Meehl, 1967; 1978) are no doubt correct in asserting that the null hypothesis is always false (at some level); however, *in practice,* we need some way of determining when a hypothesis of no difference, if not exactly true, is close enough to being true to represent an uninteresting difference. NHST can help with that decision.

Why are Type II errors so likely to occur? The answer is that researchers have not been conducting statistical analyses with enough power to detect a difference that is really there (e.g., Cohen, 1962). As noted previously, the probability of correctly rejecting a false null hypothesis is called the *power* of a statistical test. Power is symbolized as $1 - \beta$, that is, "1.00 minus the probability of a Type II error." Refer again to Figure B.1.

Consider those microscopes you have used in biology classes. You might remember that the power of microscopes varies. The more powerful the resolution, the more likely you were to see whatever was in that slide you so carefully inserted into the microscope. Most of us have had the experience of looking through a microscope and not seeing anything until we switched to a microscope with sufficient power. When that happened, we were often able to see a specimen that we could not see before (although it was always there). Analogously, statistical power is the ability to see evidence of a true difference. When power is too low, we do not see evidence of an effect (although it is really there). It is generally agreed that researchers have often been using statistical microscopes that have insufficient power to see what they are looking for.

TYPE II ERRORS, POWER, AND EFFECT SIZE

No doubt another reason why researchers have not traditionally paid much attention to Type II errors, even if they did recognize their importance, is because the specific probability of occurrence of a Type II error isn't easily determined. In contrast, a Type I error is equivalent to α and is set by the researcher. It's as simple as that. As alpha decreases (e.g., from .05 to .01), the probability of a Type I error decreases but the probability of a Type II error increases. It was generally assumed that .05 was a good "balance" between Type I and Type II errors (although, in hindsight, on what basis this was assumed is not necessarily clear). The probability of a Type II error, or β, is a function of the size of the true difference associated with the alternative hypothesis. The probability of beta is, in other words, directly linked to the effect size. Many investigators assumed that effect sizes weren't known until the research was conducted. After all, that is why you are doing research: to determine the effect of your treatment. As we will see, this thinking has changed dramatically in the last few decades.

The points we have made about Type I and Type II errors, power, and effect size can be best understood by a careful examination of Figures B.2, B.3, B.4, and B.5. Let us lead you through a discussion of these figures. This discussion is important because it provides a background to help you understand the computation of power and its application for a statistical test.

Look first at Figure B.2. Assume that the researcher is comparing two means based on performance from an experimental group and a control group, and that a nondirectional test was used. (See Chapter 9.) When two means are being compared and the researcher does not specify the direction of the difference associated with the alternative hypothesis, we can formally state the null and alternative hypotheses as follows:

$$H_0: \mu_{\text{Experimental}} = \mu_{\text{Control}}, \text{ or } \mu_{\text{Experimental}} - \mu_{\text{Control}} = 0$$

$$H_1: \mu_{\text{Experimental}} \neq \mu_{\text{Control}}, \text{ or } \mu_{\text{Experimental}} - \mu_{\text{Control}} \neq 0$$

Figure B.2 shows hypothetical distributions of scores for both the experimental and control groups. The figure indicates that population means are different. Specifically, the mean of the experimental population is greater than that of the control population. Assuming that Figure B.2 represents a true state of affairs, then the alternative hypothesis is correct. But of course the researcher does not know this as he or she begins to do research; otherwise, there would be no reason to do the research. Remember, a researcher works with samples, not populations. The distributions overlap because the true difference between the population means is not that great and the variances of the distributions are relatively large. (One might imagine a *very* large effect, or very small variances, that would lead to non-overlapping distributions, but most of the time we will discover that the population distributions of scores overlap.) The researcher's task is to decide whether a particular difference between two *sample* means is large enough to warrant confidence in the alternative hypothesis. This is done by referring to a sampling distribution of differences between two independent sample means. (See Chapter 9.)

Figure B.3 describes the theoretical sampling distribution of differences between independent sample means under both the null hypothesis and the alternative hypothesis (the latter, in this case, we know to be true). Under the null hypothesis, the sampling distribution of differences between means has a mean of zero, whereas, under the alternative hypothesis,

FIGURE B.2 ■ Hypothetical distributions of populations of scores for both an experimental and a control group. Although the distributions overlap, the mean of the experimental group is greater than the mean of the control group. The difference between the means is the effect size for this comparison.

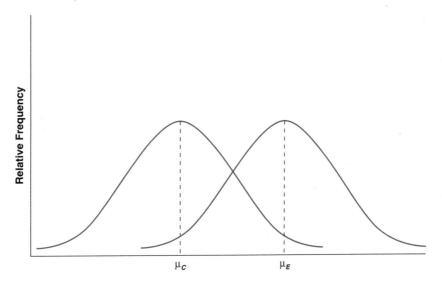

FIGURE B.3 ■ Sampling distributions of differences between independent sample means under both the null and alternative hypotheses (nondirectional).

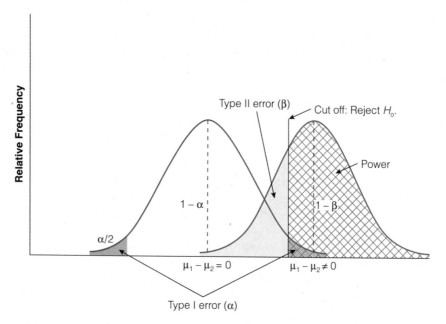

the distribution of differences between means has a mean greater than zero. Here again we see that there is overlap in the distributions, and it is for the same reasons that the populations of scores overlapped: the difference between the population means is not large relative to the standard deviation (i.e., the standard errors are large). Because it was a nondirectional test, $\alpha/2$ is in each tail and defines the critical regions. If the difference between the two sample means is large enough, the researcher would reject the null hypothesis.

Looking at Figure B.3, consider carefully the darker blue corresponding to α (Type I error) and the lighter blue that corresponds to β (Type II error). (In the figure, $\alpha/2$ is shown because a two-tailed test was used.) Alpha defines the **critical region;** a test statistic falling in this area leads us to say that the difference between the two means is "statistically significant." The outcome would lead us to reject the null hypothesis. Be sure to note that the darker blue associated with alpha is within the sampling distribution associated with the null hypothesis. Remember that, when using NHST, we gather evidence for the alternative hypothesis indirectly. We ask, *if* the null hypothesis were true, what is the probability of obtaining the test statistic (e.g., t, F)? If the probability is low assuming the null hypothesis, we would suggest that the difference between the sample means did not come from a sampling distribution of differences between means that has a mean of zero (as would be the case if the null hypothesis were true); instead, we would suggest that the difference came from a distribution of differences between means that has a mean greater than zero.

When the alternative hypothesis is true (as it is in this case), the differences between sample means actually come from a sampling distribution of differences between means that is in accord with the alternative hypothesis. Thus, we must now refer to a distribution that reflects the alternative hypothesis. Note in Figure B.3 that the lighter blue represents the area under the alternative hypothesis that would lead to *not* rejecting the null hypothesis. The lighter blue represents differences between means that came from a distribution based on the alternative hypothesis, but we would not know this on the basis of our statistical test. This area (and probability) corresponds to a Type II error (β). A Type II error results when an observed difference between sample means is actually from a distribution of differences that does not have a mean of zero, but we have not found sufficient evidence to say so.

Again referring to Figure B.3, note what happens if we decrease or increase alpha. Decreasing alpha (e.g., .05 to .01, the cutoff point moving to the right) will increase the area associated with a Type II error. However, increasing alpha (e.g., .05 to .10, the cutoff point moving to the left) will decrease the area associated with a Type II error. Therefore, one way to reduce Type II errors is to increase alpha; but, by increasing alpha, we increase Type I errors. Nevertheless, in some applied situations, it may be desirable to examine alpha with the probability of Type II errors in mind (e.g., Lipsey, 1990; Posavac, 1998).

Figure B.3 also contains a description of power. Power ($1 - \beta$) is shown in Figure B.3 by the cross-hatched area (including α). Power is that portion of the distribution that would correctly lead to a rejection of a false null hypothesis. Anything to the right of the cutoff associated with the critical region would lead a researcher to correctly reject the null hypothesis.

It is important to note in Figure B.3 that power is a function of the distance between the means associated with null and alternative hypotheses. Consider what would happen as the difference between the means of the theoretical sampling distributions is increased. You should be able to see that β would get smaller, and consequently power, defined as $1 - \beta$, necessarily would get larger. This is shown in Figure B.4 where the difference between the theoretical sampling distributions has been increased. The larger the effect size, the greater is power.

Finally, we can illustrate how power is affected by variability and sample size. The standard error of the sampling distribution of differences between two means is equal to the

FIGURE B.4 ■ A greater difference between sampling distributions leads to greater power.

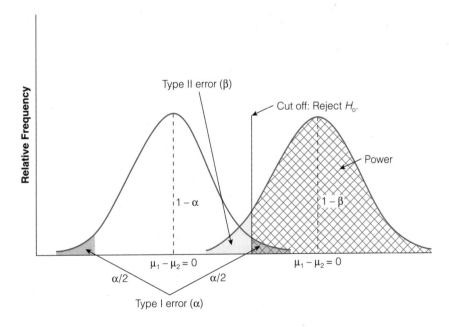

FIGURE B.5 ■ Power increases as the standard errors of the sampling distributions decrease. Given the same effect size (difference), a larger sample size produces less overlap in the sampling distributions and consequently greater power.

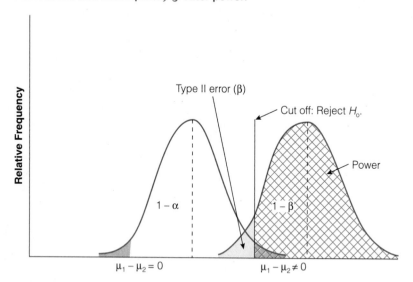

square root of the sum of the two population variances each divided by the respective sample size, i.e., when $n_1 = n_2$. (See Chapter 9.) Increasing sample sizes (n) reduces the standard error of the sampling distribution, which has the effect of reducing the overlap between the sampling distributions. Figure B.5 illustrates how β gets smaller and power, defined as $1 - \beta$, consequently gets larger as the standard errors of the sampling distributions get smaller. Note that the distance between the means is approximately that shown in Figure B.3. Given the same effect size (difference), larger sample sizes (or smaller σ^2) produces less overlap and greater power.

HOW DO YOU INCREASE THE POWER OF YOUR STATISTICAL TEST?

Suppose you have been rummaging through your great grandmother's attic and came upon what looks like a treasure map. Discreet investigation on your part suggests that it really is a treasure map and that the treasure, if still there, is worth a lot of money. Unfortunately, the treasure is located in a far-away country and you do not have the resources to mount an expedition to search for the treasure. You need to raise money, buy supplies, hire guides, and do all the other things that will make this adventure possible. You decide to approach people and ask for money and resources in trade for some share of the treasure (and of course ask them to keep quiet lest others learn about the treasure). It goes without saying that your potential shareholders will want to know two things:

(a) Is there really a treasure there (and how much is it worth)?

(b) What will it take to get the treasure?

You have no way of knowing whether the treasure is there anymore, but you can gather evidence for its existence. For example, the simple fact that no one has ever claimed to find a treasure in this area provides at least some indirect evidence that it is still there, and that your great grandmother recalls talk of such a treasure may be other evidence. A case can be made that there is something worth finding. As to what it will take to find the treasure, you must make estimates based on what others have done who traveled to these areas and what obstacles they encountered. Clearly, if you are not sufficiently prepared, the expedition will fail. You may never learn more about the treasure because your expedition didn't make it to the spot where it can be found.

For many scientists, the research process is not unlike a search for hidden treasure. Past research findings and published theories point an investigator in (hopefully) the right direction. A case can be made that there is something worth finding. But research "expeditions" can take considerable time and effort, and they often consume many resources. In other words, much is frequently invested in a research enterprise. Thus, it would behoove the investigator to assess the odds of finding what he or she is looking for and mount an expedition that has a reasonable chance of success. Insufficient resources or inadequate preparation may lead to failure. A researcher may never discover something because the research study was not capable of getting to the point where something interesting may be found. In research parlance, a researcher should seek to make sure that there is sufficient power to detect a difference if there is one.

As we have alluded to previously, many research endeavors in psychology have been ill fated because they were begun without a sufficient assessment of the power of their statistical tests. Something interesting may have been there to find, but the research study did not detect it (Type II error). As we have seen, recent critics of the research process have warned researchers about this state of affairs and have suggested ways to increase the power of statistical tests.

Our discussion of Type I and Type II errors, effect size, and power, was meant to help you identify those factors that influence the power of your statistical test and which you might manipulate to increase power. The four major contributors to the power of a statistical test are the effect size, population variance, alpha, and sample size. Although technically a researcher can exert some control over any of these factors, in practice, *the most effective way to influence power of a statistical test is through adjustment of sample size.*[1] Increases in sample size have a direct effect on power of a statistical test by, as you have seen, reducing the standard error of the sampling distributions and consequently decreasing the overlap of the distributions. (See Figure B.5.) *Increasing sample size will increase the probability that a false null hypothesis will be correctly rejected; that is, increasing sample size will increase power.*

---

[1]Of course, alpha is easily altered, and increases in alpha reduce Type II errors (β) which leads to greater power ($1 - \beta$), but, because Type I errors increase when alpha increases, most researchers do not take this path. Population variances may be reduced by careful adherence to research procedures or by the selection of relatively homogeneous populations, but the former is usually attempted (and usually contributes only a small reduction in error) and the latter may be done but it potentially threatens the generalization of results. Effect sizes may be manipulated by choosing independent variables that previous research (or common sense) indicates have a strong effect on behavior, but such choices would appear to guarantee that the results of a study would not be that interesting to the scientific community.

HOW MUCH POWER IS NEEDED?

For many years, researchers were under the impression that a "large sample" was sufficient to achieve reasonable balance of Type I and Type II errors. But what is a large sample? Many of us were taught in statistics classes (and we later taught other students) that a large sample was 30 (or thereabouts), with the reason being that changes in the critical values associated with t or F distributions do not change that much after 30. For example, if you look carefully at Table A.2, you will see that the critical value of t with 28 degrees of freedom $(30 - 2)$ and alpha equal to .05 (nondirectional) is 2.048; with infinite degrees of freedom, it is 1.960 (a difference of only about 0.09). But such considerations (and pronouncements) were typically focused on achieving statistical significance without any consideration of effect size or, in other words, what it is that a researcher was looking for.

The late statistician Jacob Cohen (1962) examined the published psychology literature and found that the typical effect size was 0.50. (See Chapter 8.) He suggested that effect sizes of 0.20 and 0.80 be considered small and large effects, respectively. As we noted in Chapter 8, Lipsey (1990) examined mainly applied research findings and reported that the median effect size was 0.40, which is somewhat smaller than that obtained by Cohen. Our point was that the only way to determine whether an effect is small or large is to compare it with effect sizes in a similar area of research. Even then, one must not dismiss small effects or applaud large effects until other factors are considered. For example, a large treatment effect size may have little practical value if the cost of implementing it is prohibitive. And a small effect size may be of importance if it is produced with a minimal effort (e.g., Prentice & Miller, 1992), or affects life-and-death decisions for millions of people (e.g., Rosenthal & Rosnow, 1991).

What Cohen and others demonstrated is that effect sizes can be estimated even when a study has not yet been conducted. Before beginning a study, an investigator can review previously published findings in a particular research area to determine what is a small, average, or large effect size. By carefully examining the nature of the independent and dependent variables used in earlier studies (and their similarity to variables under consideration in the proposed study), the researcher can estimate what is likely to be an effect size in the proposed study. *Once an effect size is estimated for a proposed study, the researcher can then determine the sample size needed to obtain statistical significance for that effect.* Let us illustrate.

Consider the research situation we previously used in this appendix to illustrate the relationship among Type I errors, Type II errors, and power. A researcher is interested in conducting a study with two independent groups. The data are measured on at least an interval scale, and a t test of independent groups is deemed appropriate to analyze the results. As introduced in Chapter 9, the t statistic for the difference between two sample means is calculated as

$$t_{obs} = \frac{(M_1 - M_2)}{s_{M_1 - M_2}}$$

where $s_{M_1 - M_2}$, the standard error of the difference of means, is calculated as

$$s_{M_1 - M_2} = s_{pooled} \sqrt{\left[\frac{1}{n_1} + \frac{1}{n_2}\right]}$$

Rearranging this formula for t_{obs}, we can show that

$$t_{obs} = \left[\frac{M_1 - M_2)}{s_{pooled}}\right][\sqrt{(n/2)}] \quad \text{NOTE: When } n_1 = n_2$$

Examine carefully this newly ordered formula for t_{obs}. The first quantity should be familiar. It is the formula for Hedges' g as first introduced in Chapter 8.

$$\text{Effect size } (g) = \frac{M_{\text{experimental}} - M_{\text{control}}}{s_{\text{pooled}}}$$

Therefore, the formula for t_{obs} can be written as

$$t_{obs} = [\text{Effect size}][\sqrt{(n/2)}]$$

Once an effect size is known (or estimated), the only factor left to vary is sample size. Thus, this formula may be translated loosely as

$$t_{obs} \approx [\text{Effect size}][\sqrt{\text{Sample size}}] \qquad \text{(See Rosenthal \& Rosnow, 1991.)}$$

When the formula is expressed this way, we can see that, given a particular effect size, one can determine whether a particular sample size will yield t_{obs} that is statistically significant. For example, assume an estimated effect size for a study is 0.50, which is an average effect under Cohen's guidelines. Further assume that a study is proposed with two independent groups, each with n equal to 31. We can then find

$$t_{obs} = [\text{Effect size}][\sqrt{(n/2)}] = [0.50][\sqrt{(31/2)}] = [0.50][3.94] = 1.97$$

With degrees of freedom appropriate for an independent groups t test $[(n_1 + n_2) - 2]$, or 60, the critical value for a nondirectional test with alpha equal to .05 is 2.00. (See Table A.2.) To determine statistical significance, we compare the observed t with the table or critical t. If t_{obs} is greater than t_{crit}, we may reject the null hypothesis. In this case, we can see that if the proposed study had been done with these sample sizes and $t_{obs} = 1.97$, this obtained result would not have been statistically significant (i.e., $t_{obs} < t_{crit}$). What many of us were taught is that a "large" sample size (i.e., ≥ 30) would not have produced statistical significance for the typical effect size in the psychology literature! As you saw in Chapter 10 (see Figure 10.1), given these data, an effect would be missed in a little more than half of the exact replications.

Keep in mind that the power of a study is the probability that a false null hypothesis will be rejected. Using the logic we discussed previously and reviewed in Figures B.2 through B.5 (see especially Figure B.4), the statistical power for a study can be calculated based on a particular effect size, sample size, and alpha level. Such calculations have been done and are referred to as **power tables.** (See, e.g., Cohen, 1988.) Power tables exist for the major statistical tests in psychology. Once an effect size is estimated, an appropriate power table can be consulted to determine the probability of obtaining statistical significance at a given level of alpha and for a specific sample size. With only a little preparation, the resources required to find a statistical treasure can be determined.

POWER ANALYSIS BEFORE AND AFTER
A STUDY IS COMPLETED

Power analyses are conducted for two reasons. The first, as we have suggested, is to determine the sample size that is sufficient to obtain statistical significance for a specific effect size and alpha level. A second reason to determine the power of a research study is to evaluate a study that is already completed (e.g., Rosenthal & Rosnow, 1991). Performing a power analysis after a study has been completed but when statistical significance has not been achieved can help determine whether the failure to find a statistically significant effect was due to small sample size. (See, e.g., American Psychological Association, 2001). What is the probability, in other words, that statistical significance would be obtained given this sample size? If the probability is low, a researcher may want to consider that an effect was likely missed and that a Type II error was committed.

For example, suppose that a researcher conducts a study with two independent groups ($n_1 = n_2 = 12$) and reports the following:

$$t_{obs}(22) = 1.50, p > .05.$$

The difference between the two sample means was not statistically significant with alpha equal to .05. By rearranging the terms in the equation given earlier, the effect size for this study can be calculated as

$$t_{obs} = [\text{Effect size}][\sqrt{(n/2)}] =$$

$$\frac{t_{obs}}{\sqrt{(n/2)}} = \text{Effect size} = \frac{1.50}{2.45} = 0.61$$

The effect size is somewhat larger than average based on Cohen's guidelines but was not detected with the sample sizes of 12. Given these sample sizes, what was the probability that statistical significance at the .05 level would be obtained? Consulting the relevant power table (presented and explained later in this appendix), it can be determined that power in this case is only about .30. The chances of rejecting a false null hypothesis in this case are approximately 3 in 10. The effect will be missed 70% of the time! Reporting the power of the study would help readers to judge whether the result is most likely a Type II error. The researcher in this case may wish to repeat the study with a much larger sample. How much larger? We get to that in a few paragraphs.

CALCULATING THE POWER OF A STATISTICAL TEST

Despite the attention given to power analysis in the past few decades, not all researchers take the time to properly compute the power of their studies prior to conducting them or to report the results of power analyses when statistical significance has not been achieved. Cohen (1992) was persuaded that one reason for this neglect is the difficulty that researchers sometimes experience wading through complicated power tables and that simpler "rules of thumb" would be helpful. (See also Dunlap & Myers, 1997.) In what follows, we present an abridged—and hopefully simple—view of power analysis for the major statistical tests we have discussed in this book. A much more extensive presentation can be found in Cohen (1988). For each statistical test, two brief power tables are presented: the first addresses the question of sample size necessary to achieve statistical significance, and the second addresses the question of power for a failed test of significance. Although both questions may be answered from a single table, we hope that presenting the information in separate tables will make the researcher's task easier.

Power analysis relies on an estimation of effect size, and, as we have seen in earlier chapters, there are various measures of effect size, both for a particular statistical test and for different tests. Calculation of an effect size is illustrated for each test before showing how a power analysis is conducted. When addressing the question of sample size, effect sizes are estimated from an examination of findings from related studies. Ideally, results of several studies are examined and an average effect size is determined for this type of study. If this is not feasible, a conservative estimate of the necessary sample size may be obtained by assuming that the effect size will be small or at best average.

In this abridged presentation, power analyses are reviewed only for alpha equal to .05 and for nondirectional tests of significance. Cohen (1992) suggests that *as a general rule, power should equal .80.* Power less than .80 leads to too many Type II errors; achieving power much greater than .80 is practically difficult given the very large sample sizes that must be obtained.

POWER ANALYSIS FOR A *t* TEST FOR INDEPENDENT GROUPS
How Large Should My Samples Be to Achieve Power Equal to .80?

Step 1: Calculate an effect size. Two popular effect size measures for the difference between two means are **Hedges' g** and **Cohen's d.** (See Chapter 8.) For the same data, Hedges' g will be slightly less than Cohen's d, with the difference decreasing as sample size increases. (See Box 8.1.) Because Cohen's power tables are based on the effect size measure, d, we suggest that this measure be used when determining group size for an independent groups t test. The following formula introduced in Chapter 8 will be helpful:

$$d = \frac{M_1 - M_2}{\sigma_{pooled}}$$

where

$$\sigma_{pooled} = \sqrt{\frac{[n_1 - 1]s_1^2 + [n_2 - 1]s_2^2}{(n_1 + n_2)}}$$

Should Hedges' g have been calculated, it can easily be transformed to d based on

$$d = g\sqrt{[(n_1 + n_2)/df]} \qquad df = n_1 + n_2 - 2 \qquad \text{(See Rosenthal \& Rosnow, 1991.)}$$

Step 2: Given the effect size, *d*, use the information in Box B.1 to find the group size (*n*) required to obtain statistical significance at the .05 level with power equal to .80. Group sizes are presented for small, medium, and large effect sizes. To determine the approximate required group size for estimated effect sizes that fall between small and medium or between medium and large, you will need to make adjustments based on the distance that your estimated effect is from small, medium, and large effect sizes. Note, however, that the relationship between effect size and group size is not linear.

BOX B.1 ■ A *t* Test for Independent Groups: How Large a Sample Should I Use to Obtain .80 Power?

	Small	Medium	Large
If my estimated effect size, *d*, is	.20	.50	.80
then size (*n*) of each group should be	393	64	26

[Based on Cohen (1992).]

BOX B.2 ■ A *t* Test for Independent Groups: What Was the Power of This Test?

		Small	Medium	Large
If the effect size, *d*, was		.20	.50	.80
then, for a given sample size, power was				
	10	.07	.18	.39
Size (*n*)	15	.08	.26	.56
of each group:	20	.09	.33	.69
	25	.11	.41	.79
	30	.12	.47	.79
	35	.13	.54	.91
	40	.14	.60	.94
	100	.29	.94	.99

[Based on Cohen (1988).]

For example, if the *d* observed had been 0.50 and 20 people had been in both groups, there is only a 33% chance of being able to reject the null hypothesis across many replications.

Given an Observed *t* That Is Not Statistically Significant, How Might I Evaluate the Power of the Study?

Step 1: Calculate effect size, *d*, based on results obtained from the study. Cohen's *d* can be simply calculated from the outcome of an independent *t* test as follows:

$$d = \frac{2t}{\sqrt{df}}$$ (See Rosenthal & Rosnow, 1991.)

Step 2: Use the information in Box B.2 to determine the power of the study given the sample size that was used. If the specific group or effect size is not given, to determine an approximate power estimate select values that are closest to the those used in the study.

POWER ANALYSIS FOR A SINGLE-FACTOR ANOVA FOR INDEPENDENT GROUPS

How Large Should My Groups Be to Achieve Power Equal to .80?

Step 1: Calculate an effect size. There are several popular effect size measures for the difference among means in a single-factor independent groups design. In Chapter 12, we introduced a measure of effect size—called **eta squared (η^2)**—that is independent of sample size and that is appropriate when the comparison involves two or more means. Eta squared is formally a measure of the *strength of association* between the independent and dependent variables (e.g., Kirk, 1996). It is a measure of the proportion of variance in the dependent variable accounted for by the independent variable.

Eta squared in a single-factor, independent groups design is easily calculated based on the sums of squares components from the ANOVA. (See Chapter 12.) It can be defined as

$$\text{eta squared } (\eta^2) = \frac{SS_{bg}}{SS_{tot}}$$

Cohen's power tables, however, make use of another measure of effect size called **Cohen's** f, which is a standardized measure of effect not unlike d, except for more than two means. It is defined as

$$f = \frac{\sigma_m}{\sigma} \qquad \text{where } \sigma_m \text{ is the standard deviation of means and}$$
$$\sigma \text{ is the population standard deviation}$$

Fortunately, f can be easily obtained from eta squared (Cohen, 1988). The translation is

$$f = \sqrt{\frac{\text{eta squared}}{(1 - \text{eta squared})}}$$

The suggested interpretation of f differs from that of d. (See Cohen, 1988.) Specifically, f values of .10, .25, and .40 refer to small, medium, and large effect sizes, respectively. (Note: Do not confuse f, a measure of effect size, with F, the ratio of variances obtained from ANOVA.)

Step 2: Given the effect size, f, use the information in Box B.3 to find the group size (n) required to obtain statistical significance at the .05 level with power equal to .80.

BOX B.3 ■ **Single-Factor ANOVA for Independent Groups: How Large a Sample Should I Use to Obtain .80 Power?**

Estimated group sizes vary with the number of independent groups (i.e., levels of the independent variable). The table shows suggested sizes for two through five groups.

		Small	**Medium**	**Large**
If my estimated effect size, f, is		.10	.25	.40
then size (n) of *each group* should be				
	2	393	64	26
Number of groups	3	322	52	21
	4	274	45	18
	5	240	39	16

[Based on Cohen (1992).]

Given an Observed F That Is Not Statistically Significant, How Might I Evaluate the Power of the Study?

Step 1: Calculate effect size, f, based on results obtained from the study. As indicated previously, Cohen's f can be simply calculated from the outcome of a single-factor, independent groups ANOVA by first calculating eta squared and then translating eta squared to f. In the preceding example, eta squared was calculated using the between groups and total sums of squares from the ANOVA. These terms can usually be obtained from the results section of a study; however, another way to obtain eta squared is as follows:

$$\text{eta squared} = \frac{F(df_{bg})}{[F(df_{bg})] + (df_{wg})}$$

where df_{bg} is equal to one less than the number of groups (k), or ($k - 1$), and df_{wg} equals $k(n - 1)$ when ns are the same

For example, if the results $F(3, 76) = 2.55$, $p > .05$ were reported, eta squared may be calculated as

$$\text{eta squared} = \frac{(2.55)(3)}{[2.55(3)] + 76} = \frac{7.65}{83.65} = .09$$

Cohen's f can then be obtained by using the previously given translation:

$$f = \sqrt{\frac{.09}{1.00 - .09}} = \sqrt{.099} = 0.31$$

Note that, because equal group sizes are assumed in these power analyses, the group size in this example must be 20. Given three degrees of freedom for the between-groups variability estimate, we know that the independent variable has four groups or levels. Each of the four groups must have 20 subjects given that the degrees of freedom for the within-groups variability estimate are 76. Recall that the degrees of freedom for the error term are $k(n - 1)$, or, in this case, $4(20 - 1) = 76$.

Step 2: Use the information in Box B.4 to determine the power of the study given the sample size that was used. If the specific group or effect size is not given, to determine an approximate power select values that are closest to those used in the study.

In the preceding example, a study yielded $F(3, 76) = 2.55$, $p > .05$. We found eta squared to be .09 and f equal to .31, which is somewhat larger than a medium effect according to Cohen's guidelines. Size in each of four groups was 20. Looking at Box B.4, we find that, with four groups and a group size equal to 20, power is .43 for a medium effect size (.25) and .85 for a large effect size (.40). Therefore, we can estimate that power in this study was greater than .43 but less than .85, roughly in the neighborhood of .60 to .70, which is somewhat less than the .80 recommended by Cohen (1992). (More-exact power estimates can be found in Cohen, 1988.)

POWER ANALYSIS FOR SIGNIFICANCE OF A CORRELATION COEFFICIENT (r) AND THE DIFFERENCE BETWEEN TWO INDEPENDENT CORRELATIONS

In Chapter 16, you learned how to apply NHST to decisions about a single correlation (r) and to test the difference between two independent correlations. In what follows, we show how power can be analyzed for these two situations.

BOX B.4 ■ Single-Factor ANOVA for Independent Groups: What was the Power of This Test?

Power estimates are given separately for studies with two, three, four, or five groups.

Two Groups

		Small	Medium	Large
If the effect size, f, was		.10	.25	.40
then, for a given sample size, power was				
	5	.06	.11	.20
	10	.07	.18	.40
Size (n)	15	.08	.26	.57
of each group:	20	.09	.34	.70
	25	.10	.42	.80
	30	.11	.49	.87
	35	.12	.55	.92

Three Groups

		Small	Medium	Large
If the effect size, f, was		.10	.25	.40
then, for a given sample size, power was				
	5	.06	.11	.22
	10	.07	.20	.45
Size (n)	15	.08	.29	.64
of each group:	20	.09	.38	.78
	25	.10	.47	.87
	30	.12	.55	.93
	35	.13	.62	.96

Four Groups

		Small	Medium	Large
If the effect size, f, was		.10	.25	.40
then, for a given sample size, power was				
	5	.06	.12	.24
	10	.07	.21	.51
Size (n)	15	.08	.32	.71
of each group:	20	.10	.43	.85
	25	.11	.53	.93
	30	.13	.61	.96
	35	.14	.69	.98

continues

BOX B.4 ■ continued

Five Groups

		Small	Medium	Large
If the effect size, f, was		.10	.25	.40
then, for a given sample size, power was				
	5	.06	.12	.26
	10	.07	.23	.56
Size (n)	15	.09	.36	.78
of each group:	20	.10	.47	.90
	25	.12	.58	.96
	30	.13	.67	.98
	35	.15	.75	.99

[Based on Cohen (1988).]

WHEN TESTING SIGNIFICANCE OF A SINGLE CORRELATION

How Large Should My Sample Be to Achieve Power Equal to .80?

Step 1: Calculate an effect size. A t test for correlations may be used when applying NHST to test the statistical significance of r. We will consider only the case in which the test is nondirectional and r is compared with a population value (ρ) of .00. (See Chapter 16.) The test asks how probable it is that the difference between r and .00 is due only to sampling error. The degrees of freedom are N minus 2 where N refers to the number of pairs of scores (or sample size).

Because the correlation coefficient is not affected by sample size, it may be considered a measure of effect size, and thus we can speak of an **effect size r.** Cohen (1992) suggested that correlations of .30 be considered medium and correlations of .50 and .10 be considered large and small, respectively. Thus, one needs only to know the value of r to use the power table in Box B.5.

Step 2: Given the effect size, r, use the information in Box B.5 to find the sample size (N) required to obtain statistical significance at the .05 level with power equal to .80.

BOX B. 5 ■ Testing the Significance of a Correlation (r): How Large a Sample (N) Should I Use to Obtain .80 Power?

	Small	Medium	Large
If my estimated effect size, r, is	.10	.30	.50
then sample size (N) should be	783	85	28

[Based on Cohen (1992).]

BOX B.6 ■ Testing the Significance of a Correlation (*r*): What Was the Power of This Test?

		Small	**Medium**	**Large**
If the effect size, *r*, was		.10	.30	.50
then, for a given sample size, power was				
	10	.06	.13	.33
Sample size (*N*):	15	.06	.19	.50
	20	.07	.25	.64
	25	.08	.31	.75
	30	.08	.37	.83
	35	.09	.43	.88
	40	.09	.48	.92

[Based on Cohen (1988).]

Sample sizes are presented for small, medium, and large effect sizes. To determine the approximate required sample size for estimated effect sizes that fall between small and medium or between medium and large, you will need to make adjustments based on the difference between your estimated effect and small, medium, and large effect sizes. Note again, however, that the relationship between effect size and sample size is not linear. Remember that *N* refers to the number of pairs of scores or sample size.

Given an Observed r That Is Not Statistically Significant, How Might I Evaluate the Power of the Study?

Step 1: Obtain the effect size, *r*, based on results obtained from the study.
Step 2: Use the information in Box B.6 to determine the power of the study given the sample size (*N*) that was used. If the specific sample or effect size is not given, to determine an approximate power estimate select values that are closest to those used in the study.

WHEN TESTING SIGNIFICANCE OF THE DIFFERENCE BETWEEN TWO CORRELATIONS

How Large Should My Samples Be to Achieve Power Equal to .80?

Step 1: Calculate an effect size. Again, we will consider only the case in which the test is nondirectional and alpha is .05. As you saw in Chapter 16, a *z* test is used to test for differences between two independent correlations. The test asks how probable it is that the difference between *r*'s is due only to sampling error. The first step is to transform each *r* to Z_r using Table A.4. The **effect size *q*** is then easily calculated as

$$q = Z_1 - Z_2$$

Cohen (1992) suggested that *q* values of .30 be considered medium, and values of .50 and .10 be considered large and small, respectively.

BOX B.7 ■ Testing Significance of the Difference Between Two Correlations: How Large of Samples Should I Use to Obtain .80 Power?

	Small	Medium	Large
If my estimated effect size, q, is	.10	.30	.50
then size (n) of each group should be	1573	177	66

[Based on Cohen (1992).]

Step 2: Given the effect size, q, use the information in Box B.7 to find the size of each group (n) required to obtain statistical significance at the .05 level with power equal to .80. Group sizes are presented for small, medium, and large effect sizes. To determine the approximate required group size for estimated effect sizes that fall between small and medium or between medium and large, you will need to make adjustments based on the distance your estimated effect is from small, medium, and large effect sizes. As before, keep in mind that the relationship between effect size and sample size is not linear. Remember that n refers to the number of pairs of scores in each group.

Given That the z Test Is Not Statistically Significant, How Might I Evaluate the Power of the Study?

Step 1: Obtain the effect size, q, based on results obtained from the study.
Step 2: Use the information in Box B.8 to determine the power of the study given the group sizes (n) that were used. If the specific sample or effect size is not given, to determine an approximate power estimate select values that are closest to the those used in the study.

BOX B.8 ■ Testing Significance of the Difference Between Two Correlations: What Was the Power of This Test?

		Small	Medium	Large
If the effect size, q, was		.10	.30	.50
then, for a given sample size, power was				
	20	.06	.14	.30
Size (n)	25	.06	.17	.38
of each group:	30	.07	.20	.45
	35	.07	.22	.52
	40	.07	.25	.58
	60	.08	.36	.76
	80	.10	.46	.87
	100	.11	.55	.94

[Based on Cohen (1988).]

POWER ANALYSIS FOR CHI-SQUARE GOODNESS-OF-FIT TEST AND TEST OF INDEPENDENCE (OR CONTINGENCY)

How Large Should My Sample Be to Achieve Power Equal to .80?

Step 1: Calculate an effect size. In Chapter 18, we introduced the phi (ϕ) coefficient as a measure of effect size or, more specifically, the degree of association for 2×2 contingency tables. A more general measure is the **effect size w,** which may be used for both the chi-square goodness-of-fit test and chi-square test of independence (or contingency) and is not limited to tests with only one degree of freedom. (See Cohen, 1988.) It is defined as

$$w = \sqrt{\Sigma[(P_E - P_O)^2/P_E]}$$

The formula states that w is equal to the square root of the sum (over all cells) of the square of the difference between expected proportions (P_E) and observed proportions (P_O) divided by the expected proportion. (See Rosenthal & Rosnow, 1991.) Small, medium, and large effect sizes are, according to Cohen's guidelines, .10, .30, and .50, respectively.

Let us illustrate with sample data from Chapter 18. Recall that a hypothetical study was conducted to see if there were an association between mothers who do or do not drink beer and their children's preference for the smells of beer and bubble gum. Two hundred and fifty children were tested: 164 had a mother who drinks beer and 86 had mothers who do not drink beer. The results for this 2×2 contingency table are as follows (see also Chapter 18):

Group	Preference for Beer Smell	Preference for Bubble Gum Smell	Total
Mother drinks beer	75/164 = .46	89/164 = .54	164
Mother doesn't drink beer	24/86 = .28	62/86 = .72	86
Total	99	151	250

Note that proportions in each of the cells have been calculated for the *observed frequencies*. To obtain the effect size measure, w, the expected proportions for each cell must also be calculated.

Expected *frequencies* in each cell can be calculated according to

$$\frac{(\text{marginal row total})(\text{marginal column total})}{N}$$

Once the expected frequencies for each cell are determined, the expected proportions for each cell can then be calculated. The following table shows both the expected frequencies and expected proportions for each cell:

Group	Preference for Beer Smell	Preference for Bubble Gum Smell	Total
Mother drinks beer	$O = 75(.46)$ $E = 64.94$ $64.94/164 = .40$	$O = 89(.54)$ $E = 99.06$ $99.06/164 = .60$	164
Mother doesn't drink beer	$O = 24(.28)$ $E = 34.06$ $34.06/86 = .40$	$O = 62(.72)$ $E = 51.94$ $51.94/86 = .60$	86
Total	99	151	250

We now have the proportions needed to calculate w. (Note that, unlike the calculation of chi-square, the calculation of w depends on proportions not frequencies.) For each cell, we subtract the observed proportion from the expected proportion, square that value, and then divide by the expected proportion. These quantities are then summed before taking a square root. Therefore, first find the sum of these quantities:

$$\Sigma \frac{(P_E - P_O)^2}{P_E} = \frac{(.40 - .46)^2}{.40} + \frac{(.60 - .54)^2}{.60} + \frac{(.40 - .28)^2}{.40} + \frac{(.60 - .72)^2}{.60} =$$

$$.009 + .006 + .036 + .024 = .075$$

Then, obtain the square root of the sum:

$\sqrt{.075} = 0.27$; that is, $w = 0.27$, which is approximately an average effect size.

Step 2: Given the effect size, w, use the information in Box B.9 to find the sample size (N) required to obtain statistical significance at the .05 level with power equal to .80. Sample sizes are presented for small, medium, and large effect sizes, which are, as we saw, according to Cohen's guidelines, .10, .30, and .50, respectively. Suggested sample sizes vary according to the degrees of freedom for the chi-square test. For a goodness-of-fit test, the degrees of freedom are number of groups (categories) minus 1. For a chi-square test of independence, the degrees of freedom are number of columns minus 1 times the number of rows minus 1, or $(r - 1)(c - 1)$.

To determine the approximate required sample size for estimated effect sizes that fall between small and medium or between medium and large, you will need to make adjustments based on the distance your estimated effect is from small, medium, and large effect sizes. Note once again, however, that the relationship between effect size and sample size is not linear.

BOX B.9 ■ Chi-Square Tests of Significance: How Large a Sample Should I Use to Obtain .80 Power?

		Small	Medium	Large
If my estimated effect size, w, is	.	.10	.30	.50
then sample size (N) should be				
	1	785	87	26
Degrees of	2	964	107	39
freedom	3	1090	121	44
	4	1194	133	48
	5	1293	143	51
	6	1362	151	54

[Based on Cohen (1992).]

BOX B.10 ■ Chi-Square Tests of Significance When *df* = 1: What Was the Power of This Test?

		Small	**Medium**	**Large**
If the effect size, *w*, was		.10	.30	.50
then, for a given sample size, power was				
	25	.08	.32	.70
	40	.10	.47	.89
Sample size (*N*):	60	.12	.64	.97
	80	.15	.76	.99
	100	.17	.85	.99+
	200	.29	.99	.99+
	400	.52	.99+	.99+

[Based on Cohen (1988).]

Given an Observed χ^2 That Is Not Statistically Significant, How Might I Evaluate the Power of the Study?

Step 1: Calculate effect size, *w*, based on results obtained from the study.

Step 2: Use the information in Box B.10 to determine the power of the study given the sample size that was used. Estimates of power are provided only for chi-square tests with one degree of freedom. To assess power for tests with more than one degree of freedom, see Cohen (1988).

If the specific sample or effect size is not given, determine an approximate estimate of power select values that are closest to those used in the study.

Key Concepts

power	$1 - \beta$	eta squared (η^2)
Type I error	critical region	Cohen's *f*
alpha (α)	power tables	effect size *r*
Type II error	Cohen's *d*	effect size *q*
beta (β)	Hedges' *g*	effect size *w*

References

Abelson, R.P. (1995). *Statistics as principled argument.* Hillsdale, NJ: Erlbaum.

———. (1997). On the surprising longevity of flogged horses: Why there is a case for the significance test. *Psychological Science, 8,* 12–15.

American Psychological Association (2001). *Publication manual of the American Psychological Association* (5th ed.). Washington, DC: Author.

Atkinson, R.L., Atkinson, R.C., Smith, E.E., Bem, D.J., & Nolen-Hoeksma, S. (1996). *Hilgard's introduction to psychology* (12th ed.). Fort Worth, TX: Harcourt Brace & Company.

Babbie, E. (1989). *The practice of social research* (5th ed.). Belmont, CA: Wadsworth.

Bandura, A. (1997). *Self-efficacy: The exercise of self-control.* New York: Freeman.

Beck, A.T., Emery, G., & Greenberg, R.L. (1996). Cognitive therapy for evaluation anxieties. In C.G. Lindeman (Ed.), *Handbook of the treatment of anxiety disorders* (2nd ed.) (pp. 235–260). Northvale, NJ: Jason Aronson, Inc.

Campbell, D.T., & Stanley, J.C. (1963). *Experimental and quasi-experimental designs for research.* Chicago: Rand-McNally.

Carr, E.H. (1962). *What is history?* New York: Knopf.

Cohen, J. (1962). The statistical power of abnormal-social psychological research: A rerview. *Journal of Abnormal and Social Psychology, 69,* 145–153.

———. (1988). *Statistical power analysis for the behavioral sciences* (2nd ed.). Hillsdale, NJ: Erlbaum.

———. (1990). Things I have learned (so far). *American Psychologist, 45,* 1304–1312.

———. (1992). A power primer. *Psychological Bulletin, 112,* 155–159.

———. (1994). The earth is round ($p < .05$). *American Psychologist, 49,* 997–1003.

Cortina, J.M., & Dunlap, W.P. (1997). On the logic and purpose of significance testing. *Psychological Methods, 2,* 161–172.

Dawes, R.M. (1994). *House of cards: Psychology and psychotherapy built on myth.* New York: Free Press.

DeCarlo, L.T. (1997). On the meaning and use of kurtosis. *Psychological Methods, 2,* 292–307.

Dunlap, W.P., & Myers, L. (1997). Approximating power for significance tests with one degree of freedom. *Psychological Methods, 2,* 186–191.

Estes, W.K. (1997). On the communication of information by displays of standard errors and confidence intervals. *Psychonomic Bulletin & Review, 4,* 330–341.

Everitt, B.S. (1999). *Chance rules: An informal guide to probability, risk, and statistics.* New York: Springer-Verlag.

Facts and figures. (1999, April). *Consumer Reports,* pp. 60–65.

Friedrich, J., Buday, E., & Kerr, D. (2000). Statistical training in psychology: A national survey and commentary on undergraduate programs. *Teaching of Psychology, 27,* 248–257.

Funder, D.C. (2001). *The personality puzzle* (2nd ed.). New York: Norton.

Gibson, E.J., & Walk, R.D. (1960, April). The "visual cliff." *Scientific American, 202,* 64–71.

Good, I.J. (1983). *Good thinking: The foundations of probability and its applications.* Minneapolis: University of Minnesota Press.

Gould, S.J. (1978). Morton's rankings of races by cranial capacity. *Science, 200,* 503–509.

Gravetter, F.J., & Wallnau, L.B. (2000). *Statistics for the behavioral sciences* (5th ed.). Belmont, CA: Wadsworth.

Greenwald, A.G., Gonzalez, R., Harris, R.J., & Guthrie, D. (1996). Effect sizes and p values: What should be reported and what should be replicated? *Psychophysiology, 33,* 175–183.

Hays, W.L. (1994). *Statistics* (5th ed.). Orlando, FL: Harcourt Brace.

Hoaglin, D.C., Mosteller, F., & Tukey, J.W. (Eds.). (1991). *Fundamentals of exploratory analysis of variance.* New York: Wiley.

Howell, D.C. (2002). *Statistical methods for psychology* (5th ed.). Pacific Grove, CA: Duxbury.

Hunter, J.E. (1997). Needed: A ban on significance tests. *Psychological Science, 8,* 3–7.

Hunter, J.E., & Schmidt, F.L. (1990). *Methods of meta-analysis: Correcting error and bias in research findings.* Newbury Park, CA: Sage.

Kahneman, D., Slovic, P., & Tversky, A. (1982). *Judgment under uncertainty: Heuristics and biases.* Cambridge: Cambridge University Press.

Kenny, D.A. (1987). *Statistics for the social and behavioral sciences.* Boston: Little, Brown.

Keppel, G., & Zedeck, S. (1989). *Data analysis for research designs.* New York: Freeman.

Kirk, R.E. (1996). Practical significance: A concept whose time has come. *Educational and Psychological Measurement, 56,* 746–759.

Krosnick, J.A. (1999). Survey research. *Annual Review of Psychology, 50,* 537–567.

Lipsey, M.W. 1990. *Design sensitivity: Statistical power for experimental research.* Newbury Park, CA: Sage.

Lipsey, M.W., & Wilson, D.B. (1993). The efficacy of psychological, educational, and behavioral treatment: Confirmation from meta-analysis. *American Psychologist, 48,* 1181–1209.

Loftus, G.R. (1993). A picture is worth a thousand *p* values: On the irrelevance of hypothesis testing in the microcomputer age. *Behavior Research Methods, Instruments, & Computers, 25,* 250–256.

———. (1996). Psychology will be a much better science when we change the way we analyze data. *Current Directions in Psychological Science, 5,* 161–171.

Loftus, G.R., & Masson, M.E.J. (1994). Using confidence intervals in within-subjects designs. *Psychonomic Bulletin & Review, 1,* 476–490.

Meehl, P.E. (1954). *Clinical versus statistical prediction.* Minneapolis: University of Minnesota Press.

———. (1967). Theory-testing in psychology and physics: A methodological paradox. *Philosophy of Science, 34,* 103–115.

———. (1978). Theoretical risks and tabular asterisks: Sir Karl, Sir Ronald, and the slow progress of soft psychology. *Journal of Consulting and Clinical Psychology, 46,* 806–834.

Miles, M.B., & Huberman, A.M. (1994). *Qualitative data analysis* (2nd ed.). Thousand Oaks, CA: Sage.

Mosteller, F., & Bush, R.R. (1954). Selected quantitative techniques. In G. Murphy (Ed.), *Handbook of social psychology.* Reading, MA: Addison-Wesley.

Mosteller, F., Fienberg, S.E., & Rourke, R.E.K. (1983). *Beginning statistics with data analysis.* Reading, MA: Addison-Wesley.

Mulaik, S.A., Raju, N.S., & Harshman, R.A. (1997). There is a time and place for significance testing. In L.L. Harlow, S.A. Mulaik, & J.H. Steiger (Eds.), *What if*

there were no significance tests? (pp. 65–115). Mahweh, NJ: Erlbaum.

Murphy, K.R., & Davidshofer, C.O. (1994). *Psychological testing: Principles and applications* (3rd ed.). Englewood Cliffs, NJ: Prentice Hall.

Myers, D.G. (1992). *The pursuit of happiness: Who is happy—and why?* New York: W. Morrow.

Myers, D.G., & Jeeves, M.A. (1987). *Psychology through the eyes of faith.* New York: HarperCollins.

Nickerson, R.S. (2000). Null hypothesis significance testing: A review of an old and continuing controversy. *Psychological Methods, 5,* 241–301.

Posavac, E.J. (1998). Toward more informative uses of statistics: Alternatives for program evaluators. *Evaluation and Program Planning, 21,* 243–254.

———. (2002). Using *p* values to estimate the probability of a statistically significant replication. *Understanding Statistics 1,* 101–112.

Posavac, E.J., & Carey, R.G. (2003). *Program evaluation: Methods and case studies* (6th ed.). Upper Saddle River, NJ: Prentice Hall.

Potts, M. (2000, January). The unmet need for family planning. *Scientific American, 282,* 88–93.

Prentice, D.A., & Miller, D.T. (1992). When small effects are impressive. *Psychological Bulletin, 112,* 160–164.

———. (1993). Pluralistic ignorance and alcohol use on campus: Some consequences of misperceiving the social norm. *Journal of Personality & Social Psychology, 64,* 243–256.

Rosenthal, R. (1990). How are we doing in soft psychology? *American Psychologist, 45,* 775–777.

Rosenthal, R., & Rosnow, R.L. (1991). *Essentials of behavioral research: Methods and data analysis* (2nd ed.). Boston: McGraw-Hill.

Rosenthal, R., Rosnow, R.L., & Rubin, D.B. (2000). *Contrasts and effect sizes in behavioral research: A correlational approach.* Cambridge, UK: Cambridge University Press.

Rosnow, R.L., & Rosenthal, R. (1989). Statistical procedures and the justification of knowledge in psychological science. *American Psychologist, 44,* 1276–1284.

———. (1999). *Beginning behavioral research: A conceptual primer* (3rd ed.). Upper Saddle River, NJ: Prentice Hall.

Rossi, J.S. (1997). A case study in the failure of psychology as a cumulative science: The spontaneous recovery of verbal learning. In L.L. Harlow, S.A. Mulaik, & J.H. Steiger (Eds.), *What if there were no significance tests?* (pp. 175–197). Mahweh, NJ: Lawrence Erlbaum Associates.

Schmidt, F.L. (1996). Statistical significance testing and cumulative knowledge in psychology: Implications for training of researchers. *Psychological Methods, 1,* 115–129.

Schmidt, F.L., & Hunter, J.E. (1997). Eight common but false objections to the discontinuation of significance testing in the analysis of research data. In L.L. Harlow, S.A. Mulaik, & J.H. Steiger (Eds.), *What if there were no significance tests?* (pp. 37–64). Mahweh, NJ: Erlbaum.

Schroeder, J.E., & Dugal, S.S. (1995). Psychological correlates of the materialism construct. *Journal of Social Behavior and Personality, 10,* 243–253.

Shadish, W.R., Cook, T.D., & Campbell, D.T. (2002). *Experimental and quasi-experimental designs for generalized causal inference.* Boston: Houghton Mifflin.

Shaughnessy, J.J., Zechmeister, E.B., & Zechmeister, J.S. (2003). *Research methods in psychology* (6th ed.). Boston: McGraw-Hill.

Stigler, S.M. (1999). *Statistics on the table:The history of statistical concepts and methods.* Cambridge, MA: Harvard University Press.

Strauss, A., & Corbin, J. (1990). *Basics of qualitative research.* Newbury Park, CA: Sage.

Tabachnick, B.G., & Fidell, L.S. (2001). *Computer-assisted research design and analysis.* Needham Heights, MA: Allyn and Bacon.

The World Almanac. (2000). Mahweh, NJ: World Almanac Books.

Thompson, B. (1999). If statistical significance tests are broken/misused, what practices should supplement or replace them? *Theory & Psychology, 2,* 165–181.

Thorndike, R.M., & Dinnel, D.L. (2001). *Basic statistics for the behavioral sciences.* Upper Saddle River, NJ: Prentice-Hall.

Tufte, E.R. (1983). *The visual display of quantitative information.* Cheshire, CT: Graphic Press.

Tukey, J.W. (1977). *Exploratory data analysis.* Reading, MA: Addison-Wesley.

Wilkinson, L., & the Task Force on Statistical Inference. (1999). Statistical methods in psychology journals. *American Psychologist, 54,* 594–604.

Zechmeister, J.S., Zechmeister, E.B., & Shaughnessy, J.S. (2001). *Essentials of research methods in psychology.* Boston: McGraw-Hill.

Index